AF361283

IMPERIAL URBANISM IN THE BORDERLANDS

Kyiv, 1800–1905

Imperial Urbanism in the Borderlands

Kyiv, 1800–1905

SERHIY BILENKY

UNIVERSITY OF TORONTO PRESS
Toronto Buffalo London

ISBN 978-1-4875-0172-3

Library and Archives Canada Cataloguing in Publication

Bilenky, Serhiy, 1975–, author

Imperial urbanism in the borderlands : Kyiv, 1800–1905 / Serhiy Bilenky.

Includes bibliographical references and index.
ISBN 978-1-4875-0172-3 (cloth)

1. Urbanization – Ukraine – Kiev History – 19th century.   2. Urbanization – Ukraine – Kiev – History – 20th century.   3. Kiev (Ukraine) – History – 19th century.   4. Kiev (Ukraine) – History – 20th century.   I. Title.

DK508.935.B55 2018   947.7′7   C2017-903717-X

This book has been published with the help of a grant from the Federation for the Humanities and Social Sciences, through the Awards to Scholarly Publications Program, using funds provided by the Social Sciences and Humanities Research Council of Canada.

University of Toronto Press acknowledges the financial assistance to its publishing program of the Canada Council for the Arts and the Ontario Arts Council, an agency of the Government of Ontario.

Contents

Part Three: Peopling the City

Part Four: Living (in) the City

Illustrations and Tables

Maps 1 to 6 are on pages xvi–xxii and maps 7 to 12 are on pages 230–6.

Illustrations

Chart

Tables

Acknowledgments

In the fall of 2013, while I was wrapping up the research for this book, peaceful protests against a corrupt Ukrainian government broke out on Kyiv's main square – Independence Square (once known as Khreshchatyk Square, later Duma Square, and today simply the Maidan). In January and February 2014 those demonstrations were marred by unprecedented levels of violence unleashed by the ruthless regime of President Viktor Yanukovych against the largely peaceful protesters; more then one hundred of them were killed by riot police, mysterious snipers, and government-sponsored thugs. Suddenly, historical Kyiv seemed far removed from this new city of televised death and heroism, a city in which my family members and close friends risked their lives and some were injured. Writing a book seemed an absurd notion at a time when civilians on Kyiv's streets were suffering through a horrifying spectacle, one that might have been painted by a postmodern Hieronymus Bosch. But then I realized why I had to finish this book – if only to remind readers of the fortunes of this great city, a place where the human spirit rebelled against oppression and that has become a monument to human perseverance in the face of political adversity, urban fragility, and (not always favourable) change. A project that I began with the city's shape in mind has evolved into one about humanity itself; the tragic events of January and February 2014 offer a sombre drum beat for an ongoing discussion of Kyiv as a place and as a community.

This book is deeply indebted to my many academic and non-academic friends who struggled for freedom on the barricades of the Maidan and on other Kyiv streets. The courage and determination of these and other fellow Kyivites inspired me to think about the city as a *living* cluster of spatial and social, built and human, historical and contemporary qualities.

I want to thank Roman Szporluk for encouraging me to think seriously about Kyiv's unique place in Eastern European history. Serhy Plokhii patiently listened to my rough ideas during a few hot summers in Cambridge, Massachusetts. I thank Douglas Donegani for his never-ending hospitality in Toronto and for helping me "search for the right metaphors." Olena Betliy and Olia Martyniuk stimulated my research by inviting me to the excellent conference on Kyiv's historical urbanism in December 2015. Faith Hillis offered generous advice and shared her precious archival materials (as well as numerous insights from her brilliant book). My own book would not have been possible without the constant care of Richard Ratzlaff of the University of Toronto Press, who enthusiastically guided me through a complex and at times obscure editorial process. I also thank Richard and his colleague Peter Kracht of the University of Pittsburgh Press for inviting me to the annual conference "Recovering Forgotten History: The Image of East-Central Europe in English-Language Academic Textbooks," which notwithstanding its "academic" title was a pure pleasure. While there I was honoured to have Andrzej Nowak, Ostap Sereda, and John Merriman as attentive readers and insightful critics of my manuscript. I also want to thank Frances Mundy, Stephen Shapiro, Matthew Kudelka, and the entire staff at the University of Toronto Press for making sure that the words are right and images are in the right places in my manuscript. I am especially grateful to the Ukrainian Studies Fund and personally to Roman Procyk for funding my research work. My project would have been impossible without Frank Sysyn's wise advice and kind support. My special thanks go to Dmytro Vortman for his excellent maps of Kyiv and for several very helpful suggestions regarding the city's cartography and its past in general. Regarding illustrations, a number of them have been generously supplied by Kyiv's famed publishing house "Mystetstvo" (a personal thank you to Nina Dmytrivna Prybieha). I am also indebted to Mykhailo Kal'nyts'kyi for his unrivalled expertise in Kyiv's past and for his help with illustrative material. My book has also benefited greatly from many discussions with my friend Olga Klimenko, whose master's thesis from Central European University was a pioneering study of Kyiv's sociospatial history. I am always grateful to Taras Koznarsky for his friendship and expertise in literary and visual sources. Paul Robert Magocsi provided a stimulating academic environment at the University of Toronto and also offered precious editorial advice. I thank Kateryna Ruban for the time spent on our urban drifting in Kyiv and New York and for conversations on various urban topics. Vova Vorotniov was an excellent guide to Kyiv's daily urbanism. Jessica Zychowicz inspired me with her vision of Kyiv's contemporary arts scene and social activism. Finally, by way of cliché, all the flaws in this book are solely my responsibility and can be blamed only partly on bad weather in Toronto and Kyiv.

K E Y

Churches:
- ☦ Orthodox
- ⚰ Roman Catholic
- ⚰ Lutheran

- 🕎 Synagogue
- 🕍 Bell tower
- ⛰ Industrial enterprise
- ▪ Other buildings
- ▲ Monument

Residential area:
- high density
- low density

- Industrial area
- Park, forest

Cemetery:
- Christian
- Jewish

- Rampart

Boundary:
- –·––·– city of Kyiv
- ·········· district
- ×××× esplanade

Names of :

PODIL district

KUDRIAVETS' locality

Maps 1–6 prepared by Dmytro Vortman.

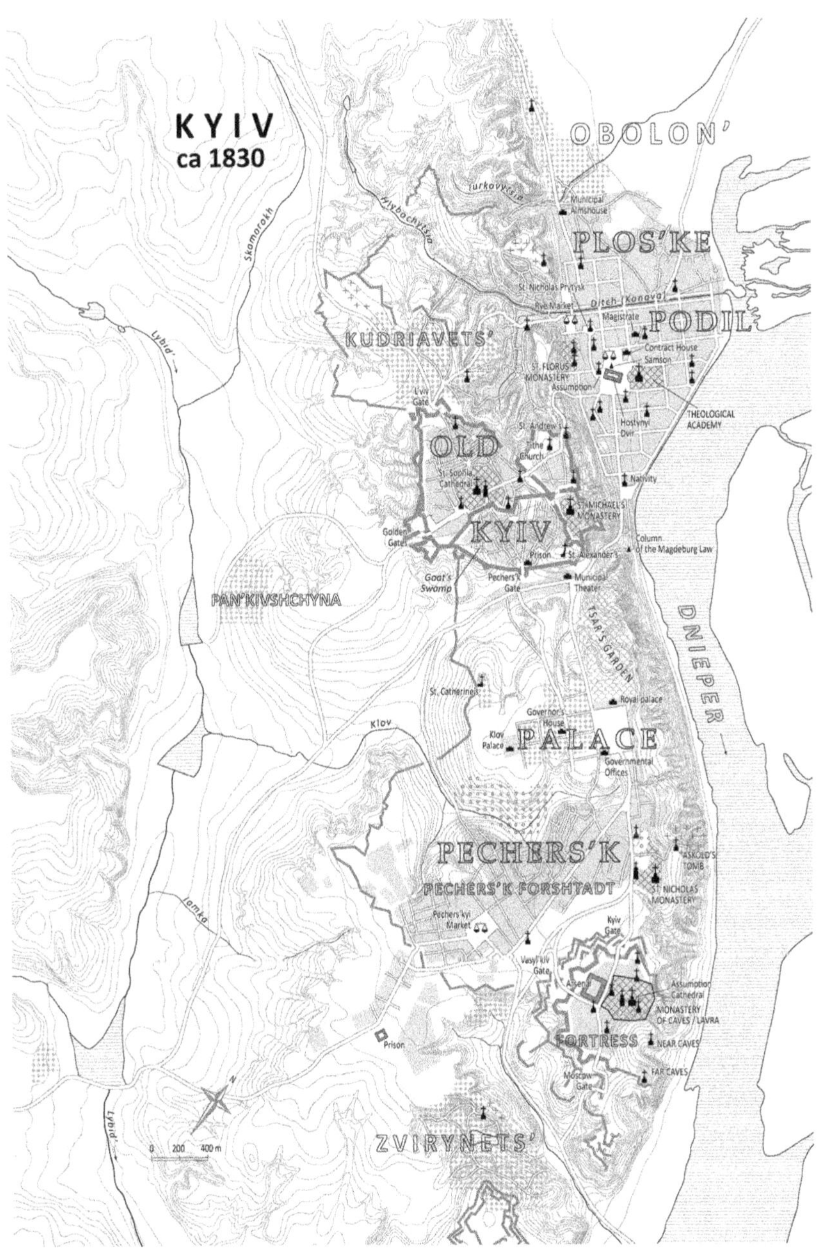

Map 1   Kyiv, circa 1830

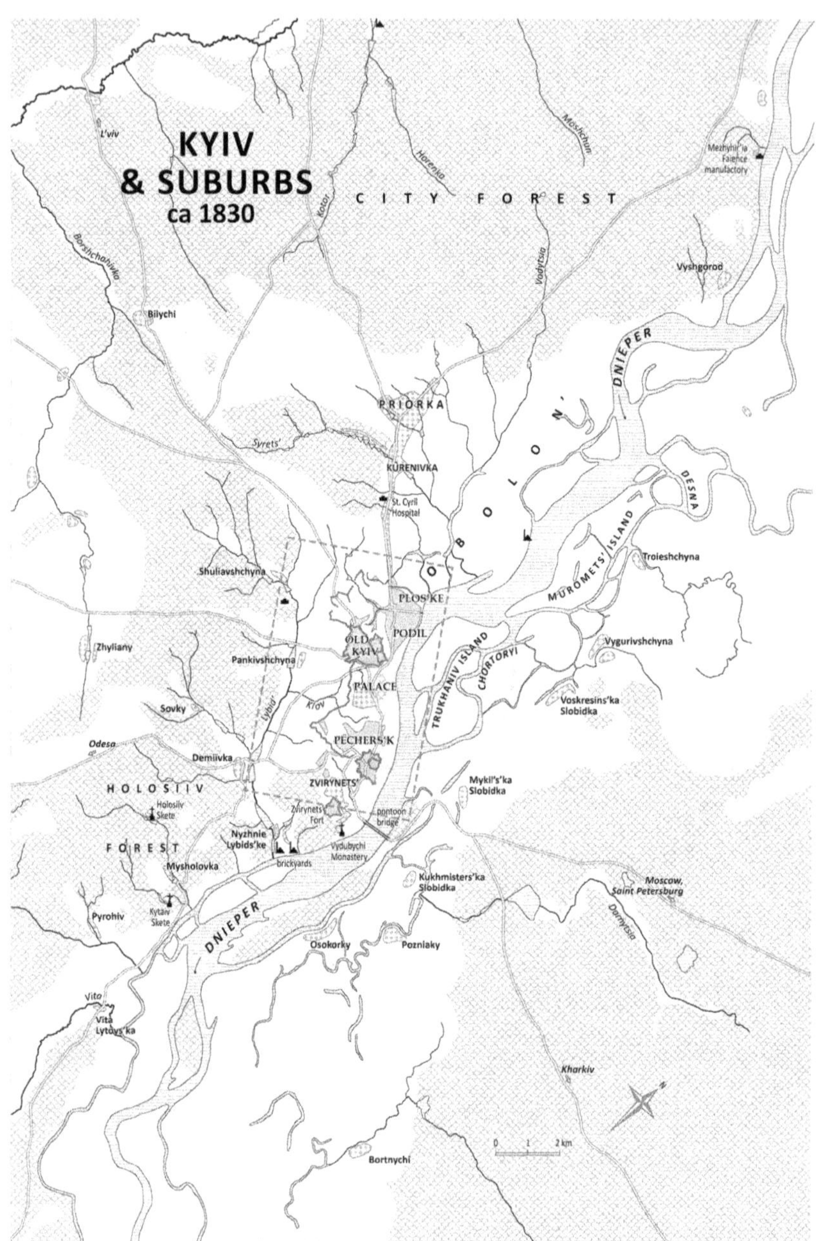

Map 2 Kyiv and suburbs, circa 1830

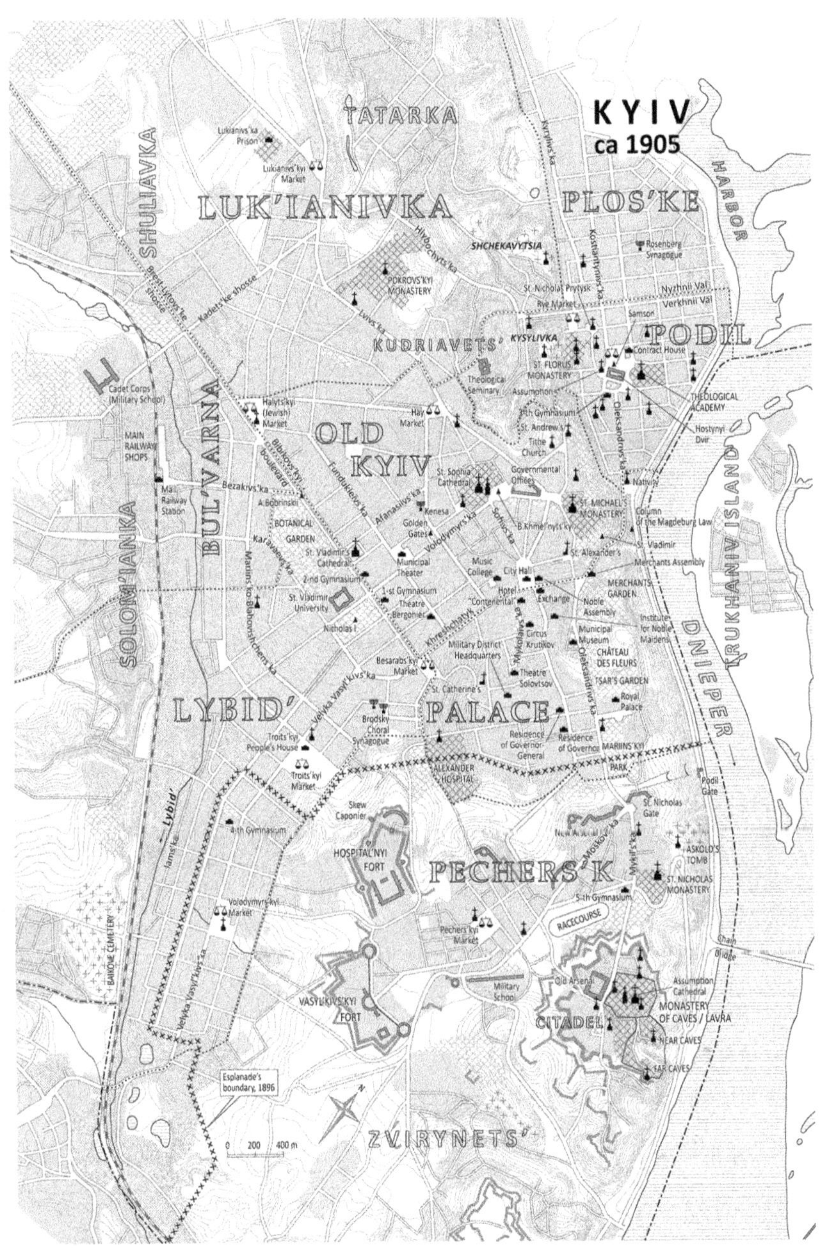

Map 3 Kyiv, circa 1905

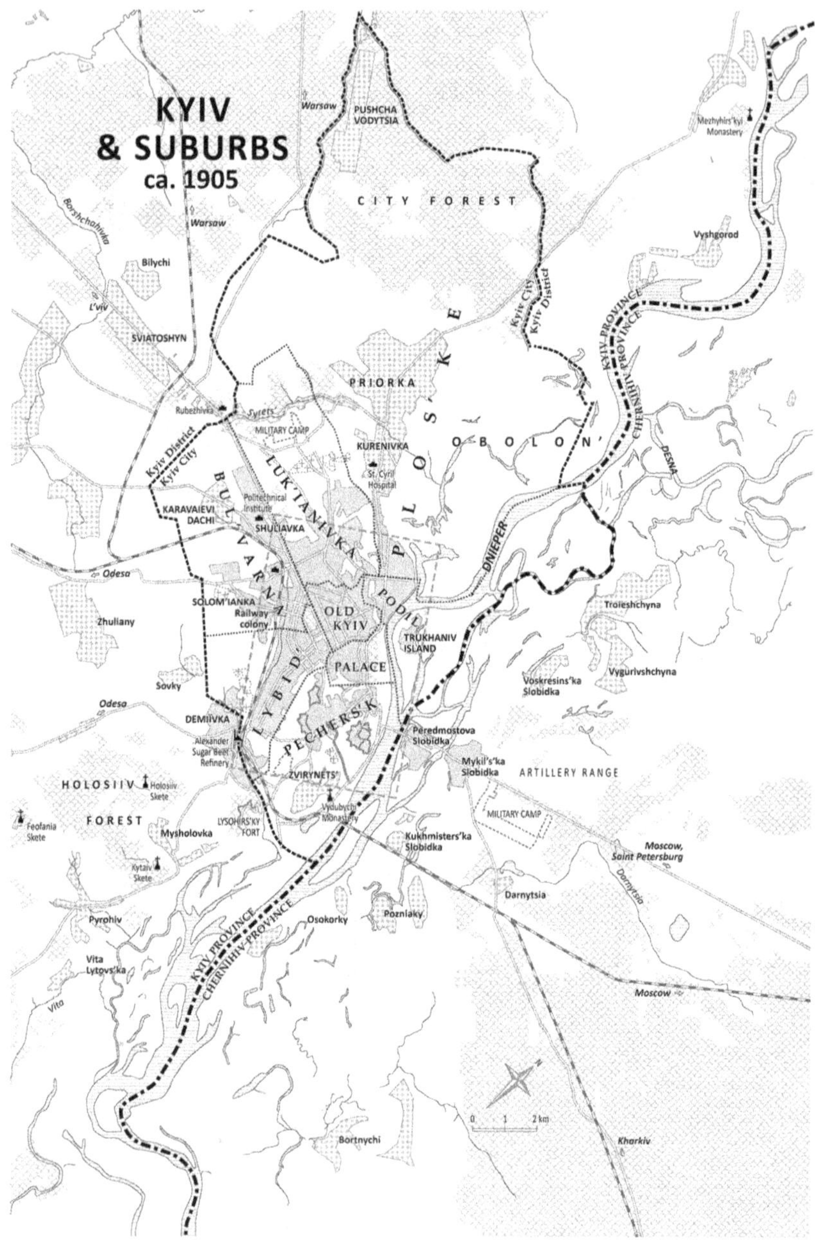

Map 4 Kyiv and suburbs, circa 1905

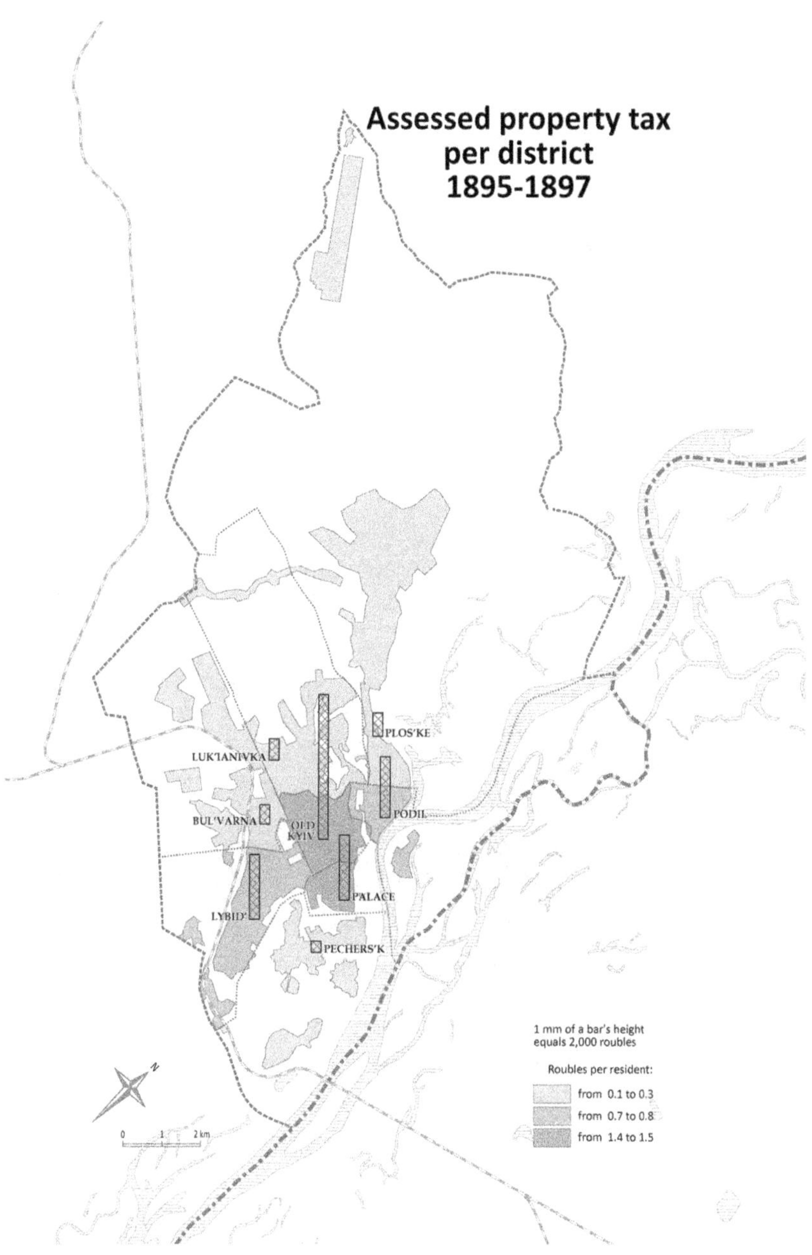

Map 5 Assessed property tax per district, 1895–1897

Map 6 Kyiv's population, 1897

IMPERIAL URBANISM IN THE BORDERLANDS

Kyiv, 1800–1905

Introduction

Why should an English-speaking audience read a historical study of imperial Kyiv, a city that in many respects has all but vanished? Today's Kyiv, a city of more than 2.8 million people and the capital of a large European state, is struggling to retain its cultural identity amidst numerous challenges. Over the past ten to fifteen years, the city has been devastated by ongoing mismanagement by the municipal government, which has allowed cowboy capitalists a free hand in the city's urban redevelopment. It has not become the Detroit of Eastern Europe (although that dubious honour might well go to other cities in Ukraine); Kyiv's main problem is *over*development rather than lack of development, especially with regard to real estate speculation. Besides all this, the city lacks proactive urban planning of the sort that might have addressed some of the acute issues it faces such as traffic, pollution, poor public transit, overdevelopment, and loss of green space. Historical preservation has been disastrous as well: many architectural landmarks have been disfigured by ugly renovations such as plastic windows, glassed-in balconies, and sheet metal front doors. Even worse, a number of historic buildings, supposedly under the state's protection, have been demolished by unscrupulous developers and replaced by new, and mostly bland, commercial and residential structures. For generations, the city had been been admired by residents and visitors alike for its almost ideal cityscape – that is, the harmony between its picturesque landscape (the iconic "city on the hills") and its built heritage. But in only a few years, those hills have disappeared from view, trees have been cut down, landmarks have been demolished, and open spaces have been densely developed. These changes have been a shock for all sensitive and sensible Kyivites. So in a sense, this book is about a city that has been lost.

Changes, especially rapid changes, are often traumatic, even if well-intended and rationally engineered. And well-intended changes can be especially painful. I will be arguing in this book that the changes the city experienced at various times *before* 1917 were no less dramatic and traumatic than those inflicted on Kyiv by the modernizers of Communist and post-Communist times. Historians of Soviet cities tend to forget this – to exaggerate the scope of changes that occurred after the advent of Communism and to downplay those that happened earlier. Similarly, those who study cities in post-Communist times tend to represent post-Communist developments as unprecedented. Yet in terms of architecture, town planning, and sociospatial form, Kyiv changed more radically during the long nineteenth century than it did after the advent (and, later, the collapse) of Communism. As a rapidly growing borderland metropolis, Kyiv absorbed better than most other Russian cities new trends in urbanism. This book contributes to the developing field of studies of urban form and life in the Russian Empire by exploring Russian imperial urbanism in the multiethnic borderlands.[1]

The specific geopolitical setting for this study is the southwestern borderlands of the Russian Empire (Right-Bank Ukraine, in present-day terms), a traditional contact zone between Eastern Orthodox and Western Catholic influences. In the course of the nineteenth century, Kyiv became a place where historical Russia, Poland, and Ukraine met – a meeting place of social classes, ethnicities, political cultures, and ideologies. Some of that complexity is present to this day and is reflected in the city's form and built environment. In this book I explain urban change by placing space and social relations in Kyiv within a broader framework of economic trends, public policies (imperial and municipal), and debates about the city's past. I also put forward a theory of Russian imperial urbanism in the borderlands by focusing on a handful of factors: the state's role in planning the city's external form; relations between the imperial government and the city; the role of municipal elites; the evolution of the city's sociospatial form; and the tensions between cosmopolitan demographics and borderland politics. I offer four main theses, one for each section of this book.

First, the best way to assess how people experienced and perceived urban change is through literary and journalistic sources. In the case of imperial Kyiv, these were written by Russians, Ukrainians, Poles, and Jews throughout the long nineteenth century. These sources may also reveal a form of urbanism that was constructed from daily life. "The accounts of the ways in which the city was incorporated into the lives of the inhabitants, both new arrivals and settled residents," writes historian Daniel Brower, "tell a story as significant as those of the proclamations and statutes of officials or the visions of educated Russians."[2] While most of these accounts were written by educated observers, many of them allude to the experiences of a broader segment of urban dwellers. I will be arguing that the changes that transformed Kyiv into a cosmopolitan metropolis were represented and sometimes anticipated in literary sources of various genres (chapter 1). By analysing these sources, we are able to approach the human edge of history and explore the human dimension of grand social processes. This in turn allows us to deconstruct various myths of modernity and of the past, some of which have continued to define Kyiv's image and the identities of its inhabitants to this day.

Modern Kyiv presents something of a paradox, in that unlike most Eastern European cities, it has been constructed through recurrent references to its past – references that are often mythological and always ideological (chapter 2). This conservative vision of the past has been based on specific politics of memory that have long nurtured the myth of the Holy City of Kyiv – a myth that has enabled Orthodox Russians and Ukrainians[3] to assert themselves but has also alienated Catholic Poles and Jews. This historical myth was politicized in the early 1830s, fuelled by Russians' fears (justified or not) of Polish territorial ambitions. Those fears led the Russian authorities to sponsor research into Kyiv's past as a way of proving that the city was indeed ancient, Russian, and Orthodox – the true spiritual capital of Russia. Indeed, the city was filled with supposedly ancient churches and monasteries, and these defined the city's "representational space" as an Orthodox Holy City, Russia's "new Zion." That image combined imperial ideology and secular knowledge with Christian cosmology.[4] This space became the strongest argument for Russian imperialists and nationalists in their struggle against real and imagined threats, whether they emanated from Poles, Jews, or Ukrainians.

Paradoxically, this reactionary attention to the past was related to various proactive socio-economic policies pursued by the Russian imperial authorities. Some of these policies, influenced by the prevailing myth, helped transform Kyiv into a modern metropolis as a counterweight to other regional centres such as heavily Polish and Jewish Berdychiv, which was the financial capital of the southwestern borderlands until the mid-nineteenth century.[5] Yet one might argue the opposite – that the conservative utopia of the Holy City of Kyiv halted social and economic modernization of the city, for example, by discriminating against Jews and Poles. Economics aside, it can be argued that rapid development actually *helped* Kyiv strengthen its status as an "ancient" city, if only by emphasizing contrasts between old and new.[6]

Second, Kyiv's pattern of urban growth was different from that of a great many Central and Eastern European cities, which in the modern period evolved from multiethnic into national centres in which one ethnic group indisputably dominated (as in Budapest), or which saw a bloody rivalry between two distinct nationalities (as in Prague and Lviv).[7] Kyiv followed a different pattern – indeed, a rather rare one for that region's main cities: from a small frontier town dominated by Ukrainian burghers, Cossacks, and the local Church, it developed into an imperial *multiethnic* metropolis under the umbrella of Russian modernity. In chapters 3, 4, and 5, which are structured chronologically, I focus mainly on urban planning and spatial change in the city and show how modern Kyiv as a territorial and administrative unity was created by Russian imperial authorities, sometimes in cooperation but often in confrontation with local municipal institutions. In this process, a new urban shape encroached on the imagined space of ancient Kyiv, which at one time had been the fabled capital of Kyivan Rus'. This largely imagined city remained at the centre of Christian Orthodox cosmology as the Holy and Blessed City of Kyiv (*svatyi bohospasaiemyi hrad Kyiv*). The coexistence of modern and (largely imagined) *ancient* and *holy* Kyiv was not always harmonious, and the tensions between these two were often depicted in the literary fiction and journalism of the time.

Another tension was between two different types of urban modernity: one represented by a self-governing city, the other brought about by the Russian imperial authorities. Regarding the first of these, Kyiv was ruled by a largely Ukrainian oligarchy until 1835; after a hiatus of thirty-six years, self-government was reintroduced in 1871, this time in the guise of an autonomous city council (the duma), which was dominated by multiethnic professionals and businessmen. In a metaphysical sense, the history of Kyiv in the nineteenth and early twentieth centuries can be viewed as a collision between the spirit of empire and the spirit of a city.[8] The sides were not equal, however: the self-governing city (i.e., before 1835 and after 1871) lacked the financial, technical, and human resources to run its own affairs, and meanwhile, the state was prepared to impose its own agenda, often to the city's detriment. These complex relations between city and state turned Kyiv into a unique case of imperial urbanism in the borderlands.

The city on the Dnieper experienced a distinct form of modern urban planning earlier than many Western and Central European cities. There are several reasons for this. First, the Russian Empire was one of the first polities in Europe to introduce comprehensive urban planning pursued by public authorities. This began with the construction of Saint Petersburg under Peter I (inspired by the Dutch), and it continued during the reign of Catherine II with the neoclassical planning of New Russian cities, among them Katerynoslav (Ekaterinoslav), Kherson, and especially Odessa, all in what today is southern Ukraine. It was Catherine who first introduced an international planning competition in 1763, with the goal of producing a comprehensive plan for Saint Petersburg.[9] Second, for far longer than other European powers, Russia retained an absolutist state apparatus that was at odds with free market capitalism, and as a consequence, public authority at the central *and* local levels held the upper hand in all matters related to urban planning and construction.[10] Put differently, for much of the period under consideration in this book, market forces were too weak in imperial Russia to challenge central or even local authorities. Third, Russian imperial architects and planners had no choice but to apply a comprehensive planning approach to Moscow, Russia's other capital, after that city was almost completely razed in 1812 during the Napoleonic invasion.[11] Daniel Brower calls fires "a useful tool of urban renewal."[12] The rebuilding of Moscow led directly to new laws and practices in the fields of construction and urban planning, and this had a long-lasting impact on all regions of the empire. Finally, Kyiv itself, owing to a fateful combination of geopolitical factors (especially the construction of a fortress) and local cataclysms (fire and floods), became a testing ground for various facets of modern urban planning, such as urban renewal, slum demolition, city extension, and street improvements.

Third, Kyiv's growth was accompanied by various attempts to count and name its changing population. Counting and naming became instruments not only for describing social reality but also for disciplining the city's borderland demographics. In chapter 6, I explore the changing language of class, religion, and ethnicity as reflected in various statistical surveys. All the while, Kyiv's "urban regimes" and municipal leaders also changed; in the first three decades of the nineteenth century, they were predominantly Ukrainian; by mid-century, they were ethnic Russian; by late-imperial times, they were multiethnic, and cosmopolitan professionals dominated the city government (chapter 7).

Fourth and finally, modernity affected both *how* and *where* people lived in the city. Spatial and social change came about hand in hand, fostering the city's "sociospatial form." One can also talk of the "social life of urban form" – a concept that refers to how cities are structured "as spatial environments around, and through social relations, practices, and divisions."[13] I therefore argue that imperial urbanism redefined the relationship between social status and spatiality in Kyiv, especially in the last quarter of the nineteenth century (chapter 8). Everywhere in the world, including in Kyiv, urban modernity reshaped sociospatial relations by introducing zoning, social segregation, and real estate speculation. It also brought *nationality* into play and place. As a result, public space became a *contested* space reflecting a political as well as symbolic struggle between various groups in which the weapons at hand were architecture and the raising of monuments (see chapter 9).

Reactions to, and perceptions of, change in Kyiv in various local traditions (Russian, Ukrainian, Polish, and until recently Jewish) have not been sufficiently addressed in the scholarly literature. Still less attention has been paid to the ways in which modern urbanism changed the city's spaces – physical, social, literary, and other. There are only a few English-language works on imperial Kyiv.[14] Arguably the most comprehensive of these is Michael Hamm's general survey of Kyiv's modern history, which tells the story of the coexistence of the different communities – Ukrainians, Russians, Poles, and Jews – that have comprised the city's diverse population to this day.[15] In contrast to Hamm's still relevant book, mine focuses on spatial and social relations and on how these were represented in various narratives that reflected a city in transition. In other words, I intend to explore how various agents *changed* the city (or "produced" space, in Henri Lefebvre's terms) and at the same time how they *represented* spatial, social, and ethnic changes that Kyiv experienced during the long nineteenth century.

Two other English-language authors – Natan Meir and Faith Hillis – address particular aspects of late-imperial Kyiv: Meir, Jewish communal organization, and Hillis, Russian conservative circles and municipal politics, which were largely defined by these circles. Both these authors' accounts are well researched and have been indispensable to my own research. While the three of us deal with different aspects of Russian urban history, Meir's and Hillis's accounts as well as my own all point to the growing importance of the study of imperial Kyiv – a study that has long been neglected.

We can complain about the scarcity of English-language writings on imperial Kyiv, but when it comes to general works on the same subject by Russian and Ukrainian historians the situation does not look much better. The best general survey of Kyiv's history written prior to 1917 is Vladimir Ikonnikov's classic account.[16] Unfortunately, Ikonnikov continued his history only up to 1855. Another problem with his book is its confusing structure; still another is his attention to minor details at the expense of important events and developments. *Kievskaia Starina* (Kyiv's Antiquities), a periodical published in Russian between 1882 and 1906, devoted itself to the history of Ukraine and Kyiv in particular. It contained a range of materials pertaining to the city's history up to the mid-nineteenth century. Most of those materials, however, were not scholarly articles but narrative sources, and they were often published without sufficient commentary.

In the 1920s, Ukrainian scholars, under the auspices of Soviet academic institutions, produced arguably the most important research on imperial Kyiv.[17] Unfortunately, their promising work was abruptly terminated by Stalinist terror. After the Second World War the biggest contribution to studies of pre-revolutionary Kyiv was made not by historians but by architects, builders, art historians, and urban planners.[18] A crowning achievement of Soviet historians of Kyiv was the three-volume academic work *Istoriia Kieva*.[19] This was an official product of Soviet Ukrainian historiography and was produced under intense political pressure; it was full of various facts of political, socio-economic, and cultural importance, but as a whole it was irreparably damaged by ideological dogmas. A new history of Kyiv has recently been published by the same Institute of History of Ukraine's Academy of Sciences.[20] This one is free of Soviet-era ideology, but it is also much sketchier, packed as it is into one illustrated volume. Over the past ten to fifteen years there have also appeared a number of publications dealing with various aspects of imperial Kyiv – architecture, streetscape, housing, daily life, prominent personalities, and so on.[21] The most comprehensive of these concerns itself with the architecture, urban planning, and urban economy of late-imperial, "capitalist" Kyiv, from the reintroduction of municipal self-government in 1871 to the revolution of 1917.[22] Regrettably, no comprehensive work such as this exists for the decades prior to 1871. There are indeed "known knowns" in studies of imperial Kyiv, but the number of "known unknowns" and "unknown unknowns" remains inexplicably high, which makes this city's past largely uncharted territory for historians. I can only hope that with the renewed political visibility of Ukraine's capital during the last few years, a scholarly treatment of its history – both in Ukraine and abroad – has gained a new momentum.

My project is situated at the nexus between the spatial and the social. It has been influenced by the stimulating ideas of French urban thinker Henri Lefebvre, who once argued that space is never a neutral or homogenous locus of social relations. Rather, it is "produced" by social and political practices, which in turn are defined largely by the existing mode of production.[23] This is all the more true for the city, which is a combination of physical and social spaces. There is one significant difference, however, between these two types of space: natural (physical) space juxtaposes and disperses by putting places and their occupants side by side, whereas social space "implies actual or potential assembly at a single point, or around that point."[24] The space of the city is especially revealing of many basic features of social space. "Urban space," continues Lefebvre, "gathers crowds, products in the markets, acts and symbols. It concentrates all these, and accumulates them." Not less importantly, each epoch and each particular society produces its own specific space, "fashioned, shaped and invested by social activities during a finite historical period."[25] To illustrate his point, Lefebvre uses various examples, from a Greek *polis* and ancient Rome to the medieval city to Renaissance Venice to Soviet Russia of the 1920s and 1930s.

His reconstruction of the spatial practice of a Greek *polis* is a good example of how a particular space is produced and represented:

> A unity was achieved here between the order of the world, the order of the city and the order of the house – between the three levels of segments constituted by physical space, political space (the city along with its domains), and urban space (i.e. within the city proper) … The founding image of Greek space was a space already fully formed and carefully populated; a space in which each focal point, whether that of each house or that of the polis as a whole, was ideally placed upon a well-chosen, well-situated eminence, sunlit and close to an abundant source of water. The Greek city, as a spatial and social hierarchy, utilized its meticulously defined space to bring demes, aristocratic clans, villages, and groups of craftsmen and traders together into the unity of the polis. At once means and end, at once knowledge and action, at once natural and political, this space was occupied by people and monuments. Its centre – the agora – served as focus, as gathering-place. At the highest point of the acropolis, the temple presided over and rounded out the city's spatio-temporal space.[26]

Lefebvre saw the space in a modern – capitalist – city through a dialectical triad or "three moments of social space": (1) spatial practice, or *perceived* space – a space navigated by residents in their daily routines;

(2) representations of space, or *conceived* space – the space of experts (planners, urbanists, social engineers, etc.); and (3) representational spaces, or *lived* space – the space of inhabitants who make symbolic use of the objects found in physical space.[27] Some aspects of the "perceived," the "conceived," and the "lived" will be addressed in Parts I, II, and IV of this book respectively.

Inspired by Lefebvre's comprehensive approach to space, I raise my own *historical* questions: What kind of space was produced by social groups, urban planners, and authorities in imperial Kyiv? And what kinds of sociospatial relations developed there? A wider geopolitical context should also be taken into account. Kyiv was a centre of Russia's southwestern borderlands, and its spatial setting – both natural and political – determined how space was produced *within* the city.

Kyiv began to appear in various sources as early as the ninth century, first as a crucial frontier town on important trading routes, later as the capital of a medieval patrimonial empire, then as a spiritual centre of Eastern Christianity within the Catholic orbit, still later as a cultural centre of Cossack Ukraine, and finally as a Russian imperial outpost in a largely hostile region. After the second partition of Poland in 1793, the city was reattached to its hinterland on the right bank of the Dnieper, and thus it attracted numerous Polish and Jewish newcomers.[28] Subsequently, Kyiv shared several demographic, social, and cultural patterns with other cities in the empire's western borderlands. It can also be argued, however, that strategically and symbolically, Kyiv was *the* most important of these cities. It was especially unique because the Russian political and cultural imagination viewed it as a Holy City and as the physical and spiritual bastion of Russian Orthodoxy for the entire western borderlands. This predetermined much of its urban shape and sociospatial pattern. Kyiv was an emerging imperial metropolis, but paradoxically, it was defined by its distant past, which was often mythological besides being infinitely recyclable. Modernity and the past often collided in Kyiv. Yet as the nineteenth century progressed, the city changed dramatically. Major agents of change included Russian imperial institutions, the city government, private entrepreneurs, intellectuals, and various technical experts. All of these brought change through public policies and debates, urban planning and building, technical innovations, statistical surveys, "invented traditions," research, and so on. Therefore, my goal here is to *deconstruct* traditional mythologies centred on Kyiv and at the same time to *reconstruct* changes associated with urban modernity.[29]

Was there a common pattern of modernization in Europe? Some argue that there were a few specific patterns of urban modernity, ranging from the more classical cases of Britain, Germany, and France to those of Austria-Hungary and Russia.[30] Should we perceive the developments in Eastern Europe as an aberration from normative urban modernity as it developed in Western Europe (most notably in Paris)? Or should we speak about a *Sonderweg*, a special way of the "other" Europe, in which "backwardness" and "belatedness" were norms and major cities were constantly trying to catch up with the "developed" West but always failing to do so? It is most likely that these Central and Eastern European cities developed distinct regimes of urban modernity. They were not more backward; rather, they developed slightly different modern responses to their unique historical legacies as well as to the universal challenges of modernization. According to this logic, imperial Kyiv represented a pattern of urban modernity, one that partly reflected the "normative" Western type but that was shaped more by Russian imperial urbanism and specific borderland politics. Rapid population growth, technological progress, and architecture put Kyiv in a group with Western and Central European metropolises, but at the same time, social and political factors – such as the narrowing of the municipal voting base and (especially) the dominance of conservative elements in municipal politics – set this borderland metropolis apart from many European and even major Russian cities, in which liberal and left-leaning figures were far better represented on city councils.

Another important issue I attempt to address in this book is the nature and pace of change in a city known primarily for its past and seen largely through the metaphors of antiquities and cemeteries. Cities like Kyiv have found it difficult to embrace and adapt to change, whether this involves urban renewal, modern architecture, industrialization, or technical innovations. Despite massive changes in its demography, sociospatial form, and built environment, Kyiv never became an industrial powerhouse like Moscow, Saint Petersburg, Warsaw, or Odessa. This was partly a result of its "industry of the past" – a cluster of conservative images, practices, and agents that opposed the transformation of Russia's *Holy City* into an unholy hotbed of "satanic mills." There were also various economic reasons for the city's limited industrialization.

Even so, the city grew rapidly, especially after the 1850s. For much of the century it grew thanks to the "transport-cost advantages" provided by waterborne commerce along the Dnieper River. For decades, Kyiv remained a transit centre for the grain and timber trade.[31] As Edward Glaeser has shown, many successful cities (among them Buffalo, Chicago, and New York) "grew on spots where goods had to be shifted from one form of transportation to another."[32] Similarly, Kyiv experienced a transportation and marketing revolution after the building of the first railways in 1870; one of these linked the city with Odessa via Balta on the right bank, another linked it with Kursk over the Dnieper on the left bank. Located as it was on a navigable river, Kyiv benefited greatly from the new means of transportation. After 1870 the city's waterfront, including its terminals for steamships carrying passengers and commercial goods, was linked by rail (albiet indirectly) to the agricultural hinterland. This cemented the city's role as a transshipment point for agricultural products on their way to seaports from the southwest and northeast. Also, railways and waterways carried goods through Kyiv to the German and Austro-Hungarian empires via the town of Brest.[33]

Apparently, though, Kyiv wasted some economic opportunities. First, there was no direct connection between the central railway station and the district of Podil with its busy waterfront, and this logistical failure contributed greatly to the district's demise as a commercial and residential hub. Second, the city lacked a modernized river port, which was built only in 1899, after prolonged bickering between the city and the Russian government.[34] Gradually, the railway replaced the river as a major source of the city's revenue. During the sugar boom, sugar was transported by rail, not river, thus bypassing Podil, which for centuries had been the city's commercial heart. Even so, the grain trade continued to be important to the city's commerce, benefiting Podil in particular. Grain was transported along the Dnieper and then stored in several large elevators on the riverbank. In the early twentieth century, Podil's waterfront was the site of a steam mill with a large elevator, a technically advanced enterprise owned by the Jewish entrepreneur Lazar Brodsky, one of the largest grain producers in the Russian Empire. It is hard to point to a single event that drove the city's continued growth in late imperial times; other factors besides the grain trade included the abolition of serfdom in 1861, the new strategic importance of Kyiv after the Polish uprising of January 1863, the construction of railway in 1870, and (perhaps) the restoration of municipal autonomy in 1871. That said, agricultural trade was clearly crucial. In the late nineteenth and the early twentieth centuries, the city's economy was spurred by railways and improved infrastructure, and it continued to be driven by the trade in grain and sugar, which attracted countless new migrants each year. The result was a building boom and the rapid development of the service sector (banking, insurance, legal services, etc.). All of this made Kyiv a modern and cosmopolitan metropolis on the eve of the new century.

To summarize, this book describes how urban change was anticipated, depicted, and implemented by examining literature, scholarship, sociospatial relations, urban planning, building, and public policies.[35] There are several ways to write about a modern city; the relevant topics range from imperial urbanism to interethnic struggle to public and private spaces to the "language" of architecture, to name but a few.[36] I contend that a combination of diverse themes, sources, and methods is the most rewarding way to write about the modern city. Admittedly, Kyiv cannot rival Paris or Vienna in terms of academic prominence, but I am positive that this iconic city on the Dnieper hills will proudly take its place alongside its Eastern European peers such as Thessaloniki, Odessa, Prague, Vilnius, and Lviv.

Note on spelling:

Russian	Ukrainian	Polish	English
Kiev	Kyïv	Kijów	Kyiv

Major streets and squares mentioned in the book:

Ukrainian	Russian	Present name if changed
Khreshchatyk	Kreshchatik	
Universytets'ka, 1835–7	Universitetskaia, Bol'shaia	Volodymyrs'ka
Velyka Volodymyrs'ka, 1837–69	Vladimirskaia, Desiatinn aia+Vladimirskaia+Nizhn	
Desiatynna+Volodymyrs'ka+ Nyzhnia Volodymyrs'ka, 1869–1901	ievladimirskaia Bol'shaia Vladimirskaia	
Velyka Volodymyrs'ka, 1901–22		
Velyka Vasyl'kivs'ka	Bol'shaia Vasil'kovskaia	
Oleksandrivs'ka	Aleksandrovskaia	Sahaidachnoho and Hrushevs'koho
Bibikovs'kyi boulevard	Bibikovskii boulevard	Taras Shevchenko boulevard
Mariïns'ko-Blahovishchens'ka (before Velyka and Mala Zhandarms'ka streets)	Mariinsko-Blagoveshchenskaia (before Bol'shaia and Malaia Zhandarmskaia streets)	Saksahans'koho
Mykolaïvs'ka	Nikolaevskaia	Arkhitektora Horodets'koho
Karavaevs'ka (before Shuliavs'ka)	Karavaevskaia (before Shuliavskaia)	L'va Tolstoho
Fundukleïvs'ka	Fundukleevskaia	Bohdana Khmel'nyts'koho
Sofiïvs'ka	Sofievskaia	
Khreshchatyts'ka, later Dums'ka ploshcha	Kreshchatitskaia, later Dumskaia ploshchad'	Maidan Nezalezhnosti
Mykil's'ka	Nikol'skaia	Ivana Mazepy and Lavrs'ka

PART ONE

Representing the City

Part I of this book examines travellers' accounts, journalism, and literary fiction written by Russians, Poles, Jews, and Ukrainians who resided in or visited Kyiv (in reality or imagination) during the "long" nineteenth century. By describing the city as they saw or imagined it, observers of different backgrounds and loyalties often sought to appropriate it by asserting the rights of their respective communities to Kyiv's legacy. Therefore, the treatment of Kyiv's past in travellers' accounts, private and government-sponsored research, public commemorations, and street names will also be examined. To own the past is to claim the present.

There has been almost no study of how Kyiv and its spaces – ideal, topographical, social, and ethnic – have been represented in various literary traditions. Kyiv's identity (if a city can have an "identity") was a contested space mapped differently in Russian, Polish, Ukrainian, and Jewish literatures and travel accounts. As my initial research shows,[1] by the mid-nineteenth century Kyiv had been mapped on three separate mental geographies – Polish, Russian, and Ukrainian, with Poles being the first to produce well-developed literary images of Kyiv. Poles also placed Kyiv on the mental map of the partitioned Poland as its eastern-most centre.[2] Another question to ask is how Orthodox observers – be they Russians or Ukrainians – perceived their long-time competitors, the Poles, who continued to constitute a sizeable and affluent minority in Kyiv up until 1917. The images of Kyiv's Jews in gentile literatures (Russian, Ukrainian, and Polish) will be analysed in connection with the growing anti-Semitism experienced by the local Jewish community, which culminated in the pogroms of 1881 and 1905. Representations of Kyiv had a direct bearing on the political imagination of Eastern European literati, igniting conflicts among Polish, Russian, and Ukrainian mental geographies, for they all claimed Kyiv as part of their "ideal fatherlands."[3]

Contemplating the city is an act of both *vision* and *division* (to use Pierre Bourdieu's terminology). By examining Kyiv's physical appearance, observers sought to define its features, map it within their mental geographies, and eventually appropriate it, thus symbolically dividing the space. What visitors and residents tended to notice was often predetermined by their identities and expectations. Some indeed found what they had expected to see, and others were struck by the unexpected, but for most, Kyiv presented a puzzle. Perhaps it was the political *divisions* that defined changing *visions* of Kyiv. As a result of partitions of Poland, in 1797 Kyiv returned politically to where it had belonged geographically from the time of its founding – that is, to the adjacent hinterland. In that year Kyiv became the administrative capital of a province (*gubernia*) comprising two former palatinates of the now defunct Polish–Lithuanian Commonwealth, which were situated on the right bank of the Dnieper. Kyiv became the main political, economic, and cultural centre for an entire region, today known as Right-Bank Ukraine, but then called the Southwestern Region (or *Iugo-Zapadnyi krai* in Russian).

My main goal in chapter 1 is to trace the changing visions of Kyiv as anticipations or reflections of radical divisions in social, ethnic, and physical spaces in the city during the "long" nineteenth century. I focus on representations of social, ethnic, and spatial relations in literary fiction, travellers' accounts, and journalism, reading my sources as an urban historian rather than a literary scholar. Cities can also be viewed as sites that mediate between global social processes and lived private experience.[4] It is literary sources that best reflect the "territorial imagination" – that is, how individuals think about their city, how they position themselves in space, how they relate to one another, and how they experience the city in daily life.[5]

Other important questions include these: How was the city appropriated through the *work* of vision? Did Russians, Poles, Ukrainians, and Jews have different visions of Kyiv and its spaces? What did they tend to see, and what did they chose to ignore?

Chapter 2 focuses on the scholarly study of Kyiv's antiquities. One of the first people to take up that research was the Orthodox metropolitan of Kyiv, Evgenii (Bolkhovitinov). Only after the 1830s, with the founding of Kyiv Imperial University named after St Vladimir, did studies of local urban history become consistent and professional. From that time on, Kyiv's past became increasingly contested, with Ukrainians and

Russians launching their own research enterprises, and with each claiming Kyiv's past as part of an exclusive national historical narrative. After the Polish November uprising of 1830–1, local Poles were deprived of institutional means to appropriate Kyiv's past. The city, they claimed, had become part of Poland in the eleventh century, under the King Bolesław the Brave. But the Catholic Poles lacked deep spiritual connections with the city, whereas for Orthodox Russians and Ukrainians, Kyiv was primarily the Holy City, the centre of Orthodoxy. Even so, they felt the urge to prove this through scholarly research. But even by the 1850s, Ukrainians and Russians perceived the holiness and history of Kyiv in different ways: for the former, Kyiv was a spiritual centre of Cossack Ukraine; for the latter, Kyiv was the "mother of Russian cities" and as such had to be defended against various enemies, above all Poles and Jews. In what follows I study the ways in which Russians and Ukrainians used the formula of a holy and ancient city to boost their exclusive claims to Kyiv and a surrounding region. I will also explore how a reactionary attention to the past and the defence of a conservative utopia of an ancient and holy city clashed with modernization and Kyiv's increasingly cosmopolitan demographics.

Chapter One

Mapping the City in Transition

Kyiv as an Ideal City

Town planners, builders, architects, and philosophers have been searching for an ideal city from the very beginning of urban civilization. Most
ideal cities are, however, cities on paper only.[1] Regarding those that
were actually built, the "ideal city" can refer to an urban layout, as a
"union of aesthetics and functionality," or to a skyline, as an image of
buildings on the horizon.[2] The town plan of nineteenth-century Kyiv
was far from reflecting aesthetics and functionality, so travellers had
no choice but to turn to its skyline. Well into the twentieth century, that
skyline was dominated by hills and churches rather than by factory
chimneys or functionalist structures. The first real rivals to this traditional cityscape – tall residential towers – have appeared on Kyiv's skyline only recently, in the first decade of the twenty-first century. In any
case, Kyiv may indeed have been perceived as an ideal city thanks to
its picturesque skyline and its role as the Holy City in the contemporary
Orthodox imagination.

There were at least three ways to view Kyiv as an ideal city through
the prism of its picturesque skyline. One could take in the city from afar,
enjoying a panoramic view. Or one could look at it up close, focusing
on one element (e.g., the church cupolas or the hills) and then transfer
this picturesque impression to the entire cityscape. Or one could simply *not* look – that is, not travel to the city – and instead read romantic
poems, medieval chronicles, or the lives of local saints from the comfort
of one's home.

In the nineteenth century, the picturesque churches on the green hills
along the Dnieper became widely accepted as an iconographic image

1.1 Sazhin, *A View of Kyiv from the Left Bank of the Dnieper* (image courtesy of Mystetstvo)

of Kyiv.³ The experience of this picturesque landscape could enhance the religious fervour of those who came to see the city's Orthodox holy places. Indeed, the magnificent "golden-domed" city invoked mystical feelings.⁴ Many Russian travellers experienced this visual excitement. In 1800 the sentimental traveller Vladimir Izmailov exclaimed: "A golden dome of the Caves Monastery had glittered. Here is Kiev, I said to myself, here is Kiev ... I see the amphitheater of mountains ... the seven-headed [*sedmiglavuiu*] Caves Monastery, and the Church of St. Andrew ... Indeed, it is a powerful picture!"⁵ It is worth noting that for Izmailov "the golden dome of the Caves Monastery" was a metonym for Kyiv itself. Prince Ivan M. Dolgorukii, who travelled to the city a few years later, drew a similar picture: "Kiev is situated on the hills: under it flows the Dnieper which embellishes the city's image. There is nothing more pleasant than the view from beyond the river ... The entire range of Kiev hills is full with picturesque beauty [*krasot*]."⁶

Another option was to enjoy the city from a high vantage point – be it a hill, a belfry, or any tall building.⁷ Nineteenth-century Kyiv offered plenty of natural elevations for an interested visitor, and Prince Dolgorukii chose one of the most spectacular of these: St Andrew's Hill, on which the magnificent Baroque St Andrew's Church had been built in 1754. The panoramic view of Podil district from that church stunned him: "There is nothing more beautiful than this spectacle [*zrelishche*] ... I think that in the whole of Russia there is nothing similar to it."[8] This picturesque, "unrivalled" city was also eulogized in more serious narratives dealing with the past. One of the most prominent authors of such works – Mykola Sementovs'kyi – left an ecstatic description of Kyiv in which he compared it favourably with other Russian cities: "True, Kiev is exceptionally rich in diverse picturesque sites, and there are only a few cities in our country that can compete with it. I visited almost all large cities in Russia ... but Kiev, unrivaled Kiev, is superior to them all as regards natural beauty."[9]

Those who approached the city from beyond the Dnieper could not but feel the excitement. In the words of yet another observer: "We saw Kiev; saw and got surprised at the powerful sight of a high and steep hill, on which, among numerous golden-domed churches and a town that was hardly seen from a distance, there rose a collosus of a tremendous size."[10] After contemplating "the golden cupolas of the Caves Monastery and ancient Kievan churches," the hero of a short story written in 1830 exclaimed: "'You do not know Kiev? Then I will tell you that no other Russian city makes as powerful impression on one's heart as does this city.'"[11] For the Romantics, Kyiv indeed was the city of the heart, a place legendary for its "sacred heights" and magnificent vistas.

Kyiv's visual aesthetics were also the subject of poetry – in Russian, Ukrainian, and Polish. Nineteenth-century Russian poetry knew the three recurrent *topoi* of Kyiv: the Dnieper, the hills, and the churches.[12] The city's iconographic image was explored by the great Ukrainian poet Taras Shevchenko, who in "Varnak" (The Prisoner) wrote: "I see, / As if from heaven hangs / Our great and Holy Kyiv / With holy miraculousness shine / God's temples, as if they spoke with God himself / ... / In Kyiv it's like being in Heaven."[13] The most vivid image of the ideal Kyiv was created by another Ukrainian poet, Ievhen Hrebinka, in his Russian-language prose poem *Machekha i pannochka* (A Stepmother and Young Lady):

How beautiful you are, my native Kiev! ... What the sun among the planets is, what czar among the people is, Kiev is among the cities. It stands on a high hill, surrounded by green gardens, topped by golden domes and churches' crosses as if by holy crown; under the hill, the vivid waves of the Dnieper – the feeder widely ran away ... My God, this is so beautiful.[14]

This image of an ideal/Holy City remained present in Ukrainian poetry and prose throughout the century. It suffices to turn to one of the most famous Ukrainian prose writers of all time, Ivan Nechui-Levyts'kyi (1838–1918), and his "urban" novel *Khmary* (Clouds), published in 1874. The following passage contains all possible attributes of a holy and ancient city: "Before their eyes, beyond the Dnieper, there opened up a magical, astonishingly magnificent view of Kyiv. On the high hills, everywhere there were churches and bell towers, looking just like the candles burning against the clear sun with their golden tops." The narrator then lists the usual set of Kyiv's sacral attractions, among them the Caves Monastery "shining with its golden tops and crosses like a bouquet of golden flowers." There was also the renowned Baroque Church of St Andrew, and there were the legendary medieval temples – St Michael's and St Sophia, among others. This idyllic setting was dominated by the hills, which "were as if deliberately flowered [*zakvitchani*] with green gardens and bouquets of golden-domed churches."[15] No doubt, for writers from Ukraine, this ideal city was emphatically Ukrainian, for the hills were "flowered" with churches by the "immortal Ukrainian history, as if by the hand of one great artist." All of these botanical metaphors and folkloric allusions further removed Kyiv from historical time and placed it within nature and cosmology. Anyone writing about the city could not avoid resorting to the same platitudes.

Defined by its proverbial holiness and visually dominated by its "sacred heights," this ideal city survived the advent of modernity with its agents of change – industrialization, urbanization, and the building boom, which tended to reshape skylines everywhere in the world.[16] As an example, in the early twentieth century, Aleksander Kuprin's heroes, approaching the city by train, experienced almost exactly the same vista as Vladimir Izmailov and Prince Dolgorukii one hundred years earlier. In fact, the writer, famous for his naturalistic style, resorted to Romantic clichés:

In the distance, in the pink festive fog of the sunset there shined the golden cupolas and crosses. High on the hill white slender churches seemed to swim in this colorful magical haze. Curly woods and bushes ran from above and advanced over the very ravine. And the vertical white cliff, while bathing its foot in the blue river, was completely furrowed, as if with green veins and warts, with accidental shoots. It was as though a fabulously beautiful ancient city itself was approaching the train.[17]

In Kuprin's long novel about the ills of prostitution, the above description of Kyiv's skyline seems almost out of place. Perhaps his purpose was to contrast the city he admired with the modern society he lamented.

One might think that the image of an ideal city was accessible only to the Orthodox – to Russians and Ukrainians. But one did not need to be a devout Orthodox Christian to see a beautiful, picturesque Kyiv, with its skyline dominated by the churches and crosses. Józef Ignacy Kraszewski, a prominent Polish writer of the mid-nineteenth century, wrote in his novel *Latarnia czarnoksięska* (Magic Lantern, 1843): "On the last station before Kijów, a hill dissected by road promises mountains, on which Kijów is built. It was morning when our travelers saw first a tower of the Pechery Lavra [Caves Monastery], pointed high into the sky, then golden, green, motley, glittering domes of different shapes and sizes of numerous Kijów churches."[18] Kraszewski, who in 1842 visited the famed Kyiv *kontrakty* (trade fair), wrote to his parents about "a huge and beautiful city": "The situation of Kijów on high mountains, covered with trees and huge buildings with [a] thousand golden domes by the Dnieper shore, is so very charming [*przepyszne*]. How must it look in the summer, if it is so nice in the winter ... There are many new, colossal buildings."[19] The renowned Polish writer Józef Korzeniowski, a professor at Kyiv University in the 1830s, offered another panoramic view of the city in his Romantic novel *Emeryt* (Emeritus, 1849):

On the hills above the Dnieper he saw scattered houses and [the] rising domes of numerous churches. On the right side he saw beautiful hills covered with the most diverse forest, through the leaves of which ... there were visible, from a distance, [the] white walls of the Vydubychi monastery. Right in front of him he saw a mass of ever rising fortress walls, among which the tower of Lavra soared a hundred and something meters above the ground, glittering from afar in this height with the golden cover of its roof and the shining cross on it. [20]

Besides this panoramic, picturesque Kyiv, which was accessible to all, whatever their confessional loyalty, there was another facet of the ideal city, at times not so benign. A literary scholar has referred to it as Kyiv's "semantic and ideological" function.[21] At the level of myth, Kyiv was perceived as the Holy City;[22] ideologically, in addition, it was seen as the centre of Russian Orthodoxy. In the late eighteenth century and the first decades of the nineteenth, Russians came to view Kyiv as a prime destination for Orthodox pilgrims.[23] For Ukrainians *and* Russians, Kyiv was much more than a picturesque city: it was the "cradle of our faith."[24] Prince Dolgorukii asked rhetorically: "Where else does Faith more convincingly show its glory than in Kiev? It is here where the crowds of martyrs inundated [*orosili*] with their blood the entire land."[25] In Kyiv, "our ancestors received an initial idea of the almighty Creator."[26] For all Orthodox writers, be they Russian or Ukrainian, Kyiv was *the* Holy City, "our new Zion."[27]

Thus Kyiv played a powerful transformative role in the imagination of Orthodox authors, as the threshold of heaven on earth and as a place to begin a new and purer life. In the late 1850s an imaginative traveller described his own mystical transformation as he approached the city: "As I approached Kiev I felt as if I was crossing over to another world; the air itself seemed to have changed; the infinite grace of God was spreading around me."[28] Kyiv's power to transform lives touched wrongdoers as well: the city was often imagined as a place where one could repent one's sins or crimes – so much so that in the early nineteenth century, exile to the city's holy places could substitute for actual imprisonment.[29] In "Varnak," Taras Shevchenko brilliantly expressed this faith in the transformative power of Kyiv's holy places. The poem's hero, a thief and a murderer, after seeing Holy Kyiv and hearing its church bells, chooses to repent: "As if he were born anew [...] / He looked around himself / And, crossing himself / Went quietly to Kyiv / To pray to the Saints, / And for a trial, a human trial / To ask from humans."[30] Similarly, in the chilling tale "Strashnaia mest" (A Dreadful Vengeance), Gogol tells of a repentant sorcerer who rushes to Kyiv's holy places demanding that a monk pray for his soul.[31]

Poles did not necessarily share with the Orthodox their mystical belief in the city, but they accepted that Kyiv/Kijów was the cradle of Christianity in Rus' and its "holy city." Thus, Korzeniowski mentioned Khreshchatyk spring as a place where "Rus' was baptized [*Ruś chrzest przyjęła*]."[32] Kraszewski described the Caves Monastery as the "Jerusalem of Rus [*Jeruzalem Rusi*] [to which] so many devout pilgrims were driven for centuries, in order to kiss the feet of the saints resting in peace there."[33] Even a Catholic priest who travelled to Kyiv in 1840 called the Caves Monastery the "Capitolium of Kijów."[34] This was a flattering metaphor, if not a completely Christian one.

Kyiv's "holy" function had direct political implications aimed at curbing Polish cultural and social influence in the city and in all of Right-Bank Ukraine (the Southwestern Region). By the 1830s, Kyiv was firmly fixed on the mental maps of the empire's subjects as a fount of Russian Orthodoxy. Perhaps this was a response to the growing Polish presence in Kyiv and the region. In 1837, Mykhailo Maksymovych, a Ukrainian loyal to the empire and a professor of Russian literature at Kyiv University, envisioned Kyiv as the centre of Orthodoxy, alongside Moscow as the centre of Nationality and Saint Petersburg as the centre of Autocracy; this reflected the notorious ideological formula "Autocracy, Orthodoxy, Nationality" as set out by Russia's education minister, Sergei Uvarov.[35] The trope of Kyiv as the Holy *Russian* City, with its strong anti-Polish implications, can be found in its most condensed form in Aleksei Khomiakov's signature poem "Kiev" (1839). For Khomiakov, ancient Kyiv was "the cradle of Russian glory" and "the baptismal font [*kupel'*] of Rus'." Kyiv was symbolically important as Russia's "east," a metaphor that highlighted the Orthodox holiness of the city. The poet also emphasized that Kyiv was the principal destination of Orthodox pilgrims, one that attracted "a host of praying children" from "remote countries," from "unknown steppes," and from "deep northern rivers." He also accused Poles of "burning" and "seducing" Galicia and Volhynia – lands that had once been Orthodox – and he called upon Kyiv to intervene in the fate of its "fallen children." Here, poetry was serving as a geopolitical weapon.

As the century unfolded, pious Russian patriots increasingly turned the trope of the Holy City against Poles and Jews. In the early 1860s, one author posed this rhetorical question: "How can people who are totally alien to Kiev, unconnected to it by any patriotic memories, whose hearts have never beat fast at the sound of the Lavra's bell, ringing in the depths of the caves ... hope to master Kiev? Its name and memory are alien to those who do not carry the name Russian."[36] Natan Meir assumes correctly that in the quoted text, the term "alien" (*chuzhie*) refers to both Poles and Jews. In the 1870s, Andrei Muraviev – arguably *the* expert on Kyiv's sacred places – linked the issue of preserving Kyiv's sacred monuments to that of the Jewish commercial presence, which he contended was detrimental to the spirituality of local Christians.[37]

Besides being repressive with regard to non-Orthodox and non-Christians (especially Poles and Jews), the formula of the Holy City, when confronted with Kyiv's urban reality, often fostered feelings of disappointment (as will be shown below). This formula partly explains why, for many educated Russians and Ukrainians, Kyiv was more a symbol than an actual place.[38]

The Real Kyiv versus the Ideal: The Mud, the Trade Fair, and the Poles

Reality can disappoint. Real Kyiv often meant ever-present mud, a chaotic street plan, a sea of wooden huts, a dearth of antiquities, and the presence of Poles (if you were Russian), the presence of Russians (if you were a Pole), or the presence of Jews (if you were Russian, Ukrainian, or Polish).

As travellers approached Kyiv, the spatial and cultural distance that enabled them to enjoy the picturesque/Holy City gave way to many unpleasant realities. They began to notice a great many unpleasant things that clashed with the ideal city. The contrasts between the idealized panoramic view and the real city could be jarring: "The city was so remarkable because it presented contrasts everywhere – poverty and luxury, its countless temples with golden, heat-shimmering [*goriashchimi*] domes were surrounded by low huts that were hardly visible above the surface," wrote Russian memoirist Baron Vigel', who grew up in Kyiv at the turn of the nineteenth century.[39] Vladimir Izmailov wrote around 1800 that in Kyiv "there are no brick buildings, no order in structure, no regularity, and [no] architecture." In addition, "the streets are unpaved, covered in sand."[40] Another observer commented that all fascination with Kyiv disappeared as soon as one entered the "shabby town."[41] It seems that the contrasts had not disappeared by 1830:

> The outscirts of the city are curious, impressive, and charming if one sees them either from the fortress hill or from the main square, or from St. Andrew's mountain. Despite this, I must confess that Kiev's interior disappointed me. There are a number of wretched, half-ruined huts in the districts of Podil, Old Kiev, and Kreshchatik … When deprived of its illustrious cathedrals, monasteries, buildings within the fortress, the administrative quarter, gymnasia, and a couple of dozens of private houses, Kiev [is] a shabby city.[42]

According to Larry Wolff, these striking contrasts pointed to a city – indeed, a whole country – that was stuck somewhere between civilization and barbarity, between Europe/West and Asia/East (hence the very concept of Eastern Europe).[43] This same mental scheme proved quite handy for those who sought to define Kyiv's geographical (or rather *quasi*-geographical) situation, for it was not actual geography but rather Kyiv's perceived historical and cultural identity that defined the city's location on the map. Many observers – Orthodox and Catholic alike – viewed Kyiv as a frontier town on the border between two conflicting worlds – Russian Orthodox (Eastern) and Polish Catholic (Western). But as long as the imagination of these observers was dominated by the image of the "holy and blessed city of Kyiv," or at least by a historical myth of Kyiv as *the* place where Rus' was baptized, Kyiv almost by default belonged more to the East than to the West, these latter categories themselves belonging to religious topography.

This omnipresent understanding of Kyiv as a mythical city only heightened the contrast with the actual city. A prominent element of this "shabby" city was mud (or dust in the summer), which was an ever-present topic in many accounts of Kyiv until the very end of the nineteenth century. "[With] the smallest rain or thaw there is an impenetrable mud, while the dust in the summer is intolerable," wrote a man who accompanied Empress Catherine II on her visit to Kyiv.[44] As late as 1837, professors at Kyiv University were complaining about the awful, "indescribable mud," which could almost never be avoided. The mud made it nearly impossible to cross Kyiv's streets on foot in the spring and fall, and sometimes most of the winter, and in the summer as well after a heavy rain.[45] Mykola (Nikolai) Kostomarov, a prominent Slavic scholar and Ukrainophile, strongly supported the view that Kyiv was an awkward, muddy, and poorly planned city, especially compared to Kharkiv, where he had studied:

> [The district of] Pechersk was the center of trade activity; in the district that was now part of the fortress were the rows of shops most frequented by the public. The university stood almost in the countryside, among slopes and sand hills that were hard to cross. The Old City was unpaved, filled with ugly shops and huts, and also contained large empty lots. Kreshchatik did not have back then either shops or stores, nor hotels. Most buildings were wooden, there were no paved roads, and during precipitation there was a deep mud and slush. The banks of the Dnieper in Podol by the mountain were literally impossible to cross … The city had a poor lighting so that night walks were a true trial.[46]

And of course, the mud was even more striking when juxtaposed with the picturesque churches and holy sites of Kyiv.

Kyiv did not *look* like a city. Indeed, Catherine II could not see a *city* there; instead she found herself trapped in what resembled a series of suburbs.[47] Traditionally, Kyiv had three parts, which in the first decades of the nineteenth century could still be viewed as three separate towns. These were Old Kyiv (Upper Town), Pechers'k (with the Caves Monastery), and Podil (or Lower Town).[48] To these, later observers would add so-called New Kyiv, a rapidly expanding district around the new university (inaugurated in 1843).[49] The problem was that the three traditional parts were so poorly connected that travellers (like Catherine II) even denied Kyiv the name of a city, as did Vladimir Izmailov around 1800: "It seems that you see three different settlements. I say settlements because the entire Kiev harldy deserves the name of a city."[50] More than four decades later, the already quoted Kostomarov seemed to agree with these earlier opinions.

With all this abundance of Russian and Ukrainain travel narratives and memoirs about Kyiv, it seems surprising that the real Kyiv – that is, its actual urban space (not only the mud) – became an object of literary attention for Russian and Ukrainian writers only towards the end of the nineteenth century.[51] Even more surprising is that Kyiv as a modern urban experience was first mapped in the *Polish* literary consciousness. In novels of Kraszewski and Korzeniowski, the heroes move to and live in Kyiv, visit friends, conduct business, and have love affairs, all in a topographically *real* city. For example, Kraszewski describes his hero August moving through the city from the Upper to the Lower Town (Podil):

August from afar pointed to the more remarkable [churches] for Stas: St Sophia Cathedral, St Andrew's Church, churches of St. Nicholas, St. Michael … a building of a Catholic church, full of humility, struck their eyes … Behind it, rows of trees rose up, with a wide street, densely packed houses, buildings, and churches – Pechers'k district, a second city after Podil but rather the only city during the year … On the right was the Old Kijów, that famous ruin of the Golden Gate, small houses attached to the deep ravine, farther in the valley was the Khreshchatyk, farther away were the domes of St Sophia Cathedral, famous for its mosaics and Iaroslav's tomb.[52]

Kraszewski also brilliantly described Kyivites – their appearance, their homes, and especially the district of Podil.[53] His literary contemporary Korzeniowski, too, through the eyes of his hero, *pan* Roman, offered a picture of Kyiv's districts and attractions, such as the

1.2 Sazhin, *A View of Podil from St Andrew's Hill* (image courtesy of Mystetstvo)

Vydubychi Monastery, the Pechers'k district, the aristocratic quarter of Lypky (an "elegant part of the town"), and the university quarter, at the time "an open field" to which the yards and small houses of a growing city were attached. His detailed description of Podil[54] was the first of its kind in modern literary fiction:

> From a long, sloping and paved street linking Podil with Khreshchatyk and Pechers'k, one goes to a big square called the square of Samson. From there, to all sides, even, wide enough streets spread out, with more-than-one-storey brick houses built closer to the square. Then there are small wooden houses, which almost all have similar shapes and same sizes … In the very middle of the square there is a large assembly of stores, sort of a trading court.[55]

He tells his readers that Podil was the "pantry of the entire city," a neighbourhood where "from time to time boils trade and where beginning in mid-January rumbles the trade fair [*kontrakty*]." His descriptions of Kyiv and its districts are almost photographic, from a distant view to a series of close-ups that point to striking contrasts in a generally picturesque setting:

> This totality slowly ... gave way to a number of details as *pan* Roman entered the city and noticed nearby the large government buildings, small wooden houses, the streets ... wide and straight but some unpaved and some having more fences than houses. Yet all these shortcomings were compensated by the view of the fortress, by the arsenal's beautiful building that appeared from behind the moats, by Lavra's golden domes ... by the crosses of seven lesser churches that seemed to have gathered under the protection of mother Lavra, but first of all by the Dnieper ... shining ... wide and blue as a sky ribbon ... [that] quietly and conscious of its force and usefulness flows majestically and rubs proudly against the banks that it feeds and embellishes.[56]

Korzeniowski's urban topography is so precise that he even mentions a hotel on a particular street (Borysoglebska, in Podil), where Krystyna, *pan* Roman's love interest, is staying.[57] His Polish characters navigate Kyiv's spaces with ease, as if the city were indeed *theirs*, despite the presence of Russian authorities and merchants. Polish writers often described Kyiv's sociospatial form as a conglomeration of Polish landlords, Russian merchants and carters, and "Ruthenian" townspeople. They also presented the city's public space as a site of interethnic competition between Poles and Russians. For example, the Catholic priest Chołoniewski proudly described the "victory" of Poles over Russians on Kyiv's streets on the occasion of the emperor's visit to Kyiv. He was especially happy that Polish carriages outnumbered Russian ones.[58] Horsemen, most of them Poles, were aware of their numerical advantage and seemed to congratulate one another proudly on their victory. The same street traffic during Kyiv's celebrated trade fair – the *kontrakty* – with the visible presence of Poles, is also described by Korzeniowski.[59] At the time of the *kontrakty*, perceptive observers saw socio-economic relations, spatial pattern, and moral order as intrinsically linked:

> On 10 January began an unusual commotion on the streets of Podil; and the bells of Krakow horse collars rang ... Each day the sound of a whip became more frequent, a whip that clapped over the heads of five brave grey horses or four bay or dappled horses; a whip which gladdened the

hearts of homeowners as an echo heralding the ducats ... Each day more
and more six-horse carriages set on sledges carried grave-looking mothers
with their marriageable daughters; or tasteful sledges in a form of carriages, landaus, or carts if they belonged to young, elegant women, who
used them for making visits; or huge sledges with leather booths from
within which one could see the unkempt mustaches of a noble capitalist,
who sat on a bale of receipts and bills of exchange while keeping his feet
on a fitted casket full of ducats and banknotes: all of them passed under
the windows of *pan* Roman. Amidst these heavier carriages were lighter
sledges of husbands, who had managed to convince their wives to stay at
home and who thus went alone.[60]

Kyiv, then, was a place where the new capitalist economy, conspicuous consumption, romantic affairs, and vanity all mingled, at least in
January. Kyiv fair was a true vanity fair. During the fair, the image took
hold of a noisy multiethnic crowd: one could hear "curses in different languages, solid conversations in Russian, noisier intimations in
Polish about business, German and Jewish muttering, Turkish whis-
pers, Transcaucasian screeching, Armenian nasal murmurs, and Tatar
gesticulations." Like Chołoniewski, Korzeniewski described in bright
colours the Polish and Russian carriers as they made their way from
Pechers'k to Podil ("Samson's Square"), shouting in Polish and Russian
as if competing with one another. Like many other Polish visitors to the
city in January, the hero of Korzeniowski's novel, *pan* Roman, was mixing romance and business, a combination that Balzac explored so masterfully in his novels about bourgeois Paris. In that proverbial capital
of modernity, an obsession with money rendered literary protagonists
increasingly incapable of intimacy. Something similar happens in the
Kyiv of Korzeniowski's novel, whose real hero is neither *pan* Roman
nor his beloved Krystyna. Rather, it is the trade fair itself, which drains
people of money, emotions, morality, and sexual desire. Not surprisingly, *pan* Roman, although he spends most of his time in Kyiv with
Krystyna (shopping, concert going, partying), does not marry her in
the end: the *kontrakty* proves fatal for their relationship, deceiving their
feelings and separating them in the end.

  Although he moves about freely in Kyiv's physical space, *pan* Roman
feels alienated from the city, especially from its higher social echelons.
The space itself rejects a Polish Romantic intruder. He walks alone down
Kyiv's streets: the city's high society consists of "people of different
habits, different language"; the city is "a purely Ruthenian [*ruskie*] city"

in which, surprisingly, the upper classes do not differ from the lower.[61] Yet the author (through his hero) "admired the character of the nation that despite such a long subordination to the neighboring state [Poland or possibly Muscovy-Russia] has preserved its native mark and has not erased a baptismal cross from its forehead."[62] Korzeniowski also reveals his knowledge of Kyiv's recent history as a self-governing Ukrainian town. When describing the renowned *Kontraktowy* (Contract) House, he mentions the last of Kyiv's elected mayors, Hryhorii Kyselevs'kyi, and the city festivities known as the "Makovii" (Maccabee), a solemn civic ceremony during which burgers dressed in *"kontusz* [ceremonial costumes], with swords, on horses and by foot," walk through Podil as the municipal guard.[63] Yet most other Polish descriptions of Kyiv focus less on Ukrainian images than on its new "Russian" features, represented predominantly by merchants and officials.[64]

Kyiv's trade fair attracted a few thousand visitors each year,[65] including Poles, Jews, and Ukrainians, but also Russians. Most of the latter came to Kyiv to see the sights. This became a sort of ritual for every educated Russian; and all the while, commoners visited Kyiv's holy places as pilgrims. In contrast, Poles visited Kyiv mainly during the *kontrakty*. The best literary descriptions of mid-nineteenth-century Kyiv were written by Korzeniowski and Kraszewski, both of whom visited during the fair. The inauguration of this "Polish fair" in 1798 considerably enriched the city. V.H. Anastasevych, a Kyivite, commented in 1801 that

> Kiev has greatly improved in terms of its buildings for the last four years, especially due to the transfer of the Polish "kontrakty" there from a town of Dubny, for which a brick house was built quite well ... "Kontrakty" occur on the eve of the holiday of Epiphany [*trzech królów*]. The gathering on this occasion can be very big, from all over Poland, and many foreign traders come with different goods.[66]

Prince Dolgorukii reported that the transfer of the fair to Kyiv had improved the city considerably, having "increased the beauty of the city and facilitated its renovation."[67] While Kyiv's broad streets seemed almost empty in the summer, in the winter during the fair "it is difficult to walk on the streets due to the flood of people walking and riding." So wrote Polish noblewoman Henrieta "z Dzialyńskich" Błędowska.[68]

Many Polish noble families, among them the Działyńskis, attended the *kontrakty* every year to conduct real estate business during the day and to attend concerts, balls, masquerades, and theatrical performances at night.[69] To be sure, Kyiv's fair was above all a highly intense business event where landlords sold, mortgaged, and purchased real estate and serfs – something that was brilliantly grasped by Polish dramatist Karol Drzewiecki. One of his heroes noted that the "kontrakty is [the time] when everybody's hands strike ten deals a day."[70] Kyiv's fair was criticized by some observers as a site of speculations, crooked deals, and risks: "So many violent emotions, tears, and impressions are contained in the very word *kontrakty*, so many miseries and guilts ... So many screams, cries, and gnashing of teeth [*zgrzytania zębów*] that one can hear everywhere upon the mere mention of the *kontrakty*."[71] Another Polish observer wrote about the "artificial concerns" among nobles before their journey to the Kyiv fair.[72]

But the *kontrakty* meant many other things besides business, such as gambling, shopping, marriage arrangements, literary gatherings, entertainments, love affairs, and sightseeing, some of which were as risky as the business deals themselves. This was the only time of the year that Kyiv became a solidly Polish city; as Prince Dolgorukii put it, "Poles come in hordes from everywhere for their sales, exchanges, rents, and pay-offs. Piles of gold slip out of their pockets; I saw those houses, which bring unbelievable revenue to their landlords."[73] It was not by chance that among the crowds at the *kontrakty*, Poles were the most visible: "Covered in an overcoat, in a tam there walks a magnate of an old Poland ... Then the scene changes in a moment, the music pounds and charming Polish ladies are dancing magically a mazurka."[74]

For many casual visitors the Kyiv trade fair offered an opportunity to "refresh oneself" while milling among the crowds. Korzeniowski's heroine, Krystyna, "looked for entertainment outside the home,"[75] while Karlgof's Russian officer "wanted to refresh himself ... in a whirl of Kiev's *kontrakty*."[76] Kraszewski pointed to the entertainment associated with the fair: "One spends the entire time of the *kontrakty* on entertainment, musical evenings, reasonable gambling in a whist only, readings, literary discussions etc. ... Even those who do business have free evenings for concerts, theater, and friendly entertainment."[77] Polish writers paid particular attention to the multiethnic crowd, in which could be heard Polish, Russian, German, Yiddish, Turkish, Armenian, and so on,[78] but mainly one saw "a mass of [Polish] noble faces."[79] Observers well realized that the *kontrakty* were mainly Polish in character, as was the entire city in January.

The main cultural purpose of the Kyiv fair was to spread Polish culture throughout the southwestern Russia and among Poles all over the empire. The Polish memoirist Józef Drzewiecki assessed the fair's role in terms of the distribution of Polish books: "From the *kontrakty* there came to our neighborhood a number of Polish books: if eyes allowed, it would have been possible to spend a whole year reading them ... which is all the more surprising because this occurred when [the Polish] language itself had no particular help for its development."[80] Juliusz Słowacki in 1832 sought a way to transport more than sixty copies of his latest work to a book fair in Kyiv.[81] Korzeniowski wrote that buying books at the fair was seen as "proper style" among Polish nobles.[82] Kraszewski confirmed that at the Kyiv fair, "even if a lot of dry candies are sold, so too are many books."[83] Finally, and perhaps most importantly, Kyiv's fair in the 1830s and 1840s was one of the main gathering places for Polish writers alongside Warsaw, Vilnius, and Krakow.

Kraszewski visited the *kontrakty* in 1842 and enjoyed the company of other prominent literati, such as Michał Grabowski and Henryk Rzewuski: "There were quite a lot of us, such lords-literati ... Thus we spent the *kontrakty* at readings, talks, debates, dinners, and breakfasts."[84] Kraszewski was considered a rising star of Polish literature. "I was received better than I deserved," he wrote in a letter. "Everybody wanted to get acqainted with me, dinners after dinners, evenings after evenings, toasts after toasts etc. – my entire time was filled." He even arranged a reading from his newest novel *Mindaugas* (Mindows) for a selected audience.[85]

The Polish cultural milieu in Kyiv was not limited to three weeks of January; it flourished there throughout the year. Polish writers were able to map the *real* Kyiv before their Russian and Ukrainian counterparts because, for Poles, the city was a vivid urban experience. Poles were Kyiv's first *flâneurs*. The *kontrakty* showcased Kyiv as a *multiethnic* imperial metropolis, but it was the Poles who dominated the city economically, socially, and not least culturally. For many decades of the nineteenth century, the *kontrakty* was the most prominent symbol of change in Kyiv, and of modernity itself, for it brought together its various forces such as the capitalist economy, new forms of leisure, conspicuous consumption, and sightseeing, to say nothing of an unprecedented mixture of ethnicities and races. During those decades, Kyiv's public space mixed genders, classes, and ethnicities into a truly complex society in which Poles and Jews were the most visible minorities. Images of the *kontrakty*, of the Poles, and of the Jews were the most tangible antidote to the Holy Orthodox City. Indeed, many Orthodox felt that *their* city was being threatened by the alien intruders. Not surprisingly, most Russian and Ukrainian literati looked at Kyiv through the prism of its holiness, its myths, and its ideological functions. For these Orthodox observers, the holy places, the *ideal* city, concealed the *real* city. Whenever they looked past that mantle of holiness, they were disappointed. They could not enjoy the city as did the *flâneurs*. Many simply could not acknowledge the reality of Kyiv as an ordinary town filled with "aliens," hawkers, beggars, and prostitutes. It would be several decades before Russians and Ukrainians learned to admire the city for what it really was or was about to become: a city of contrasts and complexity filled with the signs of imminent modernity.

"Russian Officials and Polish Landlords": Kyivites under the Romantic Gaze

Who actually lived in this city-in-transition? How did Russian, Ukrainian, and Polish writers describe Kyiv's demographics in travelogues, literary fiction, and memoirs? Perhaps the most striking feature of many Russian and Polish texts from the first decades of the nineteenth century was that they almost completely ignored Kyiv's Ukrainians. That much is clear in Izmailov's celebrated travelogue, in which he stripped Kyivites of their ethnic peculiarities. When he described Kyivites around 1800, he did not attribute to them any ethnic categories at all, instead emphasizing their patriarchal, "natural" and somewhat primitive traits. Compared to the people of Moscow, Kyivites were only beginning to overcome their backwardness. He did not mention the Polish presence in Kyiv, and he applied the term *Little Russians* only to peasants from the nearby countryside.

Yet at the time, Ukrainians were a strong presence in the city. True, in the late eighteenth and early nineteenth centuries Kyiv's upper class began to change its ethnic profile. The city's elite, hitherto solidly Ukrainian, now added many Polish and Russian names to its ranks as more and more Polish nobles and cosmopolitan aristocrats migrated to Kyiv from neighbouring localities and from abroad.[86] Baron Vigel', himself a Russian of Finnish descent, gave a colourful account of 1811–12 in which he described the open house of the Ukrainian-speaking noblewoman Iuliia Veselyts'ka. She reportedly attracted to her salons the city's Ukrainian *and* Russian elites: "in her home all Kiev was seen."[87]

Prince Dolgorukii, a famous Russian traveller, noted the city's complex demographics. On his two visits to the city, in 1810 and 1817, Kyivites struck him as "sort of foreigners." In Kyiv, he and his Russian friends felt like expatriates, far from their motherland and lacking any ties with the locals.[88] Dolgorukii confessed that he could not understand the Ukrainian language and thus found himself outside the borders of his "native country."[89] In his Kyiv narrative, Poles appeared only in connection with the *kontrakty*, although he constantly noticed Poles among the inhabitants of Kyiv *gubernia*, which was "filled with all kinds of folk": "there are Poles, Little Russians, and Russians in it."[90]

Russians often viewed Kyiv through the prism of social stereotypes. The poet Aleksei Griboedov reported in 1825 that Kyiv consisted of "Russian officials and Polish landlords"[91] – an image applied, obviously, to city's upper classes. This social divide pointed to a broader cultural divide, one that would often appear in Russian accounts. For example, Aleksei Khomiakov, another poet, in 1839 imagined Kyiv as a "frontier" town situated between the Polish Catholic and Russian Orthodox civilizations.[92] Thus, Kyiv became an important prize in the game led by Russian Orthodox crusaders. Even so, Russians did not always seem confident about the "Russianness" of Kyiv; they had to reassure themselves that Kyiv was indeed a Russian city, like the heroes of Vilgelm Karlgof's short story: "'Count – this is Kiev, this is a Russian city, does not your heart beat?' […] 'True,' responded the Count, 'it is reassuring to see after the fierce days of war a Russian city.'"[93] But as we will see, even for the heroes of this short story, Kyiv was not a completely Russian city.

Some Orthodox observers, both Russian and Ukrainian, were struck by the presence of Poles in the late 1830s, when the authorities uncovered a Polish "conspiracy" among Kyiv University students. Poles were jarringly alien to the iconographic image of Kyiv cultivated by generations of Orthodox observers. Mykhailo Maksymovych, a professor at Kyiv University who was born in Left-Bank Ukraine, found himself in a city "where there are so many Poles";[94] and Innokentii, the rector of the Kyiv Academy and an ethnic Russian, admitted that while Kyiv was "the mother of Russian cities," due to the spirit of its inhabitants Kyiv was hardly suited to be even Russia's stepmother as long as its population remained mixed. With a population consisting of "a mixture of Russia, Poland, and Little Russia how can one be filled here with Russian spirit?"[95] As late as the 1850s, Kyiv's mixed population astonished observers, who could not define the city's identity. Ivan Serdiukov, a local observer, commented that Kyiv was a "mixed" city: "scholarly" due to its university, "holy" due to its monasteries, "military" due to its fortress, and "commercial" due to its river port. In terms of nationalities, the city seemed quite diverse, consisting of Poles, Little Russians, Jews, and Russians, all of whom dressed differently. He also noticed Polish cliques among the nobles and students, who regarded "all Russians with condescension."[96]

But it was the presence of Poles in Kyiv that most distressed tourists from Moscow and Saint Petersburg. The botanist Stepan Maslov visited Kyiv in 1839 and left a shocking account: Kyiv, it seemed to him, was a *Polish* city in which only Orthodox holy places testified to the presence of Russians:

> The mixing of Poles with Russians seemed quite strange to me; even on walks it was noticable that among them there was not yet uniformity. Generally, Kiev in its civil life reflects Polish mores: here there is a Polish [rider] with spurs, one coachman with a whip without a *foreitor* steers four horses, with the long reins connected only to the forward [horses]. Among the citizens one more often hears Polish than Russian language. If it were not for the fact that Kiev was a Russian holy place whose holiness dominated in it and attracted the hearts of Russians, then it would have been simply a city conquered from Poland. But the remnants of the Saints, the magnificent Lavra, and God's temples so much occupied the minds of those who came here for pilgrimage that no one pays any attention to the fortress walls, Polish mores, a single Catholic church, and a house for the *kontrakty*. All this seems to be secondary, tiny. The real might of Kiev is its religious holiness that attracts to itself the hearts of all Russians.[97]

Count Buturlin, a Russian aristocrat who lived in Kyiv from 1834 to 1836, left a no less striking picture of the interactions among Polish, Russian, and Ukrainian aristocrats, much like Vigel's account of Veselyts'ka's house. Buturlin's saw Kyiv as an international salon hosted or attended by Poles such as Count Tyszkiewicz, Maurycy Poniatowski, Count Gustaw Olizar, and the legendary beauty Countess Ewelina Hańska, the "star of the Polish and of the entire society of Kiev"[98] and a future wife of Balzac. Buturlin added that the "Polish element got along well, as a rare exception, with the Russian one in Kiev's high society."[99] Another Russian aristocrat, the prominent Decembrist Prince S.G. Volkonskii, recounted the revolutionary contacts between Russian and Polish nobles during the Kyiv fair on the eve of the Decembrist uprising of 1825.[100]

Only rarely did Russians pay attention to Ukrainians in contemporary Kyiv.[101] And some were quite disappointed by what they saw. For example, Karlgof's hero recognized that there was only "young life" in Kyiv and that the songs of Kyiv's women had nothing to do with "thoughts and feelings of Old Rus'." In their habits, "everything reminds [one] of Poland and Magdeburg laws."[102] This quasi-Ukrainian image of Kyiv resurfaced with much more clarity in Pushkin's "Husar," a Romantic poem imbued with Gogol-like clichés, such as Ukrainian traditional foods and "black eyebrowed" beauties who sometimes turned out to be witches: "Kiev is another thing! It's such a land! / The dumplings fall [by] themselves in[to the] mouth, / The wine is abundant, / And young girl[s] are young indeed! / It is worth giving up a soul / For the look of a black-eyebrow beauty."[103]

Andrei Muraviev, a leading expert in Orthodox antiquities, noticed and indeed enjoyed the picturesque images of Ukrainians in Kyiv – an attitude rare among Russians. In his account of Kyiv (1844), he linked poetic images of old princes to those of Zaporozhian Cossacks and contemporary Ukrainians.[104] Thus, a nineteenth-century Dnieper fisherman sang not about the heroic deeds of Old Rus' princes but about Cossacks and their wars against the Poles: "These are the two epochs, separated by centuries, but united here in one voice of a fisherman and a river!"[105] He compared Kyiv's Ukrainians with the Arabs of Palestine and called ancient Kyiv "our Zion"; his imagination even carried him to Jerusalem.[106] But not until 1882 did a topographically real Kyiv of the 1840s and 1850s, with strong Ukrainian connotations, appear in Russian literature; this was through Nikolai Leskov's literary output (analysed later in this chapter).[107]

For Ukrainians, Kyiv was undoubtedly Ukrainian,[108] ancient, and holy (the two last characteristics they shared with Russians). For Shevchenko, Kyiv was "our beautiful Kyiv"; for Gogol, Kyiv was "ours," not "theirs" (i.e., not Russian) and was linked to "our old days."[109] These writers associated Kyiv with smells, nature, and a distinct cuisine: Gogol even imagined which fruits were sold in the Kyiv market.[110] Gogol voiced his impressions even though he lacked any concrete knowledge of the city; later, he asked his friend and compatriot Maksymovych to describe what Kyiv and Kyivites actually looked like: "Please, write me more substantially about Kiev ... what kind of a city it is and [what] populace [is] living there: officers, Poles, our scholarly folk, trading women, and monks."[111] Note that Gogol grasped the city's diverse demographics, again despite lacking first-hand knowledge of the city. In 1834 he actually planned to buy a house with a garden and settle down in Kyiv as a professor of world history.[112] At the time, the young writer was actively rediscovering his Ukrainian background, and Kyiv was right in the heart of his native country.[113]

By interesting coincidence, in 1832 the great Polish Romantic Juliusz Słowacki also planned to settle in Kyiv with his mother and uncle, calling it "a cheap and nice city."[114] His famous contemporary, Kraszewski, in 1835 also planned to settle there as a professor of Polish literature at Kyiv University.[115] The following year, he even won a job competition, but he was not appointed due to his reputation for being politically suspect.[116] After 1834, with the founding of Kyiv University, the city became for Poles an educational centre. Noble parents sent their children there, or they moved there themselves, "for the education of a son."[117]

But after Kyiv University was founded, for many Poles the city did not become more Polish and did not replace the abolished Polish lycée in Kremenets'. Gustaw Olizar, a prominent Polish landowner, put it sarcastically: "with unheard arrogance we were told that Charków and Kijów are the same as Wilna and Krzemieniec for the use of the same citizens."[118] Kyiv's identity was hard to define, however. It was neither Polish nor an "arch-Russian city" (*arcy-moskiewskie miasto*). As an elected leader (*marszałek*) of the Kyiv provincial nobles, Olizar referred to Kyiv as "our capital," although he also admitted that before the 1830s there had been no significant Polish community in the city.[119] For Kraszewski, Kyiv was not a traditional Polish town like Zhytomyr, because the city lacked Jews, who "make a city Polish."[120] Kyiv was a gathering place for Polish nobles from all over the Southwestern Region, but for many Poles it was above all the headquarters of repressive Russian authorities and even a place of exile and imprisonment.[121] Nevertheless, Polish émigrés, such as the democrat Jan Czyński, who lobbied for the rights of Polish urban dwellers, included Kyiv on his list of prominent *Polish* cities, a list that also included Warsaw, Vilnius, Cracow, and Poznań.[122]

For many Russians and for some Ukrainians, Kyiv was a predominantly Polish city, yet for Poles it was predominantly a Russian city, a place where Poles could "overwhelm" Russians only on particular occasions, like the Kyiv fair, the arrival of the Russian emperor, or state festivities at which Polish nobles arrived en masse (and even on these occasions, Polish polite society was incomplete due to the lack of Polish noblewomen resident in the city[123]). The Catholic priest Chołoniewski proudly described the "victory" of Poles over Russians on Kyiv's streets on the occasion of the emperor's visit to Kyiv.[124] Korzeniowski described the same street traffic during the Kyiv fair, including the visible presence of Poles.[125] But for his hero, *pan* Roman, Kyiv was "a purely Russian city."[126] It seems that Korzeniowski did not separate the Ukrainian majority from the Russian ruling minority. Aside from recognizing a distinct municipal tradition, Polish descriptions of Kyiv's population focused mainly on its "Russian" features, which could be found primarily among merchants and shopowners from Pechers'k.[127]

In his prose, Kraszewski cast Kyiv's inhabitants and their homes, as well as the city's churches, in eclectic, glittering, and even kitschy colours that had Oriental connotations: regarding homes, "the colors of the world mingle on the walls, floors, and ceilings"[128]; regarding churches, "beautiful and perhaps too flashy external decorations consist of all colors of rainbow, silver and gold are also somewhat eastern."[129] Henrieta Błędowska also saw Kyiv with its multicoloured church domes as a "completely Oriental" city, very different from European cities.[130] Oriental imagery served different purposes for Poles and for Russians. For Poles, these Oriental features of Kyiv emphasized their visual and ideological alienation from the city, while for Russians the "East" meant Kyiv's Orthodox Byzantine legacy.[131] Russians, who harboured raised expectations of Christian Kyiv, were trying to squeeze the *real* city into an *imagined* Eastern Byzantine model. Obviously, Poles were the main visual obstacle, and this caused great disappointment among Orthodox observers, Russians and Ukrainians alike.

One can argue that, precisely because they were largely free of the conservative mythology centred on Kyiv, Poles were able to map the *real* city, in which they also managed to organize a viable literary milieu.[132] From the late 1830s through the 1840s, Russian and Ukrainian cultural life there could not match that of the Poles. Ukrainians, while often as anti-Polish as the Russians, succeeded in building their own myth of a holy city, one in which "ancient" Rus' coexisted in harmony with early modern Cossacks (see chapter 2). Russians, however, held the political monopoly on myth-making in the empire, and this may have prevented Poles from developing a more elaborate Polish myth of Kyiv (although some Polish émigrés attempted to do so). As a consequence, only Orthodox Russians and Ukrainians had sufficient credentials and symbolic capital for a more convincing representation of Kyiv's identity, and they developed a strong Kyivan mythology. The competition between Ukrainians and Russians for symbolic control of Kyiv is quite another story that this book only partly explores.

The Russian tendency to ignore Ukrainians in Kyiv outlived Russian Romantic nationalism and continued well into the twentieth century. Later in this chapter we will see how the writer Aleksandr Kuprin, who lived in the city for several years – long enough to become acquainted with its demographics – in his seminal novel *The Pit* (Iama) avoided almost entirely any references to Kyiv's Ukrainians. He did include a few comical episodes that stereotypically depicted the *locals* engaged in drinking, singing, and dancing – a set of common clichés that generations of Russian writers resorted to when representing ethnic Ukrainians.

Holy Sites as Tourist Sights: Kyiv's Spiritual Industry

The Holy City of Kyiv existed alongside the ordinary city, the city of Poles, Jews, Ukrainian commoners, and the *kontrakty*. Most Orthodox travellers, however, visited the city to discover its ideal side, not the seedy and greedy streets of the real city. If anything, these travellers tried to ignore reality. By the beginning of the nineteenth century, Kyiv was the culmination of a "Little Russian Grand Tour." People from all walks of life travelled to Kyiv as if they were going abroad, to see the "ancient capital" of Russia and to make a pilgrimage to its holy places.[133] There were several types of pilgrimages – religious, antiquarian, landscape-driven, and so on[134] – but all were focused on a nearly invariable set of objects, most of them religious and historical. Mainly, these were the churches and monasteries associated with Old (Kyivan) Rus'. Also, there were several sites within or just outside the city boundaries that had links to Kyiv's earliest history. The principal sights included the Caves Monastery complex (especially the caves themselves and the Dormition Cathedral), St Andrew's Church, St Michael's Monastery, St Sophia Cathedral, the ruins of the Church of the Tithes, and the district of Podil.[135] All of these had been established in the times of Old Rus' (except for St Andrew's Church, built in the mid-eighteenth century). Newer Cossack Ukrainian or Imperial Russian sites could also be added, such as the Kyiv Academy and Gymnasium,[136] the Brotherhood Monastery, and the Mezhyhir Monastery.[137]

1.3 Unknown, *The Kyiv Caves Monastery / Dormition Cathedral* (image courtesy of Mystetstvo)

1.4 Shevchenko, *St Alexander's Cathedral* (image courtesy of Mystetstvo)

It is worth noting that Poles followed the same tourist path, with Lavra's "famous caves" as the culmination of the tour.[138] "The tower of Lavra" amidst "Kyiv's thousand bell-towers" served as an apt metaphor for Seweryn Goszczyński in his Romantic poem.[139] The difference was that the Poles usually added to their list of sights the Roman Catholic St Alexander's Cathedral and the newly founded St Vladimir University (established in 1834, moved to its present building in 1843).[140] Korzeniowski's hero *pan* Roman

toured the city, visited a fortress, was in Lavra and in the caves; saw Iaroslav's tomb and ancient mosaics at St. Sophia; prayed passionately in the Catholic church ... examined the university and in its library recalled [Tadeusz] Czacki and Krzemieniec/Kremenets' [Lyceum]; when returning from there to Old Kyiv, he stopped by the Golden Gate, saw the golden letters of the inscription and, after having put in his pocket a piece of an ancient brick glazed by age, sat there to rest ... [He] stood long in deep thought on the shores of the Dnieper, by the column where for the first time in the name of Father and Son the sanctified water flowed from the the foreheads of the people renewed/reborn by the divine light; [he] was in the gallery surrounding St. Andrew's Church from where he saw far below his feet the district of Podil and the wide Dnieper, flowing from the ruins of Olga's residence, and beyond it – the darkening forest of the Chernihiv bank.[141]

Kraszewski, not a fictitious character but the writer himself, appreciated the "understated beauty" of the Catholic St Alexander's Church more than the "motley" and "glittering" colours of Orthodox churches. "[A Catholic] church indeed, appears so beautiful in its humility, in a grey-yellow skirt with an ash-like roof," wrote the Pole, contrasting the Catholic holy place to local Orthodox churches, which appeared "glittering, bright, painted like pictures, golden and motley."[142] Korzeniowski's hero, *pan* Roman, prayed in the Roman Catholic cathedral for the soul of the founder of such a "beautiful shrine," and as he looked at the university he recalled the Polish Lyceum in Kremenets'.[143]

There were at least two ways to appreciate the holy places: the common people were usually concerned with satisfying their basic spiritual needs; the literati examined Kyiv's ruins and antiquities as material traces of the past. For them, Kyiv's churches and monasteries, and ruins such as the Golden Gate, were not merely material or even devotional objects – they were also signs of history. The Romantic cult of the dead, of ruins, and of memory inspired many pilgrimages to Kyiv. The Russian poet Alexander Griboedov revealed these feelings in a letter of 1825: "In Kiev I lived with the dead, [princes] Vladimir and Iziaslav completely possessed my imagination ... Nature is splendid; plants, poplars, winegrapes, which you [in Russia] do not have ... In addition, there is the holiness of ruins and the darkness of caves. How shuddering [*trepetno*] it is to walk in the darkness of the Caves Monastery or the St Sophia Cathedral."[144] Some, like the local academic Mykhailo Maksymovych, used the metaphor of the cemetery to underscore the antiquity of the city and to sharpen the contrast between the past and the present and the future of Kyiv. As he walked through Old Kyiv, he reminisced: "Here was the cradle of Rus' life ... Today, here is the great cemetary of ancient Rus' life, on the edges of which there are St Sophia's and St Michael's cathedrals rising above all new, as the two imposing monuments."[145] This "great cemetery of ancient Rus' life" would become the focus of lovers of antiquities when they described ancient Kyiv. Travellers of the late 1830s could add to their tour another ancient church – that of St Irene,[146] the remnants of which had been excavated by the amateur archaeologist Kindrat Lokhvyts'kyi in 1833.[147]

This archaeological attitude towards historical monuments had taken root only in the 1820s with the work of Kyiv Metropolitan Ievgenii (Bolkhovitinov) and other local amateur antiquarians. Before then, tourists from Moscow and Saint Petersburg like Prince Dolgorukii and Metropolitan Platon had been disappointed by the dearth of real antiquities in Kyiv. "Kiev is old but its antiquity is not as visible, not as tangible as that of Novgorod," wrote Prince Dolgorukii. "There [in Novgorod] there are hundreds of years on each church building ... Here, everything is new, there is more fashion here than antiquity."[148] "Ancient" Kyiv no longer existed, or at least was not as visible as travellers expected. The city was stuck between two epochs. Only as a result of work done by Kyiv's own archaeologists did the city acquire, or rather re-experience, its own antiquity. Thereafter, Kyiv was universally perceived as an *ancient* city, and this fostered an archaeological approach to Kyivan monuments. Count Buturlin, resident in the city from 1834 to 1836, blamed the destruction of Kyivan antiquities not on the legendary evildoers – Poles – but rather on Kyiv's governor general, Levashov, whose vandalism destroyed "to its foundations a part of the defensive wall of an old Kiev" and "part of an ancient moat [*vala*]" that surrounded the St Sophia Cathedral and St Michael's Monastry. All of this was done "under the pretext that it [the wall] impeded a passage."[149] Clearly, for Buturlin, even mid-eighteenth-century Kyiv had become an antiquity itself worthy of preservation.

Most archaeological and historical studies of Kyiv (including those of Maksymovych[150]) carried an explicit political meaning: many religious sites served as testimony to the city's ongoing Russian Orthodox history; for Russians, this underscored Kyiv's role as the centre of Orthodoxy and the source of the Russian collective memory.[151] So it is no surprise that Kyiv became an important destination for all Russian nationalists seeking ideological inspiration.

Another function of Kyiv's religious tourism was more mundane: many Kyivites, both secular and clerical, made their living from serving pilgrims. A number of clerics in Kyiv benefited directly and materially from the pilgrimages. Nikolai Leskov, a Russian, in his literary memoir *Pecherskie antiki* (1883) described this side of Kyiv's "spiritual industry" through the example of priest Iukhym (Efim) Botvinovs'kyi, who was notorious for his love of drinking parties, card games, and hunting. During the summer months, when Kyiv was flooded with pilgrims, his sexton, Konstantyn (or Kotyn), would hatch elaborate schemes to "catch pilgrims." Iukhym's church – St John the Baptist – was situated on the pilgrims' route halfway between the Caves Monastery in Pechers'k and the many churches of Podil, on a road that passed by St Andrew's and Tithes churches in Old Kyiv (Upper Town). Exploiting this strategic position, Iukhym's resourceful sexton sat on the bank of the stream "catching pilgrims" so that they could not reach Podil or the Church of the Tithes until Kotyn "had shaken them a bit out." His task was to extract alms from the pilgrims, and this deprived other churches of their share of income. Kotyn invented his own method for attracting the pilgrims. When he saw pilgrims approaching, he would start shaking the money in his alms box while skilfully talking them into entering his church, promising that they would see an incredible "sacred thing" (*sviatynia*): "Come, come inside the sacred shrine, I will show you one sacred thing that you won't see anywhere else." Usually he succeeded, and groups of pilgrims would follow him into the church, after which he would invite them into the priest's yard. There the pilgrims were treated with cucumbers, kvass, and bread and were allowed to rest near the barn. In return, the pilgrims were expected "to donate" as much as they could. This all looked like a customs duty paid to the priest, but many other local clerics benefited in this way from the pilgrimages.

Yet another literary work suggests a different side of Kyiv's religious economics. Ukrainian writer Ivan Nechui-Levyts'kyi, in his novella *Kyïvs'ki prokhachi* (Kyiv Beggars, 1901), described how destitute or merely resourceful Kyivites exploited the city's spiritual industry. A veritable army of local and itinerant beggars lived off the crowds of pilgrims visiting Kyiv's many holy sites, especially the celebrated Caves Monastery in Pechers'k and St Sophia Cathedral and St Michael's Monastery in Old Kyiv. Begging for alms was a traditional activity in Kyiv, a real job for many – if not respectable, then at least socially appropriate. Begging represented the other side of the Holy City. The beggars themselves reflected the diverse society of late imperial Kyiv; among them one could encounter nobles, former officials, officers, merchants, and other representatives of higher social classes. Not all of them were genuinely poor; some were professional beggars for whom the city's spiritual industry provided a decent income. For instance, a character named Denys Kmita had quit his job as a civil service clerk to become a full-time beggar, openly admitting that "it is better to become a beggar than to serve in a chancellery for fifteen roubles a month." He added that "there are bigger earnings in begging: I have done so and I have no regrets."[152] Indeed, he did quite well at it: he was able to renovate his house and save several thousand roubles as a dowry for his daughter, a recent graduate of an elite high school. People like Kmita proved that the Holy City could be a highly profitable indeed.

The City of Jews?

Nineteenth-century Kyiv was known for the presence of many Jews. For proponents of Kyiv as the Orthodox Holy City, they were a eyesore, and for that reason, the position of Jews in Kyiv was always precarious. Except for a few decades in the late eighteenth and early nineteenth centuries, imperial and local municipal laws either banned Jews outright from living in the city or sharply limited their presence there. Christian merchants and burghers saw Jews as dangerous competitors, and over the centuries they had successfully lobbied the authorities to keep them out of town. Kyiv remained a largely "Jew free" zone from the mid-seventeenth century to the late eighteenth – decades when the city was self-governing within the framework of the Ukrainian Cossack State known as the Hetmanate, which itself was politically dependent on Moscow (and, later, Saint Petersburg). In the 1790s, after the autonomous Hetmanate had been abolished and especially after Right-Bank Ukraine had been taken over from Poland by Russia, "Polish" Jews began arriving in Kyiv in considerable numbers. This time, it seems, local Christians were unable to stop them, and Jews soon became quite numerous among both merchants and common townspeople: in 1817 there were 15 Jewish merchants along with 168 trading Christians and 532 Jewish men out of around 6,000 townsmen in Kyiv.[153] Every year, more than a dozen applications were submitted by Jews (some of them baptized) seeking domicile in Kyiv. The application process was difficult but not impossible. An applicant usually wrote to the Russian civil governor, who in turn asked the magistrate to consider the application. The magistrate then asked the Jewish community (*kahal*) whether it agreed to admit the applicant into its ranks. If the *kahal* agreed and the applicant had paid all taxes owed in his original locality, he was allowed to sign up for a craftsmen's guild or choose a trade (e.g., music). After this he was considered a Kyiv burgher or merchant "of Jewish law" and a formal member of the *kahal*.[154]

Christians always noticed Jews, even if their numerical presence was insignificant. An early mention of Jews can be found in Izmailov's travelogue from around 1800, when Jews were still allowed to reside in the city: "Nowhere perhaps in Russia are [there] so many Jews as in Kiev. One encounters them on the streets; streets are populated by their houses; houses are filled with them; but it is only two years since they settled here in such numbers ... However, they live rich and are engaged in different trades."[155] In the 1820s, an overtly anti-Semitic observer could still see Jews on the streets of Kyiv: "still there are the same dust on the streets and the same, since the old days, parties of *montechis* and *capulettis* fighting each other – filthy Jews and skinny dogs."[156]

The city's Christians were unhappy about the presence of Jews. In the 1820s, under pressure from Kyiv's Christian merchants (primarily Ukrainians and Greeks), the magistrate petitioned the imperial authorities several times to have Jews removed from the city. One such petition by the city's Ukrainian merchants and burghers led to the expulsion of Jews by the imperial authorities in 1827. The authors of that petition had alleged that many Jews were residing in Kyiv illegally, were not paying taxes, and were practising trades and crafts without the approval of the magistracy and the city's Craftsmen's Board.[157] That same year, Tsar Nicholas I honoured their request, on the dubious explanation that the presence of Jews in Kyiv "is injurious to the industry of the city and to the treasury itself, and is moreover in opposition to the rights and privileges granted at various times to the city of Kiev."[158] A better explanation than the official one was that Nicholas I wanted to transform Kyiv from a trading centre into a "fortress city," a function that did not require the presence of Jewish merchants and traders.

The expulsion of Jews was officially carried out in 1835, at which time the city was excluded from the Pale of Settlement. In subsequent years, Jews disappeared from most narrative sources. The expulsion also explains why writings by Jews about Kyiv are not very voluminous and definitely not very upbeat. However, the ban on Jews in Kyiv was not total. Jewish merchants were allowed to stay in Kyiv for several days at a time, residing in special inns owned by the city. And during the famous *kontrakty*, Jews could enter Kyiv freely; for example, in 1845 some 40,000 of the fair's 60,000 visitors were Jews.[159]

But the visibility of Jews during these years certainly lessened. For instance, in the 1840s the Polish writer Józef Kraszewski saw no Jews on Kyiv's streets: "One cannot see here a Jew, he is not here anymore or if he is here, he is only in the status of a traveler and a newcomer. Jews, however, lament that they once had had a school here and lived freely."[160] This pointed to something more important for the writer: without Jews, Kyiv did not seem to be a genuinely Polish town like Zhytomyr; it seems that it was Jews who "make a city Polish"![161] Paradoxically, then, Jews became a yardstick for measuring the city's Polishness. Jews, however, did not disappear from the city. According to various sources, while attending the *kontraky*, they were visible as bankers, moneylenders, and profiteers. Vil'gel'm Karlgof, a Russian, wrote about a Jewish speculator from Berdychiv who sought to sell huge amounts of wine to a Russian trader.[162] Jews struck deals with Christians in the fair hall.[163] Another Pole, Korzeniowski, observed traditional Jews from Galicia's border town of Brody among the *kontrakty* street traffic: "[there were] carts from Brody, on wheels covered with snow, driven by a Jew in a winter hat and from which there appeared fox hats, grey or red beards of moneylenders."[164]

During the reign of Tsar Alexander II, certain categories of Jews were permitted to reside in Kyiv – at first only first-guild merchants, then later second-guild merchants, and later still artisans, ex-soldiers, and graduates of universities and institutes. Jews were permitted to settle in just two neighbourhoods: Plos'ka (also known as Plos'ke), a poor suburb, and Podil, an old residential area along the Dnieper. If they wished to reside in better parts of town, they had to apply for permission.[165] In writings from the late 1850s, Jews reappeared among other ethnic groups living in Kyiv.[166]

In the 1850s, as more and more Jews began to settle in Kyiv, Christian enmity towards them grew, especially among devout Russian Orthodox. In the early 1870s, Andrei Muraviev, a Russian speaker on behalf of Kyiv's Orthodox monuments, accused Jews of secularizing the city and transforming it into a commercial centre. According to him, greedy Jewish and Polish lawyers were littering Kyiv with the signs advertising their services. He went on to add that the despotic Jewish oligarchy had subjugated the city as they had other towns, in order "to suck out the last juices from the Christians."[167] The Jews, he contended, controlled all the industry in the city and were trying to corrupt the Orthodox with their many taverns, all the while acquiring property in Kyiv's historic centre. Muraviev warned that Kyiv was being transformed from the Holy City into the "capital of the yids." This sentiment was widespread among Russians.

Jewish residential patterns seemed to reinforce Christian fears. In the early twentieth century one Jewish resident of Kyiv described the spatial pattern of Kyiv's Jewish population, noting that certain neighbourhoods, such as Plos'ka, Podil, and Lybid', had become overwhelmingly Jewish:

> The result of such a concentration of Jews is that Kiev has streets and even whole parts of the city where not one Jew lives and it's difficult to even meet one on the street, and on the other hand there are entire quarters where the entire population is Jewish, without exception. In other words, a real ghetto. Everywhere Jewish faces, Jewish speech. We can find here the heightened competition, poverty, density of population, and unsanitary conditions that are characteristic of all kinds of other centers that are densely populated by Jews.[168]

The available social and demographic data slightly correct the narrative sources. According to Natan Meir, by 1908, almost 10 per cent of Kyiv's Jews lived in Old Kyiv, a privileged downtown district, "suggesting that a new professional class of Jewish doctors, lawyers, and engineers was taking up residence in this desirable area."[169] Another change concerned the centre of Jewish life in the city: around 1908 the most "Jewish" neighbourhood was no longer Plos'ka (north of Podil) but Lybid' in the south, an area that contained 42 per cent of the city's Jews. Yet in no neighbourhood did Jews comprise more than one-third of the population (and even in the heavily Jewish Lybid' district, they were only one-fifth of the residents). It is safe to say that anti-Semites' fears about the rapid "Judaization" of the city were greatly exaggerated. Even so, well into the twentieth century Jews were "overrepresented" in literature, memoirs, and travel accounts written by Christians (Russians, Ukrainians, and Poles).

To summarize the perceptions about Jews in Christian sources: Poles generally saw them as traditional members of the socio-economic system of Polish noble society, while Ukrainians often saw them as ruthless representatives of Polish landlords. Russians "discovered" Jews at the same time that they discovered Right-Bank Ukraine and for a long time associated them with the Polish world. Thus, all three sides saw Jews as belonging to the traditional system of Polish-dominated Right-Bank Ukraine. Because of the ban on Jewish settlement, Kyiv did not resemble a traditional "Polish" city. At the same time, Kyiv was very different from Great Russian cities, where most people never saw Jews at all. As in many other respects, Kyiv was situated between two worlds – Russian Orthodox and Polish/Jewish – and its identity puzzled many observers.

Here I will point to one curious element of that puzzle that appeared in Kyiv's anti-Semitic and anti-Ukrainian newspaper, *Kievlianin* (The Kievite). In an 1882 review of a performance of the classical Ukrainian vaudeville "Natalka-Poltavka" at the Municipal Theatre,[170] the startled reporter wrote that the event attracted a huge crowd of Jews, who "noisily welcomed" the show as if it were their own work from the "Jargon [Yiddish] repertoire." The newspaper alluded to some sort of Jewish–Ukrainian conspiracy.[171] Towards the end of the century, many Russian nationalists grew increasingly uneasy about the possibility of a Jewish–Ukrainian threat to the Russian Holy City. This paranoia would come to a head in 1905 with a savage anti-Jewish pogrom and in 1913 with the notorious Beilis trial.[172] More surprisingly, Aleksandr Kuprin, one of the more pro-Jewish Russian writers, in his seminal novel *Iama* (The Pit), set in late-imperial Kyiv, depicted Jews as the least sympathetic characters and one of them as the most villainous of them all (see below).

How did Jews themselves depict the city? Kyiv's most prominent writer in Yiddish was undoubtedly Sholem Aleichem (1859–1916), the author of wildly popular stories about Jewish urban life. Aleichem lived in Kyiv in the late 1880s and again in the early twentieth century, and he witnessed the devastating pogrom of 1905.[173] His personal and literary topography included two villages – Boiberik and Kasrilevke (both fictitious) – and three cities – Odessa, Kyiv (referred to as Yehupetz in his fiction), and New York.[174] In the *Letters of Menakhem-Mendl and Sheyne-Sheyndl* (first chapter published in 1892), Kyiv was above all the site of commercial activities centred on the stock exchange, just off Khreshchatyk Square.[175] The name of a fabulously wealthy Jewish family, the Brodskys, appears in the *Letters* a number of times, as a symbol of elusive success for Jewish newcomers to the city. The hero – Menakhem-Mendl – explains to his wife that he and his fellow Jewish entrepreneurs cannot reside in Kyiv legally, so they have to commute to the city daily and spend their nights in the suburb of "Boiberik" (probably the small town of Boiarka, just southwest of Kyiv). The city is viewed through the prism of money; as the hero puts it: "Money is everything in Yehupetz. A man is trash without it. No one cares where you come from."[176] This financial cosmopolitanism cannot conceal the uncertainty of Jewish existence in Kyiv. This is how Sholem Aleichem describes it through the voice of Menakhem-Mendl, in a typically humorous passage:

> You know I'm not supposed to be in Yehupets. Well, now and then the police show up at our boarding house to search for bad apples. We're always tipped off in advance by our landlady and away we melt like salt in water – some of us to Boiberik, some to Demyevka [Demiïvka], and some to Slobodka. This time, though, the landlady wasn't warned herself. A bad business! There we were, sound asleep in the middle of the night, when there's a knock. The landlady jumps out of bed. The cat's at the door, all mice in the straw. Naturally, there's a rush for the exits. Half of us head for the cellar and the other half for the attic, including me.[177]

This time, luckily, it is a false alarm: it is just a neighbour tapping on the window. Kyiv's Jewish community, however enticing it looks at first, proves disappointing outside the world of commerce. When Mendl's wife asks him about the *Zionites* (Zionists) in Kyiv, he responds with irony that they "are the most serious people, though not well thought of on the Yehupetz Exchange." Then he suddenly comments on linguistic matters: "I've gone to a few of their meetings [i.e., Zionist meetings] to see what it's all about, but everything was in Russian – and lots of it. You would think it would be no skin off their backs to talk to Jews in a Jewish language! My friends on the Exchange just laugh when I mention to them: 'What? The Cyanides? Dr. Herzl? You call that a business too?'"[178] The answer Menachem-Mendl soon gives is to leave Kyiv and return to his family in the village of Kasrilivke. Sholem Aleichem, for his part, left the city after the 1905 pogrom, setting out for New York. For many Jews, Kyiv indeed turned out to be Yehupetz, that is, the biblical Egypt – the land of exile.

Mapping a City in Transition: From the Antiquities to the Pit

Perhaps paradoxically, two of the authors who most vividly described the crucial changes in Kyiv's topography, daily life, and social relations were ethnic Russians. And each spent only a few years in the city. These were Nikolai Leskov and Aleksandr Kuprin, each in his own way a paradigmatic Russian writer famous for his descriptions of the borderlands.

Nikolai Leskov (1831–95), a vivid chronicler of Russian provincial life, lived in Kyiv from 1849 to 1857 and left arguably the most realistic portrayal of Kyiv in nineteenth-century Russian literature. In his literary memoirs, *Pecherskie antiki*, he describes a city in transit between a traditional Ukrainian town, with a more or less homogeneous social space, and a multiethnic imperial centre in the process of modernization, with growing social and ethnic stratification.[179] Leskov's literary Kyiv cannot rival Balzac's, Flaubert's, or Zola's Paris; even so, his text sheds plenty of light on the city's changing social relations, topography, and psychogeography. It is worth noting that one of the aforementioned Parisian literary celebrities and Leskov's contemporary – Balzac – was no stranger to Kyiv. While staying in the country mansion of his future wife, the Polish aristocrat Ewelina Gańska, Balzac visited Kyiv six times (in November 1847, November 1848, January–February and May 1849, and January–February and March 1850), at exactly the same time that Leskov was living there. In letters to his mother and sister, the French expatriate ecstatically described Ukraine as "paradise on earth" and Kyiv as an "eternal city of the North" and the "northern Rome," unequivocally alluding to the city's historical role as well as its ideological myth. But with regard to the city, he was interested less in the city's social mythology than in its "ethnography"[180] – and also in partying with local Polish socialites (among them Count Gustaw Olizar). Unfortunately, Balzac died three months after returning to France, and he never completed a literary account of his time in Kyiv.

Clearly, Balzac influenced Leskov's writings. But even though Leskov is known for his masterful depictions of various levels of society, *Pecherskie antiki* is perhaps one of his least Balzacian works. Leskov's preferred form was the literary memoir, although a "memoir" for him was only a literary device – his characters were usually invented. *Pecherskie antiki*, however, is very much a genuine memoir filled with real historical figures and real events. The anecdotes in it address all of the major sociospatial changes in Kyiv in the 1840s and 1850s. As such, they can be interpreted in Walter Benjamin's sense of *memory* as an imaginative popular alternative to the official *history*, the latter represented by a series of repressive and traumatic changes.[181] These changes were inflicted on the city by a ruthless governor general, Dmitrii Bibikov, himself a character in Leskov's memoir.

From the start, the writer laments the loss of a picturesque, even if poorly planned, city, with its devil-may-care Cossack spirit. The contrast between the city he knew when he first arrived around 1849, during the tenure of the notorious Bibikov, and the city Kyiv had become by the 1880s is rather striking:

> Kiev then differed very much from the city of today. This difference concerned not only the city's appearance, but also the customs of its residents. The appearance improved, that is, the city has been filled with good buildings, and has become more European, so to speak. But I personally regret much of the old – what was erased and destroyed by perhaps the somewhat hasty and too unscrupulous hand of [governor general] Bibikov. For example, I regret the loss of lively Pechers'k and surrounding ravines, which had been built up chaotically but very charmingly. Some of them had been populated by the remarkably distinct and peculiar people who led a disreputable and even unruly life in the ancient spirit of the Zaporozhian Cossacks. Such were, for example, Kresty and Iamki, where the shameless girls [*bessoromnyie divchata*] resided and who exemplified a curious combination of urban cultural prostitution with Cossack-style informality [*prostopletstvo*] and conviviality. These madams wore not European but national Little Russian clothes, the so-called common attire [*prostoe platie*]. They were visited by the good folk who came with their own vodka, kielbasa, lard, and fish [*horilkoiu, s kovbasamy, s salom i rybytseiu*]. The Kresty girls masterfully cooked tasty dishes from all these foodstuffs that were just brought in, and then they spent with their visitors the hours of pleasure in familial way.

In this excerpt, the post-Bibikov "European" city of "good buildings" is contrasted with a semi-rural town marked by "cultural prostitution" and intimate social relations. The city's psychogeography includes certain neighbourhoods deemed socially tawdry. Kresty had been a red-light district in Kyiv since the late eighteenth century, but became especially infamous after 1844, when prostitution was legalized and official brothels were established patterned on German models.[182] Leskov contrasts the old-fashioned trade with its Ukrainian national flavour with the regulated European industry, which has lost its exoticism as a result of Bibikov's "arbitrary hand."

Modernity's costs were not merely sentimental, and it was not just sex workers who were affected. Modernity also wrecked the lives of those Kyivites who lost their homes through the early urban-renewal projects carried out by the imperial authorities in the 1830s and 1840s. In Leskov's narrative, sentimental, esthetic, and socio-economic losses are all intermingled:

I feel also sorry for the picturesque huts set above the shoreline, which clustered on the precipices over the Dnieper cliff: they [huts] lent to the beautiful Kyiv landscape a special warm character and served as dwellings for a number of the poor. They, despite having received some compensation for their "broken homes," for this money could not build for themselves new houses in the city, and so they had knocked together nests over the cliff.

These huts, too, were later removed by Bibikov. In many Kyiv texts the image of picturesque hills overlooking the Dnieper served as an ever-present metaphor for an ideal city. Leskov dismantled that reactionary myth and mapped the city's urban topography in a radically different way. Kyiv's hills were now depicted as the sights and sites of the human cost of modernity, associated with poverty (picturesque, no doubt, like the favelas in Rio de Janiero) rather than with a glorious past.

In another respect, the city of Leskov's youth was superior to that of the modernizing capitalist project of later decades. The young author and his school peers used to spend nights in the city gardens discussing the philosophy of Kant and Hegel and "the feelings of the sublime and the beautiful." In contrast, "today," that is, decades later, people talked only about banks and how much someone was worth. Leskov wondered how this new materialism would affect adolescents' morals. As he wryly commented, "the morals ... changed even more than the buildings, and, too, not in all respects for the better." Here, the moral economy is superimposed on Kyiv's topography, with new socio-economic relations invading an idyllic space. Not surprisingly, the text is laced with nostalgia for the pre-reformed "old grey Kyiv." Imperial city planners cleared away the city's "wooden houses" and, in the process, erased its "simplicity," so cherished by the author. Markers of imperial modernity were the numerous "Bibikov's plates" on the corners of the doomed wooden houses, which read: "pull down in such-and-such a year." The iconic Old City and Pechers'k, the site of a fortress and the Caves Monastery, were especially cruelly affected by "Bibikov's plates," for those were the places where the major transformation was taking place.

These miserable huts, doomed to destruction, were very numerous. When I arrived to Kyiv and went to look around the city, "Bibikov's plates" instilled in me an unexpected sadness and gloom. You look around – [and you see] window sills, on which there are pots with red pepper and balsams, with white curtains [*firanky*] pinned on the sides; while on the roofs the pigeons are cooing and in the backyards the chickens are clucking fussily. And suddenly, for some unknown reason, some strangers will come here and will pull all this down … What is it for? And what will happen to these people and where will they go – for they probably are doing quite well and are comfortable behind their white "firanky"? It might well turn out that all this was necessary, but nonetheless this smacked of some unpleasantly arbitrary and crude despotism.

Here, as before, Leskov laments the loss of idyllic – and conspicuously Ukrainian – social and spatial patterns, which are being destroyed by "strangers" for "some unknown reason." Even decades later, the author seems unconvinced of the advantages of the rapid changes brought about by Bibikov's "crude despotism." Leskov time and time again reflects on the human cost of modernization, which is destroying old homes and displacing their inhabitants. The old, semi-rural Kyiv was a place where public and private spaces were not sharply divided, just as in the countryside, a visitor could gaze into people's yards and see clucking chickens. The market square was a focal point of Leskov's "old" city, a place where public and private, urban and rural, intermingled. In contrast, the new Kyiv was to be a city of imperial ceremonial spaces, an increasingly bureaucratic city in which public places were separated from private middle-class residences, with no sight of chickens or picturesque *firanky*. The new Kyiv was to embody imperial modernity and its institutions (governmental, educational, and cultural); the "old grey Kyiv" with its semi-rural lifestyle was doomed to disappear.

For Leskov, one sign of Kyiv's changing social and ethnic profile was the presence of new residents: the Russian Old Believers, who "came to build a stone bridge with the Englishman Vignoles." The first Chain Bridge, designed and built by British railway engineer Charles Blacker Vignoles (1793–1875) between 1848 and 1853, was the first major infrastructural project orchestrated by imperial authorities in Kyiv, and a largely non-Ukrainian workforce was hired to build it.[183]

The image of the new – imperial and multiethnic – city took concrete form when the bridge officially opened on 27 September 1853. In Leskov's account, for the occasion, Tsar Nicholas I decides to cross it on foot. Known for his rough manner, the tsar moves aside two people who are standing in his way. He shouts at the unfortunate pair: "Go away!" In Leskov's text, this incident expresses the crude force of empire as personified by the tsar himself. In fact, the writer's account is inaccurate: the tsar was not in the city on the day the bridge was opened.[184] Yet this story reflects well the political imagery and rituals of power in the minds of the Russian public even years after an event supposedly took place.

The image of Kyiv as a Ukrainian city is prominent in Leskov's literary memoir. Before coming to Kyiv, the author had heard about the "beauty" and "poetic charms of a Little Russian life" there. Kyiv's Ukrainian topography included Kyiv Mohyla Academy, known for its mischievous and free-spirited students;[185] the legendary bakeries in the city's Podil district; and female second-hand dealers (*perekupky*) from Pechers'k whose images as Leskov paints them bring to mind Gogol. Another of his Gogolesque characters – the district official Ivan Dionisovych or Dionisii Ivanovych – is a colourful remnant of the old Kyiv, an old man of Uniate (Greek Catholic) faith and a graduate of a Jesuit college. This Ukrainian-speaking man prefers to discuss prices at the Pechers'k peasant market with his colleague, a former Uniate priest, in Latin. Leskov comments wryly that "as pure aristocrats of spirit," these old men do not want to discuss prices "in the low speech of plebs."

Several other comic anecdotes in Leskov's memoir feature real figures, whom he provides, however, with fictitious characteristics. For example, there is the brave colonel Kesar' Berlyns'kyi, Bibikov himself, and his fierce mother-in-law. As if to amplify the comic effect, the direct speeches of all these characters are rendered in Ukrainian. These anecdotes mock the governor general (nicknamed "Bibik," or "the one-armed," because of his non-functional arm), specifically his unlimited power over Kyiv and its inhabitants. In one anecdote, Bibikov does not dare to demolish a poor neighbourhood because of the fearless Colonel Berlyns'kyi, a defender of poor Kyivites against the despotism of the authorities. The colonel is afraid of no one, but everyone is afraid of him, "even Bibik himself." In another anecdote, Berlyns'kyi boasts that "[Bibik] is afraid of even passing by his [Berlyns'kyi's] house." Reportedly, this story much amused Bibikov himself. Still another anecdote relates how the already mentioned Ivan Dionisovych (Dionisii Ivanovych) violates Bibikov's order not to renovate dilapidated houses. He counterfeits repair slabs using manure, sand, tar, and oats; these new slabs look perfectly "antique." "Once a so produced slab was nailed down on its place, 'Bibik' – even if he happened to pass around – would not have noticed a thing." Anecdotes like these, which mocked the all-powerful Bibikov, were the only weapons available to largely powerless citizens living under a constant threat of demolitions. Mockery served here as a popular defence against the encroachments of the modernizing imperial state.

Paradoxically, this image of a Gogolesque *Ukrainian* Kyiv was conspicuously absent from most Russian and Polish narratives of the city from the first half of the nineteenth century, when the city indeed was ethnically more homogenous. By the time Leskov mapped a Ukrainian Kyiv, for the first time in Russian literature, the city was becoming less and less Ukrainian and more multiethnic, with Russians, Poles, and Jews already dominating its spaces.

Leskov's younger Russian literary colleague, Aleksandr Kuprin (1870–1938), spent a few years in Ukraine, including Kyiv, in the late 1890s, writing for several local newspapers. Yet his most famous Kyiv-themed work, the novel *The Pit*, was finished only in 1914, while he was living in Saint Petersburg. Even though the city is never called by its name – we are told only that the story happened on "the farthest outskirts of the big southern city" – the reader has no doubt that the place itself, "the Pit," is in Kyiv. In the novel, the entire city space is reduced to a seedy area of brothels located on two small streets, Bol'shaia Iamskaia and Malaia Iamskaia. Like Leskov, Kuprin contrasts the two types of local prostitution: one traditional and *ethnographically* Ukrainian, and the other official, permitted and controlled by the imperial state. The first type is represented by "ancient familiar nests" in which "rosy and saucy soldier-widows and dark-browed juicy [*sdobnye*]" local women "secretly traded in vodka and free love." This informal ethnographic prostitution has been replaced by "the open brothels, permitted by the authorities, officially supervised, and subjected to deliberately harsh rules."[186] The routine business of this modern prostitution corresponded well to the rationality of the modern capitalist economy – a fact that seemed especially troubling for the author. Through his alter ego, the journalist Platonov, Kuprin describes the horrors of regulated prostitution: "No, horrible are the mundane, usual details, these business-like daily commercial calculations … these prosaic transactions that have been taking shape for centuries." Most horrible of all is "the dry profession, a contract, an agreement, an almost honest deal, not better and not worse than any grocery trade … Do you understand, gentlemen, the entire horror is that there is no horror! There is only philistine routine and nothing else."[187]

By associating prostitution with capitalism, Kuprin dispels the myth that there is a moral order at the root of modern society. His approach is to question capitalism's authority to make moral judgments. That is, he attacks the self-declared morality of "capitalist" society, which in reality breeds vice. In *The Pit*, the "decent" people seem even more immoral and vulgar than the prostitutes. By listing the diverse customers who visit the Pit, Kuprin shows how modern society in Kyiv comprises every possible social class, occupation, and physical type.[188] It seems that brothel visits are all that unite tsarist officials, students, thieves, writers, and anarchists:

> Here everybody frequents: half-shattered, slavering ancients, seeking artificial excitements, and boys – military cadets and high-school lads – almost children; bearded paterfamiliases; honorable pillars of society, in golden spectacles; newly-weds, and enamored bridegrooms, and honorable professors with renowned names; and thieves, and murderers, and liberal lawyers; and strict guardians of morals – pedagogues, and foremost writers – the authors of fervent, impassioned articles on the equal rights of women; and catchpoles, and spies, and escaped convicts, and officers, and students, and Social Democrats, [and Anarchists],[189] and hired patriots; the timid and the brazen, the sick and the well, those knowing woman for the first time, and old libertines frayed by all species of vice; clear-eyed, handsome fellows and monsters maliciously distorted by nature, deaf-mutes, blind men, men without noses, with flabby, pendulous bodies, with malodorous breath, bald, trembling, covered with parasites – pot-bellied, hemorrhoidal apes.[190]

The prostitutes, brothel owners, and stewards are no less socially and ethnically diverse: they constitute a truly multiethnic society that mirrors the population of late-imperial Kyiv. In just one brothel – a second-rate "two-ruble establishment" – we encounter Russians, Ukrainians, Germans, Jews, and Poles, as well as women of various social classes, from illiterate peasants to a highly educated noblewoman who is fluent in French and German. Perhaps intentionally, Kuprin represents imperial modernity in Kyiv through the image of government-regulated brothels, which are operated just like any other contemporary business, with strict bookkeeping, bonuses for overachieving workers, bribes to governmental agents, tedious and meticulously calculated financial transactions between the sellers and clients, and so on. Especially revolting are the descriptions of the most upscale brothel in the Pit, an establishment whose operation most fully resembles that of a "decent" business. A girl working there – who does highly accurate accounting – prefers prostitution to other jobs such as housekeeper, sales clerk, or governess. She hopes to marry her boyfriend, whom she says she has never betrayed (she is just doing her job!). On hearing this, a visiting celebrity, the singer Rovinskaia, cannot but exclaim: "I could not even imagine a bigger degradation!"

What makes this story even more striking is that the brothel is run and staffed exclusively by Baltic Germans, a community legendary for its loyalty to the Russian imperial family and for its military, civil, and academic service throughout the empire. Precisely because they were so prominent and ubiquitous as military officers, administrators, technical experts, scholars, and skilled artisans, Baltic Germans were hated and envied by many Russians. In Russian and Ukrainian literatures, from the Decembrists to Gogol and Shevchenko to Dostoevsky, Germans signified the mechanical, heartless, even diabolical nature of modern Russian society and bureaucracy; they also signified the non-Russian character of the imperial dynasty and public sphere (especially in Saint Petersburg). Clearly, Kuprin had taken these anti-German views to heart.[191] With this in mind, we should not be surprised that the nastiest character in the novel is Emma Eduardovna, another German and a cruel housekeeper in the brothel owned by Anna Markovna in which much of the story takes place.[192] By way of literary stereotypes, Kuprin has Emma Eduardovna say the following Russophobic words: "Discipline is *über alles* ... above all. It is a great pity that the Russian people are lazy, filthy, and stupid…"[193]

The world of Kuprin's novel, late-imperial Kyiv, is multiethnic. The city's various ethnic groups, however, are not viewed as equal in merit. Thus, Germans are thoroughly bad. Jews are *rather* bad, represented as they are by a vicious human trafficker, by an unattractive daughter sold into prostitution by her parents, and by her cowardly and greedy boyfriend, who does not rush to buy her back from the brothel. We do not know for a certainty the nationalities of most of the characters in *The Pit*, but we can assume that they are Russian, judging from their surnames and their speech. Curiously, in Kuprin's novel there is almost nothing Ukrainian about the city and its people. As with so many Russian writings about Kyiv and Ukraine, "Ukrainian-ness" is represented through Ukrainian songs: first, a group of picnicking students "had been singing sonorous Little Russian songs" before ending up in a brothel; then the author inserts a stock description of a feasting crowd in a Podil market, one that might have been written by Gogol himself. In this "naïve and dear spectacle that can be seen only in the blessed south of

Russia," a dozen Ukrainian market women are drinking, dancing, and singing festive folk songs. Characteristically, Kuprin uses this setting to comment on Ukrainian national topics by showing his character – the student Likhonin, a self-proclaimed anarchist (of questionable morals) – proclaiming "three silly speeches": on the independence of Ukraine, on the "significance of Little Russian kielbasa in connection with the beauty and family values of Little Russian women," and "on economy and industry in southern Russia."[194] Clearly, Kuprin has a solid understanding of the social status of Ukrainian speakers and the subservient role of Ukrainian culture in late-imperial Kyiv.

The great merit of Kuprin's novel is that it deconstructs the intimate links between prostitution and capitalism. It also reveals how spatial patterns reinforce the moral order of the modern city.[195] The prostitutes he writes about seem trapped in the zone of regulated prostitution, in the Pit. It is likely that they do venture out in the city, but Kuprin never shows them doing so. Even though all kinds of people visit the Pit, the contacts between the urban spaces are dangerous, especially for the prostitutes. Representatives of other spaces (customers, lovers, brothel doormen, police, etc.) regularly inflict physical and mental harm on the women.

Especially dangerous for the female inhabitants of the Pit are their attempts, although permitted by the law, to leave their ecological niche: for this transgression, dire consequences inevitably follow. For example, Luba, the most naive and innocent of the girls, is lucky enough to be "saved" from a brothel by the student Likhonin. Her happiness, however, does not last long: finding her earthly love burdensome, her saviour gets rid of her, and she must return to her former space, to the brothel. For other girls, the only way of the Pit is death (the beautiful and rebellious Zhenia commits suicide because she has contracted syphilis; "naïve, gullible, and amorous" Verka is killed by her lover in an attempted murder-suicide; "naïve, risible, meek, and scandalous" Man'ka is killed in a drunken brawl), or insanity (sex-addicted Pasha dies in a madhouse), or jail (mysterious and well-educated Tamara is arrested with her criminal lover for pulling a heist in Moscow). Yet the prostitutes themselves are capable of striking back, of using their bodies as "biological weapons" against the representatives of other spaces. After learning that she has been infected with syphilis, Zhenia pledges revenge: "But I'm deliberately infecting these two-legged scoundrels, infecting every evening from ten to fifteen men. Let them rot, let them carry syphilis over to their wives, lovers, mothers … Let them all vanish, true scoundrels."[196]

Paradoxically, however, a brothel is also a place where the city lays itself bare, stripping itself of lies and disguises, and where both life and the city reveal the "naked truth." This is precisely what Kuprin's alter ego, the reporter Platonov, means when he says that in prostitution "there are no lies, no hypocrisy, no sanctimony, nor any deals with public opinion, or with the obtrusive authority of ancestors, or with your own conscience. There are neither illusions nor embellishments."[197] This "naked city" is remarkably modern: the sights and sounds of modernity – an electric streetcar, a new sewage system, the building boom, a stock exchange, music halls, and, most important, the "moving and shouting crowd" – enliven the world of Kyiv. Kuprin was writing at precisely the time when Kyiv was beginning to resemble a European city. As the novel's arch-villain puts it: "This is a remarkable city, a totally European city! If you only knew what streets, electricity, streetcars, and theaters [it has]. And if you only knew what cabarets [*kafe-shantany*]!"[198] The fact that a notorious human trafficker is praising the city so highly seems rather suspicious here. But it is also probable that Kuprin, like any other modern *flâneur*, found it possible to enjoy the city in its complexity. Indeed, he was the first *major* writer to describe Kyiv from the *flâneur*'s perspective, without simply denouncing its vices or praising its progress.[199]

Sometimes Kyiv's spatial topography as Kuprin describes it reminds us of legendary descriptions of urban spaces, especially poor residential neighbourhoods in earlier writings such as Dostoevsky's, or in Nikolai Nekrasov's almanac *Physiology of Petersburg*.[200] Prominent in Kuprin's subterranean city are "shabby hotels," "remote streets," "semi-darkened hallways," and dark attic rooms that reek of "mice, kerosene, yesterday's borscht, dirty linen, and old tobacco smoke." These spaces indeed look as if they have been drawn from the claustrophobic world of the former student Raskolnikov, reminding us that some things in the city have not changed despite all the technical progress and that the city Kuprin is writing about could be Kyiv or Saint Petersburg or any other modernizing metropolis facing acute social problems.

Ukrainians in the "Shining Babylon"[201]

It was Polish and Russian writers, from Józef Korzeniowski to Aleksandr Kuprin, who left the most realistic, even naturalistic depictions of nineteenth-century Kyiv. But it was a Ukrainian who was the first to use this increasingly hybrid city as the principal setting for a novel. In 1871,

Ivan Nechui-Levyts'kyi (1838–1918), then still an apprentice writer, finished his lengthy novel *Khmary* (Clouds). It was published in Kyiv in 1874, after the censors made numerous cuts to it.[202] Nechui-Levyts'kyi's Kyiv is highly recognizable and realistic, although the city's topography and symbolic order are rather clichéd in his handling of them, permeated with sentimental formulas that make the city feel somewhat more conventional than it does in Leskov's and Kuprin's writings. In his novel, Nechui-Levyts'kyi presents Kyiv as a "traditional" ideal city: its picturesque hills are topped by no less picturesque churches and bell towers that "flamed like candles with their golden heads against the bright sun."[203] This image is often repeated: "What beautiful poetic hills these are! Kyiv must have been founded and built by ancient poets if [the founders] had chosen such a splendid poetic site." So exclaims the novel's main protagonist in a moment of poetic transport.[204] This static idyllic picture is rendered more convincing by the city's actual urban topography – by specific hills (Kysylivka and Shchekavytsia, among others), secular and religious landmarks (the baroque Samson-and-the Lion monument, the St Vladimir monument, St Andrew's Church, St Michael's Monastery), educational institutions (the Kyiv Academy, the Institute for Noble Maidens, St Vladimir University, the Kyiv Gymnasium), shopping and entertainment districts (trendy Khreshchatyk Street and the Château des Fleurs, a public garden offering theatrical and musical performances), and particular neighbourhoods, each with its own "psychogeography" (Podil, Pechers'k, Old Kyiv, Lypky). Against the backdrop provided by this topographically believable city, heroes are shown engaged in various urban activities such as studying, shopping, trading, promenading, crowd-watching, or just aimlessly drifting in the style of *flâneurs*.

What makes Nechui-Levyts'kyi's Kyiv even more urban is the proximity of the Ukrainian countryside, against which the city itself and the novel's characters are constantly weighed. For example, the countryside boasts the "splendid and sympathetic, truly people's spirit," whereas the city lacks an authentic "folk poetry," even though its middle classes still speak Ukrainian and retain their "nationality."[205] In this latter respect the Ukrainian village is superior to cosmopolitan Kyiv, where a new generation of townspeople, educated in Russian institutions, feels increasingly alienated from "people's poetry" and from the Ukrainian nation in general. For visitors from the country, Kyiv is a "shining Babylon," a city of "thieves and robbers," and not least a place of terrible food, where the borscht tastes "as though [it were made] for the pigs or for the dumpster." One young noble girl from the countryside declared that her estate is "ten times better than Kyiv, let alone Paris." The townspeople for their part despise the peasants, "placing themselves, beyond measure, above peasants, distinguishing themselves from peasants as something different and infinitely better than the rednecks [*seliuky*]."[206] Finally, the city is a place where Russian institutions are located and where people of various ethnicities reside shoulder to shoulder (Russians, Ukrainians, French, Poles, Jews, Greeks, etc.).[207]

Making the town even more different from the countryside are the ubiquitous crowds, the unceasing traffic, the pedestrians, carriages, and transport wagons. The novel is full of images of resting, shopping, and promenading crowds: "entire swarms of townspeople gadded about smaller alleys" (in city's main, Tsar's, garden); "many people sat on the hills above the Dnieper" watching "the splendid picture of the quiet Dnieper"; "young gentlemen ... boldly ogled young ladies who were passing by"; "the public crawled like ants"; "on a highway loomed passengers and passers-by ... flickered people, small like dolls, [and] rolled carts"; "figures on a highway moved all the time, just like dolls in a puppet show booth [*vertep*]"; "on the hills near St Vladimir monument, in the Tsar's garden, on a highway, everywhere there roamed the public: Kyiv promenaded, catching a breath of fresh air"; and so on.

Nechui-Levyts'kyi's Kyiv is also full of references to business, banking, and trade, which are represented as emphatically *urban* and *modern* activities.[208] And throughout, the writer points to the collapse of sentimental and romantic concepts of the city. The rational economics of modern Kyiv have made it difficult for the protagonists to maintain close relations. In sentimental and romantic writings it is only cruel people (often parents), cruel fate (death), or heroes' own mysterious hearts (a new love) that can stand in the way of marital bliss; in this novelist's positivist world, other, more mundane factors come into play. The beautiful Olga, granddaughter of the merchant Sukhobrus, turns down a marriage proposal by Pavlo Radiuk, a recent university graduate, even though she is passionately in love with him.[209] In doing so she uses rational arguments against romantic love: Radiuk is neither especially rich nor socially promising and thus does not correspond to Olga's ideal of a "respectable husband" – a social fantasy she developed while attending the Institute for Noble Maidens (310–13). In a sense, Olga's rejection symbolizes a widening gap between the (Ukrainian) countryside and the (Russified) city. Although educated at

Kyiv Gymnasium and the city university, Radiuk was born and raised in a Ukrainian-language environment, on his father's farmstead, while Olga was raised in a Russified family in Kyiv. More importantly, in a modern urban setting, traditional social differences are less important than social fantasies and new cultural hierarchies: Olga is of non-noble origins but has been acculturated into Russian social and cultural mythologies, so she feels herself superior to Radiuk, who is a noble by birth but who speaks the "yokels' language" (i.e., Ukrainian)[210] and vehemently opposes Russification.

It should come as no surprise that Nechui-Levyts'kyi, the son of a village priest and renowned primarily for his depictions of the Ukrainian countryside, even in his most "urban" work represents rural social relations more vividly and sympathetically than he does Kyiv with its alienating social intercourse. His main protagonist, Radiuk, belongs to the noble "middle class" of the village, as does his would-be wife Halia (who unlike Kyiv-born Olga shares his political and cultural views). Also characteristically, the novel does not include a single sympathetic character born in Kyiv, let alone a member of an urban social estate (of merchants or burghers). True, there is the colourful old merchant Sukhobrus, but he clearly belongs to another time and falls out of the picture early in the novel. The only other purely urban character – the student Kovan'ko, a hereditary Kyiv merchant – is shown to be a shallow, pathetic figure, more preoccupied with his business (a public bath) than with grand sociopolitical ideas. None of the leading Ukrainian intellectuals and activists of the time belonged to the category of burghers or merchants, and Nechui-Levyts'kyi was probably reflecting a commonly held prejudice among the educated public against specifically urban occupations and ways of life.[211]

Yet all of this city–country discord should not be exaggerated. Around the early 1860s a sort of dynamic diffusion began to develop, such that villages were no longer fully Ukrainian and Kyiv was not yet predominantly Russian. When Radiuk visits his estate during summer vacations, he is shocked to see a few cultural hybrids gaining a foothold. Among them is a "new type from the people," a semi-literate peasant's son named Tereshko Bubka. He tries to speak Russian (and speaks in fact "some crippled language") and is dressed in a bizarre way – neither like a peasant nor like an urban dweller. Radiuk is puzzled by Tereshko's social identity and wonders whether he belongs to the townspeople or to the Cossacks. Obviously, Tereshko belongs to neither. Rather, he is trapped in a social vacuum – he has rejected his peasant roots but is unable to assume a new social and cultural identity. In this, he mirrors a similar urban type, one that includes those who do not want to remain Ukrainian but who cannot become proper Russians. Cities, however, provide anonymity for such people, while in the countryside someone like Tereshko is doomed to failure, since everyone knows who he is and who he is not.

Kyiv, as a consequence of demographics and its popular culture, retained links to the surrounding countryside. The village was very much present in the city. One curious trace of this could be found in Kyiv apartments, in which there were icons in the corners wrapped in folksy embroidered towels (as in Radiuk and Halia's newly rented home). And in elite residential districts like Lypky could be found the homes of wealthy Ukrainian landowners from Poltava and Chernihiv provinces. The novel's characters include the Dunin-Levchenko family, Ukrainian-speaking aristocrats whose old house "resembled proprietors' houses in the countryside, on rich noble estates."[212] Besides all this, many Kyivites shared the language and folklore of Ukrainian villagers. An educated minority went even further. In the 1830s, but especially after mid-century, some students and scholars began espousing new radical ideas about the national unity of urban and rural dwellers, about the role of the intelligentsia in people's "enlightenment," about the need to protect popular vernacular and culture, about the women's rights, and so on. Nechui-Levyts'kyi's novel is above all about the nascent intelligentsia. But it is also about the fate of *Ukrainian* Kyiv and Ukrainian nationalism as well as rising national tensions in the changing city.

Russification had been making serious inroads in Kyiv since the 1830s, through educational institutions, as a reaction to the Polish November uprising of 1830, and to the exposing of a Polish national conspiracy led by Szymon Konarski in 1837.[213] In the novel, the daughters of the merchant Sukhobrus attended a boarding school during the 1830s where they "learned to speak Great Russian" and to sing sentimental Russian romances. Yet they still knew some Ukrainian songs and spoke Russian with a thick Ukrainian accent. But already their daughters – among them Radiuk's beloved Olga, who studied at the elite Institute for Noble Maidens – were totally alienated from Kyiv's Ukrainian environment, referring to all those who did not match their social fantasies as "boors" and even "Kirghiz." Here, education played a crucial role. Schools lifted people out of their social and cultural setting and turned them – so it seemed – into standard Russian citizens. For example, the

1.5 Lauffer, *A View of Khreshchatyk Square with the Institute for Noble Maidens* (image courtesy of Mystetstvo)

Institute for Noble Maidens looked even spatially removed from the city: with its enclosing walls and dark rows of windows it resembled a "fortress" or even a "jail." The Kyiv Gymnasium, an elite high school for boys, served a similar purpose: while there, the young Radiuk "lost any trace of Ukrainian nationality and language" (218).

Nechui-Levyts'kyi seemed to believe that in the early 1860s, Russification in Kyiv could still be stopped and even reversed thanks to the noble youth from the countryside who called themselves "nationals" (*natsionaly*). They often dressed in elaborate Cossack fashion, shocking not only Kyivites but also their own families. In the novel, one such a group of students resting in a park catches the attention of Olga, who has recently graduated from the Noble Maidens' Institute. She is stunned to discover that the clothes some students are wearing, including their funny straw hats, are not "Tyrolean" but "boorish."

Instead of celebrating imperial modernity in Kyiv, Nechui-Levyts'kyi sided openly with the alternative version of progress advocated by young "nationals." That vision paradoxically combined adoration for an idealized Ukrainian peasant commune (*hromada*) with a conservative attachment to the rural life of the Cossack nobles, in addition to new social ideas associated with positivism and the European Enlightenment.

Russification was anathema to this novelist's socially progressive (indeed utopian) world. From the very first pages, Nechui-Levyts'kyi laments the influx of Russian clerical students into Kyiv, labelling them "coarse Great Russians." They have brought with them "alien Great Russian spirit, alien learning, [and] alien language" (104). Even more brazenly, he concludes that these Russian clerics "implanted Muscovite centralization in the ancient democratic Ukrainian Church" (109). The interethnic tensions in Kyiv are also expressed through the less than cordial relations between two students: quiet and poetic Vasyl' Dashkovych (Ukrainian) and ruthless careerist Stepan Vozdvizhenskii (Russian), who vehemently opposes anything Ukrainian. Later, both marry daughters of the merchant Sukhobrus and become professors (Dashkovych at Kyiv University, Vozdvizhenskii at the Academy); in this way they represent opposing factions of a nascent Kyiv intelligentsia.

The author makes it clear that his sympathies fall with the likes of Dashkovych, Radiuk, and his university soulmate Dunin-Levchenko rather than with the anti-Ukrainian careerist Vozdvizhenskii or the superficial student-trader Kovan'ko. This may strike us as a strange subject for a writer known for his many quirks. For example, he believed that Ukrainians did not *need* Russian literature, plain and simple. At the same time, he despised one particular Ukrainian letter that had recently been introduced to distance even further written Ukrainian from Russian. To make matters worse, he never touched a drop of alcohol in his life, never married, and always went to bed, no matter what, at ten p.m. (needless to say, alone). Ironically, this reclusive man became the first literary sociologist of the Kyiv intelligentsia and of that city's urban life in general.

Especially vivid were his depictions of the major cultural and socio-political ideas championed by Ukrainian nationalists from the 1830s through to the early 1860s. If the armchair scientist Dashkovych represents a melancholic Romantic type devoted to the study of Ukrainian culture, then Radiuk embodies the fiery radical populist, equipped with the latest positivist and scientific ideas from Darwin and Spenser to Renan, Feuerbach, and Proudhon, all of whom are mentioned in the novel. In contrast to Dashkovych, Radiuk sees his mission as to actively serve the "people" by organizing Sunday schools for Kyiv's working-class Ukrainians and Saturday "readings" for its Jews. In fact, Nechui-Levyts'kyi, through his character Radiuk, was among the first gentile intellectuals to reach out to Jews, so as to "engage them in the common work in *Ukrainian* society" (emphasis added).[214] Radiuk's ideas are not limited to popular education; he preaches them to all his friends and family members and even on occasion to Russian church and civil dignitaries. In one of his speeches he sets out his democratic nationalist credo:

We protest, with our peasant clothes [*svyta*], against despotism which fell upon our Ukrainian nationality, our language, our literature, our life. With this we protest against any despotism and take a stand on the side of our people, defending it against the lords, especially alien lords, against the influence of alien languages, alien faith, against the influence of all the devils and evil spirits who dared to put their hostile hand on our well-being, on our people.[215]

With even more rage, Radiuk attacks Russian colonialism and the entire social system: "We don't need Turkestan, the army, and the lords!" On another occasion he shocks his beloved Olga, a shallow and narrow-minded figure, with his feminist message: he demands equal rights for women in education and employment and wonders why "women should not be doctors and lawyers" (294). It is no surprise that Kyiv's Russian authorities and its salons reject Radiuk and his radical message. Eventually he must leave the city for the Caucasus. It seems that Kyiv, which has by then been reshaped by imperial modernity, is not ready for young Ukrainian nationals.

Over the next several decades, more and more youths like Radiuk would arrive from villages and small towns and settle in Kyiv. But at the same time, the city would become more different from the utopian Ukrainian countryside than ever before, so much so that authors like Kuprin would be able to write about the "large Southern city" without seriously considering its links to Ukraine. In Kuprin's world, nothing reminds his readers of Ukraine except for the comical toasts of the student Likhonin. Those toasts themselves can be interpreted as inversions of fiery speeches delivered by Likhonin's Ukrainian counterpart, Radiuk.

In 1883, the same year that Leskov published his literary memoirs, the Ukrainian dramatist Mykhailo Staryts'kyi – who happened to be Nechui-Levyts'kyi's friend and co-author – wrote *Za dvoma zaitsiamy* (Running after Two Hares), a comedy about the lives of burghers in late imperial Kyiv. This play, one of the key Kyiv texts of all time,[216] was the stage adaptation of an earlier piece by Nechui-Levyts'kyi, who referred to it a "burghers' comedy."[217] Focusing on the middle- and lower-middle classes, the comedy casts a critical look at the consequences of the capitalist modernization and cultural Russification that Kyiv was experiencing in the second half of the century. The main character – a barber named Svyryd Holokhvostyi[218] – seeks to advance himself (we learn that he went broke) by marrying Pronia Sirko, a rich but ugly bourgeois girl. At the same time, he is wooing poor but pretty Halia. By using Kyiv's typical sociospatial realities, Staryts'kyi in this play was addressing the growing social and cultural inequality that characterized the city in transition. In doing so he mercilessly deconstructed the myth of the civilizing mission of the Russian state and Russian culture in Ukraine, illustrating this with the example of local burghers caught up in the process of acculturation. This marriage of imperial Russian culture and local Little Russian burghers often produced *enfants terribles* like Holokhvostyi, a homegrown cultural Frankenstein.

Another offspring of that relationship was even more monstrous. This hybrid cultural milieu would soon give rise to the Russian Empire's most notorious chauvinist, anti-Semitic, and extreme right-wing movement of the late nineteenth and early twentieth centuries.[219] People like Holokhvostyi, with their comical speech (a mixture of Russian and Ukrainian known today as *surzhyk*) and their social ambitions, would pack the Kyiv Club of Russian Nationalists, although that club's agenda was anything but comical. In this sense, Staryts'kyi's comedy was prophetic.

Za dvoma zaitsiamy is about the failures of imperial modernity and its political mythology with regard to local social relations and public space. The fundamental imperial myth was that Kyiv's people were "Russian," albeit somewhat different from other Russians because of their Little Russian *couleur locale*. This seemingly inclusive myth, however, came with underlying contradictions that limited the options for most Little Russians. As upwardly mobile locals knew, their "Little Russian" qualities were not good enough for them to participate in the imperial public sphere, so they were expected to improve themselves by adopting the speech and manners of proper Russians. That opportunity, however, was available only for the minority who had access to education and – most importantly – who had the means to enjoy a middle-class or aristocratic lifestyle. In Kyiv's hybrid sociocultural milieu, those without education and means sometimes sought to imitate (foolishly) the speech and manners of proper Russians. The barber Holokhvostyi, a tragicomic figure, well illustrates these local relations.

By dressing and behaving above himself, he pretends to be someone he is not (and *cannot* be): a proper Russian bourgeois. He even changes his name from the plebeian Holokhvostyi to one that sounds Russian and more respectable – Galakhvastov, which has no trace of the "bare tail" that had been attached to him through his original surname.

But in social terms, he finds himself in a precarious situation, as does his rural analogue Tereshko, a social transgressor from Nechui-Levyts'kyi's novel *Khmary*. Both have tried to escape the social station into which they were born, but they cannot legitimately rise to a higher status, and thus they are stuck in social limbo. This is exactly how other young burghers "decode" Holokhvostyi: "[He] had renounced the burghers but did not join the gentlemen."[220] Yet thanks to the anonymity that a large city like Kyiv can provide in the 1880s, Holokhvostyi seems to have succeeded in presenting himself (or rather performing) as socially superior, at least in the eyes of poorer burghers. Also, he has been accepted as a social equal and as upwardly mobile by some wealthy burghers (including the family of Pronia Sirko, his candidate for a marriage of convenience, a girl who just like him is culturally challenged). As a con man, Holokhvostyi is more successful than Tereshko because traditional social mores break down in big cities much more easily than in villages, in which people who break the social rules can rapidly become pariahs.[221] But how can this urban social transgressor pull it off so convincingly, and why does he eventually fail?

The answer can perhaps be found in what Richard Sennett has noted regarding modern public space, which over the course of the nineteenth century was becoming less public and more personal. As he points out,[222] modern times were marked by increasing difficulty judging people by their appearance (and at the same time, by a strong urge to do so). Guessing the social station and even the character ("personality") of a stranger by his or her appearance (through the details of clothes, facial expressions, or manner of speech) became a nightmarish obsession for modern city dwellers. Personality was a new concept and was thought to be visible through clothes, speech, and gestures. Conversely, by donning new clothes and imitating someone else's speech and manners, one hoped to assume a new personality, not just a higher social status.[223] The trick was to learn as much as possible by "reading" others in the crowd without disclosing too much about oneself. In other words, the fear of disclosing one's own personality went hand in hand with the temptation to "decode" the personalities of others.

Although himself neither a Balzac nor a Sennett, Staryts'kyi in his prophetic comedy nonetheless put his finger on something important: the changing social and cultural landscape in late-imperial Kyiv. That is why the image of Holokhvostyi so well reflects the modern fears and temptations of its author and his audience. By rejecting the descriptor of "barber" (*tsyliurnyk*) and recasting himself, more fashionably, as a "hairdresser" (*parikmakher*), the new man Holokhvostyi seeks to defy his inherited social status of a modest burgher. He also does this, as did many other men in Europe, by wearing stylish clothes, speaking what he thinks is proper language, and trying to marry a bourgeois girl. As if to illustrate what Marx wrote about "commodity fetishism," fashionista Holokhvostyi sings a paean to contemporary fashion in his inimitable Russian–Ukrainian twisted speech: "Now you think that the clothes is just anything [*lish by shto*], but the clothes are the prime thing because they greet you according to your clothes."[224] Following Marx, Sennett writes that in modern capitalism, commodities – especially items of clothing – are thought to reflect the buyer's personality and thereby acquire personal characteristics. This is precisely the fashion philosophy of our barber-turned-hairdresser. "Let's take, for example, trousers," he lectures his less sophisticated peers. "They stand like a pipe, as if they were molded, in a purely English fashion. But if you don't add something [to them], then they no longer will have a physi-ognomy. Or here is a waistcoat – it seems like a trifle – but it is a tricky thing: just miss a little bit and already there's a wrong fashion and no sympathy."[225] The words he uses – *physiognomy* and *sympathy* – clearly reflect the basic vocabulary of commodity fetishism whereby clothes became expressions of individual personality. Moreover, clothes pro-vide Holokhvostyi with a *new* personality (that of Galakhvastov), if only for a brief time.

But the odds are against him. Perhaps what betrays him is his lack of education, his poor taste, his gibberish speeches, and his foolish language – in short, his incomplete acculturation. But there is also something beyond his personal control, something that paradoxically introduces personality into the public world. Precisely because Staryts'kyi grasps the new social relations, he is able to show how the forces of modernity, which have made Holokhvostyi's new personality possible, inevitably undermine it. The people around him are no longer content to accept his "higher" status on the basis of his gentlemanly appearance, no matter how convincing that appearance may be. They keep questioning his authenticity, trying to find out who he really is (is he in fact the son of a barber "from beyond the Ditch," as well as a nephew of burgher Svynarenko?[226]). Finally, the author makes it clear that Holokhvostyi's entire appearance – his speech, his ideas, and even his clothes – shows his flawed *personality*: he is a scoundrel. In this regard the new culture of personality can be said to have destroyed his new personality. The play ends with him being detained by the police.

Nechui-Levyts'kyi seems to be sceptical about the very possibility of, as well as the need for, the social and cultural integration of Ukrainian Kyivites into modern society if the latter is capitalist and Russian. It is only logical that such integration produces scoundrels and cultural freaks. Staryts'kyi's play, then, is surprisingly conservative, especially his message about social and ethnic ecologies: one should stick to one's own roots because crossing social and ethnic boundaries can lead to a ridicule, bankruptcy, and jail, and worst of all, to the loss of personality altogether.

Conclusion

I have tried to show that all the major changes that transformed Kyiv into a multicultural metropolis were represented and often anticipated in literature of various genres – from travelogues to poetry to novels – written by diverse observers in several languages (predominantly in Russian, Polish, and Ukrainian). Literary sources bring us closer to the "human edge" of history, allowing us to explore how humans experienced urban change. Literature also allows us to confront various myths of the past, some of which have continued to define the city's image and the identities of its inhabitants to this day. Some writers, among them Leskov, Kuprin, and Staryts'kyi, confronted various myths of modernity by showing both the limits of modernity and the threats it posed – the social, political, and personal. For many decades, various images of Kyiv clashed, and so did different experiences of change – all of this depending on the social standing and the ethnic background of those who lived through them. Travellers' impressions were different from those of locals, but together they allow us to arrive at a fuller understanding of Kyiv as an urban form and social practice.

Representations of Kyiv had a direct bearing on the political imaginations of Eastern European literati. The result was ongoing tensions that ignited conflicts among Polish, Russian, and Ukrainian mental geographies, all of which claimed Kyiv as an inherent part of their "ideal fatherland." Yet Kyiv's identity escaped decisive appropriation by any side. Both Russians and Poles felt that Kyiv was in many respects an "alien" city, despite their efforts to focus on the signs of their presence – churches and pilgrims for Russians; Polish noble society and a single Roman Catholic church for Poles. In one respect, however, Poles were more confident than most of their Orthodox peers. For Polish travellers and residents, Kyiv was a real, mundane experience, a city of commerce and entertainment (during the famed *kontrakty* and beyond), even though it remained foreign on the ideological and spiritual levels. In contrast to the Poles, Russians for a long time felt estranged from the real city, despite enjoying political hegemony. Perhaps as compensation, Orthodox authors presented the city as a myth, as the Ancient and Holy Kyiv. That myth in turn was the very reason why these Orthodox observers, especially Russians, felt alienated from the real city, which was so obviously alien to their religious imagination. For the same reason, Russians became obsessed with fabricating their connections with Kyiv's distant past, when the city was presumably pure Russian and Orthodox. This exploration, fabrication, and use of the past is the subject of the next chapter.

Chapter Two

Using the Past: The Great Cemetery of Rus'

Literary Struggle: "Old Russians" versus Ukrainian Cossacks

If writing about the *ideal* Kyiv placed Orthodox Ukrainians and Russians on one side of a divide and Catholic Poles on the other, then the depiction of its past separated Ukrainians from Russians, leaving Poles altogether out of the picture.

The image of Kyiv as a cradle of Christianity and the Holy City was directly linked to the city's remote past. All seemed to agree that Kyiv was a very old and ancient city. As convincingly demonstrated by Oleksii Tolochko, Ukrainian authors ceased to feel any substantial connections with Kyivan Rus' in the eighteenth century, constructing their identity instead on the Cossack tradition to which these authors genetically belonged.[1] It is this Cossack past that effectively separated Ukrainians from Russians, while the legacy of Kyivan Rus' was appropriated by Russian literati. Most Russian authors who chose to write about the city chose themes about Old Rus' and princely Kyiv, while Ukrainian writers almost never looked to that period – or, if they did, they wrote in Russian.[2] It is not surprising, then, that Russian travellers and writers sought in Kyiv their own, Russian history and tried not to take notice of the city's Ukrainian connection.[3] For them it was the "ancient capital" of Russia, filled with "monuments of antiquity precious for every Russian."[4]

The modern Russian literary treatment of Kyiv's past took shape in Pushkin's early poetry, particularly in *Ruslan i Liudmila* (Ruslan and Liudmila, 1818–20) and *Pesnia o veshchem Olege* (The Tale of Oleg the Seer, 1822).[5] The first poem was essentially a heroic epic and a fairy tale all in one, featuring fictitious characters, some of them from Russian folk tales. Pushkin starts his poem (its first "song") with an image of Vladimir the Great (here – Vladimir the Sun) partying with the "crowd of his mighty sons," presumably in Kyiv, as later the author mentions "the Dnieper's happy shores." From this time on the poem's geography becomes effectively magical and Oriental,[6] having nothing to do with the physical and political geography of medieval Rus'. Towards the end, the "bright" and "golden-domed" Kyiv is mentioned a few times again, along with Vladimir the Sun and Kyivites "clustering on the city wall." In the final scene, Kyiv is shown besieged by the nomadic Pechenegs (*basurmane*), only to be saved by the poem's hero, Prince Ruslan. Now happy, Vladimir can resume partying with his kin. Pushkin's second poem is about another legendary old Rus' figure – Prince Oleg (Helgi of Scandinavian sagas) and his highly poetic death from a snakebite. The plot is based on a medieval account (in which the story of the prince's death is also fictionalized).[7] The poet imitates the style of both Kyiv's Primary Chronicle and a popular epic tale; the result is one of the most famous Romantic poems ever written in Russia. Not surprisingly, we do not find in it any traces of historical Kyiv, except perhaps for a highly generic "hill on the Dnieper shore" and Igor and Olga "sitting on the hill" (was it the same hill?) after Oleg's death. In both poems, Kyiv is so "ancient," or rather primordial, that it has almost nothing to do with reality, either historical or topographical.

Young Pushkin was more interested in the epic; his slightly younger literary peer Aleksei Khomiakov was more driven by ideology. Better than anyone else, this prominent Slavophile expressed the links between Kyiv's past and its "holy" function in his famous poem "Kiev" (1839). In describing Kyiv as "the cradle of Russian glory" and "the baptismal font [*kupel'*] of Rus'," the poet places an image of the Holy City in the context of ongoing Russian struggles against the Poles, thus politicizing the past. In reaction to the Polish November uprising, Pushkin himself turned to ideology in his "geopolitical" poetry of the early 1830s.[8]

Polish observers recognized Kyiv/Kijów as the "ancient capital" of Rus'. So did the writer Józef Kraszewski.[9] So we should not be surprised that even Andrei Muraviev, a Russian expert on Kyiv's historical monuments, was not immune from mixing epic and history. One way of doing this was through the use of Romantic poetic clichés. For instance, one night he was so animated by his own imagination that he saw how "ancient Kiev, covered with moonlight in a shadow of its past glory," was sleeping alongside another "old man," the city's "old friend," the Dnieper River, which was also asleep. Another time, an excited tourist seemed to hear the river singing as "if it were the ancient bard Baian at the court of a grand prince." The Dnieper (or was it the "ancient" Baian?) sang about "the beautiful girls – the princesses of Rus' and about the battles of the princes of all Rus'."[10] These moonlight meditations on the Dnieper shores became popular in Russian poetry starting with Ivan Kozlov and his poem "Kiev" (1824):[11]

> […] How often I in my dreams please my eyes
> With your holy beauty!
> I forget the earth by Lavra's walls
> And I walk above the Dnieper in the darkness of night:
> In my eyes, all fair Russian
> Is beautiful, great, and holy
>
> The moon already stood up; Lavra is shining […]
> Vladimir's shadow is flying over it; Its facets speak about glory,
> I see in remoteness – everywhere my dream is with me,
> And everything is breathing with dear antiquity.[12]

In this extract from Kozlov's poem we can see how the *topos* of "ancient Kiev" served the purposes of a nascent Russian Orthodox nationalism. Vladimir Benediktov's poem "Kiev" (1840) did not sound as explicitly nationalistic, although it also contained the *topos* of the holy, ancient, golden-domed "Old-Wise-Man Kiev":

> In the garments of holiness and glory,
> Covered with antiquity,
> Old-man Kiev before me
> Is standing, golden-headed:
> Hello, a glorious old man!
> Hello, a holy labourer.[13]

In the bygone world of both poems there is no place for Poles or even for Ukrainians with their supposed Cossack ancestry. The visible signs of an ancient princely city are presumably old Kyiv's churches, monasteries, and historical sites, as well as urban topography known from medieval annals. These "ancient" signs lend themselves easily to a panoramic view:

> From the one side, there is the Pechers'k fortress with its suburbs … set on
> a high hill above the Dnieper; from the other, on several hills along with

> St. Michael's Monastery and St. Sophia Cathedral, as if castles with houses
> and gardens, there lies Old Kiev; on the bottom, toward the Dnieper itself,
> like the pointed cape, by the foot of a high hill one can see Podil, embel-
> lished as well with a number of buildings. [14]

This repertoire of "ancient" sites remained almost unchanged in most Russian "Kiev texts" of the time. Interestingly enough, not only Russians but also Poles visiting Kyiv paid attention almost solely to the oldest period of the city's history. When the "ancient" churches and monasteries turned out to be not that old, many travellers felt painful disappointment. Nonetheless, entire poems were devoted to the particular sights of Kyiv. In Russian poetry the most typical of this genre were two poems bearing very similar titles, published the same year (1828), and written by second-rate poets of non-Russian ethnic origins – Andrei Podolinskii (Andrii Podolyns'kyi), a native-born Kyivite, and Baron E.F. Rozen, a Baltic German from Tallin. Podolinskii was among the very few Kyiv natives (although as a Ukrainian noble he had an estate in the country) who wrote about the city, either as writers or as scholars. In his brief poem "Na razvalinakh Desiatinnoi tserkvi" (On the Ruins of the Church of the Tithes),[15] neither Kyiv nor the "ruins" of the Church of the Tithes are even mentioned. Rather, they are used as hidden devices for conveying an atmosphere of fashionable gloom; this hearkens back to the baroque genre of *vanitas*, which in turn goes back to the "apocalyptic text of Rome."[16] In Rozen's slightly longer poem "Razvaliny Desiatinnoi tserkvi" (The Ruins of the Church of the Tithes),[17] in alluding to the fate of Rome, the author mentions a concrete historical event – the fall of Kyiv during the Mongol Invasion of 1240: "You fell, but gracefully fell, / The stately Kiev, the honor is with you!"

Throughout the century a clear pattern emerged in the literary treatment of Kyiv's past. Most Russian authors, as well as those Ukrainians who wrote in Russian, focused on the city as an old ("ancient") capital of Rus', populated presumably by Old Russians. Needless to say, this literary image contrasted sharply with the contemporary Kyiv populated by Ukrainians, Jews, and Polish nobles. It took several decades for an explanatory theory to be developed (in the 1850s), according to which Kyiv was originally populated by Russians who then migrated northeastward to escape the Mongol onslaught. In other words, the contemporary Ukrainians came to Kyiv only after the fourteenth century.[18] Whatever the reason, Russians generally tended *not* to write about Ukrainian Kyiv, be it a Cossack city or a contemporary one.

Russian lovers of ancient Kyiv could not, however, completely ignore the Ukrainian and Cossack links to Kyiv if they were attentive (or curious) enough to study the interiors of the presumably ancient churches. For example, Vladimir Izmailov found in the Caves Monastery's Dormition Cathedral "the portraits of great men of *our Fatherland*" (emphasis added), who happened to be Ukrainian Hetmans and other early modern figures from Ukraine. "Here is he, the glorious Khmelnitskii [Khmelnyts'kyi] who managed to liberate his compatriots from a Polish yoke; it is he to whom Little Russia owes its salvation."[19] He also mentioned Prince Kostiantyn Ostroz'kyi, "who deserved the gratitude of the Little Russian people," and the Cossack leader Severyn Nalyvaiko, "who also defended the rights of his compatriots before the Poles with the passion of a Demosthene and courage of a Khmelnitskii."[20] It is worth noting that these, probably, were his only mentions of Poles and Ukrainians (paradoxically in tandem!) in connection with Kyiv, since the real contemporary Kyiv was for Izmailov populated by quite abstract "Kyivites" (*kievliane*). This scheme in fact became the rule when representing Poles in many other Kyiv narratives: when Poles were not noticed as antagonists in the present, they appeared as evildoers in Kyiv's history.[21]

Polish visitors to Kyiv usually did not associate the city with Ukrainian history (except in historical writings such as those by Michał Czajkowski). In travelogues, however, the only explicitly "Ukrainian" association arose from the very same portraits of Ukrainian hetmans from the Dormition Cathedral. Unlike Izmailov, however, the Polish writer Józef Kraszewski experienced a feeling of angst and anxiety rather than of patriotic joy when he saw on a church's wall "the portraits of several Cossack hetmans, the figures as dark as the past, dead as it was, serious and scary." He could not but feel fear when he saw these "faces with moustaches, black eyes, and motionless and pale features." These hetmans were "the guardians of the Rus' arch" (*stróże arki ruskiej*). [22]

For Ukrainian authors and for some Russian ones, Kyiv's connections to Ukrainian history were not confined solely to the interiors of churches. These connections became visible to them when they heard about early modern clergymen like Petro Mohyla or visited specific churches and monasteries that had been established under Cossack rule or protection. Muraviev, the author of a description (1844) of Kyiv's Orthodox sites, specifically mentioned the role of Metropolitan Petro Mohyla and other Kyivan church and Cossack dignitaries (including Hetman Ivan Mazepa and the Zaporozhian leader Petro Kalnyshevs'kyi) in the building and renovation of Kyiv's holy places.[23] He also included in his list of Kyiv's holy "attractions" a clearly Ukrainian creation – that is, the Brats'kyi (Brotherhood) Monastery in Kyiv's Podil district, which had no direct association with Kyivan Rus'. Like Izmailov and Kraszewski before him, Muraviev could not avoid describing Dormition Cathedral, where he made note of the graves of Orthodox Polish-Lithuanian princes like the Ostroz'kyi family and of "Little Russian hetmans."[24] All of this established a visible link between Kyivan Rus' and contemporary Ukrainian Kyiv. It was not surprising that for Muraviev, Kyiv was "our native Zion." More surprisingly, he did notice Ukrainians in Kyiv, but for him they looked as exotic as it gets: they reminded this seasoned traveller of "Arab boys and girls" from Palestine, while the Dnieper itself provoked Italian associations, reminding him of the Tiber.[25] Despite this exoticism, which reflected an imperial mentality, Muraviev was one of the few Russians who noticed similarities between "ancient" Kyiv from historical annals and the contemporary city populated by exotic Ukrainians. Thus the poetic images of princely Kyiv were naturally related to the poetics of Zaporozhian Cossacks and modern-day Ukrainian residents (however much they might have have resembled Arabs). A nineteenth-century Dnieper fisherman sang not about the heroic deeds of Old Rus' princes but rather about Cossacks and their wars against the Poles: "What two epochs [that have been] pulled apart by ages merge here in one voice of a fisherman and of the river!"[26] According to an already established scheme, Muraviev, who did not seem to notice Poles in contemporary Kyiv, wrote at length about the struggle of Orthodox Kyivites against past Polish oppression.

With the remarkable exception of Kondratii Ryleev, Russian poets were not drawn to Kyiv's history beyond its Old Rus' incarnation. In Ryleev's poem *Nalivaiko* (1825), about the late-sixteenth-century Ukrainian Cossack leader Severyn Nalyvaiko, Kyiv lacks any historical features of an early modern city except for the presence of Polish evildoers: "Having just emerged from the dust, / With a semi-damaged forehead, / As a prey of the impudent Pole / Kiev is getting old above the Dnieper."[27] Inna Bulkina, an expert on Russian poets' treatment of Kyiv, has recently noted that Ryleev's metaphor for Kyiv was the cemetery,[28] which also figured prominently in essays and scholarly works on "ancient" Kyiv written by the poet's younger contemporaries (including Mykhailo Maksymovych). Unlike Podolinskii and Rozen, who viewed the city's past through the prism of Rome, Ryleev in *Nali-vaiko* featured an early modern city and evoked an image of Jerusalem – after the destruction of the temple and of faith.[29] This gloomy present contrasted sharply with an illustrious ancient Kyiv, an image that even by the 1820s had become a literary cliché and an Orientalist fantasy: the city once "beamed with oriental luxury in a rich land"; it boasted "noisy markets" (*shumnye torzhishcha*), "shining splendid palaces," and "domes of Caves Monastery that lightly ascended to heaven." This idyllic picture would later be erased by waves of internal and external enemies: feuding princes, invading Mongols and Lithuanians (personified by Khan "Batyi" and Prince Gediminas respectively), and, finally, the "fatal rule of the Pole." After this, Kyiv disappeared from the poem, which went on to describe how its hero, Nalyvaiko, set out to defend "oppressed" Ukrainians against "impudent" Poles and Jews.

Like the poets, Russian prose writers turned their attention to early modern or Cossack Kyiv only rarely. But here, too, there was an exception: Fadei Bulgarin (or Tadeusz Bułharyn in Polish), a Pole who became a famous Russian writer and journalist,[30] presented in his novel *Dimitrii Samozvanets* (1830) a vision of early-seventeenth-century Kyiv based on Beauplan's *Déscription d'Ukraine*. This picture was not very different from the descriptions of "ancient" Kyiv in travellers' accounts except for some elements: a castle guarded by Polish soldiers, and four Catholic churches, which by 1830 no longer existed.[31] Bulgarin being a Pole, he wrote about the affinity between Ukrainians and Poles: "Ukrainians and Cossacks are drawn to Poland more than they are to Moscow. Just destroy the [Church] Union today – tomorrow the entire Cossackdom will devote body and soul to Poland."[32] This was a rare Russian-language Kyiv text in which Poles were not viewed negatively, as they were so often in Russian literature on Kyiv.[33]

It is no surprise that Ukrainians (even those writing in Russian, like Gogol) preferred to depict an essentially Ukrainian/Cossack city. For them, Kyiv was both holy and Ukrainian. Nor is it surprising that they could easily find these features in the past. In the most famous Ukrainian historical novel, *Chorna Rada* (The Black Council), written by Panteleimon Kulish in the 1840s, Kyiv is depicted as the spiritual centre of the Left-Bank Hetmanate, where all the most important events in Ukrainian history took place and where the novel's heroes go on pilgrimage. In both Kulish's novel and Shevchenko's "The Monk," it is in Kyiv that an old Zaporozhian Cossack leaves the secular world for a monastery. Kulish begins his Kyiv novel during the times of

Old Rus', although he "Ukrainianizes" it by incorporating it into the Ukrainian historical tradition. One can say that Kulish reclaimed a Kyivan Rus' legacy from the Russians:

> It is both nice and difficult to recall you, our old man Kyiv! Because both a great glory often shined on you and great troubles gathered around you … So many princes, knights, and hetmans gained glory fighting for you; so much Christian blood was spilled on your streets, on those ancient walls, and church cemeteries! There is not even a need to recall those Olehs, those Sviatoslavs, and that enslavement by Cumans. That glory, those troubles were forgotten due to godless Tartars when Batu-khan broke into your Golden Gate.[34]

Kulish's description of early modern Kyiv's historical topography was more realistic than Bulgarin's:

> At that time almost all of Kyiv was situated in [the district of] Podil. [The district of] Pechers'k did not yet exist, while the Old or Upper city was empty after the Khmel'nyts'kyi uprising. There were some brick houses in Podil while the rest was wooden, including the walls with towers around Podil and the castle on the Kysylivka Hill. The streets were narrow and curvy; there were also some squares built by no one, with nothing on them but grazing geese.

For Kulish (and for some Russians and Poles), churches and monasteries were the most visible markers of Kyiv's Ukrainian past. In particular, the Brotherhood Monastery provided a direct link with Ukrainian Cossack history. Kulish also tried to imagine what the monastery looked like at the time it was founded by Hanna Hulevych and Hetman Petro Sahaidachnyi, who "had built a church and established the Brotherhood monastery with schools." Izmailov and Kraszewski were especially impressed by the portraits of hetmans inside the Dormition Cathedral, whereas Kulish mentioned the depictions of Ukrainian Cossack history on the walls and fences of the Brotherhood Monastery. Those paintings no longer existed by the time of Kulish's writing, so the writer indulged his patriotic imagination, contrasting the bleak present with the glorious past: "Everything that was written in the Bible was lively depicted by a monk all over the monastery. Alongside the saints our Cossack knights were depicted all over the fence so that the people could see and remember what was going on in the time of our grandfathers ... It was painted in such a way that everybody knew about the [Cossack] knights in Ukraine."[35] In describing the paintings on the walls of the Dormition Cathedral, Kulish – in contrast to his Russian and Polish colleagues – was underscoring visual signs of a Ukrainian presence that had already been erased. He was imposing a national character on the city; his Kyiv had *always* been a Ukrainian city.

In Shevchenko's and Gogol's works, Kyiv emerges as a traditional town integrated into early modern Ukrainian society and populated by Cossack officers, wealthy lords, townspeople, market traders, and students from the Kyiv-Mohyla Academy (students/*spudei* in Gogol's "Vii," *bursatstvo* in Shevchenko's "The Monk"). While literary Kyiv had its focal points – a market and the Academy (in Gogol's "Vii") – the city remained the spiritual centre of Ukraine, a place of repentance (Gogol's "Strashnaia mest'" and Shevchenko's "Varnak"), and of monastic life (Shevchenko's "Chernets'"), as well as a place where one could always find an aspiring priest ready for a dangerous assignment (Gogol's "Vii").

Kyiv's Past as Symbolic Capital and Its "Ideological Function"

The image of Kyiv as an "ancient" and "holy" city was central to a conservative and at times plainly reactionary mythology about the city, one that had been cultivated by generations of Orthodox Russians and Ukrainians. That image was shaped largely by local experts – professionals and amateurs alike – and facilitated by political figures such as Tsar Nicholas I and his loyal servants, including Sergei Uvarov, Russia's education minister. Kyiv's past thus became a prism through which the city was universally viewed throughout the long nineteenth century, and conservative forces often used that past to block or at least modify any unwanted change in the city. The authorities also resorted to scholarship and antiquities to promote their own vision of history, to claim the city and the southwestern borderlands culturally, and to place limits on the concept of new Kyiv as a means to control and discipline minorities. The city's past, often imaginary and ideological, sometimes clashed with modernity. In 1804 a reverend guest from Moscow, Metropolitan Platon, noted in his diary:

> It is quite remarkable that although the churches of St. Sophia, Pechersk, St. Nicholas, and others ... are ancient and some are more than seven hundred years old, in which we could expect to find traces of antiquity, yet we clearly see that in all those churches the icons, iconostases, and painted

walls – all do not manifest signs of antiquity, but rather reveal that they
have been painted or wrought recently or in the seventeenth or eighteenth
centuries.

He added that clearly, "various enemy devastations destroyed everything ancient and forced [us] to construct everything anew."[36] Several
years later, another Russian traveller gained a similar impression:
"Kiev is old but its antiquity is not that visible, not that tangible as
in Novgorod. There are centuries on every church building [there] ...
Here there is always something new, more fashion, less antiquity."[37]
Another ardent proponent of antiquities, Count Nikolai Rumiantsov,
visited the city in 1821 and left a sceptical note about the attitudes of the
locals towards the city's past: "In Kiev, the heart grieves when it sees
so much negligence with respect to our antiquities there, that no one is
interested in them, and almost everyone avoids any talk about them."[38]
Until the 1820s, most visitors to Kyiv were disappointed by the number
and quality of "ancient" monuments, partly because of their heightened expectations, and partly because of the actual lack of antiquities.
Most travellers had not come to the city to enjoy the monuments of
the Ukrainian Baroque Era of the seventeenth and eighteenth centuries,
which had dramatically recast what had once been a medieval city.

Visitors' impressions began to change only in the 1820s, when a new,
more proactive attitude towards Kyiv's "ancient" monuments and
ruins emerged. The cause of this was the arrival in 1822 of a new Orthodox Metropolitan, Russian-born Ievgenii (Bolkhovitinov). He presided
over a coterie of local amateur archeologists, known as antiquarians.
Thanks to their activities a few *authentic* historical sites emerged in
the city (most of them were ruins). People were gradually learning to
admire "ruins" and archaeological sites as real *signs* of the past, which a
small group of enthusiasts were excavating, exploring, and presenting
to the public.[39]

In 1824, Ievgenii himself excavated the foundations of an important
medieval monument – the Church of the Tithes, which held the sarcopha-
gus of Vladimir the Great, perhaps the most famous Grand Prince of Kyiv
(died in 1015), who converted medieval Rus' to Byzantine Christianity
in 988 and was canonized as a saint in the thirteenth century. Another
amateur archaeologist – a retired official named Kindrat Lokhvyts'kyi –
claimed to have found no less impressive objects both mythological
and real. The most impressive of these (and also the most dubious) was
the remnants of St Andrew's Cross. According to a legend, the apostle

2.1 Sazhin, *Excavations of the Ruins of St Irene's Church* (image courtesy of Mystet-stvo)

Andrew had journeyed up the Dnieper and erected a wooden cross on the hills where a great city with a multitude of churches was to emerge – Kyiv. More reliable discoveries included the remnants of St Irene's Church (in 1833) and the famous Golden Gate (in 1832–3), which ever since has been an iconographic image of Old Kyiv. Lokhvyts'kyi took a mystical approach to archaeology; for him, "ancient" monuments had sacred meanings. He no doubt collected enough evidence to place Kyiv within Christian cosmography as an Orthodox *Holy City* founded by Saint Andrew himself. In contrast to Lokhvyts'kyi, Metropolitan Ievgenii cared more about fact checking than about dubious mysticism; and he did not shun secular publicity – quite an unusual stance for a Russian cleric.[40]

To the surprise of the locals, the learned Metropolitan personally conducted the excavations – something that made him a rare bird among the largely obscurantist Orthodox clergy.[41] His discovery of the Church of the Tithes foundations signified the beginning of archaeology as a respectable activity in Russia, if not yet a profession and academic discipline. Also, Ievgenii was the first modern student of the history and archaeology of Kyiv Caves Monastery,[42] a site that drew many thousands of religious pilgrims, beggars, and secular tourists to Kyiv each year. Thanks to Metropolitan Evgenii and his circle, beginning in the 1820s, Kyiv slowly but steadily acquired – or, rather, re-experienced – its "antiquity." For Kyiv, being a city meant being an *ancient* city. The Romantic cult of ruins also helped raise the city's symbolic profile. From this time on, Kyiv would be defined through its past, and no matter how rapidly the city changed, it would be represented in literary and visual sources as above all an "ancient" city.

Kyiv's antiquity often exerted a conservative force as a symbolic and ideological counterweight to the rapid modernization that the city began to experience in the second half of the century. The more multiethnic and cosmopolitan the city became, the more this utopian past was used to represent Kyiv as a Russian and Orthodox city, Russia's spiritual capital. As a consequence, the non-Orthodox – above all, Jews and Catholic Poles – were denied any legitimate claims to the city's historical legacy. In this way, history and memory were placed at the centre of the cultural and political wars that would rage in Kyiv right up to the very end of the Old Regime in Russia.

Events in the early 1830s – specifically, the Polish November uprising of 1830–1 and the opening of Kyiv Saint Vladimir University in 1834 – catalysed both history and politics. This new imperial university became the main proponent of historical and archaeological research in the empire's southwestern borderlands. Not surprisingly, archaeological excavations and historical research focused on medieval Kyiv, once the heart of Kyivan Rus', which according to the official narrative was the cradle of imperial Russia. A special unit named the Temporary Committee for Antiquity Search was established in 1835 and brought together archaeology, history, and ideology. Along with seasoned amateurs from Metropolitan Ievgenii's circle such as Lokhvyt'skyi and Maksym Berlyns'kyi, several university professors led by Professor Mykhailo Maksymovych formed the committee. University-sponsored excavations legitimized the reinvention of Kyiv as an "ancient" city. Archaeology and history, both funded by the Russian imperial state, became important tools in the Russian rediscovery of Kyiv, whereby the city was mapped on the cultural and geopolitical imagination of the empire's subjects.[43]

As a result, by the 1830s visitors to Kyiv were able to satisfy their expectations by visiting a number of visible monuments, archaeological sites, and places of ancient topography. Most of these "places of memory" were known from medieval chronicles, but in the 1830s they were made visible and popularized through historical narratives and illustrated guidebooks.

Arguably the first professional historian of Kyiv was Maksym Berlyns'kyi, a graduate of Kyiv-Mohyla Academy, a long-time resident of the city, and a renowned educator. He began to compile his legendary description of Kyiv and its antiquities as early as 1803 (the first parts of his work were published in 1811). His major work, however, remained unpublished. This was the first "modern" history of Kyiv, which the author submitted to a committee of censors in Saint Petersburg around 1800.[44] That was well before any general survey of Russian, Polish, and Ukrainian history had been published.[45] Thus Berlyns'kyi's work reflected the standards of history writing as they existed in the eighteenth century, which was the era of learned amateurs. The son of a country priest, born far from Kyiv, Berlyns'kyi paradoxically became the most vocal spokesman for the city's own burghers, who left no significant literary, scholarly, or political legacy.

Berlyns'kyi's pioneering book was largely a history of Ukraine from medieval times. However, he placed the city of Kyiv at the centre of his narrative. He divided his work into eight parts, each corresponding to a certain period of Ukraine's history. The book's principal strength was its depiction of the seventeenth and eighteenth centuries, based on archival sources, many of which (like those from the Kyiv magistrate) have since vanished. The author was an ardent advocate of Kyiv self-government and of the city's proud burghers. Unlike most contemporary Ukrainian writers, who were linked to the Cossack leadership or gentry, this first historian of the city sided with the local burghers, often against the Cossack authorities, who tended to encroach on municipal autonomy. Proudly and meticulously, perhaps even excessively, he enumerated all of the possible "privileges" and "rights" conferred on the city by various rulers – Lithuanian, Polish, and Russian.[46] In particular, he celebrated the recent restoration of Kyiv autonomy by his favourite Russian ruler, Paul I, in 1797, noting that the Kyiv magistrate "was to maintain all its rights, privileges, municipal revenue and benefits which the city of Kyiv always enjoyed by virtue of the most supreme charters issued by the serene ancestors of his Majesty the Emperor."[47] Berlyns'kyi refused to mention (he did so only once!) his least favourite ruler – Catherine II – who largely ended Kyiv's municipal autonomy, along with the political autonomy of Cossack Ukraine.

Berlyns'kyi's role was crucial in another respect: he legitimized the concept of a united city of Kyiv, which had only recently been amalgamated by the Russian authorities. History helped him fathom this modern city in the making, with the medieval city providing a model. Here and there he writes about "Kyiv-Podil" (*Kievopodol*) or Pechers'k as separate "towns"; but he also writes that the "city of Kyiv is naturally divided into three parts" – Podil, Old Kyiv, and Pechers'k. The latter, as a seat of the Russian authorities, was to become "the main *part* of the city" (emphasis added).[48] He also correctly ascribed the key role in forging the *united* city to the Russian authorities – in terms of administration, jurisdiction, city beautification, and not least communications. Kyiv's governors, who were often Russian military figures, were instrumental in linking the separate towns by contructing new roads (the first of these around 1702, when Governor Famendin [von Mengden] laid a road linking Pechers'k with Podil, today known as St Vladimir's Slope). It was Catherine II who extended the authority of the Kyiv magistrate to burghers and merchants residing outside of Podil (in Pechers'k and Old Kyiv), paradoxically after she had abolished much of Magdeburg autonomy.[49] As he described all of these developments, Berlyns'kyi celebrated the amalgamated modern city, even if it was largely the creation of figures such as Catherine, whom he clearly loathed. He ended on a positive note, however: his beloved Emperor Paul had just restored Kyiv's autonomous institutions, which were now spreading to other parts of the city.

More importantly, in Berlyns'kyi's mind the past did not contradict the modern city; rather, the past was organically *present* in that city, either as "ancient" churches and ruins or as institutions like municipal self-government. This was especially noticeable in a condensed version of his unpublished history, *Kratkoe opisanie Kieva* (A Brief Description of Kyiv), published while he was still alive in 1820, in which he revisited the city some twenty years after his first attempt.

Thanks to the activities of people like Ievgenii (Bolkhovitinov), Berlyns'kyi, and Maksymovych, Kyiv's secular historical and sacral monuments made an indelible impression on pious Orthodox tourists. But even before that, the most imaginative visitors had been able to mix history and the present in their visions of the city. Nature and mysticism greatly contributed to this mental map of Kyiv. Prince Dolgorukii, an early Russian fan of the city, conveyed well this urban blend of history, myth, and nature while standing on St Andrew's Hill overlooking Podil:

From here one can see the entire Dnieper and on the other side – ... an open road to Moscow, [and] to the right ravines, gullies, and precipices that surround the [burying places] of the Saints and their peaceful dwellings in chilly caves; to the left, near the Dnieper waves, there is a view of Podil with all its architectural beauties, showing you the city [reflected] in water. This is a perfect optical illusion [*obol'shchenie vzora*]! Was it here where Jesus was tempted by the devil when the latter, just for one bow to himself, promised Him everything that he was showing from the height?[50]

St Andrew's Church, although associated with the purported visit of Saint Andrew to Kyiv, was a relatively new site in the first decades of the nineteenth century, having been constructed in the mid-eighteenth.[51] St Andrew's Hill and Church appeared in Kyiv texts relatively late, first in Vladimir Izmailov's travelogue: "How beautiful is the sublime St. Andrew's Church – a thousand poles touch the clouds, as if uniting Heaven and earth" and God with man.[52]

A later example indicates especially clearly the role that the past, including the newly discovered antiquities and monuments, began to play in the consciousness of educated Russians. Stepan Maslov, a botanist from Moscow, travelled to Kyiv in 1835, mainly to visit the city's antiquities. For him, Kyiv was "a living monument of ancient pre-Christian events" but was primarily an *Orthodox* holy place that attracted Ukrainian and Russian pilgrims from all over the empire. He mentioned some religious sites that had only recently been discovered or studied by local scholars: the Caves Monastery, St Michael's Monastery, St Sophia Cathedral, and the ruins of the Church of the Tithes.[53] It was where the legendary princes Askold and Dir were buried and where visitors could gaze upon reminders of Princess Olga and the heroic battles with steppe nomads. Here "came to life, on sites of past events, all ancient tales about the origins of the Russian State, about Kiev." Maslov specifically mentioned the significance of Kyiv's historical topography: although the city's remote past had long been erased, it still "spoke to your heart in a language preserved in historical names of ancient tracts [*urochishch*] of Kiev." "There are so many sacred memories in Christian Kiev!" – exclaimed this botanist turned historian, as if he himself had experienced the events he was recalling on the spot. In fact, a significant number of these "sacred memories" had been assembled only recently by professional and amateur scholars. By the mid-1830s the educated imperial public could "remember" those memories as their own past – ancient, Russian, and Orthodox. In this way, archaeology shaped the nascent Russian myth of Kyiv. Ukrainian intellectuals and travellers (like writer Panteleimon Kulish) might have envisioned Kyiv as an eternally Ukrainian city, but at the same time, quite a few of them contributed to the Russian imperial understanding of the city, at least until the mid-nineteenth century.

Several motifs in Maslov's discourse emphasized the myth that Kyiv was an ancient and holy city, Russia's spiritual capital. Among the key elements of that myth were the following: the antiquities themselves (churches, monasteries, ruins); Orthodox spirituality (sacred sites and pilgrims); "memories" (highly ideological narratives of the city's past); and, last but not least, borderland politics (the city as a "fortress" against the Poles and all potential invaders). This conservative myth presupposed the existence of antagonists, although who they precisely were varied from author to author and from period to period – from Poles to Jews to Ukrainians to impersonal market forces to the radical left.

The myth of Kyiv as Russia's *ancient* and *holy* city laid the foundations for a larger imperial project with distinct colonialist overtones – that of the "rediscovery" of Kyiv by Russian intellectuals and statesmen. Maslov was one of the first observers to grasp the sheer variety of elements of the nascent Kyiv myth – historical, spiritual, and political – all of which, by the mid-1830s, seemed to clash with the city's more mundane economic functions. He pointed specifically to some of Kyiv's new functions: (1) a fortress "important in strategic regards": a project started by the Russian government in the early 1830s in an attempt to turn Kyiv into a "fortress city"; (2) the annual trade fair – the famous *kontrakty*, which brought thousands of Poles and Jews to the city; and (3) a university that was intended to "reconcile Poles with Russians." A holy city, a military fortress, a trade fair, and a "Polish-Russian" university seemed incompatible, but together they buttressed the new political mission of Kyiv as a Russian Orthodox fortress in the borderlands. Kyiv St Vladimir University was to become a *spiritual* fortress.

To grasp the role assigned to the university in the imperial project of rediscovering Kyiv, let us examine the symbolism and rhetoric behind its founding. In his decree establishing Kyiv University, Nicholas I stated that he had chosen Kyiv as "once the cradle of the holy faith of our ancestors and also as a first witness of their civil sovereignty."[54] One can only guess where the cradle of Nicholas's own German ancestors was situated and what kind of the "holy faith" they practised. Official rhetoric, however, tended to falsify origins and distort continuities. Tsar Nicholas symbolically united with the community of Orthodox Russians who believed that Kyiv had belonged to them since time immemorial. It is curious that the university was granted "primarily to the citizens of Kyiv, Volhynia, and Podolia provinces" – that is, to the predominantly Polish-speaking and Catholic nobility of Right-Bank Ukraine. The emperor also recognized their "hereditary pursuit on behalf of education" and the fact that the former Polish lyceum in Krzemieniec (Kremenets') had been transferred to Kyiv. How is one to interpret such paradoxical logic? The best explanation may be that in fabricating a *pre*history of Kyiv University, the government was attempting to conceal the lawlessness behind the opening of the school. It was a way to forget its violent origins, which reminded everyone of the Polish uprising and its brutal suppression. This was precisely why the imperial authorities created the myth that Kyiv had been entitled to host a university "since olden times." This sort of rhetorical continuity underscored historical *discontinuity* and pointed to the arbitrary and accidental origins of the new university, which had its roots in the government's repressive policies.

So we can argue that anti-Polish factors played a major role in the founding of a university in Russia's southwestern borderlands. Several scholarly projects, such as Kyivan academics' systematic archival research in Right-Bank Ukraine, were linked to this cultural war on Poles.[55] Tsar Nicholas took a special interest in discovering and preserving Kyiv's antiquities; this seems to have been his response to the perceived Polish cultural and political threat in the region. But this attention to local history was not solely political; it also reflected the tsar's genuine passion.

For example, he was behind the creation of the Archaeographic Commission in Saint Petersburg in 1834, followed by the Temporary Committee for Antiquity Search in Kyiv in 1835 and by the Imperial Archaeological Society in Saint Petersburg in 1846. All three bodies were devoted to the study of written sources and "antiquities" – remnants of medieval churches, secular buildings, and treasure hoards. During his 1832 visit to Kyiv, Nicholas was impressed by the newly excavated remnants of the Golden Gate. He passed through the walls and declared them "a monument worthy of preservation."[56] The locals heeded his words and began to preserve Kyiv's antiquities (and also the local fruits – the tsar was known to be partial to the local preserves). The Golden Gate was the earliest embodiment of Kyivites' new project,

2.2 Sazhin, *The Ruins of the Golden Gate* (image courtesy of Mystetstvo)

and to preserve it, an architecture professor from Kyiv University (a Pole by birth) inserted iron bars into it.[57]

Most importantly, and this time with an explicit political goal in mind, the tsar, through his loyal lieutenant Dmitrii Bibikov, established the most prominent research institution in imperial Kyiv – the Kyiv Temporary Commission for the Examination of Ancient Documents (*Vremennaia kommissiia dlia razbora drevnikh aktov*), or, simply, the Kyiv Archaeographic Commission, which lasted until 1919. When he visited Kyiv again, on 25 May 1843, he placed all the historical and archaeological research in Kyiv and in the Southwestern Region under the auspices of that commission. Its members, most of them historians and legal scholars from St Vladimir University, collected (or rather confiscated) historical documents from Polish aristocratic homes and Roman Catholic monasteries all over the region. These sources, both published and unpublished, formed the collection of Kyiv Central Archive of Ancient Documents (today, the Central State Historical Archive of Ukraine), founded in 1852. The commission itself was established under the chancellery of Kyiv governor general, and as such it was an integral part of Russian government. It was financed by the state from provincial taxes (500 roubles from each of the three provinces), which indicates that the state was beginning to take the past seriously. Also, history and archaeology became an essential part of imperial borderland politics.[58]

Bibikov himself was an active player in this geopolitical game, in which the leading roles were played by Kyiv historians, who were often ethnic Ukrainians, and most of whom were newcomers to the city. This seems paradoxical – Ukrainians were infiltrating a crucial Russian imperial institution – but it would become a sensitive issue only much later. For the time being, scholars of Ukrainian background (and often with a distinct Ukrainian cultural agenda) were at the forefront of the cultural war. Orthodox Russia was combatting Catholic Poland in what many perceived as a centuries-long war.[59] But it was not just politics that moved Bibikov. A notorious womanizer with a particular weakness for women of pleasure,[60] his other passion was archaeology. He too developed into an ardent amateur archaeologist, even setting the fashion for antiquities – written sources and material culture alike – among the local educated society.[61] This fashion became so irresistible that even the Polish landlords took part in the work of the commission, whose goal was to prove that the Southwestern Region had been "Russian" and "Orthodox" from time immemorial.[62] It was as if Bibikov's main interest with regard to the governance of Kyiv was collecting materials for the Archaeographic Commission – indeed, that may be close to the truth. In the event, historical research together with borderland politics maintained the myth of Kyiv as Russia's ancient capital and holy city. This would be a cornerstone of conservative ideology for many decades to come.

Kyiv University fostered the natural and exact sciences, which were often taught by non-Russians (mostly Germans), but it was also a leading ideological institution. As such it was entrusted with the promotion of the Russian cultural presence in the borderlands. Russia's minister of popular enlightenment, Sergei Uvarov, a self-trained classicist, had an appreciation for ruins and ancient monuments. Also, he had learned from the German Romantics the importance of history and archaeology for national identity. Equipped with these ideas, he took a special interest in Kyiv University, which was to serve as a successful experiment in cultural politics. Known for his ideological triad that emphasized Orthodoxy, autocracy, and nationality as the three pillars of the new

Russian identity, Uvarov helped raise Kyiv's profile in the empire's public sphere. He did this by injecting a geopolitical and ideological emphasis into the previously literary and historical discourse on Kyiv. Not surprisingly, the university stood at the vanguard of both academic and ideological reassessments of the city.

The participants in the opening of the university were well aware of the symbolism that linked Kyiv to St Vladimir (the patron of the university) and through him to Nicholas I, his self-proclaimed successor. Kyiv University represented a visible link between Vladimir, the Christianizer of Rus', and the Russian tsar, thus turning Kyiv into a cornerstone of imperial political genealogy and Russia's own *translatio imperii*. The university's first appointed curator (*popechitel'*), Egor Von Bradke, expressed this with bureaucratic clarity: "The founding of the university named after St Vladimir who enlightened Russia with the light of the holy Christian faith will forever unite in this country the name of Vladimir with the name of Nicholas I, the great renovator of enlightenment in the region from where it had streamed all over Russia."[63]

Another product of imperial ideology and cultural politics in those years was the growing cult of St Vladimir: his impressive monument was unveiled on Kyiv's picturesque hill in 1853 (the idea for it was first broached in 1832). This was the very first monument to any historical figure in the city.[64]

The university with its political symbolism raised Kyiv to prominence. In Uvarov's own words, a key political goal of Kyiv University was "to efface those characteristic features by which Polish youth differed from Russian … to bring them increasingly together with Russian ideas and mores, [and] to imbue them with the common spirit of the Russian people."[65] An immediate consequence of these cultural politics was an emphasis on the Russian and Orthodox history of Kyiv and the surrounding area; this led to the flourishing of regional studies. This increased public attention on Kyiv also provided local scholars with greater symbolic capital and material resources, which could be used to further enhance Kyiv's profile.

Kyiv's own Mykhailo Maksymovych (1804–73), born in Left-Bank Ukraine but educated in Moscow, became the first professor of Russian letters at St Vladimir University. Already known for his studies of Ukrainian folklore and language, he was also the first to articulate systematically the historical and spiritual functions of Kyiv, thus raising the city's visibility in the imperial public sphere.[66] Well-connected in Moscow and Saint Petersburg, Maksymovych promoted whenever he could the idea of Kyiv as Russia's spiritual capital, not just a border-land outpost that happened to have been annexed from Poland. Especially important was his university speech "On the Participation and Importance of Kiev in the Common Life of Russia," which he delivered on 2 October 1837. In it he combined the city's historical and spiritual importance with a new imperial ideology known as "official national-ity," a formula created by Sergei Uvarov, who was conveniently present at the speech.[67] "Kiev until today is the main site of the Russian holi-ness" and of "the national authenticity of the Orthodox Rus'," preached Maksymovych.[68] Maksymovych summarized all of the most important elements of Kyiv's myth: spiritual (the centre of Orthodoxy), historical (the "ancient" city), and ideological (the regenerator of collective mem-ory and a guardian against Polish Catholic influence). All of this greatly heightened Kyiv's profile in the decades to come and firmly planted its image in the minds of the imperial public. The most conservative features of the myth, which Maksymovych unintentionally helped pro-mote, would be used by Russian imperialists and nationalists (includ-ing Moscow-based Slavophiles and pro-governmental conservatives in Saint Petersburg) to buttress their claims to Kyiv.[69]

Maksymovych was the most influential student of Kyiv's past and its ideological functions. He was a prominent contributor to argu-ably the best scholarly work on Kyiv and its province to appear in the mid-century – *The Statistical Description of Kyiv Province.*[70] That three-volume work's official editor was Kyiv civil governor Ivan Funduklei (1804–80), the son of a wealthy Greek merchant who had relocated to Russia from Istanbul.[71] Funduklei also sponsored and edited two other seminal publications dealing with Kyiv's past and present.[72] Like Mak-symovych and other lovers of local antiquities, Funduklei was not a native-born Kyivite. He was born in Saint Petersburg and served in various governmental offices in the capital before moving to Odessa in 1831. There he continued to climb the bureaucratic ladder. In 1837 this ambitious son of a foreigner was ennobled, and two years later he was appointed Kyiv civil governor, an office he held until 1852.

Funduklei was clearly an oddball, for instead of embezzling public funds – a practice favoured by other imperial officials – he used his own private capital to invest in Kyiv's shaky infrastructure and to support various charitable causes, especially schools.[73] Suffering from an "incur-able and disgusting lichen" (perhaps psoriasis), he avoided high soci-ety and instead mixed with artists and scholars. In the 1840s he became the largest private sponsor of historical and archaeological research in Kyiv and in the province, having joined the circle of local amateur and professional students of antiquities, among them Maksymovych, Berlyns'kyi, Lokhvyts'kyi, and the rector of Kyiv Theological Academy, Innokentii (Borisov). Maksymovych and Funduklei also collaborated in a more formal group – the Kyiv Archaeographic Commission, with the former providing expertise and the latter financial resources.

In 1847, Funduklei published in Kyiv the first of three scholarly studies of the city and its region – all three bearing his name – *Obozrenie Kieva v otnoshenii k drevnostiam* (A Review of Kyiv with Respect to Its Antiquities). His friend Maksymovych wrote the introduction, appropriately titled *Ocherk Kieva* (A Sketch of Kyiv). In that sketch the underemployed (and soon to be reclusive) academic presented the first, even if idealized, history of Kyiv; this was a better written and briefer account than Berlyns'kyi's much earlier *History of the City of Kyiv*. (The latter remained unpublished.)

In Maksymovych's sketch, Kyiv was an *amalgamated* city under a single authority – that of the Russian civil governor, who was supervised by governor general. The territorial shape of the contemporary city – that is, of 1840s Kyiv – was a major point of reference for studying earlier periods of its history. For example, by the time the legendary Prince Oleg conquered Kyiv in 882, the city "comprised hardly a fourth part of the present-day Old Town [Old Kyiv]" – that is, only the northwestern part of the Old Kyiv hill (i). Using available archaeological and narrative sources, Maksymovych reconstructed a gradual expansion of settlement to other areas: from Old Kyiv to Podil and to Pechers'k. He was well aware that Kyiv shrank a great deal spatially in late medieval and early modern times, so much so that the city proper was reduced to Podil, while Old Kyiv remained the site of a castle, ruins, and temples (viii). Maksymovych accurately traced the city's growth during the eighteenth and nineteenth centuries. In general, *Ocherk Kieva* was more Kyiv-centric than previous historical and topographical accounts of the city; its author paid comparatively little attention to external political developments, apart from mentioning prominent rulers and the states to which Kyiv belonged at different times.

Maksymovych's approach to the city's history was both more scholarly in method and more pro-Russian in outlook, at least when compared to Berlyns'kyi's writings. It seems that the former professor could not stress enough the importance of Kyiv's Russian connection. Specifically, he celebrated the fact that Bohdan Khmel'nyts'kyi "expelled from Kyiv all the non-Orthodox" and "returned" the city to within the "common boundaries of the Russian state"; he also emphasized the "restoration of church unity of Orthodox Rus'" in 1686, when the Ukrainian Orthodox Church was placed under the authority of the Moscow patriarchs (viii). As a local patriot, however, he took great pride in the fact that in the seventeenth and eighteenth centuries Kyiv, especially its famed academy, provided "spiritual workers" for "entire Rus'." In the same vein he mentioned the most remarkable churches and secular buildings built in the city by Cossack authorities, under Western European influence. Yet he also credited the Russian emperors with rebuilding Kyiv on a grand scale. For example, Tsar Peter established a fortress and facilitated a settlement in Pechers'k, while Empress Elizabeth revitalized Old Kyiv by laying the foundations for St Andrew's Church in 1744; she also envisioned the Palace district by building a royal palace in the area in 1753. Like Maksym Berlyns'kyi, Maksymovych disliked Catherine II. He only mentioned that she had approved a new city plan for Kyiv and chosen the Palace district as a new site of imperial administration (the civil governorship and various boards). His loftiest praise was reserved for the last two tsars – brothers Alexander I and Nicholas I. The latter was especially praiseworthy for giving Kyiv a new general plan and university (both in 1834). Maksymovych finished his sketch with brief but accurate commentary on each particular district and up-to-date topographical and population data.

A major draw of Funduklei's publication, however, was not Maksymovych's comprehensive sketch but its account of Kyiv's "antiquities." This was a wildly eclectic subject that brought together diverse genres, including archaeological studies, a tourist guidebook, and a literary travelogue. More importantly, the book contained sixty-two splendid drawings printed in Paris, which made those antiquities even more tangible. One chapter dealt with Kyiv's toponymy and included eighteen sites (among them such famous ones as Khreshchatyk, Obolon', Klov, and Askold's tomb), almost all of these dating back to ancient Rus'. As a consequence, the remote past, even if legendary, was now legible through modern place names, provided that people knew how to *read* the city. The longest chapter was devoted to Kyiv's many architectural monuments (primarily churches and monasteries), some of which did not survive until the nineteenth century (such as the famous Church of the Tithes, destroyed by the Mongols in 1240). With its illustrations and user-friendly content, this pioneering book was used to promote Kyiv as an ancient city and a prominent tourist destination. What previously had been narrated in travelogues was now visualized, serialized, and made readily available for all kinds of travellers. Kyiv could even be represented in a series of images-as-*logos* – be it Kyiv's picturesque skyline, St Sophia, the Caves Monastery, or the iconic ruins of the Golden Gate. Funduklei, a marketing genius, made Kyiv's past both *visible* and *legible*, and pitched images and texts to a growing audience of imperial consumers hooked on antiquities. The enterprising civil governor was the first office holder who knew how to sell Kyiv's past and how lucrative historical and religious tourism could be for the city. Unfortunately, a host of subsequent governors were enterprising only when it came to lining their own pockets.

Arguably, *The Statistical Description of Kyiv Province* was the single greatest contributor to the natural historical, statistical, and demographic study of Kyiv and its province. Although published under Funduklei's name, most of it was compiled and written by the skilled statistician and economist Dmitrii Zhuravskii. This was a grandiose collaborative effort; local authorities and private citizens (landowners, estate managers, and industrialists) sent numerous reports to Funduklei as governor. The project's actual executor, Zhuravskii, was born in present-day Belarus', studied in Saint Petersburg, and then worked in the civil service under Mikhail Speranskii, who oversaw the publication of Russia's *Svod Zakonov* (Code of Laws). In 1845, Zhuravskii relocated to Kyiv as an official for special missions under Funduklei.[74] His principal "mission" was to collect and edit all kinds of statistical data pertaining to Kyiv province.[75] As most of this dense work deals with the human and animal inhabitants of the province rather than with the city per se, I will mention only a few things related to Kyiv's past.

The book started with prehistory – with the mysterious *anthropophagi* (cannibals) mentioned by Herodotus and with the founder of Kyiv prince Kyi and his Polianians – equally mysterious people but most likely not cannibals – mentioned in the Rus' Primary Chronicle. The timeline goes on to include all the usual suspects – Rus' princes, Mongols, the Kyiv princely family of Olel'kovyches, hetman Bohdan Khmel'nyts'kyi and his Cossack state, and hetman Ivan Vyhovs'kyi and his "independent Grand Duchy of Rus'" – as well as various administrative divisions of Kyiv region in the past, from a Cossack regiment to the Russian imperial *guberniia*. This was not a truly historical introduction, but it firmly placed Kyiv within a continuous historical narrative. References to Kyiv's past also appeared when geographical or meteorological features were discussed (such as the devastating rainstorm of 26 May 1839 that flooded Kyiv's main streets, including Khreshchatyk, where the water "flooded the ground floors of many houses," and the even more destructive flood of 1845). Humans as the subject of description – past and present – then gave way to the plants, insects, and animals of Kyiv province.

Humans reappeared in Part II of the book, which contained population statistics (the subject of chapter 6 of the present book). One of the best *historical* segments of the volume dealt with the nobility of Kyiv province. The author accomplished a sensitive task: he drew the Polish Catholic nobility of the region, still socially dominant in the 1840s, into a broader historical context that seemingly proved that Orthodox and Russian (or rather Ruthenian) nobles had been present in the province much longer than their Catholic peers. He stressed that the elite of the medieval Kyiv principality had been "native Russians" and that it was from "these *Russian* landlords that the mass of local nobility originated and preserved for a long time their initial national character, until the very incorporation of Lithuania into Poland in 1569."[76] Then around 1630 the entire nobility of the Kyiv palatinate enrolled in the Kyiv brotherhood, an Orthodox pressure group. By the mid-seventeenth century, the Kyiv nobility had become more "heterogeneous," for it now included both Poles and "Russians." It was only when the Kyiv region was ceded back to Poland later in that century and Cossack officers evacuated to the left bank that the Polish nobles "began to prevail there." This historical sketch left a strong impression that this "prevalence" of Polish nobles had been only a brief episode in a largely *Orthodox* and *Russian* history of Kyiv and its region. By the 1840s, Polish Catholics still comprised a majority of the region's landowners, but there were also Orthodox – "Russian and Little Russian" – families, each group retaining its "national peculiarities." All in all, the contemporary landed nobility was "diverse by origin" but united through their "common landed interests" – a phrase that underscored that the imperial nobility, irrespective of its origins, was the backbone of Russia's sociopolitical order. It was only the events of 1863 that would prove this reassurance wrong.

Another lengthy historical excursus was devoted to Jews, from the time they settled in Kyiv, purportedly in the tenth century, until 1827, when a tsarist decree barred them from residing in the city because they were "harmful for local business." The volume's objective style did not completely conceal a specific use of history. As with the Polish nobles, history was being used here to show that Jews were an alien and unwelcome element in the city. Inevitably, both communities were regulated and disciplined by the Russian imperial authorities.

Besides a historical introduction (see above), the volume included another historical segment about Kyiv's history. Its author (Zhuravskii?) divides the city's history into three epochs: first, prior to the Mongol invasion of 1239; second, the time of "dependence" on Lithuania and Poland; and third, the "Russian" era. The author reflects the traditional Russian view that Kyiv was the capital of all Rus' only until the mid-twelfth century, when a "grand princely throne" was transferred to the northeast, to the town of Vladimir-on-Kliaz'ma. The author reconstructs the topography of medieval and early modern Kyiv with remarkable precision (based on archaeological and written sources); his general historical scheme seems much sketchier. He makes no mention of the autonomous Kyiv principality under the Olel'kovych dynasty (from the mid-fourteenth century until 1470), although he does mention that "during the Lithuanian-Polish epoch the citizens of Kyiv received privileges" related to municipal self-government (the Magdeburg Law). After referring briefly to the "Cossack wars" and Bohdan Khmel'nyts'kyi, the author writes about Kyiv's "transfer" to the "authority of Russia" in 1654 and the subsequent expulsion of Poles, Armenians, and Jews from the city. In keeping with the volume's legalistic approach to history, he also emphasizes that the new rulers confirmed all of Kyiv's "privileges and rights."

The author imagines Kyiv as a recently amalgamated city, crediting imperial rulers with extending it and with connecting its previously separate parts, including Pechers'k and Podil. He emphasizes that the imperial government played a crucial role in replanning several districts, specifically Podil in the 1730s and 1740s: a city hall (*ratusha*) was completed, and "major streets were paved, canals were laid, and hospitals, armouries, powder magazines ... were built."[77] Also discussed is the city's self-government. For example, this is how the author explains the somewhat confusing coexistence of several jurisdictions within the city, alluding to the fact that Kyiv historically had been split into a number of distinct territorial communities:

As regards subordination, with the establishment of the Kyiv Viceroyalty [in 1782] Kyiv was placed under supervision of the Kyiv treasury board [*kazennaia palata*] in economic matters; policing and executive powers were given to the Kyiv governor; military – to the commandant of Pechers'k fortress; while legal procedure and internal governance were left to citizens themselves on the basis of the Magdeburg law which ... had applied, from its very introduction, to the inhabitants of Podil only. Meanwhile,

Upper Town [Old Kyiv] was always administered directly by voivodes and governors. But then until 1782 the issue of the Magdeburg Law was constantly changing for more than a hundred of years, together with general changes in regional administration. For the most part, however, the city depended on the Little Russian government, while Kyiv governors used to have only limited supervision over citizens, without meddling in internal affairs of the magistrate.[78]

In contrast to Berlyns'kyi and Maksymovych, who ignored Catherine II, the author (or authors) of the 1852 book commended the empress for her role in redeveloping Kyiv. Specifically, she approved the "first regular plan of the city," according to which Podil was to be erased, with its inhabitants resettled in Old Kyiv and Pechers'k. Although convenient for the military, this plan proved to be "contrary to the benefits of burghers and the needs of trade" and thus was revoked in 1797. This historical sketch ends on an upbeat note: it calls the city's rebuilding during the first four decades of the nineteenth century the "epoch of Kyiv's greatest development." It is no surprise that the author, himself a state official, attributed this "greatest development" to his own employer – the imperial state that was bringing urban modernity to the borderlands.

Regarding more popular treatments of Kyiv's past, two writers cannot be ignored. One wrote in the more academic style of a historical-archaeological study; the other offered "light reading" – a blend of travelogue and tourist guide. The first was Mykola Zakrevs'kyi (1805–71); the second, Mykola Sementovs'kyi (1819–79).

Zakrevs'kyi was a native-born Kyivite – an extremely rare bird among the many amateur and professional experts on the city's past. He was born into a noble family from Poltava region. He graduated from the local *gimnaziia* and went on to study at Kharkiv and Derpt (Tartu) universities, the latter located in what is now Estonia, where he spent a number of years teaching Russian. He settled in Moscow in 1859, where he worked as a clerk at Moscow University and at the local public (Rumiantsev) museum. His first piece of writing about Kyiv's past was the brochure *Ocherk istorii Kieva* (A Survey of Kyiv's History), published in 1836 in Revel (Tallinn). His most important work, *Letopis' i opisanie Kieva* (A Chronicle and Description of Kyiv), appeared in 1858, sponsored by his Ukrainian compatriot Osyp Bodians'kyi, who was a professor at Moscow University and the editor of a prestigious journal.[79] The book was very well received; even so, the author immediately started work on a revised and expanded edition. This one, titled *Opisanie Kieva* (A Description of Kyiv), was published in 1868 in two volumes in Moscow, funded by the president of the Moscow Archaeological Society, Count Aleksei Uvarov.[80] This may have reflected not so much the well-connectedness of the author, a humble clerk, as the growing importance of Kyiv and its antiquities for the empire's public. The two versions of Zakrevs'kyi's seminal work were separated by the Polish January uprising of 1863, a critical event that helped rekindle interest in Kyiv's past besides intensifying the struggle over the southwestern borderlands.

Although not a professional historian, Zakrevs'kyi was a skilful researcher who often cited primary and secondary sources in various languages. He even doubted the conventional story about Saint Andrew's journey to the Dnieper and his prophecy about the founding of Kyiv – an apocryphal tale that still had its proponents among the "experts" on Kyiv history (including Maksymovych). Nor did his critical spirit spare another mainstay of the local tradition – the story about the city's legendary founders, the brothers Kyi, Shchek, and Khoryv and their sister Lybid', whose names are mentioned in the Primary Chronicle and reflected in local toponymy. He dismissed that tale as an "invented fable," adding that "the fate of almost all cities famous for their antiquity is the same where their origins are concerned."[81] He pointed to the examples of Athens, Rome, Constantinople, and other great ancient cities. Nor could Zakrevs'kyi pass up an opportunity to slam his rival Sementovs'kyi, whose popular book appeared in 1864. The literary feud between these two foremost experts on Kyiv antiquities took on the familiar comic overtones of Gogol's "Tale of How Ivan Ivanovich Quarreled with Ivan Nikiforovich." In an unusually long footnote, Mykola Vasyl'ovych (Zakrevs'kyi) accused Mykola Maksymovych (Sementovs'kyi) of various sins, from ignorance to plagiarism.[82] In particular, the former reproached the latter for taking the "tale" about Kyi, Shchek, and Khoryv (and similar tales) literally, as if they were historical fact. More seriously, Sementovs'kyi was accused of plagiarizing Zakrevs'kyi's work (his 1836 *Ocherk istorii Kieva*). All in all, Zakrevs'kyi considered his rival's works to be "contrary to common sense" – an even stronger insult than the epithet "goose," which had so terribly offended one of the quarrelling landowners in Gogol's famous story.

Notwithstanding all this, the author of *Opisanie Kieva* largely follows Nestor the Chronicler when describing the city's medieval history and topography, although he also quotes some Latin sources, besides assessing various publications of the Primary Chronicle. Kyiv rivalled European capitals in its glory but also shared their fate in its decay. After the death of Prince Iaroslav "the Great" in 1054, the capital on the Dnieper suffered the same fate as Aachen after the death of Charlemagne – the great ruler's "weak and cowardly successors" destroyed the city's "happiness" and "the might of Russia." "With the death of this monarch," laments Zakrevs'kyi, "there began a great tragedy that lasted for around 300 years, which plunged our fatherland into impotence." As if anticipating a rivalry with ethnic Russians, Zakrevs'kyi stresses that the term "Rus'" was applied in the twelfth and thirteenth centuries almost exclusively to Ukrainian lands, or "southwestern Russia." In the same vein, he mentions that Prince Andrei of Vladimir-Suzdal, whose troops plundered Kyiv in 1169, "had already for a long time looked at Kyiv's dominance with indignation." With overt populist fervour, the author writes that on the eve of the Mongol Invasion in 1240, Kyivites "in time of danger were not blessed by the presence of a single prince who would have shared with them their labors and terrible fate."[83]

The political climate in the Russian Empire in the 1860s was relatively liberal; despite this, the Moscow-based writer accepts the notion of Kyiv's "return" (*vozvrashchenie*) "under the Russian state" in 1667. He also parrots the common (albeit incorrect) view held by most Russian historians that during the fourteenth and fifteenth centuries Kyiv was no more than a "poor village." But he does mention the "Kyiv revival" of the mid-fifteenth century associated with the princely Olel'kovych family – in particular, the restoration of the Assumption Cathedral at the Caves Monastery. "Ukrainians" and "Little Russians" appear in this scrupulous survey of Kyiv history quite unexpectedly, right after the author's comments about the abolition of the Kyiv principality in 1471 and, more predictably, in the context of Polish social and religious oppression. Also rather conventionally, he associates Ukrainians with the Zaporozhian Cossacks:[84]

> The persecution [at the hands of] Polish nobles and clergy of the Orthodox faith was on the rise. In the meantime, Little Russians, who sought refuge from their tyrants, found such in Kyiv, and thus the city was getting more populous ... As a result, Kyiv-Podil grew to be the largest district. Other Ukrainians, who were persecuted in Poland and Lithuania for their Orthodox faith and were ravaged by Tatar raids, found refuge on the Dnieper islands where they laid the foundations of the Zaporozhian Sich.

Then Zakrevs'kyi proceeds to do what he knows best – he quotes from various primary sources, ranging from Royal (Polish and Lithuanian) Charters and "privileges" to Latin- and Polish-language treatises and chronicles to "universals" of Ukrainian hetmans and charters of Russian tsars. In doing so he seeks to depict socioeconomic relations in the city, which he does quite believably. Like Maksym Berlyns'kyi before him, Zakrevs'kyi, a proud Kyiv resident himself, pays special attention to the Magdeburg (or "Ottonian") Law, which supposedly had been obtained by the residents of Podil in 1499, and was expanded by Polish kings and then confirmed by the Muscovite government in 1654.[85] That law guaranteed self-rule and trading privileges to Kyiv's municipal community, which was based in Podil, where the magistrate was located. The Magdeburg Law, the author stresses, separated Kyiv from Russia in crucial legal ways: "All these charters, laws, and the so-called privileges, a part of which must have been the Magdeburg Law, little by little separated Kyivites from their native brother Russians. So there appeared among Kyiv citizenry a new order, alien to Rus', that removed all of those former laws and customs which contradicted the German law."[86]

Then, suddenly, the author lashes out at the Jews. By quoting a royal privilege of 1619 banning Jews from residing permanently in Kyiv, Zakrevs'kyi shows himself to be an outspoken anti-Semite and an opponent of the 1860s liberal reforms that permitted certain categories of Jews to return to the city. He assures his readers half-heartedly that he is not a bigot and that he respects the "human rights" of Jews; he then adds that a decree similar to the one from 1619 "would be quite useful in our own times, because the interests of Jews, due to their religion, character, and a distinct nationality, always were and shall always be *incompatible* with those of Christians."[87] This statement exposes the typical narrow-mindedness of native-born Kyiv burghers.

Quite expectedly, among all the historical personalities of the volatile seventeenth century, the author chooses to discuss two Cossack hetmans and one church dignitary. They are Petro Konashevych Sahaidachnyi, Bohdan Khmel'nyts'kyi, and the Orthodox Metropolitan Petro Mohyla, all three of whom embodied a stereotypical narrative of the Kyiv Orthodox community's struggle against Catholic Poles. For Kyiv this centuries-long struggle ended happily in 1686, when "Providence returned to Russians their ancient and holy heritage." Historians often resorted to this cliché when describing the Russo-Ukrainian connection, at least until around 1900, when Mykhailo Hrushevs'kyi, then a professor in Lviv, began to "unmake" Russia's dominant historical scheme.[88] Although no stranger to clichés, Zakrevs'kyi was one of the most critically minded writers on Kyiv, certainly much more so than Berlyns'kyi, Zhuravskii, and Maksymovych. For instance, his general assessment of much of the legacy that various dignitaries, including the Russian tsars, left in Kyiv was overtly sceptical: "Piety or vanity, good will or politics of Princes, Tsars, and Hetmans filled the archives of the magistrate and monasteries with charters and privileges, but very little was done for the education of local residents and the development of the city."[89]

Especially when it comes to the eighteenth to mid-nineteenth centuries, Zakrevs'kyi's well-referenced work has been indispensable for all subsequent historical studies of Kyiv (including Vladimir Ikonnik-ov's classic survey of 1904). Here I mention only a few of the author's favourite themes and rulers. Remarkably, unlike other writers about Kyiv, Zakrevs'kyi did not worship all Russian tsars, and he limited their presence in his book to descriptions of their visits to Kyiv (Peter's in 1706 and 1709, Elizabeth's in 1744). For Ukrainian authors, Elizabeth was by far the most beloved ruler, and Zakrevs'kyi was no exception to this, calling her "[Peter's] generous daughter who did so many favors to this city and to the entire Little Russia." Her successor Catherine II, so deeply detested by Berlyn's'kyi, is accorded a far more prominent role in Zakrevs'kyi's version of Kyiv's past. During her "glorious" reign, he asserts, the city acquired its contemporary municipal order, and "there occurred many changes which had beneficial consequences." Strangely, we do not learn what those "consequences" were.[90] Instead we learn a great deal about the 1781 visit of Grand Prince Pavel Petrovich – Russia's future Emperor Paul I, Catherine's son, whom she famously disliked. In his meticulous descriptions of the visits of Catherine and Paul, the author shows Kyiv's proud burghers in their collective glory. In doing so, he celebrates municipal self-government by visualizing for his readers the elaborate rituals of the past.

Perhaps the highlight of the volume's historical section is the author's personal account of the fire that devastated Podil in 1811 (see the next chapter). He credits the Russian government and private donors with donating substantial sums of money to the fire's victims, although he adds that this financial help was distributed unevenly. His own family, for example, lost a house and became so destitute that his father soon "died of sorrow."[91] Yet by 1812, the city architect Melens'kyi had laid out the new regular blocks and streets in Podil. Zakrevs'kyi attributes the city's greatest transformation to the rule of Nicholas I, Russia's conservative monarch, who for better or for worse was obsessed with Kyiv – with its history and its geopolitical role. Although he was a native-born Kyiv resident, Zakrevs'kyi was strikingly terse about the abolition of Kyiv's Magdeburg rights in 1835, devoting only one sentence to this development. His overall assessment of the radical changes that Kyiv experienced in the first half of the century was rather negative; he lamented the loss of historical landmarks and the inadequate improvement of the city's districts.

Zakrevs'kyi's main interest was not social or political history; rather, it was historical toponymy to which he devoted the largest part of his two-volume publication. Compared to an earlier publication by Funduklei and Maksymovych (*Obozrenie Kieva v otnoshenii k drevnostiam*, 1847), Zakrevs'kyi's 141 toponymic entries are much more detailed, and they are arranged in alphabetical order (from the mysterious place name Azagorium to the church of St Theodosius); in this way, they serve as a comprehensive encyclopedia of Kyiv antiquities. His work is also distinguished by its academic character. If Funduklei made antiquities visible, thereby stimulating the city's tourist industry, Zakrevs'kyi made them speak – primarily to a learned audience.

Following in Funduklei's footsteps, Zakrevs'kyi's younger contemporary and rival Mykola Sementovs'kyi targeted a much wider audience. He perfected the genre of the popular guidebook. Compared to Zakrevs'kyi, he had a more traditional biography for a student of Kyiv's antiquities. Like many experts on the city's past, Sementovs'kyi was born in the countryside, on his father's estate in Left-Bank Ukraine. He studied at the famed Nizhyn Lyceum, Gogol's alma mater. After 1843 the young Ukrainian, like the famous writer before him, migrated to the imperial capital. While in Saint Petersburg, he transformed his hobby – Ukrainian history and folklore – into a highly prolific career as a writer and historian. In 1849 he moved to Kyiv, where in 1852, the same year that Funduklei left office, he found employment in the chancellery of the Kyiv civil governor. Sementovs'kyi's first important work about Kyiv was a travelogue about his deeply personal encounter with the city and its most prominent historical landmarks.[92] Despite this book's popular appeal, or perhaps because of it, it brought its author many official accolades, ranging from a golden snuffbox awarded by Tsar Nicholas's two sons to a diamond ring awarded by Nicholas himself. That same year, this modest bureaucrat turned writer was elected a corresponding member of the Imperial Archaeological and Numismatic Society.

What was it about his book that was so appealing to the empire's political and academic establishments? Part spiritual journey, part guide to antiquities, the book was a dramatized account of a journey the author and his brother made from Left-Bank Ukraine (the town of Pereiaslav) to Kyiv, on their way visiting sites associated with Old Rus' and the Ukrainian Cossacks, who were still a fashionable subject for the imperial public.[93] The book's poetic style is evident in the following description of the road to Kyiv. This passage is heavy with Romantic notions of nostalgia, remembrance, and forgetting:

> It is a pleasure to ride along this way so rich in historical events. On every step of the way memory brings forth recollections that lure [one's] imagination to the past ages. Here every rampart, every hill and burial mound among the fields – built by human hands and soaked with human blood – bear witness to numerous events of the past and give birth to both memories and imaginings. In the green fields, which now stand in beauty of splendid crops, in the old days there often shone the weapons of the Cumans, Varangians, Pechenegs, Turks, Tatars, Poles, Zaporozhians, and Ukrainian warriors. The soil here is abundantly washed with the blood of Christians and pagans. But today all these events have disappeared, all has passed like a dream or a fleeting apparition, having left the rich fields in the middle of the autocratic Russian realm that began to extend its present immense limits precisely from these places.[94]

The past may have become a dream or even an apparition, but it could be reconstructed with the help of the imagination, through which "thousand-year-old events repeat themselves in every detail."[95] The final product has little to do with secular science – the author continually makes reference to Christian cosmology and the next world. For example, as soon as he sees the dome of the "holy Lavra," he immediately envisions biblical characters: the shepherds and the Magi guided by the Star of Bethlehem, the latter symbolized by the dome itself. "I began to think about afterlife," admits Sementovs'kyi in mystical fervour, and he adds that in Kyiv he can feel divine grace. This biblical setting reflects an overall transcendental treatment of Kyiv's past, sprinkled with a heavy dose of Russian Orthodox nationalism in the present. The image of omnipresent pilgrims flocking to the Caves Monastery symbolizes the unity of all "children of Russia" worshipping at the "native shrine." Sementovs'kyi believed the myth of Saint Andrew, according to which the apostle travelled along the Dnieper and erected a wooden cross on the hill where Kyiv would later rise. "This is how in the person of the apostle God granted His blessing to the creation of Kyiv and then to the birth of the mighty Orthodox Russian realm," he writes, underscoring his imperial political correctness.

By combining personal narrative, popular history, brazen religious fervour, and imperial ideology, Sementovs'kyi seems to have found a perfect recipe for a bestselling guidebook. He ideologically sterilizes all historical events and turns them into imperial souvenirs. While visiting the Caves Monastery, he creates a Kyiv-centred version of the imperial historical canon in which Kyivan Rus' princes, Ukrainian hetmans, local church dignitaries, and Russian monarchs and aristocrats are mentioned side by side, either as benefactors of the monastery or as deserving of a burial place there. Predictably, hetman Mazepa is mentioned not as a benefactor but as the man who executed two Cossack officers buried in the monastery. Later, walking through Podil, Sementovs'kyi in the same breath mentions Grand Prince Vladimir the Great, the Cossack hetman Sahaidachnyi, an eighteenth-century Ukrainian traveller, and even local Gogolesque market women, while also quoting from a popular Ukrainian folk song. In his descriptions of Podil's numerous churches, he exaggerates or imagines their origins in the remote past, during the age of Kyivan Rus'. In this way, he ascribes to Kyiv's burgher heartland an *all-Russian* significance that transcends the district's Ukrainian flavour of the last few centuries.

The genre of the walking tour, which is more travelogue than academic study, allowed Sementovs'kyi to attach historical accounts to particular monuments and sites.[96] This eclecticism in terms of themes and characters was offset by uniformity in ideology: from medieval princes to Zaporozhian Cossacks, "eternal" Kyiv was at centre stage in an epic struggle waged by the Orthodox against their various enemies – steppe nomads, Muslims, Catholics, Uniates, and other "alien people." Like Maksymovych before him but speaking to a wider audience, Sementovs'kyi extolled Kyiv as the fount of Russia's spirituality and power. As he stands at one historical site in Old Kyiv, once the political heart of Kyivan Rus', he exclaims: "It is here where Rus' was born – its Orthodoxy, its nationality, its invincible might, greatness, and its autocracy. This place is sacred for every Russian."[97] Kyiv was so significant because it had preserved its "imperishable holiness," thus proving that "faith and shrines" outlive all else in the world.[98]

But no other publication could rival Sementovs'kyi's immensely popular historical guidebook *Kiev, ego sviatynia* (Kyiv and Its Holiness), which had gone through seven editions by 1900.[99] In many ways this new work was an updated version of the author's earlier guidebook, but this time the narrative was much more academic, structured as it was around the city's six districts. In it, in a rather dry, academic voice, he describes various religious and secular sites in each district. His ideological stance, which embodies the spirit of the notorious "official nationality," is most obvious in the book's two epigraphs, both from Russian emperors: Nicholas I called Kyiv "the cradle of the holy faith of our ancestors"; Alexander II described the city as the "Jerusalem of the land of Rus'."

Aside from this and few other popular guidebooks and illustrated albums that presented Kyiv as Russia's Jerusalem and were filled with ideological and visual clichés,[100] there were more academic treatments of Kyiv's past. Volodymyr Antonovych was a long-time professor at St Vladimir University,[101] known primarily for his studies of early modern Ukraine. But he was also an expert on historical Kyiv.[102] He approached the city's past from a Ukrainian standpoint (albeit cautiously), emphasizing a continuity of local history from the end of Kyivan Rus' to the advent of Polish rule in the region in the sixteenth century. His views, however, were not entirely new. By the mid-nineteenth century the history of Kyiv had turned into a battleground between Ukrainian and Russian authors, although they were often friends or worked in the same institutions.

Mikhail Pogodin, a conservative historian from Moscow, contended that Kyiv and its environs were originally populated by Great Russians who migrated north after the Mongol Invasion of the mid-thirteenth century. Only after this migration, he argued, did the "Little Russians" or Ukrainians come to the area. Pogodin's close friend, Mykhailo Maksymovych, refuted the thesis that Ukrainians were later arrivals in Kyiv.[103] As Serhii Plokhy recently put it, "at stake was the question of Russian and Ukrainian historical identity and which of the two East Slavic nations had the better claim to the legacy of the Kyivan Rus' princes."[104] So generations of Ukrainian historians, from Maksymovych through Antonovych to his most celebrated student Mykhailo Hrushevs'kyi, pointed to a continuous Ukrainian presence in Kyiv and to the city's uninterrupted significance as a commercial, spiritual, and political centre.

This view found its fullest expression in *Kievskaia Starina* (1882–1907), a journal overseen by a group of local academics and civic activists sympathetic to the Ukrainian cause. The editors published many materials about the city's eighteenth- and nineteenth-century history. Their journal did much to promote civic spirit among Kyivites by elucidating the history of local self-government and its legal tradition, which had been based on the Central European Magdeburg Law until it was ended by the Russian authorities in 1835. Arguably, however, the greatest achievement of academic historiography on Kyiv was the 1904 survey of the city's modern history written by Vladimir Ikonnikov (1841–1923), a Kyiv-born historian who taught at St Vladimir University.[105] Ikonnikov was a specialist in eighteenth-century Russian history; this particular survey, though, dealt with the most sensitive period of local history, from 1654 to 1855 – two hundred years marked by a gradual decline in the city's autonomy, especially after the mid-eighteenth century. Ikonnikov's survey was ideologically neutral and took a positivist approach, providing an assortment of facts and quotations gathered from a multitude of sources, ranging from archival legal documents to memoirs. His inclusive vision was that of a city shaped by various political forces and sustained by different historical traditions.

The exploration of Kyiv's past was undoubtedly part of the Russian rediscovery of the city and the surrounding region – a political project spearheaded by the imperial government. Kyiv was thus subjected to the notorious "imperial gaze," and most of the active participants in this were born outside the city. Agents of empire of various ethnic backgrounds and of different occupations (among them officials, academics, and travellers for pleasure) found themselves in a politically charged "contact zone" in which no knowledge could remain neutral.[106] Also, knowledge of Kyiv's past was used differently by Ukrainian and Russian scholars as early as the mid-nineteenth century, during the Pogodin–Maksymovych debate. But as Faith Hillis recently showed, the boundaries between Russian and Ukrainian intellectuals remained blurred until well into the twentieth century.[107] It was only after the 1917 Revolution that a specifically Ukrainian treatment of Kyiv's past became fully established.

New Kyiv vs Old Kyiv: The Cemetery, the Bridge, and the American Speed

It has been assumed that Kyiv as a city was always somewhat reluctant to embrace change. Anything jarringly new in this city of the past was frowned upon. Kyiv was symbolically stuck in the past, and many contemporaries were not ready to recognize its right to change.[108] With the rise of the modern city, the voices of the past grew more belligerent.

Yet the most ardent defender of old Kyiv against change was not in fact a Ukrainian, nor was it even someone born here; rather, it was a northern tourist who became passionately attached to the city's holiness and antiquity. This was Andrei Muraviev (1806–74), a Russian-born advocate of Kyiv's Orthodox legacy, who spent his later years in the city campaigning for the preservation of local antiquities.[109] In 1859 he purchased a large house in Old Kyiv just across from the Baroque masterpiece of St Andrew's Church. For the next ten years he visited his second home annually for recreation and meditation. In 1868 he settled in Kyiv permanently, and from his home on St Andrew's Slope he began to harass various public authorities with multiple complaints. He even managed to antagonize Kyiv's highest clergy by constantly finding fault with local religious practices. This pious Orthodox crusader, also known for his vigorous struggle against the sex trade in the city,[110] was perhaps the single most important defender of old Kyiv against various forces of change, be they the railways, Jewish capitalists, Polish lawyers, or Russian generals intent on transforming the city's historic core into a huge fortified camp.

This conservative romantic launched an onslaught against the contemporary city. But the real target of his harangues was urban change in general, with the Jews and the railways being only its most visible and annoying representatives. More than anyone else before or since, he decried the coming of the new Kyiv:

One doesn't need to be a Kyiv old-timer to be able to see how much [the city's] original character has changed. In the course of some ten or fifteen years there has disappeared all this patriarchal character which comprised [Kyiv's] defining feature and was perhaps its best adornment, second only to the beauty of its natural setting! "Old things have passed away; behold, all things have become new,"[111] but is this all for the better? Although all this is considered as progress, this very word is still not adopted by our speech. Kyiv was a cradle of our faith, situated on the hills where there began to shine for us the enlightenment, and not secular but religious. Kyiv was a depository of native prayers from the early centuries of our Christianity, and remained a bastion of Orthodoxy during the middle ages of our history. Now [Kyiv], in appearance and in spirit (which is even sadder), has changed itself from the holy mother of Russian cities into the one like all the others. It doesn't stand out anymore, and if it were not for its ancient temples on picturesque hills, which are attended more by visiting pilgrims than by locals, then it would have been impossible to see in it our native Jerusalem – so much it has lost its poetic and legendary character.[112]

From the position of Orthodox fundamentalism, he attacked the coming of the railway to the city. In the good old days, the mass of pilgrims had travelled on foot to the local holy sites; now, by contrast, "everyone is rushing by, on the steam wings of the railway, as if there were nothing in Kyiv which could hold back this hasty rush." This grumpy old man proceeded to complain about "the whistles of steamers or railways" at all hours of the day and night, which somehow made people forget about the "sacred meaning" of Kyiv. He even seemed to think that pilgrimage to the city by railway was sinful! In a tone worthy of Savonarola, he castigated Kyivites, especially their "high society," for preferring theatres and a noisy entertainment park where "music roars and rockets burst." Even the clergy was guilty for distorting "church canons" by cancelling morning services. But, as he sarcastically put it, who cared about morning services "under the whistles of railways and steamers"? The city that Muraviev longed for and whose loss he lamented so much was a utopian city of holy relics, devout pilgrims, and prayer meditations – a city untouched by modern communications, urban planning, and military installations (like the infamous fortress). While this utopian city of Orthodox saints had never actually existed, the city of Orthodox anti-Semites was very much alive.

An obsessive anti-Semite, Muraviev was no fan of cosmopolitan demographics in general. He perceived all the non-Orthodox in the city as the embodiment of perilous modernity, on par with the whistles of steamers and trains. Poles may have been an eyesore in the Orthodox cityscape, but "despite the Polish speech … the strong hand of those in power was able to keep everything in due order, and the Russian spirit predominated over the alien element." Jews, however, were much more detrimental to the utopian Kyiv of Orthodox fantasies. He blamed the "Jewish scourge" (*iazva Evreiskaia*) for the supposed fact that Kyiv "has lost its primeval Orthodox character." He rejected outright "loud phrases about the equality of all faiths before God and all national rights in society," instead lamenting Kyiv's "Egyptian bondage." This time, however, the slave masters were Jews themselves. He wrote these lines at the very end of his life in 1874, as if Jews were a much bigger concern for him than the eternity he was about to face. He was convinced that the despotic Jewish oligarchs "suck out the last juices from the Christians," thus managing "to subjugate all [Christian] inhabitants in villages and towns."[113] The Jews had already "invaded" Kyiv's "best neighborhoods" and taken over "all industries." In addition, the greed of Jewish and Polish lawyers has littered Kyiv with the signs advertising their services. Kyiv, the utopian city that Muraviev so cherished in his free-ranging reveries, was clearly doomed:

> Thus Kyiv gradually is being transformed from a holy center of our Christianity into a Jewish capital; and soon it will be subjugated, together with the entire Southwestern Region, by these incorrigible enemies of Christ, who have become in it not only homeowners but also, by posing as renters, real landowners, even though they [Jews] are much more detrimental than the Polish magnates in all respects – industrial, moral, and religious.[114]

To the list of enemies of old Kyiv, such as Jews, Poles, lawyers, railways, commercial signboards, loud music, and theatres, Muraviev added another element – the newly introduced municipal self-government. The problem with it was that the new city executive (*uprava*) was filled with academics, "men of progress," rather than with "experienced old-timers" who would cherish the past and the "tales of ancientry." As a fiscal and social conservative, Muraviev attacked the city for raising taxes, selling the "splendid University square" for "Jewish housing," and ignoring the alcoholism and rampant filth that plagued the city. However absurd all of this was, Muraviev did win some battles in his one-man war. He did not stop the building of railways, nor did he prevent Poles and Jews from "littering" and "subjugating" Kyiv. But he did manage to halt some plans of the Russian generals.

The city had been struggling for years with a very cumbersome esplanade[115] when around 1869 the local military authorities decided to extend the fortifications even farther. Even the university quarter would have been affected by this proposed expansion. As a defender of Kyiv's historic monuments, Muraviev was greatly alarmed. He later recalled that "the critical moment came for Kiev ... This would have destroyed both the Old City and the new areas around the Botanical Garden, of which the best parts were being allocated for the fortifications; the city, which was under construction in those parts, would have been completely demolished ... Kiev in regard to economics would have fallen altogether." Reportedly, only Muraviev's personal influence among Russian statesmen spared Kyiv from this destructive military urbanism.[116] Clearly, the Holy City of Kyiv was at times stronger than the imperial military. A second plan, this one developed by military engineer Eduard Totleben to encircle Pechers'k fortress with twenty-seven forts, was also abandoned.[117] That plan, however, was realized in

Warsaw, where by 1886 more than thirty forts surrounded the city core, as if to emphasize that city's far greater strategic importance.[118]

As a self-proclaimed spokesman for the Orthodox city, Muraviev "invented" one of the most important traditions in imperial Kyiv, one that forged continuity between the pre-1835 self-governing city and the amalgamated imperial city of the 1860s. Specifically, he revived the public cult of Saint Vladimir, already a saintly patron of Kyiv University, whose monument had adorned one of Kyiv's picturesque hills since 1853.

Apparently on Mid-Pentecost (an Orthodox holiday celebrating the Small Blessing of the Waters), Kyivites used to conduct a cross procession. On that day they proceeeded down towards the earliest of Kyiv's monuments dedicated to Saint Vladimir (in fact commemorating the confirmation of the city's Magdeburg rights by Tsar Alexander I in 1802). The procession, however, had no a fixed date, so the ceremony – initially a celebration of civic pride – was all but forgotten after municipal self-government was abolished in 1835. Soon after, the monument deteriorated as well. Years later, in 1861, Muraviev, who enjoyed the respect of Russian military and civil authorities, as well as of Orthodox hierarchs, decided to move the cross procession from Mid-Pentecost to Saint Vladimir's day (15 July). In the run-up to this, "some burghers" renovated the monument, while Muraviev himself founded the Saint Vladimir Brotherhood, an Orthodox advocacy group whose aim was, aside from assisting parish schools, to "strengthen Orthodoxy" in the Southwestern Region. In practice, this meant missionary activity among the non-Orthodox, above all Jews, for which purpose this Orthodox crusader opened a special shelter and school for recent converts.[119]

The laying of the foundation of St Vladimir Cathedral in 1862 completed the formation of the public cult of Vladimir the Great in imperial Kyiv.[120] Regarding the renewed procession, Kyiv's conservative Russian newspaper *Kievlianin* produced an ecstatic report. Needless to say, this "invented tradition" was viewed as an explicit refutation of Polish claims to Kyiv and its historical legacy:

And after this celebration one can't help asking: whose city is it – Polish or Russian? This magnificent multitude of Orthodox clergy in holy attire, these sounds of holy songs flowing together with the sounds of military music, these crosses and banners of Orthodox churches accompanied by Russian military flags and tens of thousands of people [praying] in the common native Russian language: what the solemn – and spontaneously appealing to anyone – affirmation of primordial rights of Kyiv to the name of a *three times Russian* city![121] (emphasis added)

This and other invented traditions only underscored the tensions between the old and new elements in Kyiv's image. Those tensions were already apparent by the 1820s, with the inception of the antiquarian activities of Metropolitan Ievgenii (Bolkhovitinov) and his circle. As early as 1820, the first historian of Kyiv, Maksym Berlyns'kyi, left an eyewitness report:

The Kyiv of today does not resemble [the city of the] past. Even its hills and valleys on which it rests, as well as the waters surrounding it, all are changed; except for its ancient name, everything in it is new. All ancient is erased and effaced by previous centuries, while new ages renewed it [Kyiv] again, especially today's age, the age of education and civilization, under the benevolent care of the blessed authorities [...]. One can see everywhere taste, perfection, industriousness, care, [and] pursuit of the new best.[122]

Others felt less upbeat about the radical change. As we already know, one Russian expatriate in the city, Count Buturlin, who resided there in the 1830s, witnessed a heavy-handed implementation of the new urban plan in the city core. He attributed the destruction of many of Kyiv's antiquities to the actions of Governor General Vasilii Levashov, whose "vandalism" destroyed "to its foundations a part of Old Kyiv's defensive wall" and "part of an ancient moat" that surrounded St Sophia Cathedral and St Michael's Monastery. All of this was done "under the pretext that it [the wall] blocked a passage."[123] Whether or not the count knew that the "ancient" rampart was largely a product of the eighteenth century, in his eyes the old city had to be defended against ruthless government authorities.

Arguably the most important intellectual in Kyiv in the middle decades of the century was the already mentioned Mykhailo Maksymovych, a newcomer to the city, who arrived there from Moscow in 1834 (although he was born just east of Kyiv). Like his fellow Muscovite Stepan Maslov, Maksymovych was a botanist and natural scientist; he became interested in antiquities while still at Moscow University. Maksymovych's interests, however, were more specific: his first love was Ukrainian folklore and Cossack history. Besides being Ukrainian (in the sense of regional identity), he was the most important *Russian* secular intellectual in Kyiv, which was still a border town in many respects. As a result, his views largely defined both Russian and Ukrainian visions of Kyiv during much of the nineteenth century.

His thoughts on Kyiv history remained influential for decades. Despite what he said about Kyiv's significance for all of Orthodox Rus' in his university speech in 1837, he continuously emphasized the city's Ukrainian connection. What the Ukrainian writer Panteleimon Kulish did in fiction, Maksymovych did in his scholarly writings. He shared his local Ukrainian patriotism with his close friend, the renowned Russian writer Nikolai Gogol.[124] Both men symbolically appropriated Kyiv for Ukraine even before setting foot in the city. Hoping to take the chair of world history at the projected Kyiv University, Gogol called Kyiv "beautiful, ancient, [and] promised," filled with "plentiful gardens" under the "southern beautiful and marvelous sky."[125] In another letter to Maksymovych, Gogol exclaimed: "There, there! To the ancient and beautiful Kyiv! He is *ours*, not *theirs*, isn't he? There or nearby the acts of *our antiquity* were done" (emphasis added). Thus for these and many other imperial intellectuals of Ukrainian origins, Kyiv was "ours" (Ukrainian) and "ancient," as opposed to "theirs" (Great Russian). According to Maksymovych, the ancient city was threatened not just by ethnic Russians and Poles, but most importantly by the advent of the modern city, the "new" Kyiv.[126]

This "new" Kyiv referred both to the emergence of completely new districts and to the destruction/reconstruction of older ones. In both cases the perception of urban modernity was ambiguous. Kyiv had long been split into the three historical parts: Old Kyiv (or Upper City), Pechers'k, and Podil (or Lower City), each containing numerous antiquities dating back to medieval times. After the mid-1830s, one could also speak about New Kyiv, the district emerging around Kyiv University, whose main building was completed in 1843. Some expected, with justification, that the university would change the city entirely: "The poor huts crammed alongside each other in remote parts of the city will turn into huge, beautiful edifices; new, beautiful buildings and wonderful promenades will arise on the expansive empty spaces separating one part of the city from another, which create so many difficulties for the citizens, greatly hindering the city's internal development."[127] This optimistic observer, a Greco-Roman historian, also hoped that the university would bring about an increase in the urban population and a growth of education among "all classes of society."

Despite his devotion to antiquities, Maksymovych, too, was able to appreciate the coming of the "new" city. He was a conservative but not a retrograde like Muraviev. In 1839 he specifically mentioned Khresh-chatyk (later Kyiv's main thoroughfare) as a "quite nicely constructed ... part of Kyiv" that linked Old Kyiv with Pechers'k. But even Old Kyiv was already marked by modernity: this historical part was "currently being rapidly renovated," with new "straight streets and squares" being constructed and new houses built "in place of worn-out huts and narrow curving alleyways that like labyrinths used to cover the ancient ruins of Old Kyiv during the centuries of its neglect."[128] So for Maksy-movych, the 1830s were years of radical urban renewal in Kyiv.[129] Like Leskov, Maksymovych did not celebrate the coming of urban moder-nity without reservations. The discourse of the old and new Kyiv gen-erated a rather melancholic view of the city's past, a vision that did not ignore the advantages of imminent modernization. The first to articu-late this melancholic optimism was Maksym Berlyns'kyi, whose nostal-gia for the past allowed for some praise for modernizing forces.

While this celebration of modernity and authority was shared by many of Maksymovych's contemporaries, he, more than any other intellectual, lamented the loss of Kyiv's historical artefacts. And unlike Count Buturlin, he was able to date them correctly. Under the new cul-tural layers, "soon it would be impossible to discern those few places on which still in the seventeenth century there were the bare ruins of Rus's antiquity," he complained in 1840. He did not assign blame to anyone in particular. The guilty were the Kyivites themselves, who used for their new dwellings the "debris of ancient buildings ... while the rest has been covered with the new layers of soil."[130] After listing the lost medieval monuments, Maksymovych coined a bitter metaphor for the historical Kyiv – the cemetery: "Walking through Old Kyiv and remembering its past, here was the cradle of Rus´ life ... Today here is the great cemetery of an ancient Rus' life."

The metaphor of the cemetery was popular among Romantics, for it alluded to both death and the potential for resurrection. The old city was contained within a new one (albeit as a cemetery), awaiting his-torians and antiquarians whose task would be to excavate the past, to preserve it, and finally to consecrate it. Kyiv could reclaim its "antiq-uity" by making it more visible, even tangible. Yet however much they adored the past, Maksymovych and his university colleagues belonged to the *new* city that was being created by imperial modernity. Old Kyiv *needed* new Kyiv in order to (literally) resurface.

The amateur historian Mykola Zakrevs'kyi could still find a few signs of "eternal" Kyiv in the 1860s – and in this regard, he pointed to the presence of Ukrainians and Jews, among others. "There are the same charming hills, the same sacred golden-domed shrines … the same simple-hearted Little Russian type of the majority population, and the same restless Jews as there were 35 years ago!" He concluded that the city was the same *"eternal* Kyiv, our *Roma aeterna!"*[131] But he also articulated a growing tension between old and new Kyiv. For him, change was both destructive and insufficient. It was destructive with respect to the city's past and insufficient in terms of urban renewal and overall city improvement. (Here, he mentioned Podil's "fathomless filth" and Khreshchatyk as a "parody" of Nevsky Prospect in Saint Petersburg.)[132]

A handful of critical voices aside, after the mid-nineteenth century the celebration of modernity in Kyiv began in earnest. In 1852, Funduklei in *Statistical Description of Kyiv Province* presented an image of a progressively developing city in which the past had been all but erased:

> Kiev is quite an ancient city, but today one can hardly notice in it anything decrepit, except for a few wooden houses designated for demolition. In general, it looks like a comfortable, developing city that is being transformed into other, more capacious and regular forms. This movement is closely related to the previous changes that had an impact on the expansion and layout of the city.[133]

In 1853 the city finished its most ambitious technological achievement to date – the Chain Bridge. In most contemporary accounts, two cities – one modern, the other wedded to the past (with its mythological and spiritual images) – coexisted harmoniously. The following passage comes from an official (and at the time, the *only*) Russian newspaper published in Kyiv:

> The year 1853 can justly be called the golden year for Kyiv. We hardly have time to contemplate and to adore its countless [new] buildings, its beautifully laid-out roads, and its slopes and ravines levelled so artfully. Kyiv today is nice, but in ten years it will be beautiful. This forefather of the Russian cities will get younger and perhaps only slightly will lag behind our capitals Saint Petersburg and Moscow in terms of architecture. Our famous bridge over the Dnieper, thanks to the tireless work of the Englishman Vignoles, is already completed. Curious people every day come to see this graceful product of engineering

2.3 Timm, *The Chain Bridge* (image courtesy of Mystetstvo)

[*inzhenernogo iskusstva*] … It is said that all the iron for this bridge was brought from England where it is notable for strength and impeccable smoothness. In a word, Kiev's [Chain] Bridge will be among the most famous in Europe.[134]

This journalist smoothly linked new urban planning and British engineering with the traditional imagery of Kyiv as *the* centre of Russian Orthodoxy. He went on to describe the monument to Saint Vladimir, also erected in 1853. Apparently forgetting all the technological wonders brought from England, he took up the usual rhetoric of militant Orthodox nationalism, which had become somewhat standard during the reign of Nicholas I. "The common, true Orthodox faith has united the tsar and the nation into one family and has been a bastion against all the enemies," he wrote. "In the current century, especially during the happiest reign of our Majesty Emperor Nicholas Pavlovich, Russia rose to the highest degree of its might and glory, and all this has been the product of [our] faith, preserved in all purity since the times of Saint Vladimir." The past was being evoked here not to mitigate the rush of change but to emphasize yet again Kyiv's unique place in the imperial political imagination and in the tsar's own geopolitical fantasies. Thus, at least in official discourse, technological progress and the advance of the modern city did not contradict Kyiv's traditional image as a city of the past, the centre of Orthodox spirituality, and, by extension, the bastion of Russian Orthodox nationalism.

Urban progress could also relate to more prosaic matters. For example, progress was embodied in the "butcher's shops of New York." Such was the topic of a report from 1853 in Kyiv's official newspaper:

> The meat is cut in regular tetragonal pieces and is placed there on nice plates made of tin, faience, and porcelain. The plates are put on long tables covered with snow-white tablecloths. At the table sits a female owner, dressed in clean clothes and white apron ... Each piece has already been weighed, so the customer is served right away ... The owner's hands are always clean because she never touches meat with her hands but rather takes it and serves it with a fork that is constantly being rinsed and washed. We think that this example is worthy of imitation.[135]

Here, at least, meat was not being directly linked to Russian Orthodox nationalism. Clean food was a much less controversial hallmark of progress than urban renewal, changes in topography, or even technological wonders like the railway. In the local press, whatever the paper's ideological stance, America in general became a constant point of reference symbolizing a new world power, just like Russia itself. Kyiv newspapers (and the conservative *Kievlianin* in particular) were packed with stories about the United States – its democracy, the power of its journalism, its skyscrapers, its urban growth, its transportation networks, the criminal deeds of the Italian mafia, and so on. Some of these American developments were treated as mere curiosities; others were deemed worthy of imitation; and still others seemed threatening. In 1905, for example, *Kievlianin* reported on the astonishing growth of Chicago, whose population had reached two million less than a hundred years after its founding. The report specifically mentioned traffic jams so severe that many streets had become impassable.[136]

Writing in 1897, at the height of Kyiv's first building boom, a local journalist could not help raising American associations. Pointing to one of Kyiv's latest "skyscrapers," he commented: "Such *American buildings* are most likely the result of the building fever that has plagued Kyiv, thanks to which we have seen as of late the rise of one building after another at a truly *American speed*" (emphasis added).[137]

If, indeed, late-imperial Kyiv suffered from a "fever," then "American speed" was simply the most noteworthy symptom of the same modern disease – laissez-faire capitalism. Among its more unpleasant symptoms were speculation, rising urban rents, and homeowners' indebtedness to the banks. The main victims of this quite possibly incurable disease were nature, the old city, and many individual residents. Some, like Muraviev, criticized all of this from a religious conservative standpoint; others did so from socioeconomic, preservationist, and even ecological perspectives. The best example of the latter criticism can be found in the memoirs of Oleksandr (Aleksandr) Pataleev – an unlikely critic, given that he was a wealthy merchant. Even so, he credited the railways with spurring Kyiv's economic growth, which had given rise to mortgage banks and a building boom. More perceptive citizens with means began acquiring urban estates in the city centre, which later became a major source of their fortunes. As a consequence, rents rose dramatically: a shopkeeper who in the early 1860s paid 300 roubles per year to a property owner was likely paying around 2,000 by the middle of the next decade. This rapid increase generated enormous profits for a small group of shrewd property owners, but it also caused a great deal of collateral damage, ranging from poor-quality housing to a sharp rise in prices to the loss of green space. Pataleev, who had a strong social conscience, confronted these negative consequences head-on:

There has begun speculation in houses in Kyiv; there have appeared speculative builders who build hastily and crudely [*na zhivuiu nitku*] for resale. While arranging beautiful staircases, parquet floors, and splendid stucco ceilings, they introduced harmful cost savings – regarding foundations, wall thickness, the quality of building materials, etc. ... Adequate supervision over buildings by the municipal government has yet to exist. One needs only an architect's signature on plans, which can be obtained for around 50 roubles. Many have taken advantage of this situation and abused it. Collapses of houses are not infrequent ... There were human casualties.[138]

Speculation led not only to poorly built houses – many of them death traps – but also to more wide-ranging economic and ecological losses, as well as to an overall change in the city's sociospatial form:

The more populous Kyiv became, the more expensive life was in it. The apartments, which previously cost 300–400 roubles [to rent], have doubled in price. Chasing higher profits from houses their owners began to destroy old fruit orchards, stables, barns, and cellars. All this has been remade into living quarters bringing in an income. Small businesses and artisanal shops could no longer pay higher rents and were relocating to second-rate streets.

The new, more comfortable lifestyle led to changes in the city's "moral economy": the more residents grew accustomed to new standards (such as bathtubs), the more this created a demand for comfort. This proved very costly. Comfort became something of a drug for many Kyivites, who, while chasing it, "went beyond the bounds of their modest budgets." As a result, many went bankrupt.[139] This "luxury economics" was sustained by the mortgage policies of new banks, which in turn raised concerns that were even discussed in the city duma in 1887. Someone naively remarked that before the expansion of credit, "everybody was content with what one had." Banks started lending money to individual Kyivites, who began building "large houses," and as a consequence, more and more of them became buried in personal debt. "If an apartment stands half a year or a year unoccupied, the homeowner will be totally lost," complained one city councillor.[140]

But who were the lucky ones? That is, who benefited the most from speculative building and laissez-faire capitalism? Who were the faces of the "new" Kyiv? We know that most of them were newcomers to the city. A good example is Olexandr Pataleev (quoted earlier), who did well navigating the new economy. In 1867, his family, which had relocated to Kyiv from nearby Chernihiv in 1855, purchased from a local burgher a large plot in city centre. This was a typical urban homestead consisting of a modest house, a few outbuildings, and a splendid orchard.[141] Then in 1879, long before the first building boom of the mid-1890s, the Pataleev family hired the municipal architect Vladimir Nikolaev[142] to redesign their home. The result was a large, three-storey brick house, an impressive building that still stands. It seems that these recent newcomers to the city had no trouble raising the money for this. The elder Pataleev was head broker (*gofmakler*) of the Kyiv stock exchange and thus was closely associated with the new capitalist economy. In 1873 he opened a banking office that bought and sold all kinds of government securities, issued loans with those securities as collateral, and conducted all the other sorts of business that bankers usually do. A document dated 1882 indicates that the banker's family lived confortably on a large urban estate priced at 9,000 silver roubles (around 36,000 paper roubles), a value typical of other upper-middle-class homes. The Pataleevs' property was among the largest rental apartment houses in the city, containing two seven-room apartments on each of the three floors, most of them reserved for tenants.

Whether or not this was the effect of an embarrassment of riches, Kyiv's new wealthy class often combined business acumen with an appreciation of the arts. The elder Pataleev, for instance, surrounded himself with famous actors and helped arrange theatre performances and concerts, often in the hall of the Kyiv stock exchange.[143] His son Oleksandr participated in the performances of Kyiv drama society, while his own business reflected his cultural affinities: from 1894 on, he sold imported pianos through stores in Kyiv, Odessa, and even Berlin. Despite his obvious love for Kyiv, in the early twentieth century he relocated to Saint Petersburg, possibly because of the worsening political atmosphere in the city after the violence of 1905.

As a memoirist, Pataleev was unique among the merchants of Kyiv; but as a wealthy man interested in arts and antiquities, and as someone born outside of the city, he was rather typical. He represented a growing class of wealthy newcomers, many of them ethnic Russians, who came to the city in several waves, some before 1835 but most after the abolition of municipal self-government. "New" Kyiv was indeed represented by new men and the *nouveaux riches*. Various sources enumerate the most important of the commercial families, referred to as "firms"; they included the Protazanovs, Bugaevs, Popovs, Dekhterevs, Pirozhnikovs, Bogatyrevs, and Shyshkins, almost all of them ethnic Russians from central Russia, who dominated Kyiv's economy after the 1850s.[144] Even more striking was the rather modest social background of many of these merchants before their arrival in Kyiv. For instance, Iuda Bogatyrev was a peasant, and Ivan Shyshkin a simple burgher; both were from Tula province.[145] Many of these "new" Kyivites were Old Believers, religious dissidents well-known for their social conservatism as well as their business acumen. In the Russia of Nicholas I, the Old Believers were a persecuted group, but in the 1830s and 1840s they were encouraged to settle in Kyiv by tax breaks and other financial incentives, as a way to counter the socioeconomic influence of Poles and Jews.[146] In chapter 7 I will discuss the Old Believers and other wealthy families in more depth, in the context of Kyiv's new "urban regime." That regime, which established itself after the Magdeburg rights were abolished in 1835, raised to prominence a number of Russian *nouveaux riches*. A few matters, however, should be mentioned here.

A community of Old Believers in Kyiv developed in the early nineteenth century. In the first half of that century, it never exceeded 400 members; by 1900, however, it had grown to 1,500 members. Most of them came to the city from the Old Believers' communes of Chernihiv province in northern Ukraine and from Kaluga province in central Russia, taking advantage of the tax benefits granted to Russian merchants. By 1850, half of the ten wealthiest first-guild merchants in Kyiv were Old Believers; the most prominent of them were the cousins Timofei and Rodion Dekhterev.[147] Rodion owned the earliest steam-driven industrial enterprise in the city – the cast-iron foundry, which produced equipment (such as cauldrons and presses) for sugar refineries. He also manufactured rams for the pile drivers used in the construction of the city's Chain Bridge.[148] Even though the city prospered economically from the Old Believers' enterprises, the Russian government returned to persecuting the community in the 1850s. In 1853 the Old Believer merchants were allowed to remain in guilds only temporarily, and in 1856 they were barrred from the guilds altogether; this led to the decline of their business community in Kyiv.[149]

The persecution of Old Believers could be viewed as an attack not only on the tight community of religious dissidents and entrepreneurs, but also on the new city in general. Clinging to a reactionary political mythology, Tsar Nicholas wanted to set limits on the concept of new Kyiv, whose growth seemed to be spinning out of control after 1850.[150] His Kyiv was to exclude (substantially, if not completely) the danger-ous "Other" – Jews, Old Believers, and Poles – no matter how beneficial their presence. They were to be kept at a distance from the city, which Nicholas viewed as a fortress (spiritual no less than physical) intended to protect him from all his enemies (internal no less than external). In his mind, economic interests ran second to geopolitical fantasies. Metaphorically speaking, Nicholas allowed "old" Kyiv to take revenge against the new city – the city of human mobility, entrepreneurship, and dangerously blurred social boundaries.

But the tsar's vision of Kyiv allowed some space for local (and loyal) Ukrainians, who were quite numerous among the city's new men. The Symyrenko, Iakhnenko, Khanenko, and Tereshchenko families were among the wealthiest in Kyiv, and they too were newcomers, most of them from modest rural backgrounds.[151] Together with their Russian and Jewish counterparts of no less humble descent, they comprised the commercial and municipal elite of the new Kyiv.

An interesting way to look at the relationship between old and new Kyiv is by examining the attitudes of these wealthy newcomers towards the city's past. Russians, Ukrainians, Poles, and Jews often participated in the same public projects.[152] The most notable of all these was the Kyiv Municipal Museum (also known as the Museum of Antiquities and Arts), which was sponsored by a group of wealthy Kyivites, many of whom were born outside the city and had spent much of their lives elsewhere. They were the faces of new Kyiv after mid-century, just like Funduklei and Maksymovych were a generation before.

More than half the amount needed to build the museum was provided by the Tereshchenko family, which contributed 108,000 roubles.[153] The Tereshchenkos were an entrepreneurial Cossack family from Hlukhiv in northern Ukraine. They started out poor but grew rich by trading in bread and lumber and, finally, by investing in the expanding sugar industry.[154] Nikola, the son of a Cossack entrepreneur, grew too large for Hlukhiv, having leased and acquired lands and sugar refineries from landowners who had been hit hard by the emancipation of the serfs in 1861. From 1851 to 1872, he was also a Hlukhiv town head, and in 1870 he received the highest imperial honour: his father and all his descendants were elevated to the hereditary nobility. By then the owner of an industrial and commercial empire, Nikola relocated to Kyiv in 1874, after a short stint in Moscow.[155] Despite their wealth, the Tereshchenkos had never owned real estate in Kyiv, so they had to buy an appropriate home for their large family.[156] It is surprising how quickly and how deeply these newcomers involved themselves in local charitable causes. By 1894, Nikola, who had received only a primary education, his son Oleksandr, and his brother Fedir were founding members of the museum committee, the city's most prominent cultural institution, as well as its biggest patrons. Nikola donated to the museum his collection of portraits of Kyiv historial figures and purchased for it a large collection of antiquities.[157]

Other notable patrons of the museum were Bohdan Khanenko and Lazar' Brodsky, the uncrowned king of Kyiv's Jewish community.[158] The Brodsky and Tereshchenko families participated together in various Jewish and Christian charitable causes. This perhaps was a consequence of the close working relationship between the Tereshchenkos and the Brodskys in the sugar cartel, which these two influential *nouveau riche* families helped establish.[159] Belonging clearly to the *common* public sphere, the Municipal Museum provided the best evidence that new Kyiv was able to unite people of different backgrounds, not only at work but also at leisure. The Ukrainian historians Volodymyr Antonovych and Oleksandr Lazarevs'kyi and the Russian art critic Adrian Prakhov provided the museum with expertise. All of these people could be considered new Kyivites, in that they were born elsewhere.

Apart from the Tereshchenko family, the single most important donor to the museum was Bohdan Khanenko. In contrast to Tereshchenkos, who were of modest background, Khanenko was a descendant of the Ukrainian Cossack aristocracy, born on his father's rural estate in Chernihiv province. He studied law in Moscow and then worked as a government employee in Saint Petersburg and Warsaw before relocating to Kyiv in 1881, where he was active in the financial and industrial sectors.[160] Having married the daughter of Nikola Tereshchenko, after 1896 he managed the industrial enterprise of Tereshchenko brothers. His other passion was the Municipal Museum, to which he contributed time and money, as well as art and antiquities. The latter accounted for more than half of museum's archaeological collection. It was Khanenko who solicited various government agencies and figures (including Nicholas II) for subsidies to cover the building costs. In the end, the Ukrainian oligarch could celebrate: in 1897 the tsar allocated 50,000 roubles from the state treasury for the museum, which was finally completed in 1901.[161]

With regard to Kyiv's past, nothing better illustrated the attitudes of the city elites than the fundraising for the monument to Bohdan Khmel'nyts'kyi, the Ukrainian hetman who triumphantly entered Kyiv on Christmas 1648. His descendants, however, were not as generous as had been expected. In 1872, Kyiv's conservative newspaper *Kievlianin* published a lengthy article that accused local Ukrainian notables of not contributing enough for the monument.[162] By then, total contributions had reached 20,000 roubles – a meagre sum, given that original estimates had been that 145,200 roubles would be needed to complete the monument (later lowered to 95,700 and finally to 57,964 roubles).[163] The largest contributions came from institutions of local self-governments (*zemstva*), clergy, and peasants, primarily from Right-Bank Ukraine, but also from Great Russia. Remarkably, the largest donations arrived from Orlov *zemstvo* (500 roubles) and from the Saint Petersburg and Moscow municipal governments (500 and 200 roubles respectively). The Kyiv self-government gave 150 roubles, while Ukrainian peasants from Podolia province gathered more than 300 roubles. The article's author noted that it was peasants, not nobles, who had donated the most funds across Russia. He criticized Kyivites and Ukrainian nobles for sabotaging the fundraising. He had expected that among the largest donors would be "Little Russian landowners" – the "descendants of those heroic fighters for the Orthodox faith and fatherland, who, together with father Bohdan, broke the then strong Poland." Alas, except for 200 roubles offered by the Poltava *zemstvo*, "the indifference about the monument on the part of Little Russians proper proved complete." Some "Little Russian landowners," the reporter alleged, in their "wild speeches," even suggested that the hetman "did not do much to enrich Little Russia."[164]

True or not, there could have been other reasons for the sluggish fundraising besides political sabotage. According to a later financial report, the flow of donations had almost ended by 1875, primarily due to the Russo-Turkish war of 1877–8 and the ensuing economic crisis.[165] However, the same source indicated that Kyiv's notables (mainly the newly rich but also some aristocrats) began to donate more actively in the 1880s. Thus on the list of donors we see the names of industrialists Nikola and Fedir Tereshchenko (300 roubles each); another sugar baron and peasant's son, Ivan Kharytonenko (1,500 roubles); an aristocratic supporter of Ukrainian culture, Vasyl' Tarnovs'kyi (700 roubles); another Ukrainian aristocrat, Hryhorii Galagan (100 roubles); a historian and landowner, Mykola Rihel'man (1,000 roubles); a merchant and Kyiv mayor of Greek descent, Ivan Tolli (1,000); and others,[166] almost all of them born outside Kyiv. Many of them also supported a number of other cultural causes (both Ukrainian ones and those focused on Kyiv).[167]

Setting aside the prominent role played by new Kyivites in preserving Kyiv's past, the city was affected by modernity in some very drastic ways. As will be shown in chapter 5, laissez-faire capitalism destroyed many physical remnants of the old city that had survived even the most reckless redevelopment schemes pursued by the imperial authorities from the 1830s to the 1850s. This changed Kyiv both as a mental image and as an urban form. But the two cities – old and new – continued to coexist. Indeed, the coming of modernity to Kyiv helped emphasize its historical and spiritual image, cementing the conservative myth that this growing borderland metropolis was an "ancient" and "holy" city. Consequently, the present was bound to retain visible or easily imaginable indicators of the remote past. Technological, economic, and demographic changes only reinforced the conservative reaction among the proponents of old Kyiv, from Russian authorities who routinely censored modernity to the openly anti-Semitic and anti-Catholic religious right, whose most refined intellectual voice was Andrei Muraviev. In their eyes, Kyiv – *ancient* and *holy* – had to remain a crucial bastion of Russian Orthodoxy in the borderlands, and all innovations had to be subordinated to that higher function.

Conclusion

This chapter has explored the treatment of Kyiv's past through various narrative sources – literary fiction, travellers' accounts, journalism, and scholarly research sponsored by public institutions. Just like fiction, scholarship on Kyiv reflected an ongoing struggle among different communities for the prize of representing the city and claiming its legacy. The scholarly study of local antiquities began in the first quarter of the nineteenth century; its first practitioners were amateurs, some of whom were more adept than others. Among those enthusiasts who were better suited to do research were several newcomers to town, particularly the Orthodox Metropolite of Kyiv Evgenii (Bolkhovitinov), who was an ethnic Russian. Another prominent student of Kyiv's past and antiquities was Mykhailo Maksymovych, the first rector of Kyiv St Vladimir University, born in Left-Bank Ukraine but trained as a botanist at Moscow University. Beginning in 1834 and over the following few decades, he was a leading specialist in local written tradition and material culture, cementing what would later become known as *kyievoznavstvo*, the historical study of Kyiv and its region. With the founding of Kyiv's St Vladimir University in 1834, studies of local urban history became more professional. But from their very inception, those studies had a clear political purpose, which was to refute Polish claims to Kyiv's historical legacy. Much of the research, then, was fuelled by growing Russian fears of an imminent Polish (later Jewish and Ukrainian) threat, be it putative or real. These fears led Russian authorities to sponsor research into Kyiv's past as a way of proving that the city was ancient, Russian, and Orthodox and was filled with sacred antiquities (supposedly ancient churches and monasteries). The city's "representational spaces," including long-known sites and newly discovered antiquities, would greatly influence both the production of the new imperial space and the conservative mythology of the city.

One can argue that if it were not for the Poles and Jews, Kyiv would not have been mapped as an ancient and holy Orthodox city. Jews and Poles served as catalysts of the conservative Kyiv myth, which emphasized the city's role as Russia's historical and spiritual capital, especially after the 1830s and 1840s. When the Polish threat reappeared again in the 1860s, and when certain categories of Jews were allowed to settle in the city, Kyiv's image as an ancient and holy Orthodox city was further strengthened, this time with more aggressive xenophobic overtones. Ukrainians, too, were increasingly alien to this myth, which by the end of the century had united all the most loyal "children of Rus',"[168] who were anti-Semitic, anti-Polish, and anti-Ukrainian in outlook. As both holy and ancient, Kyiv became the strongest argument for Russian nationalists in their struggle against real and imagined threats – Polish, Jewish, Ukrainian, or revolutionary, the last of these often perceived as instigated by "aliens" (*inorodtsy*). This reactionary attention to the past and a conservative politics of memory also contributed to more specific socioeconomic policies pursued by the public authorities, imperial and municipal alike. Accordingly, the development of Kyiv as a modern metropolis was accompanied by recurrent references to its past, which were often mythological and always ideological.[169]

This conservative myth proved surprisingly enduring and has recently been resurrected in Russia by the highest clerical dignitaries. They are actively pushing the agenda of the so-called *Russkii mir* (Russian world), a clear substitute for the nineteenth-century political concept of the all-Russian nation. Unfortunately, backed by Russia's political establishment, the myth has acquired highly dangerous revanchist overtones.

PART TWO

Making the City

In this part I will deal primarily with two topics, each exploring a crucial aspect of imperial urbanism in the borderlands: (1) various urban planning and city improvement schemes, including the changing concepts of the city centre and peripheries; and (2) the dynamics of spatial change, with a special focus on relations between the city, the Russian state, and private agency. The material in this part is split into three chapters, each exploring a particular period of urban history: the self-governing city beween 1800 and 1835 (chapter 3); the imperial government's dominance over the city between 1835 and 1870 (chapter 4); and the restoration of municipal autonomy between 1871 and 1905 (chapter 5). Even though the imperial government played an important role in Kyiv's physical development, the state consistently exhibited an anti-urban bias.

The major changes in Kyiv's cityscape came with the reign of Nicholas I (r. 1825–55) who wanted to transform the city from a small trading hub into a "fortress city." That vision would strongly skew the city's development, affecting its ethnic and social profiles, its planning, its architecture, and last but not least its ideological and strategic functions in the empire. Nicholas may have been "a bland, philandering tsar, an ignoramus and a cad, whose entire reign was not worth a single foot of Pushkin's verse" (such was the unflattering characterization by writer Vladimir Nabokov). But there is no denying that he loved Kyiv and invested heavily in its redevelopment. Two of his governor generals, who supervised military and all of the most important social and political matters in Russia's Southwestern Region (comprising Kyiv, Volhynia, and Podolia provinces), resided in Kyiv and orchestrated much of the change in the city. These were Vasilii Levashov (1832–8 in office) and Dmitrii Bibikov (1837–52 in office), both of whom were energetic administrators – perhaps a bit *too* energetic. It is hard to identify in the history of modern Kyiv a single factor that explained this modest frontier town's dramatic transformation into an imperial metropolis. In mid-nineteenth-century Kyiv, there was no construction of wide boulevards as in Paris or Brussels; there was no energetic and reform-minded mayor (similar to Baron Haussmann in Paris); there was no laying down of a spectacular thoroughfare encircling an old town (like Vienna's celebrated Ringstrasse). In fact, the situation in the capital of Russia's Southwestern Region was quite different from that of European cities, where dynasties and militaries were surrendering more and more ground – ideological, political, and urban – to the rising middle classes. In Kyiv, it was the imperial authorities and the military that were taking over more and more space from urban communities and social corporations. In Vienna, the Ringstrasse, announced by the emperor Franz Joseph in 1857 as the central feature of that city's reorganization, came to symbolize the triumph of the liberal bourgeoisie over absolutism and the military; whereas in Kiev, the dominant architectural project was a huge military fortress, hardly a symbol of liberalism.[1] Thus, over the coming decades the main agent of modernity in Kyiv would be the Russian government, whose militaristic and conservative agenda would dominate imperial urbanism in the southwestern borderlands. Perhaps only Warsaw could rival Kyiv as a city where military architecture (a citadel and defensive forts) dominated civil urbanism while also restricting urban growth.[2]

Prior to the 1830s, Kyiv consisted of three historical districts, which over the centuries had functioned more like three separate towns: Old Kyiv (or Upper Town), Podil (or Lower Town), and Pechers'k.[3] Because of this, Kyiv exhibited what urbanist Spiro Kostof, following Aristotle, called "synoecism" – that is, an urban form reflecting "[the] coming together of several proximate villages to form a town."[4] Until the late eighteenth century, Kyiv strongly resembled ancient cities along the middle Niger in West Africa or in northern China that "consisted of a cluster of residential communities in close proximity, each physically discrete and socially specialized according to occupation or status."[5] Cities like this did not have a clearly defined centralized institution, although they contained various corporate groups interacting with one another, among them the elites. Kyiv retained some features of Kostof's model far longer than most other European cities. Until 1835, what would become the city of Kyiv was not united in administrative terms: since the fifteenth century, the Podil district, where most townspeople resided, had enjoyed self-government based on the Magdeburg Law, a legal system that had taken hold across much of urban Eastern and Central Europe. Under this system, basically all socioeconomic, fiscal, and judicial power belonged to the elected mayor (*viit*) and a group of municipal councillors and judges.[6] In the 1750s, the Russian government began trying to curtail the autonomy of Podil's burghers,[7] but the city's elite managed to defend its privileges until the mid-1830s.

Other historical parts of Kyiv – Old Kyiv and Pechers'k – were never granted Magdeburg autonomy[8] and instead were governed by other elites, who often clashed with one another. Old Kyiv was administered by St Sophia Cathedral and St Michael's Monastery, which since 1654 had shared their authority with the Russian garrison stationed there. Curiously, from the late-sixteenth century through to the mid-seventeenth, Old Kyiv contained at least two self-governing burgher corporations that seemed to rival Podil's magistrate.[9] In 1782, Russian officials assumed full fiscal and administrative control over the district, although the Church continued to participate in administration. Similarly, Pechers'k, a district famous for its medieval Caves Monastery (*Pechers'kyi*), until 1782 was administered jointly by the monastery, the Russian governor general, and the Ukrainian Cossack state known as the Hetmanate.[10] With the latter's abolition in 1782, the Russian government assumed full control over the district, which remained the seat of a governor general until the mid-1850s. The district early on became a model for the entire city to emulate: a "fortress town" set against external and internal enemies, closely administered by Russian civil and military authorities and populated by Russian officers, soldiers, artisans catering for military needs, monks, and ethnic Russian merchants, and last but not least by aristocrats of various backgrounds (Russian, Polish, Western European, and occasionally Ukrainian).

The impact of this administrative diversity was felt as late as the 1840s by numerous observers, especially when it came to urban layout and communications within this newly united city. During much of the year, movement between its parts was almost impossible because of poor roads and adverse weather – mud, snow, or floods. Yet the Russian imperial authorities did something that no other government, Lithuanian, Polish, or Ukrainian Cossack, had managed to do after the mid-thirteenth century – it forged Kyiv into a territorial, administrative, and symbolic unity. It took the Russians a few decades, but by the mid-1830s they had succeeded in joining the separate towns and suburbs under their civil and military power.

The following three chapters also tell the story of two types of urban modernity: one embodied in a self-governing city, before 1835 and, again, after 1871; another associated with the Russian imperial authorities. The first type, which existed until 1835 under a largely Ukrainian oligarchic leadership, resurfaced in 1871 in the guise of a self-governing city council (*gorodskaia duma*), this time dominated by multiethnic professionals and businessmen (of mostly ethnic Russian, German, Greek and occasionally Ukrainian, Polish, and Jewish descent). The city sometimes clashed with the imperial authorities, as did the two versions of urban modernity. The transformation of Kyiv into a multiethnic metropolis was at times painful, laced as it was with multiple contradictions. This process was exacerbated by the city's perceived borderland status, its ideological functions, and its spiritual importance. The latter was often used as symbolic capital by various agents struggling to represent the city and the surrounding region.

In the previous chapters, I attempted to *deconstruct* traditional and modern mythologies; my next goal is to *reconstruct* the municipal and governmental policies that affected Kyiv's topography, demography, and architecture in fundamental ways. The physical forms of the city, as reflected in things such as housing stock, public and private spaces, and population distribution, are first of all the products of social, economic, and political designs before they are shaped by architects and technical experts.[11] In this part I focus specifically on spatiality and urban planning. I am well aware that terms such as *town planning, city planning, Städtebau, Städteplanung, urbanisme,* and *gradostroitel'stvo* all came into a common use only between 1890 and 1914.[12] But planning institutions and experts (architects, military and civil engineers, land surveyors) had become an important presence in cities well before 1890, and Kyiv was no exception. By "urban planning" I therefore mean "the deliberate ordering by public authority of the physical arrangements of towns or parts of towns in order to promote their efficient and equitable functioning as economic and social units, and to create an aesthetically pleasing environment."[13] The relations among the various agents of public authority responsible for urban change – representing either the city or the Russian government – will provide a political context for the chapters that follow. Finally, I will touch on what Henri Lefebvre called "representations of space," which played a substantial role in the production of space in the city by way of construction and architecture, the latter seen as a "project embedded in a spatial context."[14]

Chapter Three

Municipal Autonomy under the Magdeburg Law, 1800–1835

"Yes, the Tradition Was Alive!"

On 16 February 1802, proud and elegantly dressed urban notables ("registered citizens") and a crowd of simple burghers took part in a ceremonial procession from the magistrate building towards the Assumption Cathedral in Podil, in celebration of a very special event: the restoration of Kyiv self-government by Tsar Alexander I. To the music of the city's own brass band and under the magistrate's golden banner, Kyiv's mayor (*viit*) Heorhii Rybal's'kyi, together with two members of the magistrate, carried the tsar's charter, which had been placed on a golden velvet pillow, into the church, where the Kyiv Metropolitan blessed the precious document. The city went on to celebrate for three days, and afterwards, it was decided to erect a stone monument and a fountain on the so-called Khreshchatyk spring, at the spot where the sons of Prince Vladimir the Great were believed to have been baptized. The city fathers also decided to establish on 15 July an annual solemn procession, with crosses and banners, to the projected monument, "in order to remind the future generations about the tsar's favors given today to this city as an ancient capital."[1]

The monument, a Tuscan column, officially raised in 1808, was provided with the following inscription: "By the diligence of Kyiv citizens, for the confirmation of privileges of this ancient capital by the All-Russian Emperor Alexander I."[2] While it glorified the tsar, it was not devoted to any particular hero; rather, it honoured the city itself. It had been erected to commemorate the restoration of Kyiv's municipal autonomy based on the medieval Magdeburg Law. For several centuries, Kyiv had been a self-governing city, administered by the magistrate on the basis of municipal laws that protected local burghers, most of them Orthodox and Ukrainian,[3] against the intrusion of outside forces – Polish and Ruthenian magnates, Jewish traders, Ukrainian Cossacks, and, finally, the Russian military, merchants, and artisans – into the city's economic, judicial, and administrative affairs.[4] The 1802 event was a celebration of civic pride, but it was not the only one. Solemn processions of Kyiv's proud burghers took place twice a year, but some of these – including one to mark the opening of the Kyiv Gymnasium (elite college) on 30 January 1812[5] – were intended to showcase the dignity and wealth of the city's ruling elite. Michael Hamm has drawn a composite picture of one such civic holiday – Maccabeus Day on 1 August – on the basis of several narrative sources:

> Men dressed in Cossack attire, and those with fevers swam in the river. Maccabeus also marked a holiday for all the guilds. Guildsmen assembled at the Samson Fountain, built in Podil in 1808 on the site of the old city well.[6] Sitting high in their Cossack-type saddles, the burgher cavalry assembled at the Assumption Cathedral. Dressed in their traditional green ceremonial cloaks (*kuntushy*) decorated with golden cord, red long coats (*zhupany*) and tall golden-tasseled, crimson Astrakhan velvet hats, they awaited the procession, sabers hanging from their silk sashes, a pair of pistols from their saddles. Guildmasters drew their sabers as the procession, led by the magistracy's brass band, moved toward the Florivsky (Florovsky) Monastery. After concluding the church service, clergy blessed the waters in the Samson Fountain. Then, amid the brass fanfares and pounding of drums, the procession fanned out to appointed spots, and a meal was shared by prominent clergy and burghers at the Contract Hall. The festival ended with a great roar: a cannonade set off by the barbers' guild; the firing of weapons of all kinds; the collective cheer of Podil's inhabitants, many bearing jars of blessed water; the ringing of church bells; loud music; and the neighing of frightened horses … For the remainder of the night burghers were allowed to fire their guns from their yards.[7]

Reportedly, the ceremony's participants were extremely proud of their role in this dramatization of Kyiv's self-governing spirit. One contemporary proudly described Ivan Mazhnyi, a commander of the municipal militia: his splendid attire, his expensive horse, and his majestic brigade.[8] Another later recalled: "When I'd sit on my horse, my blood began to flow, and I could scarcely recognize myself"; he felt "almost like a general; even the *moskali* [here Russian soldiers] were afraid of me. Yes, the tradition was alive!"[9]

The tradition might have been alive, but it would not be for much longer. The ceremony had practically *become* what it was supposed only to *represent*: an autonomous city. The ceremony might have been growing, but the city's rights and privileges were shrinking. The restored and partly invented tradition[10] in fact served as dubious compensation for lost powers. Even so, it is hard to overestimate the role such ceremonies played for the maintenance of civic spirit. Decades later, similar medieval urban ceremonies would help Habsburg Austria's most popular (and also most controversial) politician, Karl Lueger, cement his grip on Vienna's lower middle classes. These were the descendants of once proud guildsmen, who since the 1880s had felt more and more threatened by "liberal capitalism," a phenomenon they associated with large Jewish enterprises.[11] Just like the late-nineteenth-century Viennese, Kyivites prior to 1835 felt that their self-government was being curtailed by the Russian authorities; economically, many Kyivites believed they were losing ground to their more skilled and aggressive Russian and Jewish competitors operating outside of the guild system. In addition, most burghers were being increasingly exploited by the local oligarchy, which was misusing the magistrate and other municipal institutions for personal gain. Ceremonies like the one just described were in fact a swan song for the proud Kyivites, who had found themselves on the losing side of history. Unlike their later Viennese peers, they had no one to represent their interests – there was no figure on their side with the stature of Mayor Lueger. Kyiv might have lacked *der schöne Karl*, but there were plenty of influential anti-Semites among the city's Christian burghers and merchants, and in 1827, they finally persuaded the tsar to sign a decree banning Jews from the city.[12] Ironically, the burghers' autonomy did not survive the final expulsion of Jews that occurred in 1835. It was mainly Russian (but also German) merchants and artisans who took advantage of the disappearance of Jews and the abolition of Kyiv's self-government.

Whatever its weaknesses, municipal self-government had a strong impact on Kyiv in the first decades of the nineteenth century. In this chapter I explore the role played by Kyiv's municipal institutions prior to 1835 in various transformations of the city's space – a role largely unexplored by Ukrainian and Russian historians. Historians have generally overlooked the workings of Kyiv's municipal self-government in the first three decades of the century, dismissing the magistrate and its institutions as mere puppets of the Russian authorities or as a corrupt clique of oligarchs.[13] I argue that on the contrary, Kyiv's self-governing institutions, located in Podil, had enough leverage and negotiating power to participate in the city's socioeconomic, topographic, and demographic changes. Kyiv's self-government was functional, the presence of crooks notwithstanding. And despite certain tensions between the magistrate on one side and the Kyiv governor-general and civil governor on the other, we should not view Kyiv's sociopolitical history during this time as a government-versus-city or Russians-versus-Ukrainians conflict but rather as a complex constellation of power relations. We can speak about urban modernity (or, at least, imperial urbanism) in Kyiv as a *co-product* of Kyiv's municipal (largely Ukrainian) leadership and local imperial authorities. The latter had many economic and personal ties with the municipal oligarchs.

Before discussing the role of municipal and imperial institutions in Kyiv's evolving urban space, we should look at the space itself as it appeared on the first "official" plans of Kyiv, prepared around 1800. The 1803 plan, prepared by the city architect Andrii Melens'kyi, shows what the city looked like before the devastating fire of 1811 that destroyed most of Podil, then a major residential district of Kyiv, and also before the dramatic changes that Kyiv underwent starting in the 1830s (see map 7, pages 230–1). On the plan you will notice what you may already have gathered from literary sources and travelogues – namely, that Kyiv was indeed a poorly planned and badly connected city, or rather a loose assemblage of separate settlements.

The most populous of those settlements was low-lying Podil, on a floodplain below the city's hills along the Dnieper. Old Kyiv or Upper Kyiv, on a steep-sided plateau overlooking Podil, in the early nineteenth century was still the site of a Russian fortress and was encircled almost entirely by ramparts. Those same ramparts crossed the area roughly through its centre, bypassing the St Sophia complex (on the map, the ramparts are shown with thick black lines).[14] Even after centuries of topographic change, Old Kyiv retained its traditional radial-concentric street plan,[15] although it had been severely disrupted by the ramparts, which were built largely in the early eighteenth century. The land in the area was owned by the Church and by private citizens; its plots and houses were of diverse sizes and shapes, reflecting an irregular city form in the extreme. Not until the 1830s did the authorities begin to tear down the ramparts and straighten the streets.[16] Notice that the links between Old Kyiv and Podil were poor, despite their physical proximity to each other. Then, just as today, the shortest route between the two – and the only direct one – was via Andriïvs'kyi uzviz (St Andrew's Slope), which in those times was little more than a steeply curved lane, impassable for much of the year.[17]

3.1 Sazhin, *St Andrew's Slope* (image courtesy of Mystetstvo)

The streetscape in Podil – Kyiv's main residential area at the time – was even more peculiar. Most streets were unpaved and irregular, and the houses along them were situated haphazardly, with many set back from the street, in the middle of a plot. Often it was not a house but some outbuilding that faced the curving street (see map 7, pages 230–1). One contemporary, the local historian Maksym Berlyns'kyi, described the Podil streetscape in this way: "In Podil there are more than 130 streets and alleys which, for the most part, are narrow, with only main ones paved with logs … The houses, for the most part, are wooden, low, and usually [consist] of only one floor, situated in the city without any symmetry."[18] For all this spatial chaos, the street layout was not as disorderly as it may seem. Until the end of the eighteenth century, Podil was the heart of Baroque Kyiv, whose focal points were the Kyiv-Mohyla Academy and the magistrate (both in Podil) and the print shop of the Caves Monastery in Pechers'k. The principal religious and secular structures in Podil (including the magistrate) were built of stone in the baroque style, and this lent the city a certain integrity. Baroque Kyiv "seems to have crystallized around the points embodying municipal Self-government, learned Brotherhood [academy and print-shop], and a newly legitimized Orthodoxy."[19]

So, logic and even harmony could be found in the seemingly undisciplined layout of Podil. As in other medieval "organic" towns, the district's streets were oriented towards churches, a few public buildings (the magistrate and the academy), markets, and so on. For instance, among the major streets of Podil were Uspens'ka (leading towards the Dormition Cathedral),[20] Rozhdestvens'ka (named after the local Nativity Church), Prytys'ko-Mykil's'ka (leading up to Mykola Prytyska Church), and others named after local churches. Also, it is not surprising that Podil's main square was called the Market Square (also known as the Town Hall Square), where the magistrate was located and where important trade fairs took place three times a year.[21] The adjacent quarters were the most prestigious in the city: magistrate's officials, merchants, and clergy lived close to the market.[22] The prices for some stone houses on the Market Square could be staggering (as high as 8,000 or even 15,000 roubles, compared to just 95 roubles for the hut of a master potter in a modest area near the Dnieper).[23] In the late eighteenth century, wealthy oligarchs owned around one-third of the residential properties in Podil,[24] renting out most of them to those who had the means but could not legally own land in the city (Russian and Jewish traders, local peasants, foreigners, etc.). This socioeconomic diversity explains the severe fragmentation of Podil's townscape (i.e., the variations in the shapes of building lots and houses), although, as we have just seen, that fragmentation was not completely irrational. Just as in many other river cities, several of Podil's principal streets ran along the Dnieper, following its arc. This reflected the city's preoccupation with the river trade.

For Russian imperial planners and architects, this traditional streetscape was an eyesore. The concept of spacing buildings along the streets was developed by Baroque Era city planners, who in the eighteenth century "everywhere urged, or legislated when they could, that street-defining buildings be brought to the edge of their lots in a straight line, and further, that they be given identical façades."[25] In the Russian Empire, this alignment of houses along streets was enforced for the first time by Peter the Great during the construction of his new capital, Saint Petersburg.[26] Applying his proverbial iron will, fiscal penalties, and even confiscations of incorrectly located houses, by the 1720s he had succeeded in forcing property owners and developers to align their houses along the "red line" of the street.[27] Many of these measures, though, were limited to Saint Petersburg. Not until the reign of Catherine II were broader planning measures applied to Russia's other cities, including Kyiv.[28] The ambitious young empress, a German "import," set out to assign a plan for every city in her empire. In so doing she established the core principles of imperial urbanism as part of her autocratic power – a power that, as Daniel Brower put it, "used the material and human resources of the empire to construct outposts of a peculiarly autocratic vision of civilization."[29] In 1762, a Building Commission was established to oversee planning in Saint Petersburg and Moscow; in 1763, Catherine signed the decree "On making special plans for all cities, [of] their buildings and streets, separately for each province." This measure targeted 500 cities; however, it would take almost thirty years for the government's planners to prepare the hundreds of plans this entailed.[30]

Regarding Kyiv, Catherine had a wider agenda. By 1785 she had largely ended its self-government and allowed ethnic Russians and Germans to settle there. She also made plans for sweeping changes to its urban space.[31] In 1787, on her way to the Crimea, she stopped in the city for several months, where she frequented the Caves Monastery and paid her respects to the magistrate, which, for all practical purposes, she had just eliminated.[32] Noting that "the local city is bizarre as it consists of fortifications and suburbs," and confessing with irony that she had yet to actually find the city itself, she urged her engineers to come up with the first "regular plan" for Kyiv. That plan, which she signed five days before leaving the city, was developed by military engineer I. Miller and Count A.P. Shuvalov.[33] It called for the city to be moved up to the hills, stretching from the Pechers'k fortress to Old Kyiv; at the same time, low-lying Podil would be demolished, for that district did not correspond to the new rational requirements of urban planning. But this "regular" plan would require extraordinary human and material resources, which the state could not provide, and as a result, a few years later, in 1797, the decision to relocate Podil was revoked.[34] The only element of Catherine's grand plan that was realized was the Arsenal (constructed between 1784 and 1798), across from the Caves Monastery complex in Pechers'k, a huge building that would become the single largest manufacturer in Kyiv. Most measures called for by Catherine's planners were not carried out; even so, the 1787 plan had an impact insofar as it launched a new era in local planning – that is, it was the start of the classicist replanning of Kyiv, which would go on for half a century and give the city its current shape.[35]

The new century brought a number of changes to Kyiv's urban space. The major creative force behind these changes was Andrii Melens'kyi, Kyiv's chief architect between 1799 and 1829, who was in charge of designing a general plan of the city in 1803.[36] For the first time ever, Kyiv's urban space was considered as a totality. Melens'kyi, who had worked in Saint Petersburg with the celebrated architect of the Imperial Court, Giacomo Quarenghi, from 1787 to 1792, transferred his invaluable experience in planning and classical architecture to Kyiv, an old city with an "organic" layout (in the sense suggested by Spiro Kostof[37]). At the time the young Russian architect arrived there in 1799, the city was split into various jurisdictions[38] and lacked any consistent strategy in urban planning. Basically, there was *no* planning worth mentioning. To make matters worse, since the death in 1785 of its major "civil" architect, Ivan Hryhorovych-Bars'kyi,[39] who had been employed by the self-governing district of Podil, Kyiv had gone fifteen years without any notable architect. Indeed, in the late eighteenth century there were only a few builders in Kyiv, most of them military engineers. Because the city was situated on the border with Poland–Lithuania, the Russian government's main focus was on the fortress (the so-called Old Fortress, established around 1706 by Peter the Great in Pechers'k, near the monastery).

Thus Melens'kyi became not only Kyiv's first chief architect but also its planner.

He treated Kyiv as a space that so far lacked unity and that needed to be bound together by picturesque avenues. In bringing this about, he took into account the city's complicated terrain.[40] According to a contemporary expert on Kyiv's architecture, "by laying out new neighborhoods he [Melens'kyi] began to 'glue' separate parts of Kyiv, designing a new centre of the city – Khreshchatyk Street."[41] Initially a dusty road connecting Podil with other parts of the city and with the countryside, Khreshchatyk would evolve into a major commercial artery of the modernizing imperial metropolis. Around 1803, Melens'kyi began distributing parcels of land for construction there, and between 1804 and 1807 he built the first professional theatre in Kyiv (with a capacity of around 470), in one of the mansions located at the foot of the street, on what today is European Square. It should be emphasized that the theatre was a symbol of the pride and influence of the local Ukrainian oligarchs. Since it was to be built by private citizens (by "the society of most venerable citizens") as a joint venture, "both revenues from the building and expenditures should belong to the [private] society, not to municipal assets."[42] The theatre building served as a nucleus; more development soon followed nearby, helping transform Khreshchatyk into a fashionable residential and later commercial area.

Between 1802 and 1808 the Kyiv magistrate commissioned Melens'kyi to erect the already mentioned Column of the Magdeburg Law, a symbol of the restored local self-government, on the Dnieper bank between Podil and Khreshchatyk. Podil, as seat of the magistrate, would remain the largest and most densely populated part of Kyiv until well into the nineteenth century. Indeed, Podil *was* Kyiv, and certainly it was the district where most burghers lived. According to data from 1785, Podil had by far the largest number of houses owned by the townspeople (*mishchany*). However, for the wealthier merchants and for other social and ethnic categories that were *not* part of the traditional urban community (among them Russian soldiers, peasants, and lower service elements known as *raznochintsy*[43]), Pechers'k was in the lead.[44] Ten years later, Podil still had the largest share of private houses in the city (2,068 versus 1,098 in Pechers'k and 506 in Old Kyiv).[45] But Podil's demographic and administrative pre-eminence would not last much longer. On 9 July 1811, it was almost completely destroyed by a huge fire.[46] An eyewitness, the urban historian Mykola Zakrevs'kyi, left a moving account of this catastrophe:

3.2 Sazhin, *A View of Theatre Square* (image courtesy of Mystetstvo)

At that time the summer was hot and dry; hence the wooden roofs of houses easily flared up from falling sparks. An ever growing fire upset the balance of atmosphere and caused a storm that ... spread the fire with such speed that within three hours Kyiv-Podil turned into a sea of fire. Those who were not able to escape in advance, running along the narrow streets, now could not find a way out and fell victim to the fierce elements. Many perished in the cellars or churches ... The Old Kyiv rampart from the church of St. Andrew to the corner of St Michael's Monastery, above Khreshchatyk, was covered with a few thousand residents of Old Kyiv and Pechers'k who from here could comfortably watch the misery of their brethren, for human help was then powerless. The waves of fire passing from one part of the Lower Town to another, strong winds carrying on all sides burning slabs, a thick smoke, the falling houses in the extent of three quarter *versts*, and the distant cries of victims – all this looked extraordinary and horrible ... Our homestead ... was filled with a great many soldiers and a mob in rags. These Vandals looked quite busy. I then turned six, therefore I could not be a proper eyewitness, but I took notice that these people were breaking off locks on our storerooms, taking our jars with preserves which they were eating immediately, and breaking our tableware while fighting. The same happened to the drinks as well. In a word, within a few minutes our storerooms and cellar were completely empty. Then they turned to our other belongings ... With difficulty we could make our way through curvy and narrow streets blocked up with furniture, people, and carriages. From all sides there was fire, smoke, noise, and cries that horrified me. Finally we reached the Dnieper shore and stopped at Obolon' [area]. Here an incredible amount of belongings were thrown about in great disorder on the sand. The people were bustling about, many half-dressed. A shared sorrow ruled in this kingdom of plunder. Some people cried bitterly, witnessing the death of the city and the riot of fire, an image that seemed even more horrible at night. It burnt almost for three days ... On July 10 Kyiv-Podil was already transformed into stinking ruins that were burning or fuming. The streets were unrecognizable.[47]

Almost all of the district's churches and monasteries were destroyed by the fire. In fact, most of Podil burned to the ground, except for the area beyond the Ditch (*Kanava*), later known as the district of Plos'ka (or Plos'ke if a wider rural locality was concerned). For a time, the victims of the fire found refuge in the suburb of Obolon', where they lived in rude shelters. Despite some financial help provided by the government and private benefactors, many could not rebuild their houses – they included Zakrevs'kyi's own father, who died of a broken heart shortly afterwards.

This disaster, however, proved beneficial in at least one respect: almost immediately after the fire, Podil became a laboratory for urban renewal in Kyiv. The man entrusted with this was, not surprisingly, Melens'kyi. His major achievement was the new plan for Podil, which combined orthogonal classicist features with the traditional Baroque-inspired radial layout.[48] Considered by some to be one of the best classicist plans in the history of urban planning, it used surviving stone churches as its spatial "landmarks."

Unfortunately, Melens'kyi's elegant plan was not fully implemented. Podil was soon rebuilt, but in the much more monotonous grid we see today (see map 8, page 232). After the fire, Podil increasingly became an object of imperial regularization. The imperial law even prescribed (although this was not always enforced) the sizes of building plots, which were grouped into three categories: large (1,000 square *sazhen*), medium (600), and small (300), each with a house of corresponding size. Each house's main façade was of a defined length (ten to fifteen *sazhen*) and had to face the street; outbuildings and (often) gardens were to be behind. This meant that Kyiv's buildings now formed perimeters, with green parcels within each block. Another novelty was the introduction of a hierarchy of streets and types of a housing stock.[49] In 1806 the Kyiv governor declared that "the places designated for [new] settlement should be defined by large open streets," along which "houses of the first range" were to be built. On the smaller streets, "the houses of the second range" could be built, while in "closed lanes," the governor allowed "the houses of the third range." After 1810, the government also began to enforce "exemplary" façades in private construction, so that between 1813 and 1818, of the 7,889 newly built dwelling houses with approved façades throughout the empire, more than 400 were built in Kyiv province (and most of those in Kyiv).[50]

The redevelopment of Podil allowed Melens'kyi to express himself fully as a talented architect. He designed or supervised numerous private and public structures. Among his chief projects was the modernized Market Square, built between 1812 and 1828, which was dominated by a new commercial centre, Hostynyi Dvir (shopping arcades for retail traders), and by the new Contract Hall, built in 1815–17 for famous annual *kontrakty* (Contract Fair). Despite this remarkable reconstruction, something had been lost in the devastating fire and in a series of natural misfortunes that followed it: Podil had gradually but steadily ceased to be Kyiv's main commercial and residential centre; many of its residents had chosen to settle in other areas after the fire of 1811 and a series of floods.[51]

Meanwhile, the local police, who were subordinate to the commandant of Kyiv fortress but financed through the municipal budget, pressed for further unification of the city.[52] In 1810 the commandant submitted a proposal calling for the expansion of police personnel and the division of Kyiv's three historical districts (Podil, Pechers'k, and Old Kyiv) into five police districts (two in Pechers'k, two in Podil, one in Old Kyiv), which in turn would be split into twenty-one smaller sub-districts. Each sub-district would have from seven to nine sentry boxes, each staffed with five guards (210 men for a total of forty-two boxes). One justification for this system was an urgent need to keep "malign people" under surveillance: for "many people having settled in Kyiv recently from Polish and other remote provinces ... give refuge to malign people, thus forcing police to act."[53]

For reasons of security, among others, the Russian imperial authorities chose to reside outside of noisy Podil filled with "malign people." Yet that part of the city, despite various disasters and a demographic downturn, continued to be the seat of Kyiv's self-governance institutions until 1835. Even after municipal autonomy was abolished, the new city duma was still located in Podil, in a house purchased from a local merchant.[54]

Even before the fire that devastated Podil, Melens'kyi was applying his planning skills to other parts of the city, building not only for the municipal commune but also for Kyiv's imperial masters residing elsewhere, in the emerging district of Lypky, adjacent to Pechers'k *forshtadt* (from the German *Vorstadt* – "suburb"). Here, between 1803 and 1810, Kyiv's chief architect and planner designed the Palace Square, in front of the mid-eighteenth-century royal palace, where the governmental offices (*prisutstvennye mesta*),[55] a governor's mansion, and the Noble Assembly (a representative organ of provincial, mostly Catholic and Polish-seaking, nobility) were now located. The square was also designed to serve as a parade ground for imperial troops. Lypky, the area across from the square, which was laid out on an "orthogonal-grid" pattern, became the city's new administrative centre as well as its first elite residential district.[56] Until the mid-1830s, Kyiv retained the following spatial balance of power: the new imperial centre was in Lypky, while its old municipal centre remained in Podil. This uneasy coexistence reflected the final stage of the city's acquisition by imperial authorities. The space itself seemed to reflect the unequal power relations. Podil's main street, Oleksandrivs'ka, led all the way up to the Palace Square. Despite being an unpaved road through ravines and virgin hills for much of the way,[57] it perhaps symbolized the magistrate's increasing dependency on the Russian governor, who even spatially was situated *above* the local burghers.

So did autonomous Kyiv become a "lame duck" by the early nineteenth century? Was its civic pride irreparably wounded by imperial prejudice? Before answering this, let me raise a few more specific questions. What was the role of Kyiv's self-governing institutions in planning, financing, and executing the redevelopment of Kyiv prior to 1835, while Melens'kyi was the city's chief architect and planner? What does this tell us about the advent of modernity in Kyiv? And finally, what was the relationship between municipal institutions and imperial authorities during those years? By answering these questions, we may be able to ascertain the degree to which the Russian authorities constrained the powers of municipal institutions and imposed their own "imperial" or "Russian" agenda on the city. In the end, I will attempt to answer a somewhat more controversial question: Can we speak about a distinct – "Ukrainian" or local – version of modernity as opposed to the "Russian" one, the latter presumably imposed on Kyiv from the outside by ruthless imperial authorities and their economic agents – Russian merchants and artisans?

Historians usually agree that after the 1780s (with the implementation by Catherine II of the 1785 Charter to Towns), despite the restoration of the Magdeburg Law in Kyiv in 1802, Kyiv's autonomy had been curtailed in a number of important ways. How true is that?

It is true that the magistrate – the traditional executive and judicial organ of the autonomous city – was restored in 1802. But it is also true that a few years later the local Russian authorities established an additional institution, the Kyiv City (or Communal) Commission (or simply the municipal commission), to manage revenues and expenses. This institution was authorized by Tsar Alexander I on 3 September 1806.[58] The commission duplicated some of the functions previously reserved for the magistrate, specifically in matters related to the city budget and sources of municipal revenue. More importantly, the new commission was required to report regularly to the governor and to a local treasury board (*kazennaia palata*).[59] This was a clear sign that local self-government was being subordinated to imperial authorities. Also, the Kyiv governor was required to confirm all the elected members of the commission. Another task of the commission, and perhaps the most important one, was managing the city's capital – private and public – and thus it functioned as Kyiv's first bank. The city's capital was put into circulation, with interest rates on loans between 8 and 12 per cent per year.[60] Wealthy burghers, members of other social estates, and even institutions (such as the magistrate of the town of Vasyl'kiv) deposited money in the commission's account, reportedly at "moderate interest."

The commission had been established by the government, but it was run by the mayor (*viit*) together with his plutocratic colleagues from among the burgomasters. Of the four initial members of the commission, which represented several strata of urban dwellers – "distinguished citizens" (*imenitye grazhdane*), merchants, "registered fellows" (*reiestrovi tovaryshi*),[61] and the largest but humblest groups of "guildsmen" and simple burghers – two would later be accused of embezzling public funds.[62]

Reportedly, the informal power of the *viit* was so great that he alone selected the "elected" members of the commission; the "respected citizens" had no choice but to go along. In another respect, the magistrate's influence not only did not wane, but rather increased over time, for this major organ of municipal self-government gradually took over all the banking operations as they related to the commission's funds. It was the *viit* who endorsed all loan commitments. If someone did not pay a debt on time, the debtor was brought to the magistrate's court, which was conducted in the presence of the commission's own secretary. Most of the debtors were burghers and merchants who owned real estate in the city; among the investors were many non-burghers and non-Kyivites. More remarkably, despite the obvious conflict of interest, the city commission served as a bank for the magistrate itself, with the *viit* presiding over both institutions. In fact, the magistrate borrowed heavily from private creditors (who usually invested at 6 per cent interest), supposedly to balance the city budget. What the magistrate owed to individuals and legal entities had then to be paid off from the municipal commission's funds (basically from the city budget). Thus as early as 1807 the magistrate owed a handful of people more than 130,000 roubles – an enormous sum at the time, roughly equal to the city's annual revenue![63] Most of the major creditors were Kyiv merchants (some had loaned the magistrate between 10,000 and 11,000 roubles), and, astonishingly, one of them, Ivan Kyselevs'kyi (the father of Kyiv's last *viit*), was also a member of the magistrate.[64]

It is hard not to notice a huge elephant in the room – the city's financial affairs were so tightly bound up with the personal affairs of municipal leaders that it was almost impossible to separate public monies from private interests. Certainly, many of the plutocrats running the city deliberately confused public with private, especially when it came to revenues (although where the municipal debt or mismanaged funds were concerned, our heroes were quick to disassociate themselves from the city and its financial woes).

In light of all this, it is no surprise that the city fathers later claimed that all of the documents held by the municipal commission featuring the names of the creditors and the sums they had deposited on commission's account had been lost without a trace in the 1811 fire. Moreover, the documents of the commission between 1817 and 1827, when it was run by another plutocrat, burgomaster Pylyp Lakerda, had mysteriously disappeared as well. Even the investigating officials' powers, which had been vested in them by the imperial state, failed to procure financial evidence (except for a short retrospective note written by a staffer).[65] So much for this early exposure to banking and for the power of the Russian state, the latter clearly exaggerated by later historians. This first experience with financial capitalism would prove fatal not only for the plutocrats themselves but also for the city they acted as if they owned.

But first let us look at how the city spent money – or rather, how it was supposed to spend it, given the huge embezzlement of public funds and the more than questionable bookkeeping. The scale of irregularities shocked even the most seasoned imperial bureaucrats, who themselves were renowned for their shady financial practices. Many important aspects of the city economy, including planning and city beautification, have long been overlooked by historians. For all the government's efforts to supervise the city, especially its revenues and expenses, that supervision was sporadic at best. Hence the task of the Kyiv municipal commission was to balance the city budget, whose looming deficit had been a constant concern for the local Russian authorities since at least 1803.[66] Yet as we have already seen, the commission became a playground for plutocrats linked to the magistrate through their private and professional interests. Admittedly, the commission had to follow the guidelines (an estimate of the city's revenues and expenses), first "confirmed" by the Kyiv governor in 1806 and enforced for a number of years. All incidental expenses (i.e., those exceeding the estimate of 1806) and new taxes had to be approved by the governor on an ad hoc basis.[67] In addition, after the mid-1820s the city was required to submit each September a report on municipal expenditures to the governor and the local treasury board (*kazennaia palata*) – another clear sign of Kyiv's growing dependency on the government.[68] Yet, as becomes clear from the correspondence between the city and the governor in 1824,[69] the state had great difficulty extracting financial reports from the magistrate.[70] One can only agree with the historian of Kyiv self-government Ivan Kamanin that the supervision the government officials exercised over the city was ceremonial rather than strict.[71]

We have a rather rare occasion to study official data on city revenues and expenses for the various periods. These particular numbers come from the report the municipal commission submitted in 1827 to the local imperial authorities. This important document compared city revenues and expenses for two years – 1806 (the starting date for the commission) and 1826 (the latest figures the report used).[72] These data were later confirmed by another joint government–municipal organ – the Temporary Committee on the Reorganization of Kyiv.[73]

Creative accounting notwithstanding, in both years the biggest source of municipal income was the "spirits charge" (*vynnyi zbir*). Kyiv burghers had long enjoyed the exclusive right to produce and sell alcoholic beverages in the city.[74] This also happened to be the most lucrative (and hence open to various irregularities) activity for the city's plutocrats, the most plutocratic of whom attempted to privatize this city monopoly. The scandal surrounding the sale of alcohol was (and still is) nothing surprising, given that Kyivites had always loved to drink (especially spirits made *in* the city), but the scandal that erupted in the 1820s was unique in that it led to enormous reputational and financial losses. It even contributed to the demise of Kyiv self-government as such. According to the investigators, in 1810 a group of plutocrats (among them Pylyp Lakerda and Hryhorii Kyselevs'kyi) journeyed to Saint Petersburg to renew the *vynnyi vidkup* – essentially a harvest of revenues from the production and sale of alcohol in the city. What was supposed to be conducted by the city as a legal entity (through the magistrate) was in fact carried out by a group of plutocrats on their own behalf. Indeed, they borrowed for this purpose 50,000 roubles from the municipal commission, that is, from the city.[75] The contract was for four years, with an annual payment to the state treasury of 371,500 roubles. Soon, forty more people joined the enterprise with a pledge to invest an additional 250,000 roubles.

As it turned out, the family of burgomaster Lakerda misappropriated the money (later estimated by the municipal commission at around 300,000 roubles!); only 135,000 was returned to the city after a series of audits conducted in the 1820s. A number of people, including some members of the Lakerda clan, were prosecuted and some even went to jail; others had to auction off their property to satisfy the public authority's financial claims. Whatever the personal consequences, Kyivites had proved in their own way that alcohol can indeed be bad for you.

In the short run, however, alcohol proved to be very good for the city. In the 1820s the alcohol monopoly brought to municipal coffers real money – 110,000 roubles in 1826, making it the city's largest source of revenue.[76] Another important source of city revenue was the leasing of city-owned hayfields to wealthy private Kyivites, which reminds us that at that time, the city was more than just streets and buildings – it included a vast agricultural belt.[77] It goes without saying that among the largest leaseholders of those hayfields were wealthy plutocrats such as the already mentioned Hryhorii Kyselevs'kyi, who, despite his involvement in the alcohol scandal, was elected Kyiv's *viit* in 1826.[78] Another wealthy plutocrat and burgomaster (in 1815 and 1818), Mykhailo Hotsaienko, rented not only the second largest hayfield but also one of the three city-owned houses (in which he operated an inn).

Again, a close relationship between private interests and public service in self-governing Kyiv is glaringly obvious. That Kyiv was not yet a modern metropolis is clear from the meagre income (420 roubles) the city derived from a few small factories (mostly brickworks and soap and tile factories) and a (virtually absent) residential property tax. The leasing of municipal property (such as fifty-eight shops, many on Hostynyi Dvir,[79] and a few marketplaces) brought in significant income (around 18,000 roubles), but that amount was clearly less than it ought to have been owing to corruption and financial mismanagement. Another large source of revenue for the city was harbour fees (12,050 roubles), which indicates that river traffic still played a major role in the city's economic life, as it had for centuries. By this time, several sources of revenue that the governor and the city had established in 1806 had ceased to yield any returns or yielded less than expected.

Even so, in 1826 the city's revenues (157,853 roubles) exceeded its expenditures (155,592 roubles). The following year the budget looked even better: 173,298 in revenues versus 170,704 in expenditures.[80] This was achieved not least by introducing a few new "capitalist" taxes – for example, on promissory notes used in all real estate transactions; on all deals between the owners of commercial real estate (such as the sale or lease of a house, a store, or a barn) in which a broker was involved (with one rouble from each such deal going to the city budget); and on all auction sales (with 2 per cent of the proceeds going to the city). Another new source of municipal income was fees and excise duties (*aktsyzy*) paid by all non-resident merchants and manufacturers.[81] Bizarrely, circus performers and actors (*ekvilibristy* and *shtukmaistry*) who visited Kyiv "to show to the public performances and rarities they brought with them" were specifically mentioned as an important *new* source of city revenue.[82] Nothing more signalled the coming of fiscal modernity in Kyiv than did this entertainment tax.

The main item of municipal expenditures in 1826 was street improvement and city beautification (a staggering 55,376 roubles),[83] clear evidence that the autonomous city, whether under pressure from the government or not,[84] was not ignoring the muddiest (literally!) issue that Kyiv faced. The city fathers seem to have jumped on the bandwagon of urban modernity, which would later be hijacked by the imperial authorities. In fact, the municipal commission had to justify these large expenses to the government by citing the growing need for "street, road and canal improvement," for street fixtures such as lanterns, and for the maintenance of "city-owned houses, Dnieper ferry and a bridge." It appears that the city itself initiated, financed, and carried out much of this city beautification agenda, which was not limited to Podil; it also included other areas of the expanding city such as Lypky, Khreshchatyk, and Old Kyiv.[85] What did this early city beautification agenda include?

It seems that in the 1820s the most pressing concern, pursued jointly by the city and Russian governors, was the paving of major streets and roads. Previously the magistrate had rejected the notion that each homeowner should pave the street in front of his or her house. The new governor had discovered a better way to do the job at the city's cost – by hiring contractors.[86] By 1826 a few major streets had already been paved with stone, among them Moskovs'ka Street in Pechers'k and Oleksandrivs'ka Street in Podil. After this, the joint committee established the priorities for the street improvement scheme, which included Khreshchatyk (as a main route connecting Podil with Lypky), St Andrew's Slope (a winding road linking hilly Old Kyiv with low-lying Podil), and the future Velyka Vasyl'kivs'ka Street, then an important road out of town. Another urgent project was the cleaning and regulating of a notoriously filthy ditch in Podil known as the Kanava (or simply the Ditch), an eyesore separating Podil proper from its former suburb, now the city's newest district of Plos'ka.

The authorities might have decided to bear the cost of *paving* the major streets, but their *maintenance* (cleaning and repairing) was not a priority either for the city or for the government. In Pechers'k and Podil and in the Khreshchatyk valley, the homeowners themselves were expected to maintain the streets and roads in front of their houses. In Old Kyiv, however, the residents reportedly lived in "absolute poverty" and could not afford such maintenance. There, the city agreed to take on the task, which was otherwise considered a private concern. The governor and the city also put forward several proposals with respect to more comprehensive planning (while recognizing their own limitations). So in Pechers'k, with the expansion of the fortress and its esplanade, a number of houses (around 280) were to be relocated to the valley of the Lybid' River; in this way, "Pechers'k could merge with Khreshchatyk" (which turned out to be an unrealistic expectation).

By contrast, in the case of Old Kyiv the authorities sounded too pessimistic, admitting that they were unable to regularize the district, which "by its very situation does not offer either convenience or means to improve itself as regards regularity of streets and buildings." Only one major postal road leading from the suburbs to St Sophia and a few smaller streets were to be widened, and this would require the demolition of several "small homesteads" (*dvorikov*). Ten years later a much more ambitious planning agenda would be introduced in the city, and Old Kyiv would become a main laboratory of change.

Before the mid-1830s, however, of all of Kyiv's districts only Podil was being totally made over, given that it was still recovering from the 1811 fire. Planners noted that Podil was developing according to the 1812 plan, and many plots had been already rebuilt. Yet many remained empty and had not even been "being fenced off," due to the poverty of their owners. The authorities then did something that they would not often do again, especially during the ruthless urban regimes of the 1830s through to the 1850s: they mercifully allowed Podil residents to ignore a previous requirement to build *only* stone houses along some of Podil's major streets. Instead homeowners could build wooden houses on stone foundations (with the caveat that they should start building in the course of the *current* year – otherwise they would lose their plots). Finally, with respect to Plos'ka, just north of Podil, a district that had escaped the fire, the planners applied a hands-off policy, noting specifically that the area would be allowed to develop according to the "[economic] circumstances of its residents." Unfortunately, this mild and perhaps even socially conscious version of urban planning was coming to an end, along with the fortunes of the self-governing city.

Until the early 1830s, however, the city was very much tied to a planning agenda. This can be illustrated by the figure of architect Melens'kyi. He worked mainly for the municipal commune, and it was the city that paid his salary, by allocating to his office 2,040 roubles – more than went to the city jail and hospital and almost as much as the Kyiv municipal commission received for its own deliberations.[87] In this capacity, Melens'kyi was at the vanguard of Kyiv's municipal agenda (planning, improving, and building), although he also participated in projects carried out by the Russian imperial authorities, as a founder of the Kyiv provincial drafting office and a member of the committee that worked on a new city plan in 1832.[88]

So far the range of activities of the city fathers seemed quite broad, if not sufficiently independent. Those activities included everything from embezzling public funds to beautifying the city to milking municipal property. Another important piece of city business was the distribution of land parcels and the supervision of private construction.[89] The major occasion for redistributing land in the city arose after the catastrophic Podil fire of 1811. After the new plan of the district had been prepared (with the active participation of Melens'kyi), the municipal authorities began to distribute plots to all those who wanted one and who could build for themselves a stone or wooden house. However, the streets would be regulated and the houses would have to have the right façades and be of the correct size. In 1812–13, according to a general plan, for each of around 150 sub-districts (*kvartaly*), the authorities prescribed a certain number of houses – for example, six stone and four wooden (as in sub-district no. 2),[90] with the governor giving approval for individual building plots. But there was a catch to all this redevelopment: the public authority did not care much about the poorer burghers who could not raise enough money to rebuild a house. In most of the sub-districts, around half the residents appeared to be "unable to build" (*nesostoiatel'nye k postroike*). In addition, wealthier Kyivites (plutocrats and merchants, among them Pylyp Lakerda) were taking advantage of the fire by acquiring, for an extra charge,[91] neighbouring plots that their previous owners were unable to develop. An examination of the distribution of land parcels points to another important consequence of the 1811 fire: afterwards, Podil acquired a much stricter spatial ecology whereby some quarters attracted almost exclusively the rich and powerful.[92] Poorer elements disappeared from certain areas, with the result that they became more socially homogeneous.

For the next decade or even longer, dissatisfied burghers bombarded municipal institutions with various demands for monetary payments or land allotments as compensation for lost property (houses or shops).[93] From a document dated 1832 we learn that a number of private land parcels in Podil (more than 140) remained undeveloped or had been built up incorrectly, that is, outside the approved plan.[94] Among the leading causes of this were lack of sufficient funds or outright poverty, unfortunate natural circumstances (Dnieper floods, springwater), or some judicial reason ("debtor's claim," an imminent trial, etc.). More unusually, among those who had failed to build houses were a number of merchants and notorious plutocrats, among them the merchant Denys Barshchevs'kyi (whose two stone houses "were in pledge" for debts), merchant and plutocrat Anton Lakerda (who had built a house without a plan), and "citizen" and plutocrat Vasyl' Tokhai (his property

3.3 Kul'zhenko, The View of Podil (Podil redeveloped), *Vidy Kiev*

had been confiscated by the police in anticipation of public sale). It appears that some of these men were under investigation for corruption and other offences and had been forced to sell their properties in order to pay what they owed to the state and the city. It is important to emphasize here that the ultimate authority for enforcing the quite strict building regulations[95] belonged to the Russian state, not to the autonomous city. So in 1832, the governor authorized the police to "force" property owners to start building immediately and according to the approved plans – otherwise their plots would be redistributed.[96] This was another clear sign of the imperial authorities' growing impatience with local plutocrats and with the autonomous city in general.

One Man's War against the City and the End of Autonomy

At the beginning of the new decade, the 1830s, the government began to act more decisively with respect to the city's many topographic and spatial issues. New city plans were prepared, and new municipal boundaries were delineated, and these measures were initiated largely by the state rather than by the city. Political factors, such as the Polish November uprising of 1830–1 and a subsequent plan to build a new fortress in Pechers'k, no doubt contributed to the total makeover of Kyiv.[97] This was a government-driven change that essentially belongs to the next period of history. Here, let us consider a few harbingers of that change.

In 1830 a new general plan of Kyiv was prepared by the newly appointed city architect Pavlo Dubrovs'kyi, in collaboration with several government-employed experts.[98] The plan showed both what the city looked like at present and what it was going to look like in the future. It outlined five existing parts of the city and envisaged a few new directions for city expansion (see map 9, page 233). Unfortunately, the names of the streets were not shown on the plan, but we can still detect a few main arteries. Aside from unnamed streets, the map identified a few old exit roads, among them the road to the town of Vasyl'kiv and one to the village of Shuliavka.

On this plan we also see that one of the few planned areas in Kyiv was Podil, formerly the least regulated part of the city. Just north of it (to the right of it on the map), beyond the Ditch (Kanava), was the sprawling and largely unregulated district of Plos'ka, recently incorporated into Kyiv as Part V of the city.[99] Farther north and north-west lay vast green zones surrounding a few older suburbs (such as Luk'ianivka, Kurenivka, and Priorka, the latter two in the valley of the Syrets' River, where Kyivites owned farmsteads and often leased them to non-residents). The historical district of Old Kyiv (Part III of the city) remained the most "organic" in terms of its layout, with military fortifications still visible in the centre near the site of St Sophia (no. 53 on the map). Khreshchatyk was still an unpaved and unregulated road rather than a major thoroughfare, and what was later to become Khreshchatyk Square was merely the site of a military jail (*ostrog*) and barracks (no. 57). St Sophia was flanked by a relatively thin residential belt, and the Golden Gate ("newly discovered," as we are informed by the map's legend) was in the middle of an empty space (no. 61). Huge areas to the west, all the way up to the village of Pan'kivshchyna (near the map's upper margin) are shown on the map as devoid of significant settlements; instead they are speckled with various topographic marks indicating ravines, dunes, brushland, and forests. Nowhere does the map indicate that in fifteen years a whole new district would emerge there centred on the university. Pechers'k, by contrast, was still a fairly dense residential area, without a more and more sprawling fortress. Finally,

the most regulated part of the city was Lypky (Part II), a centre of imperial power and an elite residential district. The map shows a number of
important buildings there, such as the Kyiv Gymnasium and its "grape
garden" (no. 46), a parade square (*plats-parad*) surrounded by provincial government offices (*prisutstvennye mesta*, no. 40), the residence of
the governors general (no. 49), and the royal palace (no. 41).

The government was ready to ensure that the 1830 general plan
did not remain a fantasy. The Kyiv civil governor in 1833 urged the
municipal architect Dubrovs'kyi to inspect the new neighbourhood
in the Lybid' Valley so as to "prevent any irregular construction [that
may appear] contrary to the plan that was approved by the highest
authorities."[100] All of the houses constructed without regard to a particular plan or without a prescribed façade and those that were located
on "unsuitable places" were to be removed. This needed to be done not
least "for the benefit of beautification [*blagovidnosti*]" of the city. In the
end it was decided that a few houses would have to be demolished to
make way for new buildings, this time in accordance with the plan.[101]
(For the projected changes on the city plan see map 10, page 234). The
government's increasing attention to urban planning and construction
in Kyiv was spurred by the wider political developments.

Not surprisingly, Poles were to blame for this and other changes.
In the early 1830s Kyiv once again suffered collateral damage as a
consequence of Russian–Polish armed conflict. In the aftermath of
the Polish November insurrection (1830–1) the imperial government
launched an aggressive centralizing campaign aimed at curbing Polish influence in the region. Eventually this policy was applied to all
sociopolitical, administrative, and judicial features in the empire's
Southwestern Region. An immediate outcome of this campaign was
the founding, on 22 January 1832, of a governorship-general based
in Kyiv, whose jurisdiction would extend to all three "formerly Polish" provinces: Kyiv, Volhynia, and Podolia.[102] The first head of the
highest regional office was General Vasilii Levashov (in office 1832–5);
between then and 1914 he would be succeeded by thirteen other military figures entrusted with the highest military and administrative
authority in the region. Although he was a soldier and had no roots in
Right-Bank Ukraine, Levashov turned out to be a committed lobbyist
for Kyiv's interests, at least as he understood them.[103] It seems that he
also encouraged provincial authorities to involve themselves more in
municipal affairs and to bypass as much as possible the Kyiv magistrate and the local plutocrats.

Evidence of this new trend in the city's affairs is a report submitted to Levashov by a military engineer, Colonel Savych, a local Ukrainian employee of the provincial building board. His 1832 report sharply criticized planning and city beautification practices (or, rather the lack thereof) in the capital of the southwestern borderlands. Savych's report also contained a surprisingly irreverent ad hominem attack on Kyiv's *viit*, as if its author felt confident that Levashov would receive his views with favour. The civic-minded colonel opened his report with a brief philosophy of city beautification, presenting it as a citizen's duty rather than a matter of immediate concern for the public authorities. Savych was one of the first to critically address the topic of planning and city beautification:

> In all well-organized [*blagoustroennykh*] towns and even villages of Russia every inhabitant does his best to keep buildings in due order, every inhabitant keeps the streets, moats, bridges, stones, and sidewalks in good repair, putting them in order along with [their] houses. In all villages of Little Russia where there are only clay [*mazannye*] houses these are coated [with clay] and whitewashed several times a year – both for comely looks and for the usefulness of coating, for it preserves the walls from rottenness and dampness, while also retaining the heat. It is only in Kyiv that public and citizens' own benefit is not protected – and this is more because of laziness and bad habit and furthermore because of the bad example of the *viit* himself, whose houses differ from others by their ugliness![104]

Savych then launches his own agenda with regard to urban planning and city beautification, in which he reveals his military mindset: he would force private residents to participate in his improvement schemes:

> 1) Order police to induce residents to finish the streets, each in front of his own courtyard, according to exemplary ones; that is, each resident should make a signed statement that they would maintain in front of their courtyards sidewalks, stones [for tethering a horse or a cart], and bridges, as well as drain water and level streets by filling in with sand, etc. Those places which would require considerable planning ... should be regulated at treasury's expense.
>
> 2) Order police to oblige residents to mend immediately fences and gates, to repair roofs, to paint the new ones, and to plaster, coat, paint, or whitewash the walls.

3) Order the municipal commission to put, in appropriate places, lamp poles and align them with stones ...

4) Order the city architect to amend, in all four parts of the city, everything that has been put in this budget estimate that I have corrected.[105]

Clearly overestimating the powers of the police, as well as his own, Savych hoped, too optimistically, that most of the work indicated in his proposal could be finished within several weeks, "provided that there will be active supervision." One cannot call this a *Russian* attack on a *Ukrainian* city, for Savych almost certainly belonged to the Ukrainian noble class from Left-Bank Ukraine. Most probably his report, filled as it was with military decision-making, reflected the hostile attitude of a new group of Russian imperial bureaucrats towards local administrative practices. Those practices were increasingly being perceived as detrimental to the sort of progress associated with centralization and stricter control over local affairs and private citizens in general, especially in the tense political atmosphere that plagued Kyiv after the Polish November uprising. In the event, Levashov ordered provincial and municipal institutions to implement the colonel's suggestions. Officials, however, refused to put too much pressure on homeowners, who "should feel free to look for [building] materials and workers."[106] Even so, Levashov and his subordinate Savych had introduced a new, militaristic approach to urban planning and city beautification in a city that officially remained self-governing.[107]

As part of a series of measures taken by Levashov, in 1833 Kyiv was finally split into five (later six) police sections. The local police had been lobbying for this for years.[108] Levashov also launched a large-scale redevelopment of Kyiv with the help of a government-funded building committee. In March 1833 he submitted to the committee his general proposal concerning urban planning and city beautification; in doing so, he explicitly bypassed the magistrate and the municipal commission.[109] Levashov's proposals reflected both the growing intrusion of the Russian government in municipal affairs and his personal involvement in the minutiae of urban life to a degree unprecedented for any previous imperial official. Of his eleven points, the first was a follow-up to an earlier proposal by Colonel Savych, who wanted private citizens to play a more active role in maintaining the pavements in front of their houses. Levashov confirmed that it was indeed a homeowner's duty to maintain sidewalks and roads. He also urged the city to exercise tighter control over public construction by "issuing advance orders" and by drawing detailed estimates of works. Confident in his new role as the city's true master, Levashov demanded to know in advance which works in the city had to be carried out in the coming spring and summer. He did not shy away even from more technical issues such as how to prevent Khreshchatyk from being inundated with rainwater streaming down from the surrounding hills. Among other urban renewal issues, Levashov pointed to those that required more comprehensive planning, such as the resettlement of Kyivites to higher ground from the marshy Lybid' River valley (which had to be drained) and from the bank of the Dnieper (which was often at risk of flooding). Finally, the tireless governor general suggested opening a public library in Kyiv. In 1832, as it carried out Levashov's program, the city spent an astonishing 98,986 roubles on various planning, beautification, and renewal projects.[110]

Not surprisingly, this ambitious agenda had its dark side. In particular, Levashov oversaw a controversial development in Lypky on the site of a linden grove popular among Kyivites. He could easily be a poster boy for today's ruthless developers who have imposed so much unwanted change on Kyiv over the past ten to fifteen years. As if inticipating the cowboy capitalism of much later times, in 1833 Levashov had the linden trees cut down to make way for private housing, an action perceived by many as barbarous.[111] One disaffected observer commented on the military-style urban planning practised by Levashov: "In his front-line zeal to follow a straight line as much as possible, Levashov levelled bumpy slopes of one of the hilly streets. This work was done so fast and as it seems so unexpectedly that in one place, as I was informed, one unfortunate pharmacist reportedly lost any access to his house because of the precipice of a hill coming right to his porch."[112]

Perhaps even more notorious was the governor general's role in the demise of Kyiv's municipal autonomy: in 1835, he reportedly convinced Tsar Nicholas to abolish the Magdeburg Law in Kyiv.[113] But the demise of Kyiv's "ancient" self-government could be blamed only in part on an imperial government that sought to reduce local privileges and tighten its centralizing grip. A more immediate cause was one man's war against the city.[114]

Vasyl' Kravchenko, a butcher, was an honest man but clearly a quarrelsome one (characterized by one contemporary source as a man of "a restless disposition"[115]). In 1821 he was present during the election of Kyiv's artisanal executive (*remisnycha uprava*), held at the magistrate. Kravchenko was unhappy with the outcome and confronted *viit*

Mykhailo Hryhorenko and burgomaster Pylyp Lakerda, an omnipo-
tent plutocrat who had long been implicated in much of the corruption and backroom dealing involving a number of city fathers. The
butcher filed a complaint with the Kyiv governor about an unlawful
collection of taxes by the magistrate from burghers (in addition to the
poll tax), a complaint that was supported by a group of forty other
burghers. An investigation by the provincial authorities ensued. The
magistrate insisted on its exclusive right to collect taxes from Kyiv
burghers, a claim the plutocrats backed by making references to the
Magdeburg Law and to seventeenth-century charters of Polish kings
later confirmed by the Russian Senate. The plutocrats also claimed that
Kravchenko had somehow coerced forty other men into supporting
his complaint. So the local administration dismissed his accusations
as unfounded. In addition, the magistrate launched a smear campaign
against the forty co-signers, insinuating that they "have lost trust of the
society" and eventually banning them from municipal elections. Some
were declared bankrupt, others were accused of "lecherous behavior,"
and still others were dismissed for being under trial for "their illegal
actions."[116]

The Don Quixote of Kyiv did not give up. For years he bombarded
Russian authorities with numerous other denunciations against the magistrate, the municipal commission, and individual members of the Kyiv
plutocracy. To Kravchenko's forty signatures the magistrate responded
by collecting those from 650 burghers (out of a total of 6,000 male
burghers),[117] the "most venerable society," who supposedly supported
the testimony of the city fathers. As it turned out, many of them had
signed under duress.

In 1827 the authorities (now at the central level) resumed the investigation, and the plutocrats started implicating one another, although
most of those who were made scapegoats for what they *all* had done
were dead by then (among them Pylyp Lakerda and *viit* Hryhorenko).
Thus, many still living got away with fleecing the city. Not coincidentally, the post of Kyiv prosecutor went to the son of the newly elected
viit, Hryhorii Kyselevs'kyi. To no one's surprise, the prosecutor con-
spired with the plutocrats, and together they succeeded in sabotaging
the investigation. In the end, the state decided not to prosecute most
members of the magistrate. Many, however, had to return various sums
to the city, and some had to stand trial, as a result of which they were
deprived of voting rights.[118] Kravchenko's denunciations had no doubt
opened a Pandora's Box of wide-ranging accusations that eventually

undermined the entire municipal self-government. The investigation also revealed the extent to which a handful of families of city plutocrats had monopolized urban affairs and used public resources for private gain. However, we should avoid the temptation to reduce the entire history of Kyiv's self-governing commune to corruption and cronyism.

Despite a noticeable weakening of Kyiv's autonomy since the late eighteenth century, the magistrate and its ruling plutocrats still had plenty of leverage regarding various municipal matters such as land distribution, tax collection, construction and urban planning, the admission of new members to the urban community, and the administration of credit through the municipal commission. Supervision by the imperial authorities was rather sporadic and often retroactive; evidence for this was the long and bumpy investigation into allegations of corruption and embezzlement that surfaced in 1821. The misuse of funds and other irregularities perhaps lasted for decades, and the investigation itself took many long years. What is more, the investigators found it difficult to obtain basic financial and fiscal documents from the city's chief officers, who represented a handful of families – *de jure* elected but *de facto* self-appointed city leaders. They had once treated Kyiv as their property, constantly mixing public with private affaris. These informal power relations were not necessarily corrupt in modern sense, because the law too, ambiguous as it was, safeguarded Kyiv's self-governing status, in which public authority was not strictly separated from private interests.

Conclusion

Until 1835 Kyiv retained several significant features of autonomy. It was governed by the formally elected magistrate and by informally selected plutocrats, whose base was the traditional economic heartland of the city – Podil. The key figure in urban policy during those years was the architect Andrii Melens'kyi, who worked primarily for the municipal commune. He was instrumental in designing and implementing Kyiv's municipal agenda (planning, improving, and building). At the time, municipal economy and planning were the result of a partnership – albeit increasingly unequal – between the self-governing municipal commune and the Russian imperial authorities ("Russian" in the political rather than the ethnic sense). Also, several high-ranking imperial officials had personal, sometimes family ties with the leading plutocrats. In this sense the city had become a "family business." Allusions to a mafia notwithstanding, a number of urban changes were initiated, financed, and implemented by the city (through the magistrate and the municipal commission). Despite corruption and inefficiency in the city's institutions, there was a relatively viable version of a nascent urban modernity in Kyiv. A self-governing municipal commune was the last remnant of administrative autonomy in Russian-ruled Ukraine.

This all changed after 1835. Over the next several decades, modernity in Kyiv was driven almost exclusively by the Russian imperial authorities (both civil and military) and their economic agents – ethnic Russian merchants, who came to dominate the city's economy and municipal affairs. In this respect, 1835 separated two different cities, one representing a Ukrainian tradition, the other a Russian imperial one. These cities were different in terms of institutions, leadership, dominant culture, and political symbolism. An intricate structure rooted in medieval Magdeburg Law gave way to a new institution – Kyiv's city duma – which, just as in every other Russian city, was tightly controlled by a governor. In the decades to come, Kyiv's spaces and social and ethnic relations would be changed forever, and in the process the city would develop into a prime example of imperial urbanism in the borderlands.

Chapter Four

Planning a New City: Empire Transforms Space, 1835–1870

The Grief of the Kyivites

During the first three decades of the nineteenth century, changes in Kyiv were largely a by-product of municipal and imperial institutions. However, all strategic decisions concerning the *entire* city were taken in Pechers'k and Lypky, where the Russian military and civil authorities were located at the time. The imperial authorities also provided major resources for larger infrastructural projects, thus "preserving" the bulk of municipal revenue in the provincial Office of Public Care (*Prikaz obshchestvennogo prizreniia*).

The year 1835 brought a dramatic change in municipal leadership and in the overall demographics of Kyiv. It seems that this transition was lamented by Kyivites, especially by those who had a stake in municipal autonomy.[1] The abolition of the Magdeburg Law in Kyiv inspired an anonymous author (most likely a former staffer at the magistrate) to write a lengthy Ukrainian-language poem lamenting the resulting loss of "privileges" and the victory of ethnic Russians over local Ukrainian plutocrats.[2] Written shortly after 1835, this text was arguably the sole Ukrainian literary reaction to the dramatic shift in Kyiv's fortunes. Besides being radically anti-Russian, the poem was an extraordinary discourse of civic rights and pride, in which the author blamed Kyiv's Ukrainian oligarchs for squandering away the self-governing city.

The poem opens with an unusual gathering of Kyiv's municipal elite before Governor General Levashov, who is about to announce the "new statutes." According to the "rumor – something bad is going to happen to us" (*chutka – shchos' pohane z namy!*). The rumour turns out to be true: the "bad" is the abolition of the Magdeburg Law. The procession itself is ominously different from past municipal ceremonies: there is no marching band, nor is there a mounted municipal guard ("registered fellows"); instead there are rows of Russian police officials. The author then makes a few surmises about who caused this commotion: Was it perhaps the butcher Kravchenko, the notorious challenger of the local plutocrats? But no, the author rules him out ("Oh, it was not his work!"). Others must share the blame, among them the last *viit*, Kyselevs'kyi, who is mentioned twice in the poem:

> And this Sunday at the church
> So spoke Pryzenko [plutocrat Illia Pryz],
> After getting intoxicated,
> That it was Kysil' [Kyselevs'kyi] who has done it
> It was him, who messed things up,
> He said something to Levashov
> Who must have believed him
> And then he stirred up the whole town.

Another rumour has it that Kyselevs'kyi will not be a city head anymore, for he and other plutocrats are standing trial. The author proceeds to the next important question: "Who are going to be our judges?" The answer is a scathing portrayal of the Russian (Great Russian) merchants who are about to become Kyiv's new municipal elite[3]:

> They are not from common people but from the puffed up [*nadutykh*]
> And from Russians with the beards,[4]
> That is, the goat [*tsap*] coming from Tula
> Or from Briansk, from the woods
> Who once used to mold cannons and bullets?
> Or manufacturer Khodunov[5]?
> [...] Now another one is coming,
> Levashov himself appointed him –
> He who has lots of money,
> Dekhterev, residing by the Dnieper shore.[6]
> And their horde seems so big,
> Where do they all come from? From Kaluga –
> No good will come out of it
> They will make it hot for us [...]

They will all become lords,
Even though they have untidy hair [*v patlakh*] and beards
Someone who used to loiter about selling bread,
Will become a city head.

A rapid consequence of this massive Russian immigration anticipated by the poem's patriotic author will be the loss of Kyiv's rights and privileges and, last but not least, its municipal ceremonies, those vital symbols of the autonomous city. And indeed, the latter's sudden cancellation would be the most painful and visible sign of Kyiv's changing fortunes: the anonymous author specifically laments the disappearance of Kyiv's ceremonial "golden banner," the drills of the municipal guard, and the parade ceremonies. He dryly comments: "When we squandered away our rights / We should forget about our army." Then, as if anticipating Taras Shevchenko's critical poetry, the amateur poet makes a biting social and national commentary about the new order brought about by Russian *nouveaux riches*:

For what will *Pylypon*[7] say?
He will give us a different thought
How to establish his law,
[…] And he will give us such an education
That even in Paris is unheard of,
He will show us the instruction,
How to caracole in blast shoes [*u laptiakh*][8]
Everybody will become a lord,
You won't even detect a priest,
For after mixing with the Jews
All will look like goats.

The last two somewhat cryptic stanzas mentioning Jews and goats are perhaps meant to emphasize the visual confusion that has accompanied the social change in the city (although Jews were all but absent in Kyiv after 1835). The author continues to make ironic fashion statements, focusing primarily on facial hair:

We should no longer shave either beards or mustaches
We should rather grow long hair [*patly*]
To look like goats [*tsapy*].

The last part of the poem is a passionate condemnation of Kyiv's Ukrainian plutocrats, among them the already mentioned Hryhorii Kyselevs'kyi (here referred to simply as Kysil'):

> They drank away all the rights for nothing,
> Kysil' squandered them at cards
> Or they wasted [*proïly*] them all to pieces
> And themselves they went to hell [*da i samykh ïkh did'ko vziav*].

The Ukrainian plutocrats, however, did not perish; they simply "made fools of themselves," having lost out to their Russian competitors. In an explicitly anti-Russian rant, the indignant author prophetically envisions an "invasion" of multitudes of Russians who "like jackdaws fly to us [...], without a shirt, without a purse" – an allusion to the initial poverty of many Russian newcomers and also to their economic appetites. The poem's conclusion is quite distressing; the author suggests flight rather than fight, in the end adorning his newly found prophetic zeal with a Biblical reference:

> Leave your house, leave your wife
> Follow your nose and flee [...].
> They squandered away our rights
> And now the Muscovite will decide.
> This all looks quite bad for the Kyivites
> This all is like the Exodus of Israelites.

But unlike the Biblical Israelites, the Ukrainian Kyivites did not leave their city.[9] Except for a few plutocrats who had to auction off their property, most retained their houses and their wives, contrary to the pessimistic predictions of the poet-bureaucrat. As we will see later, even the most notorious plutocrats, who seemed to have lost so much power and wealth to the victorious Russians, remained in the city, often whiling away the rest of their lives as country gentlemen on their suburban estates.

The central government issued a decree abolishing Kyiv's Magdeburg autonomy on 23 November 1835. In that document, Tsar Nicholas specifically noted that Kyiv's old self-government "does not correspond to the essential benefits of the city," and that of the rights once given to the city, "some have long since expired, while others, in the course of time ... turned into the detriment and burden of the entire composition of municipal society."[10] So in place of the municipal commission, the government was reintroducing the city duma and reducing the magistrate to a purely judicial organ.[11] Curiously, the abolition of the municipal mounted guard was justified by its uselessness from the standpoint of city beautification. The contemporary historian Vitalii Shul'gin summarized this sweeping change in the following passage:

> the former magistrate, subordinate directly to the Senate, has been renamed the city duma, [an organ] put in a position of dependence on local provincial authorities; the position of a lifelong *viit* was replaced with that of a city head; the old offices of a *ratman*, *shafar*, *lavnyk* and *instigator* are all gone; the fellows of the golden banner along with municipal militia are also gone; the city ceremonial processions on the day of Epiphany and on the Maccabees day, in which this militia ... continued to show its old bellicosity, are gone too.[12]

It seems that the former *viit* and several ex-members of the magistrate refused to cooperate with the new magistrate, as if to protest the change in the city. The new members complained to the governor that Kyiv's old-timers had "retired from their offices" without leaving any financial reports and inventories of municipal documents. This inquiry lasted at least until 1840.[13]

Tsar as the City's Supreme Planner and His Fortress

How did radical institutional changes affect Kyiv's cityscape? What new practices did the Russian government introduce in local urban planning after the suppression of the Polish November uprising in 1831 and the abolition of the city's autonomy in 1835? What was the impact of military architecture on the city's overall development?

Most European capitals and large cities experienced ambitious planning and urban renewal schemes in the nineteenth century, especially after 1850.[14] Kyiv was becoming a modern city more slowly and less visibly, perhaps due to its impossible terrain. Nonetheless, many contemporaries were overwhelmed by the pace of change. This happened not least because of the notorious borderland policies of Russian absolutism, which ensured that Kyiv experienced more government supervision than most other cities in Western and Eastern Europe, including perhaps Saint Petersburg.[15] But despite close attention from above to this growing city, Kyiv, in its urban layout and architecture, for much of the century resembled a minor provincial town, albeit spread out over a large territory somewhere between 45 and 48.6 square kilometres.[16]

Also, Kyiv was bypassed by a dominant trend in nineteenth-century planning practice. International planning competitions radically changed the face of Europe's major cities; Kyiv never enjoyed this sort of attention. Most preserved plans of the city showed an *actual* urban space rather than projected grand changes and often dealt with minor local alterations (such as the linking of two streets, or the extension of a single street). That said, there were a few more comprehensive proposals – so-called "general plans" (*obshchii plan*) for the city – that dealt with the entire city or with large parts of it that were to be replanned or incorporated. Besides an ambitious but not fully realized plan drawn up by the architect Melens'kyi in 1812, there were three later general plans that were more successful, if less aesthetically pleasing.

A general plan of 1837 featured a proposed southwestern extension of the city, towards the Lybid' River (see map 11, page 235). This reflected imminent changes in urban space and in power relations during the reign of Nicholas I. Two other general plans were tabled in 1861 and 1874, the latter remaining in force until the First World War. Various subsequent changes in the city's space were usually shown on the official copies of the last (1874) general plan of Kyiv. Remarkably, even the slightest changes projected by the *autonomous* city after 1871 were to be marked out on an official copy of the 1874 plan. Such a copy was usually prepared and approved by the provincial authorities through their own technical expert (an architect or engineer).

For much of the period under consideration, urban planning in Kyiv meant street improvement: widening, paving, cleaning, and landscaping a few major streets and roads. Planning on a grander scale was always checked by the city's complex natural setting and by a highly complicated planning ritual, for even the slightest changes required the approval of the central authorities before they could be put on the city's "general plan." In addition, like most other hill towns, and in contrast to towns built on flat ground with a rectilinear shape,[17] Kyiv grew spontaneously, with its streets determined by its topography. Thus the mere maintenance of Kyiv's streets posed a difficult logistical challenge for various authorities. Even so, between the 1830s and the 1850s Kyiv experienced a number of remarkable changes, at times so dramatic that they could rival those brought about by the Soviet regime in the 1930s. In fact, imperial traditions of public control over city planning, and a long-standing practice of rigorous regulation of construction in Kyiv, anticipated the exclusive role the Soviet state would play in planning and building.[18]

Tsar Nicholas himself aspired to be the supreme city planner, and he launched a number of planning measures on the spot during his many visits to the city from the 1830s to the 1850s.[19] Few cities in contemporary Europe, except perhaps Paris under Napoleon III, have experienced such heavy-handed transformations orchestrated by a despotic regime.[20] The tsar's grandiose vision of Kyiv's cityscape was neoclassical in form but also rooted in Baroque visual aesthetics, or in what Spiro Kostof aptly called the Grand Manner. "Perceived as an expansive pattern of sweeping vistas, its relation to topography and prior urban arrangements is arbitrary, its effects often grandiloquent," wrote the scholar of urban forms. "Typically, behind designs in the Grand Manner stands a powerful, centrist State whose resources and undiluted authority make possible the extravagant urban vision of ramrod-straight avenues, vast uniformly bordered squares, and a suitable accompaniment of monumental buildings."[21] Russian absolutism was at its peak during Nicholas's reign, so the state could apply its power (unlimited) and material resources (somewhat limited) to make the tsar's grand vision a reality in Kyiv. "The visible manifestations of tsarist urbanism," wrote Daniel Brower, "were embodied in city plans and in the regulations governing urban construction and public activities."[22] Consequently, the governors and the police became responsible for the "orderliness and cleanliness of the streets, squares, and markets" and for the enforcement of "the approved [city] plan and rules for building façades." Architecture was thus to become the symbolic representation of public order. Saint Petersburg was the supreme embodiment of this urban vision. A version of façade planning "was inserted within the larger political project of tsarist urbanism throughout the empire and was the centerpiece of this policy."[23]

But it was not easy to insert northern aesthetics into the prevailing natural and architectural background of Russia's "first" capital. In this city of ancient domes and picturesque hills, which had for centuries served as its visual dominants, local baroque and imported classicism were not easily compatible. During these few decades, the empire gave Kyiv another spatial order: it replaced the traditional aesthetics of the Ukrainian Baroque that respected the city's complex topography with a new style favoured by Nicholas. That style was known as "Russian classicism," and while it looked organic on Saint Petersburg's flat northern terrain, it seemed strange on the hilly right bank of the Dnieper.

As a result, architecture became the symbol of empire and of autocratic power.[24] "The classicist redevelopment tries to regularize [in Kyiv] all that is alive and independent," wrote a historian of Kyiv's architecture. "The city endures it as a forced illness."[25] So the terrain was levelled, streets were straightened, and ramparts were erased. Neighbourhoods hitherto separated were now joined together by new straight arteries, and sometimes by vistas, and meanwhile, the city itself was expanded by adding new gridded districts. Finally, during the tenure of Nicholas and his loyal governor general, Dmitry Bibikov, Kyiv saw built several of its most recognizable architectural landmarks, almost all of them public buildings, such as the university (1843), the Institute for Noble Maidens (1842), the First Kyiv Gymnasium (1852), the monument to St Vladimir (1853), and the Government Offices (*Prisutstvennye mesta*, 1857). Today we can still see elements of the Grand Manner in much of the city's public architecture and urban layout from the 1830s and the 1850s. In what follows I focus on several major elements of Kyiv's Grand Manner.

The new local power relations and the change of elites helped Nicholas implement much of what was planned. By abolishing Kyiv's autonomous institutions and restoring an obedient city duma – a Russian imperial institution – the authorities largely ended any opposition from the city's once powerful oligarchs. Kyiv had experienced a duma in the 1780s, when Catherine II sought to "reform" local administration,[26] but her successor, Paul I (1796–1801), had restored the city's self-government based on the Magdeburg Law. In 1835, Nicholas, acting in Catherine's spirit, again returned to Kyiv an institution that was designed in 1785 and whose legal definition and actual practice were very confusing. However ineffective the city duma may have been, the Russian imperial authorities clearly preferred it to the seemingly unreliable institutions of Kyiv's self-government – the magistrate and the municipal commission. We can agree with Soviet historians that "the duma's entire activity completely depended on tsarist administrative organs – governor, the police, [and] various commissions. The biggest part of revenues obtained by municipal treasury the duma spent on the maintenance of the police, fire department, governmental offices, and municipal buildings, with only a small sum allocated for the beautification of streets."[27]

Almost by default the new/old city dumas came to represent "city dwellers in particular" (*gorodskie obyvateli v osoblivosti*), that is, merchants, townspeople, and artisans – "urban" social estates that dominated municipal politics in almost all cities and towns of the Russian Empire.[28] Other social groups, such as the nobility, clergy, professionals, foreigners, and peasants, lacked both the means and the incentive to participate in municipal self-government, however limited it was. Although the duma's executive was supposed to consist of representatives of all six social estates, in practice it included only merchants and townsmen, or only merchants.[29] The fact that the governor's bureaucrats exercised so much control over the duma's daily business could also be explained by the personal characteristics of the new municipal players: many merchants elected as mayors and town councillors were simply illiterate.[30] The governors of various provinces complained to the interior ministry that the nobles had been removed from running the cities and that as a result the cities were being managed by incompetent and often illiterate people (burghers and merchants).[31] In this respect, it seems that Kyiv was not very different from a great many Russian towns.

As already noted, Kyiv by the early 1830s was still very much a loose assemblage of disparate settlements that functioned more like separate towns than as districts within a unified city. However, with the abolition of municipal self-government, its disparate parts were increasingly more integrated by the imperial authorities into a common administrative and economic unit, which from now on would be more tightly controlled by the civil governor. Kyiv's spatial structure also underwent several major changes.

In particular, mention should be made of Pechers'k and Old Kyiv in its extended form, although other parts of the city were also affected. A new part adjacent to Podil – Plos'ka – had been added to the city. That neighbourhood, just beyond the notorious Ditch (Kanava), had long been a semi-rural suburb where more affluent burghers owned farmsteads or rented them out to peasants. In 1844, Plos'ka was planned, redeveloped, and added to the city as its newest district.[32] Around the same time, many inhabitants of Podil and Plos'ka, after suffering through the devastating flood in 1845, began to resettle on the higher ground, in the suburb of Kurenivka. These ecological factors notwithstanding, the main topographical and social changes occurred in Kyiv as a direct result of the grand strategic vision of Tsar Nicholas. He wanted to transform the city into a fortress against all possible enemies, both external and internal, among them Polish and Russian revolutionaries.

Nicholas chose Pechers'k as the site for a new fortress, a fateful decision that signified the first major redevelopment of the city.[33]

He ordered its construction in 1830, in response to the Polish November uprising of 1830–1. That work continued until 1852; after the Crimean War broke out in 1853, it was never completed as planned. Nonetheless, the fortress swallowed almost the entire district of Pechers'k, and this would lead to a number of changes in the city's urban layout and demographic profile.[34] During the 1830s and 1840s, most private houses in Pechers'k were demolished, and their inhabitants – mostly soldiers, non-commissioned officers (*unter-ofitsery*), and poor townspeople – were relocated elsewhere.[35] The government paid some compensation to those whose houses were to be demolished, and most of their owners resettled in the valley of the Lybid' River, in the area that came to be known as the New Building (Novoe Stroenie).[36] A contemporary described the process with the impartial voice of a social scientist:

> In 1830, during the construction of new fortifications near Pechers'k fortress it proved necessary to move aside from it the closest parts of a local settlement. Therefore, many private houses along the entire streets or parts of the streets, which were to become part of fortification lines, had to be gradually demolished. The owners of these houses were to be relocated to the plots [situated] between the Lybid' river and the old fortress; there a suburb of the new fortifications has emerged. To cover the expenses, such as the dismantling of houses that were to be demolished, their transportation and their erection, as well as the losses from the spoiling of materials, the treasury reimburses homeowners financially after [property] assessment.[37]

So between 1832 and 1846, 533 houses were demolished (131 of these in 1832 alone), and 270,133 silver roubles were paid to the owners from the imperial treasury. Among all other major imperial cities, only Warsaw suffered more damage, caused in that case by the construction of its notorious citadel and forts, which became the most important military installations in the empire's western borderlands.[38] Similarly, Kyiv's earliest urban renewal was an immediate consequence of Nicholas's private phobias. Mykhailo Maksymovych, a local and loyal intellectual, had an excellent sense of the geopolitical, xenophobic, and urban planning considerations behind the city's redevelopment. Around 1847, he wrote in *Ocherk Kieva*:

> [Pechers'k], in place of previous small houses and huts, has received each year big and beautiful buildings belonging to the fortress. Before this construction began and as a result of the Tsar's Ukase of 2 December 1827,

Jews were at last removed from Kyiv, where they had attempted to settle, especially in Pechers'k, when it began to get settled in the last century. Other residents of Pechers'k were relocated primarily to the Lybid' River [valley], and this marked the beginning of the so-called New Building [Novoe Stroenie] in 1834. This Lybid' part of the city, centred on the magnificent building of St. Vladimir University for which the foundations were laid on 31 July 1835, grows bigger each year. Soon it will certainly become one of the most populous parts of Kyiv, which in all fairness might be called New Kyiv.[39]

Maksymovych was correct about the New Building (and the Lybid' district in general): it would soon become the core of New Kyiv, a new imperial city that had begun to grow under Tsar Nicholas. Another immediate consequence of the tsar's beloved project – the Pechers'k Fortress – was the emergence of an elite residential neighbourhood – the Palace district (in Russian, *Dvortsovaia*; in Ukrainian, *Palatsova*), adjacent to the fortress. We have already seen that the Palace district began its steady development at the beginning of the century, after governors began distributing large parcels of land there to aristocrats and generals. But it was only after the 1830s that the area acquired the status of the most exclusive part of the city. In 1847, Maksymovych could describe the Palace district as the "main and most beautiful part of the city," especially in reference to its newest section, known as Lypky (named after a linden grove that once grew there).

The construction of the fortress required immense material resources and commitment, and this led to a rethinking of what kind of city Kyiv was and was about to become. For the first time in centuries, Kyiv was being treated as a truly unified space under a single authority (although most of Pechers'k and large swathes of land around it – the so-called "esplanade" – were administered directly by the military). The newly established city duma (in 1835) might not enjoy the autonomy and civic pride of its predecessors (i.e., the magistrate and the municipal commission), but the authority it did have reached throughout the city. Now, though, the real power unambiguously belonged to the office of the civil governor and its various boards, which were staffed with technical, economic, and policy experts, who dealt with all of the most pressing urban issues, from overall planning to architecture to street improvement. As before, the governor general was entrusted with strategic oversight, and his involvement in civic affairs depended on his personality.

For example, Dmitry Bibikov (in office in 1837–52) was a notorious control freak who exercised unprecedented influence over the daily lives of Kyivites and even more over urban planning and political affairs in the entire Southwestern Region. He did not establish a totalitarian regime, but he came as close to it as one could get in a relatively small city by practising a modernizing absolutism. There was at least one very convincing reason why many observers liked how he ran Kyiv. One of his supporters recalled:

> The city was extraordinarily well-ordered and tidy, but here the police were given so much power that [they] did not enjoy anywhere else ... Riding around in a coach-and-three, accompanied by two mounted policemen, the head of the police department himself administered justice and meted out punishment. At night the guards were always around, as well as the mounted patrol. Theft and robbery were extremely rare occurrences in Kyiv, almost unheard of. The citizens enjoyed perfect safety.[40]

It may well be that Kyivites, even those who dared oppose Bibikov's micromanagement, were won over by his security policy. His personal influence no doubt exceeded the formal authority vested in his office. Symbolic of these local power relations was the building of the first permanent bridge over the Dnieper between 1848 and 1853. The Chain Bridge would eventually be hailed as a spectacular showcase for the empire's growing industrial prowess and for its capacity to bring off ambitious engineering projects – a clear sign that Kyiv was becoming a crucial regional centre of a modernizing state.[41] But this same project revealed another, more traditional side of Russian governance – rampant corruption. One technical expert soon came to grasp that the head of Bibikov's own chancellery, Nikolai Pisarev, a man notorious for his omnipotence and corruption, was on the take. Before the Chain Bridge was built, for much of the year hundreds of carts and other carriers had to form huge line-ups on the left bank of the Dnieper, waiting their turn to cross the river by boat or ferry. Many paid bribes to jump the queue, and the contractor who operated the river crossing was said to have paid a portion of those bribes as kickbacks to Pisarev.[42] Reportedly, Bibikov turned a blind eye to his aide's corrupt practices in exchange for Pisarev remaining silent about the governor general's disreputable sex life, including his affair with Pisarev's own wife.[43]

From the start, a permanent bridge over the Dnieper was viewed as a "national" project rather than a municipal one, with technical expertise and material resources to be provided by the state. Tsar Nicholas himself suggested a bridge in 1829, and he would closely supervise its construction. But even this ruler, an infamous despot, could not easily overcome the multitude of technological, socio-economic, and local topographical issues that stood in its way. Finally, he chose an English engineering "celebrity," Charles de Vignoles, to design the project and supervise its construction.[44] For want of local Ukrainian master builders, Vignoles imported Russian guest workers, many of them Old Believers. This engineering miracle cost the central and provincial governments the staggering sum of 2,350,000 roubles, far surpassing all other previous architectural and infrastructural projects in Kyiv. Another expensive project that the government undertook – this time with the city – was the construction of an embankment running from the Chain Bridge along Podil at a cost of several hundred thousand roubles.[45]

Needless to say, all of the most important planning in Kyiv was done by the local imperial authorities, not by the city or by private entrepreneurs. All major changes to the city plan had to be approved by the highest authorities in Saint Petersburg (be it the responsible minister, or the Senate, or the tsar himself). This strong centralization made the city's redevelopment a cumbersome affair. However, because so much of Kyiv was sparsely populated, planners enjoyed almost unlimited opportunities to lay down streets without infringing on the rights and interests of local property owners. By contrast, in many densely populated European cities, private owners were often able to thwart even the most modest planning schemes.[46] Also, the authorities in Kyiv did not need to dispense enormous amounts of cash to private owners in order to purchase their lands or existing structures. There was enough unoccupied land, although Pechers'k was rather an exception to this.

But this sheer volume of undeveloped space had its negative side. Clearly, in order to turn Kyiv into a modern city, new connecting roads and streets would have to be cut through hilly and sandy terrain and new districts would have to be laid out over a sprawling wasteland. This task would require considerable material resources. Did the city have enough money to attend to its own needs? As we know, before 1834 the still autonomous city had to send reports about its revenues and expenditures to the civil governor. After 1834 the budgets of *all* cities in the empire had to be reviewed by the interior ministry in Saint Petersburg,[47] a clear sign of the absolutist state's triumph over an increasingly powerless city.

Kyiv entered a new era of its history with a relatively small budget. That budget, though, was similar to those of other Russian imperial cities of comparable size. And most importantly, it did not have a budget deficit. According to the data submitted to the ministry, in 1834 Kyiv's revenues were 192,706 roubles, while its expenditures were 189,928 roubles – a surplus, then, of almost 3,000 roubles.[48] After we compare these numbers with those from the 1840s, we can safely say that Kyiv's economy had quite smoothly survived the end of the Magdeburg Law and an abrupt change of municipal elites (for more on this change, see chapter 7). Indeed, by 1840, Kyiv (population 47,400) was among the most profitable cities in Russia, in the same league as Astrakhan' (46,000), Odessa (60,055), and Nizhnii Novgorod (31,900).[49] Kyiv's Office of Public Care had accumulated the second-largest capital fund in Russia after Saint Petersburg (the former 2,690,592, the latter 2,825,418 silver roubles). Furthermore, the state had increased the annual fund for the construction of public buildings in Russian cities (general amount allocated, 984,525 roubles).[50] By the early 1840s, however, the cities with the highest revenues (including Kyiv) also faced the greatest expenditures, and they had all begun running budget deficits. There are various possible reasons for these deficits, including limited revenue sources for Russian imperial cities, the disorderly state of municipal property, and the lack of strict accountability.[51] For example, in 1843 the budget deficit in Kyiv grew to a staggering 22,994 roubles – perhaps the largest among Russian imperial cities.[52]

To understand how much the Kyiv duma could spend on urban planning and city beautification, we must look at the city budgets from the years of intense urban redevelopment, from the late 1830s to the 1860s. Tables 4.1 and 4.2 show the city budgets and expenditures, each year representing a decade between 1835 and 1871 (provided that the data are available).

Table 4.1 Kyiv budgets, 1837–68 (in roubles)

Budget	1837	1846[53]	1853	1859	1868
Revenues	320,324	82,234	127,533	186,927	151,506
Expenditures	271,445	75,104	125,195	182,090	160,781

Table 4.2 Main expenditures in Kyiv, 1837–68

Expenditures	1837	1846	1853	1859	1868
Municipal administration (including police and fire departments)	95,594[54] (72,130 police and fire brigade)	39,764 (29,491 police and fire brigade)	37,046	61,247 (24,109 police; 21,867 fire brigade)	80,935 (38,309 police; 29,239 fire brigade)
Municipal property, city planning, and beautification	88,542	27,738	42,462	84,382	60,348
Paying off debts			8,613	31,343	5,176
Charitable and educational institutions	4,000	5,255	2,199	2,317	6,297

Sources: DAK, f. 17, op. 4, spr. 2713 (1837); spr. 2819 (1853); op. 5, spr. 443 (1859); op. 5, spr. 492 (1868); Funduklei, *Statisticheskoe opisanie Kievskoi gubernii*, pp. 398–400 (1846).

This structure of expenditures in Kyiv reflected a general picture of expenditures in all Russian cities at the time.[55] Perhaps the most noteworthy trend over these decades was the growing costs of police and fire departments. In Kyiv, expenditures for the police skyrocketed especially in the 1860s, in the aftermath of the Polish January uprising in 1863. In this regard, 1868 is especially revealing: revenues had markedly decreased compared to 1859, but the costs of municipal administration had grown by one-third. It seems that the sums allocated for city planning and beautification varied wildly from year to year and often were assigned to "extraordinary" or "lump sum" costs (*edinovremennye zatraty*) – that is, they were sporadic and not envisaged in the estimates of yearly expenditures.[56] Nonetheless, these sums remained high – for example, paving the roads with stone was among the largest expenditures (often as high as 20,000 to 30,000 roubles).[57]

Yet the quality of most of the public works financed by the city or by the state was inadequate, no matter how large a budget was allocated for urban planning and city beautification. Also, the actual thought behind planning was underdeveloped. Most of the city plans from the 1830s through to the 1860s that we can examine today look rather static; they emphasize natural topography as well as specific objects – such as churches, monuments, and public buildings – rather than arterial connections, new squares, or traffic nodes. True, a few new thoroughfares were cut, as well as several larger and smaller through-streets, but these were not the key elements in those plans. Kyiv was not unique in this respect: many major European cities neglected to develop adequate communications between existing districts and those being planned.[58]

Overall, Kyiv's planners only slowly adopted the concept of circulatory and respiratory systems – for example, arteries and open spaces specifically intended for traffic and sanitation respectively. In large European cities, street improvement was often driven by traffic concerns;[59] in Kyiv, traffic seemed to play less of a role in planning schemes. Also, Kyiv experienced something between the "regularization" that Paris did during the tenure of that city's legendary (and controversial) prefect Baron Haussmann and the "extension" that Barcelona did with the famous Cerdá plan.[60] Kyiv was even more an example of fragmentary efforts: the regularization of several (usually new) quarters and the unsystematic opening of a few main arteries.[61] Similarly, squares in the city were not modern traffic nodes but rather traditional enclosed plazas, used mainly as sites for agricultural markets.

One exception, perhaps, was Khreshshatyk Square (today the famous Independence Square, or simply the Maidan), which came to serve several functions: a marketplace, a traffic node, and later a ceremonial ground (after 1876 it was also the site of the city duma). Until the early nineteenth century, the square was the site of a "goat's swamp" – *Kozyne boloto* (hence Kozynobolotna street nearby) – and a flour mill.[62] The fate of Khreshchatyk would finally be sealed by Kyiv's topography. Topography almost always defined the subsequent urban form, in that it encouraged an "organic," concentric, or gridiron street layout. Also, when a town is situated on two or three hills, its main square or communal centre usually emerges on open land between hills, at the confluence of two or three directional arteries. Such was the case with medieval Siena and its celebrated square, the Campo.[63]

Similarly, Khreshchatyk Square developed in the valley between the hills on which the city's historical districts were located – Old Kyiv (or Upper Town) to the west and Lypky and Pechers'k to the east. In Kyiv, again as in Siena, it took several centuries for a new centre to emerge. The network of through-streets that linked the aristocratic residential neighbourhood of Lypky (and by extension the military-administered Pechers'k) with Old Kyiv began to emerge in the 1830s and 1840s, during the neoclassical makeover of the city. All of these streets ran to and from Khreshchatyk, thus making it a crucial transit zone.[64] However, no artery *crossing* Khreshchatyk was ever laid down, so the city did not

4.1 Sazhin [?], *Khreshchatyk Square* (image courtesy of Mystetstvo)

receive its central cross-axes, perhaps due to its complicated terrain and inadequate planning resources.

Khreshchatyk and its square became the focus of planners' attention in 1834, when the hyperactive Governor General Levashov decided to regulate this increasingly important but neglected transit hub.[65] Khreshchatyk had to be "planned": the earth removed, the surface levelled, the street paved, and its southern end linked with the old exit road running towards the town of Vasyl'kiv. The square awaited a similar fate: its most notable landmark – a military prison – and the eighteenth-century ramparts were to be removed, the ground paved with stone, and the wooden market stalls rearranged "along the lines of the square."[66] This was one of the most ambitious urban planning proposals the city had seen so far. As no private contractor was willing to do the job, the authorities had to carry out the task on their own. A staggering sum, 63,213 roubles, had to be found in the city budget. Municipal officials contended that they could not provide the requested sum, and this triggered a conflict between the governor and the autonomous city. In the end, the governor conceded, and allocated funds.[67] Aside from some financial and technical difficulties, the planning of Khreshchatyk was a relatively simple task, for it did not involve a *new* street cutting through an *old* district.

The new street had both geographic and symbolic significance in that it connected three very old parts of the city – Podil, Old Kyiv, and Pechers'k.[68] In 1839, Mykhailo Maksymovych specifically mentioned Khreshchatyk as a "quite nicely developed part of Kyiv now" that linked Old Kyiv with Pechers'k.[69] In 1847 he added that Khreshchatyk, which had been "almost uninhabited" in the late eighteenth century, "in the last years has turned into one of Kyiv's best streets that is already becoming the heart of the local business life."[70] Another contemporary, the historian Mykola Sementovs'kyi, commented in 1852 that Khreshchatyk was indeed "the best street in all of Kyiv, built up with magnificent and colossal houses that are covered with various commercial signboards." He emphasized the street's importance as a traffic artery linking Podil with the south end of the city, which was located in the valley of the Lybid' River.[71] The growing importance of Khreshchatyk is confirmed by the value of real estate there: by the early 1860s the street became Kyiv's most expensive residential and commercial area. Building lots there cost between 20,000 and 48,000 roubles and often featured two-storey brick houses with shops located on the ground floor.[72]

By the early 1850s, Khreshchatyk was widely viewed as the city's main promenade – Kyiv's *corso*. A local newspaper informed its readers that "the busiest part of the city at noon" is Khreshchatyk, where the "cream of our high society" (*luchshii tsvet obshchestva*) was always promenading. Two new large brick houses were being constructed on the street.[73] Yet as late as the early 1860s, thirty years after Khreshchatyk and its square had been regularized, the street remained an eyesore and a health hazard, especially whenever nature went berserk. One contemporary recalled:

The terrain profile of the pavement on Khreshchatyk looked like a gutter [*zhelob*] along which during rains and in early spring the water flowed full-width. In the courtyards of houses lining the street, wooden bridges on wheels have been stored for such occasions. Yardmen and policemen rolled out these bridges into the street, so that people could cross over them from one side of the street to the other. Back then an underground drainage system did not yet exist. And then during heavy showers the rainwater with torrential flows rushed from the streets such as Kozebolotnaia [today Kreschatik Lane], Sofievskaia,

4.2 Timm, *The View of Old Kyiv from the Iaroslav Rampart* (image courtesy of Mystetstvo)

Zhitomirskaia, Mikhailovskaia, Kostel'naia, Institutskaia, Liuteranskaia and Kadetskaia [today Fundukleevskaia],[74] carrying away all the bridges, and forming a wide deep river that whirled away at full speed towards the ravines situated beyond the Besarabka market [at the far end of Khreshchatyk].[75]

Also in the 1830s, Old Kyiv attracted the attention of imperial planners. Rebuilding it would be a challenge, considering its long history, hilly terrain, and residential density. In contrast to Podil, which was populated by modest burghers, the residents of Old Kyiv were much more diverse, with nobles and officials comprising 23.5 per cent of the neighbourhood's homeowners – the second-largest group after burghers (25 per cent).[76] This made the acquisition of private properties there for the purpose of urban planning more difficult than elsewhere in the city. Also, the existing street layout in Old Kyiv was complicated by landownership patterns – there was an assortment of ecclesiastical, private, and military owners – and by various fortifications that would have to be demolished. A major landowner was the Church, represented by St Sophia Cathedral and St Michael's Monastery.

Despite various geographical and legal challenges, the core of the new imperial city was gradually moving towards this hilly neighbourhood, once the heart of medieval Kyiv and for centuries the ecclesiastical centre of the city where the residence of Orthodox Metropolitans was located. Changes were becoming apparent by the late 1830s. Mykhailo Maksymovych, an ardent defender of the city's antiquities, could not help but admire the new urban planning. Old Kyiv was his favourite district, and it was already marked by modernity: it was "currently being rapidly renovated," with new "straight streets and squares" constructed and new houses built "in place of worn-out huts and narrow curvy alleyways that as labyrinths used to cover ancient ruins of Old Kyiv during the centuries of its destitution."[77] Thus Old Kyiv looked "more open" and was becoming "much more convenient for residence and more suitable for further improvement."[78] Maksymovych was among the earliest proponents of the radical urban renewal being imposed on Kyiv by the new imperial masters (such as governors general Levashov and Bibikov) and "experts" (among them the architects Beretti, father and son).

Mykola (Nikolai) Kostomarov, an academic peer of Maksymovych, was much more critical. He arrived in Kyiv in 1844, *after* an early urban renewal scheme had been implemented. Even so, he saw Kyiv as a dirty provincial town filled with ugly clay huts and wooden houses and lacking even the most basic infrastructure.[79] We should take his words with a grain of salt, however. Old Kyiv had become the city's main architectural focus by the late 1830s, and the emerging thoroughfare Khreshchatyk had been partly incorporated into that district.[80] Adjacent to Old Kyiv was the developing quarter around the university (finished in 1843), which formally belonged to yet another neighbourhood, Lybid'. The university quarter and the New Building (Novoe Stroenie) comprised what Maksymovych called "New Kyiv." Actually, this never became the official title for any district in the city. Old Kyiv had been an emerging neighbourhood since the 1830s, and it soon became the core of the *new* imperial city. Put differently, Old Kyiv came back as truly "new" Kyiv.

So it is not surprising that Old Kyiv was chosen to become the new administrative centre of an amalgamated imperial city. The Government Offices (*Prisutstvennye mesta* in Russian), previously located in Lypky near the fortress, had been demolished in 1853. In 1854 the foundations for a new building were laid, on the spot between St Sophia Cathedral and St Michael's Monastery. Except for the location, there was nothing

4.3 Orda, *Khreshchatyk Square and the Government Offices in the background* (image courtesy of Mystetstvo)

especially noteworthy about this spot, which at the time of construction was largely a wasteland.[81] Completed in 1857, the new office block was home to a number of executive boards of the Kyiv provincial administration. Like many other large architectural and planning projects in Kyiv, this one was financed from the state treasury, and it cost the impressive sum of 400,000 roubles. Designed in the Neo-Renaissance style by a local architect (who heavily "quoted" Russian Classicism), the block became the symbol of imperial power and the model for subsequent city planning in Kyiv.

This new block and the square largely dictated the development of the surrounding area, which for centuries had been dominated by St Sophia Cathedral to the south and St Michael's Monastery to the north. Yet the square remained empty for a number of years, until the 1870s, when Kyiv's autonomous city council began selling parcels of the wasteland in front of the Government Offices to private buyers.

The choice of this site for the Government Offices suggests that the secular authorities wanted to ensure their own visibility (and perhaps legitimacy) amidst traditional symbols of religious power in a city that throughout its history had been known largely for its role as the centre of Orthodox spirituality. Kyiv, now, was also a *visible* centre of secular power. As another sign of the growing importance of Old Kyiv, a new stone theatre opened its doors on Volodymyrs'ka Street in 1856, financed jointly by the state and the city.

The Italian Job

Kyiv's other modern focus, at the opposite end of Old Kyiv, had begun to take shape even earlier, around the imposing new building of St Vladimir University, erected in 1843. It was designed by the architect Vikentii Beretti, the son of an Italian expatriate who had settled in Saint Petersburg in the 1780s. Unlike his fellow Italian Ludovico (Liudvik) Stanzani, who had served as Kyiv's city architect from 1833 to 1848, Beretti came to Kyiv only in 1836 and never worked for the municipal commune. Formally, he was the chief architect of Kyiv St Vladimir University and a member of the university building committee. Yet his imprint on Kyiv's architecture and overall planning turned out to be considerably more significant than that of Stanzani (even though the latter had also worked on Kyiv's general plan).

Beretti's major architectural project was the main building of Kyiv St Vladimir University, the first of the few public buildings constructed (or designed) during the reign of Nicholas I. Its site was an open field; leading to it would be the city's first and only boulevard, which in 1869 would be named Bibikovskii (after the governor general).[82] Rivalling Khreshshatyk as the first modern straight street in the city, it had as its focus the monumental university building, built in Classicist style.[83] Bibikovskii Boulevard did not lead straight to the university, instead running slightly to the right of it, but this did not obscure the monumental view, which opened at the very foot of this tree-lined vista. The boulevard was a crucial element in the grandiose redesign of Kyiv under Nicholas I and Governor General Bibikov. Not surprisingly, it was later named after Bibikov, its political planner, although the design itself has been attributed to Beretti.

In Europe, a boulevard (from the Dutch *bolwerc*, bulwark) usually meant a tree-lined promenade, usually built on the site of former fortifications. (For example, in northern Paris the boulevard ring was first

4.4 Shevchenko and Sazhin, *Kyiv St Vladimir University* (image courtesy of Mystetstvo)

opened in the reign of Louis XIV.)[84] Later it also meant a road running around a town, often replacing the fortifications encircling a city (such a road was proposed for Vienna as early as the eighteenth century). In other cities, however, boulevards had nothing to do with former fortifications. For example, in Athens in 1833, a broad, tree-lined street that was to surround the centre of the new city in the form of a rectangle, was also called a "boulevard," although it was not on the margins of the town and was not replacing any fortifications. In Barcelona, "boulevard" was used in the more traditional sense of a monumental ring road (similarly to Vienna's Ringstrasse). It was in Paris that the term "boulevard" acquired a new meaning – a tree-lined main street – as a result of Baron Haussmann's redevelopment of the city. There, three main arteries forming a north–south axis in the *grande croisée* were called Boulevard de Strasbourg, Boulevard de Sébastopol, and Boulevard de St Michel. Apparently, this new meaning of "boulevard" took root only in Paris, and later in Brussels, where "boulevard" has been the term for a new street through the centre of a town. Thomas Hall stresses that outside France and Belgium, "this connotation does not seem to have spread, apart from one or two isolated instances." In Kyiv, as in Haussmann's Paris and in Budapest, *bul'var* came to designate a diagonal thoroughfare rather than a ring.[85]

Kyiv's first boulevard was also designed to address military and public security concerns.[86] Bibikov himself reportedly insisted on making the new street as broad as possible, although he did not leave any official explanation for this. According to a contemporary anecdote, however, the ever suspicious governor-general widened the streets so as to make it more difficult for rebels (especially Polish ones) to erect barricades.[87] Also, the straight, wide streets – particularly the boulevard – would make it easier to move troops through the city. Conveniently, the military barracks and training grounds were just west of the city, along the old exit road – Brest-Lytovs'ke *shosse* (highway), which was effectively an extension of Bibikovs'kyi Boulevard.

Under Bibikov's tenure, all major streets were to be straight and wide. In terms of overall significance, only one street proved to be more important than the *bul'var* that connected the city with the military grounds. This new street became the permanent address of Kyiv St Vladimir University, with its façade set parallel to Khreshchatyk. Named after St Vladimir, the patron saint of the university, Velyka Volodymyrs'ka became another key artery, one that linked the new imperial centre of learning with the Government Offices and the seat of the Kyiv Orthodox Metropolitan, both located in the heart of Old Kyiv. Bibikovs'kyi Boulevard and Volodymyrs'ka Street served as the city's main cross-axis, even though these two streets were *not* centrally located at the time. In envisioning this new spatial focus for Kyiv, Beretti most fully expressed his creative genius.

A historian of Kyiv architecture has aptly characterized Beretti's classicist urban design:

> The architect who had grown accustomed to building on the clear plan of Saint Petersburg, knowing for certain where ... to place his buildings, made [a] technical effort ... to transfer to Kyiv the orderliness of the imperial capital ... In preparing the site for the university just south of Old Kyiv, V.I. Beretti planned a district that soon would carry off the palm from Pechers'k. The main axes of the new planning design became Velyka Volodymyrs'ka Street and the Boulevard, and it is near the point of their intersection that the university square was sited.[88]

Most of the iconic streets that have defined the urban face of Old Kyiv to this day (among them Volodymyrs'ka, Mykhailivs'ka, and Zhytomyrs'ka) were planned between 1837 and 1848,[89] with the active participation of Beretti. Yet his masterpiece was undeniably Kyiv University and its surroundings.

Kyiv St Vladimir University was a groundbreaking project in a number of important respects, all of which reflected radical shifts with regard to the functions of space, architecture, and planning after Kyiv lost its autonomy in the mid-1830s.

First, the project began as an entry in an architectural competition, an approach that at the time was unprecedented in the history of local architecture and planning. Commissioned by the imperial education ministry, the competition was held among the professors of Saint Petersburg's Academy of Arts in 1834–5.[90] Four leading professors submitted projects, although all of them seemed to have missed the deadline, initially set for May 1834. Only a year later did the president of the academy sent all four projects to the education minister; after that, it took several more months for the minister to choose the winner – Vikentii Beretti. Remarkably, his project was approved before any realistic budget could be established. This was precisely why Beretti was asked to relocate to Kyiv in the summer of 1836. While there, he was to "obtain the data necessary for the budget," procure local building materials, supervise the work, submit reports, compile working drawings, and perform various other roles of a metropolitan expert banished to the province. Beretti moved to Kyiv and would remain in the city until his death in 1842. Thus, ironically, it was Kyiv rather than Saint Petersburg that became the showcase for Beretti's neoclassical designs, which were inspired by the monumental architectural idiom of Russia's northern capital, a model quite alien to Kyiv's hilly and baroque-dominated cityscape.

Second, the building itself became Kyiv's most remarkable example of Russian monumental neoclassicism (known simply as "Russian Classicism"). Beretti and his team had a number of models to imitate; however, they also had to solve numerous technical difficulties, ranging from the arrangement of the internal main walls to the innovative use of cast iron for decorative purposes to the external colouring of the building. The university they erected was (and still is) a large tetragonal building with an enclosed internal courtyard – a design typical of military barracks, arsenals, and large public buildings during the reign of Nicholas I, who was an ardent fan of military aesthetics. The long

4.5 Kul'zhenko, Kyiv St Vladimir University, *Vidy Kieva*

three-storey façade was dominated by a portico of eight Ionic columns; the interior was marked by a somewhat eclectic combination of Greek Doric and Roman Doric columns in the main vestibule and second storey respectively. This monumentality was a standard homage to neoclassicism. Both the façade and the interior conveyed a strong message of discipline to students and professors alike. The tsar never trusted the intellectual professions, preferring professional soldiers, to whom he entrusted the supervision of education and teaching at his universities. Kyiv University in particular became both an instrument and an object of supervision; discipline was its reigning virtue.

The building was monumental but also simple, and this too served the purpose of discipline. The same could be said of many public buildings of that time. Even its colour acquired some political symbolism. Beretti had wanted to paint it either yellow (with white paint for the cornices) or "with splashes," in imitation of granite, so that it would like as if it were made of "solid stone."[91] Even on this question, however, the highest imperial authorities involved themselves. Bibikov, for all his authority, could not solve the issue of paint colour, so he forwarded it to the education minister, Uvarov, who suggested a model to imitate – the Winter Palace in Saint Petersburg. Tsar Nicholas agreed to this on 15 August 1842, adding that "the color of the Winter Palace imitates rough [*dikii*] stone and therefore it is the most appropriate for a grand edifice, depriving it of any mixture of colors [*pestrota*]."[92] But the story was not over yet. It turned out that no one in Kyiv knew the ingredients of the tsar's favourite colour, so Beretti himself had to travel north to acquire the magic formula. On his way back to Kyiv, all his luggage was stolen, including the paint samples, with the result that Kyivites had to wait another year for the new samples to arrive. Then it turned out that the local grey lime, an important ingredient for the paint, was different from what had been used for the Winter Palace.[93] But the question was eventually settled, and in October 1843, Kyiv University acquired its signature brownish-reddish colour. When the Bolsheviks became the new masters of the city, even they did not dare to change its traditional colour to "apricot," as was suggested in 1935.[94] This story reminds us that the supreme developer of the new Kyiv was Tsar Nicholas himself, a micromanager who treated soldiers, students, and paint with the same captiousness.

As we have already noted, Kyiv University established the parameters for an entire new urban quarter in Kyiv, around the city's major cross-axis at the intersection of Bibikovs'kyi Boulevard and Velyka Volodymyr'ska Street. In this sense, the university was arguably the earliest example of what Thomas Hall has called "local design planning," by which he meant "the inclusion of monumental accents such as squares or streets, generally within an existing urban structure" in an attempt "to create an architectural setting round a building or a group of buildings."[95] Practised for centuries, this type of planning performed primarily ceremonial and aesthetic functions, in that it created a splendid setting for a ruler, a governmental institution, or the city itself. In addition to this, Kyiv University's main building influenced the building fabric and planning of the surrounding area. In other words, the monumental façade of St Vladimir University became a main reference point against which other things were measured and to which they were subsequently added (such as large classical buildings, regulated streets, and planted greenery).[96] The planning of Volodymyrs'ka Street on a large scale, the creation of a neoclassicist ensemble in the new centre, and the direction of

Bibikovs'kyi Boulevard were all immediate outcomes of the university project.[97] The problem was that on its completion in 1843, the university stood in the open field, away from any contiguous built-up area. The main building with its impressive eight-column portico faced Khreshchatyk, but that street at the time was still a backwater, and the sprawling three-storey block of the university weighed rather gloomily on the entire New Kyiv, like a mirage in the desert.

Some were disconcerted by the sight of this monumental temple of gloom surrounded by wasteland. In 1839, one early observer, a traveller from Moscow named Stepan Maslov, was rather sceptical about the prospects for Kyiv University, which was so far from the "city centre" (whether that was for him Pechers'k or Podil):

The current university is being built on a new spot, beyond Khreshchatyk, on the edge of the city. The building will be capacious and magnificent; the only pity is that it is so distant from the city center. This is a serious inconvenience for the students and auditors residing outside of dormitories, who will have to commute to classes from opposite ends of the city. How much waste of time [going from] here and there and how much extra fatigue in studies requiring fresh energy this [commute] will take! In this regard, Moscow University, situated downtown, will always have an advantage over Kyiv.[98]

Another observer from the 1840s, writing at the time when the area was already developed, also noted the building's magnificent solitude. He described the difficult (and at times dangerous) trip he used to make as a young student from Podil to the university and back:

Right before my eyes, through the hills surrounding the city, which perhaps then played the role of ramparts of a fortress [in Old Kyiv] and through the ruins, still huge, of St Irene's Church, they were laying Volodymyrs'ka Street. ... Just behind the Golden Gate the road descended along the ramparts into an open field, and so walking in this field we would get to the university, passing by some military or quartermaster's barns. There was nothing yet in this area – either the First Gymnasium or Levashov's boarding school. In the middle of this empty space the university building alone spread out magnificently on all sides. In front of the building there was a field, pock-marked with bumps and hollows, in which the sappers seemed to have done some extensive work, while drilling "in the country" [za gorodom] ... When returning from the university event, I, in order to shorten the way, didn't walk through the Golden Gate but struggled forward amidst the bumps where [the future] Volodymyrs'ka Street was already marked out and where a single house was built along the line [of the street].[99]

As late as 1860, the university square was still empty – "unfenced and unkempt." Passing through the square even in broad daylight was unsafe because of the "large packs of hungry stray dogs that attacked the passersby, tore their clothes, and at times inflicted serious wounds." The ones who suffered the most were children going to the elite secondary schools situated nearby.[100]

These observers witnessed the prolonged process of planning the new area, which had become known, locally, as the University quarter or the New Building (Novoe Stroenie). Notwithstanding some sceptical voices (like those of Maslov and, to a lesser extent, Kostomarov[101]), the choice of location for the new university seemed prophetic. Although sited along the axis of the new quarter and the adjacent square, the building was considerably indented in relation to the "red line" of projected Volodymyrs'ka Street. The purpose of this was to emphasize the prime location of the university and its dominant role in the development of the "new" Old Kyiv.[102] Abandoning the usual practice of "ribbon building" (by means of perimeters with contiguous façades), the square followed the principle of "sporadic building" in which a free-standing university disrupted the monotonous "red line" of the street; this allowed for the inclusion of greenery in the streetscape. This same principle would be followed in later years, when other large buildings in Kyiv were sited. The visual unity of the university quarter was maintained by combining several elements such as vistas, straight lines, columns, parkland, and the uniform planting of trees. More importantly, the architecture of the university was expected to be visible from afar, including from the slopes of Pechers'k.

In designing the university quarter, Beretti displayed his outstanding planning skills. Following the principles of classical urban planning, he attempted to build the city as a whole ensemble, in such a way that individual structures were subordinate to an overall composition of streets, squares, and the city.[103] What Melens'kyi had started in the first decades of the century (albeit with more limited municipal means), Beretti perfected in the 1830s and early 1840s, taking advantage of much greater financial and technical resources provided by the state. Another important difference between Melens'kyi and Beretti was aesthetic: the former brought to Kyiv a more intimate Empire style, imported from

Moscow, while the latter brought there the classicism of Saint Petersburg with its more monumental features.[104]

The final important change wrought upon the city with the opening of St Vladimir University was geopolitical: spatially and ideologically, it *refocused* Kyiv. As a site of modern power/knowledge, Kyiv now presided not only over Right-Bank Ukraine but increasingly over the entire western part of the empire, insofar as the Polish-inhabited Vistula lands and the German-dominated Baltic provinces were viewed more and more as culturally alien and politically suspect. The siting of the new university and its monumental classical design closely reflected Kyiv's new geopolitical role. The city was also refocused spatially: its new section, on the border between Old Kyiv and the recently settled New Building, had become a cultural and educational centre of the growing imperial metropolis.

An appropriate addition to this classical makeover of Kyiv was the Institute for Noble Maidens, a neoclassical building magnificently sited on a hill just off Khreshchatyk Square. Built largely between 1839 and 1842 by Vikentii Beretti and completed by his son Alexander in 1845, the institute "served as a certain 'connector' to the Old City in the common body of the New Kyiv," as one local expert put it.[105] More impressively, the two Beretti buildings entered into a visual dialogue with each other: the university and the institute were built on hills at opposite ends of Kyiv's new centre, which created a picturesque vista between the two. Unfortunately, after 150 years of redevelopment in the area, this vista of hills – at one time an undeveloped space intentionally closed at both ends by Beretti's classical edifices – is now almost invisible, at least without mental "Photoshopping" to erase a few layers of the building fabric.

The elder Beretti's role in Kyiv's redevelopment was not limited to a few public buildings, however magnificent, and to his engagement in 1837 with the general plan of the city. Shortly before his death in 1842, he designed perhaps his most ambitious project (unfortunately unrealized) – a plan for grand changes in the layout of central Kyiv.[106] At the core of his proposal was an impressively long and picturesque diagonal – an avenue (*prospekt*) – that would have linked the Government Offices, still located in Lypky, with the new university. In the words of the architect himself, "a new avenue, beginning from Mykil's'ka street [in Pechers'k], through the Grape Garden between the two towers of a fortress under construction, and through the round square situated at the borders of the Grape and Mulberry gardens ... From there [it goes] right to the middle of the university in front of which a square is being laid out."[107] He also planned another quarter nearby in which only stone buildings were to be erected (and which would be built years later). His avenue would have allowed an unrestricted view of the university and the newly developed quarter "from different points in the city," thus forming another prominent vista. Probably his main aesthetic goal was to make the university visible from Pechers'k in much the same way that it was already visible from the Institute for Noble Maidens. As it turned out, no diagonal artery was ever constructed. Had this plan been realized, Beretti's new avenue rather than Khreshchatyk might have become Kyiv's main thoroughfare.

Apparently what stood in the way of such a spectacular vista were private interests and the city's land acquisition practices. The building committee blocked Beretti's proposal and argued against the demolition of twenty private houses. Most likely the homes belonged to the rich and powerful, whose interests were protected by the local administration.[108] This was one of the few cases in Kyiv where private interests effectively stopped imperial planners and architects.

But as a planner, Beretti was lucky elsewhere. As we already know, he played a crucial role in planning Kyiv's main cross-axis – Volodymyrs'ka Street and Bibikovs'kyi Boulevard (then known as Bul'varna Street); in that case, there were no private interests with which to reckon. His son Alexander completed his father's projects – the university, the institute, and the observatory. In the classicist spirit of his father, the son also built a few other major buildings, including the university's anatomical theatre, the First Gymnasium, and Madame Levashova's boarding school, all situated in Kyiv's new centre, within walking distance of the university. This centre, largely designed by Italian expatriates from Saint Petersburg (Ludovico Stanzani and father and son Beretti, among others),[109] became the embodiment of the new imperial Kyiv, given that it contained the city's most important institutions of power/knowledge. While various economic and strategic factors contributed to the rise of Old Kyiv and the New Building *at the expense* of Podil and Pechers'k, the role of rational urban design was no less important.

One last important aspect of the plan for the new imperial Kyiv was the systematic use of a grid pattern for new neighbourhoods. The grid was applied everywhere when older, "organic" city forms were being extended,[110] and Kyiv was no exception. The grid fit very well with the spirit of regularization championed by Nicholas I, who was notorious for his attention to the minutiae of street fixtures and home designs and who tried to enforce the construction of private houses *only* according to plans drawn beforehand by city architects. And the latter did not have a completely free hand when designing private properties, for they had to choose one of the "typical" façades published in series in Saint Petersburg.[111] The government allowed only the poorest of retired soldiers to ignore prescribed façades, in the process legalizing the construction of dugouts. This, however, was only a minor departure from an overall tendency to regularize and supervise private and public construction in the city.

The first area to be regularized in Kyiv was Podil after the devastating fire of 1811. In the end, it was rebuilt in the form of a rather unassuming chequerboard (although the architect Melens'kyi initially suggested a more creative orthogonal-radial pattern). The first of the *new* neighbourhoods where the grid reigned supreme was the Novoe Stroenie (New Building), just south of Old Kyiv. The inhabitants of Pechers'k were resettled there in the 1830s, following the construction of the new fortress in that ancient district. In the 1837 plan, the vast area south of Old Kyiv – the New Building and the entire Lybid' district – was split into rectilinear blocks cut by the straight lines of existing and projected streets (see map 11, page 235).[112] This general plan was Kyiv's first and most ambitious outline of the areas to be added and developed. Compiled by a team of local architects and land surveyors led by the municipal architect, Ludovico Stanzani, with the participation of Vikentii Beretti, and approved by the tsar himself, the plan outlined new areas for city expansion as well as major arteries linking those new quarters with the old ones.

It is worth noting that within each of the five districts, the map indicated with separate colours several types of quarters: (1) those already developed according to a plan (for Podil, designed in 1812); (2) those that were still non-regularized and contained "old lanes" (as in Plos'ka); (3) those that were to be pulled down to make room for the construction of the fortress in Pechers'k; (4) those that were situated "on the [Dnieper] shore, on the hills, and in the ravines" of Podil, whose inhabitants were to be relocated to safer ground; and (5) undeveloped quarters reserved for the resettlement of citizens who had lost their houses elsewhere (predominantly in Pechers'k or in Podil). In most cases, the homeowners from Pechers'k, compelled to move by the military, and from Podil, threatened by nature, were resettled in Lybid' and Plos'ka districts. The plan's structural centre was the intersection of Volodymyrs'ka Street (then known as Universytets'ka) and Bul'varna Street (the future Bibikovs'kyi Boulevard), the first modern

4.6 New building area (photo from the 1870s, from the collection of Mykhailo Kal'nyts'kyi)

streets to be designed for the emerging imperial metropolis. We can also see what Beretti suggested for the university area: a huge military parade ground was to be replaced by a square and a residential quarter delimited by new straight streets.

In general, the 1837 plan treated Kyiv as a functional totality, and as such it largely reflected the most advanced planning theory in contemporary Europe. The links between the new, gridded extensions and the "organic" core of the city were done quite seamlessly, via Volodymyrs'ka (aka Universytets'ka) Street, a newly planned artery running from the northern edge of Old Kyiv to the heart of the New Building. For much of the century, however, the street was formally split into several parts, each with its own name. The plan specifically provided for the regularization of Volodymyrs'ka (Universytets'ka) Street and surrounding quarters, with building lots now aligned in straight rows along the red line of the street.[113] The rugged and sandy terrain, quite visible even on the old map, posed significant technical challenges for the planners. But the areas on both sides of the projected street were sparsely populated, and this allowed Stanzani and others to largely avoid having to expropriate private lands through eminent domain.[114]

Besides incorporating new areas, the plan presupposed the further integration of older parts of the city such as Pechers'k, Old Kyiv, and Podil with one another via Khreshchatyk Street, which was to connect all major parts of the city. Hence the 1837 plan contained a few cross-sections of major streets, among them Instytuts'ka, Sofiïvs'ka,

Oleksandrivs'ka, and parts of Khreshchatyk together with Khreshchatyk Square.[115] The latter thus became a vital traffic node, from which several radial streets branched out in all directions. Clearly, the circulation of people and commodities had finally drawn the attention of city planners.

When we compare the 1837 plan of Kyiv with that of 1861, we can see that the developments envisioned by Beretti and Stanzani in the mid-1830s were largely realized. A new centre had indeed formed around the university quarter (although it was not yet built up), and Old Kyiv had received its own major artery, Volodymyrs'ka Street. Another major axis – Bul'varna Street (aka Bibikovs'kyi Boulevard) – had been considerably extended, running as a highway beyond the city limits towards the village of Shuliavka. New quarters had been laid out northwest of Podil, most importantly Luk'ianivka. Podil and Plos'ka were the most regulated parts of the city – each resembling a chequerboard – but they had ceased to be hubs of economic, social, and cultural life. Pechers'k was still the site of a fortress and was surrounded by a long, wide esplanade, inside of which, and in the vicinity of which, permanent settlement was severely limited.

The plan of 1861 introduced another crucial novelty that survived until the First World War – the division of Kyiv's streets into four ranks, each marked with a separate colour. A product of the bureaucratic mind, this street hierarchy and zoning did not change much over the decades. By the early 1860s, Kyiv had largely filled in its "natural" borders: the Dnieper to the east and the rivers Lybid' and Syrets' to the west. These natural features effectively thwarted urban sprawl.

Conclusion

After 1835 the city became increasingly dependent on policies crafted by imperial experts in the offices of the civil governor and the governor general. This period was largely defined by the personal role of Tsar Nicholas I (r. 1825–55), whose policy was to transform Kyiv from a small Ukrainian town into a "fortress city." This vision affected not only urban planning and building in the city but also its ethnic and social profiles. Two governors general implemented Nicholas's grand vision for the city – Vasilii Levashov (1832–5 in office) and Dmitrii Bibikov (1837–52 in office). As a result, for the first time since the thirteenth century, Kyiv emerged as a unified city, with all of its districts ruled by a single authority (although different social groups continued to be administered by different bodies). The imperial state expended significant material resources on refashioning Kyiv's physical space. Someone who saw Kyiv around 1870 after thirty years' absence would not have recognized it. The most diverse and promising neighbourhood – Pechers'k – was gone. The traditional burgher heartland, synonymous with the "city" itself – Podil – was in decline. The pride of the Kyivites – the self-governing magistrate – had been abolished. A new *imperial* centre of the city had been developed around St Vladimir University. Finally, a new commercial thoroughfare – Khreshchatyk – had replaced the traditional centres of commercial activity, such as Moskovs'ka Street in Pechers'k and the Town Hall Square and Oleksandrivs'ka Street in Podil. The grand urban planning schemes implemented in Kyiv under the city's energetic governors general had laid the foundation for the miraculous transformation of a frontier town into an imperial metropolis, the administrative, economic, and cultural capital of a huge region. The city could now boast new governmental, educational and cultural institutions, a few decent hotels and restaurants, a real boulevard, the cutting-edge Chain Bridge over the Dnieper, and even a few streets paved with granite. This was indeed a fairy tale, a spectacle of empire and autocratic power. Yet Kyiv was something of a Potemkin village: its grand imperial façade – all this Russian and international architecture – hid numerous traces of a small Ukrainian town. To use another metaphor, during a few middle decades of the century, a local – largely Ukrainian – audience was invited to watch a grandiose spectacle staged by a cosmopolitan cast of actors – governors, architects, technicians, merchants, and other masters of imperial ceremonies.

Chapter Five

Municipal Autonomy Reloaded: Space for Sale, 1871–1905

"The Animals Often Graze There"

In the last quarter of the nineteenth century, most Ukrainian traces would be all but erased. In 1871, Kyiv got a chance to exercise self-rule for the second time in its history. This time, municipal autonomy was not the result of a prolonged struggle between a burgher commune and a feudal ruler (as had been the case with the medieval Magdeburg Law); rather, it was the outcome of grand social reforms decided elsewhere, in the high offices of Saint Petersburg, and then imposed on most cities and towns across the empire. This second coming of autonomous Kyiv was increasingly Russian and cosmopolitan in spirit. In this sense, the imperial stage of a Potemkin village changed places with the audience: while the latter (Kyivites) were becoming ever more cosmopolitan, the Ukrainians were now reduced to theatrics. This happened literally insofar as public expressions of Ukrainian identity became possible only on the theatre stage.

Unlike the previous Kyiv city duma, which had existed between 1835 and 1870, the new duma was a reformed institution staffed by merchants and professionals, most of whom were of Russian, German, Greek, or Polish background. The new duma was supposed to represent the city as a whole (unlike the previous duma, which had been a representative organ for a few urban groups only). As such, the new city duma had been granted autonomy in a number of socio-economic and fiscal matters, a model first tested in Moscow (in 1862) and Odessa (in 1863).[1]

The urban reform of 1870 sought to introduce in Russia organs of municipal self-government based on economic classes rather than feudal estates. The reform established a municipal council (*duma*), whose executive (*uprava*) was headed by an elected mayor. The authority of dumas remained limited to local economic matters such as city beautification, local trade and industry, public health, education, sanitation, and fire safety. The city budget was raised mainly through taxes on municipal real estate, trade, manufacturing, baths, and slaughterhouses, in addition to state contributions. Most cities, however, ended up with significant budget deficits (with the exception of Moscow and Saint Petersburg). Arguably the most important new source of revenue was the "assessed property tax" (*otsenochnyi sbor*) – a tax on private real estate that the city began to exact after 1871 and that grew seven times between 1894 and 1911.[2] This tax would be a perennial source of controversy, for it was not clear what it was actually based on: Was it property's relative value (usually insurable value)? Or was it net income derived from tenants (minus upkeep costs)?[3] In Russian cities, most expenditures went to cover the costs of policing, prisons, military barracks,[4] and fire safety (60 per cent), while beautification and infrastructure received 15 per cent, education – 13 per cent, and public health only 1 per cent of the budget.[5] Yet the police were not even controlled by municipal councils.

Tables 5.1 and 5.2 show the city budgets and expenditures, each year representing a decade between 1871 and 1901 (provided that the data are available).

Table 5.1 Kyiv budgets, 1871–1901 (in roubles)

Budgets	1871	1880	1890	1899	1901
Revenues	268,632	796,496	1,400,000	2,585,166	3,531,516
Expenditures	228,565	803,288	1,400,000	2,633,000	3,512,096

Table 5.2 Main expenditures in Kyiv, 1871–1901 (in roubles)

Expenditures	1871	1880	1890	1899	1901
Municipal administration	25,724	64,883	100,000	174,879	192,713
Police and fire departments	46,000 (police); 19,755 (fire)	112,000	140,000 (police)	218,329	164,061 (police)
Municipal property, city planning, building, and beautification	41,160	199,812	100,000 (paving only)	489,000	696,241
Paying off debts	10,076	21,424	?	109,000	791,039
Charity, medicine, sanitation, and education	17,778	87,881	244,000	327,000[6]	1,073,687

Sources: DAK, f. 163, op. 47, spr. 18, pp. 83–86 (1871–80: a report based on the materials of the Senate audit); *Zaria*, 1880–2; V.D. Bublik, *Putevoditel' po Kievu i ego okrestnostiam*, 2nd edition (Kyiv, 1890), p. 21; *Kievskoe slovo*, 4628 (1900), p. 2.

The costs of policing grew steadily, and this, more than the billeting of troops, angered both liberal and conservative observers within the municipal administration and in the press.[7] Russia was indeed a police state, and Kyiv was a police bastion in the southwestern borderlands. Municipal administration itself was becoming increasingly costly. For example, journalists alleged that in just the first ten years of the new municipal order (i.e., between 1871 and 1882), the costs allocated for Kyiv duma's executive (*uprava*) increased by 170 per cent, or almost threefold, from 25,607 to 69,070 roubles. This was viewed as out-of-control spending.[8] The construction of the Kyiv duma's own building on Khreshchatyk Square, a project started in 1874, drew even more criticism. The liberal *Zaria* alleged that the overall construction costs ranged somewhere between 300,000 and 400,000 roubles (far exceeding the municipal loan of 180,000 roubles).[9] All the while, the autonomous municipality was spending ever larger sums on urban planning, street improvement, education, and charitable institutions.[10] As late as 1904, however, most of the city's streets remained unpaved, especially in peripheral districts such as Lybid', Luk'ianivka, and Plos'ka.[11]

The municipal reform was not completely democratic, for it introduced property qualifications (based on taxes paid to the city treasury) for participation in municipal elections and politics, a system borrowed from Prussia's municipal order. That system was based not on property values but on the sum of taxes paid to the city.[12] Obviously, the wealthiest one-third of taxpayers dominated the masses of poor voters. Kyiv's liberal paper *Zaria*,[13] in its first year of circulation, published a scathing critique of the narrow social base of the new city duma. The reporter concluded that the duma did not care about the common people. In another article, the writer expressed shock that professionals and members of the "intelligentsia," who dominated the new duma, were preoccupied not so much with public health, social welfare, or education as with real estate.[14] The liberal press continuously accused the city government of indifference towards poor Kyivites, especially those on the city's periphery, and of favouring downtowners as well as glitzy public projects such as the Municipal Theatre.[15]

In the late nineteenth century it was wealthy downtowners who benefited the most from the proliferation of a new form of residential real estate. New multistorey apartment buildings first rose downtown and then spread across the city. Spurred by rapid economic development, especially in the sugar beet industry, population growth in Kyiv presented a serious quantitative and qualitative problem for town planners and city politicians. They responded by erecting large apartment buildings, widening streets, installing new forms of transit (the first electric streetcar in Russia), and increasing population and residential densities, among other ways.

Kyiv experienced two building booms, one from 1895 to 1901, and another from 1907 to 1914, as a result of which more than 1,000 multistorey apartment houses were built. These rental apartments generated stable incomes for their owners (which were often corporations).[16] Large apartment buildings brought about a revolution in Kyiv's real estate market, which for centuries had been dominated by single-family detached houses, usually situated in private gardens. Commenting in 1897 on one of the latest "skyscrapers," a local journalist evoked American associations: "Such American buildings are most likely the result of the building fever that has plagued Kyiv, thanks to which we see as of late the rise of one building after another at a truly American pace."[17] This notorious "American pace," however, arrived in Kyiv rather slowly and rather late in the century.

Until the 1890s, most families of the various social classes (simple townspeople and nobles alike), depending on their means, of course, lived in private houses and kept livestock – smelly and noisy herds of cows, oxen, pigs, and chickens – on their homesteads, often in the heart of downtown. This traditional ecological order, however, was increasingly becoming an eyesore to the local educated public. A number of comical and sometimes outright bizarre stories about the roaming cattle on Kyiv's streets circulated in local press. One reader shared this story in 1872: "While passing along [the central] Volodymyrs'ka Street, I saw many times in the square, just in front of the City Theater, cows and calves which ... imperturbably had lunch and broke branches of trees and bushes." Concerned about the city's "beautification" (*blagoustroistvo*), this citizen tried to alert the policeman, who happened to spend his working hours at a nearby tavern. "To my request to chase away the cattle, he responded that the animals often graze there and that he cannot watch over that matter."[18] In another account, someone complained that near the Golden Gate, in the vicinity of the city's major church, St Sophia, "one cannot pass without coming across a cow," and that cows routinely intimidated decent ladies who were walking towards fashionable Khreshchatyk Street.[19] Even in the square across from the Government Offices one could encounter grazing cows and horses.[20] In one story, a particularly wild one, a female servant was fatally mutilated by the horns of some roaming beast on one of the main (or rather, mean) streets of the city.

Until the first building boom of the mid-1890s, small wooden houses predominated in Kyiv. In 1856, out of a total of 4,873 houses, only 371 (7 per cent) were made of the famous local bricks. In 1863, despite a considerable increase in the number of brick houses (592), their share in Kyiv's built environment was still minuscule (8.8 per cent); and out of a total of 6,747 dwelling houses, 5,916 were still wooden structures, and 239 were dugouts inhabited by the poorest Kyivites.[21] Even in the early 1870s, of the newly built several hundred houses, 295 were wooden and only 117 were of brick.[22] Those who did not own their own houses – among them newly appointed public servants, visiting merchants, peasants, soldiers, officers, and the like – rented rooms or apartments in private one- or two-storey houses. Wealthy merchants usually owned two or more houses and often rented them out entirely to one or several families. Even priests in Kyiv supplemented their income with rents paid by tenants.[23]

The first buildings designed specifically as rental apartment houses appeared in the late 1840s, many of them on Khreshchatyk.[24] Initially they were relatively small – only two or three stories. One such house, in which later the family of the writer Mikhail Bulgakov lived as tenants, was built in 1888 and contained only two apartments, a larger one (with seven rooms) taking up the second floor, and a smaller one (with five rooms) occupying the first. The owners rented out the larger apartment and lived in a smaller one, while also renting out a small shop on the ground floor. In Kyiv at that time, "a provincial town with established conservative traditions," this was the most typical living arrangement.[25]

The proliferation of banks and the availability of credit in Kyiv after the early 1880s made it easier for citizens to build houses specifically for rent or sale. This new development anticipated the coming of capitalist modernity whereby the "provincial town" became an "industrial city." "The urban landscape was fundamentally transformed when urban land came to be seen as a source of income, when ownership was divorced from use, and property became primarily a means to produce rent," wrote urbanist Spiro Kostof.[26] For a long time, land had been regarded as a "collective amenity"; now, it had come to be viewed as a "commercial good."[27]

Another consequence of the "land-rent gradient" was the segregation of uses in the city, a process encouraged by the capitalist economy. This happened in Kyiv later than in many other European cities. When the "land-rent gradient" finally came to dominate the local urban economy in the last quarter of the nineteenth century, Kyiv's "town plan," its "land use pattern," and especially its "building fabric" changed more rapidly and more dramatically than anywhere else.[28] Urban historian Oskar Handlin described the rise of urban rent in this way:

> Precious urban acreage was withdrawn from farming. And the distribution of population by income levels permitted a rational valuation of space in terms of an abstract, calculated, rent. Speculation was the incidental by-product, rather than the cause, of this development. Space was reallocated with an eye toward its most profitable use; and buildings directed toward a single function – trade, industry, or residence – went up with ruthless efficiency. The process of differentiation created demands for services which theretofore had been unneeded or had been supplied within a household, for fresh foods, milk, water, waste disposal, light, transportation, and recreation. In the frenzy of construction, the city was entirely recast and its ties to the past obliterated.[29]

This process reared its head in Kyiv in the 1890s. With regard to urban planning, the city experienced a tension – felt everywhere in the industrialized world – between the idea of active public authority and that of free economic competition that emphasized private ownership of all factors of production, including land. The idea that the public authority could exercise control over private land in towns was not easily accepted.[30] But because of the Russian government's long history of being the sole voice in urban development, even during the height of laissez-faire capitalism in the early twentieth century, the position of the public authority in the city remained remarkably strong.

"The City's Appearance Became Unrecognizable"

Thanks to the first building boom, which began in 1895, and the attendant massive capitalization of real estate, new apartment houses popped up like mushrooms after the rain. In the words of a contemporary expert, "the land downtown was taken by force, the old houses that were still livable were completely demolished and instead there emerged the giant structures of the new type. The number of brick plants increased, the prices of bricks almost doubled, the banks issued loans right and left, [and] the city's appearance became unrecognizable."[31] As a result, almost 1,000 new apartment houses were built between 1898 and 1901 – an unprecedented figure. This increased the proportion of brick buildings in the city's total building stock to around 20 per cent.[32] Credit and interest were perhaps capitalist "fictions" (to quote David Harvey's famous Marxist dictum), but they were real enough to have changed the social and architectural landscape of late imperial Kyiv.

The role of credit institutions was indeed crucial in the new urban economy, for they enabled both building booms in the city.[33] But this rapid real estate development had its dark side: the increasing indebtedness of homeowners to the banks. This matter was debated in the city duma as early as in 1887. An early critic of Kyiv's "land-rent gradient" nostalgically and perhaps naively remarked that before the proliferation of credit and loans, life had been easier for homeowners, for "everybody was content with what one had." Once pledges and mortgages were introduced, Kyivites started building "large houses." This drew more and more people into debt. "If an apartment stands half a year or a year unoccupied, the homeowner will be totally lost," said a concerned councillor, who added, however, that this did not apply to Khreshchatyk, a commercial artery where real estate was always profitable.[34] Yet we know that even Khreshchatyk experienced difficulties with respect to the new speculative real estate. Many old-timers wondered whether large apartment houses were actually profitable. Others were simply afraid of living in "high-rises" (i.e., above the second floor), anticipating the imminent collapse of these buildings.[35]

Profit-seeking citizens were also confronted with the strict building regulations that were enforced, however haphazardly, by the public authorities. We should remember that until the early twentieth century, Kyiv was a "fortress city." The area occupied by various military establishments (the fortress, esplanade, barracks, training grounds, gardens, etc.) almost equalled the city's settled area administered by the municipal authorities.[36] For years after 1871 the autonomous city duma engaged in lengthy negotiations with the imperial authorities on the question of municipal land and the urgency of lifting the cumbersome esplanade rules. Those rules were first enacted in the mid-nineteenth century and were enacted again several times thereafter, remaining in force until 25 July 1909.[37] In 1872 the government significantly relaxed the esplanade rules, freeing large portions of the city from the restrictions. Indeed, most city areas (such as Podil, Plos'ka, Lypky, Khreshchatyk, most of Old Kyiv, and part of the New Building in Lybid' district) were freed from building restrictions. But in Pechers'k, in much of Lybid', and in parts of Old Kyiv and Lypky, private construction was either banned altogether or strictly limited with regard to size and form (to one-storey wooden houses).[38] In the large Luk'ianivka district, where big chunks of land had remained empty for decades due to the esplanade rules, the restrictions were lifted only in 1880–1.[39]

The persistence of an esplanade for so many decades inhibited the city's expansion and limited building activities; it also brought down the value of land and real estate in much of the city. Furthermore, it undermined the overall profitability of construction in Kyiv. By banning construction altogether in some areas and by limiting the size and the form of structures in others, the esplanade rules discouraged potential buyers from investing in real estate. What is more, the military in charge of Kyiv fortress and its esplanade began leasing lands they had previously appropriated from the city to private holders, thereby depriving the city once again of municipal property.[40] The municipal authorities repeatedly complained about this injustice to the minister and to the Senate, but to little avail.

Besides all of this, there were two other highly contentious issues in the relations between the city and Russian government. The first of these was the rate of real estate tax that Kyiv's homeowners paid to the state treasury. The sum of this tax was established in advance based on Kyiv province's total economic and demographic indicators. The problem was that state officials often overstated the property tax for the city because of their inflated assessments of the provincial economy. Also, because all state, public, and charitable properties were exempt from the tax, the entire burden of taxation fell on private homeowners. In response to this widely decried injustice the city submitted several formal complaints to the state authorities about the excessive tax burden.[41] Reportedly, the city itself abused its right to assess property values by understating the profitability of municipal property, and this added to the burden faced by private owners, who had to contribute more to the total sum established by the province's tax officers.[42]

Another contentious issue was the billeting of imperial troops, an ongoing concern for the city both before and after 1871. For decades, the municipal authorities had been selecting particular homesteads for quartering troops – a very burdensome duty for residents, many of whom (if means permitted) chose to pay a fee to avoid a billet. At the same time, the state itself funded the construction of military barracks (first in Pechers'k from the 1830s to the 1850s, then in suburban Syrets' in 1869), without, however, abandoning the practice of billeting in private homes. It seems that after 1874 a new, more balanced system was established: the city provided quarters for the garrison by building barracks or by renting private houses (paid by local taxpayers, to be sure); for this, the military contributed financially. Even so, conflict between the city and the military persisted. The question now concerned the complex economics of the deal. It turned out that the money the military offered (the so-called *kvartirnyi oklad* or "billeting pay") was not enough to rent decent accommodation, for Kyiv's homeowners were reluctant to rent their properties at prices substantially below the market price.[43] This meant that the city had to step in by paying the remainder, again from taxpayers' money. Some parts of the city remained under a dual burden: homeowners had to pay fees for building/renting the military accommodation in the city even while continuing to billet troops.[44] Eventually the city focused on the best possible solution – building military barracks at its own expense, because it could not find enough private developers willing to provide cheap accommodation for the military.[45] Despite the relatively high cost of building and maintaining all the military establishments (the expenses ranged from paying state taxes on municipal property to insurance fees to renovation costs to cleaning to barrack "accessories"),[46] this ultimately proved extremely profitable for the city coffers.[47]

In another field – control over planning and construction in the city – the imperial government and the autonomous city duma divided their spheres of competence relatively smoothly. Both central and local authorities had attempted to regulate private construction in Kyiv. This started with an official mania for "exemplary façades" and for private plots of predetermined sizes during the reigns of Alexander I and especially Nicholas I. This policy of state control culminated in 1861 in the publication of local "building regulations" initiated by the office of the Kyiv civil governor. That document would rule much of subsequent urban planning in Kyiv.[48] That these regulations were updated in 1872 (and confirmed in 1874) indicates how little success the city had in implementing its own policies. Nonetheless, these planning and building principles were remarkable in several major respects.

First, although self-government had been restored in Kyiv, the most important strategic document that defined the "building fabric" and "land use pattern" in the city had been crafted by state officials. Second, the regulations did not bring an end to the esplanade rules, but rather prolonged a festering war between the military and the city. Third, the regulations were quite arbitrary, based as they were on abstract aesthetic principles, and as such they paid little heed to the mass of homeowners and their needs or means. Finally, through these building regulations the local state authorities has strongly shaped Kyiv's new commercial and residential centre. Thus it was the state, not the city duma or the business elites, that defined the city's modern centre. On the eve of the twentieth century the free market would somewhat correct the formal "hierarchy" of streets in the city. But the overall planning philosophy, once formulated in 1872, remained deeply entrenched in the commercial practices of Kyiv developers. As late as 1913 the decades-old "building regulations," including the division of the city's streets into four categories, were reissued with only a few minor changes.[49]

According to the regulations of 1872 (which largely remained in force until the First World War) all city streets were divided into four categories: (1) main ones; (2) secondary ones; (3) streets of lesser importance; and (4) "the rest."[50] On the streets of the first category it was permitted to build (both along the streets and within the plots) "only stone structures covered with iron." Along major streets in Old Kyiv, the Palace district, and Podil, as well as on Volodymyrs'ka Street in Lybid', structures had to be built "along the lines of the streets," and houses had to be at least two storeys high. On streets of the second category, it was permitted to build wooden houses on stone foundations or "semi-floors." On streets of the third category, one could build also one-storey wooden houses on wooden foundations, but with "improved façades." Remarkably, the buildings in the first three categories were expected to be approved by the governor's construction office. On streets in the fourth category, wooden houses "with façades without particular embellishments" could be built, and it was the responsibility of the municipal architect, not the governor's office, to supervise the construction of these. The 1872 regulations made it explicit that stone structures in the third and fourth categories had to conform to the esplanade rules.[51]

The first category clearly delineated Kyiv's new centre as it was envisioned by government officials. At its heart was the district of Old Kyiv, which was old only in name. The Government Offices (built in 1857), located between St Sophia Cathedral and St Michael's Monastery, were the *administrative* heart of the new city, while Khreshchatyk was its *commercial* hub and its major promenade.[52] Most streets in Old Kyiv belonged to the first category. They included most of Bibikovs'kyi Boulevard (its right side), most of Fundukleïvs'ka and Volodymyrs'ka Streets, and several radial streets leading from Khreshchatyk Square to the Government Offices, as well as all major squares (such as Khreshchatyk Square, Tsar's, St Michael's and St Sophia's Squares). In total, in Old Kyiv twenty streets and squares belonged to the highest category.

In Lypky, an elite residential area, six streets were assigned to the first category, among them Khreshchatyk (left side), Oleksandrivs'ka, and Instytuts'ka. But the designation of the streets in Lypky did not take place without a struggle, this time between an influential city councillor and the office of the governor general. Why would anyone oppose to the elevation of streets to the top category? The arguments submitted by Professor Rennenkampf cited economic considerations and seemed to have represented the position of local homeowners. Specifically, he argued against the attribution of several streets (among them Bankova) to the first category because (1) these streets were "distant from all the commercial and manufacturing centers, as well as from educational institutions," and (2) these streets "are built up with modest single houses and wings [*fligeliami*]" and were populated by families that sought quiet living quarters "free from cohabitation with other people."[53]

He then put forward an economic argument against the government's aesthetic considerations: the homeowners would have difficulty finding tenants for the two- and three-storey stone houses, the construction of which was prescribed by the new regulations. The local homeowners – most of whom were officials and pensioners – were generally not very affluent and would not be able to afford to build stone houses. In the end, he suggested designating only three streets as first-class – "the main streets connected directly with Khreshchatyk" – with the other three remaining in the second class. Rennenkampf viewed his role as city councillor in a radically new way: he saw himself as an advocate for his constituents' interests. He declared outright that building regulations must serve not only the interests of fire safety and beauty but also the needs of city dwellers.

Yet the state continued to exert pressure on the city duma.[54] The arguments of the governor general reflected primarily aesthetic concerns. "In the present situation [with the mitigation of the esplanade rules], the Palace district [Lypky] obviously cannot remain in the third cat-egory: there are a number of governmental and public buildings in it, such as the Imperial palace, a commercial bank, a stock exchange, the Institute for Noble Maidens, the governor-general's house, a school for girls of clerical origins, houses of the charitable society, the Lutheran church, and numerous private stone buildings, so that further permis-sion [to build] wooden structures would not conform to the orderly improvement [*blagoustroistvu*] of this part of the city."[55] These argu-ments proved more convincing than those of Rennenkampf.

This story also reflected different views of the modern city. The gov-ernment was more concerned about public order and aesthetics; city dwellers voiced their opposition to changes. Conservative homeown-ers did not yet favour the large-scale commercial redevelopment of the downtown. For their part, the imperial officials enforced changes in the cityscape, ignoring the needs of local residents.

This same situation developed in other districts as well. In Lybid', six streets and quarters were assigned to the first category, among them the entire university quarter with its botanical garden, Volodymyrs'ka Street, and the portion of Bibikovs'kyi Boulevard closest to the uni-versity. In Podil, eight streets and squares were assigned to the first category, among them Oleksandrivs'ka Street and Square, Verkhnii Val (Upper Rampart), and the Rye Market Square (*Zhytnietorz'ka plosh-cha*). In the poorer and more populous Plos'ka district only four streets were designated as first-class, all of them adjacent to Podil, among them Nyzhnii Val (Lower Rampart). These categorizations provoked another councillor, the old-school Podil merchant Fedir Voitenko, a brother of the previous city head, to submit to the duma an even more wide-ranging criticism.[56] His constituents resided in Podil and Plos'ka. Voitenko's overall assessment of the building regulations was that they punished the poor. The rules favoured houses of higher catego-ries instead of helping homeowners improve existing houses, many of which were "semi-ruined huts with ragged roofs in which the walls are always wet from rain."

All of these new planning guidelines were reflected in the general plan of the city approved by the central authorities in 1874.[57] The plan defined the shape of the city for many years to come and would remain in force until 1914. The streets in each category were in sepa-rate colours – red for the first, yellow for the second, blue for the third, and green for the fourth. The Cyrillic letters from A to I scattered all over the city indicated the spaces of an esplanade according to the new

regulations of 1872 and 1873. The city was split into six police districts –
Old Kyiv, Pechers'k, Palace, Lybid', Podil, and Plos'ka – and a few "suburbs" (*predmest'ia*) and "outskirts" (*urochishcha*) such as Luk'ianivka,
Hlybochytsia, and Iurkovytsia.[58] The new heart of the city was unques-
tionably Old Kyiv and parts of the adjacent Lybid' and Palace districts
(see map 12, page 236), while Pechers'k was enclosed by the esplanade
and Podil was effectively cut off from the new centres of commerce and
culture by the lack of adequate communications.

Symbolically, in the centre of this *new* Kyiv (technically within the
district of Old Kyiv) stood the new city hall – the Kyiv city duma
(not yet built; on the plan of 1874 it was marked by the letter *A* – see
map 12). With its opening in 1876, Kyiv saw yet another example of modern local planning, and also the realization of a highly ambitious public
construction scheme.[59] During Vienna's Ringstrasse era all major public
buildings (including the Rathaus) had been financed through the sale of
nearby plots to private owners; by contrast, the new home of Kyiv's self-
governing municipality was financed through a municipal loan of 180,000
roubles.[60] The square in front of the building, known as the City House,
became one of the principal civic places in the city, and its main building
would influence the form of the surrounding built environment.

The 1874 general plan underscored the former economic and
demographic prominence of Podil, a district that by 1874 had only
14,518 residents – significantly fewer than Lybid' and Plos'ka, each
of which had more than 20,000 inhabitants, and even Old Kyiv and
Pechers'k, each with around 20,000 people.[61] Yet Podil was second
only to Old Kyiv if judged by the number of first-class streets
and squares (eight, compared to twenty in Old Kyiv and six each
in Palace and Lybid' districts).[62] The two most populous districts –
Plos'ka and Lybid' – were also the most regularly planned in all of
Kyiv, consisting of uniform blocks (rectangles in Lybid' and squares in
Plos'ka). Remarkably, these most highly regulated spaces were largely
populated by the city's poorest inhabitants (although some parts
of Lybid' closest to the university contained residences of the new
professional and enterpreneural elites). Perhaps this orthogonal layout
somehow facilitated the sale and redevelopment of plots during the
first and second building booms, when the city was inundated with
apartment houses. Finally, the map showed that by the early 1870s,
Kyiv had filled in the geographical space bounded by the Dnieper on
one side and by the Lybid' and Syrets' rivers on the other, this historical
shape emphasized by the railway since 1870.[63]

Another pressing issue was the lack of funding for private renovations. The city duma had used to issue small loans (up to 600 roubles) to homeowners; banks did not provide such loans. For lack of funds, modest homeowners were unable to meet the new building and zoning regulations. Apparently even the second category of houses (requiring stone foundations) was beyond the means of most residents of Podil and Plos'ka. The already quoted councillor who represented Podil's voters also argued against the equal treatment of streets in different districts. For example, the first-class streets in Old Kyiv and Palace districts could not be compared with those of the same category in Podil and Plos'ka because in these poorer areas, revenues from rents were considerably lower. Therefore, the councillor insisted, most streets outside of Old Kyiv and Palace districts should be reassigned to the second class, including some more outlying streets in Old Kyiv (such as the farthest portion of Bibikovs'kyi Boulevard). Similarly, a number of the second-class streets should be downgraded to lower categories due to the quality of the soil, which made the construction of larger houses with stone foundations practically impossible. Of all these suggestions, the city duma supported only one, concerning the prohibition on building basement apartments in Podil and Plos'ka, "due to the quality of soil and the proximity of spring water."[64]

A persistent concern of Kyiv's municipal self-government was the supervision of private construction in the growing city, where more and more people wanted to invest in commercial real estate. Around 1871 the duma's executive, the *uprava*, issued a special directive on private construction, according to which all building and renovation projects would henceforth require permits issued by city officials as well as detailed plans. Homeowners, however, would be free to divide their plots for sale "without limitations."[65] The new Municipal Statute of 1892 further strengthened the city's prerogatives with regard to private construction: the Building Department of the Kyiv provincial board (*gubernskoe pravlenie*) would now oversee the construction and maintenance of *public* and *state-funded* buildings in the city and in all of Kyiv province. Also, state officials could inspect private construction in Kyiv.[66]

In theory, the construction of *every* home required a permit from the city, as did any major reconstruction or minor renovation. Only towards 1910 did municipal control over private construction in Kyiv decrease, owing to the enormous volume of construction work. Indeed, the volume was so high that in 1911 a journalist complained that no one seemed to be overseeing construction in the city. Municipal officials, he wrote, usually limited their involvement to the approval of building plans.[67] Although the city tried hard to impose order on private construction, a number of irregularities occurred even before 1910. Some buildings even rose miraculously without *any* permit.[68]

It seems that the city had failed to put an end to arbitrary and spontaneous construction on private homesteads, a long-standing practice despite decades of imperial regulations prescribing plans and "exemplary façades." The municipal authorities, however, did not give up their fight against non-human urban dwellers – chickens, pigs, and cows (although cowsheds were allowed). For example, municipal regulations specifically banned the keeping of pigeons, dogs, and cats in the yards of new apartment houses,[69] apparently a persistent custom among many old and new Kyivites. Also, although it had abandoned the early-nineteenth-century practice of controlling the form and size of private homesteads, the autonomous city continued to regulate the space *inside* the plots. For example, it prescribed a minimum size for empty spaces within courtyards, so as to maintain hygiene and prevent fires.[70]

Yet many owners managed to "condense" built-up areas for the sake of maximizing their profits.[71] This was especially the case with multistorey apartment buildings, which often replaced owners' old houses. Sometimes a new property was built next to an existing house, the owner's residence, with the result that two or three buildings stood randomly on a single plot. In such cases, building density could reach 95 per cent, meaning that the plot was almost completely built up. This dense redevelopment of urban homesteads in Kyiv was caused not only by greed but also by topographical and jurisdictional limitations.[72]

A typical homestead in Kyiv consisted of a small one- or two-storey house and one or two outbuildings (where people kept livestock). Multistorey apartment buildings began to appear on such plots in the last quarter of the nineteenth century. When the second building boom began in the early twentieth century, single plots were too small to accommodate the growing ambitions of many developers, so they often had to acquire neighbouring plots. Such was the case with the tallest building in Kyiv at the time, the so-called "Ginzburg's skyscraper," built between 1910 and 1912 on two adjacent homesteads.[73] Most developers, however, could not afford to build on two or more plots, so the density of individual plots greatly increased over time. Consequently, the placement of houses on a redeveloped homestead became even messier. Homesteads in Kyiv varied greatly in size and form, and as a result, apartment houses were built in wildly diverse shapes and with floor plans just as diverse. Most American cities, for example, had been divided *in advance* into monotonous rectangular parcels in order to facilitate the sale of individual plots (the Commissioners' Plan for Manhattan of 1811 being the most famous example); by contrast, Kyiv's chaotic land use pattern resulted in a very diverse "building fabric."[74] Depending on the plot, individual buildings acquired different shapes – from simple rectangular- and Г-shaped to mid-sized Т-Г-П- and H-shaped to large and complex buildings taking up entire blocks.[75]

But unlike many European cities, and much like most American cities, Kyiv enjoyed this advantage: it possessed large swathes of a sparsely populated land. So until the very end of the nineteenth century the developers could still find, even in the city centre, undeveloped plots, both private and city-owned. Perhaps the largest undeveloped estate in downtown Kyiv belonged to Fedor Mering/Möring (1822–87), a popular doctor and professor of medicine at Kyiv University. His fame was so universal that, in the words of Sergei Vitte, then a resident in the city, "every dog here knew him."[76] The wealthy doctor treated the poor (especially poor Jews from Podil) for free, and a number of grateful Jewish brokers helped him buy and sell real estate for profit. By the end of his life he had accumulated an enormous landed estate just east of Khreshchatyk, with a total area of 10.5 hectares, consisting of several brick and wooden houses, vegetable gardens and orchards, greenhouses, a large pond, and a bathhouse.[77]

The redevelopment of Mering's extensive property was without a doubt the most spectacular experiment in modern urban planning and architecture in late-imperial Kyiv. Also, this was one of the very few *documented* cases where a private owner, not the public authority, initiated the laying out of new streets in the city. This was also a story of an urban landowner who possessed a huge property in Kyiv's precious downtown but who failed to capitalize on it and eventually went bankrupt. Capitalism as it worked in Kyiv rewarded neither the location nor the size of a plot but rather an owner's ability to redevelop, sell, and/or rent commercial real estate at a maximum profit.

After the professor's death and with the start of the first building boom in the mid-1890s, Mering's huge but rather "empty" estate began to look anachronistic: it was an old-fashioned rural mansion in the heart of a modernizing city. In 1894, Mering's son, now the sole owner of his father's estate after he had bought out his siblings' shares

5.1 Mering's estate before redevelopment, 1880s

in the property, made the city an offer it could not refuse. Mikhail Mering planned to lay out four new streets and a square on his property
and then turn them over to the city "in perpetual ownership."[78] One
of the streets, not surprisingly, would bear the name Mering. The city
and Mering, however, could not agree on the width of the streets (he
wanted narrower) and on who would pay for the streets' paving, maintenance, and lighting. The city kept pressing Mering until he agreed
to the conditions put forward by the municipal authorities. In January 1895, he pledged to plan the streets, to drain subterranean waters,
and to build the gas pipes, all at his own expense. He also agreed to
finance the paving, maintenance, and lighting of the streets, as well as
the costs of extra police personnel "until the plots will be built up and
the city will receive the assessed property tax from the new houses."[79]

After making this deal with the city, Mering was ready to proceed
with building, but another problem arose: he did not have enough
funds to redevelop his property. The only option was to sell the estate to
a joint-stock company.[80] The Kyiv Home Building Society was founded
in 1895 specifically to redevelop Mering's extensive properties; this

5.2 Mykolaïvs'ka Street, Hotel Continental (postcard)

included executing the contract with the city. Conveniently, the son of the late professor and his sole heir became the "honorary" head of the society's board, while its real founder was the famous architect and banker Georgii P. Shleifer (who also designed some of the area's major buildings).[81] Among other board members were representatives of Kyiv's new business and professional elite, such as the entrepreneur Vasilii I. Tolli – the son of Kyiv's former mayor, of Greek descent – and David S. Margolin, a wealthy Jewish merchant. The redevelopment of Mering's estate would involve significant changes to the city plan, and this would require approval from the central authorities. That approval was soon granted by the Building Department of the Russian interior ministry.[82]

The old estate was now split into eighteen smaller plots. Most of them were sold to private developers (companies and individuals).[83]

The profits from these new parcels (the upscale Hotel Continental, the Industrial Bank, restaurants, and a number of chic apartment houses) were to be shared by numerous shareholders (a total of 3,600 shares were issued, worth 500 roubles each); the city for its part received four new streets and a square.[84] The new quarter's principal street, Mykolaïvs'ka (Nikolaevskaia), became one of the most fashionable residential and commercial streets in the city. Arguably the most iconic modernist structure in Kyiv's architectural history – the house of architect Vladyslav Horodets'kyi (Polish-born Leszek Dezydery Władysław Horodecki) – was built on the edge of Mering's former property in 1902.[85] Most of the new plots were sold by the Kyiv Home Building Society to private and corporate owners; only a couple of new structures, such as Hotel Continental and a theatre, remained in the company's ownership. This was a spectacular redevelopment, but something went terribly wrong for the joint-stock company and for Mering's heir in particular. Because of the rising costs of labour and construction materials and also because the company had failed to sell several plots (around twenty completed houses), the land that still belonged to the company was mortgaged, first to the Kyiv Credit Society and then to the firm owned by sugar baron Lazar Brodsky.[86] To make matters worse, Mikhail Mering got involved in dubious financial practices and ran up debts exceeding 700,000 roubles – funds he had "borrowed" from the joint-stock company's capital. As could only be expected, the company failed to pay off the mortgage, and the Kyiv Credit Society auctioned off its property. While a few homeowners continued to derive benefit from the redeveloped area, a number of shareholders went bankrupt, including Mering himself.[87]

The city itself was among the main beneficiaries of Mering's estate, for it gained possession (for free!) of several streets that would generate significant tax revenue from new commercial real estate. The city, it seems, generally avoided acquiring private land for municipal purposes such as cutting new streets or widening existing ones. In one such early case dating from 1872, a duma resolution cited the enormous expenses that would be involved "for acquiring privately owned land, planning, and paving a new street, whereas the city cannot find funds to maintain the existing streets."[88] In Kyiv, in contrast to London, the investor-developer was usually the owner of the plot of land on which he was going to build.[89] So the city was happy to cooperate with Mering in the redevelopment of his extensive property.

Garden City, Kyiv Style

Regarding urban form and the city's relationship with the suburbs, Kyiv stood out among major European and Russian imperial cities. In the last quarter of the nineteenth century the city finally filled in its natural borders, a space it had occupied in medieval times. Because of its complex geography, the city avoided the urban sprawl that was so typical of European and American cities at the turn of the twentieth century (London being the prime example). This is not to say that suburbs did not emerge outside the city core, but they never encircled it, nor did they absorb a significant amount of the population. Most importantly, there always remained strict legal borders between the city of Kyiv and various satellite settlements, most of which belonged to the village administrations of Kyiv district (*uezd*) or to the neighbouring districts of Chernihiv and Poltava provinces (e.g., the settlements north and east of Kyiv, on the left bank of the Dnieper). Consequently, the city largely abstained from incorporating the suburbs. The suburbs themselves often opposed the plans of incorporation proposed by the Kyiv municipal authorities.

The earliest suburbs lay just north of the city, on the northwestern fringes of Podil. The farmsteads, forests, and agricultural holdings of Podil burghers (usually the more affluent ones) had been located in Kurenivka, Priorka, and Syrets' for centuries. These were the first – and among the very few – settlements to be incorporated into the city. This happened as early as 1799, by order of Emperor Paul I.[90] Some of these lands later evolved into fashionable recreational communities; others turned into industrial zones, with workers' housing close by. All three neighbourhoods developed along the old road leading from Podil to the ancient town of Vyshhorod, just north of Kyiv. The most popular spa town for Kyivites – Pushcha Vodytsia – was founded along this road around 1900. It was directly linked by a streetcar (first steam-powered, later electric) with Khreshchatyk, via Kurenivka and Priorka, and this facilitated the spa's beautification. Pushcha Vodytsia eventually had an artfully designed park, a theatre, retail stores, a restaurant, and various other modern amenities, including telephone service.[91]

It is quite easy to detect some patterns in the formation of suburbs. Older suburbs took root along the old roads leading from Kyiv radially in all directions; newer industrial settlements grew around sites where railways intersected with traditional highways (see map 5, page xxi). Among the former were the already mentioned old "suburbs" such as Kurenivka, Priorka, and Syrets'; among the latter were two of the most important commercial and industrial settlements in the vicinity of Kyiv – Demiïvka, on a southern road running towards the town of Vasyl'kiv, and Shuliavka, on a road leading west to Zhytomyr.[92]

Initially an agricultural village in Kyiv district (*uezd*), in the second half of the nineteenth century Demiïvka became a major source of labour and the site of several industrial plants. The largest of these was the Alexander sugar beet refinery, which employed more than 2,000 workers and which, by the 1880s, had become the Russian Empire's largest sugar refinery.[93] This village soon lost its agricultural character and became a crucial commercial and industrial hub closest to Kyiv. As part of Khotiv *volost'* of Kyiv district, Demiïvka was within the Jewish Pale of Settlement, and this made the village exceedingly attractive to Jewish entrepreneurs and artisans. They could not legally reside in Kyiv, but they could commute daily to the city, especially after 1892, when a streetcar line opened between Demiïvka and Khreshchatyk.

Kyiv city councillors were split over the issue of Demiïvka. Those in favour of annexing it pointed to the potential revenue, also emphasizing that the majority of local residents were not peasants but "free settlers." Furthermore, the latter owned most of the trading and manufacturing establishments, which could become a major source of tax revenue for the city. "Without this merger," argued proponents of annexation, "Demiïvka will always exist and develop its strength at the expense of the city."

The arguments against annexation were as follows: the revenue from Demiïvka would not cover the expenses of its beautification; the local peasants could secede and organize a new "Demiïvka," which would have a harmful impact on the city's revenues; and finally, if the suburb was incorporated the local Jews would be forced to leave Demiïvka, thus depriving the city of significant revenue.[94] Despite several attempts by city councillors, Demiïvka had not been incorporated into Kyiv when the Old Regime collapsed in 1917 – it remained officially a village.[95] It was a social curiosity, populated mostly by artisans, traders, entrepreneurs, and workers (both Jewish and Gentile), where peasants were a minority. The government sided with the peasants, who opposed the merger. If anything, this situation revealed an enduring anti-urban bias at various levels of Russian imperial government.[96]

The case of Shuliavka was very similar to that of Demiïvka, except that the former was even more heavily industrialized and had far fewer Jewish residents.[97] This last factor perhaps led to another

5.3 Kul'zhenko, Demiïvka suburb, *Vidy Kieva*

difference – namely, Kyiv city councillors spoke out more decisively in favour of incorporating Shuliavka. But this suburb too was far more multiethnic than Kyiv itself, which perhaps was a significant deterrent for many zealous Russians on the Kyiv city council and in the government. More importantly, the city could not annex any territory that formally belonged to a rural district unless it had the consent of the imperial government. When in 1887 the Kyiv mayor asked the civil governor whether the city could annex the area known as Shuliavka, the latter responded that he needed more time to study the issue.[98] In the meantime it turned out that part of Shuliavka had in fact belonged to the city since 1851 and that the issue of incorporation concerned only a village commune, also called Shuliavka.

This was hardly a village, however, for no more than ten of its seventy homesteads were owned by peasants. Most of these belonged to townspeople, merchants, and retired soldiers. There were also more than twenty-three dachas belonging to Kyivites.[99] In February 1888 the Kyiv duma decided unanimously against the merger, the reason being (as with Demiïvka) that the city would likely spend more on local amenities and beautification than it would receive in revenues.[100]

Several years later, however, in 1894, the new duma established a new commission, this time dealing with both Shuliavka and Demiïka. Unexpectedly, the commission members voted unanimously to annex both suburbs. Of the two, Shuliavka generated less controversy. Supporters of annexation pointed to the "indissolubility of interests and life" of the inhabitants of Shuliavka and those of Kyiv; they also cited the "privileged position" the suburbanites supposedly enjoyed over Kyivites with respect to commercial and industrial activities, arising from the fact that the former "used, on a par with the latter, all the amenities of urban life, without paying the equal taxes."[101] A petition from the locals – signed by a few nobles, officials, and merchants – also demanded incorporation into Kyiv, mentioning security concerns, the lack of police services, and the urban character of Shuliavka's population. So on 27 February 1896, the city duma voted to annex Shuliavka (unanimously) and Demiivka (by an overwhelming majority of votes).[102] The governor, however, blocked the motion, most likely due to loud opposition by the local peasant communes. The peasants feared the loss of "their communal administration," the confusion that would result regarding taxes and loans, and the introduction of a municipal property tax. As the government wanted to avoid any fiscal confusion, the decision dragged on for many years.[103]

In general, there were several types of suburbs around Kyiv: industrial (among them Shuliavka); residential/commercial (Demiïvka); recreational (Pushcha Vodytsia and Sviatoshyn); and educational (Rubezhivka and a section of Shuliavka where the Kyiv Polytechnic Institute was founded in 1899). Most of these suburbs were near transportation hubs. Their quality of planning, services, and utilities was uneven. For example, those suburbs that the city had purchased from district authorities for a specific purpose (among them Pushcha Vodytsia and Sviatoshyn) fared the best in terms of planning and services provided by the city. Those that grew spontaneously, especially as working-class communities (particularly Shuliavka and Solom'ianka, where many railway workers lived), suffered from high crime rates, poor public hygiene, and a lack of the most basic utilities. There was no clear geographic pattern in determining rich and poor suburbs (although the poorer, working-class suburbs tended to emerge at the intersections of railway lines with major exit roads).

As already noted, the city itself was often reluctant to incorporate suburbs, typically citing the financial burden of providing services from the city budget. It seems that fiscal conservatives in Kyiv's municipal government almost always had the upper hand.[104] Be that as it may, it is still incredible that until the end of the Old Regime the city incorporated only a few suburbs, most notably Solom'ianka in 1910, Karavaievi Dachi in 1912, and finally Shuliavka in 1912–14.[105]

The issue of Solom'ianka reveals much about Russian imperial urbanism. Its industrial credentials were even stronger than those of Shuliavka, besides which it was strategically important as a transportation hub. The neighbourhood emerged around the city's main railway station and the Main Railway Shops (est. 1867) which soon became Kyiv's largest employer.[106] As in many European cities (like Berlin, London, and Paris), the railway tracks and the station itself were located on what at the time was edge of the densely built urban area.[107] This explains why the tracks often functioned as barriers separating new areas of expansion from the city proper. The case of Solom'ianka also suggests why suburbs themselves opposed incorporation into the city. The power of the modern city, and the limits on that power, are well illustrated by the following story.

In 1900, apparently in order to avoid municipal taxation, a group of the residents of Solom'ianka and surrounding areas (formally part of Kyiv's Bul'varna district) submitted to the central authorities a petition asking for special status for their communities.[108] In January 1901 the imperial Senate officially recognized Solom'ianka as a village belonging to Khotiv *volost* of Kyiv province (just like Demiivka farther south). Aside from lower taxes, another advantage of separate status for the locals was that they acquired the opportunity to privatize their landholdings, which until then had been owned by the city and had only been leased to Solom'ianka residents. In 1903 the emboldened local residents petitioned for the creation of a brand-new town out of Solom'ianka and neighbouring communities. The town would have been named Oleksandriia (Aleksandriia in Russian) after Nicholas II's wife, and it would have covered more than 4.8 square kilometres and comprised more than 13,000 inhabitants. But after winning a battle, the residents of the would-be secessionist town lost the war. The Kyiv city fathers somehow managed to win over Prime Minister Petr Stolypin to their side, and as a result, Oleksandriia's independent existence came to an abrupt end in 1909–10. The community was incorporated into Kyiv (albeit on preferential terms), and its new royal name reverted back to the old one, Solom'ianka. This story shows not only the reluctance of some suburbanites to join the city but also the city's growing determination to incorporate its suburbs at the beginning of the new century. Kyiv now treated the surrounding communities as its own backyard, and the municipal authorities sought to "prevent the loss of municipal lands."[109] The fate of the failed town of Oleksandriia also testified to the growing power of the city of Kyiv in the eyes of the high imperial authorities, who now had to reckon with the interests of the large metropolis.

So Oleksandriia was stillborn. But it was resurrected to some degree through the most original piece of urban design ever developed in pre-revolutionary Kyiv. Although unrealized, the 1912 plan by Kyiv civil engineer Hryhorii Dubelir masterfully applied the Garden City philosophy of the British urbanist Ebenezer Howard. A professor at the recently created Kyiv Polytechnic Institute, Dubelir proposed a large new neighbourhood that would overlap spatially with what a few years earlier had been imagined as the town of Oleksandriia.[110] As this project exceeds the chronological limits of my book, I will mention only a few things. First, the new neighbourhood would have stretched from Demiivka to Shuliavka on an elevated plateau with a huge area of 750 hectares. Second, the neighbourhood would have been as much as possible in harmony with the hilly landscape, extending along the right bank of the Lybid' River. Third, Dubelir planned to lay out streets according to their functions, separating vehicular traffic (including streetcars) from pedestrian streets.[111] Fourth, instead of levelling the heights, he called for the planting of gardens and public parks in the ravines, while reserving the heights for public buildings. Finally, the population of the neighbourhood was expected to reach 100,000 people in fifteen years. In contrast to Ebenezer Howard, however, Dubelir had as his goal not to establish a separate town or a cluster of towns, but rather to transform chaotic and slumlike working-class colonies into green suburbs. In envisioning green suburbs for Kyiv, Dubelir was in keeping with most American, British, and continental European interpretations of the Garden City.[112] He wanted to turn the new suburbs into "orderly green spaces offering to the city health and beauty."[113] It seems that Kyiv's own urbanists, while giving credit to the Garden City movement with its emphasis on "health and beauty," nonetheless remained deeply *urban* thinkers devoted to the growth of the modern city.

As we have already seen from the debates about Demiivka and Solom'ianka, the arguments for and against incorporating suburbs revolved around two facts: suburbs functioned as tax havens for those who did not want to pay higher taxes *within* the city; and while benefiting from the city's market, they did not contribute enough to its treasury.

Fiscal and more irrational social fears of incorporation were not the expression of some primordial "Russian soul," anti-urban by nature.

Instructive here are examples from Central European metropolises, which were better known for their rational urban minds than for their mysterious rural souls. Paralleling the situation in Kyiv, within the Prague agglomeration the most populous working-class suburbs successfully resisted incorporation into the city proper, contrary to the desires of the Czech urban elites.[114] The imperial authorities sided here with the "proletarian" suburbs against the "bourgeois" city of Prague – the Habsburgs (and the local German elites in Bohemia) were not ready to support the creation of a united Greater Prague as a Czech *national* metropolis. Likewise, Berlin did not grow spatially after 1861, initially because the middle-class elites opposed the incorporation of the poor industrial suburbs, and then in the 1890s because the state was reluctant to strengthen a potentially *socialist* metropolis.[115] In Warsaw, annexation of the suburbs was blocked by the two rings of military installations (forts) around the city proper.[116] In the imperial capital of Vienna, the Habsburg administration acted differently and from early on facilitated the incorporation of the inner and outer suburbs – the *Vorstädte* and *Vororte* – with especially large absorptions taking place in 1890 and in 1904–5.[117]

By the early 1900s, Kyiv more closely resembled Vienna than Prague or Berlin, for the Russian imperial authorities had embraced a more pro-urban policy, one that permitted the city to incorporate some of the larger suburbs. This did not mean, however, that irrational fears disappeared: the authorities continued to fear the influence of the Jewish bourgeoisie, and that attitude proved detrimental to the city's development. These fears were especially noticeable when it came to suburbs like Demiïvka, where Jews – particularly those engaged in trade – formed a near majority. It can be argued that the presence of Jews was the principal factor precluding the incorporation of this suburb into the city.

Another crucial matter to consider is what defined the *extent* of Kyiv's municipal borders in modern times and what distinguished this city from other imperial centres in terms of the relationship between the city core and its peripheries.

The territorial growth of Kyiv in the second half of the nineteenth century was greatly facilitated by railways and highways, which paradoxically provided the means for the city's expansion even while it controlled urban sprawl. The role of the railways was particularly important in this puzzling development. Railways required a wide radius of action as well as distance from residential areas – conditions that could only be found in river valleys.[118] So it is not surprising that the first railway line was laid out in 1870 along the valley of the Lybid' River, just southwest of the city, while the second line was constructed thirty years later in the valley of the Syrets' River, northwest of the city. "Therefore the railway underlined even more strongly the circle of natural boundaries which delimited the regularly planned Kyiv of the 19th century," wrote the city's own urban historian.[119] On the east, the Dnieper had always served as Kyiv's *natural* border; on the city's other sides, the natural frontiers were shaped by small rivers (such as the Lybid' and Syrets') and then reinforced by the railway and supplemented by a quite broad industrial "band."[120] Consequently, the railway became the new "natural and [simultaneously] artificial" factor that preserved the specific features of urban topography. This combination of natural and technological conditions caused Kyiv to grow differently than other Russian imperial cities: most of them developed industrial belts *around* the centre, whereas in Kyiv, industrial and other specialized suburbs emerged *along* major highways without forming a continuous circle around the city.[121] This saved Kyiv's middle classes residing in the city core from being stifled by "dangerous" working-class suburbs.

Also, the construction of the railway in the valley of the Lybid' River and particularly the opening of Kyiv's central railway station in 1870 changed the spatial distribution of trade and economy in the city by forcing more and more people to relocate from Podil to the areas closest to the railway. A late-nineteenth-century observer wrote about the city's pre-railway social topography, noting that in the 1860s the centre of Kyiv's trade and industrial life was still in Podil, while the area around the university (the New Building) was exclusively an administrative and educational zone, with no commercial significance. It was only with the construction of the railway that these large areas on the margins of old Kyiv became the most densely populated and built-up urban districts. "Kyiv's commercial and industrial life has been moving ever closer to the railway," he concluded.[122]

It should come as no surprise, then, that the first *comprehensively* planned community in the city emerged around the central railway station and the Main Railway Shops. The "Railway Colony" was established in the 1870s in the suburb of Upper Solom'ianka according to a well-designed plan that for the first time in local planning history applied the principle of functional zoning.[123] The production shops and warehouses of the Main Railway Shops were located in the southern part; in the centre there were rows of single-family wooden and brick houses, each surrounded by a garden; a few public buildings were located in the west (among them a hospital, an orphanage, and a chemical laboratory). The colony also contained a railway college, a boarding school, and three parks.[124] It seems that by the early twentieth century the colony's inhabitants enjoyed a far better quality of life than most Kyivites. The expansion of railways in Kyiv also solved a perennial issue: the physical alienation of the city proper from its southwestern suburbs, which had long been separated by the Lybid' River. Between 1902 and 1907, thanks to the construction of a local goods station, a few bridges and overpasses were built over the river, thus enabling a city extension in that direction.[125]

The railways and rivers also performed some of the functions of a ring road, which imperial Kyiv lacked. According to Thomas Hall, the system of outer and inner rings in European cities (such as Berlin, Brussels, Vienna, Paris, Budapest, Copenhagen, Madrid, and Stockholm) served several major purposes. First, by embracing the greater part of the built area, rings "reflected the still persistent perception of the town as a closed physical unit, with a definite boundary between itself and the surrounding countryside." Second, they served fiscal purposes by making it easier to collect tolls and to guard against smuggling. Third, they facilitated traffic, especially if combined with the radial streets, which often followed the routes of the old exit roads and linked old and new parts of a town (Budapest being the best example, with its three ring roads and many exit routes).[126]

"Natural and artificial" frontiers effectively separated Kyiv from the neighbouring "suburbs" and communities, which legally belonged to rural districts. In a fiscal sense, the railways and rivers also delineated the boundaries between the city of Kyiv and rural areas, where taxes were lower. As regards traffic, however, Kyiv was at a disadvantage compared to large European and American cities, which developed some combination of "radial" (diagonal) and concentric arteries.[127] Kyiv had acquired a main cross-axis when Volodymyrs'ka Street and Bibikovs'kyi Boulevard were laid down, but that axis for a long time was peripheral, and those arteries did not fully link the city's more remote neighbourhoods, nor did they facilitate traffic.

The closest thing to a diagonal street that Kyiv ever knew was Bibikov'skyi Boulevard and its long western extension – an old exit road to Zhytomyr. The artery linked the old city core with new districts

and suburbs and more importantly with military training grounds and
barracks just outside the city. Brest-Lytovs'ke *shosse* (or highway), as it
became known in the late nineteenth century, led straight from downtown (via boulevard) to Shuliavka, a crucial industrial suburb. It seems,
however, that no other *major* diagonal or radial artery was constructed
in late-imperial Kyiv. It is true that by the mid-nineteenth century, Old
Kyiv had been linked with new parts – the so-called New Building
(*Novoe Stroenie* in Russian) and the entire Lybid' district – via Khreshchatyk and its southern extension, Velyka Vasyl'kivs'ka Street, an old
exit road running towards Demiïvka and the town of Vasyl'kiv – hence
the name. But communications between the hilly and low-lying parts
of the city remained inadequate and often indirect.

Conclusion

The late imperial city planners added little to the network of arteries
that had existed for centuries and were then refurbished (straightened,
paved, and in some cases extended) in the first half of the nineteenth
century, especially during the time of Nicholas I (r. 1825–55). For centuries, Khreshchatyk had connected, albeit not very adequately, Podil,
Old Kyiv, and Pechers'k,[128] and no new (diagonal) arteries linking
these old districts with one another and with new parts such as Lybid'
or Luk'ianivka were created in the last decades of imperial rule. Old
Kyiv had no direct links with Lypky, situated just across Khreshchatyk;
Instytuts'ka Street stopped at the low-lying Khreshchatyk Square,
which was dominated by the huge duma building after 1876. The few
narrow, winding streets leading from there up to Old Kyiv hardly facilitated modern traffic. Old Kyiv also did not have any immediate connection with Pechers'k, and *no* street crossed Khreshchatyk, the city's major
north–south artery, which meant that Kyiv had no *central* cross-axis.[129]
Podil fared worst in terms of connections to other parts of the growing city. For centuries, the district's only link to Lypky and Pechers'k
remained the congested Oleksandrivs'kyi (Alexander's) Slope and
Oleksandrivs'ka Street, while its only link to Old Kyiv was hilly, winding Andriïvs'ka Street (aka St Andrew's Slope). Another cause of Podil's
marginalization and economic decline was the city's failure to build a
railway spur between the river port and the main railway line.[130]

Arguably, the last decades of Romanov rule in Kyiv did not bring
anything particularly new to the city shape, which had largely been created by urban planners over the previous decades, most notably from

the 1830s to the 1850s. That being said, the decades after the reintroduction of municipal autonomy dramatically refashioned architecture, urban infrastructure, and sociospatial relations in the city, turning Kyiv into the most remarkable showcase of Russian imperial urbanism in the borderlands. As the city became truly cosmopolitan, public authority and urban policy in general were increasingly defined by laissez-faire capitalism. The myth of the "holy and blessed city of Kyiv" lent historical legitimacy to the modern city, which otherwise kept erasing its tangible links to the past.

If the task of the modern city has been "to provide clean water while safely removing human waste," as urbanist Edward Glaeser has recently suggested,[131] then the Kyiv municipal authorities had achieved moderate success by 1905. Yet many critics, both at the time and later, accused the city fathers of not doing nearly enough to improve the city's infrastructure and the living conditions of the poor. This, and the persistence of conservative elements in the local Russian administration with its militaristic and xenophobic outlook, defined much of imperial urbanism in Kyiv both before and after 1905.[132] Despite its self-governing institutions and the triumph of capitalism, Kyiv as the principal city of the southwestern borderlands remained entangled in the Russian imperial agenda with its pronounced anti-urban bias and deeply rooted mistrust of change.

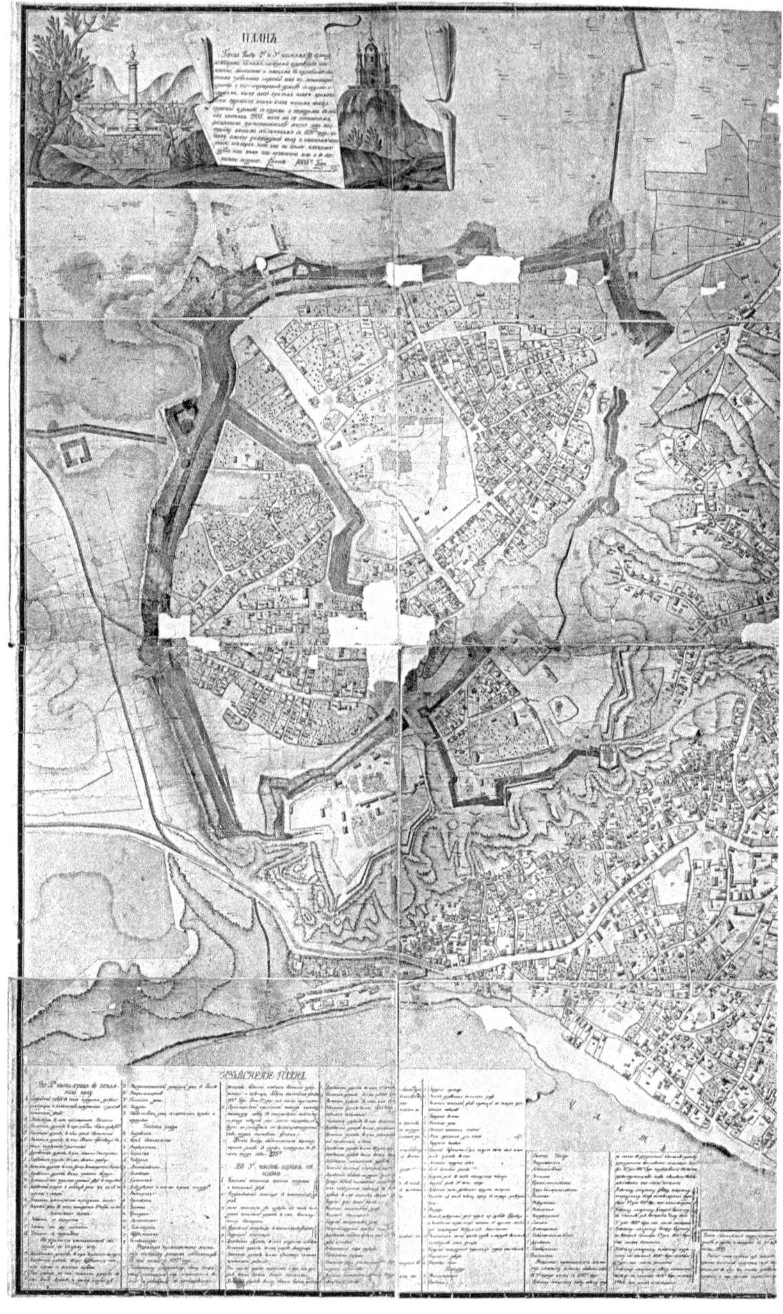

Map 7 Plan of Kyiv, 1803 (above and opposite, http://photohistory.
kiev.ua)

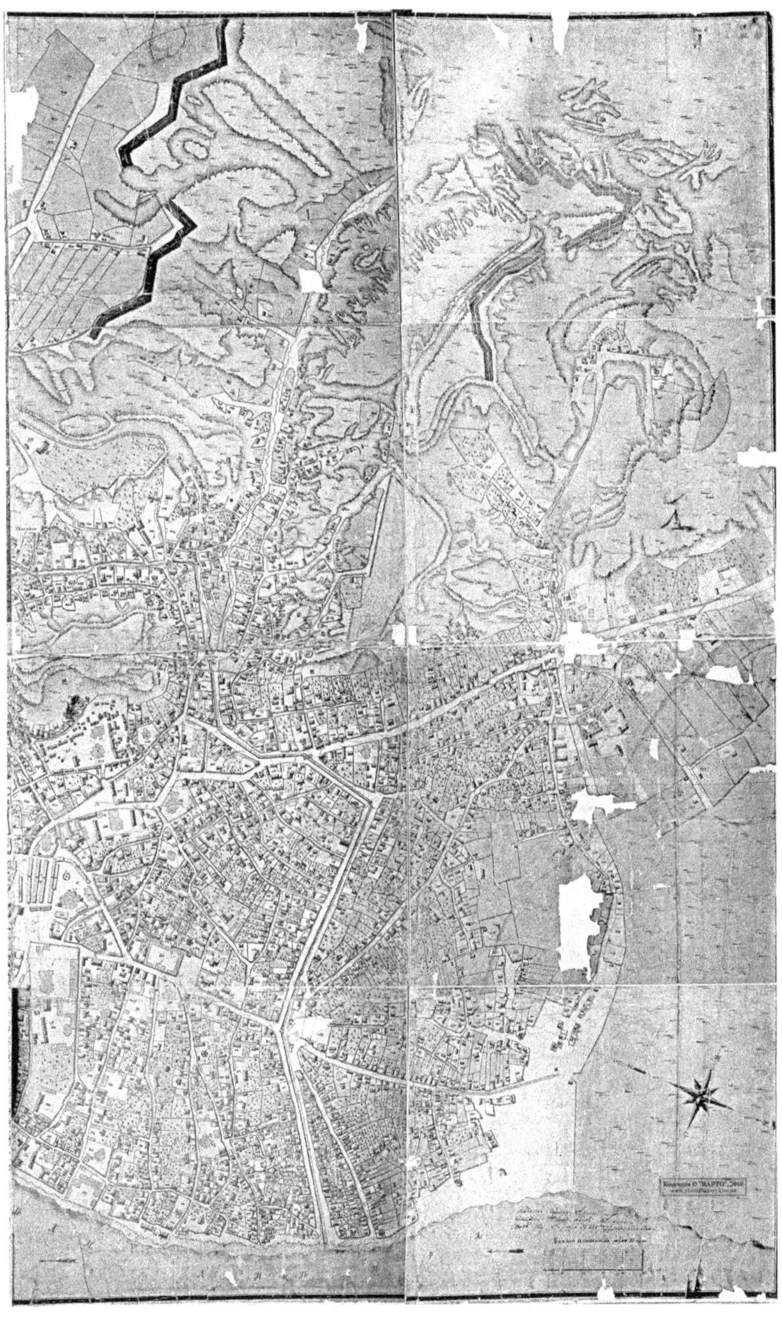

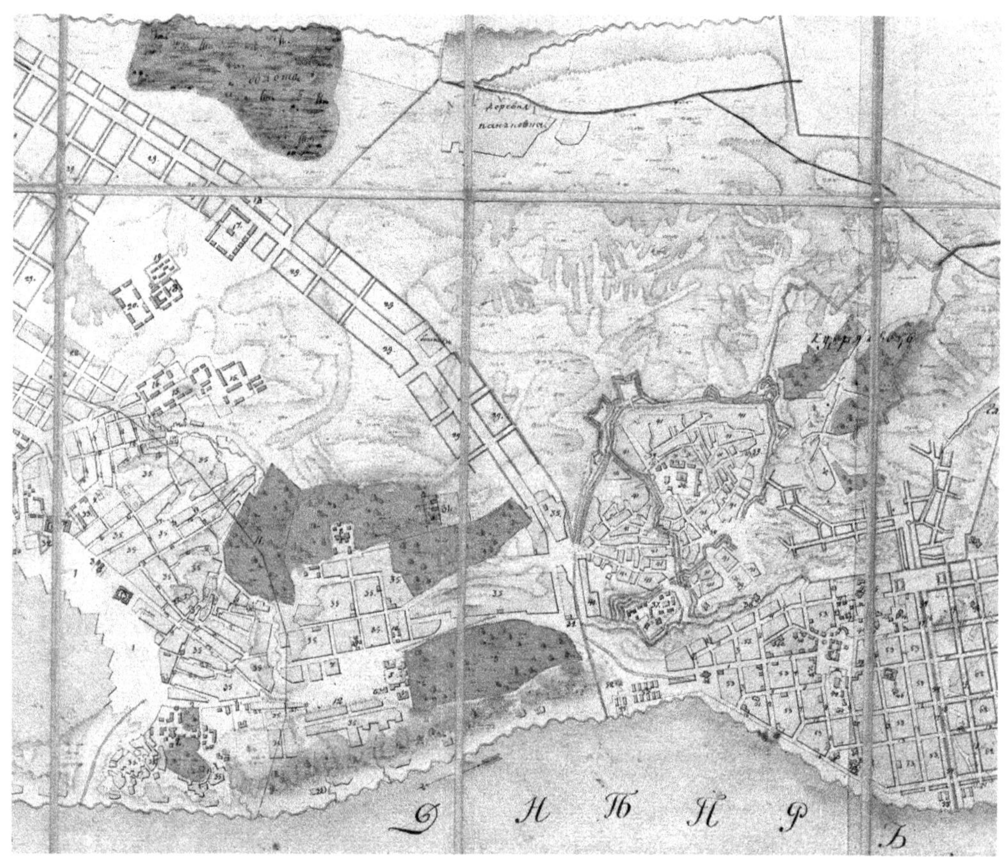

Map 8 Plan of Kyiv, 1812 (courtesy of the department of cartography of the Vernadsky National Library of Ukraine)

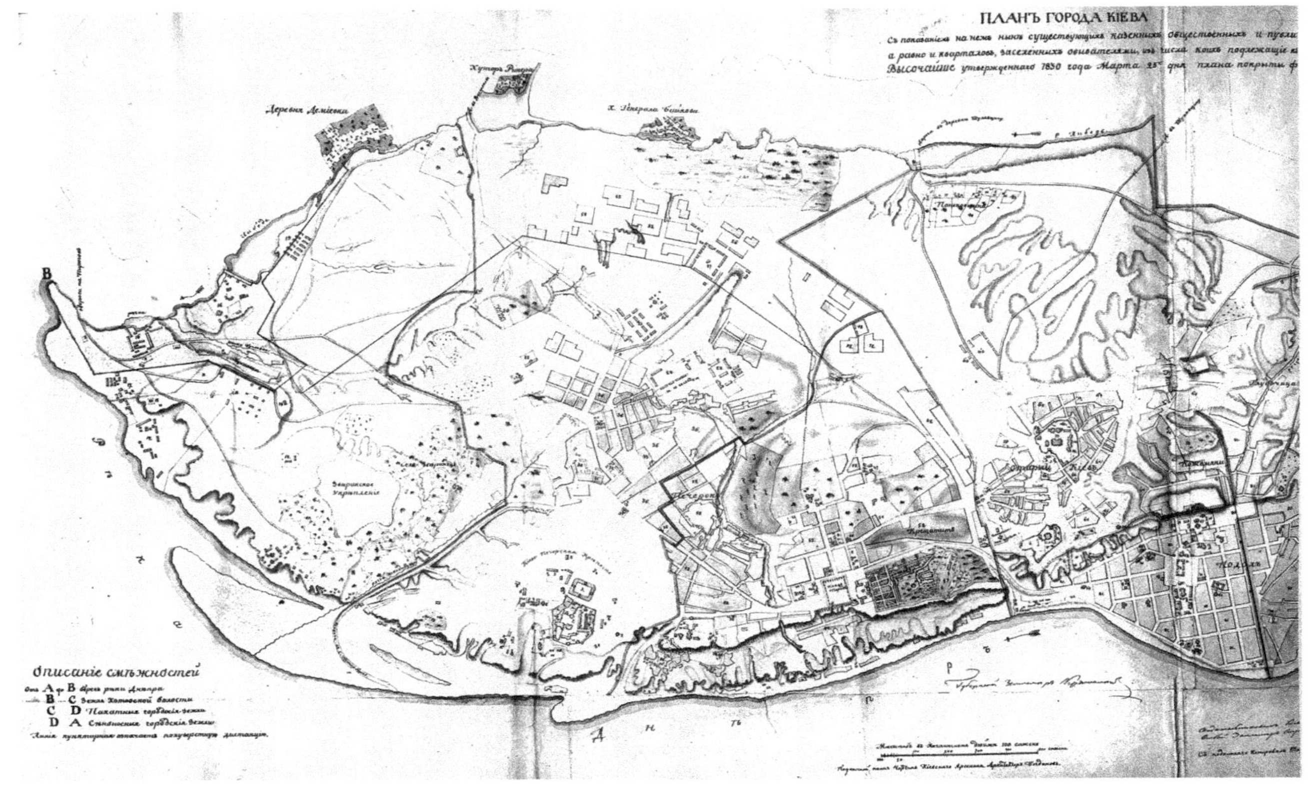

Map 9 Plan of Kyiv, 1830 (courtesy of the State Archive of the City of Kyiv, f. 239, op. 1, spr. 1a, p. 5)

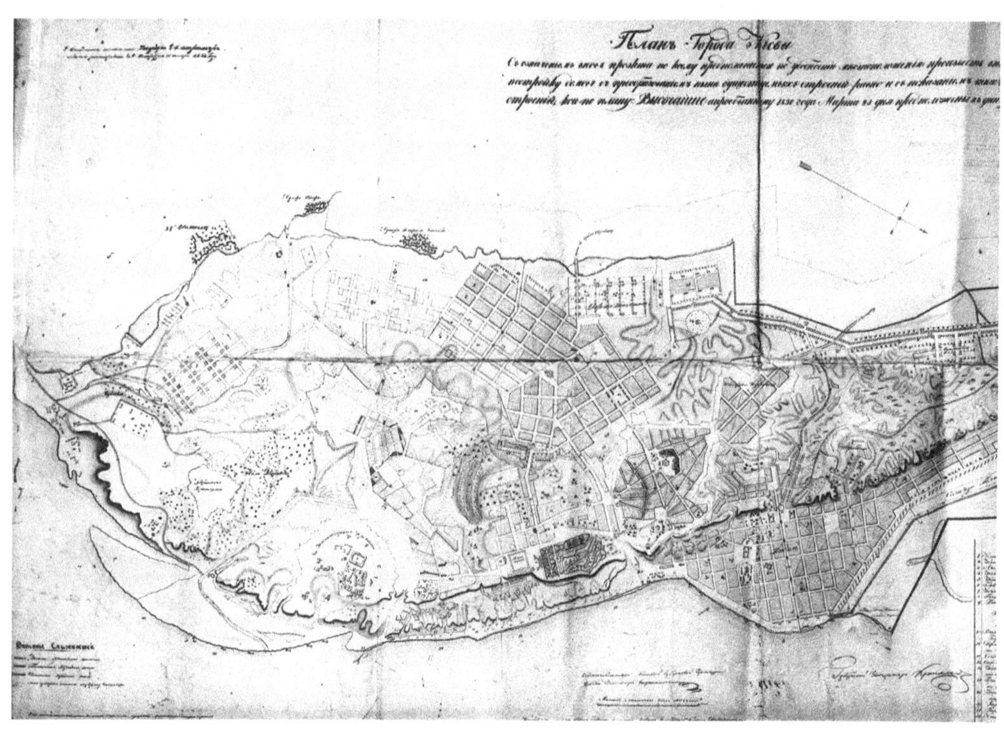

Map 10 Plan of Kyiv, 1833 (courtesy of the State Archive of the City of Kyiv, f. 239, op. 1, spr. 1a, p. 7)

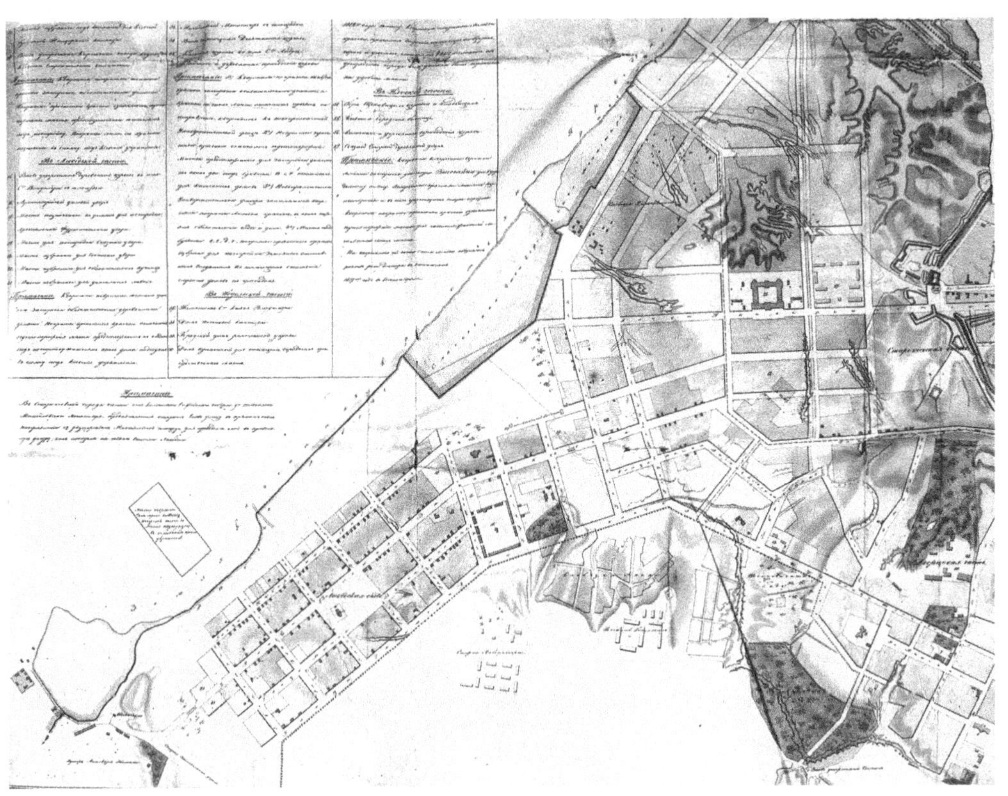

Map 11 Plan of Kyiv, 1837 (courtesy of the State Archive of the City of Kyiv, f. 239, op. 1, spr. 1a, p. 11)

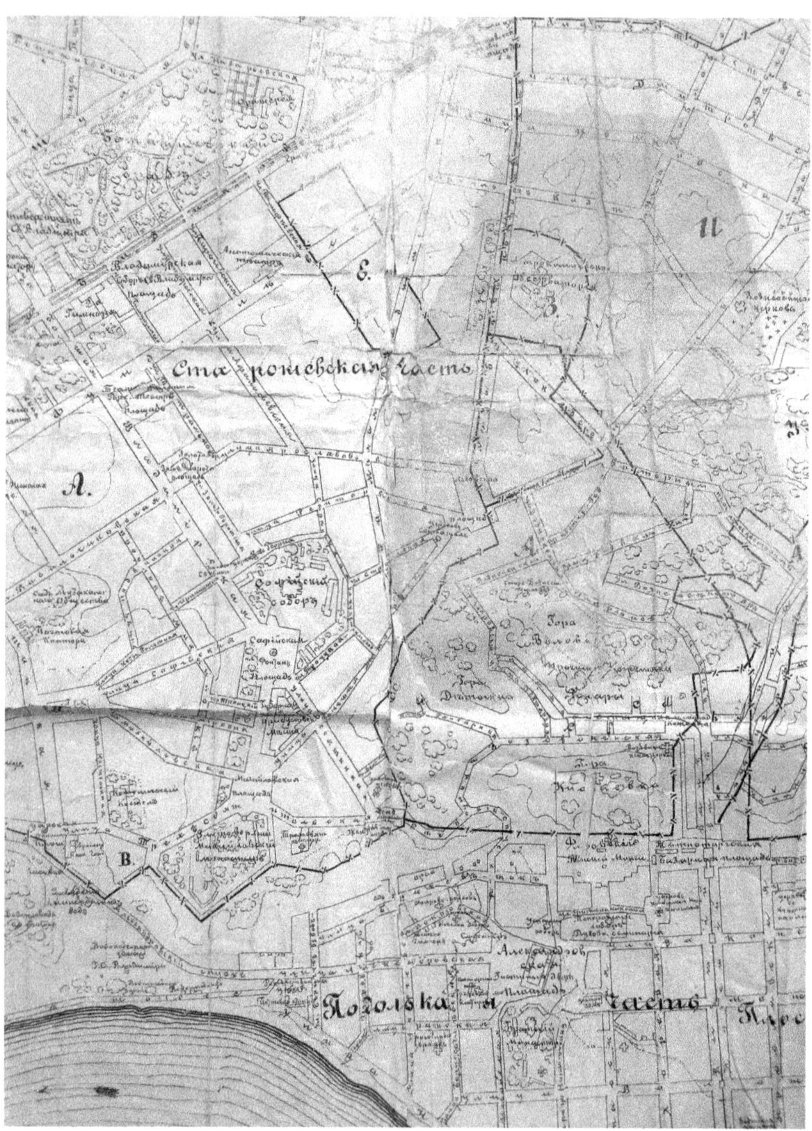

Map 12 Plan of Kyiv, 1874 (courtesy of the State Archive of the City of Kyiv, f. 163, op. 41, spr. 4545, p. 1)

PART THREE

Peopling the City

In this part I will deal first with categories and classificatory schemes used by police officials, statistical experts, scholars, and census takers to describe Kyiv's population in social, religious, and ethnographic terms.[1] The data produced by all these agents ascribed to the city dwellers their identities. It would be a mistake, however, to take these data at face value – that is, as if they were hard facts – without questioning the very classificatory schemes that produced particular categories and numbers. Can we *really* know who the Kyivites were, or even how numerous they were? What did all those social, occupational, and ethnic categories mean, and how well did they reflect social reality?[2] Perhaps we will never find comprehensive answers to these questions, but we will at least try to deconstruct both the *words* and the *numbers* that were used to describe Kyivites.

What is certain is that our knowledge about Kyivites is extremely uncertain. For a start, the very words and numbers that have routinely been used with respect to the city's population are themselves the products of highly incomplete and often unreliable sources. Those sources were usually compiled by bureaucrats, scholars, and enthusiasts with different and often incompatible loyalties and skills. Consequently, many of the sources, such as property assessment lists, statistical surveys, and scholarly writings, used very random categories and shaky classifications that were hardly compatible with one another. Therefore it is very difficult for us to form our own – scholarly – understanding of Kyivites in social and ethnographic terms, let alone reconstruct the self-perceptions of those who were classified, taxed, and assessed. If in chapter 1 we started with general impressions left by travellers, writers, and journalists who tried to grasp the elusive *personality* of the city and its diverse residents, here we will confront that impressionistic evidence with numbers and words found in major statistical sources.

Speaking of personality, both individuals and collectives could now claim some unique characteristics. Kyivites as a whole might have had one too, disclosing it to various outsiders from the beginning of the century. "Kievites are still only approaching the development of all their moral abilities that constitute a human being in a highest sense of the word."[3] These words of Vladimir Izmailov, a Russian traveller to Kyiv at the very beginning of the nineteenth century, undoubtedly referred to the "personality" of the Kyivites. He was among the first to introduce the concept of "Kyivites" into the public discourse on Kyiv. But while sentimental travellers seemed to know who the Kyivites were, the official sources presented a more complex picture: often instead of picturesque Kyivites they saw a few distinct social, occupational, and religious groups, each with a different status and jurisdiction. These groups had hardly anything to do with one another. Unlike the insightful travellers, the local experts for a long time did not perceive Kyivites as a unifying category at all.

Another important "demographic" issue to consider is that of urban elites and the "urban regimes" in Kyiv between 1800 and 1905. The concept of urban regime – famously used by Clarence Stone in his study of post–Second World War Atlanta[4] – seems incompatible with pre–First World War Kyiv, but some of Stone's urban insights may well be applicable to Russian imperial cities. The three periods in the history of imperial Kyiv can also be represented as three different urban regimes. A closer look at the structure of municipal elites will allow us to understand the nature of change in the city, which experienced abrupt discontinuities in both "formal workings" and "informal arrangements," which in turn shaped urban regimes there for over a century. Most of these issues have not been sufficiently explored by historians and urbanists dealing with modern Kyiv.

Chapter Six

Counting Kyivites: The Language of Class, Religion, and Ethnicity

Chinese Encyclopedia

The earliest "experts" in urban statistics were most likely local police officials. The official and semi-official sources they created indeed contained (or rather *produced*) certain social and religious characteristics of Kyiv's population. Although limited in scope, these sources shaped the city's social structure on the ground. Until the middle of the nineteenth century the overall understanding of who could be considered Kyivites remained quite inadequate. The situation changed markedly only with the advent of positivism, which paved the way for the creation of a comprehensive conception of Kyivites in terms of a set of measurable categories – social, cultural, occupational, and ethnographic. This new, "scientific" understanding of city residents found its fullest expression in two censuses: one semi-official, conducted by local pro-Ukrainian scholars in 1874; and the other official, the first and only imperial census of 1897.

The key category for all statistical and impressionistic visions of Kyiv's population remained religion, which played a prominent role in *all* statistical data collected by imperial officials and scholars alike. This can be seen either as a vestige of a pre-national world or as a veiled reference to more modern differences (ethnic or national). The Russian Empire long preserved numerous features of a pre-national dynastic state; after the middle of the nineteenth century, however, Russians more and more viewed themselves as a ruling *nationality* that united all Orthodox Eastern Slavs (in today's sense Russians, Ukrainians, and Belarusians). Thus any emphasis on ethnic (national) particularities was viewed as a threat to both the "all-Russian nation" and the empire in general.[1]

One should perhaps start with the tax assessments (*revizii*) conducted regularly by the local Russian authorities. Like any other colonial authorities, Russian imperial officials were perplexed by local realities and tried to squeeze Kyiv's complex demographics with its peculiar social categories into a rigid frame of imperial tax assessments. So when we look at the early *revizii*, we find ourselves in a truly Borgesian world. In his famous essay "The Analytical Language of John Wilkins" (1942), Jorge Luis Borges describes a non-Western catalogue – an alternative taxonomy of the animal world, supposedly taken from an ancient Chinese encyclopedia titled *Celestial Emporium of Benevolent Knowledge*. That catalogue lists a number of wildly incompatible things, at least to our own analytical tastes, mixing together animals that "belonged to the emperor," the "embalmed ones," "those that are trained," "suckling pigs," "mermaids," the "fabulous ones," "stray dogs," and others.[2] Just like this fictional Chinese encyclopedia, most local sources until at least the 1850s used highly peculiar categories and lacked the concept of Kyivites as a community of *all* residents (although there were some attempts to count Kyivites as early as the 1820s).

Kyiv's tax collectors cared only about the "urban" classes – burghers and artisans – and left aside other taxpayers (such as peasants living in the city) and those who did not have to pay the poll tax (primarily nobles and priests). Merchants were usually included on lists of Kyiv residents even though they paid "guild duties" instead of the poll tax. So nobles, priests, peasants, and soldiers, many of whom were permanent residents of the city, were not counted. A typical *reviziia* very much resembled the *Celestial Emporium of Benevolent Knowledge* in that it mixed social, religious, and occasionally ethnic categories (such as Gypsies), although no mermaids were ever recorded among the diverse groups of local residents. By contrast, suckling pigs, stray dogs, and cows were perhaps as numerous in Kyiv as humans. The following is a typical account of Kyiv's demographics dated 1817 (only men were counted). That year, "in Kyiv and its environs, according to the *reviziia*, there were 168 merchants of Christian religion; 15 of Jewish [religion]; 5,463 Christian burghers; 48 Gypsies; 532 Jews [burghers and artisans]; 10 foreign guests [merchants]; 53 Christian captives who have been enjoying a ten-year tax benefit (along with 5 Jews); 146 foreign expatriates enjoying a six-year tax benefit; or 6,440 men in total."[3]

One social scientist later took it as a fact that Kyiv's permanent residents in 1817 numbered 23,514.[4] All of the categories used in such assessments – from "burghers – the guild artisans" to simply "burghers" to "registered fellows" – mixed the Russian social system (with its

rather strict division into burghers and merchants) with Kyiv's autonomous tradition (which, for example, included the category of "registered fellows").[5] After 1835, Tsar Nicholas I, who was obsessed with
discipline and military parades, decided to inject modern bureaucratic
order into the tangled borderland society.

It should also be noted that Russia's social system preserved a number
of feudal vestiges in such a way that *legally* defined social estates hindered
the development of modern *economic* classes and capitalism in general.[6]
By tradition, Russia's urban population was split into several social estates
that enjoyed different rights. This system was introduced in Kyiv at the end
of the eighteenth century. For most of the following century the burghers
proper (*meshchane*) were a minority in most cities of the empire, numbering
fewer than two million men in mid-century, or one-third of all those living
in a urban environment. The rest were peasants who traded in the markets or worked in crafts (outside the guild system), or they were nobles,
officials, merchants, soldiers, and so on. Catherine II, in the late eighteenth
century, was the first to create "townspeople" as a legal category – one that
had, quite ambiguously, both modern economic and more traditional legal
connotations. Born and raised in Germany, Catherine brought to Russia
a typically European concept of the urban middle classes by introducing
the category of "urban dwellers in general,"which included all those who
resided in cities and engaged in trade, crafts, arts, and sciences – that is,
most non-nobles and non-peasants. This was an attempt by an enlightened
autocrat to bring Russia closer to Europe by incorporating an idea of the
third estate into her vast domain.

The social reality, however, proved much more complicated. Hence
Catherine's law was full of contradictions. For example, the law retained
a narrower feudal definition of "townspeople" as a distinct social estate
consisting of petty traders, shopkeepers, artisans, and beggars.[7] Law and
practice then separated burghers (*meshchane*) from merchants (*kuptsy*), a
privileged urban bourgeoisie with capital greater than 500 (later 1,000)
rubles, who were not subject to the poll tax. The situation was also
marked, in the words of historian Daniel Brower, by an "extraordinary
degree of disarray and disregard for both legal norms and state-imposed
regulations." In this sense, nineteenth-century Russian urbanism encompassed both a "caste-like hierarchical order and disorder."[8] This confusing social reality complicated the language used in official sources for
describing Kyiv's population.

The linguistic confusion and mental uncertainty of imperial classifi-
ers affected Kyiv's municipal elite in particular. Merchants, as a legally

defined trading group, were prominent in the administrations of all Russian pre-reform cities. In Kyiv, however, the municipal elite was broader, consisting of an informal coalition of merchants and other related social groups, such as *grazhdane* (roughly translated as "citizens"). The latter were an elite group that included, at different times, wealthy merchants, wholesale traders, professionals, and all those who had ever held elected office in the municipal government. As we will see later, in Kyiv prior to 1835 all eligible voters (merchants, *grazhdane*, prominent artisans) comprised a vaguely defined category of *pochetneishee gradskoe obshchestvo* (the most venerable municipal society), a close-knit group of municipal elites that numbered around 200 members.[9]

Before the abolition of the Magdeburg Law, "non-urban" social groups, including the nobles, played no significant role in municipal affairs. This reflected a general Russian practice. Nobles who owned real estate in cities formally belonged to the "true urban dwellers" (a category introduced by Catherine II in 1785), but legal and administrative practice tended to exlude nobles, peasants, and all those who could be considered professionals from municipal society. Instead, that society was comprised of three obvious "urban" groups: merchants, burghers, and guild artisans (*tsekhovye*). The members of other social groups were labelled "non-urban estates" and as a consequence were excluded from municipal governance almost everywhere in Russia. According to a report by Russia's interior minister, a significant proportion of city dwellers, despite owning some urban real estate, was "almost totally excluded" from participation in municipal government.[10] The municipal commune encompassed predominantly the lower social estates. In this situation, urban pursuits (including municipal service) did not enjoy much respect among the empire's educated public.

To illustrate some of the points stated above, we will take a look at real estate assessment lists compiled by imperial officials from the 1830s to the 1860s. The earliest preserved materials are from 1835 and 1836 and list all homeowners in the city, whatever their gender, class, occupation, religion, and ethnicity.[11] The lists are still Borgesian in style, but they often apply alphabetical order and divide large neighbourhoods into smaller quarters (*kvartaly*). Where Borges (or rather John Wilkins) lists diverse animals, our files list no less diverse humans; they also provide information so peculiar that any modern classification seems virtually impossible. For example, in the file from the Lybid' district, we find that a fellow named Andronov is a glass cutter "serving" in the

Kyiv military hospital, that his wife, Avdot'ia Osipovna, sells fruit at a local market, and that they most likely built (rather than purchased or inherited) their house. Mikhail Bubnov is a third-guild merchant who owns an empty plot but resides elsewhere (in Podil). Semen Bondarevs'kyi, an official of the ninth rank, is married, has five children, lives in a new house, and serves in an institution with a cryptic name – the Kyiv Commission's Commissariat Depot (which, quite prosaically, turns out to be an office responsible for supplying Russian troops stationed in the region). Ivan Demiev is a fifty-five-year-old old retired soldier, married, with two children; his wife "bakes and sells bread." And the list goes on, providing the names of 260 other owners – many soldier's widows, a few nobles, a couple of dozen arsenal workers (with particular occupations – locksmith, blacksmith, or simply "factory hand"), and numerous non-commissioned officers (often listed with a specific rank).

We also encounter more uniform lists. For instance, in one private real estate register, from Plos'ka district in 1836, all noble owners – from the lowliest civil servants and non-commissioned officers to generals and wealthy landowners – are listed *separately*, as members of a privileged social group ("officials and nobles"), setting them apart from "urban classes," peasants, and all plebeian homeowners.[12] In general, however, ownership of private property increasingly united all social categories, however different they were, so as to form a modern concept of urban residents – that is, Kyivites.

To be sure, the bureaucratic authors of all these lists were concerned first and foremost about particular houses and their values. People appeared on the lists only insofar as they were municipal taxpayers, and for the purpose of taxation any further classification may seem redundant. Still, it is surprising how much unrelated information was given about each particular homeowner. Perhaps the goal was to better locate taxpayers in space and in society; if so, it explains why police officials gathered as much information as possible about all potential wrongdoers. In a way, taxing *was* policing. Later in the century, when the police became more effective – not least as a result of Bibikov's personal intervention – the police records were separated from taxation records. As a result, the real estate listings from 1849, 1863–4, and 1869 eliminated much of the irrelevant information about individuals while also expanding entries on individual properties – their market value, the taxes paid (or still owed) on them, and their location, along with detailed descriptions. Information about homeowners, by contrast, was reduced to names and very generic social ranks (official, official's widow, soldier, etc.).

With the rise of positivist scholarship in Russia around 1860, a few attempts were made to provide scholarly statistical information about Kyivites. The first attempt at counting Kyivites for scholarly rather than restricted fiscal purposes was made much earlier by the city's own biographer, Maksym Berlyns'kyi, first in 1799 and then again in 1820. In his unpublished but pioneering history of the city, Berlyns'kyi approached modern Kyiv as an administrative unity of its historical parts, a concept made possible by the centralizing policies of the Russian imperial authorities. Yet in 1799 he still struggled with the concept of an amalgamated city as he counted and characterized residents of each historical part *separately*. He even sometimes called each of those parts – Podil, Old Kyiv, and Pechers'k – a "town."[13]

Describing the "original residents of Kyiv-Podil [*Kievopodol*]," he wrote that they were "largely Little Russian by descent and partially Polish [here, natives of the ex-Polish Right-Bank Ukraine], which is why in their mores, customs, behavior, and clothes they are similar to these nations."[14] They spoke pure Ukrainian even though most of them were migrants to the city ("a rare household could trace their roots back more than 100 years"). Most of them dressed in Ukrainian fashion (*kaftany, cherkesky, bekeshi,* and *kuntushi*) and had traditional haircuts. Not surprisingly, Podil contained the largest number of private houses (2,135) and was the most populous of the three city parts. Its inhabitants – most of them burghers, with some merchants – were administered by the magistrate. Podil, however, was becoming more socially diverse, and by the time Berlyns'kyi gathered his statistics more than 200 households belonged to *raznochintsy* (non-burghers and non-nobles), who did not fall within the jurisdiction of the magistrate. All in all, Podil was home to 12,596 "souls" of "all conditions [*vsiakogo zvaniia*] and both genders."

Compared to Podil, the populations of Pechers'k and Old Kyiv were much more diverse, described by Berlyns'kyi as "*raznochintsy*, out-of-town, and recently settled, always different from Podil [residents] by clothes and customs." Pechers'k in particular had a large population of Russian merchants, Jews (newcomers to the city), the military (retired and on active service), and officials. This neighbourhood, the seat of the Russian imperial authorities, was second-largest in terms of private housing (1,058 households) and population (5,446 "souls"). A third historical part of the recently amalgamated city – Old Kyiv – was still dominated by two ancient religious institutions – St Sophia Cathedral and St Michael's Monastery. The district was also populated by a mix of people – primarily retired officers and soldiers, but also petty officials, burghers, and state peasants. This part contained 536 private households that housed 2,534 "souls."[15] Berlyns'kyi avoided giving an aggregate number of Kyiv residents (20,576), perhaps because Kyivites, for him, were still unfathomable as a social and demographic concept.

Twenty years later, in his classic work *Kratkoe opisanie Kieva* (Brief Description of Kyiv), he provided a number for the civilian population – "residents of all estates and of both genders" – 23,514. This total included several social groups – clergy (435), nobles of male gender (1,164), merchants (279), burghers paying taxes (5,956 men), and serfs (580).[16] But he did not know what to do with other categories of Kyiv residents – monks and nuns, all the military, state officials without their own houses or residing temporarily, their servants, non-residents such as students and journeymen, and finally all the Jews, that is, all those "whose one-time number is impossible to establish." Using more detailed birth and death data from church records, Berlyns'kyi concluded that the real number of *only* Orthodox Kyivites had to be no less than 42,000 and perhaps more than 45,000 (again excluding Jews and other "aliens").[17] Although these numbers were most likely exaggerated, his overall approach to Kyiv's demographics pointed to the new understanding of the city as a spatial, historical, and social unity.

In 1847 appeared the statistics in Ivan Funduklei's edited volume *Obozrenie Kieva*. In its introduction, Mykhailo Maksymovych presented Kyiv population data, most likely based on police records. So he wrote that there were about 50,000 permanent residents of both genders. To that figure he added another 6,000 people residing in the city temporarily, coming there "for work and business," and 13,500 military personnel billeted in the city. And to this he added religious pilgrims who visited the city during the summer months, numbering somewhere between 50,000 and 80,000.[18]

The Rise of Scholarly Statistics

The next significant step in the statistical assessment of the city's population was largely the work of a single man, the trained statistician and economist Dmitrii Zhuravskii, who compiled "The Statistical Description of the Kyiv Province" (published under the name of the Kyiv civil governor Funduklei, who had commissioned the work).[19] The author even tried to reconstruct population data for previous years, going back to the late eighteenth and early nineteenth centuries. Based on municipal tax records, he estimated that Kyiv's "permanent residents" in 1798 numbered 19,000 souls. It appeared that 68 per cent of these people (13,041) were real estate owners (*khaziaeva*) and their families; tenants, servants, and workers together numbered 6,040, or 32 per cent of the population. This could only mean that the city's economy was still dominated by small owners – artisans and traders – and that the number of hired workers was small. In addition, there was an unknown number of temporary residents and visitors, such as pilgrims, Jews, military men, workers, and merchants. Judging from the birth and death rates among permanent and temporary residents, Zhuravskii estimated that in the period 1796 to 1800 there were around 30,000 people in the city.[20]

An extremely valuable section of the volume compared Kyiv's population statistics for 1835 and 1845. The language of description was still quite traditional, based largely on social estates, but the approach to the numbers was scientific rather than narrowly fiscal. Kyiv's entire population was split into permanent, temporary, and peripatetic, each category containing different social estates and economic groups, from wealthy landowners to day labourers. The permanent population included all city residents and also troops permanently quartered in the city. Apart from the military, it was estimated that in 1845 there were 50,137 permanent residents in the city compared to 29,000 in 1835.[21] Together with the permanently stationed military (13,339 soldiers and officers),[22] the total number of permanent residents in 1845 was 64,000. The social data also included the "temporary" civilian population – merchants, peasants, and all other migrant workers with valid work and residence permits (*pasporta*) – 56,971 civilians in total (or 71,000 if we add permanent military residents). Table 6.1 reflects both the language of social description and the most important changes the local society experienced during the decade between 1835 and 1845.[23]

The changes were remarkable: despite their notable numerical growth, the shares of nobles, merchants, and burghers in Kyiv's overall population had dramatically decreased, while the shares of peasants and clergy had markedly increased. Yet the percentage of nobles, officials, and clergy in Kyiv was remarkably high, which set this centre of the southwestern borderlands apart from other Russian cities.[24] This was certainly not a sign of modernization, although the dramatic rise in the percentages of peasants, *raznochintsy* (the kernel of a nascent intelligentsia), and discharged soldiers in Kyiv's population pointed to growing opportunities in the private and public sectors – opportunities ranging from domestic service to teaching jobs to manufacturing and

Table 6.1 Social and economic groups in Kyiv, 1835 and 1845 (%)

Socio-economic groups	1835	1845
I. Clergy and church servants		
Orthodox	728 (2.5)	2,091 (3.7)
Catholic	8	9
II. Nobles		
Hereditary	3,477	4,533
Personal	2,379	4,768
Total nobles	*5,856 (20)*	*9,301 (16)*
III. Trade and crafts		
Merchants I guild	0	32
Merchants II guild	35	160
Merchants III guild	570	1,133
Total merchants	*605 (2)*	*1,325 (2)*
Burghers and artisans	17,440 (60)	21,851 (38)
IV. Various ranks		
Raznochintsy	557 (2)	3,232 (5.7)
Freed serfs	39	752
State peasants	405	2,084
Serfs	687	1,544
House serfs	972	2,714
Former magistrate peasants	223	288
Total peasants	*2,287 (8)*	*6,342 (11)*
Discharged soldiers and their families	710 (2.4)	4,518 (8)
Foreigners	542	866
Students in various schools		3,546

Source: Funduklei, *Statisticheskoe opisanie Kievskoi gubernii*, 349–50.

retail.[25] The city was becoming increasingly attractive to newcomers,[26] and this would strongly challenge the traditional social vocabulary. From now on all bureaucratic experts would struggle with words as they tried to define and classify an ever-changing urban society.

Besides providing the aforecited table based on social ranks, Funduklei boldly attempted to present a more nuanced social profile of Kyiv's workforce around 1845, mixing the categories of social estate, economic class, and occupation. First, he estimated that around 34 per cent of the population (17,000 permanent residents) belonged to the upper classes either by income (the owners of "commercial and industrial enterprises") or through their social estate (nobles and priests), with their income derived from real estate and government salaries. The majority of Kyivites, however, belonged to the "middle and poor classes [*sostoianiia*]" and earned their living with their hands, primarily in crafts, agriculture, gardening, carting, and day labour.

The detailed table grouped all artisans into six classes of trade and also divided them into locals and non-residents (*inogorodnye*).[27] The total number of artisans was 7,148, with non-residents comprising almost half of all artisans (3,189), the best evidence that Kyiv already was very attractive to outsiders. Most of these outsiders – 2,868 masters, journeymen, and apprentices – were employed in construction as carpenters, masons, plasterers, and so on. Construction was heavily dominated by "non-residents" (96%) – that is, by seasonal workers, often serfs from Great Russia, where they formed cooperatives (*arteli*) on their landlords' estates. In all other branches, non-residents were clearly minorities: 5 per cent in the food industry, 9 per cent in the clothing industry, 10 percent in the making of adornments and luxury articles, 13 per cent in the production of various household items. Most artisanal workshops were small enterprises in which the owner/master was the sole worker (exceptions to this were certain labour-intensive crafts such as tailoring, shoemaking, and blacksmithing). It was likely that crafts supported around 15,000 Kyivites of both genders and of all ages. The remaining 18,000 Kyivites made a living as farmers, market gardeners, carriers, day labourers, servants, and workers. Some of them, especially freight carriers, could grow quite rich.

The most pressing social and (sociological) issue facing imperial experts for decades was the presence of a large military population in the city. Men in uniform – permanently residing in barracks and private apartments, as well as temporarily "gathering in camps" – easily outnumbered the city's permanent civilian residents: around 62,000 military to 50,137 civilians in 1845, not including the staggering number of soldiers and officers (around 62,000) "passing through the city" (but often staying for a time in people's houses).[28] As the principal city in the Southwestern Region, a borderland confronted with real and imaginary dangers, Kyiv had been overwhelmed with soldiers and officers, especially after it had been designated a city-fortress. Hence no one could agree on the exact size of Kyiv's population and whether permanent military residents were to be included.

The first comprehensive census of Kyiv's population addressed some of these issues. Conducted in 1863 by the officials of the Kyiv provincial statistical committee, that census was unprecedented in scope and revolutionary in intent.[29] But it still described the local demographics in traditional terms – social and religious – ignoring any ethnic and linguistic categories. Following in Funduklei's footsteps, the statisticians represented Kyiv's population as a community of permanent and temporary residents – the Kyivites – not simply as homeowners attached to their properties or as members of distinct social estates. The total number of residents amounted to 70,341 (53,251 permanent, 17,090 temporary).[30] This approach to census taking was as scientific as one could get in Kyiv at that time. The statistical committee sent out a uniform questionnaire to every house, asking both homeowners and tenants (another novelty!) to fill out the form; this task had been largely completed by 20 January 1863.[31] A clear sign of the modern times was that those homeowners who permanently resided outside Kyiv were to be included in the category of temporary residents, while tenants absent from the city for only a short time were to be counted as permanent residents. This was a timely recognition of tenants, who, whatever their social estate, often were frowned upon as not quite full urban citizens.

So the census takers imagined Kyiv's population as divided along several major lines: social estate, gender, temporality, religion, and locality. Social estate remained a major category of description, although compared to previous attempts (like Zhuravskii's), the 1863 data gatherers used more general entries. The census included several entries denoting social status:[32] nobles (12,207, or 17 percent); clergy of all denominations (4,034, or 5.7 per cent); "urban estates" (23,589, or 33.5 per cent); "rural estates" (11,086, or 15.8 per cent); "military estates" (17,815, or 25 per cent)[33]; foreigners (897, or 1 percent); and those who belonged to none of the above (511, or 0.7 per cent). The percentage of nobles in the city remained remarkably high; this included the many nobles from the provinces who had flocked to the city to find employment in the public service. The relatively small percentage of peasants in Kyiv pointed to a fact that the city was still mainly an administrative and military centre in which trade and manufacture played a lesser role.

The 1863 census confirmed Funduklei's finding that the city contained an enormous number of troops. It should be mentioned, however, that many of those who belonged to "military estates" – especially retired servicemen and their wives and children – in their lifestyle and daily pursuits were indistinguishable from the mass of Kyiv burghers and peasants. In this regard, the Russian imperial army was very much a people's army.[34]

In terms of gender, the city's population was rather heavy with men (39,328 men to 31,013 women). Again, this can be explained by the huge number of servicemen stationed in Kyiv (including the retirees).

Regarding permanent and temporary residents, the census takers chose a very sensible approach, defining the former (47,479) as those who engaged in "full-time specific pursuits" and the latter (20,945) as those who had permanent residence elsewhere but who stayed in the city for a limited period of time (e.g., for casual employment). Importantly, Kyiv residents were now defined through a new set of socio-economic criteria – property, residence (even if temporary), and daily pursuits that linked various private individuals to the city. Religion was perhaps still important, but it was only one of several categories. The census included all possible religious denominations that could be encountered in European Russia.[35] As expected, the Orthodox were the largest group, claiming 58,910 men and women (84 per cent); Roman Catholics came second with 8,604 believers (12 per cent); Jews, who had just been allowed to settle in Kyiv, numbered 1,411 (2 per cent); Lutherans accounted for 973 people (1 per cent). There were two branches of Old Believers – the so-called *edinovertsy*, numbering 48 men and women (0.6 per cent), and the Dissenters (pejoratively known in Russia as *raskol'niki*), numbering 380 (0.5 per cent). Muslims and Karaim also made the list, with the total of 12 men. Thus Kyivites were represented as a truly diverse community of municipal taxpayers and all those who were connected to the city through residence, real estate, service, trade, crafts, and casual employment. A rich Jewish merchant who had recently moved to the city from a *shtetl*, a Polish landowner, a peasant selling produce at Podil market, and a Kyiv-born beggar – all were now Kyivites in the eyes of a positivist social scientist.

But the traditional social estates were still alive and kicking. As has been already shown, the pre-1870 municipal system was confusing and almost completely dependent on government supervision. Social reforms, particularly the new municipal statute of 1870, had addressed many of the contradictions of the previous urban regime and had opened it up for the participation of nobles and professionals. This was a way for the government to counter the influence of uncultivated merchants, many of them Old Believers.[36]

The greater participation of nobles could only be achieved at the expense of other social groups. The government, therefore, sought to limit the involvement of both poor burghers who owned little more than a rundown shack and wealthy merchants who dominated the pre-reform urban regimes in most cities of the empire, including Kyiv. The reform was not intended to change ownership patterns or to abolish social estates in cities. Rather, the purpose was to "reset" the municipal order so as to allow the "educated classes" to participate in urban affairs through elections and governance. Nobles and government officials were very well represented among the electoral category of homeowners, a voting block that comprised somewhere between 60 and 90 per cent of all eligible voters in large and medium-sized cities. The government, however, miscalculated the electoral activities of its favoured citizens. Due to the very low activity (absenteeism) of "homeowners" (the category to which most noble voters belonged), the majority in most municipal councils still consisted of merchants and burghers.[37]

Socialism, Sociology, Census

In the early 1870s, Kyiv was growing at an unprecedented pace and its society was changing rapidly. The city's social and ethnic profile was also changing, to the constant dismay of conservative imperial observers. But it was liberals, not conservatives, who embarked on the most daring statistical enterprise to date: a comprehensive census of the Kyiv population conducted on a single day in March 1874. Organized by the Southwestern (Kyiv) branch of the Russian Imperial Geographic Society, the 1874 census grasped a city in transition from a frontier outpost to an emerging imperial metropolis whose rapid growth was being facilitated by the sugar beet industry and not least by the expansion of the railways.[38] And this time (in contrast to the 1863 census), the men behind the numbers and the words were not loyal imperial officials but suspect Ukrainian activists who would later be accused of infiltrating a respectable research institution.[39] Besides being pro-Ukrainian, some of the census organizers were prominent socialist thinkers in the Russian Empire.[40] Statistics at the time was a young science that was attracting many radically minded scholars, who viewed the study of numbers as part of an important social mission to improve the lives of the common people. Many conservatives, not without reason, openly accused statisticians of stirring up trouble. Numbers could be just as dangerous as words.

Yet as the official story goes, the initiative to conduct a census in Kyiv came from the local governor general, Aleksander Dondukov-Korsakov, in 1873.[41] In response, a prominent historian and a member of the Kyiv branch of the Russian Geographic Society, Volodymyr Antonovyh, who happened to be a leading Ukrainian activist, suggested that the society could take it upon itself to conduct the census. A special commission was established, one that included several scholars with strong

Ukrainian sympathies, such as Antonovych, the ethnographer Pavlo Chubyns'kyi, the teacher and archaeologist Volodymyr Berenshtam, and others, who would act as census supervisors in the city's few districts. There were also 450 local volunteers, mostly students at Kyiv St Vladimir University and the Kyiv Theological Academy, who would serve as census "foot soldiers," gathering data through house-to-house visits.

The real head of the enterprise, albeit informally, was the economist and statistician Mykola (Nikolai) Ziber, a university instructor and a pioneering Marxist scholar.[42] According to one contemporary source, it was Ziber himself and his radical colleagues who suggested a one-day Kyiv census; only later was the idea adopted by the governor general.[43] These activist-scholars changed the whole agenda of statistical questioning by introducing Marxist and nationalist discourses.[44] The former was reflected in the particular attention paid to the workforce, economic classes, and residential poverty; the latter was masked by a series of entries about language and the geographic origins of various social and occupational groups of Kyivites. The issue of language was controversial in itself and provoked heated criticism from the right.[45] More importantly, in their positivist zeal the organizers treated the census as a scholarly enterprise rather than an attempt at fiscal control or policing (although it proved difficult to convince the anxious population that the census was not about heavier taxation, stricter passport controls, or the expulsion of Jews). Another revolutionary decision by the organizers concerned the treatment of space: it was decided that the census would cover both the city and its closest suburbs such as Demiïvka and Solom'ianka, populated largely by urban residents, many of them Jews.

In these and in many other respects the 1874 census was different from the one conducted by provincial statisticians in 1863. Another important difference concerned the size of the result: it was huge. It was also detailed to an unprecedented degree – 400 pages long and with hundreds of tables.[46] Yet another significant difference was its far greater use of spatiality as an integral part of the city's demographic profile (discussed more fully in chapter 8). Here I will touch on only the most important thematic tables that described Kyiv's population with regard to gender, religion, social status, language, and ethnicity. The census organizers pointedly avoided dividing the population into permanent and temporary residents, perhaps because in the modernizing metropolis it had become almost impossible to maintain that division.[47] Also, the census was affected by the two most pervasive of all modern

Table 6.2 Kyivites' places of birth, circa 1874 (%)

Kyiv	Ukraine	Russia	Belarus	Kingdom of Poland	The Baltic	Caucasus	Siberia and Central Asia	Abroad
36,005 (28)	57,865 (45)	16,872 (13)	10,515 (8)	2,371 (1.9)	761 (0.6)	270 (0.2)	189 (0.1)	2,170 (1.7)

political mythologies – that of class and that of nationality. Finally, the Kyiv population was represented as a municipal commune, united by residence, employment, and municipal politics.

Both the language of description and the city's demographics had changed drastically in numerical and qualitative terms since the previous census of 1863. The language tried to catch up with the growing complexity on the ground. The population of Kyiv had almost doubled since 1863; it now totalled 127,251 (71,848 men, 55,403 women), and showed a gender imbalance considerably higher than before; this can be explained by the ever-growing number of male workers in the city.[48] The 1874 census raised the spectre of nationality (see table 6.2), disguised as the "division of population according to a place of birth and ethnographic regions."[49] Place of birth and "ethnographic region" did not necessarily refer to a certain ethnicity/nationality, but these categories well reflected the fashion for "ethno-schematization,"[50] a pattern of spatial imagination that sought to map ethnicity in cartography and beyond.

The language used by the census takers does not allow us to establish the national composition of Kyivites with any precision, but we can make a few safe assumptions. First, by the early 1870s Kyiv had become a city of migrants; an overwhelming majority of residents (more than 70 per cent) were born outside the city. Second, a large majority were born in what is now Ukraine,[51] and most of them were almost certainly ethnic Ukrainians (minus a few thousand Jews and Poles). Third, ethnic Russians were a clear (if visible) minority – an undisputable fact that the Ukrainian census organizers were only happy to emphasize.[52] The category of "ethnicity," however, was conspicuously absent from the census.

Another way to describe this proverbial elephant in Kyiv's municipal room was through language and religion. Religion had for centuries been a mainstay in censuses and was perhaps the earliest category that had been used to classify Kyiv's population. The religious labels in 1874 were slightly different from those used in 1863, but generally they

referred to the same communities. The largest group united the Orthodox with Armenian-Grigorian believers, and together they comprised
98,698 people in the city and its suburbs (more than 77 per cent).[53] Jews
came second with 13,803 men and women (almost 11 per cent of the
entire population). Catholics trailed in third place, with 10,409 people
(or 8 per cent). Other notable groups included Protestants (2,740, or
2 per cent) and Old Believers (*staroobriadtsy*) and Dissenters/*raskol'niki*
(1,182, or 0.9 per cent). There were also *edinovertsy*, Uniates, Karaim,
Muslims, and, most exotic of them all, the "Heathen," each of these
groups comprising fewer than 200 people.

The category of "language" was more problematic. In Russian geographical and statistical works, "language" had long been used to
indicate the dominance of "Russians" in the Russian Empire.[54] This
time, however, the category of language was more controversial,
for pro-Ukrainian scholars were applying it to show the presence of
Ukrainians and Belarusians. The organizers came up with an idea that
was awkward in terms of scholarship but politically brilliant: they
split the conventional Russian language (*russkii iazyk*) into several
unconventional categories – three "dialects" (*narechiia*) and, more
bizarrely, one entirely new "language" (*iazyk*).[55] Those who spoke the
"Russian language" in Kyiv and its suburbs formed a clear majority –
98,205 people, or 77 per cent of the population, a number that almost
equalled that of Orthodox believers. This seemed to confirm a widely
shared belief that the empire's Orthodox were "Russians" and that the
true Russians indeed *were* Orthodox. The authorities could only welcome such findings. Beyond that point, however, words and numbers
began to diverge from the expectations of Russian nationalists and
imperial loyalists.

Of the three *narechiia*, the one most commonly spoken in Kyiv
appeared to be Ukrainian (or "Little Russian," in the politically correct usage of the census takers), which was used by 38,553 Kyivites
and suburbanites (or more than 30 per cent of all residents). The Great
Russian "dialect" was spoken by a small minority – only 9,736 people
(or 7.6 per cent of Kyivites). The White Russian or Belarusian "dialect"
was a distant third, with 1,479 people (1 per cent) claiming to speak it.
Arguably, this linguistic consciousness depended on the social status,
occupation, and residence of the respondents. Most people, however,
were not accustomed to defining their group identity through language
and ethnicity, at least not apart from their belonging to Orthodox Rus'.
So the actual number of people who were of Russian, Ukrainian, or

Belarusian descent was probably greater and could not be measured by the three "dialects" defined by census takers.

Specifically for these "non-aligned" residents, the census takers created "Newspeak" – a language they imaginatively called "all-Russian" or "common Russian" (*obshcherusskii*). What really was this language? What was it for the residents themselves and for the census takers who invented its name? And finally, how different was this language supposed to be from the Great Russian, Little Russian, and White Russian "dialects" of the "Russian language"? We can only guess now what this pre-Orwellian Newspeak was. Michael Hamm thought this language to have been a misnomer, encompassing "Ukrainians, and to a lesser extent Belarusians and Poles, who could speak enough Russian to be counted as Russian-speakers in the census."[56] I would only add that this Russian Newspeak was probably chosen as a spoken or first language[57] by all those who were educated enough to claim some knowledge of the Russian *literary* language, or who shared the "all-Russian" identity.[58] Or perhaps the organizers assigned to this category all those whom they had failed to interview personally (among them soldiers, as well as patients in local hospitals). Speakers of the "all-Russian language" comprised the largest single linguistic community in the city – 48,437 people, or 38 per cent of all residents.[59] In any case, the scholars who stood behind the census were well aware of the political sensitivity attached to any of the linguistic labels.

It comes as no surprise then that the linguistic creativity of the census takers was met with sharp criticism from the right.[60] An anonymous critic cast doubt on the feasibility of dividing the "Russian language" into several groups. Specifically he wrote that the "people would not understand" such a division and that a Great Russian "dialect" was not a mere dialect but rather the "all-Russian" literary language per se. Hence it did not make any sense to distinguish between the "Russian language" and the "all-Russian literary language" because the two were virtually the same. This critic argued that all the speakers of the "literary dialect" should instead be reassigned to the category of speakers of Great Russian, "which alone, by the force of history, developed into a literary language."[61] For this undercount of Russian speakers the conservative critic was ready to blame the pro-Ukrainian organizers of the Kyiv census.[62] To add insult to injury, the number of those who claimed to speak Great Russian in Kyiv (9,736) turned out to be even lower than that of Yiddish speakers (12,917). It is therefore not surprising that the same newspaper later alluded to a "Jewish-Ukrainian" conspiracy.[63] Other rivals – Polish speakers – lagged far behind, numbering only 7,863 (or 6 per cent of Kyivites).

The relationship of language to religion seemed more direct. In fact, one could learn from the census that "Russians" were Orthodox and that almost all Orthodox spoke "Russian." When it came to Catholics, however, the census takers clearly made an effort to dissociate the Catholic religion from any single nationality.[64] The Ukrainian intellectual tradition also acknowledged the presence of *non-Polish* Catholics in the region, and the data seemed to confirm this: Polish-speaking Catholics were only 6,936 (or 76 per cent) of the 9,155 faithful in Kyiv and its suburbs. A significant portion of Kyiv Catholics – 1,472 people, or 16 per cent of the Catholic body – turned out to be "Russian" speakers. In reality, however, this whole category remained somewhat imaginary, for these "Russian"-speaking Catholics, not least because of the lack of Russian church services at Kyiv's only Catholic church, continued to be part of the Polish world and were treated as such by the authorities. Other religions were linked more straightforwardly to a single language: virtually all Old Believers spoke Russian; most Protestants, German; and Jews, "Jewish" (Yiddish).[65]

Nothing indicated the social standing of the various religious and ethnic communities more clearly than the number of literate and illiterate residents within each. As could be expected, the most literate groups were the Protestants and Catholics (78 and 74 per cent literate respectively); these were religious communities with a truly elite membership of nobles, state and municipal officials, professionals, and new entrepreneurs. The high rate of illiteracy among the Orthodox and the Jews (55 and 58 per cent respectively, if the numbers are accurate), pointed to the low social standing of many in those communities – poor artisans, small traders, beggars, factory workers, and specifically Jewish hawkers and *Luftmenschen*, among others.

The 1874 census grasped another big change in Kyiv's social landscape: a very specific tension between (largely acquired) economic class and (largely ascribed) "feudal" social estate. Soviet Marxists used to talk of the triumph of the capitalistic economic class over a feudal social estate in post-reform cities; but in reality, until at least 1905, *legally* defined social estates coexisted, often antagonistically, with *informal* economic classes.[66] The social terminology, however, lagged behind, continuing to refer to nobles, officials, clergy, burghers, merchants, venerable citizens, and peasants. The scholarly language of the 1874 census retained the flavour of Borges's Chinese encyclopedia, but its attention to detail reflected the rise of the new social science. The words and numbers in 1874 were as follows: hereditary nobles (10,565, or 8 per cent); non-hereditary nobles and officials (9,128, or 7 per cent); clergy, including monks and priests with their families (3,506, or 2.7 per cent); venerable citizens, both hereditary and non-hereditary (1,420, or 1 per cent); merchants (4,362, or 3.4 per cent); burghers (41,421, or 32.5 per cent); peasants (22,342, or 17.5 percent); "lower military ranks" (29,451, or 23 per cent); foreigners (2,449, or 2 per cent); and "other estates" (2,607, or 2 per cent).[67] One thing related to Kyiv's growing social complexity is particularly striking – the number of those who could not be ascribed to any of the old social estates, a clear sign that Kyiv was indeed undergoing modernization.

Yet the links between social estates, language, and religion were rather traditional.[68] The most notable change was the rise of Jews among the social estates of merchants and burghers. Here, preference for a particular language was indicative of that person's actual or aspired cultural allegiance.

As it turned out, most members of the "privileged estates" (nobles and officials combined) spoke the "Russian language," with a large minority speaking Polish (16 per cent); this was more than twice the percentage of Polish speakers among the Kyiv population overall. A combined group of citizens and merchants were much less "Russian"-speaking, with almost one-third of those engaged in trade speaking "Jewish." Kyiv burghers were perhaps the most "multiethnic" social group, in which at least four linguistic communities each exceeded 1 per cent. Peasants were by far the most homogeneous group in terms of language: almost all were "Russian" speakers, and probably most in fact spoke Ukrainian. The members of "lower military ranks" (soldiers, non-commissioned officers, and their family members) were largely "Russian"-speaking, although the share of Jewish men and women was remarkably high (6 per cent), a fact that rejected the stereotype about a massive Jewish evasion of military service. Finally, out of 2,307 foreigners included in the table, most spoke German (50 per cent), Polish (16 per cent), or "other West European languages" (15.5 per cent).

The division of social estates based on religion was almost identical to the one based on language,[69] which only confirms our preliminary assumption that as a rule, a religious community in Kyiv was at the same time a distinct linguistic and ethnic community. This overlap was most evident in the case of Jews, Catholics/Poles, and Orthodox "Russians." The most culturally diverse social estate comprised "citizens

Table 6.3 Social structure of Kyiv's major religious communities, 1874 (%)

Religion	Privileged	Citizens and merchants	Burghers	Peasants	Military	Foreigners	Other
Orthodox	17,407	2,889	28,339	21,005	24,316	267	1,917
96,140	(18)	(3)	(29)	(22)	(25)	(0)	(2)
Catholics	4,122	278	2,140	656	1,794	953	227
10,079	(41)	(2.7)	(21)	(5.6)	(18)	(9)	(2)
Jews	20	2,087	9,320	214	1,743	110	346
13,840	(0)	(15)	(67)	(1.5)	(12.5)	(0.8)	(2.5)
Protestants	589	278	511	70	209	1035	62
2,754	(21)	(10)	(18.5)	(2.5)	(7.6)	(37.6)	(2)

Source: *Kiev i ego predmistia*, 66–73 (table XIX).

and merchants," groups engaged in large-scale trade, in which Jews by language and religion accounted for more than one-third of all members. Burghers were the second most diverse social estate, within which Jews were the largest minority. Regarding the "privileged," the ruling classes in the Russian Empire were always cosmopolitan, encompassing members of various ethnic descents who spoke different languages and practised all major religions. Kyiv was not an exception to this; the Catholics and Poles in particular had established a prominent presence there since at least the late eighteenth century. Despite the persecution of Polish Catholics following the January uprising of 1863, the share of Catholics (18.6 per cent) and Polish speakers (16 per cent) among the city's elite was still impressive, far surpassing the percentage of Polish speakers and Catholics among Kyiv's total population.

Although the census included no ethnicity/nationality entries in its main sections, it is still possible to arrive at some tentative conclusions regarding particular ethnicities by looking at the social characteristics of Kyiv's major religious and linguistic communities. Which were the most privileged of the city's major communities, and which were the humblest? Table 6.3 attempts to visualize a communal pecking order in Kyiv.

As the religious and language data show,[70] certain religious and language communities were almost identical in terms of social structure, so much so that we can speak about four sets of "twins": the Orthodox and "Russian" speakers; Catholics and Polish speakers; Jews and Yiddish speakers; and Protestants and German speakers. This structural similarity most likely revealed the existence of particular nationalities.

The Catholics and Polish speakers clearly overlapped, in the process disclosing the Catholic Poles; Jews were visible as a religious *and* ethnic community; Protestants and German speakers alluded to the presence of "Germans," however, their Germanness was more problematic[71]; and finally, the Orthodox and "Russian" speakers, as many believed, formed the "all-Russian nation," a ruling and numerically dominant community in the empire. The existence of this nation, however, was cast into doubt by the very activity of the census takers, who made a case for a distinct Ukrainian nationality. Likewise, a number of Polish intellectuals and even some Russian imperial officials argued against the Catholic interpretation of Polishness. The 1874 census very much reflected an uneasy coexistence of various visions of community and social relations, a situation in which the traditional concepts of social estate and religion clashed with modern notions of nationality and class.

Despite these real and imaginary tensions, we can still make several important observations about the *traditional* social structure of Kyiv's major communities. First, Catholics and Polish speakers (or *Catholic Poles*) were the most privileged religious and linguistic community and were greatly overrepresented among Kyiv's bureaucracy and leisure class. Within the closely related communities of Catholics and Polish speakers, members of privileged estates comprised up to 47 per cent of all those who were counted. Not even German-speaking Protestants could rival Polish Catholics.[72] Second, Jews were the most "bourgeois" community, comprising almost one-third of Kyiv's commercial elite – the citizens and merchants group. In addition, quite a few Jews were listed as artisans but were *not* artisans; they had merely purchased – illegally, to be sure – artisans' certificates permitting them to reside in Kyiv. In fact they were engaged in trade, the legal profession, or money-lending. Despite these numerous cases of upward mobility, most Kyiv Jews were humble burghers, many of them destitute, among them beggars, hawkers, *Luftmenschen*, and sex trade workers. Third, the Orthodox "Russians" (including ethnic Ukrainians) were the most socially diverse group, providing the city with most of its masters and their servants, soldiers, artisans, and workers almost in equal measure.

With a little imagination we can animate a series of possible social encounters in Kyiv during a single day in 1874. It is highly likely that an official you bumped into near the Government Offices in Old Kyiv was an Orthodox and a Russian speaker, but his colleague from the same department, just passing by, was most likely a Polish-speaking Catholic.

While walking down towards St Alexander's Cathedral (occasionally fending off an attack by a roaming cow), you would encounter a Catholic parishioner, probably a landlord visiting or residing in the city on fashionable Khreshchatyk Street. If, for some reason, while ambling down Khreshchatyk, you chose to stop at a garment store, the merchant owner was probably Jewish, while a neighbouring merchant trading in hardware was likely to be a bearded Great Russian, probably a pious Old Believer. If you suddenly developed a headache and needed some medicine, you would visit an apothecary owned by a wealthy German Protestant merchant. On your way there you would see quite a few barefoot milk peddlers, all women dressed in Ukrainian peasant attire. If you continued along Velyka Vasyl'kivs'ka Street you would pass by a number of small artisanal shops, almost all owned by Jews, who themselves were the sole employees there. Several times you would be accosted by poor Jewish hawkers selling cheap hardware or brushes. And you might well see a district policeman, a heavy-set, middle-aged man born in the countryside, chasing away one poor hawker with curse words uttered in the inimitable local speech – a mixture of Ukrainian and Russian known today as *surzhyk*.

Such an imagined picture would necessarily have both social and ethno-cultural overtones, all of them quite ambiguous. Along with "feudal" social estates, our imaginary traveller in time would have noticed new "capitalist" economic classes. Thanks to an acute social awareness and the rigorous academic training of its organizers, the census once again grasped the tension between old and new in Kyiv society. Much of the census was devoted to an analysis of new economic classes. Kyivites were divided into three classes, based partly on their relationship to the means of production (in Marx's sense) and partly on particular occupations. Each class – "industrial and artisanal" (*promyshlennyi i remeslennyi klas*), "those engaged in transportation, trade, credit, and insurance operations," and "those who serve popular enlightenment" – encompassed residents belonging to all social estates. Mykola Ziber, the creative mind behind the census, saw society and economy through the Marxist prism of production, consumption, and human labour as a cost unit.[73]

In fact, the "industrial and artisanal class" contained two new classes: the working class and that of capitalist owners. The former included journeymen and factory workers, the latter the owners of the means of production (master artisans and factory owners). Can we speak then about capitalist exploiters and an exploited proletariat? The picture, it seems, was not so antagonistic. Among all those engaged in crafts and industries (17,820 men and women) the "workers" indeed comprised the largest single group – 8,403 people, or 47% per cent; but self-employed masters working in their own shops (*khoziain-odinochka*) were still a significant social force, amounting to 6,341 people, or 35.6 per cent of all engaged in crafts. By contrast, the number of employers (*khoziain-predprinimatel'*) was rather low (1,817, or 10 per cent).[74] These data show that the times of Kyiv's proud master artisans were long gone but that numerous self-employed manufacturers, both master artisans and small employers, still held on to their independent, if often uncertain, existence. Most of these loners worked in traditional crafts, such as dressmaking (tailors, seamstresses, shoemakers), furniture making (joiners, furniture makers), and small-scale metal work (blacksmiths, locksmiths). Likewise, most employers and most wage earners were concentrated in the same crafts. So the highest number of business owners and workers could be found among the carpenters (94 and 1,301 respectively), shoemakers (266 and 834), joiners and furniture makers (73 and 738), blacksmiths (209 and 374), and locksmiths (95 and 227).[75] These last data also indicate that most employers were small business owners, often working themselves and employing one or two workers, and thus were hardly ravenous capitalist sharks. Indeed, they were in a precarious social position, a little bit above the "proletarians" but well below the proverbial "capitalists."

For all its industrial growth, Kyiv at this time almost entirely lacked large enterprises and heavy industry. Most employment was concentrated in traditional crafts rather than in more technological fields such as machine building. Perhaps the newest category of employment was to be found in a handful of areas connected to modern technologies – railways (the largest single employer in the city), steamship lines, river navigation, the telegraph, and so on.[76] In social terms, these positions were situated on the occupational scale between those held by skilled craftsmen in the old *trades* and those of technical experts/engineers in modern *professions*.[77] Spurred by the sugar beet industry in the countryside and by the city's new economic functions, managers, entrepreneurs, and service sector employees formed the nucleus of Kyiv's modern middle class, whatever their social estate. There were 3,787 shopowners, brokers, business agents, and the like, both men and women, who employed 2,081 shop assistants and salesmen and more than 700 workers and day labourers. In addition, there were four bank owners and 102 moneylenders. Class was born, but occupation rather than property was still more important for Ziber and his left-leaning peers.

Table 6.4 Share of social estates in crafts and trades, 1874 (%)

Privileged	Urban	Rural	Soldiers	Foreigners	Other	Total
1,098	8,253	5,081	4,436	406	114	19,388
(5.7)	(42.5)	(26)	(23)	(2)	(0.6)	(100)

Source: *Kiev i ego predmistia*, 124–37 (table 3).

The census also pointed to the dissolution of social estates, in that the privileged and the wretched toiled in the same (sweat)shops. For example, in the food trades (beekeeping, dairy husbandry, farming, baking, etc.), men and women from "privileged estates" comprised 7 per cent of the 2,681 workers, alongside burghers and merchants (51 per cent), peasants (26 per cent), and soldiers (11.5 per cent).[78] Nobles and officials comprised 8 per cent of all those engaged in dressmaking (especially in tailoring, sewing, embroidery, and shoemaking). Peasants were overrepresented in construction, accounting for 46 per cent of the total workforce and dominating the ranks of carpenters and glaziers.

Table 6.4 shows that the share of various social estates in crafts and trades roughly corresponded to the social estate structure of Kyiv's total population (although the percentage of nobles and officials in manual occupations was lower, while that of peasants and burghers was higher than their respective shares among urbanites). Kyiv's other class – "those engaged in trade, transport, credit, and insurance operations" – was markedly more aristocratic and middle-class. For example, the "privileged" comprised the largest single group among railway staff (29 per cent) and telegraph employees (32.5 per cent) and the second largest, after "urban estates," in Dnieper steamship companies (30 per cent) and among the personnel of Kyiv's means of communication (28 per cent). In addition, nobles and officials dominated credit and insurance societies, accounting for 48 and 66 per cent respectively. Trade per se (shopowners, commissioners, brokers, etc.) was dominated by merchants and burghers (62 per cent of 6,580 men and women).

Table 6.5 shows the dominance of "urban estates" in these most urban occupations and economic activities. Remarkable also was the presence of nobles and officials in trade: shopkeepers from the "privileged estates" formed the second-largest group after burghers and merchants. This pointed to a new class of commercial bourgeoisie and a further dissolution of distinct social estates. Many nobles and officials now had more interests in common with their plebeian peers than with

Table 6.5 Share of social estates in trade, transport, credit, and insurance, 1874 (%)

Privileged	Urban	Rural	Soldiers	Foreigners	Other	Total
1,240	5,513	2,000	1,546	290	23	10,612
(11.7)	(52)	(19)	(14.5)	(2.7)	(0)	(100)

Source: *Kiev i ego predmistia*, pp. 180–3 (table VII).

Table 6.6 Share of social estates in arts, crafts, and related businesses, 1874 (%)

Privileged	Urban	Rural	Soldiers	Foreigners	Other	Total
313	693	156	307	108	31	1,608
(19)	(43)	(10)	(19)	(6.7)	(2)	(100)

Source: *Kiev i ego predmistia*, pp. 198–9 (table XI).

other members of the "privileged estates," who continued to serve the state or stayed in the countryside.

A third class, "those who serve popular enlightenment" (table 6.6), was an obvious misnomer for it had nothing to do with education. Instead it pulled together skilled artisans, artists, "artsy" shopowners, and the creative intelligentsia – all of those who were engaged in arts and crafts and related businesses, which signified the professionalization of culture. It comes as no surprise that nobles and officials were very prominent in this class of literati and the artisanal elite (hence the illiterates within the class were a small minority – 165 people, or 10 per cent).[79]

There was also the fourth class, reserved for those who "served" in various capacities. This group comprised government officials, clerics, "lower military ranks," and simple servants in public service. Of its 16,930 members, most (12,389) belonged to the "lower military ranks." Government employees numbered 3,038 (18 per cent), and most of them served the Church (931), local administration (780), or education (466).[80] Ironically, the census takers added some prisoners to the total number of government officials, which prompted a scathing remark from a critic: any criminal might now claim, referring to the authority of the census, that when roaming the streets in search of a victim he was preparing for state service, and when he was finally sent to prison this would mean he had been awarded with a state office. Instead, this critic ironically remarked, the prisoners should have been assigned to the category of "teachers and students," because prison was just like

Table 6.7 Birthplaces of Kyivites by economic classes, 1874 (%)[82]

Workforce	Kyiv	Ukraine	Russia	Belarus	Kingdom of Poland	Baltic region	Siberia and Central Asia	Abroad
I class	5,390	6,021	3,670	1,366	397	152	?	483
19,388	(28)	(31)	(19)	(7)	(2)	(0.8)		(2.5)
II class	2,520	4,516	1,760	894	296	121	?	290
10,612	(23.7)	(42.5)	(16.6)	(8.4)	(2.8)	(1)		(2.7)
III class	416	681	117	100	43	23	?	109
1,608	(26)	(42)	(7)	(6)	(2.7)	(1)		(7)
IV class	881	6,781	5,303	1,438	495	254	?	45
15,392	(5.7)	(44)	(34)	(9)	(3)	(1.6)		(0)
Population	36,005	57,865	16,872	10,515	2,371	761	189	2,170
total	(28)	(45)	(13)	(8)	(2)	(0.6)	(0.1)	(1.7)

Source: *Kiev i ego predmistia*, 110–23 (table 2), 176–9 (table 6), 196–7 (table 10), 210–11 (table 16).

school.[81] Despite this unintended comic relief, these data show that service to the state (ranging from church to school to prison) remained an essential breadwinner for Kyivites, being the most common alternative (after crafts and trades) to a life of crime.

What were the links between class and nationality? The word "nationality" (*natsional'nost'*) did in fact appear in the census, but it was accorded a relatively minor place in the total order. Instead, "ethnographic regions" described the regional, if not ethnic, origins of the Kyiv workforce, split as it was into four major classes.

Table 6.7 clearly shows that the "ethnographic" origins of each of the four classes almost coincided with the regional origins of Kyiv's population. There were, however, a few striking discrepancies between the Kyiv population in general and particular classes. For example, there was a far greater proportion of people born in Great Russia among state officials, soldiers, artisans, and workers (from classes I and IV), and consequently a lower share of those born in Ukrainian provinces among the city's emerging working class. Specifically, people born in Great Russia almost completely dominated construction trades such as carpentry, plastering, and glazing, but also such exotic food specialties as "loaf baking" (*pecheniie bulok*). Even more striking was the very low percentage of Kyiv-born state employees and soldiers (class IV), a clear sign that the growing borderland metropolis was tapping largely external human resources for key positions in education, the military, local administration, and the Church (almost equally from Ukrainian and Russian provinces). Whether this was also a sign of "internal colonialism" is a matter of debate.

"Ethnographic regions," however, did not necessarily mean ethnicity. For instance, many Kyivites born in Ukrainian provinces or in the Kingdom of Poland were of various ethnic descents – Jewish, Polish, Belarusian, or Ukrainian – and the city indeed had become more multiethnic by 1897. The word "nationality" as used in the census was no less ambiguous. The census recognized the following "nationalities": Russians (without any further divisions), Poles, Jews, Germans, and "others" (for those born in Russia), and "Slavs," Germans, French, and again "others" (for those born abroad). The census showed that an overwhelming majority of "Russian" artisans were illiterate, while most Polish masters and workers were literate.[83]

Several aspects of the census data may have been even more worrisome to patriotic Russians. They could now see the growing numbers and economic strength of Jews, Poles, and Germans. And they could see how the masses of burghers, peasants, and workers surrounded from all sides the Russian imperial bureaucracy, a relatively small group. Not surprisingly, the latter felt increasingly embattled. In addition, Russians in Kyiv felt threatened by a growing Ukrainian movement. For whatever reason, the census takers became the target of a *double* attack launched by Russian conservatives on pro-Ukrainian activists *and* socialists, who were active members of the local branch of the Russian Geographic Society.[84] By 1874, denunciations had begun to appear on the pages of *Kievlianin* and in other reactionary papers. Historian and Ukrainian activist Mykhailo Drahomanov recalled that the press "began to assail the Kyiv Geographic Society ... labelling it a Ukrainophile *kahal* that smuggled in political separatism under the flag of scholarship. These attacks ... grew stronger when the mass arrests of socialists began in Russia in 1874."[85] Conservatives even insinuated that the census had no value.[86]

A self-styled socialist, Drahomanov was forced to resign his teaching position at Kyiv St Vladimir University and leave for Europe in 1875. These political reactions revealed that many in the government viewed the new positivist social science with suspicion, seeing it as a seditious *political* activity linked to socialist propaganda. Another census organizer, the early Marxist Mykola Ziber, was forced to leave Kyiv following the departure of his close friend Drahomanov.[87]

To make matters worse, people also misconstrued the word "sociology" as "socialism."[88]

But one did not need to be a sociologist or a socialist to notice ever more changes in urban society in Russia. The problem was that Russia's urban policies and laws were deliberate attempts to block social modernization by limiting municipal autonomy and by minimizing public participation in the city's affairs. As a result, urban autonomy in Russia became even more precarious in the early 1890s, when the conservative Tsar Alexander III introduced several counter-reforms. First, he increased the participation of the nobility and strengthened governmental control over rural self-government. Then, in 1892, he issued the new Municipal Statute with the goal of encouraging the participation of nobles and officials by limiting the role of merchants and poor burghers.[89]

The Imperial Census of 1897: From Language to Nationality

The reforms of the 1860s and 1870s and the changing economic circumstances did not destroy the feudal social estates (*sosloviia*) in cities. Under Alexander III the imperial government adhered to the conservative utopia of a stratified social order, which favoured nobles and bureaucrats. Peasants were feared but also revered for their productive labour and famous Russian character. The inhabitants of the cities, by contrast, were neither feared nor revered but rather despised for their "parasitic" economic activities and narrow-mindedness.[90] Throughout Russian-ruled Eastern Europe, burghers remained a socially oppressed and economically destitute social group, comprising on average only one-third of all urban dwellers. Unlike nobles and merchants, burghers could not travel freely from one city to another without a special permit. Also, they had to be registered in a particular city; they needed a special permit (a "leave pass" from their city's "municipal society") to study or enter civil service; they could not employ more than sixteen people; and so on. Only in 1906 were some of these feudal restrictions finally lifted. Some burghers transformed themselves into capitalists; many more, however, were relegated to the class of proletariat, a process already reflected in the 1874 census. Most continued to lead traditional burgher's lives as market traders, peddlers, small shopkeepers, salesmen/saleswomen, self-employed artisans, minor clerks, servants, and so on.

Most professions (doctors, lawyers, engineers, journalists, etc.) did not appear on the 1874 census. Instead they were hidden behind more

Table 6.8 Birthplaces of Kyivites, 1897 (%)

Kyiv	Ukraine	Russia	Belarus and Lithuania	"Vistula provinces" (Poland)	Baltic region	Caucasus	Siberia and Central Asia	Abroad
79,972 (32)	95,880 (38.7)	43,624 (18)	16,911 (7)	4,605 (1.8)	1,142 (0.5)	808 (0.3)	1,025 (0.4)	3,216 (1.3)

Source: *Pervaia vseobshchaia perepis' naseleniia Rossiiskoi imperii*, Vol. 16: *Kievskaia guberniia* (Saint Petersburg), 1904, 40–8 (plate VII).

general occupational and economic categories ("administration," "court," "technicians," "literature," "music," and the like). Despite some confusion, professionals (known in Russia as intelligentsia) were beginning to be taken seriously as a distinct socio-economic category, separate from officials, artisans, and the mass of wage earners engaged in physical work.

There was also a growing urgency to recognize "ethno-schematization" in official classifications of urban populations. The local organizers of the 1874 census were already sensitive about the issue of nationality. This also became an important issue for the organizers of the first and only Russian imperial census of 1897.[91] Juliette Cadiot, who studied the topic, writes that while the categories of estate (*soslovie*) and religion were officially recorded in Russian identification documents (parish registers, passports), "nationality was at best a marginal administrative or legal category in the Russian Empire." The 1897 imperial census "makes clear that the concept of nationality remained weakly defined. Statisticians, in fact, decided not to ask individuals a direct question on nationality, arguing that the population would not know how to respond to such a question, or would answer so poorly that the results would not be a true reflection of 'reality.'"[92] The census takers comprised 150,000 people across the empire, and they asked a dozen questions ranging from civic status and occupation to language, religion, and social estate.[93]

The census estimated the population of Kyiv as 247,723 people (of whom 10,265 were in the city temporarily during the census). When it came to the place of birth of Kyivites, the situation had not changed much compared to 1874 (see table 6.8).

Kyiv remained a city of newcomers, with the proportion of native-born residents (32 per cent) almost unchanged since 1874 (28 per cent).

Table 6.9 Religion in Kyiv, 1863–97 (%)

	1863	1874	1887	1897
Orthodox	58,910 (84)	91,357 (78)	127,496 (77)	187,935 (76)
Roman Catholics	8,604 (12)	10,409 (8)	19,397 (11.7)	19,230 (7.7)
Jews	1,411 (2)	13,803 (11)	15,833 (9.5)	32,093 (13)
Protestants	973 (1)	2,740 (2)	2,162 (1.3)	4,708 (2)

Sources: *Sbornik statisticheskikh svedenii o Kievskoi gubernii* (Kyiv, 1864), 25–38; *Kiev i ego predmistia … po perepisi 2 marta 1874 goda* (Kyiv, 1875), v; *Kievlianin*, 11 (1887), 2; *Pervaia vseobshchaia perepis' naseleniia Rossiiskoi imperii*, vol. 16: *Kievskaia guberniia* (Saint Petersburg), 1904, 37–8.

The most noticeable change was the decrease in migrants from Ukrainian provinces – from 45 per cent (57,865) down to 38.7 per cent (95,880), while the share of those born in ethnic Russian provinces increased from 16,872 (13 per cent) to 43,624 (18 per cent). A significant proportion of migrants from Ukrainian provinces were most certainly non-Ukrainians (Jews and Poles), but almost all those migrating from Great Russia were ethnic Russians. Migrants, particularly from outside Kyiv province, were numerous in all classes of society and comprised a majority among peasants (60 per cent) and among nobles and officials (57 per cent).[94]

In the general overview of the population of Kyiv province, the social estate remained a primary category of classification. The towns (including Kyiv) consisted of nobles (8 per cent), clergy (1 per cent), merchants (1.89 per cent), burghers (58 per cent), peasants (28 per cent), foreigners (1 per cent), and "persons belonging to other estates" (2 per cent). Regarding religion, the *urban* population of Kyiv province consisted primarily of the Orthodox (60 per cent), Jews (31 per cent), and Roman Catholics (5.6 per cent).[95] The census also included a rather clear entry on language. Among the province's overall population the absolute majority spoke "Little Russian" (79 per cent), with small minorities speaking "Jewish" (12 per cent), "Great Russian" (5.9 per cent), and Polish (1.9 per cent). In Kyiv some of these numbers were considerably different. Although religious labels changed slightly over the years, it is possible to compare the changes in religious communities over the final four decades of the nineteenth century (see table 6.9).

As we can see, the most noticeable trend was the dramatic increase in Jewish believers, largely at the expense of Roman Catholics in the city. In 1863 certain categories of Jews had just been allowed to settle in the city; by 1897, despite the continuous limitation on the types of Jewish

Table 6.10 Social estates in Kyiv, 1835–97 (%)

Social estate	1835		1863		1874		1887		1897	
Nobles and officials	5,856	(20)	12,207	(17)	19,693	(15)	14,628	(8.8)	31,309	(12.6)
Burghers and merchants	18,045	(62)	23,589	(33.5)	47,203	(37)	97,907	(60)	107,932	(43.5)
Peasants	2,287	(8)	11,086	(15.8)	22,342	(17.5)	34,265	(20.7)	96,985	(39)
Military		n/a	17,815	(25)	29,451	(23)	13,574	(8)		n/a
Clergy	736	(2.5)	4,034	(5.7)	3,506	(2.7)	1,255	(0.7)	3,772	(1.5)
Foreigners	542	(2)	897	(1)	2,449	(2)	2,229	(1.3)	4,302	(1.7)
Other estates	557	(2)	511	(0.7)	2,607	(2)	1,454	(0.9)	8,490	(3)
Total	29,000		70,341		127,251		165,461		247,723	

Sources: Funduklei, *Statisticheskoe opisanie Kievskoi gubernii*, 349–50; *Sbornik statisticheskikh svedenii o Kievskoi gubernii* (Kyiv, 1864), 25–38; *Kiev i ego predmistia... po perepisi 2 marta 1874 goda* (Kyiv, 1875), v; *Kievlianin*, 11 (1887), 2; *Pervaia vseobshchaia perepis' naseleniia Rossiiskoi imperii*, vol. 16: *Kievskaia guberniia* (Saint Petersburg), 1904, 37–8.

residents permitted in Kyiv, their numbers in the city had swelled. With regard to social estate the changes were even more striking (table 6.10).

The most obvious change was a dramatic increase in peasants in the city; there was also a notable increase in "urban estates." Whereas the growing presence of peasants was a trend found in all Russian cities,[96] Kyiv again differed markedly from other cities because of its high percentage of nobles and officials. For comparisons see table 6.11, which shows a general social profile of Russian imperial cities.

Table 6.11 Russia's urban population by social estates, 1897 (%)

Estates	Population size	
Nobles	1,048,600	(6.2)
Clergy	166,000	(1.0)
Venerable citizens	183,900	(1.1)
Merchants	225,600	(1.3)
Burghers	7,449,300	(44.3)
Peasants	6,526,100	(38.8)
Military Cossacks	171,900	(1.0)
"Aliens" (*inorodtsy*)	619,100	(3.7)
Other estates	191,100	(1.1)
Foreigners	247,300	(1.5)
Total	16,828,900	(100.0)

Source: Rashin, *Naselenie Rossii za 100 let*, 122.

Table 6.12 Languages in Kyiv, 1874 and 1897 (%)

Languages	1874		1897	
(All) Russian	48,437	(38)	n/a	(n/a)
Great Russian	9,736	(7.6)	134,278	(54)
Little Russian	38,553	(30)	55,064	(22)
White Russian	1,479	(1)	2,797	(1)
Polish	7,863	(6)	16,579	(6.7)
Jewish	12,917	(10)	29,937	(12)

Peasants migrated to cities, and to Kyiv in particular, because a city provided job opportunities ranging from trade to manual labour to domestic service to crime. But there might be another explanation for this huge numerical and proportional surge of peasants in Kyiv: military service. The 1897 census, in contrast to all previous statistical exercises, did not include the military among the social estates. The census takers included military service under a different rubric: occupations. So the number of military personnel and their family members totalled 24,512 people.[97] It can safely be assumed that most of the soldiers were peasants and burghers by social origin. The numerous retired soldiers and officers (along with their family members) were most likely listed under their original social estates.[98]

An even more important innovation in the 1897 census was its attention to the cultural and national characteristics of the local populations, as separate from the official hierarchy of estates, particularly on the ethnic peripheries.[99] The census introduced the category of separate East Slavic languages – Great Russian, Little Russian, and White Russian – still collectively referred to as the "Russian [languages]" (*russkie*).

The most significant change in 1897 was a further marginalization of Ukrainian, as seen in table 6.12. All minorities were under increasing pressure to assimilate, particularly Ukrainians, who formally were not even considered a minority like Jews or Poles. Hence even among peasants and burghers the share of those claiming to speak Great Russian was unbelievably high: 57 and 46 per cent respectively.[100] Migration from ethnic Russian provinces may have had something to do with this linguistic turn, but it is more likely that the universal appropriation of the Russian language as a norm (whether actual or desired) had led to the preponderance of "Great Russian" in Kyiv. We can also assume that in reality, considerably more people spoke Ukrainian or the Ukrainian-Russian mixture known today as *surzhyk*.

The census takers themselves added to the confusion. For instance, one early critic pointed out that they were "volunteers, who had hitherto never engaged in the census, and had never been interested in statistics, that is, these [were] people who were not sufficiently prepared for this matter."[101] Referring to the question about the "native language" on the census questionnaires, the critic wryly noted: "Often, the respondent answered 'Russian' and the ignorant census-taker … immediately counted this person as Great Russian, even though the Little Russian respondent in fact meant the Little Russian language."[102] But some respondents simply did not care, for they spoke both languages equally well. Others – who had studied at school in Russian, or who spoke Russian at home – often indicated Russian as their language, even though they were ethnically Ukrainian. Therefore, language in the census did not represent nationality. Prominent Ukrainian and Belarusian intellectuals also argued that census takers undercounted minorities (Ukrainians, Belarusians, Jews, Poles, and others) while overestimating the number of Great Russians. In general, the government and minority activists used the census data to refute each others' claims.[103]

It seems, however, that the links between language and religion were even more direct than in 1874. The overwhelming majority of "Russian" speakers (97 per cent) were Orthodox, who in turn were almost all (99 per cent) speakers of Russian, Ukrainian, or Belarusian. Among the speakers of Great Russian, 1,728 (1.3 per cent) were Old Believers and a small minority (895) were Roman Catholics. Likewise, most Polish speakers (97 per cent) were Roman Catholics, while most Roman Catholics were Polish speakers (84 per cent), with the second-largest group of Catholics being "Russian" speakers (7 per cent). This was in marked contrast to the data from the 1874 census, which revealed that Polish-speaking Catholics totalled only 6,936 (or 76 per cent) out of 9,155 faithful in Kyiv and its suburbs, where "Russian"-speaking Catholics comprised 16 per cent of the religious community. It may be that by 1897 the links between religion and language (and nationality by default) had strengthened and that "Russian"-speaking Catholics were on the decline in Kyiv, as was the imperial campaign to introduce Russian (or Belarusian) in the Catholic Church. It is also interesting to note that whereas the number of Polish speakers in Kyiv more than doubled between 1874 and 1897 (from 7,863 to 16,579) – a growth rate higher than that of the city's entire population – the number of "Russian" Catholics had decreased. Other possible reasons for this resurgence of Polish Catholics in Kyiv may have included the weakening of the anti-Polish campaign in

Table 6.13 Division of social estates by language (major languages), 1874 and 1897 (%)

1874	Estates	"Russian"		Polish		"Jewish"		German	
	Nobles and officials 22,149	17,413	(78.6)	3,583	(16)	13	(0)	435	(2)
	Citizens and merchants 5,708	3,117	(54.6)	184	(3)	1,754	(30.7)	236	(4)
	Burghers 39,457	28,423	(72)	1,621	(4)	8,789	(22)	529	(1.3)
	Peasants 21,379	20,692	(97)	411	(2)	209	(1)	34	(0)
	Military 27,406	24,220	(88)	1,333	(5)	1,660	(6)	93	(0)
1897	Estates	"Russian"		Polish		"Jewish"		German	
	Nobles and officials 31,309	23,862	(76)	6,445	(20.6)	205	(0.6)	513	(1.6)
	Citizens and merchants 10,131	6,867	(68)	246	(2.4)	2,566	(25)	318	(4)
	Burghers 97,801	63,427	(65)	5,814	(6)	26,474	(27)	1,472	(1.5)
	Peasants 96,985	90,637	(93)	3,129	(3)	790	(0.8)	683	(0.7)

Sources: *Kiev i ego predmistia*, 58–63 (table 18); *Pervaia vseobshchaia perepis'*, 260–2 (plate 24).

the 1890s, the opening up of new employment opportunities in Kyiv, and simultaneously the worsening of economic conditions for Polish nobles in rural areas. Much like Ukrainians (but in contrast to Poles), Jews felt the attraction of Russian public culture in Kyiv: 6 per cent of Jews by religion indicated Russian as their native tongue, a sign of the growing Jewish professional and business presence in the dominant culture.[104]

When it comes to illiteracy, not much changed between 1874 and 1897. The most literate groups remained Protestants and Catholics. Although the Orthodox, Jews, and especially Old Believers all made impressive progress in terms of literacy, they still lagged far behind Protestants and Catholics in this respect; no doubt this reflected their social and professional standing.

It is also worth comparing the data from the two censuses as regards the division of social estates by language (table 6.13).

As we can see, there were only a few changes in the language identities of the members of social estates in Kyiv between 1874 and 1897. The "privileged estates" (nobles and officials combined) remained largely Russian-speaking (70 per cent), with the rest of them speaking Polish (20 per cent) and Ukrainian (6 per cent). The proportion of privileged Polish speakers even increased over the two-plus decades and now was three times the share of Polish speakers among the Kyiv population

Table 6.14 Social structure of Kyiv's main linguistic communities, 1874 and 1897 (%)

Language group, 1874	Nobles and officials	Citizens and merchants	Burghers	Peasants	Military	Foreigners	The rest
"Russian"	17,413	3,117	28,423	20,692	24,220	199	1,660
95,724	(18)	(3)	(30)	(22)	(25)	(0)	(2)
Polish	3,583	184	1,621	411	1,333	366	144
7,642	(47)	(2)	(21)	(5)	(17)	(4.7)	(2)
"Jewish"	13	1,754	8,789	209	1,660	73	298
12,796	(0)	(14)	(68.7)	(1.6)	(13)	(0.5)	(2)
German	589	236	529	34	93	1,160	60
2,547	(17)	(9)	(20.8)	(1)	(3.6)	(45)	(2)

Language group, 1897	Nobles and officials	Citizens and merchants	Burghers	Peasants	Soldiers	Foreigners	The rest
"Russian"	23,862	6,867	63,427	90,637	n/a	706	2,148
192,139	(12)	(3.6)	(33)	(47)		(0.4)	(1)
Polish	6,445	246	5,814	3,129	n/a	826	111
16,579	(39)	(1.5)	(35)	(19)		(5)	(0.7)
"Jewish"	205	2,566	26,474	790	n/a	21	219
29,937	(0.7)	(8.6)	(88)	(2.6)		(0)	(0.7)
German	513	318	1,472	683	n/a	1,310	43
4,354	(12)	(7)	(34)	(15.7)		(30)	(1)

Source: *Kiev i ego predmistia*, pp. 58–65 (table XVIII) and *Pervaia vseobshchaia perepis'*, 260–2 (plate 24).

overall. Another noticeable trend was an increase of Jews among Kyiv burghers. Table 6.14 shows the social structure of language groups.

Consequently, Polish speakers remained the most elite community in the city, although the share of the privileged estates among them slightly decreased, while the share of peasants dramatically increased. The latter might be partly explained by the social origins of soldiers, who in 1897 were not listed as a separate social estate but who were quite numerous among Polish speakers in 1874.[105] From the other side, Polish-speaking peasants were part of a massive migration of people of various origins from rural areas into the city. The same was probably true of other language groups – Russian and particularly German – in which the share of peasants increased even more dramatically. "Russians" (or rather Russians, Ukrainians, and Belarusians) became the most heavily "peasant" community in the city, although most of those peasants were engaged in trades and industries, thus forming the nucleus of the city's working class.[106]

Unfortunately, the imperial census takers, in contrast to their socialist and positivist colleagues of 1874, were much less interested in socio-economic matters. Hence only a few trends can be observed. Social estates became even more obsolete, and the census takers applied a category of occupations (*gruppy zaniatii*): from administration and military to education, science, agriculture, trade, and prostitution (more than sixty entries overall). Excluding dependents, most Kyivites were employed in private and domestic service or as day labourers (35,217, or 24 per cent of the entire workforce), served in the military (22,065, or 15 per cent), were rentiers or received pensions (15,947, or 11 per cent), worked in garment production (11,067, or 7.5 per cent), or engaged in wood and metal work (8,083, or 6 per cent). They were also active in various types of trade, from grocery to armaments (around 10,000, or 6.7 per cent). There were also 153 prostitutes and 833 prisoners.[107] Unfortunately, from this list we cannot determine the number of large business owners, master artisans, employers, and their workers.

It seems that for census takers, nationality was more important than the socio-economic profile of the workforce. So we do not find the division of the workforce by social estates or by economic classes; instead we learn about the relationship between language and occupation. Here, census takers used the word "nationalities" (*narodnosti*) even though they really meant languages. So it is no surprise that such sensitive services as provincial administration, the courts, and the police were dominated by Russians (62 per cent), followed by Ukrainians (30 per cent), with Poles comprising only a small minority (2.6 per cent). The military service, by contrast, was truly multiethnic. Out of 22,065 soldiers and officers, Russians were 48 per cent, Ukrainians 31 per cent, Jews and Poles 5 per cent each, Tatars 3 per cent, and Germans 2 per cent. Private and domestic service and day labour, perhaps the most modest occupations, were dominated by Russians (55 per cent), followed by Ukrainians (32 per cent) and then Poles (5 per cent). A rather elite group of rentiers and pensioners was again led by Russians (64 per cent) and then split quite evenly among Ukrainians (16 per cent), Poles (13 per cent), and Jews (10 per cent).

In general, Russians dominated all occupations (including prostitution, with an impressive 81 per cent) and all types of trade.[108] Partly this was the continuation of a long-term trend indicating that ethnic Russian workers and traders were better equipped to succeed in a modernizing society than their Ukrainian peers. Partly, however, this apparent dominance was based on flawed language data. So "Russians" could include a number of ethnic Ukrainians and all those who chose Russian as their native language or language of public communication. Arguably most Kyivites were not sure what "language" and "nationality" really meant, while those who stood behind the census conflated these two categories.

Conclusion

Around 1897, Kyiv's population experienced a significant transformation. If from the 1830s through the 1870s only a few substantive changes occurred in the city's sociodemographic profile, by 1897 it underwent a total makeover. This was consistent with the rise of a capitalist economy that required a new workforce, both professionals and labourers. The need for the latter largely explains the huge influx of peasants into the city. Consequently, the share of nobles and state officials kept decreasing over time. This is not to say that Kyiv ceased to be the centre of bureaucracy and the military in the southwestern borderlands. Sociologically speaking, the city continued to show a strikingly high proportion of "nobles" and "officials" and a relatively modest number of peasants, especially when compared to Moscow or Saint Petersburg, where there were large industrial enterprises and commercial sectors. In those cities most industrial workers were former peasants, who by the early twentieth century already comprised the majority of residents in both.[109] While it is true that Kyiv never developed into an industrial powerhouse, by the early twentieth century it nonetheless had become a crucial commercial hub and a truly cosmopolitan metropolis.

Chapter Seven

Municipal Elites and "Urban Regimes": Continuities and Disruptions

**"If You Squeeze a Finger of One Official,
Then Everybody Will Feel His Pain"**

The cooperation between the municipal commune (whether autonomous or not), the city's mercantile elites, and local imperial authorities allows us to speak about Kyiv's "urban regimes," even though that term has usually been applied to post–Second World War Western cities.[1] The general political framework of interactions between the city and the imperial government ("formal workings") was explored in Part II of this book; here we will take a closer look at the municipal elites ("informal arrangements"). In modern democratic societies, the authority of governments is greatly limited by law and by the nation's political tradition. Local informal arrangements have assumed special importance in urban politics, and it seems that in non-democratic – often thoroughly corrupt – societies, informal arrangements in cities have long played an even greater role. This informal side of city governance was particularly well exemplified by the interactions between the local Russian authorities and the autonomous city of Kyiv prior to 1835. Corruption and clans of plutocrats were the two most notable features of Kyiv's urban regime during those years. Corrupt families of plutocrats upheld the city's autonomy even while undermining it. They upheld it by safeguarding Kyiv's economy and governance from various outside influences, whether Russian and Jewish traders or local imperial authorities. But at the same time they undermined it by creating "informal arrangements" that increasingly alienated much of the municipal commune, not least by embezzling huge sums of public funds. This eventually alarmed the imperial authorities and sealed the fate of Kyiv's centuries-old municipal autonomy.

From the police reports of the late 1820s we learn about the corporate and family ties between the self-governing city and the local imperial administration. The head of the Kyiv gendarmes, Lieutenant-Colonel Rutkovs'kyi, in one of his reports, complained about "family ties of all officials of Kyiv province with one another and with the city mayor [*viit*], as well as with some district officials."[2] He even quoted a local saying: "If you squeeze a finger of one official, then everybody will feel his pain." He recommended that all local officials be sent to other provinces, "but not to the capital, so that they would not have their agents of influence there." Indeed, the ties went all the way to the top. For instance, a newly appointed Russian military governor of Kyiv brought to the city Fedir Hudym-Levkovych, a man of Ukrainian noble descent who had served in Great Russia. It turned out that Hudym-Levkovych, besides heading the military governor's chancellery, was a relative of the Kyiv *viit* Kyselevs'kyi, as well as of two prominent legal officials – a provincial prosecutor (*gubernskii prokuror*) and a district attorney (*uezdnyi striapchii*). The military governor himself was in debt to the Kyiv civil governor, a local Ukrainian noble who had amassed a huge fortune on state service and who was in cahoots with municipal plutocrats. Needless to say, local imperial officials obstructed or soft-pedalled all inquiries into alleged irregularities within the elected municipal administration.

Ukrainian historian Volodymyr Shcherbyna reconstructed a plutocratic network based on Rutkovs'kyi's evidence. It showed that almost all senior members of the Kyiv provincial administration – salaried imperial officials – were related to municipal plutocrats. This was also an informal juncture of the imperial state and the autonomous city, of the Russian Empire and the Ukrainian urban commune. This defies traditional Ukrainian historiography, which has emphasized the conflict between Russian colonialism and Ukrainian autonomy. From that perspective, the self-governing city of Kyiv became, as it were, the latest victim of the Russian imperial state. But this sidesteps the fact that the Russian imperial state was represented at the local level by Ukrainian noble officials, who in turn were embedded in wider rural and urban societies, which produced closely knit social and political networks. The cluster of informal family ties was thus the basis of the urban regime in Kyiv prior to 1835. According to Rutkovs'kyi, these ties led to widespread injustice in the city:

Justice in this province is in a quite unfortunate situation. All in all, everybody complains about injustice, and some even send me their reports.

And this injustice comes from the fact that all provincial officials (except for those who are elected by nobility)[3] are related to each other and to the members of the city magistrate – beginning from Hudym-Levkovych, a head of chancellery of [the] military governor, who … is related to [imperial] officials and [members of] the magistrate. It is from this mutual kinship in the province that injustice and great abuse originate.[4]

These "informal arrangements" based on familial and corporate networks were strengthened by other flaws in the system: the confusion of powers in the city and the monopolistic power of the *viit* (Kyiv's elected mayor). Rutkovs'kyi also commented on these issues:

The city of Kyiv is administered by the *viit* on the basis of the most graciously granted privileges by the kings of Poland and the Magdeburg rights. This *viit* presides over the magistrate or the city duma. The *viit*, as well as burgomasters and *ratsgery* [councillors], by the privileges, are elected for life, without change until their death. According to the same privileges, the highest provincial authority has no influence over judicial proceedings in the magistrate, while the appeal against its decision must go directly to the senate. On these grounds the *viit* and the magistrate members, while being related to all provincial and major junior officials, practice exorbitant extortion.[5]

A pre-revolutionary historian of Kyiv attributed this breakdown in municipal order to the end of the eighteenth century, when the increased intrusion of the Russian government into the city's internal affairs undermined municipal autonomy.[6] A related problem within Kyiv's urban regime was confusion with regard to the functions of governance and justice, which were represented in the magistrate by the council and the judicial college (*lava*) respectively. Both institutions were dependent on the *viit*, and the same people who dealt with public finances and governance also meted out justice. This inevitably led to the confusion of private with public interests. This is what enabled the plutocrats to misappropriate the "*vynnyi vidkup*" – the farming of revenues from the production and sale of alcohol in the city. Those same plutocrats also ran the municipal commission, the city's major institution, established around 1805, which combined executive and banking functions.[7] Meanwhile, Kyiv's urban elite began to emulate the Cossack elite of the Hetmanate by acquiring noble titles. The *viits* were also assigned ranks (ninth to sixth) from Russia's Table of Ranks, which established a pecking order in the imperial service. Similarly, in the eighteenth century the members of the magistrate began to call themselves "magistrate officials," "administrative officers" (*uriadnyky*), or "administrative staff" (*uriadni liudy*). Finally, municipal service became lifelong and hereditary as clans of plutocrats secured key elected offices for their sons and relatives, thus forming closed political networks.

By tradition, the magistrate had submitted financial reports to the entire municipal commune; but after the Petrine reforms, it submitted them only to the "most venerable society." Although after 1782 these reports had to be reviewed by the local treasury board (*kazennaia palata*), these reviews were often either delayed for months or evaded altogether. The plutocrats argued that only the municipal "society" could validate expenditures, not the government. Furthermore, the growing power of the plutocrats transformed municipal elections into mere formalities, during which the elite hand-picked the winning candidates. Although the Russian authorities sometimes parachuted external candidates for the office of the *viit* (particularly during the reign of Catherine II), the municipal elites usually opposed the election of outsiders – ethnic Russians – as Kyiv city heads.

After Catherine abolished the magistrate in 1785, the city continued to be administered by local plutocrats. When the Magdeburg rights were restored in the early nineteenth century, Russian governors acquired more authority over the city. For instance, the civil governor gave official permission for the electoral meeting of the "most venerable society" – a social category borrowed from post-Petrine Russian urban practice. In this and in some other respects, Kyiv increasingly resembled Russian cities. Kyiv, however, was directly subordinate to the Senate, while other Russian cities remained under the jurisdiction of the Supreme Magistrate in Saint Petersburg.[8] Among other important changes in local urban practice were the loss of communal control over the magistrate and the introduction of the "verbal court" (for minor offences), which included two Russian merchants.

Formally, the reason why the Russian authorities meddled in Kyiv's internal affairs was the constant deficit in the city's budgets from the late eighteenth through the early nineteenth centuries. In 1803, 1822, and 1828, the Kyiv governors struck a committee "to balance revenue and expenditure" in the city. That committee included representatives of the state and the city. In addition, the municipal commission became a permanent institution attached to the magistrate. Headed by the *viit*, and staffed by members of the magistrate as well as representatives of "citizens," merchants, and burghers, this commission was tasked with supervising the city's revenues and expenditures. The commission thus became another organ of plutocratic influence in the city. The Russian authorities now had to approve all additional expenses; even so, the budget deficits did not disappear. After the 1820s, budgetary estimates were submitted to the governor for approval, but his control over city finances was random and ineffective. This was revealed by a protracted investigation into the embezzlement of public funds by plutocrats, as we saw in an earlier chapter. The government-led investigation disrupted but did not destroy the oligarchic networks that controlled municipal elections and self-governing institutions such as the magistrate and the municipal commission.

The voters were members of the "most venerable society," which united the major plutocratic clans and their clients. That "society" was not very numerous. Judging by the municipal elections of 1813 (earlier records have not been preserved), the number of voters was quite small: out of 5,517 male burghers, there were only 166 voters – 3 per cent of all full members of the municipal commune.[9] Of these eligible voters only 104 showed up on election day. According to the Magdeburg Law, electors were divided into six groups, each with a separate list of candidates. The participants voted with ballots, and the winner was decided by a simple majority.

The following table represents a slice of the Kyiv municipal elite, showing the most important *elected* positions in municipal administration. For the period 1800 to 1820 we have more or less complete lists of municipal servants (see table 7.1). Unfortunately, the sources for later years are more fragmentary, so in order to reconstruct the core group of plutocrats, I will use other sources, both primary and secondary.

In the autonomous city, the most influential plutocrats were from a handful of families, most of them engaged in trade as "merchants" and "venerable citizens." Those families intermarried, thus creating powerful networks that secured their private gains through public offices. They had no qualms about embezzling public funds. A few families were especially important, among them the Kyselevs'kyis (Ivan was an influential burgomaster, his son Hryhorii was the last *viit*), the Lakerdas (Pylyp was once an acting *viit*, while his sons Anton and Ivan were both *ratsgers* and burgomasters), the Romanovs'kyis (Ivan, Pylyp Lakerda's son-in-law, was a *ratsger* and burgomaster; his brother Pavlo was also a *ratsger* and burgomaster), and the Hryhorenkos (Mykhailo was the *viit*, his son Ivan was a *ratsger*). Perhaps the most important clan was the

Table 7.1 Kyiv municipal elite, 1799–1820

Year	Viit	Positions in the magistrate		Representatives in the police
		Burgomasters	*Ratsgers*	
1799	Stepan Rybal's'kyi (1797–1813)	Pylyp Lakerda, Mykhailo Hryhorenko	Ivan Pryluts'kyi, Ivan Kyselevs'kyi, Ivan Dolinnyi	n/a
1800		Petro Barshchevs'kyi, Ivan Mohyl'ovets'	Mykola Samochka, Pavlo Ryzenko, Ivan Atanazevych	n/a
1801		Hryhorii Balabukha, Fedir Nevodovs'kyi	Ivan Kar(a)maleia, Klyment Ternavs'kyi, Fedir Baranovych	n/a
1802		Pylyp Lakerda, Mykhailo Hryhorenko	Mykola Symochka, Iakiv Snizhko, Ivan Dolinnyi	n/a
1803		Petro Barshchevs'kyi, Ivan Mohyl'ovets'	Ivan Kar(a)maleia, Pavlo Ryzenko, Ivan Atanazevych	n/a
1804		Iakym Bars'kyi, Petro Barshchevs'kyi	Klyment Ternavs'kyi, Tymofii Zaremba	n/a
1805		Iakym Bars'kyi, Mykhailo Hryhorenko	Iakiv Snizhko, Mykola Symochka	n/a
1806		Klyment Ternavs'kyi, Ivan Kmelevs'kyi	Pavlo Ryzenko, Marko Bezsmertnyi, Ivan Atanazevych	n/a
1807		Petro Barshchevs'kyi, Marko Bezsmertnyi	Tymofii Zaremba, Oleksii Ostrovs'kyi	Iakym Kobets', Matvii Fylypovych
1808		Mykhailo Hryhorenko, Iakym Barshchevs'kyi	Pavlo Ryzenko, Ivan Ivans'kyi	Ivan Atanazevych, Iakiv Snizhko
1809		Ivan Kyselevs'kyi, Marko Bezsmertnyi	Iakym Kobets', Oleksander Balabukha	Tymofii Zaremba, Dmytro Ternaviot
1810		Petro Barshchevs'kyi, Marko Bezsmertnyi	Iakym Kobets', Oleksii Ostrovs'kyi	Tymofii Zaremba, Matvii Fylypovych
1811		Mykhailo Hryhorenko, Akim Bars'kyi	Pavlo Ryzenko, Kostiantyn Balabukha	Nazar Sukhota
1812		Pylyp Lakerda, Klyment Ternavs'kyi	Iakiv Snizhko, Oleksander Balabukha	Ivan Atanazevych, Havrylo Ivanchenko
1813	Pylyp Lakerda (1813–14), temporary *viit*	Iakym Bars'kyi, Iakiv Snizhko (after his death Marko Bezsmertnyi)	Kostiantyn Balabukha, Vasilii Pirazhkov	Ivan Atanazevych, Dmytro Ternaviot
1814	Mykhailo Hryhorenko (1814–26)	Marko Bezsmertnyi, Kostiantyn Balabukha	Pavlo Ryzenko, Hryhorii Kyselevs'kyi	Iakym Kobets', Nazar Sukhota
1815		Petro Barshchevs'kyi, Hryhorii Kyselevs'kyi	Oleksander Balabukha, Mykhailo Hotsaienko	Oleksii Ostrovs'kyi, Samson Strembyts'kyi
1816		Marko Bezsmertnyi, Hryhorii Kyselevs'kyi	Vasilii Pirazhkov, Vasyl' Tokhai	Pavlo Romanovs'kyi, Semen Balabukha
1817		Petro Barshchevs'kyi, Iakym Kobets'	Pavlo Ryzenko, Anton Lakerda	Ivan Bushev, Stepan Navan
1818		Marko Bezsmertnyi, Vasyl' Tokhai	Mykhailo Hotsaienko, Nikofor Bolotinov	Samson Strembyt'skyi, Hryhorii Iaroshevs'kyi
1819		Kostiantyn Balabukha, Hryhorii Kyselevs'kyi	Pavlo Romanovs'kyi, Semen Balabukha	Mikhail Bubnov, Ivan Smorodinov
1820	Hryhorii Kyselevs'kyi (1826 34)	Klyment Ternavs'kyi, Iakym Kobets'	Anton Lakerda, Iakiv Hrozdovs'kyi	Andrii Mazhnyi, Ivan Rybal's'kyi

Sources: DAK, f. 1, op. 2, spr. 174.

Balabukhas, who dominated municipal politics before 1835 and who would retain their visibility in the city's economy and local politics until the very end of the century. The Balabukha family was prominent in the city by the mid-eighteenth century, when Vasyl' Balabukha became a burgomaster in 1751. Another Balabukha, Semen, was a burgomaster in 1782 and a deputy of the new city duma in 1787. His sons – Semen, Kostiantyn, and Oleksandr – practically monopolized Kyiv self-governing institutions (Semen and Kostiantyn were members of the municipal commission).[10] Through their marriages, the Balabukhas were linked to other families of Kyiv notables such as the Kyselevs'kyis, Riabchykovs, and Mytiuks. Even after the Magdeburg Law was abolished, the Balabukhas continued to make a living as successful merchants, above all as the founders of the Kyiv jam empire. Some went on to become imperial officials and professionals.[11]

Other important figures came from elite artisanal backgrounds. For example, Ivan Atanazevych was an influential master artisan in the silverware guild, a head of the Kyiv artisanal board (*uprava*), and a *ratsger*.[12] Another silverware master, Fedir Korobka, also presided over local artisans and was a *ratsger*. His peer Marko Bezsmertnyi, also a silverware master, was a long-serving burgomaster, while his relative (probably his brother) Vasyl' Bezsmertnyi was a head of the city's artisanal board. The Bezsmertnyis were among the very few old families that relaunched their careers in a different setting – as officials and professionals – well into the next century. For example, Vasyl's son, Adrian, graduated from university and served in the chancellery of the Kyiv civil governor. His eldest son Volodymyr became one of Kyiv's most renowned architects and later, in Soviet times (after 1921), lectured at the Kyiv Polytechnic Institute.[13]

It is then not surprising that when in 1832 the investigators discovered that the plutocrats had embezzled 68,557 roubles of public funds, a few dozen highly placed municipal officials were to pay back various sums.[14] The senior plutocrats paid the highest amounts – the acting *viit* Pylyp Lakerda, 7,960 roubles, and the *viit* Mykhailo Hryhorenko, 8,055 roubles – while a number of burgomasters (among them Marko Bezsmertnyi, Kostiantyn Balabukha, and Hryhorii Kyselevs'kyi) had to pay 2,856 roubles each. It is noteworthy that the worst culprits (such as Lakerda, Hryhorenko, and Balabukha) were already conveniently dead. In addition, a newly appointed Kyiv prosecutor was the son of the *viit* Kyselevs'kyi, and he soft-pedalled the investigation. In the end, in 1842, after years of deliberations involving Russia's interior ministry and Senate, the plutocrats were relieved of responsibility for the embezzlement of public funds.[15]

Kyiv's traditional elite included families that had been accumulating prestige and wealth for centuries, using the city's self-governing status to their advantage. By the eighteenth century the city's wealthy office holders comprised a hereditary patrician community that aspired for noble status. These urban patricians did not welcome new members and distributed important elected offices within a closed circle of a few (often related) families.[16] Kyiv's urban regime prior to 1835 had amounted to joint ownership of the self-governing city by a few interrelated families, with no clear distinction between private (property) and public (authority). The "formal workings" of public authority were further diluted by "informal arrangements" whereby the state was represented by local Ukrainian nobles – salaried officials – who themselves were often related to municipal plutocrats.

Kyiv's urban space allowed for frequent contacts between plutocrats and officials: on the streets, in the trade hall (*Hostynyi dvir*), at public celebrations, and in church. Perhaps because they comprised only around 3 per cent of Kyiv householders, the municipal elites formed quite a tight circle. In this regard, they were similar to oligarchies in contemporary cities around the globe.[17] And much like their peers elsewhere, Kyiv's elite of traders and artisans genuinely believed that adherence to their own interests benefited all. The entrepreneur embodied public opinion and public consensus. In the words of a historian of a nineteenth-century American city, the close-knit community of urban elites "generated a general consensus about the city and helped to speed policies toward implementation."[18] In Kyiv, that "general consensus" after 1835 was embodied in the will of Russian bureaucrats, who would define the city's development for decades to come.

The Fall of "Old-Time Residents"

What happened to Kyiv's municipal elite after 1835, with the abolition of the city's autonomous institutions? How dramatic was the change in the composition of the city's elite in the years following 1835? Was there a regime change in the city? The best way to study this change is to trace the share of Russians in the ethnic profile of the municipal elite. When we examine the highest municipal office holders between 1800 and 1820 (table 7.1), we encounter only one recurrent Russian name – that of the merchant Vasilii Pirazhkov.[19] There were also three Russian

Chart 7.1 Share of Russians among Kyiv municipal voters, 1813–46[21]

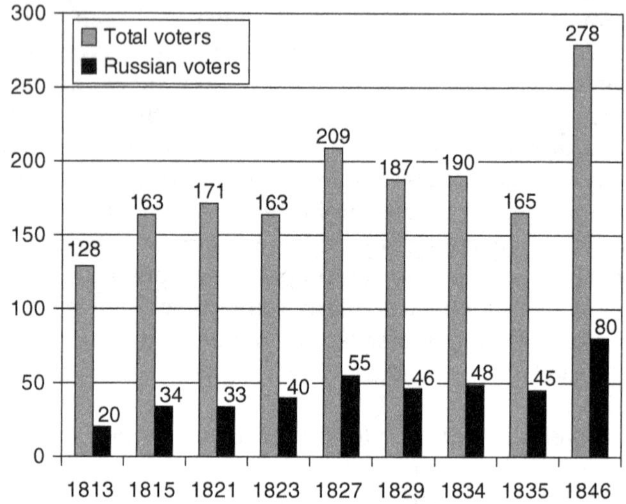

Sources: DAK, f. 1, op. 2 (2), spr. 174 (1813); DAK, f. 1, op. 2(2), spr. 296 (1815); DAK, f. 1, op. 1, spr. 283; DAK, f. 1, op. 2(2), spr. 977; DAK, f. 1, op. 2(2), spr. 1289; DAK, f. 1, op. 2(2), spr. 1710; DAK, f. 1, op. 2(2), spr. 1773; DAK, f. 17, op. 2, spr. 922. A chart created by Konstantin Nekrasov.

merchants among the city's representatives on the police and occasional Russians among the burgomasters and *ratsgers* in later years.[20] Chart 7.1 shows the share of ethnic Russians among municipal electors in a few selected years prior to the abolition of the Magdeburg rights in 1835 and ten years later.

However, when we leave out the burghers and artisans, the proportion of Russians among voters was even higher.[22] The Russians remained the second-largest voting block, and that block was still growing.

The archival data also show that after 1835, with the reintroduction of the Kyiv city duma, Russians replaced Ukrainians as "city heads" (in Russian, *gradskoi glava*) and as key municipal officials. So regime change did indeed happen: a group of Russian merchants, supported by the imperial authorities, had replaced Kyiv's "old-time residents" (*starozhyly*) as the city's new economic and administrative elite. For instance, during the first elections to the office of Kyiv city head in March 1835, the pool of candidates included five Russians (Orthodox and Old Believers) and one German, but not a single Ukrainian![23] That year the local Russian authorities rejected the lists of voters compiled by the *viit*, who was now "under trial."[24] It was mostly Russians who were elected as Kyiv "city heads" after 1835.[25] More Russians and some Western Europeans were elected to other major municipal offices, as duma deputies, burgomasters, and *ratmany* (councillors). The most remarkable of these Russians was Ivan Khodunov (1788–1853), a symbol of the new urban regime in the city between 1835 and 1870. Born in Iaroslavl' province in Russia's ethnic heartland, he established himself in Kyiv as a wealthy merchant and then served as the city head for three terms (1838–41, 1844–7, and 1851–3).

Khodunov was a typical representative of the Russian merchants who increasingly aspired to municipal leadership. A few Russian trading families had resided in the city much longer, some from the times of Peter I, as military suppliers and camp followers. Most of them lived and traded in Pechers'k, where they were protected by the Russian authorities. By 1741 there were forty-three Russian merchants in Kyiv, and some of their descendants survived in the city until the early twentieth century.[26] Among the Russians who were prominent during the time of Kyiv's transformation in the 1830s and 1840s we have encountered the names Smorodinov, Bubnov, Sveshnikov, Khodunov, Dekhterev, Eliseev, Mogilevtsev, and a few others. Among the most successful entrepreneurs were Old Believers from Russia's ethnic heartland or from their migrant communities in northern Ukraine. By around 1850, Old Believers had come to dominate the trade in iron, hardware, lumber, fish, and foodstuffs by founding large family firms.[27]

Despite the traditional prejudice against the Old Believers, the Russian government supported their businesses in the 1830s and 1840s as a way of strengthening Great Russian settlement in the region. This was expected to undermine Polish and Jewish influence in Kyiv. In other words, the change in municipal elites in Kyiv was part of a larger agenda of Russification that the imperial authorities were pursuing throughout the Southwestern Region.[28] Thus by mid-century, the Old Believers had established a strong presence among Kyiv's economic elite. With their conservative attire and long beards, they constituted a true "visible minority." Their successes were indeed remarkable. For example, in 1849, of the ten first-guild merchants in the city, five were Old Believers; they were also five out of thirty-one members of the second guild. The persecution of Old Believers, however, made a comeback in the 1850s, when Tsar Nicholas I banned these Russian religious dissidents from joining the merchant guilds.[29] Yet ethnic Russians, whether mainstream Orthodox or dissenters, continued to dominate the city's economy until the 1880s, when Jews became exceedingly prominent among Kyiv's merchant class (particularly in the elite first guild).

What happened to the Ukrainian plutocrats after 1835? A few families continued to provide cadres for municipal offices, including that of city head. In fact, between 1835 and 1870 at least three Ukrainians were elected to that office; however, only one of them was the scion of a clan that was prominent *before* 1835 – the Balabukhas. In 1844, at the young age of thirty-nine, Mykola S. Balabukha was elected Kyiv city head, but he refused the offer; in 1847 he was elected a second time – an offer he could not refuse this time – and remained in office until 1851.[30] Through intermarriage, the Balabukhas became related to some prominent Russian families: Mykola himself married a daughter of the merchant Fedor Riabchikov,[31] while his son, also Mykola, married the daughter of the Russian mogul and three-term city head Ivan Khodunov.[32] Other scions of the Balabukha clan continued their careers in public service and in business.[33] Another Ukrainian, the son of a local merchant (of lesser prominence), Hryhorii Pokrovs'kyi, was city head in 1857–60. Finally, Fedir Voitenko, city head in 1863–70, was an extremely popular figure among those "old-time residents" of Kyiv who "still had not forgotten the time of [their] self-government based on Magdeburg Law." These Ukrainian residents reportedly saw in him "a fully preserved monument [to] Kyiv's old days, so dear to their hearts" – so much so that after his death, grieving Kyivites turned his funeral into a ceremonial procession for the "old Magdeburg Kyiv."[34]

Overall, however, the most notorious plutocrats and old families fell from grace in post-1835 Kyiv. Because their economic prominence prior to 1835 had been linked to their unrivalled grip on municipal offices, their businesses all but collapsed when these clans lost their social and political monopoly. There were some exceptions, however, such as the already mentioned jam empire of the Balabukhas and the Kobets' family's famous tanneries.[35] By all accounts, the urban regime in Kyiv between 1835 and 1870 was defined by the Russian government, which tightly controlled all urban affairs. Large public works – new roads and streets, the university, schools, the Chain Bridge, and so on – all largely financed by the state, were sometimes subcontracted out to local entrepreneurs, but the role of the mercantile elites in municipal governance was rather limited. Nonetheless, these decades were the time of the new men, whether merchants or professionals.

It has been assumed that cities "offer a huge variety of job opportunities that allow poor people (indeed, everybody) to find talents they might otherwise never know they had."[36] Urban markets also create spaces where people can sell their labour to people with capital. Was imperial Kyiv such a city of opportunity? Was it a good place for newcomers? We have only anecdotal evidence. A few cases of migration – from Great Russia and from the Ukrainian hinterland – serve as good examples of the social advancement of "new" people in Kyiv on the eve of the great reforms of the 1860s.

One case is that of the already mentioned Russian merchant Ivan Khodunov (1788–1853).[37] He was born in the heart of Great Russia, but we do not know much about his life before he appeared in Kyiv sometime in the first quarter of the nineteenth century, as part of the ongoing migration of Russian merchants and smaller-scale traders of peasant background. We know that the young Khodunov started his economic rise with a modest trade in kvass, a business dominated by ethnic Russians. Prior to 1835, Khodunov had never held any significant office in the municipal government, as he probably had no connections with the local Ukrainian plutocrats who controlled the city's administration and much of its economy. Nonetheless, he got rich quite quickly, and in 1819 he was elected a "*quartiermeister* responsible for billeting troops" in the city. Other elected offices, albeit minor, soon followed. In 1825 he was elected a local trade deputy in one of the city's districts; in 1830 he was a member of the Kyiv housing commission dealing with billeting troops. In 1833 he was elected to the city pavement commission and also joined a board of prison trustees. All of these civic engagements paved his way to the highest municipal office – that of city head (*gradskoi glava*), to which he was elected in 1835 by a landslide.[38] Governor General Vasilii Levashov blocked his appointment, but his successor, Dmitry Bibikov, confirmed Khodunov's election in 1838. In all he would be elected five times and serve three terms in office.

Like his Ukrainian predecessors, he combined politics with business, in his case the production of candles and soap, as the founder of the city's first wax candle factory. In terms of urban space, Khodunov's tenure symbolized the turn from Podil to other parts of the city. His factories, businesses, and even houses were located in the new manufacturing and commercial areas such as the New Building (Novoe Stroenie), where he himself resided, and Khreshchatyk, where he built a famous hotel. Khodunov and Kyiv definitely benefited from each other. Although a migrant to the city, he surprisingly quickly won the trust of local merchants, so much so that in 1835 they sent him to Saint Petersburg for an audience with the tsar.

Khodunov's marital strategy proved no less important for the city. One of his daughters married a son of the city head, Mykola Balabukha. Another daughter wed Sylvester Hohots'kyi, a Ukrainian-born professor of philosophy at Kyiv St Vladimir University. Later she became publisher of *Kievskii telegraf* (1875–6), a liberal paper that during those years served as a mouthpiece for the Ukrainian radical intelligentsia.

The Russian-born Khodunov was arguably the most impressive example of a newcomer who thrived in the atmosphere of a city in transition. The imperial government encouraged the migration of ethnic Russians to the southwestern borderlands, and to Kyiv in particular, by issuing tax exemptions for fifteen or even twenty-five years as well as other "benefits," such as exemption from military service.[39] Soon dozens of merchants came to the city – most of them ethnic Russians, but also some Ukrainians and Greeks.[40] From the lists of merchants and burghers who enjoyed tax breaks we see that most of these Russian economic migrants came to Kyiv between 1843 and 1848, primarily from Kaluga, Moscow, and Tula provinces.[41] More remarkably, many of them settled in the traditional burgher districts – in Podil and Plos'ka – among the old-time Ukrainian residents.[42] Prior to the 1840s, Russian merchants had tended to settle in Pechers'k, closer to the Russian administration. This meant a big change for Kyiv's sociospatial relations, in which economic status and occupation mattered more than ethnicity. Russian merchants and skilled artisans seem to have benefited more than other groups from the new urban economy,[43] and they became the backbone of Kyiv's urban regime between 1835 and 1870.

Some Ukrainians, Poles, and Jews also managed to take advantage of the changing city.[44] Perhaps the most famous example of non-Russians in the city's business community was a firm founded by two Ukrainian merchants, Kindrat Iakhnenko and Fedir Symyrenko, who were based in Odessa. In 1846 they decided to establish their presence in Kyiv, where they planned to open a sugar refinery. But in the economic crisis of the early 1860s, the firm went bankrupt. Ukrainians turned out to be the least successful urban community in late imperial Russia.[45]

Kyiv Professors of "the Good Old Days"

The legislative reforms of the early 1870s brought about a dramatic change in the composition of Kyiv's municipal leadership, creating a new urban regime. The new law, which imitated the municipal systems of Prussia and Austria, granted the franchise to men twenty-five years of age and older who satisfied the property qualifications and who paid sufficient municipal taxes, either as real estate owners or as business owners. This system was based not on property values but on the sum of taxes paid to the city. As in the Prussian curial system, voters in Russian cities were split into three "classes," each paying one-third of all taxes irrespective of how many people belonged to each class.[46] The explanation for this three-class system was "not to permit the advantage of majority over minority, inevitable when all voters combined cast their votes." The first class included the wealthiest home and business owners; the second, middle-range taxpayers; the third, petty taxpayers. Thus a small minority of the largest taxpayers elected as many deputies as did much more numerous groups of voters. Most eligible voters chose not to vote in the 1870s and the 1880s. In Kyiv, for example, only around 16.4 per cent of voters came to the polling stations.[47] The share of voters was also small – in Kyiv, the 3,222 eligible voters amounted to only 4.2 per cent of the population,[48] while in Saint Petersburg, the 18,590 voters were only 3.4 per cent of residents.

Notwithstanding the very limited franchise, the reforms of 1870 meant radical change that affected both *how* the city was governed and *who* governed it. In chapter 5 I described the major political features of the post-reform urban regime, particularly the relations between the city fathers and the imperial government and the role of private actors in the "production" of (new) space in the capitalist city. Here I will describe the general characteristics of the urban regime as seen through the prism of the new municipal elite.

The new city administration represented all urban residents, whatever their social estate. This did not mean, however, that political representation had become democratic. Rather, after 1870 the municipal government represented the interests of several groups of bourgeoisie, among them industrialists, bankers, professionals, and homeowners. By taking advantage of "informal arrangements" and by accumulating various types of capital – financial, symbolic, and sociopolitical – these groups shaped the urban regime in Kyiv until 1917. As elsewhere in Europe, the petit bourgeoisie suffered along with the working classes, but at least the former found populist advocates in the city duma – mostly right-wingers, anti-Semites, and monarchists.[49]

The first elections to the reformed duma in 1871 brought about a drastic change in the composition of the elected deputies, reflecting the changes in who could vote. The total number of eligible voters had reached 3,222 – a considerable increase over the 150 to 200 voters prior to the reform.[50] Thus the first curia included the 96 wealthiest voters (40 in the homeowners' category, the rest mostly commercial taxpayers); the second curia included 532 voters (307 in the homeowners' category, 79 merchants, and 146 in a mixed category – those paying real estate taxes and showing merchant documents); and the third curia, the largest, included 2,594 people – the least affluent voters (most of them modest homeowners). Notwithstanding this clear dominance of homeowners among Kyiv's eligible voters, merchants were the most active voting block, as they were everywhere in Russia.[51] As a result, merchants comprised the largest single social group in the new duma.

Kievlianin published a breakdown of the results. Out of 72 deputies, 27 belonged to the "commercial and industrial estate"; 23 represented the learned professions (15 were university professors); and 22 were landowners, officials, or nobles.[52] The fact that more than one-third of the deputies, contrary to the government's expectations, still represented merchants and burghers, gave a pro-government journalist an opportunity to lash out at the "oligarchy." The "oligarchy," he wrote, was attempting "to demoralize voters"; by this, he obviously meant that the old mercantile elites had retained their influence in the city.[53] Who were these notorious old-timers? Among those elected in the second class were a few names that had been prominent in the city since the early nineteenth century, such as Bars'kyi, Zadolinnyi, Voitenko, and a few others. In fact, the great majority of ballots had been cast for Fedir Voitenko, Kyiv's last city head prior to the reforms of 1870. This reflected the dominant trend across Russian and Ukrainian cities – most elected deputies were merchants and burgers.[54] Although Jews were allowed to participate, not a single Jew was elected in Kyiv, which surprised even the conservative *Kievlianin*.[55]

The first city head of the post-reform city was a young and wealthy Russian socialite, Pavel Demidov (1839–85), a scion of the legendary clan of industrialists and philanthropists. Born abroad and educated at Saint Petersburg University, he served for a time in the Russian diplomatic service before relocating to Kyiv when he was thirty-one. He was elected to the office of city head primarily due to his wealth, as Kyivites believed that a rich mayor would be good for the city. His election was backed by the Kyiv governor general,[56] a sign that wealth and power still defined "informal arrangements" in the city. The young mayor at least partly met the expectations of Kyivites as he dispensed his large private funds for a variety of charitable causes.[57] But as one witness reported, Demidov was only a *formal* city head: he had hired a duma deputy – Professor Nikolai Rennenkampf – to run the city's daily affairs.[58] There was a charged atmosphere in the duma in the 1870s arising from a conflict between the old-timers (including Kyiv's former head, Fedir Voitenko) and the "newly fledged city fathers" (primarily university professors and other professionals).[59] Thus the duma's executive, the *uprava*, from its inception contained two factions – one professorial, the other mercantile.

The founding editor of *Kievlianin*, Professor Vitalii Shul'gin, unequivocally supported his university colleagues in the city duma. He was quite pleased with the second municipal elections in 1875 (he was elected). This time, he wrote, the deputies represented the "entire educated Russia"– that is, all of the city, and not only Podil and its part "beyond the ditch [i.e., the district of Plos'ka]."[60] Shul'gin, however, kept attacking a mysterious force – a "clique tightly organized by the leaders and upholders of the previous order" (probably old-time merchants), which had allied itself with "ultra-liberals" (an allusion to the liberal pro-Ukrainian paper *Kievskii telegraf*). Shul'gin was at least partly right: in the new duma, the merchants he detested comprised two-thirds of the members (46 out of 72), and almost half of all members (35) had been re-elected from the previous duma. In the new duma, the biggest difference from the old was the presence of three Jewish members (among them Israel Brodsky) and two burghers.

The duma after this one (1879–83) had fewer merchants, but they were still a majority (38).[61] There were also 15 professors, who formed the second-largest group, which increasingly defined the municipal agenda. When it came to religion, the Orthodox comprised an overwhelming majority (61), with religious minorities represented by Jews (6),[62] Lutherans (4), and a single Roman Catholic. By far the largest taxpayer was Professor Fedor Mering, the owner of a huge property just off Khreshchatyk, whose wealth could easily rival that of any merchant.

Around this time, the number of eligible voters increased considerably, to 4,157. This was primarily due to the extension of the third curia to 3,511 people. Throughout the 1880s the number of eligible voters continued to grow (although not proportionally to the growth of Kyiv's population). According to the police, Kyiv's population in 1887 was 165,461, compared to an estimated 76,979 in 1871.[63] By 1887 the number of eligible voters had increased to 5,750, but their share in the overall population had dropped to 3.5 per cent[64] (compared to 3,222 eligible voters, or 4.2 per cent of all Kyivites in 1871).[65]

By 1887 the first curia had decreased to 120 voters (compared to 155 in 1879–83). This can be explained by the imperial government's perennial desire to limit the participation of Jews and to diminish the political influence of plutocratic merchants of all faiths.[66] As the third curia had now expanded to 5,078 voters (compared to 3,800 in 1883), the city fathers decided to split the curia's electorate into five groups (in 1883) and then into six (in 1887); here, their apparent goal was to further limit the electoral clout of the most numerous and *poorest* voters. For instance, 650 voters from the curia's first group together paid 30,807 roubles in taxes and hence elected eleven deputies, while the sixth group, the most numerous one (1,673 voters, who paid 2,604 roubles in taxes) elected only one duma member.[67] Populist critics of this "reform" pointed out that the fewer members an electoral group was entitled to elect, the less enthusiastic the voters were about the elections. As a result, electoral activity among voters of the third curia decreased after it had been divided into several smaller groups.[68] One last factor restricted voter participation – tax arrears: all debtors were excluded from the electoral lists (18 voters from the first curia, 89 from the second, and 1,199 from the third). All in all, 1,306 eligible voters were excluded from the elections in 1887, and only 4,444 people were allowed to vote.[69]

The most severe curtailment of electoral rights occurred in 1892 as a result of the municipal counter-reform implemented by the increasingly reactionary imperial administration of Tsar Alexander III. While the formal workings of municipal self-government remained largely intact, the relationship between the imperial administration and cities changed. Cities were now more closely controlled by their governors and by Russia's interior ministers. For example, municipal agendas were to be approved beforehand by the governor, who could also block the implementation of *any* decision of the city duma if he deemed it "incorrect." Jews were now excluded from municipal self-government, and all *elected* municipal officials now had to be "appointed" and "discharged" by the government. More importantly, a sharp increase in the property qualification limited the pool of municipal voters to the most affluent residents.[70] Thus the number of municipal voters decreased dramatically, in some cities by more than 90 per cent. Now only somewhere between 0.4 and 1.8 per cent of urban residents in Russia enjoyed voting rights (compared to 5.3 per cent in the 1870s and the 1880s).[71] In Kyiv the number of eligible voters decreased to 1,936, or 0.8 per cent of all residents.[72] In some towns the number of elected municipal officials did not exceed that of voters! In comparative terms, the number of those who were entitled to participate in municipal politics in Russian cities after 1892 was considerably lower than in most European cities, including major cities in neighbouring Austria-Hungary.[73]

The consequences of all this in Kyiv far exceeded the expectations of the Russian government. The next electoral results ensured that the duma would be dominated by nobles and officials, including professionals and professors.[74] With 53 members (73.6 per cent) belonging to this elite group, Kyiv had the highest (after Kishinev, with 74.2 per cent) proportion of nobles and officials in the city duma among *all* Russia's cities.[75] The subsequent elections confirmed this trend. Although the number of eligible voters grew to 3,005 in 1898 and to 3,441 in 1902, their share in city's overall population remained negligible.[76] The social profile of the elected members of the Kyiv city duma also did not change much compared to 1892: nobles and the new professional class retained their grip on the city government (in 1902 the share of merchants and venerable citizens dropped even further – to 20.5 per cent, compared to 25 per cent in 1892).[77] Municipal politics in Kyiv remained a bastion of social elites until the end of the Old Regime, in sharp contrast to other major cities (such as Saint Petersburg, Moscow, Kharkiv, or Saratov). But the municipal elite in late imperial Kyiv was hardly homogeneous. It included both old and new elements, from service nobility and military officers to professors, teachers, and technical experts. Some of them also had an interest in the expanding financial sector, and this helped them run their political machines.[78]

It is almost impossible to reconstruct the political machines of Kyiv's new notables, save for a few general features of the post-1871 urban regime. A review of Kyiv's city heads reveals the rising role of professionals. Gustav Ivanovich Eisman (1825–84) best personified the new municipal politics and urban regime in general. A scion of an old German Protestant family (his father owned a famous pharmacy), Eisman studied law at Kyiv St Vladimir University, where he later held a chair in the history of Russian law. His wealth did not come, however, from his academic position, which he left in 1862, but from extensive real estate holdings that his entrepreneurial father had begun to assemble in the 1840s, such as a large plot on Khreshchatyk.[79] The young son provided his father with legal advice on how to maintain and augment his real estate empire. In 1871, Eisman was elected to the city's executive organ – the *uprava* – as a member supervising construction in the city. Soon he secured the highest municipal office – that of city head (first term 1872–3). He was elected again in 1875, and refused; and again in 1879, and accepted. He would remain in office until his death in 1884.

Eisman proved to be an authoritarian politician who followed the principle "the duma, it is I." As a legal expert well versed in the newly enacted Municipal Statute, he was able to push any of his decisions through the duma, which still included a number of barely literate members. His seemingly invincible political machine was heavily based on his chairmanship (between 1871 and 1879) of the Kyiv Municipal Mutual Lending Society.[80] That society was founded in 1868 by another professional of German descent, Professor Nikolai Bunge, for the purpose of issuing loans to its contributing members, most of whom were middle-class homeowners and developers. The society's first chairmen were almost exclusively professors at Kyiv University: Bunge, Eisman, and Heorhii Sydorenko (1882–9). A similar society, the Kyiv Credit Society (est. 1885), specialized in long-term loans.[81] Among its leading members were architects, building engineers, and duma members, such as the renowned architect Georgii Schleifer, also a German Protestant and the society's longest-serving director (1885–1913), who conveniently happened to be the head of the duma's building department (1882–1911). Another senior member of the board was Vladimir Nikolaev, Kyiv's chief architect (1873–87) and a member of the city duma for more than twenty years. A number of other famous architects worked for the credit society as experts in mortgages.[82] This expert knowledge was then translated into political influence in the city through the duma and its organs.

Thus the power of the new municipal elite had three pillars – the city duma, a prominent financial institution, and building expertise. A contemporary memoirist, a merchant unsympathetic towards the new professional and professorial elite, commented on the corrupt fusion of power, knowledge, and money, focusing on Eisman's political machine:

> In the good old days Kyiv professors, with a few exceptions, did not engage in scholarship; they delivered lectures to students from old outdated notes, and hence the professors enjoyed more than enough spare time. It is they who, being inspired by professor-millionaire Eisman and under his direct command, rushed towards various sinecures in banks and in the duma. The administration of the Kyiv Municipal Mutual Lending Society consisted entirely of professors. The chairman was Professor Eisman, his deputy – Professor [of financial law] Sydorenko who embodied the "at-your-service" attitude. Their deputies were either other professors

or Eisman's relatives ... By having seized this institution they [used it to] arrange elections to the duma of the exclusively professorial personnel.[83]

The same memoirist then called Eisman a "power-seeking and vain intriguer." Eisman's political machine was based on his ability to select loyal clients and get them elected. Apparently he "surrounded himself from all sides with his own minions obedient to his slightest wish," and he did not allow any independence in conduct and thought if these contradicted his own. His influence on voters seemed so great that whomever he ordered to elect, got elected, and whomever he did not want, did not.

This scathing criticism of Kyiv's new elite and Eisman in particular was not entirely fair, but it still provides us with a rare glimpse into the "informal arrangements" operating behind Kyiv's post-reform urban regime. A similar criticism of corruption and clientelism under Eisman's watch appeared in the liberal paper *Zaria*. Referring to the notorious sale of votes, a still optimistic journalist extolled the value of voting rights:

> Everything absolutely depends on the will and desire of the voters; it is only necessary that the voters should know their legitimate rights and use them for the common good, instead of selling their votes – their priceless civic rights – for the mess of pottage or for the promise of private gain. It is necessary that the voters, strictly abiding by legal grounds and conscience, should not elect as members of duma those people whose private gains, one way or another, are linked to the city's treasury.[84]

The same paper reported that the imperial auditor (Senator Polovtsov) had uncovered a number of irregularities in the workings of Kyiv's municipal self-government, including in its electoral system, whereby elected members "represent the interests of only a single class" (meaning the rich and powerful).[85] Allegations of corruption and of neglect of poorer residents were levelled at the city duma from left and right well beyond the tenure of strongman Eisman. In 1902 the renowned law professor Otton Eikhel'man (Otto Eichelman),[86] himself of Baltic German descent and a recent duma member, looked back at the 1898 council and came to an overall negative assessment of its legacy. He pointed to poor management, favouritism towards concessionaires, and the lack of progress in public services. More specifically he mentioned that the duma had chosen not to build a city-wide electric streetlight network; it had failed to cover the sewage ditch; it had not extended the horse tram network; and it had not taken "any measure to improve the cultural level of the masses."[87] Around the same time, strong populist criticism from the right – with anti-capitalist and anti-Semitic overtones – began to target the municipal oligarchy and the urban regime in general.[88]

Conclusion

Kyiv's saw at least three urban regimes between 1800 and 1905, which also signified dramatic changes in the composition of the municipal elites. This had the effect of displacing many long-time residents from the older parts of town to the peripheries. The changes in the composition of Kyiv's municipal leadership also reflected an overall demographic change: from a predominantly Ukrainian city to a Russian one at mid-century to a cosmopolitan one on the eve of the new century. During this last period, the city government was dominated by professionals in whose ranks "native Kyivites" were but a tiny minority. One can argue, however, that the overall quality of the city government considerably improved towards the end of the nineteenth century, when a fairly cosmopolitan group of professionals came to dominate the new city duma.

The twentieth century brought new disappointments, however. For example, arguably the most controversial of all Kyiv city heads[89] was a doctor from Podil named Vasilii Protsenko. He was Kyiv's version of Vienna's mayor, Karl Lueger – a virulent anti-Semite supported primarily by the "old-timers." These were mainly Russian and Ukrainian merchants and artisans from Podil. They rallied against their Jewish competitors, who supposedly represented large financial and industrial capital. Because of their role in the 1905 pogrom, the Kyiv city duma and Protsenko became known together as the "Black Hundred council with a hooligan mayor."[90]

All in all, however, after 1871 Kyiv's urban regime – as everywhere in the world – was increasingly shaped by financial and industrial capitalism and by the rise of a new professional class. In late imperial Kyiv, professionals of various ethnic backgrounds were well equipped with financial skills, technical expertise, and cultural capital, which together helped them end the domination of old-school merchants in municipal governance. Corrupt and reactionary at times, this new municipal elite nonetheless placed Kyiv on the map of the world's most rapidly growing cities.

PART FOUR

Living (in) the City

This exploration of imperial urbanism in Kyiv would be incomplete without a look at how people were associated with space – that is, without studying the changing social relations in the modernizing city in connection with urban space (the "sociospatial form" of the city). Admittedly, for much longer than many western European cities, Kyiv remained a rather traditional, pre-industrial town, with its spaces and population experiencing only slow change. Anthony Sutcliffe, a renowned expert on European planning history, described the difference between a traditional spatial pattern and the structure of a modernizing industrial city:

> The bigger the town, the more it tended to diverge in its economic, social and physical structures from the urban centers of pre-industrial Europe. Two related features, above all, marked it out as something new: its centrifugal dynamic of growth, and its division into areas of distinct function. In the pre-industrial town the wealth-generating institutions, among which trade and administration were very prominent, and manufacturing somewhat less so, had tended to concentrate in the center, in association with the homes of the most prosperous and powerful of the population. The poor tended to live on the outskirts. Such an arrangement, especially when combined with a static population, generated little peripheral expansion, a characteristic which was confirmed by the fortification ring which surrounded most European towns. Areal distinctions within the town, which were in any case not very marked, were usually based on the preference of various trades for particular districts, or on social divisions generated by the rivalry of great families.[1]

It was only with the rise of the capitalist economy that the city experienced marked residential differentiation and that social reproduction began to take place within particular, socially homogenous neighbourhoods. This process was conditioned by specific values, consciousness, ideology, and life experiences of city dwellers.[2] The noted urban geographer David Harvey has put forward a Marxist explanation for this modern urban development: "Residential differentiation is produced by forces external to the individual or even to the collective will of the particular social grouping. These processes stretch back over a relatively long time period, and it is probably the case that residential differentiation in the contemporary sense was well established in most major cities in both the United States and Britain by 1850."[3] One specific force responsible for residential differentiation was the activities of speculator-developers and speculator-landlords; another was the power of the financial and governmental institutions that facilitated the new capitalist order, in which the poorest had no choice of where to reside after more affluent groups had made their own choices. Residential differentiation has a mediating influence "in the process whereby class relationships and social differentiations are produced and sustained."[4]

What has been just said about the generic city can also be applied to Kyiv. As we have already seen, the city's municipal elite, especially prior to 1835, tended to reside in Podil near the Market Square, where the magistrate was located. Later, Kyiv's new "oligarchs" chose to reside on or near Oleksandrivs'ka Street, a major commercial artery leading from low-lying Podil to Khreshchatyk and then up to Lypky. A part of the Palace district, Lypky started as the centre of the Russian provincial government and soon also became the city's most elite residential area. In self-governing Podil, the rich and the poor resided very close to each other, whereas in Lypky, the social classes did not mix. Starting around 1850 the elites and the poor were increasingly separated spatially as city districts become more socially homogenous.[5] The residential differentiation in Kyiv was greatly facilitated by the building regulations enacted by the local provincial administration in 1851 and 1861 and then expanded by the autonomous municipality in 1874 and 1913. These regulations made certain streets and neighbourhoods privileged by ascribing different types of housing to different areas, which made building more expensive and taxes higher on the upper-category streets. Needless to say, only the affluent could afford to reside on these *deliberately* chosen streets. As the city grew together spatially, it grew apart socially. Even the concept of its centre radically changed, geographically, socially, and economically. This too affected the city's "psychogeography."[6]

Kyiv's residential pattern was somewhat shaped by its relatively underdeveloped industry. The city did not have a surrounding industrial belt. In many European towns, factory belts replaced former fortification rings around the inner districts, facilitated by efficient railway communications.[7] Kyiv's shape, by contrast, was defined by a combination of natural and technological boundaries – rivers and railway lines. In addition, the city's efforts to expand encountered a number of legal restrictions. Residential differentiation in Kyiv thus more resembled a patchwork than concentric circles. How exactly that patchwork developed and how it functioned needs to be explored more thoroughly. Finally, as a way to explore what Henri Lefebvre called *lived* space – the space of inhabitants who make symbolic use of the objects found in physical space (representational spaces)[8] – I will use for a case study the city's monuments, which might also be placed in the semiotic context of the "language" of cityscape.

Chapter Eight

Sociospatial Form and Psychogeography

People in Space

Space has become a social product, and all social relations have their spatial dimension. Henri Lefebvre showed how over time natural space is almost totally transformed by social relations.[1] He wrote that "any space implies, contains, and dissimilates social relationships" and that a space "is not a thing but rather a set of relations between things (objects and products)."[2] Space, then, is never produced in the sense that sugar and cloth are produced. Rather, space *itself* is a social relationship. For Lefebvre, however, it is not just any "social relationship" that matters, but the one that is inherent in property relationships (particularly landownership) and that is interwoven with the forces of production (which impose a form on that land).[3] Also, social relations and space are intrinsically linked to the moral order as a set of social mores and conventions, together comprising what David Harvey has called the "sociospatial form of the city." Referring to the American urban sociologist Robert Park, Harvey notes that "social relations were inscribed in the spaces of the city in such a way as to make the spatial pattern both a reflection of and an active moment in the reproduction of the moral order."[4] These mutual relations became more obvious with the rise of capitalism and the growing segregation of social groups in cities. Spatial segregation thus expresses various inequalities – of income, consumption, opportunities, and so on.[5]

Changes in the sociospatial form of the city were driven directly by the rise in the value of urban land. This happened in Kyiv largely in the second half of the nineteenth century. Single-family dwellings had long defined the city's spatial pattern. Most adult townsmen (and a number of their widows) in Kyiv owned real estate – often only a shack or a peasant-style hut with a thatched roof – but a few owned large homesteads with big stone houses and outbuildings. But not all of those who owned real estate in the city were "burghers" (*meshchane*) in the strict legal sense: houses were also owned by merchants, nobles, officials, soldiers, peasants, and foreigners. Later in the century they were joined by university professors, industrialists, and professionals (doctors, technical experts, lawyers, and bankers). Finally, after the 1890s the city's real estate market was driven by developers and housing entrepreneurs, who built large multistorey apartment buildings in which separate apartments were rented out to an ever larger class of professionals and employees in the public and private sectors.

Until the building boom of the 1890s, however, it was most common for a family to own a house in which two or three generations resided – the typical Anglo-American pattern.[6] Adult sons who lived under the same roof with their fathers and mothers were excluded from important municipal affairs.[7] Almost half of all listed homeowners were women. A female real estate owner was defined through the social or occupational status of her father or, most often, through that of her husband. Thus women were usually listed as "soldier's daughter/widow" (*soldatka*), "widow of a non-commissioned officer" (*unter-ofitsersha*), "official's wife" (*chinovnitsa*), "colonel's heiress," or simply as "townswoman," "noblewoman," or "female merchant." The latter category often referred to her independent commercial activities – merchant was one of the few occupations open to middle-class women.

The social and ethnic profile of homeowners varied over time and from one neighbourhood to another. The city developed a complex spatial ecology, with different social classes, occupational groups, and ethnicities tending to concentrate in particular neighbourhoods and quarters. Social and ethnic relations were indeed reflected in spatiality, even though the segregation of social and ethnic groups in Kyiv was never as rigid as in many European cities at the time.

For instance, Paris was an ethnic "melting pot" that reflected the growing power of the French state to assimilate minorities. At the same time, France's capital was a prime example of the mounting spatial segregation of economic classes, a process buttressed by and reflected in Baron Haussmann's planning schemes. In this proverbial "capital of modernity," the change in the city's sociospatial form followed the advent of new manufacturing patterns and the overall commodification of social relationships.[8] In major Central and Eastern European cities such

Table 8.1 Public, state, and private houses in Kyiv, 1817

	Pechers'k	Old Kyiv	Podil	Plos'ka	Total
Military, municipal, and public buildings	33	3	16	8	60
Manufacturing establishments	82	58	32	39	211
Shops	152	16	143	5	316
Stone houses	14	10	23	2	49
Wooden houses	1,598	957	438	926	2,919

Source: Funduklei, *Statisticheskoe opisanie Kievskoi gubernii*, 327.

as Prague, space always reflected changes in both socio-economic and ethnic relations, which led to a spatial separation of economic classes and ethnic groups.[9] Another example was Vienna, a truly multiethnic city; there, the numerous Czech migrants were overrepresented among the proletariat that resided in the outer suburbs (where they comprised nearly one-quarter of the residents in the growing industrial district of Favoriten).[10] In other words, in cities with complex interethnic relations any economic change also affected the city's ethnic composition by bringing rival nationalities into public space.

In Kyiv, just as in Prague, the links between ethnicity and spatial relations were quite visible. In Kyiv, however, ethnic segregation was much less pronounced than in Prague, and social segregation much less so than in Paris. Kyiv's ethnic and cultural divides seemed striking at times, but its public space and urban layout did not reflect interethnic dynamics as sharply as was the case in Prague, Lviv, or even Vienna (with its heavily Jewish district of Leopoldstadt, once the site of the Jewish ghetto). That being said, Kyiv's interethnic relations and spatial patterns were no less complex. A certain degree of social segregation did indeed follow from growing industrialization, as a result of which the city came to express in spatial form the dominant economic and social structures, a process facilitated by the more efficient market for urban land.[11] Also, the city experienced some form of ethnic segregation, particularly when it came to Jews and Russians, at various times during the long nineteenth century.

The earliest data revealing the city's sociospatial form come from 1817 (see table 8.1). Judging from the number of houses and shops in the four districts of the city, we can see that by 1817 Pechers'k had become the city's leading residential and commercial area, while Podil, the traditional base for self-governing burghers, was losing its edge in this competition (partly due to the devastating fire that had reduced its territory by 80 per cent). Meanwhile, the construction of the fortress in Pechers'k arrested the development of that district for many decades. Between 1832 and 1846 the authorities demolished no fewer than 533 private houses there, a planned destruction that initiated the earliest urban renewal policy in the city.

Tax records are even more useful for studying the city's sociospatial form. They listed real estate owners and revealed the distribution of social groups in space. Unfortunately, there are several potential problems with these records: (1) they listed only property owners and not the growing number of tenants; (2) they often used very fragmentary data; (3) the records have been preserved for several years only; and (4) the data for some neighbourhoods are missing.

Despite their limitations, these little-studied sources do provide invaluable insights into the spatial distribution of social and occupational groups in the city. These were social estates rather than fluid economic classes, and they retained a number of pre-modern vestiges, which meant that income did not necessarily coincide with social status and prestige. For example, military service was considered a highly prestigious occupation in imperial Russia, if not the most profitable one. Similarly, the civil service – that engine of social mobility for non-nobles – was thought to be more honourable than specifically urban pursuits such as trade, moneylending, crafts, or even a scholarly career, despite the obvious financial advantages of some of the latter choices.[12] Clearly, then, establishing the socio-economic locations of Russian imperial subjects is no easy matter. For that reason I have tentatively divided Kyiv's real estate owners into six categories based on social estates, bureaucratic ranks, and occupations featured in local property assessments. An ascribed status is much easier to detect than a person's economic position or wealth, for which we have only indirect evidence (such as the value of real estate).

The first category, the highest, consists of nobles and state servants – high- and mid-ranking officials, military officers, and professionals. The second category unites trading groups – guild merchants and "citizens" (*grazhdane*) – traditional but non-noble urban elites. The third category represents something of a departure from the first, as its occupations – non-commissioned officers (*unter-ofitsery*) and civil officials below the tenth class on Russia's Table of Ranks – are pieced together from the lower range of military officers and civil servants. The fourth category includes burghers and craftsmen (including shopkeepers and market sellers) – that is, the lower middle class, a group of urban poll

Table 8.2 Social profile of real estate owners in Kyiv by district, 1835–6 (%)

Social groups	Old Kyiv	Lybid'	Podil
I	112 (23.5)	25 (9.3)	82 (12)
II	2 (0.4)	7 (2.6)	83 (12)
III	109 (22.8)	52 (19.3)	32 (4.6)
IV	121 (25.4)	74 (27.5)	413 (60)
V	96 (20)	108 (40)[13]	60 (8.7)
VI	36 (7.5)	3 (1)	19 (2.7)
Total	**476 (100)**	**269 (100)**	**689 (100)**

Sources: Derzhavnyi arkhiv m. Kyieva (DAK), *fond* 1, *opys* 2a, *sprava* 254 (Old Kyiv); *sprava* 253 (Lybid'); and *sprava* 261 (Podil). The data concerning other neighbourhoods – Pechers'k, Ploska, and Palace – are not available.

tax payers (unlike merchants but like peasants). The fifth category consists of soldiers, Cossacks, and peasants residing in the city, legally (but not always economically) the most deprived social groups.[14] Finally, the sixth category includes church officials, from archpriests to sextons and church servants, a group always prominent in the Holy City of Kyiv. Retired officials and soldiers, as well as widows, are also quite numerous among homeowners.

Several time samples will allow us to notice the changes in the sociospatial form of the city. Table 8.2 shows the city's sociospatial form around 1835–6 on the basis of three neighbourhoods – the traditional "burgher" heartland of Podil (or Lower Town), Old Kyiv (Upper Town), and Lybid', a new quarter adjacent to Old Kyiv.

Tables 8.2 and 8.3 are certainly incomplete without the data from three neighbourhoods – Palace, Pechers'k, and Plos'ka – but even with the available data we can draw a few conclusions. Old Kyiv was the most socially diverse neighbourhood, while Podil was the most heavily "bourgeois." Lybid' was the least elite area, where peasants and soldiers-artisans comprised 40 per cent of all homeowners; most of them had been resettled from Pechers'k due to the construction of the new fortress. In terms of social groups, most nobles and officials owned real estate in Old Kyiv, a rising district with mixed demographics, while the overwhelming majority of merchants and "citizens" owned their property in Podil. The lack of data from Pechers'k especially affects our understanding of the residential pattern of homeowners belonging to the sixth category (church community), for many of them resided in the vicinity of the Caves Monastery.

Table 8.3 Residential pattern of social groups in Kyiv, 1835–6 (%)

Neighbourhoods	I	II	III	IV	V	VI
Old Kyiv	112 (51)	2 (2.2)	109 (56)	121 (19.9)	96 (36)	36 (62)
Lybid'	25 (11.4)	7 (7.6)	52 (27)	74 (12.2)	108 (41)	3 (5)
Podil	82 (37.4)	83 (90.2)	32 (16.5)	413 (67.9)	60 (23)	19 (33)
Total	**219 (100)**	**92 (100)**	**193 (100)**	**608 (100)**	**264 (100)**	**58 (100)**

Sources: The same as in table 8.2.

The evidence from the 1840s largely confirms the sociospatial patterns established in the mid-1830s.[15] These patterns changed radically only during the 1860s and the 1870s, with the rapid growth of the city and with the advent of railways. In the meantime, the most striking numerical changes affected Pechers'k, which lost a number of houses and people (primarily soldiers and peasants), who were relocated mostly in Lybid' district.[16] There was also a dramatic decrease in the rate of homeownership in Podil, particularly when it came to burghers (from 413 to 294), whereas the number of homeowners in Old Kyiv and in Lybid' almost doubled. This puzzling development can best be explained by the natural disasters that afflicted Podil, particularly the great flood of 1845, which forced many inhabitants to higher ground.[17] At the same time, the presence of wealthy homeowners in the second category increased in Podil both quantitatively and proportionally (from 83, or 12 per cent, to 121, or almost 21 per cent). By 1849, Plos'ka had surpassed Podil as the most populous district, in which homeowners-burghers predominated.[18] Palace district continued to be by far the most socially exclusive area; there, nobles and officials of all classes were the overwhelming majority among homeowners and the share of townspeople (around 15 per cent) was the lowest in the city.

Let us compare these data with the number of private houses in each district around 1845: in Pechers'k, 1,827; in Lybid', 453; in Palace, 392; in Old Kyiv, 781; in Podil 542; and in Plos'ka, 899.[19] These numbers generally confirm the spatial shift in Kyiv's demographics away from Podil and towards other, new and literally "gentrified" areas. Between 1845 and 1863 the population of Kyiv grew steadily, although the dramatic rise would occur only in the next decade (see table 8.4).

The most noticeable spatial trend around 1863 was the spectacular decline in homeownership in Old Kyiv and its dramatic rise in Lybid'. While the total number of homeowners in Old Kyiv markedly

Table 8.4 Social profile of real estate owners in Kyiv by district, 1863–4 (%)

Social groups	Old Kyiv	Lybid'	Podil	Plos'ka	Pechers'k	Palace	Luk'ianivka	Kurenivka
I	224	222	61	63	113	84	47	42
	(42.5)	(25.7)	(11.6)	(6.7)[20]	(24.8)	(64.6)	(9)	(6.6)
II	44	63	167	94	43	22	19	24
	(8.3)	(7.3)	(32)	(10)	(9.4)	(17)	(3.6)	(3.7)
III	110	229	71	72	72	12	111	39
	(21)	(26.5)	(13.5)	(7.7)	(15.8)	(9.2)	(21)	(6)
IV	70	207	181	619	101	7	235	479
	(13)	(24)	(34.5)	(66.3)	(22)	(5.4)	(45)	(75)
V	41	133	21	73	116	4	93	49
	(7.7)	(15.4)	(4)	(7.8)	(25)	(3)	(17.7)	(7.7)
VI	38	10	23	12	11	1	19	6
	(7)	(1)	(4.4)	(1.3)	(2.4)	(0.8)	(3.6)	(0.9)
Total	527	864	524	933	456	130	524	639
	(100)	(100)	(100)	(100)	(100)	(100)	(100)	(100)

Sources: Derzhavnyi arkhiv m. Kyieva (DAK), *fond* 17, *opys* 5, *sprava* 467 (Podil, 1864), *sprava* 662 (Palatsova or Dvortsovaia in Russian, 1863), *sprava* 663 (Lybid', 1863), *sprava* 664 (Pechers'k, 1863), *sprava* 666 (Old Kyiv, 1863), *sprava* 668 (Kurenivka quarter, 1864), *sprava* 669 (Luk'ianivka quarter, 1864), and *sprava* 672 (Plos'ka, 1864).

decreased (from 805 to 527) – most likely due to the secession of the suburb of Luk'ianivka – the share of nobles, civil servants, and military officers among local homeowners grew substantially (from 38 per cent in 1849 to 63 per cent in 1863). Only Palace district had a larger share of these groups among property owners (73 per cent). Lybid' grew due to its proximity to the university and because it had developed a diverse economy based on trade and manufacturing. Lybid' followed Palace and Old Kyiv as regards the share of nobles, officials, and military officers, with a total of 52 per cent (compared to 41 per cent in 1849). By contrast, the share of poor homeowners in Lybid' (soldiers and peasants) fell dramatically to 15.4 per cent, the lowest since 1835, when it was 40 per cent. Podil continued to decline, particularly in terms of the number of homeowners of burgher descent. Yet judging by the share of trading groups (merchants and "citizens"), the district was still an attractive area for commercial activities, and owners most likely chose to reside close to their sources of income. The reason for the narrowing gap between burghers and merchants in homeownership was not that society was growing wealthier but rather that fewer Kyivites could afford to own a separate home, for land in the city was becoming more expensive in an economy defined by the "land-rent gradient."

Pechers'k lost a number of homeowners to the fortress and its esplanade; even so, the district's social structure continued to reflect diverse demographics. By contrast, Palace district became even more exclusive, and now, in addition to the imperial elite, it was attracting more and more merchants. Another sign of the times was the decrease in the burgher homeownership rate everywhere in the city except in Pechers'k and in Kurenivka, a growing inner suburb where burghers formed the largest group among homeowners (75 per cent). Kurenivka was also the humblest area, with the smallest percentage of nobles and merchants among homeowners; this was reflected in the low average value of real estate there. Another suburb, Luk'ianivka, was more prestigious, with many nobles and officials owning homes there.

So, out of a total of 4,597 homeowners, members of the imperial elites – nobles, officials, and military officers – numbered 1,572 men and women (or 34 per cent of all property owners), a slight increase over 1849, when these groups accounted for 31 per cent. Burghers remained the largest single group of homeowners, at 41 per cent – a notable decrease from their share of 47 per cent in 1849. These changes in homeownership reflected general demographic changes in Kyiv between 1845 and 1863: the overall proportion of nobles *increased* from 16 to 17 per cent, while that of "urban estates" *decreased* from 38 to 33 per cent. Kyiv remained a bulwark of the Old Regime in the borderlands.

Most nobles, officials, and military officers from the first category owned their properties in Old Kyiv and Lybid' and to a lesser degree in Pechers'k and Palace (see table 8.5). Their humbler peers from the third category tended to own their homes in Lybid', Luk'ianivka, and Old Kyiv. Burgher homeowners resided overwhelmingly in Plos'ka and Kurenivka, the two poorest neighbourhoods. Merchants and "citizens" still preferred Podil and Plos'ka, although they also established a noticeable presence in Lybid', and even in the elite Palace district, where they now comprised 17 per cent of all homeowners (compared to 7 per cent in 1849). More transient and less established groups, such as peasants and soldiers, owned their property in newer, humbler, or more remote parts of town (Lybid', Pechers'k, and Luk'ianivka). Finally, by far the largest number of clerical homeowners resided in Old Kyiv – the site of St Sophia Cathedral and St Michael's Monastery – followed by Podil and Luk'ianivka.

Table 8.5 Residential pattern of social groups in Kyiv by district, 1863 (%)

Neighbourhoods	I		II		III		IV		V		VI	
Old Kyiv	224	(26)	44	(9)	110	(15.3)	70	(3.7)	41	(7.7)	38	(31.7)
Lybid'	222	(26)	63	(13)	229	(32)	207	(11)	133	(25)	10	(8.3)
Podil	61	(7)	167	(35)	71	(10)	181	(9.5)	21	(4)	23	(19)
Plos'ka	63	(7)	94	(19.7)	72	(10)	619	(32.6)	73	(13.8)	12	(10)
Pechers'k	113	(13)	43	(9)	72	(10)	101	(5.3)	116	(22)	11	(9)
Palace	84	(10)	22	(4.6)	12	(1.7)	7	(0.4)	4	(0.7)	1	(0.8)
Kurenivka	42	(5)	24	(5)	39	(5.4)	479	(25)	49	(9)	6	(5)
Luk'ianivka	47	(5.4)	19	(4)	111	(15.5)	235	(12)	93	(17.5)	19	(15.8)
TOTAL	**856**	**(100)**	**476**	**(100)**	**716**	**(100)**	**1,899**	**(100)**	**530**	**(100)**	**120**	**(100)**

Archival sources also allow us to study the geography of wealth and poverty based on the value of real estate and/or the taxes paid on it. By far the largest concentration of wealth was in Khreshchatyk, the city's rising commercial artery, which was split between two central districts – Old Kyiv (left side) and Palace (right side).[21] The largest and most lucrative properties there belonged to merchants and entrepreneurial members of the new class of professionals and occasionally to the old aristocracy. For example, Friedrich Mering (Moering), a professor of medicine and a wealthy proprietor, owned a plot assessed at 28,000 roubles, which consisted of a two-storey stone house with four shops on the ground floor as well as several outbuildings and a garden.[22] His peer and another German, professor of medicine Julian Matson (Julius Mazonn), owned a lucrative homestead assessed at 26,000 roubles; this property included several stone residential houses and a separate building with shops.[23] Two even pricier properties belonged to Ivan Kyselevs'kyi, the son of Kyiv's last *viit*: one homestead for 48,000 roubles, another for 20,000. But the most valuable property belonged to Anton Hudym-Levkovych, a Ukrainian aristocrat serving as a cavalry captain in the Russian military, who owned a large three-storey stone building assessed at a staggering 72,000 roubles.[24] This was Kyiv's legendary Hotel Europe, designed by the renowned architect Alexander Beretti, after which the nearby square was named.[25] Merchants owned a number of other valuable real estate assets on Khreshchatyk, ranging from the 50,000-rouble mansion of Ignat Bagreev to the 36,000-rouble homestead of Iakov Protazanov, an Old Believer.[26]

Outside of Khreshchatyk, the highest-priced properties were along Oleksandrivs'ka and Instytuts'ka Streets (in Palace district) and along Volodymyrs'ka, Zhytomyrs'ka, and Sofiïvs'ka Streets (in Old Kyiv).

This spatial pattern pointed to the rising residential segregation of the rich and the poor. Symbolic of this trend was Gustav Eisman, a lawyer and Kyiv mayor. In 1858–61 the architect Alexander Beretti built for Eisman's father a massive three-storey structure in the heart of Old Kyiv, at Zhytomyrs'ka Street 2 (today the Diplomatic Academy of Ukraine). In 1863 this property was valued at a mind-boggling 90,000 roubles.[27]

Wealthy merchants continued to do business and reside in Podil, particularly along its old thoroughfare, Oleksandrivs'ka Street. Here the most expensive properties belonged to Russian merchants, often Old Believers, who began to dominate local economy after the mid-1830s. Among them was the merchant Iakov Protazanov, whose property (a two-storey stone house, shops, and a one-storey annex) was assessed at 57,000 roubles. The widow of another Old Believer, and a merchant woman herself, Natalia Bugaeva, owned a few properties on this and other Podil streets (three two-storey stone houses, shops, baths, and an inn) assessed at 80,000 roubles.[28] There were still a few scions of older Ukrainian families. Judging by the properties, the wealthiest among them was Mykola Kyselevs'kyi, an official and probably another son of Kyiv's last *viit*, who owned a "two-storey stone house, an annex, and a barn" assessed at 36,000 roubles. Merchant and Kyiv mayor Fedir Voitenko owned two two-storey stone houses (worth a total of 36,000 roubles), while his predecessor in office, merchant Hryhorii Pokrovs'kyi, owned a similar property assessed at 31,000 roubles.[29] With very few exceptions, though, most Ukrainian merchants could be classified as the commercial middle class; they were no longer wealthy plutocrats.

Still, they were immeasurably better off than most Kyivites of any ethnic background in a city that was increasingly segregated by class. Some spaces became almost exclusively the domains of the poor, be they Ukrainian, Russian, or Jewish. Thus the entire Kurenivka quarter developed into a ghetto for destitute burghers. The overwhelming majority of homes there (many of them thatch-roofed huts) were assessed at 100 to 400 roubles.[30] But even there one could encounter rich merchants, who had located their factories in this remote suburb. For example, the Marr family, immigrants from Germany, owned a famous brewery in Kurenivka valued at 14,700 roubles.[31] Another German merchant, Genrikh Keln (Heinrich Koeln), owned a sugar refinery assessed at 50,000 roubles.[32] Conversely, a few poor homeowners lived in wealthy districts such as Palace and Old Kyiv, but there they were segregated, rarely mixing with more fortunate owners. For example, in

Palace the poor – mostly soldiers and burghers – lived in small wooden huts valued at 100 to 300 roubles, at the base of the Pechers'k hills, in the ravine known as Provallia.[33] In Old Kyiv the poor concentrated along Afanasiivs'ka Street (today the prestigious Ivan Franko Street), where some lived in dugouts.[34]

The data from the first official statistical survey of Kyiv's population conducted in 1863 confirms our archival findings regarding homeownership.[35] As an administrative centre of the borderland region, Kyiv had a large social and *spatial* presence of nobles and officials compared to most other imperial cities save perhaps Saint Petersburg and Warsaw. In this sense, social relations that reflected the dominant mode of production became inscribed in space and in the process *produced* that space.[36] In Old Kyiv, for example, nobles and officials owned a staggering 68 per cent of all residential buildings, although the percentage of these social groups in the district was only 35.5 per cent. By contrast, merchants and burghers, who comprised 24 per cent of the district's residents, owned only 19.6 per cent of the houses there. Old Kyiv's real estate market, however, was rather an exception as a bastion of imperial elites. Other districts were more typical of urban demographics. For example, in Lybid' three social groups – nobles and officials, merchants and burghers, and the military – each owned an equal share of residential housing (between 31 and 33 per cent). In Podil almost 70 per cent of houses were owned by merchants and burghers, who comprised more than 66 per cent of the district's homeowners but only 44 per cent of its residents.

Overall, Kyiv's space was still dominated by dwellings owned by burghers and merchants (51 per cent), who numbered 23,589, or 33.5 per cent of the city's overall population. Plos'ka and Podil had the largest shares of burgher-owned houses in their building stocks (65 and 37 per cent respectively). Houses owned by nobles and officials accounted for 25.5 per cent of all houses, thus markedly exceeding the share of these groups in Kyiv's population (17 per cent). Soldiers and their family members owned 17 per cent of Kyiv's housing stock, a low figure compared to their share in the population overall (25 per cent). Peasants were greatly underrepresented among homeowners, owning only 2 per cent of the houses although they comprised almost 16 per cent of the population – a clear indication that the peasantry was the least established community in Kyiv.

The city was still defined by single-family dwellings. Most often, these were urban homesteads (i.e., residential houses, often with annexes and outbuildings). Regarding the number of inhabitants per residential house, the average figure was six in Kurenivka quarter, eight in Plos'ka, nine in Luk'ianivka quarter, thirteen in Lybid', fourteen in Old Kyiv, nineteen in Podil, twenty-seven in Pechers'k, and twenty-nine in Palace district.[37] The average household size in Kyiv around 1863 was 13.48. In the poorest neighbourhoods, such as Kurenivka, Plos'ka, and Luk'ianivka, the household size was the smallest; this can be explained by the poor quality of the houses, which were often small shacks. In the elite Palace district, by contrast, the density was high because there, many houses were large and opulent, and the owners often rented them out to multiple tenants, often public servants. But why was the same figure so high for poor Pechers'k? The largest district by population, it contained a relatively small number of houses – fewer than in most districts. More than half the residents of Pechers'k were soldiers, who owned 51 per cent of all houses there, but many of them lived in barrack-like accomodations, which explains why so many people were crammed in one house. Also, there were a number of poor civilians in the district, so not surprisingly, of the city's 239 dugouts, almost half (100) were located in Pechers'k,[38] a neighbourhood where substandard housing predominated. The average household size in each district reflected residential density, which can be conceived of as the point at which the social and spatial in the city come together, thus revealing the social life of urban form.[39]

Summing up various statistics from 1863, we can say that the wealthiest and most prestigious residential areas in the city were Palace and Old Kyiv, both popular with nobles and officials, followed by Lybid' and by the emerging suburb of Luk'ianivka, while Podil and Plos'ka continued to be home to the lower middle classes. Pechers'k and Kurenivka were the poorest districts with the least desirable real estate. And while by number of residents Pechers'k, Lybid', and Podil were the largest neighbourhoods, poor Plos'ka had by far the largest number of houses and homeowners.

Finally, the 1863 census for the first time in the history of local statistics counted all residents according to their social status and place of residence (table 8.6).

Thus by share of nobles and officials the most elite district was Old Kyiv, although in terms of number of residents it was still modest, behind Pechers'k, Lybid', Podil, and Plos'ka. Nobles and officials also dominated the real estate market in Old Kyiv (owning 68 per cent of the houses there). Lybid', the most socially diverse district, perhaps best

Table 8.6 Sociospatial profile of Kyiv residents by district, 1863 (%)

	Old Kyiv	Lybid'	Podil	Plos'ka	Pechers'k	Palace	Kurenivka	Luk'ianivka
Nobles and	3,420	3,104	1,329	1,067	781	1,285	298	923
officials	(35.5)	(27)	(12)	(10.8)	(5)	(28.6)	(7)	(20)
Merchants	2,342	3,186	4,913	5,595	1,917	1,182	2,612	1,842
and	(24)	(28)	(44)	(56.6)	(13)	(26)	(61.4)	(40)
burghers								
Military	1,059	2,866	1,131	1,845	7,926	770	933	1,285
	(11)	(25)	(10)	(18.7)	(53.3)	(17)	(22)	(27.7)
Peasants	1,947	1,915	1,442	1,157	3,031	1,015	303	478
	(20)	(16.8)	(13)	(11.7)	(20)	(22.6)	(7)	(10.3)
Clergy	576	70	2,179	152	930	17	41	67
	(6)	(0.6)	(19.5)	(1.5)	(6)	(0.4)	(1)	(1.4)
Foreigners	289	287	167	67	271	220	66	39
and others	(3)	(2.5)	(1.5)	(0.7)	(2)	(5)	(1.5)	0.8)
TOTAL	9,635	11,430	11,161	9,883	14,856	4,489	4,253	4,634
	(100)	(100)	(100)	(100)	(100)	(100)	(100)	(100)

Source: Dinovskii, "Zapiska sekretaria statisticheskogo komiteta," p. 30.

represented the city's changing and diverse demographics, being home
to academics clustered around the university, as well as artisans (many
of them Jewish) and peasants seeking employment in the numerous
small workshops along Velyka Vasyl'kivs'ka Street. Surprisingly, the
largest share of peasants could be found in Old Kyiv and Palace districts, perhaps because many of them were employed as domestics
by the many nobles and officials who owned opulent residences or
rented large apartments. Also, a number of peasants were employed by
Khreshchatyk property owners, often on construction sites in the area.
The poor inner suburb of Kurenivka contained the highest share of
burghers, who were often priced out of the real estate markets in more
affluent parts of the city. But the real "world apart" from the rest of the
city was Pechers'k, which was populated overwhelmingly by temporary male residents (soldiers and peasants).[40] Despite these changing
demographics, Kyiv's real estate market was still dominated by traditional groups – "old-time" burghers and merchants, followed by nobles
and officials, many of whom had resided in the city for generations.

Remarkably, the census reveals the residential patterns of minorities.[41] For example, Roman Catholics (8,604 people in total) resided predominantly in Lybid' district (2,534, or 29 per cent), Old Kyiv (2,002,
or 23 per cent), and Podil (2,002, or 23 per cent). They also comprised

large minorities of the population of the two most elite districts – Palace and Old Kyiv – 23.5 and 21 per cent respectively – where they greatly exceeded their share of city's overall population (12 per cent). Many Roman Catholic Poles were officials and students and resided close to their jobs and schools. Finally, a number of Catholic artisans – most likely recent migrants from Right-Bank Ukraine – clustered together in parts of Lybid' and Podil. Jews comprised a small community of 1,411 people (2 per cent of Kyivites), and in contrast to the Poles, they lived in more modest quarters, primarily in Podil, Plos'ka, and Lybid' districts.

Between 1863 and 1874, Kyiv's population exploded. This was the first dramatic rise of the century – from 70,343 people to 127,251 (including suburbs)[42] – an increase of more than 78 per cent. An even more dramatic rise would occur between 1897 and 1905, when the city's population jumped from 247,700 to 450,000 – a rise of almost 82 per cent. How did these demographic changes affect Kyiv's sociospatial form?

Within a decade, Kyiv's sociospatial form underwent radical change, most likely in response to the rapid advent of capitalism, which brought new opportunities for migrants. The demographic rise, however, was unevenly distributed, reflecting the "distributional inequalities" typical of a modern city.[43] The most significant population increases occurred in the inner suburb of Luk'ianivka (more than doubled), in Old Kyiv and Plos'ka (doubled), and in Lybid' (almost doubled). The dramatic growth of Luk'ianivka pointed to rising urban sprawl and the flight of many nobles and officials to this nearby suburb, which had a reputation for a healthy climate. By 1863, around 35 per cent of all houses there were owned by nobles and officials (a percentage higher than in all other districts except Old Kyiv and Palace).

Like the statistical survey of 1863, the census of 1874 provided a sociospatial profile of *all* residents in every district and suburb, both owners and tenants. Judging from the tables in the 1874 census,[44] population growth affected most neighbourhoods; however, their social content remained almost the same as in 1863. There were, however, two general trends: a decrease in the percentage of soldiers in Palace, Kurenivka, and Luk'ianivka and an increase in the number and proportion of peasants in all districts except Pechers'k. This latter development no doubt reflected the peasantry's growing social and physical mobility in the aftermath of Russia's great reforms of the 1860s. Table 8.7 shows the residential pattern of social groups in Kyiv in 1874.

More than half of all nobles and officials resided in Old Kyiv and Lybid', in close proximity to the new centres of power, capitalist

Table 8.7 Residential pattern of social groups in Kyiv by district, 1874 (%)

Neighbourhood	Nobles and officials	Merchants and citizens	Burghers	Military	Peasants	Clergy	Foreigners and others
Old Kyiv	5,784	1,294	4,360	2,447	4,028	676	788
	(30)	(23.6)	(11.7)	(9)	(20)	(19.4)	(17)
Lybid'	5,013	744	5,910	3,605	3,867	267	1,502
	(26)	(13.6)	(16)	(13)	(19.6)	(7.7)	(32.5)
Podil	1,591	1,516	5,895	2,352	2,774	1,108	282
	(8)	(27.7)	(16)	(8.7)	(14)	(32)	(6)
Plos'ka	1,037	962	10,732	4,003	2,771	177	950
	(5.4)	(17.6)	(29)	(15)	(14)	(5)	(20.6)
Pechers'k	1,785	230	2,311	10,879	2,747	823	209
	(9)	(4)	(6)	(40)	(14)	(23.6)	(4.5)
Palace	1,893	411	1,439	988	1,319	265	570
	(9.8)	(7.5)	(4)	(3.6)	(6.7)	(7.7)	(12)
Kurenivka	212	82	2,971	771	478	45	105
	(1)	(1.5)	(8)	(3)	(2.4)	(1)	(2)
Luk'ianivka	1,960	240	3,523	1,982	1,770	121	210
	(10)	(4.4)	(9.5)	(7)	(9)	(3.5)	(4.5)
TOTAL	19,275	5,479	37,141	27,027	19,754	3,482	4,616
	(100)	(100)	(100)	(100)	(100)	(100)	(100)

economy, education, and culture. By contrast, burghers were scattered all over the city, although almost one-third of them resided in poor Plos'ka. The fact that so many peasants resided in central areas (in Old Kyiv and Lybid') alluded to the new patterns of urban economy – a number of rural migrants were becoming urban workers. No doubt, however, ever more peasants were engaging in trade and in domestic service.

In terms of housing stock, in the 1870s Kyiv remained a city of small wooden houses.[45] Most of the three- and four-storey houses were downtown, where most rental properties were located. Stone houses comprised a small minority (1,115, or 12 per cent) and were mostly located in Old Kyiv (338), Podil (277), Pechers'k (175), and Palace (121) districts. The number of dugouts and daub huts (*mazanki*) in Pechers'k (247), Kurenivka (230), and Plos'ka (175) indicates that acute poverty was concentrated in those districts. As regards the number of residential buildings, it is interesting to compare the data from 1863 and 1874 – before and after the demographic surge (see table 8.8).

There were 9,291 residential houses and 3,392 homeowners in Kyiv in 1874 (with some people owning more than one homestead).[46]

Table 8.8 Number of residential houses in Kyiv by district, 1863 and 1874

	Old Kyiv	Lybid'	Podil	Plos'ka	Pechers'k	Palace	Kurenivka	Luk'ianivka
1863	646	841	551	1,202	523	138	659	516
1874	1,206	1,766	1,167	1,788	1,199	444	862	859

Sources: *Sbornik statisticheskikh svedenii o Kievskoi gubernii* (Kyiv, 1864), 28–9 (1863); *Kiev i ego predmistiia: Shuliavka, Solomenka s Protasovym Iarom, Baikova Gora i Demievka s Sapernoiu slobodkoi po perepisi 2 marta 1874 goda* (Kyiv, 1875), 276 (plate 1, 1874).

The census provides fascinating data on the ethnic and social profiles of Kyiv homeowners. Out of a total of 3,392 owners, 3,072 (90.5 per cent) were classified as "Russians," 174 (5 per cent) as Poles, 72 (2 per cent) as Germans, and 39 (1 per cent) as Jews. "Russians," then, were greatly overrepresented among homeowners, while Jews were significantly underrepresented. The latter might be explained by various difficulties facing those Jews who wanted to reside in Kyiv. Most of them, even the more affluent ones, were tenants rather than owners, or owned homes through straw men of gentile origins.

In terms of the social origins of Kyiv homeowners, more than a half of them – 1,714 (50.5 per cent) – were burghers and merchants, 949 (28 per cent) belonged to the "privileged estates," 474 (14 per cent) were soldiers and their family members, and 229 (6.7 per cent) were peasants.[47] One crucial observation should be made regarding the social profile of homeowners: from the 1830s through the 1870s, it changed much more slowly than the city's overall demographics. Most newcomers to the city, especially peasants and Jews, whose numbers increased almost ten times between 1863 and 1874, did not own real estate. Also notable was a sharp rise in housing stock in Palace district, which might be explained by the rapid development on and around Khreshchatyk Street, the city's hottest commercial real estate market.

The census also provided valuable information about annual and monthly rentals in various city districts, which pointed directly to the rising number of tenants in the fast-growing city (see table 8.9).[48] The tenants, however, were distributed unevenly.

There is also evidence that the highest number of persons per homestead (*sadyba* in Ukrainian, *usad'ba* in Russian) could be found in Palace district (45.8), followed by Old Kyiv (30.8), Podil (25.4), Lybid' (22), Plos'ka (18), Luk'ianivka (15.6), Pechers'k (15.4), and Kurenivka (6.4).[49] These numbers show that the more affluent districts (Old Kyiv, Palace,

Table 8.9 Residential houses and rental apartments in Kyiv by district, 1874

	Old Kyiv	Lybid'	Podil	Plos'ka	Pechers'k	Palace	Kureniv-ka	Luk'ianivka
Houses	1,206	1,766	1,167	1,788	1,199	444	862	859
Apartments	1,908	2,799	1,424	2,073	988	577	221	969
Residents	19,377	20,908	15,518	20,632	18,984	6,885	4,664	9,806
Average number of persons per house	16	11.8	13	11.5	15.8	15.5	5.4	11.4
Rentals per house	1.6	1.6	1.2	1.1	0.8	1.3	0.2	1.1

Source: *Kiev i ego predmistiia*, 14–5 (table 2)

and Podil) contained larger homesteads and larger houses, while in poorer districts (like Kurenivka) both the plots and houses were small, populated by fewer residents (although in Pechers'k small houses contained comparatively more residents). As table 8.9 indicates, the highest rental apartment-per-house ratios were in Old Kyiv and Lybid' (although by annual rentals, Palace was ahead of Lybid'). This was a clear sign that with the rising urban rents in these central neighbourhoods, rentals had become a major source of household income. No wonder these districts would be the first to be infected by the construction boom of the mid-1890s. An important observation can be made from the predominance of monthly rentals over annual rentals in all city districts, but especially in Lybid' (2.9 to 1).[50] It meant that the city overall – and Lybid' in particular, the neighbourhood closest to the Central Railway Station – contained an increasingly transient population, including many Jews. All of these people needed short-term accommodation, and monthly rentals worked best for them.

The Palace district, which contained a relatively small number of *annual* rentals (354) – behind Old Kyiv (949), Plos'ka (765), Lybid' (713), and Podil (620) – boasted the second-highest aggregate rent (302,215 roubles), behind only Old Kyiv (655,543 roubles). Not surprisingly, the most expensive apartments, with annual rents above 3,000 roubles, were to be found only in Old Kyiv (17) and Palace (7), with combined rents of 112,593 and 34,990 roubles respectively. These two districts also contained the largest number of larger apartments (more than eleven rooms). Plos'ka contained the highest number of cheaper and smaller apartments (1 to 4 rooms) with rent below 12 roubles (71), followed by the city's poorest quarter, Kurenivka (48), and by Pechers'k (19). Lybid' and Podil took the lead in the "low-middle" category, for which the price range was from 50 to 150 roubles, while Old Kyiv prevailed in all price categories above 200 roubles. Podil rebounded in the upper categories (between 600 and 3,000 roubles), behind only Old Kyiv. This probably indicated that many members of the traditional mercantile elites still resided in Podil, while the new professional and commercial classes preferred to own and rent their dwellings in Lybid' and Old Kyiv. As new administrative, educational, and commercial institutions clustered together in these two neighbourhoods, more and more tenants and owners took up residence nearby. Both annual and monthly rentals (with central areas offering a number of luxury apartments, while Kurenivka and Plos'ka offered the cheapest)[51] indicate that because of population growth and rising economic complexity, Kyiv's housing market was becoming quite diverse.

The census also permits us to reconstruct the residential pattern of minorities. Thus the largest numbers of those born in the Great Russian provinces resided in Pechers'k (3,948, or 25 per cent) or Old Kyiv (2,779, or 18 per cent). Most of them were military and officials residing close to their employment sites. By contrast, the largest numbers of native-born Kyivites resided in the most populous neighbourhoods – Plos'ka (7,801, or 24 per cent), and Lybid' (6,024, or 18.5 per cent). The third-largest group of those born in Kyiv (4,067, or 12.5 per cent) lived in the middle-class suburb of Luk'ianivka, where they comprised more than 40 per cent of all residents.

Those who claimed to speak the Great Russian language were outnumbered by Ukrainian speakers in each district. Surprisingly, the highest number of Great Russian speakers resided in Podil (1,604, to 4,838 Ukrainian speakers), which indicates that this one-time heartland of the city's Ukrainian burghers experienced dramatic changes after mid-century. Most of the city's 7,400 Polish speakers resided in Old Kyiv (2,324, or 31 per cent) and Lybid' (1,915, or 26 per cent), a pattern unchanged since at least 1863.[52] However, the share of Polish Catholics in the population of the most elite districts had considerably decreased since 1863 and now was about 15 per cent in both Palace and Old Kyiv, largely because in the aftermath of the Polish January uprising, Roman Catholics were discouraged from residing in Kyiv.[53]

Jews, who numbered 11,662 in 1874, were forced by law to reside in three districts – Plos'ka (5,926, or 51 per cent), Podil (2,360, or 20 per cent), and Lybid' (1,891, or 16 per cent).[54] Although 28.7 per cent of Plos'ka's

Table 8.10 Assessed property tax per district (in 000s of roubles)

District	1878[55]	1882	1886	1895
Old Kyiv	2,456,800	42,503	71,870	56,376
Lybid'	1,308,500	18,025	31,450	25,376
Podil	n/a	17,685	26,553	23,630
Plos'ka	638,100	9,097	13,040	9,162
Pechers'k	313,400	5,619	8,046	4,338
Palace	1,315,300	19,161	30,004	25,462
Kurenivka	157,800	1,778	2,577	1,994
Luk'ianivka	286,200	7,202	10,979	8,490
Bul'varna	n/a	6,165	8,087	7,491
Total	**7,773,600**	**128,356**	**202,611**	**162,915**

Sources: *Kievlianin*, 98 (1878), 1; 106 (1886), 2; 229 (1895), 3; *Zaria*, 134 (1882), 2.

residents were Jewish, and some parts of the district were overwhelmingly Jewish, one can hardly talk about Jewish ghettoes in late imperial Kyiv.[56] The only important change in the Jewish residential pattern occurred in the early twentieth century, around 1908, when almost 10 per cent of Kyiv's Jews lived in Old Kyiv, a privileged downtown district, and the most "Jewish" neighbourhood was no longer Plos'ka but Lybid' in the south, an area that now contained 42 per cent of city's Jewish residents. This spatial change also pointed to a social change: the birth of a new professional class of Jewish doctors, lawyers, and engineers, who took up residence in more prestigious areas.[57]

The imperial census of 1897 does not provide any specific information on city neighbourhoods. Other sources, however, can help us trace both continuities and ruptures in the history of Kyiv's sociospatial form. One such source is the tax on private housing (*otsenochnyi sbor*), collected by the city from property owners. It also reveals the hierarchy of the city's neighbourhoods through residential property assessments (see table 8.10; see also map 5).[58]

Assessments fluctuated as a function of the market, rental prices, housing stock, and (more often) the valuation method used.[59] Despite this, we can clearly see that Old Kyiv was consistently assessed as the most expensive property market in the city, almost always followed by the Palace district, which was much smaller in size and population. The emerging district of Lybid' – much larger than Palace – was usually assessed as the third-hottest property market in the city. In general, high assessments in late imperial Kyiv were a function of *centrality*.[60] The new city was centred on Khreshchatyk – the thoroughfare with the highest property values – and on the university quarter (situated largely in Lybid' district).

Plos'ka illustrates the curse of peripherality. By 1897 it had grown to become the largest district in terms of population and the number of residential houses, but it was consistently one of the neighbourhoods with the least valuable real estate. This is confirmed by the data on the profitability of homesteads during the first building boom, in the mid-1890s. In 1898 there were 7,000 privately owned homesteads (including suburbs): 1,421 in Plos'ka, 1,333 in Luk'ianivka, 1,290 in Lybid', 749 in Old Kyiv, 673 in Bul'varna, 623 in Pechers'k, 495 in Podil, and 188 in Palace.[61] Around 1,419 homesteads – located in the "most developed districts" (Old Kyiv, Palace, and Podil) – had been mortgaged by their owners to raise funds to build rental apartment houses. But the owners of homesteads from Plos'ka and Kurenivka could not get the needed funds for redevelopment because their properties were "filled up with very poor huts of very little value."[62] Among other negative factors was inadequate access to public transportation, services, jobs, and education.

The twentieth century brought new homeownership structures, population sizes, and densities. Tables 8.11 and 8.12 show the population sizes and densities of various disricts in the late nineteenth and early twentieth centuries.

We can see that the highest densities were in central neighbourhoods (Old Kyiv and Palace) and also in the old residential hub of Podil.[63] By 1905 the population of some districts had grown substantially, and so had densities. The latter had grown especially in Old Kyiv, from 236 to 343, in Luk'ianivka, from 70 to 135, in Lybid', from 163 to 284, and in Palace, from 226 to 342 persons per *dessiatina*.[64] That poverty is not always correlated

Table 8.11 Number of residents in Kyiv's districts, 1863–1905[65]

	Old Kyiv	Lybid'	Podil	Plos'ka	Pechers'k	Palace	Kurenivka	Luk'ianivka
1863	9,635	11,430	11,161	9,883	14,856	4,489	4,253	4,634
1874	19,377	20,908	15,518	20,632	18,984	6,885	4,664	9,806
1897	39,782	35,264	35,200	49,455	33,460	16,958	n/a	26,493
1905	57,632	61,344	36,223	46,110	29,549	25,648	n/a	51,368

Sources: Sources: Dinovskii, "Zapiska sekretaria statisticheskogo komiteta," 28; *Kiev i ego predmistiia*, 3 (plate 1); Nikolai Sementovskii, *Kiev, ego sviatynia, dre`vnosti, dostopamiatnosti i svedeniia neobkhodimye dlia ego pochitatelei i puteshestvennikov.* 7th ed. (Kyiv and Saint Petersburg, 1900), 19; *Kievlianin*, 56 (1906), 2.

Table 8.12 Population densities in city districts (per *dessiatina*[66]), circa 1897–1902[67]

Districts	Population	Area (in *dessiatinas*)	Persons per *dessiatina*	Persons per homestead
Plos'ka	49,455	957	51	19
Old Kyiv	39,782	168	236	53
Lybid'	35,264	216	163	23.5
Podil	35,200	103	341	67
Pechers'k	33,460	170	197	39
Luk'ianivka	26,493	380	70	17
Bul'varna	23,099	205	112	24
Palace	16,958	75	226	72

Sources: Sementovskii, *Kiev, ego sviatynia*, 7th edition (Kyiv and Saint Petersburg, 1900), p. 19; I. Tairov, comp., *Plan goroda Kieva so vsemi zemliami, sostoiashchimi v vedenii onago po Kievskoi gubernii/* Kievskaia gorodskaia chertezhnaia (Kyiv, 1902).

with higher densities[68] is illustrated by the examples of Old Kyiv, Palace, and Plos'ka – two high-density areas and one low-density. Palace and Old Kyiv exploited their high population densities, which brought more and more people closer to transportation, jobs, schools, cultural venues, and so on. These two districts along with Lybid' absorbed the highest numbers of newcomers to the city between 1897 and 1905. The high concentration of persons per homestead can be explained partly by the relatively large average size of homesteads (for Palace) and partly by the height and number of buildings on each plot (for Podil and Palace and especially for Old Kyiv). By contrast, low-density Plos'ka[69] was far from most of the urban advantages associated with higher densities, while experiencing all possible disadvantages of its peripheral location: a lack of public services and amenities, poor sanitation, concentrated poverty, and so on. The single streetcar line running through Plos'ka had been laid out later than most – in 1903.[70] In the 1870s, Plos'ka (together with Lybid') had the highest mortality rate for Orthodox residents (30–5 per 1,000). Even thirty years later, around 1900, Plos'ka was still being described as the neighbourhood with the unhealthiest living conditions in the city – a consequence of the swampy ground and frequent flooding – and as a place in which many poor families lived in damp, airless basement apartments, sometimes two or three families to a one-room apartment. It was also estimated that Jews lived three times more densely than Christians.[71] Overall, Kyiv was a quite sparsely populated city, although almost half its residents – both Jewish and Christian – lived in high-density neighbourhoods (in Old Kyiv, Podil, and Pechers'k).[72]

Table 8.13 Residential densities in city districts (per *dessiatina*), circa 1902

Districts	Number of homesteads	Area (in *dessiatinas*)	Number of homesteads per *dessiatina*	Size of homesteads
Plos'ka	2,611	957	2.7	0.36
Plos'ka proper	769	235	3.3	0.30
Old Kyiv	751	168	4.5	0.22
Lybid'	1,499	216	7	0.14
Lybid' proper	1,217	195	6	0.16
Podil	523	103	5	0.19
Pechers'k	854	170	5	0.19
Pechers'k proper	252	39	6.5	0.15
Luk'ianivka	1,550	380	4	0.24
Bul'varna	967	205	4.7	0.21
Bul'varna proper	316	52	6	0.16
Palace	235	75	3	0.31

Source: I. Tairov, comp., *Plan goroda Kieva* [1902]

Residential densities (homesteads per *dessiatina*) painted a slightly different picture than population densities. For this part of the discussion, I will use so-called *site density*, which includes only the *residential* component of the land area – the area occupied by homesteads[73] – which excludes local roads and all non-residential land uses such as parks and schools. The result will be the most concentrated measure of density (see table 8.13).

In terms of the number of homesteads per *dessiatina*, the densest neighbourhoods were not Palace and Old Kyiv; they were Lybid', Pecher'sk, and Bul'varna (the latter two without their suburbs), where homesteads tended to be small and rather poor. Judging from population and residential densities and also from the low property values, Pechers'k was a prime example of high density combined with high levels of poverty and peripherality.[74] Lybid' was a mixed-income neighbourhood with an increasing population density and above-average residential density. During the first years of the twentieth century, construction in Kyiv came to a halt,[75] but by 1907–12, Lybid' had become the primary site for a new building boom. During those years, the neighbourhood was reshaped: smaller plots were consolidated and taller structures were built, which dramatically increased densities.[76] The largest homesteads were in the elite Palace district, where building plots tended to be larger due to the activity of commercial developers, who bought up smaller properties and built large multistorey apartment houses on them. This explains why the lowest number of homesteads per *dessiatina* and the highest number of people per homestead were both in Palace.

The average number of homesteads per *dessiatina* in Kyiv (including suburbs) was 4.8, with the average size of homesteads being 0.2 *dessiatina*.[77] It stands to reason that two central districts – Old Kyiv and Palace – with their high population densities and relatively low residential densities, must have contained taller and bigger buildings from the time of the earliest building booms. There was also continuity in terms of household size: the districts with the highest number of persons per homestead in 1902 were the same as in 1874: Palace, Old Kyiv, and Podil.[78]

Lacking sufficient data on the social profile of homeowners in the early twentieth century, we can only assume that more and more homesteads were owned by merchants and real estate speculators. As a consequence, the rate of homeownership among burghers, petty officers, soldiers, and peasants was declining, especially downtown.[79]

The relative importance of neighbourhoods can also be judged from the number of municipal voters in each district. As the electoral property qualification became much stricter, the number of voters in Kyiv decreased sharply, from 5,647 in the late 1880s to around 2,200 in 1892.[80] Most homeowners and merchants and all Jews were excluded from the electoral process. So in 1902,[81] the largest single group of voters (688) – most of them homeowners – resided in Old Kyiv, while the largest district by population – Plos'ka – had only the fifth-largest group of voters (284). Pechers'k – fifth by population – had only 134 voters – the fewest among eight districts. Podil had 334 voters, while far less populous Luk'ianivka had 438. Bul'varna and Palace – a district with a considerably smaller population – had almost equal numbers of voters – 217 and 206 respectively. As a result of all this, Old Kyiv provided 20 members of duma; Lybid', 15; Luk'ianivka, 12; Podil, 9; Plos'ka, 8; Bul'varna, 6; Palace, 6; and Pechers'k, 4. Thus, almost half of all duma members came from the centre – from Old Kyiv and Lybid', whose residents comprised only 29 per cent of city's entire population. Clearly, wealth mattered more than size in the spatial distribution of political influence in the city.

The "land-rent gradient" confirmed the new hierarchy of city districts. Around 1907 the price of a square *sazhen*[82] of urban land varied from 17 roubles in Podil to 60 in Luk'ianivka to 72 in Old Kyiv to more than 130 in Palace. By 1910 the price for a plot in the most prestigious districts – Palace (Lypky) and Old Kyiv – had grown to 200 to 300 roubles per square *sazhen*,

8.1 Kul'zhenko, Khreshchatyk, *Vidy Kieva*

while on the most fashionable streets – Khreshchatyk and the recently developed Mykolaïvs'ka – that price had reached 600 and even 800 roubles.[83] More than half of all residents now lived in the new multistorey apartment buildings. Also, a majority of the homesteads with the highest assessments (above 1,500 roubles) were located in Old Kyiv, Lybid', and Luk'ianivka. In Old Kyiv, Podil, and Palace districts these most valuable properties comprised absolute majorities of all homesteads – 88, 78, and 74 per cent respectively.[84] Another important trend during these years was the change in the social geography of elite neighbourhoods such as Palace. The invasion of the bourgeoisie had changed the real estate market there. New owners bought up properties from the impoverished aristocracy, in the process taking on the aristocratic lifestyle.[85]

To illustrate these and other crucial changes in Kyiv's sociospatial form and psychogeography, let us consider a few particular cases from fiction, the press, memoirs, and scholarly literature. The Russian writer Nikolai Leskov, who came to Kyiv in 1849 during the tenure of the notorious Governor General Bibikov, noted that significant sociospatial changes had occurred in the city by the time of his writing in the 1880s. These changes were largely a direct result of the government's active measures in urban planning. This aggressive planning strategy was augmented by a series of social, economic, and demographic policies that also affected Kyiv's cultural profile. Leskov focused on ancient Pechers'k, which had once been dominated by the Caves Monastery. In the 1820s and 1830s, Pechers'k was the centre of commerce and high living, rivalling the burgher quarter of Podil. With the construction of the new Pechers'k fortress beginning in the early 1830s, this highly diverse (ethnically, socially, and economically) urban district fell into decay until the end of the century. As a consequence, Kyiv's administrative headquarters and carriage trade districts moved elsewhere.

By 1820, Lypky had emerged as the city's first socially exclusive neighbourhood, perhaps because the seat of imperial power and noble privilege (the Noble Assembly) was there. Named after the linden trees that had once grown there, Lypky was situated between Pechers'k, now an enclosed military zone, and a new commercial district around Khreshchatyk. Lypky's aristocratic population remained diverse, mixing foreigners and locals of various descents. An informed observer wrote about the cosmopolitan atmosphere of the 1850s, one in which Russian aristocrats (Princes Kudashev and Vasil'chikov) mixed with Ukrainian (Myloradovych, Lukashevych, and Bezborod'ko) and Polish (Count Tyszkiewicz). In some of these houses "splendid feasts took place, as well as dazzling balls and receptions; at the receptions at Myloradovych and Veselyts'ka they made a show of the Ukrainian language."[86]

Iuliia Veselyts'ka (?–1822) was the widow of Petro P. Veselyts'kyi (d. 1812), a Russian imperial diplomat of Ukrainian–Dalmatian background in whose home "all of Kiev was seen."[87] The fate of their family mansion in Lypky reflects the various changes – topographic, social, and ethnic – that Kyiv underwent during the nineteenth century.[88] Since the early nineteenth century this large mansion (on more than five acres of land, or 1.45 hectares) had been owned by the Veselyts'kyi clan, which was linked to several other noble Ukrainian families. It speaks volumes about Kyiv's socio-economic structure that even in the 1820s, this mansion was still not only an urban aristocratic salon but also a farm on which oxen and probably other types of cattle were raised.[89]

When Governor General Vasilii Levashov in 1833 launched a large-scale urban planning scheme, some private properties in Lypky – among them the one owned by Mykhailo Veselyts'kyi, Iuliia's older son – were expropriated in exchange for either other land parcels within the city or monetary compensation. Veselyts'kyi opted for the money, setting a price of 7,000 rubles, and in 1834–5 the imperial authorities compensated him through an auction.[90] The remnants of Veselyts'kyi's property still appear on a tax assessment list for 1863, valued at 9,000 roubles.[91] The property remained in the hands of the Veselyts'kyi clan until perhaps the 1870s, when it was sold to an "outsider," Prince Semen M. Vorontsov, a Russian. After that, its owners were mostly non-Ukrainians, among them the family of the engineer Eduard Adelheim (in the 1880s–1890s) and the family of the Jewish sugar baron Lazar Brodsky (1890s–1911). It is worth noting that during this period the owners took advantage of the rising real estate prices in the area and profitably rented out houses divided into upscale apartments. After 1911 the new owners – the famous Tereshchenkos – split the property in several parcels to construct separate residences.

Those residences became the most visible sign of Lypky's exclusive social standing. The *osobniak* (literally "standing by itself"), somewhat analoguous to Parisian hôtel particulier, was a local type of comfortable home, usually referring to a one- or two-storey detached house occupied by a single family. This type of private residence was especially widespread in Lypky, Old Kyiv, and Luk'ianivka, and among their owners, professionals and capitalists comprised the largest groups (25 and 20 per cent respectively), followed by state officials and military officers.[92] Tenants were not welcome.[93] Because of high taxes and maintenance fees, only the rich could afford such accommodation in the historic core of the city. Lypky boasted the highest number of wealthy private residences in all of Kyiv.[94] While socially homogenous, the area remained ethnically diverse well into the twentieth century: here were the mansions of Russian statesmen (such as Kyiv's notorious governor Fedor Trepov) alongside the palaces of Jewish "plutocrats," among them Lazar Brodsky.

"These Places of Misery"

In psychogeographic terms, Lypky was universally perceived as the "healthiest" place in the city. According to a late-nineteenth century authority on Kyiv topography, "thanks to the extensiveness of homesteads, abundance of gardens, and generally clean air [Lypky] is the most favourable [area] for living in hygienic regard; that's why it is inhabited mostly by wealthy people."[95] Whether the wealthy gravitated towards other wealthy people or were attracted by the healthy climate is difficult to say. Perhaps it was both. According to various estimates, there were also private mansions-*osobniaky* outside of Lypky (Palace district) – in Old Kyiv, Bul'varna, and Luk'ianivka districts – but there they were almost invisible among the continuous blocks of multistorey rental apartment houses. In the rest of the city – in Podil, Pechers'k, Plos'ka, and Lybid' districts – the *osobniak* was a rare bird.[96] Lypky was also among the first neighbourhoods in Kyiv to have experienced a strict zoning policy: apart from a pharmacy and a few grocery stores, other commercial, manufacturing, and drinking establishments (such as inns and taverns) were not allowed there.[97] The notables and plutocrats residing in Lypky, as everywhere, liked quiet and did not want to be disturbed by the smells and noises of drinking and working folk.

The very concept of urban centrality was also defined in psychogeographic terms. In one early description, Khreshchatyk was portrayed in much the same way as Nevskii Prospekt was in Gogol's fiction, as a chimerical social carnival, or a masquerade: "Every day from 4 pm the walkers begin to gather on the main Khreshchatyk Street. And you would see here everybody ... This is a real Venetian carnival! Everything here is in full swing as in the anthill and it seems that everybody keeps oneself busy."[98] The centre was also set against the periphery – both geographic and mental – with the latter often imagined in the local press as unhealthy, miserable, and dangerous. In one article, the criminals who had taken part in the anti-Jewish pogrom of 1881 were identified with the outsiders residing on the edges of the urban core. The liberal reporter urged the police to turn their attention to those remote streets "which are populated by the migrant working folk from Great Russia: there one can possibly find much of the loot ... Passersby see there all the time children who play, among other toys, with the silver fragments of watches, even with entire piano covers and legs, remnants of broken costly furniture, chandeliers and their frames, caskets, and so on. It is these streets that provided the largest contingent of looters."[99]

Earlier the same newspaper had reported that "the main culprits, leaders and instigators of the pogrom were Muscovites who arrived in hundreds to Kyiv with a goal to plunder." Reportedly they belonged neither to the "cultivated class" nor to the workers, but rather were burghers from Moscow. The reporter added that it was obvious that these guys were "strangers who had never been to Kyiv before." But now they were gone, "as if they vanished into thin air."[100] The liberal paper was trying here to exonerate local residents and the entire urban core from any possible links to the pogrom, by locating violence within peripheral spaces and attributing it solely to one group of outsiders. It seemed that the best way to prevent any subsequent plunder was to better control the "dangerous" spaces populated by elusive "strangers." This very fact made control both essential and unfeasible.

Thus the outskirts generated a constant psychogeographical tension in urban public space. For its part, the monarchist paper *Kievlianin* reported that outsiders – ethnic Russians – had been the most active looters during the pogrom. One "eyewitness" mentioned that across the city people were telling "the most incredible tales about the hordes of *katsapy* [pejorative for Russians] who came to the city." But this depended on the area: in some places he had seen predominantly locals – artisans and day labourers – carrying loot from plundered Podil; in others, it was migrant Russian workers, "strangers."[101] Clearly, middle-class residents across the ideological spectrum preferred to associate crime with outsiders and peripheries.

In the minds of middle-class Kyivites, the suburbs were spaces of crime and violence. Shuliavka was the most notorious of them all. Paradoxically, crime was one of the reasons why some local residents thought Shuliavka should merge with the city – for policing purposes.[102] But the city was reluctant to annex the outer suburbs – officially because of the costs involved, unofficially because of the undesirable demographics. Sometimes, however, human misery was hidden just behind the main streets and affluent façades of the city centre. One social moralist drew the attention of the inhabitants of the "centre" to "such places":

There are such places in Kyiv of which the inhabitants of the "center" do not have the slightest idea and of whose very existence they are hardly aware. If somebody from these "central" residents accidentally got to one of such places, he would have been genuinely surprised at the fact that inside such a well maintained city there were such isolated areas [*zakholustia*]. These places of misery are not always clustered on the outskirts. It happens that in a short distance from any paved and lit street one encounters such places of misery. If you only turn from this "clean" street into one of the countless side streets ... you will find yourself as it were in a different country which does not resemble anything that your eyes got used to in the "clean" part of town. Especially numerous such places of misery are in the hilly part of town, which serves as a passage from Old Kyiv to Podil. These places are inhabited primarily by workers and sometimes by retired officials who, having been tempted by the idea of becoming a homeowner, build here small houses with three windows facing the street [...]. You will not see here big stone houses, and only rarely a pavement. In the summer, it is dry and dusty here, but in the fall, here stands an impenetrable filth, through which a cabby would not risk driving for all the money in the world.[103]

Thus the geography of misery could not be reduced solely to the peripheries, even if "central" residents chose not to notice it in their own backyards. But this would change when particular neighbour-hoods became more socially homogenous, especially as regards home-ownership. Another consequence of the advent of capitalism in the city was the rise of a distinct centre and peripheries, as if in opposition to each other.[104] The birth of the city centre as an image, a place on mental maps, an ideology, and a utopia was conditioned by the gradual relo-cation of the poorer classes to peripheral areas. The economics of class helped residents locate the "centre" on their mental maps. Having been scrubbed of "places of misery" – which had largely been displaced to the peripheries – the centre became more socially exclusive.

Centrality and peripherality were mental as much as physical cat-egories, and this fomented fear of peripheral spaces among the well-to-do central residents as well as envy of the centre among the poor in outlying districts. But people were slow to embrace this new psychoge-ography of the centre and its peripheries; it was as if they were reject-ing the sociospatial changes brought about by the new economy and rational planning. In 1885 a group of merchants from Podil protested the municipal authorities' decision to build a horse-drawn streetcar line that would bypass their neighbourhood. Remarkably, these merchants still considered Podil to be the "main and heavily populated part of town,"[105] although this was no longer the case. Fifteen years earlier, a decision to relocate the city duma from Podil first to the university square, then to Khreshchatyk, triggered a heated debate on where the centre of Kyiv was located:[106]

[S]ome people begin to complain that moving the city administration away from the *city center* [emphasis added] and from municipal hayfields and fisheries will harm the interests of the poor classes of population and those of trade that predominantly are concentrated in Podil. To which others reasonably respond that first, Podil does not constitute the center of the city, just as Old Kyiv does not; second, the poor people equally and even in greater numbers than in Podil live in Pechers'k, Lybid', Zvirynets' and Luk'ianivka quarters; third, the city executive is in charge of the interests of not only [the] trading estate but of all matters related to the economy and improvement of all urban residents, hence its current location in the centre of all parts of the city is probably more advantageous and convenient than the prior one. While Podil is indeed located a little closer than Old Kyiv to municipal hayfields and fisheries, the city government itself must not cut the hay nor fish (either in troubled or in clean waters). Collecting taxes from these articles is equally convenient from Old Kyiv as much as from Podil.

Referring to his source in the city government, the reporter informed his readers that the new city duma building would be erected in the *real* centre of the city – in the vicinity of European Square (in fact, it was built slightly to the south – on Khreshchatyk Square). By the early 1890s the concept of the centre of Kyiv had finally been fixed: then as today it was bordered by Khreshshatyk Square in the north and Bibikovs'kyi Boulevard in the south; this included Khreshchatyk proper, most of Old Kyiv and Palace districts, and the closest parts of Lybid' district.[107] By 1892 some duma members were already referring to Podil as the "outskirts," along with dangerous Shuliavka.[108] A few years later, several shopowners from Podil's main street – Oleksandrivs'ka – petitioned the city government for reduced taxes on commercial real estate. Their businesses were failing, they argued, and therefore their street should not be equated with Khreshchatyk in terms of taxation.[109]

For another example of how particular neighbourhoods were perceived through the prism of psychogeography, let us look at "healthy" and "unhealthy" spaces. What mattered here was not the actual statistics on disease and mortality,[110] but rather the mental images attached to particular spaces. Statistical data, however, often shaped perceptions. Thus in 1869, one writer criticized Kyiv with regard to sanitation, pointing to the city's high mortality rate – 40 persons per 1,000 residents, which was higher than in London (22) and Paris (28):

Despite the fact that our city much more resembles a big village; that the lifestyle of lower classes does not differ much from that of peasants; and that population is scattered across a huge space due to the city's natural situation – its mortality rate is considerable – much higher than that in the cities that have the worst reputation in this regard and contain the most miserable and the most short-lived proletariat ... As regards public hygiene and corporal well-being, we are still at a low stage of development.[111]

The concerned author then discussed particular neighbourhoods. It turned out that the highest mortality rate (85 per 1,000) was in Old Kyiv, followed by Plos'ka (73 per 1,000) and Podil (52 per 1,000), while the healthiest neighbourhood was the elite Palace (5 per 1,000). Old Kyiv would soon shed its reputation as the "deadliest" area in the city; Plos'ka would perennially top this negative ranking. In 1886 the same paper alleged that "about a third of all city residents live in filth."[112] Some local experts, such as the city's famous doctor and hygienist Ivan Pantiukhov, also assessed city neighbourhoods in terms of moral development, wealth, and mortality. So among the reasons for premature death and disease he listed the "uneven distribution of population," high density, ignorance, and poverty. It appeared that in areas with more affluent and "more developed" populations, such as Palace, Khreshchatyk, and the central parts of Old Kyiv, the death rate was lowest. By contrast, where residents were poor and "ignorant," the mortality rate was highest.[113] A bigger mystery for Pantiukhov was the gender of newborns in each district.[114] But if different mortality rates depended on the degree of human development in each neighbourhood, why could not some "strange local conditions" be responsible for a baby's gender?

More than a decade later, another sanitary doctor was not puzzled by local mysteries; he directly blamed the abysmal sanitary conditions of much of the city on "strangers" and Jews. Because of the rising presence of many thousands of "newcomers engaged in trade and industries," Khreshchatyk had become not only Kyiv's "main vital artery" but also its sanitation disaster. But the worst area of all was infamous Plos'ka, whose residents used manure and sand to fight against constant flooding. As a consequence, Plos'ka was "one of the dirtiest and unhealthiest parts of town," not least because it was populated by numerous poor Jews, "known for their overcrowding and slovenliness." This only worsened the sanitary condition of the district, which was "unhealthy by nature."[115]

Each city district was also known to possess a certain social character: Lypky was considered a largely "aristocratic" part of town; Khreshchatyk and Podil, "mercantile"; Pechers'k, "military"; Old Kyiv and Luk'ianivka, "bureaucratic"; and Lybid' (the New Building), "scholarly."[116] Podil was also infamous as the location of the city's skid row, which was packed with dive bars and frequented by drunks who "often, in an unconscious state, lie on sidewalks half-naked," while others verbally harassed schoolgirls as they passed by.[117] As regards other spaces of vice, such as brothels, both peripheries and central areas contained red-light districts. At different times, spaces of vice flourished in various locations, such as St Andrew's Slope linking Old Kyiv with Podil, the Ditch (*Kanava*) separating Podil from Plos'ka, the very central Kozynobolotna (Goat's Swamp) Street, just beyond the City Duma building, and Iams'ka Street on the periphery – the setting for Aleksandr Kuprin's notorious novel.[118]

What Roshanna Sylvester has noticed about the attitudes of the centre-based middle class of Odessa towards that city's crime- and poverty-ridden suburb of Moldavanka can also be applied to Kyiv. The middle-class residents of central neighbourhoods defined their identity partly in terms of their aspirations for moral virtue, which they sought in the stark opposition between a criminal periphery and the "respectable center" and thus derived "an unambiguous, reassuring image of their city and themselves." By investing the residents of the notorious suburb "with a host of negative traits, middle-class central city residents could dissociate themselves from immoral and disreputable behavior, assert control over the definition of respectability, and shore up their own tenuous claims to moral authority."[119] The middle-class residents of Kyiv's central districts felt exactly the same about "unhealthy," "filthy," and "dangerous" outlying districts and suburbs such as Plos'ka or Shuliavka.

Conclusion

I have tried to show in this chapter that spatial change is inseparable from social change and that together they form what might be called a city's "sociospatial form." With the rise of urban rent and financial capitalism, Kyiv's space came to reflect the uneven distribution of capital – social, commercial, and cultural – with the result that almost all prominent business leaders, professionals, and intellectuals were newcomers to the city from across the empire. As a consequence, many small businesses and crafts, which until the 1860s and the 1870s had been located on major streets, were crowded out to the edges.[120] This was also the time when the new concept of the Kyiv city centre was born. This was, not coincidentally, the city's hottest real estate market.

Imperial urbanism did much to alter the relationship between social status and spatiality in this borderland metropolis. In the opinion of the city's early demographer, by the early 1870s it was already difficult to find Kyiv residents whose parents and grandparents were born in the city. Their numbers did not exceed 20 per cent of all residents. This scholar made an overall pessimistic assessment of the sociospatial change that affected these "native Kyivites":

Native Kyivites, famous burghers in the 17th and 18th centuries, for various reasons have been left behind by the arriving element in terms of development, and thus were pushed to the outskirts. The majority of native burghers are in the state of profound ignorance, and hence they cannot struggle with life circumstances that are constantly changing. Having been bypassed by education and the spirit of enterprise, they grow poorer, even become beggars, fall into vices, and perish prematurely. The sanitary conditions on the outskirts undoubtedly depend mainly on ignorance, poverty, and depravity of [native] residents, while climate, soil, air, and water in this case are of secondary importance.[121]

The city's ethnic and social landscape changed significantly several times over the "long" nineteenth century. Although Kyiv's urban space was not clearly segregated along social and ethno-cultural lines, there were distinct pockets of poverty as well as areas dominated by minorities. Central districts, such as Old Kyiv and Palace, while retaining their ethnic and religious diversity, by the early 1860s were becoming more and more socially homogenous – as the wealthiest areas in the city. A distinct "ecology of classes" was taking shape, a process facilitated by the new capitalist economy, the expansion of bureaucracy and education, more comprehensive urban planning, and profitable construction. What Richard Sennett has written on post-Haussmannian Paris can well be applied to Kyiv (albeit on a smaller scale):

Whatever heterogeneity occurred spontaneously in the division of private houses into apartments in the first half of the century was now opposed by an effort to make neighborhoods homogenous economic units; investors in new construction or in renovation found this homogeneity rational in that they knew exactly what kind of area they were putting their capital into. An ecology of *quartiers* as an ecology of classes: this was the new wall Haussmann erected between the citizens of the city as well as around the city itself.[122]

The functions the defensive and later the tariff wall performed in Paris, were performed in Kyiv by topography, the fortress, and the esplanade. In both cities, financial capitalism and rational planning augmented sociospatial change. The results were similar: the "segmenting" of the city and the creation of a number of socially homogeneous neighbourhoods in place of previously diverse areas where rich and poor had lived side by side and interacted daily in the market and at work.

Chapter Nine

What Language Did the Monuments Speak?

While the relationship between language and city is crucial for our understanding of urban space, here the focus will be on just one aspect of it – the "language" of monuments. We know that Kyivites spoke various languages, but what we know much less about is how those languages were reflected in public space as *signs*. Henri Lefebvre once noted that space indeed "speaks" to us through signs but that it conceals more than it reveals. Hence, monumentality always embodies and imposes a clearly intelligible message, but it also hides a lot: its own political nature. Monumental buildings "mask the will to power and the arbitrariness of power beneath signs and surfaces which claim to express collective will and collective thought."[1] Nothing better illustrates this thesis than monuments and representational spaces in late imperial Kyiv.

Residents of multiethnic cities in Eastern and Central Europe may have shared residential (private) space, such as housing and neighbourhoods, but in public they tended to be divided along distinct social, national, and religious lines.[2] Kyiv, however, seemed to be different. There is evidence that Kyivites with different political views frequented the same places, at least before the upheavals of the early twentieth century. For example, in one of the best-known downtown restaurants during the 1870s and 1880s, run by the wealthy merchant Afanasii Diakov, a former serf from Kyiv province, there gathered famous artists, professionals, and businessmen of all ethnic backgrounds, among them renowned Ukrainian intellectuals (such as the philologist Pavlo Zhytets'kyi).[3] It is also known that Jewish and Christian civic leaders participated in the same charitable institutions – such as the Kyiv Literacy Society – which served as "neutral territory" where residents of all faiths and nationalities "could and did mingle in the pursuit of knowledge and leisure."[4] But what about the built environment – buildings and monuments? Did they too express this purported unity of Kyiv's public life?

If architecture represents the relations of production in a given society as it produces its own space,[5] then the architecture in Kyiv in the age of classical capitalism did not differ much from that in Europe, where the dominant architectural style was historical eclecticism. Carl Schorske once noted that the capitalist age had failed to develop its own original style. This failure, according to him, "reflected the strength of the archaistic current even among the urban bourgeoisie. Why, if railway bridges and factories could be built in a new utilitarian style, were both domestic and representational buildings conceived exclusively in architectural idioms antedating the eighteenth century?" Schorske's answer was that historicism "expressed the incapacity of city dwellers either to accept the present or to conceive the future except as a resurrection of the past. The new city builders, fearing to face the reality of their own creation, found no aesthetic forms to state it [...]. Mammon sought to redeem himself by donning the mask of a preindustrial past that was not his own."[6] This was as true about Kyiv as it was about Napoleon III's Paris, Wilhelmian Berlin, and Victorian London.

The past that Kyiv's architects, developers, officials, and historians made references to was in itself a problem. In some ways, the city's *historical* space was invented.[7] Many architects working in late imperial Kyiv were outsiders either from the ethnic Russian provinces or from elsewhere, and for them local Ukrainian traditions in arts and architecture were at the very least unknown or outright alien. Public buildings, especially from the 1830s through the 1850s – among them the university, the First Gymnasium, and the Institute for Noble Maidens – were built predominantly in the style of Russian Classicism, sometimes influenced by Neo-Renaissance (the Government Offices), the favourite aesthetics of Nicholas I. Another prominent public edifice (although much maligned for its form and price) – the house of the Kyiv City Duma (built in 1876) – was designed in the style of Petrine Baroque.[8] After that, during the last decades of the century, Neo-Renaissance (also known as Viennese Renaissance) dominated both in public architecture (banks, the stock exchange, the municipal theatre) and in the construction of multistorey apartment houses. This style became so popular among local developers that it was even called Kyiv Renaissance. Architectural styles often followed ideological fashions, so a number of residential and public buildings in the late nineteenth century were designed in the "Russian" style, imported from Moscow and Yaroslavl by Russian-born architects.[9] One of them was Vladimir Nikolaev, a very prolific builder employed by the city as its chief architect between 1873 and 1887.[10] The prominent feature of Kyiv's built environment was the pervasive use of locally produced yellowish bricks in open decorative brickwork – the so-called "brick style," which was often mixed with various "historical" styles. Curiously, it was only on the eve of the First World War that Ukrainian national aesthetics was revived within the Art Nouveau movement (known in Russia as *stil' Modern*).[11]

The stylistics and meanings of the monuments were different from those of residential buildings.[12] Henri Lefebvre noted that monuments convey symbols that have an "objective content, emotional effectiveness, archaic origins," through which the space of death can be negated and thereby transfigured into a living space.[13] He also argued that monuments and symbols "introduce a depth to everyday life: presence of the past, individual or collective acts and dramas, poorly specified possibilities, and the more striking, beauty and grandeur."[14] This makes them perfect media for the appropriation of space. According to another French urban thinker, Pierre Nora, monuments are the "most symbolic objects of our memory."[15] Monuments, space, society, and politics are intrinsically linked, which also means that history and memory are constantly changing in tandem with the ruling elites and the power they hold. Therefore, says Nora, by creating monuments the elites promote one dominant memory for a specific event.

More than buildings, monuments have been perceived as both physical and *aesthetic* objects that can be used to construct an explicit national or imperial narrative. "Statuomania" in Paris and the German "Nationaldenkmäler" (a series of monuments to German political figures) of the late nineteenth century established an example for all Europeans who sought to visualize their own national and/or imperial "master narratives." In his classic book about Paris, Patrice Higonnet bluntly calls monuments "texts" and adds that "various monuments form a coherent whole, a monumental grammar."[16] In Eastern Europe in the 1880s, Poles from Austrian-ruled Galicia were among the first to begin purposefully creating national "places of memory"; they did so in order to underscore the Polish character of their cities (most notably Lviv).[17] By contrast, the dominant language of Kyiv's monuments was pretty much an imperial classicist idiom that reflected the prevailing power relations as well as the tastes of governmental elites. In the early twentieth century, however, an imperial idiom that emphasized "Russian" monarchs from Saint Vladimir to Alexander III was challenged by competing national narratives – ethnic Russian and Ukrainian – as both groups strove to "nationalize" Kyiv's public space and define its "monumental grammar." But despite some incursions of these national "sites of memory" in the city's public space, the signs of empire prevailed until the end of the Old Regime.

By then, the development of modern monuments in Kyiv had taken root in local tradition. That tradition started in 1802 with the "Column of the Magdeburg Law," dedicated to the city's saintly patron, Prince Vladimir the Great, who gave the monument its alternative name, the Saint Vladimir Monument. The column commemorated the restoration by Tsar Alexander I of Kyiv's self-government based on the Magdeburg Law. This Tuscan column, which referred to the urban tradition of Renaissance Italian cities, was a powerful symbol of civic pride. It was erected at the city's expense by the still powerful municipal oligarchs.[18] According to Mykhailo Kal'nyts'kyi, the modern-day expert on Kyiv history, the monument was saturated with various meanings.[19] First, it celebrated the Magdeburg Law. Second, it marked the Baptism of Rus', for it was widely believed that at this very spot twelve sons of Prince Vladimir had been baptized in the late tenth century. Hence, the spring flowing nearby began to be called Khreshchatyts'ke (from *baptism*, or *baptize*). Above the spring the locals had built a well, in the belief that the water from it was holy. For generations, pilgrims visited the "holy site" of the spring as if to observe the baptism of Rus'. Thus the monument also celebrated the figure of Saint Vladimir, to whom the monument was dedicated: "To Saint Vladimir – the enlightener of Rus'." The monument also forged the continuity of secular power: grateful Kyivites were expressing their gratitude to Vladimir's successor, Alexander I, who had confirmed the city's rights. Symbolically, then, the monument visualized the links between the city and the imperial government, in the process erasing from public memory the history of troubled relations between the two.[20]

Another monument also celebrated Saint Vladimir, although it took the authorities almost fifty years to provide the city's saintly patron with his material incarnation. In contrast to the Tuscan column, whose message was quite ambiguous, this second "site of memory" (inaugurated in 1853) showcased Vladimir as a saint and as a prince in all his awe-inspiring monumentality. This monument to Saint Vladimir was funded by the no less monumental Russian state, which had begun to promote the myth of the Saintly Prince with the opening of Kyiv

9.1 Timm, *A Monument to the Magdeburg Law* (also known as the Lower Monument to St Vladimir) (image courtesy of Mystetstvo)

St Vladimir University in 1834. The idea for this monument was first broached in 1832, but nothing came of it immediately. Ten years later, Saint Petersburg's Academy of Arts announced a public competition for the design of a monument to Saint Vladimir.[21] The Tsar himself selected the three best entries out of twenty-two submitted – an indication that the statue was to become the prime symbol of imperial power in the borderlands. The gigantic bronze statue of Vladimir[22] was a near perfect visible embodiment of the Russian Empire, reflecting classical imperialism in politics and imperial classicism in the arts. Oddly, the bronze ruler holds in his left hand the "Monomakh cap," a headdress attributed to his grandson (Vladimir Monomakh), as if handing it over to his successors, the tsars of Muscovy and the Russian emperors. The entire monument can be said to serve as a visual representation of the dominant narrative of Russian history created by Nikolai Karamzin and Sergei Soloviev.[23] In contrast to the "lower" Saint Vladimir monument, this new one was called the "upper" Saint Vladimir monument. Ukraine's national poet Taras Shevchenko responded with sarcasm to the monument's imperial symbolism: he called it a fire-lookout tower (*pozhezhna kalancha*), from which Vladimir watched over Podil as if making sure another fire did not break out there.[24]

The next monument was rather an exception in the monotonous monumental space of late imperial Kyiv. It was a product not of the autocratic state but of a modernizing society that was celebrating Kyiv's recent economic successes. Those successes were especially indebted to the lucrative sugar refining industry. The statue of Count Aleksei Bobrinskii, the builder of the first imperial railway (linking Saint Petersburg with the suburb of Tsarskoe Selo) and a prominent promoter of sugar refineries in Right-Bank Ukraine, was opened in 1872. The bronze count was placed in the middle of Bibikovs'kyi Boulevard near the corner of Bezakivs'ka Street, which led straight to the railway station. Quite appropriately, the count was facing the station, as if reminding the visitors of his career as a railway entrepreneur and as a major investor in Russian Ukraine's first railway line (Kyiv–Balta).

At the opening of the monument on 6 February 1872, the choice of keynote speaker seemed a bit strange – Pavlo Chubyns'kyi, a prominent Ukrainian nationalist and a recent political exile. He was present here, however, not because of his dubious political credentials but because he was an expert in sugar beet production and representative of the business community. In the early 1870s he had begun to study the sugar beet industry and become a secretary of the Kyiv branch

9.2 Sazhin, *A Monument to St Vladimir* (image courtesy of Mystetstvo)

9.3 Monument to Bobrinskii (contemporary photograph)

of the prestigious Imperial Russian Technical Society. In his speech, Chubyns'kyi expressed the commercial spirit of the time: "Today, by this social monument we immortalize the memory of a man who promoted, as a private actor [*deiatel'*], the economic prosperity of our fatherland. This is our first monument to an industrial entrepreneur."[25] His speech undoubtedly resonated well with his audience – the sponsors of the monument and his own employers. Clearly, Kyiv's nascent bourgeois class had decided to erect a monument celebrating one of their own (even though Bobrinskii was an aristocrat whose father was an illegitimate son of Empress Catherine II and her minion Grigorii Orlov). In other words, with the monument to Bobrinskii, Kyiv's bourgeois were celebrating themselves – their own economic successes and prospects. Because of the nondescript Roman attire (a sort of Roman toga) that Bobrinskii was draped in, contemporaries compared Kyiv's count with Odessa's more famous duke (de Richelieu), the latter topping the equally famous stairs that today bear the name Potemkin – the battleship, not another lover of Catherine's. But unlike the modest state servitor Richelieu, Bobrinskii was an audacious capitalist who lobbied in Saint Petersburg for the interests of Kyiv's sugar barons. They in turn financed the monument. Indeed, Bobrinskii himself partly funded his own monument: he left substantial capital in a local bank so that the interest could be used for the maintenance of his bronze double. Ironically, some "entrepreneurs" repeatedly stole bronze reliefs, ornaments, and even single letters from the dedicatory inscription that adorned the monument.[26]

The optimism of the Kyiv bourgeoisie proved as short-lived as the monument's bronze reliefs. The local middle classes never developed into a triumphant liberal bastion as did their peers elsewhere in Europe. No major monument (aside from a few busts) to a prominent figure in business, liberal politics, or culture was erected in Kyiv until the very end of the Old Regime. What did change, however, was the distribution of monuments over time: bronze and stone figures began to appear more frequently on Kyiv's squares. The first and the second monuments in Kyiv were separated by almost fifty years; it took only another twenty before the third monument was erected.

The next monument was to become one of the most controversial "sites of memory" in the history of imperial Kyiv. It glorified Hetman Bohdan Khmel'nyts'kyi, founder of the Ukrainian Cossack state in the mid-seventeenth century and the man who unified Ukraine and Russia under the sceptre of the tsars of Muscovy. In the latter capacity, he was an appropriate historical figure in the imperial pantheon, a generic symbol of the loyal Little Russian. For modern Ukrainians, his image was tarnished by his submission to Moscow – a fact that accounted for their general indifference towards the projected monument. Ironically, though, the statue of this most famous hetman in history would remain for a long time the single most visible sign of Ukrainian presence in late imperial Kyiv.

The man behind this monument was Mykhailo Maksymovych, a professor of Russian literature at Kyiv St Vladimir University, who first suggested it in the 1840s.[27] At the time, nothing came of his idea. In the mid-1850s a Kyiv historian, Mykola Zakrevs'kyi, was perplexed by the absence of a monument to a "hero" equal to Russian commanders like Suvorov and Kutuzov. Ukraine's hetman also deserved a monument, he insisted, but "he is forgotten, perhaps because we are separated from him by more than 200 years."[28] Only after the suppression of the Polish January uprising of 1863 did the proposal for the monument gain momentum. That year, several Kyivites (among them Mikhail Iuzefovich, a conservative public servant from Ukraine) turned to the Russian painter and sculptor Mikhail Mikeshin, a famous liberal, widely known for his magnificent work of imperial political art – the monument of the Millennium of Rus' in Novgorod (in 1862). Mikeshin designed the project, which was approved by Tsar Alexander II in 1869.[29] That original design was never built; even so, it is worth presenting here the sculptor's vision of the monument, which is filled with striking ideological images, including several that Mikeshin's contemporaries justly viewed as utterly offensive:

[The] Hetman's equestrian statue is depicted as if flying up to the top of the unlined granite cliff. In his right hand, raised high above, there is a mace [*bulava*] pointing towards northeast, that is, to Moscow. With his left hand he powerfully reins in his wild horse. Under the hoofs of his horse there lies the body of a Jesuit covered in a torn Polish gonfalon; nearby there are the pieces of the broken chains. On Khmel'nitskii's way, behind his horse, there is the figure of a Polish landlord falling off the cliff [as he is] thrown down by the horse's hoof. Still below there is a corpse of the Jewish leaseholder, whose hands [are] brokenly ossified on the communion bread, the Easter bread, and the church utensils that he had stolen ... This granite cliff, together with all these sculptures, is to stand on the four-sided conic pedestal from Kyiv Labradorite ... On three sides of the pedestal there are three bronze reliefs: 1) the battle at Zbarazh [of 1649]; 2) the council at

Pereiaslav [of 1654], and 3) the solemn welcome of the hetman-liberator in Kyiv, near St. Sophia, by the clergy and the people [in 1649].

In the foreground of the monument, below Khmel'nitskii, there is supposed to be a group of five figures: in the center, under the overhang, sits a Little Russian singer [*kobzar'*] singing glory to the people's hero. Others listen to him thoughtfully, from the one side a Great Russian and Belarusian, from the other – a Little Russian and a Red Ruthenian [Western Ukrainian]. Just above them, on the cliff, below the equestrian statue, there is an inscription: "One and indivisible Russia to hetman Bogdan Khmel'nitskii."[30]

Here we see how Russian imperial symbolism hijacked traditional Ukrainian representations of Bohdan Khmel'nyts'kyi, together with his political role. This symbolic blend was no longer strictly either "Ukrainian" or "Great Russian"; rather it was simultaneously "Little Russian" and "all-Russian." It was Little Russian in the sense of the provincial community of the hetman's loyal descendants. These descendants were to be reminded of their historical and contemporary enemies – the same treacherous Polish "landlords" and villainous Jewish "leaseholders" – who were now the enemies of Orthodox Russians as well. The "all-Russian" significance of the monument was underscored by its caption: "One and Indivisible Russia to Hetman Bogdan Khmel'nitskii," the words symbolizing the imperial appropriation of the hetman's figure for contemporary political purposes.

In this way the historical imagery was transferred to the post-1863 Russian imperial mix of borderland politics and historical mythology, wherein Poles and Jews were consistently represented as the dangerous others. Mikeshin clearly overdid it by inserting highly provocative images into the projected monument, which quickly generated controversy. The figures of the Pole and the Jew angered Kyiv's governor general, Prince Dondukov-Korsakov.[31] In addition, the state was not prepared to fund the monument, and the public did not rush to step in.[32] Mikeshin, however, rejected "any changes whatsoever in the design of this monument ... without the supreme will of the monarch [to do so]," as he wrote in 1873.[33] This unwillingness of the local public to donate prompted a journalist from the conservative paper *Kievlianin* to remark sarcastically that local Ukrainian "patriotic nobles" showed no zeal to contribute funds for the Khmel'nyts'kyi monument (supposedly in contrast to peasants from ethnic Russian provinces, who were more generous).[34] For the lack of funds, the sculptor cut his initial budget by almost one-third, to 95,700 roubles.

9.4 Shpak and Seriakov, *A project of Khmel'nyts'kyi statue*

9.5 Kul'zhenko, Statue of Bohdan Khmel'nyts'kyi, *Vidy Kieva*

In the end, this Russian enthusiast of the Ukrainian hetman came
to an agreement with a contractor from Saint Petersburg, who would
cast Khmel'nyts'kyi's figure for 23,000 roubles. But now the tsar himself found the figures of the Pole, the Jesuit, and the Jew inappropriate
and urged that they be destroyed.[35] Mikeshin had to comply with the
tsar's wishes, so after 1878 the monument consisted of just the horse
and Khmel'nyts'kyi himself. Initially the monument was to be placed
on the margins of the urban core, in the seedy Besarabka ravine, near
a notoriously dirty market. For this purpose, an unassuming square
was renamed Bohdan Khmel'nyts'kyi Square (and would be known
as such for the next few decades).[36] However, local enthusiasts of the
monument (including Iuzefovich) opted for another location, in much
more prestigious Old Kyiv, in front of St Sophia. There, however, they
met with opposition from the Orthodox dignitaries, who reasoned
that the figure of a horse would be inappropriate if placed on such a

holy site – especially if it turned its rear to either St Sophia Cathedral or St Michael's Monastery and obstructed the view of one temple from the other.[37]

In the end, the city duma decided to shift the monument slightly so that it would not obstruct the iconic vista.[38] The question was finally settled, and in 1881 the equestrian statue of Bohdan Khmel'nyts'kyi was placed on a temporary brick base on St Sophia Square. The organizing committee had run out of money (mostly private donations) before the planned granite pedestal could be constructed. At this critical moment the Russian state decided to support the bronze hetman by contributing the needed 12,000 roubles for the pedestal. Only in 1888 was the completed monument unveiled to the public, just in time for the celebration of the nine hundredth anniversary of Christianity in Rus'. By combining these two events, the municipal masters of ceremonies had created a continuous imperial master narrative.

The next monument was erected to commemorate one of the most notorious Russian tsars: Nicholas I, who for better or for worse loved Kyiv more than any other Russian ruler before or after him. But it took Nicholas's three successors – Alexander II, Alexander III, and Nicholas II – to complete the monument to the city's informal chief planner. As early as 1869, local loyalists had suggested erecting a monument to Nicholas in front of his most notable creation, St Vladimir University, on a huge square that had been used as a military parade ground. But with the reinstatement of municipal autonomy, the cash-strapped city duma decided to parcel the lands in the area and to sell the plots to private owners. This reflected the market-oriented land policy that dominated those years. It meant that expensive downtown land could not be allocated to open spaces such as parks and gardens. Indeed, everywhere in Europe economic considerations practically dictated that such land be put to productive *building* use – in most cases for commercial real estate.[39] Kyiv's municipal authorities more than once tried to put these plots up for public sale but were dissatisfied with the prices they were offered. One city councillor (future mayor Gustav Eisman) argued against selling plots in front of the university, pointing out that the potential buyers were "almost exclusively Jews." The city, he insisted, should prevent Jews from acquiring "the best part of the [university] square."[40]

But it was not anti-Semitism that saved the university square from redevelopment; it was the unexpected visit of an exotic guest. In 1876,

while visiting Kyiv, Emperor Pedro II of Brazil addressed the city's
newly elected mayor in the presence of the governor general:

> What a beautiful city you have and what a good city mayor it has! While
> regulating the city's redevelopment, you have retained a vacant space in
> front of the university in order to set up here a large park. You are com-
> pletely right. Although you already enjoy in Kyiv a great many gardens,
> so magnificent and beautiful a building such as your university should
> have in front of it an appropriate park. Together they will form a gorgeous
> panorama, one which only rarely can be seen in a large city.

Reportedly, after these encouraging words from the Brazilian emperor,
the Kyiv governor general stared pointedly at the rattled mayor, who
hastened to remark that Don Pedro had more or less guessed the intent
of the city duma.[41] The monument to Tsar Nicholas was to become the
most important marker of the Russian imperial presence in the city,
especially given that it was to be placed in front of the imperial university; but the government was not ready to pay for this piece of political
art. As before, those who launched the idea were relying heavily on private donations. The mayor himself (the millionaire Pavel Demidov, aka
Prince San Donato) donated the largest single amount – 15,000 roubles.
Only years later, in 1885, did the city duma announce a competition
to design the royal monument. Still later, in 1889, the city allocated an
additional 30,000 roubles from its own budget to carry out the winning
design. In June 1894 the monument was at last placed on its high pedestal, consisting of nine layers of granite. But the public opening took
place only in the summer of 1896, in the presence of the new Tsar Nicholas II (in the meantime, Alexander III had passed away).[42] The large
figure of Nicholas I embodied the empire. It was "a magnificent figure
of the Emperor standing up straight, dressed in a military frock-coat,
with an uncovered head," a popular guidebook reported. "The monarch rests his hand on the … plan of Kyiv that he had once approved for
the first time and that has remained in force until today."[43]
Besides a city plan that reinforced the image of Nicholas the City
Planner (a classicist reincarnation of Peter I the Builder), the pedestal
included the bronze reliefs of buildings constructed in Kyiv under his
tenure. Among them were St Vladimir University, the First Gymnasium, the Chain Bridge, and the elite military school (*kadetskii korpus*).
The monument also explicitly evoked an imagined community of loyal
Kyivites, reflected in the inscription on the pedestal: "Grateful Kiev to

9.6 Kul'zhenko, Statue of Nicholas I, *Vidy Kieva*

Emperor Nicholas I." As a later irony, in 1939 a monument to Taras Shevchenko, the Ukrainian national poet persecuted by Tsar Nicholas, replaced the statue of his persecutor in front of the university. This was a powerful victory for Ukrainians in a prolonged war of monuments that would continue well into the twenty-first century.

Until 1905 no other major monument rose in Kyiv. Even after the 1905 revolution, statues of Russian tsars and statesmen continued to dominate Kyiv's squares. For example, on 30 August 1911 a monument to Alexander II[44] was unveiled on Kyiv's prestigious Tsar's Square (today's European Square), funded by the city (45,000 roubles) and by private donors (among whom were numerous peasants, although the most generous was the wealthy entrepreneur Nikola Tereshchenko, who contributed 25,000 roubles). The same year, another monument arose in Kyiv, this one commemorating the city's early Christian history, albeit with a Russian imperial and nationalist twist. It was part of a monument agenda known as the "Historical Path," which had been proposed by Kyiv's Russian monarchist circles as a way to commemorate imperial history with some local peculiarities.[45] Eventually, the "Historical Path" was to include a few dozen monuments, among them those to old Kyivan princes (Oleh, Sviatoslav, Saint Vladimir, and Iaroslav the Wise), the Ruthenian early modern Prince Kostiantyn Ostroz'kyi, Kyiv Metropolitan Petro Mohyla, theologian Teofan Prokopovych, Muscovite Tsar Aleksei Mikhailovich, Russian Emperor Peter the Great, and so on. Most of these monuments were to be erected in the heart of Old Kyiv, between St Sophia Cathedral and St Michael's Monastery.

It is in connection with this pompous agenda that the Kyiv municipal duma made its hugely controversial decision concerning the fate of the Taras Shevchenko monument. According to the duma's previous decision in 1909, the monument was to be erected near St Michael's Monastery, in front of a state-run technical school. In response to this decision, a curator of Kyiv's educational district sent a confidential letter to the Kyiv governor general in which he pointed out that "in front of a government-run school," instead of a monument to the dissident poet, "it would be more appropriate to erect a monument to some important figure in Russian history."[46] As an alternative, Princess Olga was suggested, and the Kyiv duma agreed. As the city head wryly put it, "a gentleman should give up his place to a lady."[47] So on 4 September 1911 a monument to the medieval Rus' princess, flanked by Saint Andrew on one side and by Saints Cyril and Methodius on the other, was unveiled on the spot previously assigned to Ukraine's national poet. The indifference of the Kyiv public towards this new work of imperial political art was evident in the meagre public donations, most of which (10,000 roubles) came from the tsar's own office. Hence the monument was made not of the usual bronze but of much cheaper concrete. Its inscription – "A Gift of His Majesty Emperor to the City of Kyiv" – only reinforced the bureaucratic idea behind the monument.

No monument better reflected Russian nationalists' efforts to hijack Kyiv's public space than the statue of the controversial Russian prime minister Petr Stolypin. His only local connection was that he had been assassinated in the Kyiv opera house by an anarchist turned police informant on 1 September 1911. This time, public donations from Kyiv alone reportedly sufficed to erect the monument.[48] The competition for this project was a true celebration of Russian nationalism. One of the kitschy designs featured a beautiful woman riding a horse – the woman (or perhaps the horse) symbolizing autocratic Russia, with Stolypin himself steering the animal. A slithering snake, a symbol of revolution, was biting the prime minister right in his heart. But on 6 September 1913, in the presence of Stolypin's widow and members of the imperial cabinet, another project was selected. This monument turned out to be no less pompous. On the pedestal, made of pale granite, stood a bronze statue of Stolypin, holding in his right hand one of his speeches. The pedestal's inscriptions flamboyantly celebrated extreme Russian nationalism. On the front of the pedestal: "To Petr Arkadievich Stolypin from the Russian People." On the right side of the statue, on the pedestal, a few words from a telegram Stolypin had sent in March 1911 to Kyiv's society of Russian nationalists: "I strongly believe that the light of the Russian national idea, which began to glow in the west of Russia, will not go out and soon will light up the whole of Russia." Another quote: "You need great upheavals, we need great Russia" – a slightly changed wording from a famous speech that Stolypin delivered in 1907 in which he attacked radicals and liberals. This hideous display of imperial kitsch was reinforced by two additional figures flanking the main one: a mourning woman on one side was dressed in Russian folk costume and symbolized Sorrow; another figure, supposedly depicting an old-Rus' warrior sporting a helmet and chain mail, embodied Strength.[49] The placement of Stolypin's monument in front of the Kyiv duma further underscored the triumph of Russian nationalism in late imperial Kyiv.

Yet there were a few other "sites of memory" in Kyiv at that time. Besides large monuments reserved for Russian statesemen, there were

9.7 Statue of Stolypin (postcard)

several modest busts dedicated to prominent cultural figures. Size here mattered insomuch as it showed who really dominated the city's public space. Culture was clearly subordinate to politics in Kyiv's urban spectacle. The first cultural figure to be honoured with a bust was Aleksandr Pushkin, a symbol of modern Russian culture. This happened in 1899 for the centennial of the birth of this most famous of Russia's famous poets. The modest but elegant monument was funded by the students of the Fifth (Pechers'k) Gymnasium and placed in front of its building. The bust's location was far from prestigious as the gymnasium itself was on the outskirts of the city, at the intersection of two exit roads, near the wasteland of the esplanade.[50] The Russian composer Mikhail Glinka was somewhat luckier: not one but two busts of him were eventually placed in front of the city's two leading music institutions. The first was placed in 1910 by the Kyiv chapter of the Imperial Russian Music Society, in front of Kyiv Music College. The second was initially planned as a full-fledged monument, to be placed on the façade of the new home of the Kyiv Municipal Theatre. Sent from Saint Petersburg as a gift to Kyiv at the very end of the nineteenth century, the statue was reportedly damaged during transportation – or, according to another version, it was simply poorly constructed (with a disproportionately short lower body and oversized feet and hands). As a solution, Glinka's torso and limbs were cut off and his bust, along with that of his fellow composer Alexander Serov, was placed on the second tier of the Municipal Theatre.[51]

More impressively, despite the growing visual presence of Russian nationalists in Kyiv, Taras Shevchenko did eventually enjoy a monumental incarnation. This became possible with the building of Troïts'kyi People's House, a project initiated by the Kyiv Literacy Society in the late nineteenth century. A public organization concerned with the expansion of popular education, the Kyiv Literacy Society since 1882 had arranged in the city and the surrounding towns public libraries, Sunday schools, lectures for the masses, and so on. In 1899 the city duma granted a plot on municipal land for the society's own house, which would include a thousand-seat auditorium, a free public library, a reading room for 150 people, a Sunday school, and a cafeteria, among other things.[52] Remarkably, the people's house became a unique example of cooperation between Christians and Jews, especially between the society's Ukrainophile leadership and Kyiv's Jewish oligarchs.[53] When the People's House was finally opened in 1902, its façade was adorned with the busts of two prominent literati – Ukraine's national bard Taras

Shevchenko, and a renowned Russian writer of Ukrainian descent, Nikolai Gogol. A second bust of Gogol was also high above street level, atop the cornice of a privately owned apartment house on the street that after 1902 would bear his name (on the fiftieth anniversary of his death).[54]

By the end of the Old Regime, Kyiv's public space was dominated largely by visual signs of empire and of an emerging Russian nationalism. In this respect, Kyiv did not look much different from a great many other Russian cities. Visitors to Kyiv in the early twentieth century could barely see anything "Ukrainian" in the cityscape. While Poles had their Roman Catholic cathedral (and another impressive church after 1909), and Jews had a few synagogues, Ukrainians could only point to a small bust of Shevchenko (after 1902), if they could notice it beneath the roof of the People's House. Of course, there was Bohdan Khmel'nyts'kyi's monument, but that had been initiated by the "Little Russian" establishment, designed by a Russian sculptor, and funded largely by the Russian imperial public, and it was perceived as the embodiment of Russo-Ukrainian unity. Later, however, Ukrainians managed to reappropriate the monument and could take great pride in the equestrian hetman. In the early twentieth century, the Ukrainian writer Volodymyr Vynnychenko depicted a humorous yet politically charged scene set around the monument. It featured a "zealous" Ukrainian engaged in a heated argument with a Russian cabbie about the merits of the monument and the signs of Ukrainianness in the city:

We took a cab and were approaching the monument of the hetman Bohdan Khmel'nyts'kyi. Daniel poked the cabbie in the back, asking him what kind of monument it was.
"That one?"
"Yes."
"That's some Ukrainian general."
"Why do you say he's Ukrainian?"
"Because if he were Russian like us, he would be sitting up straight on the horse. This one is leaning to one side. A miserable general!"
Panasenko suddenly jumped up, grabbed the cabbie's belt and shook him, shouting:
"What? Miserable? Ah, you blasted Russian! Don't you know that all your Russian generals aren't worth the soles of his boots? Ha? This is the hetman of Ukraine! Do you hear?"[55]

Conclusion

In the short story quoted above, "A Zealous Friend" (1907), by the Ukrainian left-leaning writer Volodymyr Vynnychenko, one of the characters was a representative of the 1905 generation of Ukrainians for whom the monument to hetman Khmel'nyts'kyi was the single most visible sign of the Ukrainian presence in the otherwise Russified city. In that city even cabbies spoke Russian and indeed *were* ethnic Russians. The events of 1905 changed much of the political and cultural scene in the city, but even they could not markedly refashion the cityscape, dominated as it was by buildings and monuments that largely "spoke" the Russian imperial or national idiom. In fact, Warsaw had more prominent signs of Ukrainian (Little Russian) presence than did Kyiv, among them a monument to the "Little Russian cuirassiers" fallen "heroically" in a battle against Polish insurgents on 13 February 1831; another was a monument to Prince Ivan Paskevich, a Ukrainian-born tsarist viceroy of Congress Poland, ironically a symbol of Russian oppression.[56]

A major paradox of late imperial Kyiv was that despite the city's increasingly diverse demographics, its monumental spaces largely reflected the imperial master narrative and Russian nationalism. This was one of the most effective ways to symbolically claim the city for the empire and for the nation (in this case, the "all-Russian nation"). This had direct repercussions for the city's Jews, Poles, and Ukrainians. There was, however, nothing surprising about this, since until the very end of the Old Regime it was the Russian imperial authorities and Russian (increasingly nationalist) intellectuals who controlled much of the public space in the multiethnic city.[57] Thus space in late imperial Kyiv concealed much more than it pretended to reveal.

Conclusions: Towards a Theory of Imperial Urbanism in the Borderlands

Far from suggesting a comprehensive theory of urban development in the borderlands, this book offers a working framework for a *potential* theory. Such a theory should include the role of the state in planning the city's external form and its infrastructure; the relations between the imperial government and the city; the role of the commercial class; the sociospatial form; the tension between cosmopolitan demographics and borderland politics; and so on. As a case study of Russian imperial urbanism in the southwestern borderlands, this book contributes to the growing field of studies of urban form and life in the Russian Empire. The example of Kyiv is that of a city located in one of the most contested areas of Eastern Europe, and this geopolitical setting also underscores the role that borderland politics played in the urban development of much of European Russia. But Kyiv was not just a city in the borderlands; it was *the* most important city in the west of the empire, perhaps second only to Warsaw in economic and strategic regards.[1] Warsaw's urbanism was much more shaped by military concerns than was Kyiv's.[2] But in some ways – ideologically, culturally, and historically – the city on the Dnieper was even more central for the imperial authorities and the public alike. Apart from the role of economy, however essential at times, Kyiv's remarkable growth exemplified other factors that made sociospatial changes in the city paradigmatic. While in Western Europe it was economics rather than politics that shaped "modern forms of urbanism,"[3] in Russia-ruled Eastern Europe the economy was embedded in strategic and military policies that the central authorities actively pursued in the borderlands.

Kyiv can also be viewed as what Daniel Brower called a "migrant" city – that is, a city in which most residents were born elsewhere, their migration greatly facilitated by the advent of railways. Brower was one of the first (and very few) historians of urban Russia to develop a typology of cities and to discern patterns in their development. His focus was on one particular type – the "migrant" city.[4] Kyiv, however, differed markedly from most of the cities Brower studied. While almost all of them – mainly in Great Russia – had a strong commercial class, merchants were not particularly influential in Kyiv, especially after municipal autonomy was reintroduced in 1870.[5] Due to the city's geopolitical situation – in the southwestern borderlands – and its ideological importance, it was loyal nobles, professionals, and state employees (including academics), rather than economically independent merchants, who became the city's ruling class after 1870. In this regard, Kyiv reflected the government's urban vision more than most other Russian cities, which were more "Russian" in ethnic terms. Other features of Russian imperial urbanism that were prominent in the well-studied cases of Saint Petersburg and Odessa – cities that were built from scratch – in the case of Kyiv are not so easily discernable, but they nonetheless point to certain mainstays in the relationship between cities and government, as well as in the production of urban space.[6] Before arguing that Kyiv is important to studies of Russian imperial urbanism, I should make a general observation regarding a key concept used in this book.

The concept of "imperial urbanism" refers here to two different but related groups of issues. First, it refers to the set of urban policies, interventions, and urban images applied by the imperial state to the city and its increasingly complex demographics. Second, it means urbanism as it was experienced by the residents themselves in their relations with the built environment, space, and one another. This includes the city's sociospatial form – its evolution and functions – as shaped by both public authorities and residents in their daily lives. There might arise, however, some reservations about the use of the term "imperial urbanism." The borders between the "state" and "residents" were often blurred, given that many imperial experts (architects, planners, and academics) were also residents who debated urban issues in semi-official or non-official settings and who experienced urban changes on the ground.[7] In addition, the city government – prior to 1835 and especially after 1870 – was a major agent of public policy, sometimes in competition with the imperial state. Much of local urbanism was thus a product of a delicate balancing act between "imperial" and "municipal" interventions. Empire, however, left numerous traces on the city, besides shaping its identity – through built environment, monumental spaces, urban form, demography, iconography, and so on. While certain features of Kyiv's development appear rather unique, there are also some that reveal a more general culture of imperial urbanism in Eastern Europe.[8] Here I will summarize only a few major points of intersection between empire and urbanism in Kyiv during the long nineteenth century.

First, Kyiv was in many ways an unusual place within Russia's urban geography. Russia herself was very much responsible for making Kyiv a borderland town, for it had dissected the Ukrainian Cossack state along the Dnieper into two halves between 1667 and 1686, thus leaving Right-Bank Ukraine within the borders of Poland–Lithuania. In the 1790s, when the city was reattached to the right bank, it was made the capital of the Southwestern Region (*Iugo-Zapadnyi krai*); yet it continued to be located in the borderlands. For decades, the city functioned and was perceived by many as a frontier outpost, set on the civilizational border between Orthodox Rus' (the spiritual alter ego of imperial Russia) and Catholic Poland. Until 1835 the city also represented one of the last vestiges of municipal autonomy in the empire. But even before 1835, Kyiv had come to represent Russian imperial urbanism in the entire region and perhaps even beyond. In terms of mental geography, Kyiv was paradoxically positioned on the periphery, in the southwestern borderlands (particularly as the centre of the Kyiv governorship-general since 1832), and at the same time at the centre of Russian sacral geography as the "ancient capital of Rus'," the proverbial "mother of Russian cities." Geopolitically peripheral but spiritually central, Kyiv was also unique in that much of its urbanism was shaped by mythology and historical ideology. The streetscape itself was full of markers of the past and of the city's famed "holiness": ruins, churches, monasteries, monuments, sites of memory. The myth of the Holy City and continuous references to its "ancient" past defined much of imperial urbanism in Kyiv.

This image of Kyiv as a holy and ancient city was to a large degree the product of interplay between imperial ideology and the new discipline of archaeology. By uncovering "ancient" ruins – many of them Orthodox holy sites – archaeology provided imperial ideology with plenty of evidence that Kyiv was indeed the "mother of Russian cities." Consequently, as both "holy" and "ancient," Kyiv became the strongest argument for Russian monarchists and nationalists in their struggle against real and imaginary enemies, be they Poles, Jews, Ukrainians, or revolutionaries. This largely conservative politics of memory, which emphasized a "Russian" and Orthodox history of the city, also contributed to specific urban policies pursued by the public authorities (imperial and municipal alike), such as setting limits on Jewish residential patterns, and creating Kyiv's new administrative centre in the vicinity of St Sophia Cathedral and St Michael's Monastery. Some zealous Orthodox writers even cautioned against building the railway, because it supposedly threatened the Holy City. Many conservatives bluntly pointed to the city's cosmopolitan demographics – especially its Jews – as the main threat to the Holy City (and, by extension, Holy Rus'), an argument that turned violent at times of crisis, such as in 1905. The tension between Kyiv as a holy and ancient city and Kyiv as a modern cosmopolitan metropolis continued until the end of the Old Regime.

Second, Kyiv as a unified city – spatially, judicially, and administratively – was created by the Russian imperial authorities between the 1780s and the 1830s. As it turned out, only a central government could overcome various traditional jurisdictions, clerical and secular, to create the city we know today. Hence the imperial state was instrumental in planning and building an amalgamated city. The state even managed to "correct" the city's complex topography and change its traditional spatial patterns. Originally, Kyiv followed two topographical patterns that defined its urban form: riverine settlement (Podil) and hilltop town (Old Kyiv).[9] These two patterns had resulted in two major urban clusters for much of the city's history.[10] For centuries before the 1780s, the city of Kiev was synonymous administratively, demographically, and even culturally with the Lower Town or Podil, the commercial and artisanal quarter ruled by the self-governing magistrate. Large parts of the future united city, such as Pechers'k and Old Kyiv (or Upper Town), functioned as separate towns dominated by several church jurisdictions and by secular authorities – Polish, Ukrainian Cossack, and finally Russian. Only after abolishing Ukrainian Cossack institutions in 1782 could the Russian authorities begin systematically to unite Kyiv's various parts – which had once comprised a medieval city – under their civil and military power. By abolishing the city's autonomy in 1835, the Russian government completed the task of uniting all parts of the medieval city under its authority. The state never completely renounced its tight control over the city, and even after municipal autonomy was reintroduced in 1870, much of the land within the city limits was controlled by the military. The state owned much of the riverfront and some crucial roads until the early twentieth century.

Third, in terms of urban form, Kyiv in the modern period followed a Central European pattern of urban growth: very little suburbanization, with urban sprawl checked by natural and human obstacles (mountains, ravines, moats, rivers, old and new fortifications, etc.). A few outer suburbs were indeed incorporated into the city, but mostly these were inner lands reclaimed by means of "internal colonization" after centuries of depopulation and neglect. The elites resided almost exclusively in the historical centre, not in remote rural suburbs. However, the city's rugged terrain and low population density allowed for a suburban lifestyle even in central Kyiv. For much of the nineteenth and early twentieth centuries, the authorities discouraged uncontrolled urban growth in the countryside, primarily for socio-economic reasons. For much of this period, Kyiv's growth boundaries were defined by a pastoral greenbelt, natural barriers, and a militarized frontier consisting of a series of modern fortifications and "esplanades" – swathes of vacant land controlled by the Russian imperial military. The struggle between the municipal government and the military for these lands was very much part of the city's modern history.

Fourth, as in the case of Odessa and (before that) Saint Petersburg, the imperial state played a crucial role in transforming a frontier town into a cosmopolitan metropolis. It has been assumed that the central government's role in Russia's urban development was greatest during the eighteenth and early nineteenth centuries, when imperial planners shaped cities through rational and regularized designs. By the mid-nineteenth century, these attempts had been largely abandoned, while "further administrative efforts went principally into policing migrants, who were variously perceived as vagrants, criminals, and hooligans."[11] Regarding Kyiv and western borderlands, however, the authorities continued to keep a close eye on urban development both by planning space and by policing diverse residents, not least because of the city's unique geopolitical and spiritual importance.

The Russian government's military and strategic considerations became especially prominent in the aftermath of the Polish November uprising of 1830–1, which steered much of the change that Kyiv experienced over the next decade: the construction of the fortress, the first large urban planning and renewal schemes, and the abolition of the city's self-government, followed by an overall change in the urban regime. At the same time, the Russian government began to encourage Great Russian merchants and artisans to settle in Kyiv, officially to spur its economic development, unofficially to counter the influence of the Polish landed nobility and Jewish financial capital. This is how Kyiv became a *migrant* city, although the authorities sought to control that migration by distinguishing desirable migrants from undesirable ones. Thus between 1827 and 1835 they decided to expel all Jews from the city, having judged them to be undesirable residents. They meant Kyiv to become a Russian military and *spiritual* fortress.

It can also be said that political, military, and strategic concerns often trumped economic ones as major factors in the city's development. Sometimes these concerns facilitated its growth, but more often they curbed its spatial expansion and restricted its demographics. In supporting Russian Orthodox settlers, expelling Jews, and fighting Poles, the government was mixing its rigid ideal of urbanism with borderland politics. Until the early twentieth century, the city's military installations inhibited its expansion and also limited its building activities, thereby diminishing the value of real estate in much of the city. In some areas, the strict esplanade rules blocked construction altogether, thus discouraging potential buyers from investing in real estate in those districts.

This is not to say that Kyiv did not benefit from purely economic factors, even if economic concerns often ran second to borderland politics, ideology, and historical mythology. The local economy profited at times from the imperial government's geopolitical and cultural concerns. It is precisely because of those concerns – partly *strategic*, partly *ideological* – that Saint Petersburg decided to place a cap on the development of Kyiv's regional rivals in the mid-nineteenth century – particularly in the town of Berdychiv, where the economic interests of local Polish landowners aligned with those of Jewish enterpreneurs. Until around 1850, Kyiv and Berdychiv had virtually equal populations, and the latter even had a stronger economy. Kyiv, however, was about to dwarf its rival as a consequence of the new policies that Russia launched in the southwestern borderlands after its armies crushed the Polish insurgents in 1831. After that year, Kyiv's new commercial class, consisting mainly of ethnic Russians, was systematically favoured with tax breaks and various socio-economic advantages while Berdychiv's growth slowed. A telling illustration of the new policies was the closing down of the Berdychiv branch of the Warsaw-based Polish Bank and the immediate opening of an office of the Russian State Bank in Kyiv. The second Polish uprising in the winter of 1863 emphatically decided the outcome of this regional rivalry: Berdychiv's commercial and demographic position rapidly declined following the collapse of the economic alliance between the Polish landed nobility and Jewish capitalists, who relocated to Kyiv and Odessa.

Another distinct feature of Kyiv as a borderland metropolis in the making was that its commercial class was initially created by the imperial authorities – and mainly out of recent newcomers, among whom ethnic Russian merchants, skilled artisans, and entrepreneurial peasants predominated from the 1840s through the 1860s. However, more liberal attitudes in the latter decades of the century, which accompanied the sugar boom, the rise of commercial agriculture, and the advent of railways, brought increasingly diverse demographics to the city. Despite the ongoing efforts by local authorities to control migrants, Kyiv's role as a major commercial hub in the southwestern borderlands transformed it into a genuine cosmopolitan metropolis. This led to building booms as well as to massive sociospatial changes, both driven by laissez-faire capitalism rather than by the imperial government. Thus on the eve of the new century, the economy finally emancipated itself from the military and strategic concerns that for many decades had driven state intervention in urban affairs. This in turn integrated the city more into the economy and demographics of the borderlands.

As a result of all this, Kyiv's pattern of urban growth was rather unusual for Eastern and Central Europe: from a homogenous town (albeit some minorities were well-established there by 1800), it evolved into a cosmopolitan imperial metropolis in which an indigenous, previously dominant group – Ukrainians – found itself a dwindling minority by century's end. With the ongoing marginalization of "native-born" burghers, the city increasingly reflected the diverse *borderland* demographics. This demographic diversity was partly a consequence of Kyiv being the Holy City and partly a result of its status as a fortress city. The latter explained the constant presence of huge numbers of soldiers, pilgrims, and vagrants from across the empire, who together often outnumbered city's permanent residents. As we have seen, at first the imperial authorities *chose* whom to invite to the city: after the 1790s, it was Polish nobles as local officials; after the 1830s, it was ethnic Russian merchants, artisans, state employees, and professionals; in the 1860s, it was Jewish entrepreneurs and skilled artisans; welcome at all times were Protestant Germans as military and police officers, civil servants, and professionals. These ethnic and social groups came to embody the early stages of urban modernity in the city.

Arguably the main engine of Kyiv's rapid growth in the second half of the century was the sugar beet industry. In 1887, with the government's backing, all of the major sugar producers in the Southwestern Region (among them Poles, Jews, Russians, and Ukrainians) formed a syndicate with its head office in Kyiv, and by century's end this group controlled more than 90 per cent of all production of granulated sugar in the empire. As an unrivalled centre of commercial agriculture, the city attracted numerous entrepreneurs, professionals, labourers, and criminals of all ethnic and social backgrounds. Unfortunately, this cosmopolitan metropolis also provoked an intolerant and increasingly militant opposition from the right that united numerous supporters of the Holy Russian City against the "aliens" – Poles, Jews, and Ukrainians.[12] Anti-Semitism became the most notorious reaction against urban modernity, but it was also deeply rooted in local history (after all, it was native Ukrainian burghers who, in the 1820s, petitioned the imperial government to expel the Jews). Even so, the state and the city government quite willingly turned to Jewish capital to meet various municipal needs. These included costly charitable, educational, and infrastructural projects – among them, privately funded utilities (such as sewerage and electric streetcars, both largely owned by wealthy Jewish investors) and the Polytechnic Institute (partly funded by Jewish capitalists such as Lazar Brodsky).

Then came 1905, the year of the first Russian revolution and also of a devastating Jewish pogrom. The Kyiv city government sided unequivocally with the pogrom's perpetrators. Soon afterwards, as Faith Hillis informs us, the deputies of the city duma "issued a manifesto promising that 'ancient Kiev,' 'the mother of Russian cities,' would redeem all 'Holy Rus" from the threats posed by its enemies and would reclaim for the Orthodox East Slavs the 'rights' that they deserved in their native land."[13] The damaged houses would be repaired, and many new tall buildings would be built (the tallest of them by Jewish developers), but the fragile liberal concept of a cosmopolitan metropolis, as it took shape in the late nineteenth century, was irrevocably damaged in 1905. From that point until the very end of the Old Regime in 1917, Kyiv would be haunted by the borderlands, which had once again been politicized and were increasingly viewed as spaces of religious, ethnic, and civilizational conflict.

Ironically, when Soviet Ukraine was officially proclaimed in 1919, its capital was the eastern city of Kharkiv; Kyiv was thought to be too close to hostile Poland – in the contested *borderlands* once again! Consequently, it was Kharkiv, not Kyiv, that experienced the boldest experiments in early Soviet architecture and urbanism.[14] The Soviets destroyed a number of churches and undertook a grand reconstruction of Khreshchatyk (destroyed by NKVD operatives in 1941), but beyond that, they did not

introduce any radical changes to the space shaped by imperial urbanism. Moreover, it has been argued that in post-Communist times, Kyiv
suffered more damage from greedy developers and corrupt municipal
officials than at any time during the Soviet years.[15] Many Kyivites look
back with nostalgia at pre-revolutionary times, holding old buildings
(often anything built before 1917) and imperial urbanism overall in
much higher esteem than Soviet and post-Soviet built environments.
One change, however, seems to be universally appreciated: after 1991
Kyiv has ceased to be located in the borderlands and had finally been
placed in the centre.

Notes

Introduction

1 Arguably the most comprehensive recent study of urban life in Russia is Koshman, *Gorod i gorodskaia zhizn'*. Although Koshman's research is focused on Great Russian cities, it perhaps provides useful comparisons with cities set on Russia's western borderlands.

2 Brower, *The Russian City*, 225.

3 The terms Ukrainians and Ukrainian are used here and throughout the book for the sake of convenience. I am well aware that with respect to present-day Ukrainians and Kyivites, other terms were applied more often in imperial times, among them Little Russians, South Russians, Cossacks, and Ruthenians (*Rusini* in Polish). The locals, however, clearly distinguished themselves from Great Russians and Poles. Most external observers also noticed the differences (unless they chose to ignore them for ideological purposes). In addition, Russian and Polish identities were no less ambiguous and different from what they are nowadays. See my *Romantic Nationalism in Eastern Europe*; compare Anton Kotenko, Olga Martyniuk, and Aleksei Miller, "Maloros," in A. Miller, D. Sdvizhkov, and I. Shirle, eds. *Poniatiia o Rossii. Kliuchevye obshchestvenno-politicheskie poniatiia v Rossii imperskogo perioda* (Moscow: 2012), 392–444.

4 Curiously, such a combination of ideology, knowledge, and cosmology was characteristic of medieval production of space. See Lefebvre, *The Production of Space*, 45.

5 On the rivalry between Kyiv and Berdychiv, see Moshenskii, *Finansovye tsentry Ukrainy*, 26–9; Hamm, Kiev, 133. Compare Shcherbyna, *Novi studiï z istoriï Kyieva*, 18.

6 I have shown elsewhere how a nascent modernity contributed to the "invention" of Kyiv as an "ancient" city in the Romantic age. See Bilenky, "Inventing an Ancient City," 107–26.

7 Péter Hanák has noted that as a result of rapid modernization, the populations of three Habsburg metropolises – Vienna, Prague, and Budapest – grew very rapidly and that in the process their populations were transformed "into almost homogenous German, Czech and Hungarian" respectively. See his preface to Melinz and Zimmermann, *Wien–Prag–Budapest*, 8.

8 This is how an architectural history of Kyiv is presented by the city's own architectural historian Boris Erofalov-Pilipchak in his comprehensive study of the architecture of late imperial Kyiv. See his *Arkhitektura imperskogo Kieva*, 12.

9 See Peter Breitling, "The Role of the Competition in the Genesis of Urban Planning: Germany and Austria in the Nineteenth Century," in Sutcliffe, *The Rise of Modern Urban Planning*, 33.

10 Obviously this was mitigated by chronic bureaucratic incompetency, underfunding, and corruption. On the role of public authority and the private sector in planning and construction in major industrialized countries prior to 1914, see Sutcliffe, *Towards the Planned City*. Imperial Russia seemed to have developed stringent building regulations and more comprehensive planning policy compared to the four cases studied by Sutcliffe.

11 The city lost 80 per cent of its building stock, which required both rebuilding and an overall replanning. See Bunin and Savarenskaia, *Istoriia gradostroitel'nogo iskusstva*, 376–7, 455.

12 Brower, *The Russian City*, 12.

13 The "social life of urban form" can be studied "through a set of conjunctions between social and spatial processes in the city." See Tonkiss, *Cities by Design*, 16–17.

14 Hamm, *Kiev*; Meir, *Kiev, Jewish Metropolis*; Hillis, *Children of Rus'*.

15 Hamm's book is one of the best general histories of the city written in any language (including Ukrainian and Russian).

16 Ikonnikov, *Kiev v 1654–1855*.

17 Among the most remarkable achievements were the following: Hrushevs'kyi, *Kyiv ta ioho okolytsia*; idem, *Kyïvs'ki zbirnyky istoriï i arkheolohiï*, vol. 1; Volodymyr Shcherbyna, *Novi studiï z istoriï Kyieva*; idem, "Kyïv ta Kyïvshchyna"; Ernst, *Kontrakty ta kontraktovyi budynok*; Klymenko, *Kyïvs'ka mis'ka kapela*; idem, *Tsekhi na Ukraine*.

18 See the following publications: Shul'kevich and Dmitrenko, *Kiev*, of which the first Ukrainian-language edition appeared in 1958; A.V. Kudritskii, *Kiev. Entsyklopedicheskii spravochnik*; idem, *Kyïv: Istorychnyi ohliad*. The latter publication united architects with more traditional historians and archeologists.

19 Imperial Kyiv was the subject of the second volume: Kondufor, *Istoriia Kieva*, vol. 2.

20 *Iliustrovana istoriia Kyieva*. In the tradition of Soviet patrimonialism, the editor-in-chief of this volume was at the time the head of Kyiv's municipal administration, Oleksandr Popov, an appointee of Ukraine's President Viktor Yanukovych.

21 Among the best publications are Kovalyns'kyi, *Kyïvs'ki miniatiury*, 9 vols.; idem, *Metsenaty Kieva*; Erofalov-Pilipchak, *Arkhitektura imperskogo Kieva*; Malakov, *Prybutkovi budynky Kyieva*; idem, *Arkhitektor Horodets'kyi*; Malakov and Druh, *Osobniaky Kyieva*; Druh, *Vulytsiamy Staroho Kyieva*; Hyrych, *Kyïv v ukraïns'kii istoriï*; Kal'nyts'kyi, *Zruinovani sviatyni Kyieva*. Among the more eclectic publications of an "encyclopedic" nature, see Makarov, *Malaia entsiklopediia Kievskoi stariny*; idem, *Kievskaia starina v litsakh*.

22 Kal'nyts'kyi and Kondel'-Perminova, *Zabudova Kyieva*.

23 Lefebvre, *The Production of Space*, 11, 26. On Lefebvre's philosophy of space and the city, see Stanek, *Henri Lefebvre on Space*.

24 Lefebvre, *The Production of Space*, 101.

25 Ibid., 73. For Lefebvre, however, a mode of production (e.g., capitalism) matters more than a particular historical society. See ibid., 31.

26 Ibid., 247, 249–50

27 Ibid., 38–9.

28 This also meant that after the partitions, Kyiv became integrated into the economic and social structures of the southwestern borderlands, thus ceasing to be a borderland city strictly speaking. However, the city's borderland status was reconstituted after the Polish November uprising and the creation of the Kyiv governorship-general in 1832. I am grateful to Dr Andrzej Nowak for these observations.

29 For the best analysis of modern urban mythologies on the example of Paris, see Patrice Higonnet, *Paris: Capital of the World*, in which the history of the city is narrated through the deconstruction of the most famous myths of Paris.

30 All of these issues were raised in the pioneering comparative study of "urban modernity" in the three leading cities of the Habsburg Empire – Vienna, Prague, and Budapest – by Melinz and Zimmermann, *Wien–Prag–Budapest*, 15–21 (on the discussion of the paradigms of "urban modernity" in major regions of Europe).

31 Funduklei, *Statisticheskoe opisanie Kievskoi gubernii*, 371. On the role of transportation costs in the rise (and decline) of major American cities, see Glaeser, *Triumph of the City*, 4–5, 43–6.

32 Ibid., 44–5.

33 On the role of railways and rivers in urban economic growth, see Brower, *The Russian City*, 43.

34 On the river port and the lack of a rail line to Podil, see Ievleva, "Transport," in Kal'nyts'kyi and Kondel'-Perminova, *Zabudova Kyieva*, 311–13.

35 On different interpretations of urban planning and public policy, see Suttcliffe's introduction to his *The Rise of Modern Urban Planning*, 3.

36 Alfonsin, *When Buildings Speak*; Cohen, *The Politics of Ethnic Survival*; Driver and Gilbert, *Imperial Cities*; Harvey, *Paris, Capital of Modernity*; Mazower, *Salonica, the City of Ghosts*; Schorske, *Fin-de-Siècle Vienna*; Thernstrom and Sennett, *Nineteenth-Century Cities*; Weeks, *Vilnius between Nations*; and others.

Part I: Representing the City

1 Bilenky, "Battle of Visions." Some original quotations from the article appear also in this book.

2 See, for example, what Kyiv meant for various Polish authors in Bilenky, *Romantic Nationalism*, 20, 26, 156.

3 For various "circles" of imperial hierarchy – political, social, and cultural – see the insightful essay by Kappeler, "Mazepintsy, Little Russians, Khokhly."

4 On a more theoretical level I refer here to the ideas of Lefebvre, particularly his *Urban Revolution*; see also Stanek, *Henri Lefebvre on Space*, 81.

5 Tonkiss, *Cities by Design*, 19.

1 Mapping the City in Transition

1 Kostof, *The City Shaped*, 162.

2 On the "ideal city," specifically on the search for an ideal town plan throughout history, see Smith, *City*, 37–44; on the concept of "skyline," see ibid., 13–15. Compare Kostof, *The City Shaped*, 162–5 and the entire chapter 3 (on ideal cities) and chapter 5 (on the urban skyline). Skyline is also thought to be a city space that came to define the modern urban condition. See Lindner, *Imagining New York City*, 9.

3 Kostof notes that usually there were two ways "to fix a skyline": through "extraordinary landscape features" (like a mountain), or through "pre-eminent buildings" (cathedral or church). Kostof refers to the pre-industrial skyline dominated by religious structures as "the sacred heights," an architectural arrangement whereby sacred buildings "were often situated on eminences, natural or artificial," and "their visual prominence was enhanced by sky-aspiring props." See Kostof, *The City Shaped*, 288, 290.

Kyiv's traditional skyline had an added aesthetic value: it included both "props" (a natural setting – the hills) and "pre-eminent buildings" (the numerous domes of the city's legendary churches).

4 Tolochko, "Kyievo-rus'ka spadshchyna," 320.

5 Izmailov, *Puteshestvie v Poludennuiu Rossiiu*, 96–102.

6 Dolgorukov, "Slavny bubny za gorami," 259, 284. Kostof points out that the waterfront view of the city, similar to that enjoyed by Prince Dolgorukov, is often "panoramic and progressively revelatory," showcasing "an ambience in motion." See Kostof, *The City Shaped*, 314. Another noted urbanist, Kevin Lynch, once observed that a panoramic view of a city set on the hills, often from across a river, forms a very strong and coherent city image, which he considered to be an indispensable condition for a meaningful urban experience. See Lynch, *The Image of the City*, 110.

7 Kostof, *The City Shaped*, 314. On the aesthetic function of modern skyscrapers, see Lindner, *Imagining New York City*, 35.

8 Dolgorukov, "Slavny bubny za gorami," 304.

9 Nikolai Sementovskii, *Kiev i ego dostopamiatnosti*, 183.

10 Levshin, *Pis'ma iz Malorossii*, 85.

11 Karlgof, *Povesti i rasskazy*, vol 2, 152.

12 Bulkina, "Antolohiia iak nahoda," 19.

13 Shevchenko, *Povne zibrannia tvoriv*, vol. 2, 84.

14 Hrebinka, "Machekha i Pannochka," vol. 1, 323.

15 Nechui-Levyts'kyi, *Tvory v dvokh tomakh*, vol. 1 (1985), 102.

16 On how industrialization reshaped the skyline all over the world, with smokestacks, water towers, and skyscrapers as new symbols of the city, see Kostof, *The City Shaped*, 279–82, 319–35.

17 Kuprin, "Iama," 259.

18 Kraszewski, *Latarnia czarnoksięska*, 288.

19 Idem, *Listy do rodziny 1820–1863*, 105.

20 Korzeniowski, *Emeryt*, 418.

21 Bulkina, "Antolohiia iak nahoda," 19.

22 Curiously, Kyiv functioned as the Holy City in the imagination of secular and religious pilgrims even though it lacked an orderly spatial "diagram" (to borrow Kostof's metaphor) reflecting a divine order (or Heaven) on earth.

23 Tolochko, "Kyievo-rus'ka spadshchyna," 319.

24 Mitropolit Platon, "Puteshestvie … v Kiev… v 1804 g.," in Snegirev, *Zhizn' Moskovskogo Mitropolita Platona*, 135.

25 Dolgorukov, "Slavny bubny za gorami," 285.

26 Levshin, *Pis'ma iz Malorossii*, 86.

27 Kyiv's "holy" function could be found in numerous Russian and Ukrainian writings. See, for example, Hrebinka, "Machekha i Pannochka," p. 323; Vigel', *Vospominaniia*, 19; Karlgof, *Povesti i rasskazy*, 117; Shevchenko, *Povne zibrannia tvoriv*, 54, 84; Muraviev, *Puteshestvie po sviatym mestam russkim*, 95.

28 Nikolai Sementovskii, *Kiev i ego dostopamiatnosti*, 12.

29 Tolochko, "Kyievo-rus'ka spadshchyna," 319.

30 Shevchenko, *Povne zibrannia tvoriv*, 84.

31 Gogol, *Polnoe sobranie sochinenii i pisem*, vol. 1, 211–12.

32 Korzeniowski, *Emeryt*, 419.

33 Kraszewski, *Latarnia czarnoksięska*, 295.

34 Chołoniewski, *Opis podróży kijowskiej*, 71.

35 Bilenky, "Spohliadannia mista," 21–2.

36 As quoted in Meir, *Kiev, Jewish Metropolis*, 44.

37 See Muraviev, "Zapiska o sokhranenii samobytnosti Kieva," 259–67. Compare Meir, *Kiev, Jewish Metropolis*, 45.

38 Bulkina, "Antolohiia iak nahoda," 19.

39 Vigel', *Vospominaniia*, 33–4.

40 Izmailov, *Puteshestvie v Poludennuiu Rossiiu*, 192–3.

41 V.S. Ikonnikov, *Kiev v 1654–1855 gg.*, 58.

42 Sbitnev, "Zapiski," 305–6.

43 Wolff, *Inventing Eastern Europe*.

44 See Ikonnikov, *Kiev v 1654–1855 gg.*, 58.

45 Bilenky, "Spohliadannia mista," 26.

46 Kostomarov, *Istoricheskie proizvedeniia*, 271–2.

47 Ikonnikov, *Kiev v 1654–1855*, 52.

48 Berlyns'kyi, *Korotkyi opys Kyeva*, 31; Dolgorukov, "Slavny bubny za gorami," 260.

49 Bilenky, "Spohliadanniia mista," 16.

50 Izmailov, *Puteshestvie v Poludennuiu Rossiiu*, 184–5.

51 The exception was a negligible and long-forgotten short story by Vil'gel'm Karlgof. See Karlgof (A.V. Ve – skii), "Sila privychki," 177–99.

52 Kraszewski, *Latarnia czarnoksięska*, 28.

53 Ibid., 289.

54 Korzeniowski, *Emeryt*, 418.

55 Ibid., 424.

56 Ibid., 419.

57 Ibid., 431.

58 Chołoniewski, *Opis podróży kijowskiej*, 48.

59 Korzeniowski, *Emeryt*, 423.

60 Ibid., 423.

61 Ibid., 420. The writer used the term "ruski," which at the time meant rather "Ukrainian" than "Russian," the latter usually rendered as "moskiewski" or "wielkoruski."

62 Korzeniowski, *Emeryt*, 420.

63 Ibid., 424. The writer specifically mentioned that the city ceremonies were abolished in 1836 (correctly in 1835); around the same time, Kyiv's self-government based on Magdeburg Law was abolished.

64 Kraszewski, *Latarnia czarnoksięska*, 289; Chołoniewski, *Opis podróży kijowskiej*, 75; Korzeniowski, *Emeryt*, 424.

65 It was estimated that between 1835 and 46, on average 5,165 people visited Kyiv trade fair each year, most of them from outside of Kyiv province. See Funduklei, *Statisticheskoe obozrenie Kievskoi gubernii*, vol. 2, 175.

66 V.G. Anastasevych, "Zapiska iz Polotska v Krym i Peterburg," in RNB OR, fond 18 (of V.G. Anastasevich), 4.

67 Dolgorukov, "Slavny bubny za gorami," 259–60.

68 Działyńska z Błędowskich, *Pamiątka przeszłości*, 163.

69 Ibid., 58, 128.

70 Drzewiecki, *Kontrakty*, 101.

71 Quoted from Ułaszyn, *Kontrakty Kijowskie*, 61.

72 Drzewiecki, *Pamiętniki*, 319.

73 Dolgorukov, "Slavny bubny za gorami," 259–60.

74 Karlgof, *Povesti i rasskazy*, vol. 1, 153–4.

75 Korzeniowski, *Emeryt*, 385.

76 Karlgof, *Povesti i rasskazy*, vol. 1, 153.

77 Kraszewski, *Latarnia czarnoksięska*, 293; compare Jełowicki, *Moje wspomnienie*. Writing much later, the Russian-Jewish journalist M.L. Goldstein recalled the atmosphere of the *kontrakty* in the 1880s and 1890s, specifically mentioning theatre performances ("Hamlet" and "Othello"). See Goldstein, *Vpechatleniia i zametki*.

78 Korzeniowski, *Emeryt*, 424; Drzewiecki, *Kontrakty*, 139.

79 Korzeniowski, *Emeryt*, 426.

80 Drzewiecki, *Pamiętniki*, 324.

81 Juliusz Słowacki, *Dzieła*, 105.

82 Korzeniowski, *Emeryt*, 428.

83 Kraszewski, *Latarnia czarnoksięska*, 293.

84 Quoted from Ułaszyn, *Kontrakty Kijowskie*, 72.

85 Kraszewski, *Listy do rodziny*, 103.

86 Ułaszyn, *Kontrakty Kijowskie*, 24–5; Ikonnikov, *Kiev v 1654–1855*, 82.

87 Vigel', *Vospominaniia*, 208–9.

88 Dolgorukov, "Slavny bubny za gorami," 242.
89 Ibid., 64.
90 Ibid., 260.
91 See Ikonnikov, *Kiev v 1654–1855 gg.*, 132.
92 Maksimovich, *Pis'ma o Kieve*, 16.
93 Karlgof, *Povesti i rasskazy*, vol. 2, p. 117.
94 Maksimovich, "Mysli ob universitete Sv. Vladimira," 101.
95 Innokentii (Borisov), "Zapiska o Kievskom universitete Sv. Vladimira v 1838 g.," in *Z imenem Sviatoho Volodymyra*, vol. 1, ed. Korotkyi and Ulianovs'kyi, 141.
96 Serdiukov, "Avtobiograficheskaia zapiska," 364–5.
97 Maslov, "Putevye zametki," 61.
98 Buturlin, "Zapiski," 586–7.
99 Ibid., 590.
100 Volkonskii, *Zapiski*, 400–5.
101 This is particularly surprising because Russian travelers easily noticed differences between Russian and Ukrainian peasants – in dress, speech, and customs. See Bilenky, *Romantic Nationalism*, 89–100.
102 Karlgof, *Povesti i rasskazy*, vol. 1, 153–4.
103 Pushkin, *Polnoe sobranie sochinenii*, vol. 3, pt 1, 300.
104 Muraviev, *Puteshestvie*, 142.
105 Ibid., 32.
106 Ibid., 123.
107 Leskov, "Pecherskie antiki."
108 The term "Ukrainian" refers here to the historical region of "Ukraine," located in the middle Dnieper area. The city was often viewed as Ukrainian or Little Russian as a centre of Cossack tradition, populated by ethnic Ukrainians (who might or might not have called themselves "Ukrainians" in the mid-nineteenth century).
109 Shevchenko, *Povne zibrannia tvoriv*, vol. 6, 40; Ponomarev, *Podlinniki Pisem Gogol'a k Maksimovichu*, 4.
110 Ponomarev, *Podlinniki Pisem Gogol'a k Maksimovichu*, 14.
111 Ibid., 19.
112 Ibid., 15, 19.
113 For Gogol's mental maps, see Bilenky, *Romantic Nationalism*, 67–9, esp. 261–3.
114 Słowacki, *Dziela*, vol. 11, 92.
115 Kraszewski, *Listy do rodziny*, 68.
116 Ibid., 75.
117 Chołoniewski, *Opis podróży kijowskiej*, 28; Drzewiecki, *Pamiętniki*, 312; Kraszewski, *Listy do rodziny*, 239.

118 Olizar, *Pamiętniki*, 119.

119 Ibid., 150.

120 Kraszewski, *Latarnia czarnoksięska*, 287, 289.

121 Drzewiecki, *Pamiętniki*, 34, 37; Olizar, *Pamiętniki*, 166.

122 Jan Czyński, "Do mieszkańców miast polskich," *Echo miast polskich* 1 (Paris, 20 October 1843), 1–4, as quoted in Łukaszewicz et al., *Postępowa publicystyka emigracyjna*, 417–18.

123 Chołoniewski, *Opis podróży kijowskiej*, 58.

124 Ibid., 48.

125 Korzeniowski, *Emeryt*, 423.

126 Ibid., 420.

127 Kraszewski, *Latarnia czarnoksięska*, 289; Chołoniewski, *Opis podróży kijowskiej*, 75; Korzeniowski, *Emeryt*, 424.

128 Kraszewski, *Latarnia czarnoksięska*, 290.

129 Ibid., 295.

130 Działyńska z Błędowskich, *Pamiątka przeszłości*, 163.

131 Maksimovich, *Pis'ma o Kieve*, 32; compare A. Khomiakov, "Kiev," in his *Stikhotvoreniia i dramy*, 112–14.

132 Straszewska, *Czasopisma literackie*, 45, 71, 231, 254.

133 Ikonnikov, *Kiev v 1654–1855*, 127; Tolochko, "Kyevo-rus'ka spadshchyna," 318–19.

134 Ibid., 330.

135 See various travelogues, particularly Izmailov's *Puteshestvie v Poludennuiu Rossiiu*; Levshin's *Pis'ma iz Malorossii*; and Dolgorukov's "Slavny bubny za gorami"; compare Tolochko, "Kyevo-rus'ka spadshchyna," 320.

136 Levshin, *Pis'ma iz Malorossii*, 130–2.

137 Muraviev, *Puteshestvie*, 139–4.

138 Kraszewski, *Latarnia czarnoksięska*, 295; idem, *Listy do rodziny*, 103; Korzeniowski, *Emeryt*, 420.

139 Goszczyński, *Zamek Kaniowski*, 56.

140 Korzeniowski, *Emeryt*, 420.

141 Ibid., 419–20.

142 Kraszewski, *Latarnia czarnoksięska*, 288.

143 Korzeniowski, *Emeryt*, 420.

144 Quoted from Ikonnikov, *Kiev v 1654–1855*, 132.

145 Maksymovych, *"Kiev iavilsia gradom velikim …,"* 30.

146 Maslov, "Putevye zametki," 56.

147 Tolochko, "Kyevo-rus'ka spadshchyna," 329.

148 Dolgorukov, "Slavny bubny za gorami," 259.

149 Buturlin, "Zapiski," 596.

150 On his activities, see my *Romantic Nationalism in Eastern Europe*, 270–9. On the political meaning of Kyiv's past in Russian, Ukrainian, and Polish writings, see chapter 2 of the present book.

151 Bilenky, "Spohliadannia mista," 24.

152 Nechui-Levyts'kyi, *Kyïvs'ki prokhachi*, in his *Tvory v dvokh tomakh* (1977), vol. 2, 407.

153 These are the data of the so-called enumeration lists (*revizskie skazki*) compiled by the authorities for the purpose of taxation and preserved in the State Archive of the City of Kyiv (Derzhavnyi arkhiv mista Kyieva, hereafter DAK), f. 1, op. 2, spr. 574.

154 DAK contains a number of applications from Jews who wished to become Kyiv citizens. Despite the unwillingness of the magistrate to admit Jews, in most cases their applications were approved by Russian authorities.

155 Izmailov, *Puteshestvie v Poludennuiu Rossiiu*, 183–4.

156 Sulima, "Zametki starogo kievlianina," 619.

157 The petition can be found in DAK, f. 1, op. 2, spr. 1386.

158 Quoted in Meir, *Kiev, Jewish Metropolis*, 24.

159 Ibid.

160 Kraszewski, *Latarnia czarnoksięska*, 289.

161 Ibid., 287, 289.

162 Karlgof, *Povesti i rasskazy*, vol. 1, 153.

163 Drzewiecki, *Kontrakty*, 139; Korzeniowski, *Emeryt*, 424.

164 Korzeniowski, *Emeryt*, 423.

165 Meir, *Kiev, Jewish Metropolis*, 25.

166 Serdiukov, "Avtobiograficheskaia zapiska," 364–5.

167 Muraviev, "Zapiska o sokhranenii samobytnosti Kieva," 264.

168 This was a report by one engineer, Aizenberg, about Jews of Kyiv, which he sent to the newspaper *Voskhod* (21 October 1901). The quote is from Meir, *Kiev, Jewish Metropolis*, 119.

169 Ibid., 120.

170 On Kyiv public and the Municipal Theatre, see Sereda, "Nationalizing or Entertaining?," 33–58.

171 *Kievlianin*, no. 9 (1882), 2. Curiously, *Kievlianin*'s major rival in Kyiv was the liberal newspaper *Zaria* (the Dawn, 1880–6), which supported both Jewish and Ukrainian causes. Not surprisingly, the chauvinistic editors of *Kievlianin* called *Zaria* a "Ukrainian–Jewish–Polonophile mouthpiece."

172 The literary product that expressed these Russian fears was the brochure by one A. Shmakov, *Pogrom evreev v Kieve*.

173 Dauber, *The Worlds of Sholem Aleichem*, 162.

174 See Hillel Halkin's introduction to Aleichem, *The Letters of Menakhem-Mendl*, vii.

175 Ibid., 19–20.

176 Ibid., 39.

177 Ibid., 50.

178 Ibid., 61.

179 Leskov lived in Kyiv from 1849 to 1857, staying with his uncle, a professor at Kyiv St Vladimir University. *Pecherskie antiki* are quoted here from Leskov, *Sobranie sochinenii*, vol. 10, 248–327. The work is also available at http://az.lib.ru/l/leskow_n_s/text_0300.shtml.

180 In one of his letters he wrote that "even if I had no friends living near Kyiv I would nonetheless have come to Kyiv for the sake of literature and ethnography." See Grossman, "Balzak v Rossii," *Literaturnoe nasledstvo* (Moscow: 1937), vols. 31–2, 250. See also Savchenko, "Balzak na Ukraïni (1847–1850)"; and Prymak, "Honoré de Balzac's Ukrainian Dreamland."

181 On Benjamin's (and also Balzac's) concepts of memory, see Harvey, *Paris, Capital of Modernity*, 51–3.

182 Makarov, *Malaia entsiklopediia kievskoi stariny*, 233–5. See also Kovalyns'kyi, *Kyïvs'ki miniatiury*, vol. 4, 45–8.

183 On the Chain Bridge and the role of Vignoles, see Kovalyns'kyi, *Kyïvs'ki miniatiury*, vol. 7, 406–45. On the migration of Russian artisans to the city in the 1830s and 1840s, especially as builders, see Hamm, *Kiev: A Portrait*, 88–91; compare Funduklei, *Statisticheskoe opisanie Kievskoi gubernii*, 344.

184 The last time Nicholas visited Kyiv was in October 1852, and a few times during the bridge's construction. See Kovalyns'kyi, *Kyïvs'ki miniatiury*, vol. 7, 432. The description of an actual ceremony that took place on 28 September 1853 can be found in *Kievskie gubernskie vedomosti* 40 (3 October 1853), 309–310. The reporter wrote about the "thousands of spectators" who came to watch the ceremony, which was "one of those picturesque spectacles that one can see in life only rarely."

185 Leskov specifically describes one of academy's former students and later an infamous character in Kyiv – Viktor Askochens'kyi (1813–79), who later edited a Conservative journal in Saint Petersburg. His precious "Dnevnik" (Diary) appeared in journal *Istoricheskii vestnik*, 1882, Nos. 1–9.

186 Kuprin, "Iama," 160.

187 Ibid., 212.

188 Koznarsky, "Three Novels, Three Cities," 103.

189 For some reason, the translator excluded "anarchists" from the original list.

190 See Kuprin, *Yama*, 19–20.

191 It can be added that ethnic Germans had become an important presence in Kyiv by 1850, as professionals and administrators, and took a highly active part in the resurrected municipal self-government in the last quarter of the nineteenth century

192 Conveniently, a junior housekeeper in the same brothel was Zosia, most certainly a girl of Polish descent.

193 Kuprin, "Iama," 405.

194 Ibid., 301.

195 For those interested in representations of space and social relations in literary fiction, see David Harvey's excellent analysis of spatial and social images of Paris in the 1830s and 1840s in Balzac's writings. Harvey, *Paris, Capital of Modernity*, esp. 38–43.

196 Kuprin, "Iama," 285.

197 Ibid., 232.

198 Ibid., 254.

199 As I tried to prove earlier in this chapter, the first literary *flâneurs* who mapped Kyiv were probably Poles as early as the 1830s and 1840s. It took Russians fifty years to respond: Kuprin was the first major Russian writer to have done this, and he did so more convincingly than anyone before him.

200 Taras Koznarsky insightfully notes that Kuprin's *The Pit* is also a "demonic inversion" of another famous literary model – that of Kyivan spiritual pilgrimage. The resulting text is a strange mixture of literary genres and clichés, which turns the depicted city into Kyiv-Babylon. See Koznarsky, "Three Novels, Three Cities," 104–7.

201 Michael Hamm metaphorically titled one of his short but comprehensive chapters "Ukrainians in Russian Kiev," alluding to the fact that the city was becoming increasingly "Russian" in the second half of the nineteenth century. See Hamm, *Kiev: A Portrait*, 82–116. However, what that "Russianness" meant in Kyiv remains an urgent subject of analysis. Kyiv as Babylon (a metaphor applied by Taras Koznarsky in his analysis of Kuprin's novel) may have captured the sense of late imperial Kyiv as a cosmopolitan metropolis-in-the-making even better than the adjective "Russian."

202 See the commentary by V. Pylypchenko to "Khmary," 606. On Nechui, see Tarnawsky, *The All-Encompassing Eye of Ukraine*, esp. chapter 2 on his urban visions.

203 Nechui-Levyts'kyi, "Khmary," 102.

204 Ibid., 368.

205 Ibid., 296. This is how Nechui contrasted Kyiv's townspeople to villagers. Nonetheless, he depicted a few scenes attributed to the 1830s in which the

townspeople were singing Ukrainian folk songs, an element of everyday culture they shared with villagers.

206 Ibid., p. 407. This is despite the fact that the social estates of "merchants" and "townspeople" were open for entrepreneurial peasants, who were the largest single source of growth of Kyiv's population in the nineteenth century.

207 Nechui points to a few multiethnic clusters in the city: Kyiv Academy, the earliest institution of higher learning in Kyiv, which attracted numerous foreigners (Russians, Greeks, Southern Slavs); the Institute for Noble Maidens, an imperial Russian school run by Frenchwomen (at least in the novel); and the residential district of Lypky, where Ukrainian, Polish, and Russian aristocrats resided side by side.

208 In fact, Nechui was first to emphasize this business side of modern Kyiv, which was no longer limited to the time of *kontrakty* fair, as was the case with earlier Polish and Russian writings. For example, the author described in detail the lifestyle and world view of an affluent Kyiv merchant named Sukhobrus, who had risen to prominence through a business very specific to the city: he painted icons for sale to the "thousands of pilgrims from all over Ukraine." Breaking with tradition, he kept his money not only at home but also in the bank. Furthermore, one of his practically minded daughters mentioned the revenue from her house and her intent to make a deposit in a bank ("so that the interest could grow for a daughter"). Another character, a student named Kovan'ko, was a merchant's son, who despite his university education owned a soap factory and a store; he also operated a public bath, where he himself used to sell tickets, "under the influence of new realist ideas." The author, however, explicitly mocked Kovan'ko's career choices, morals, and attitudes.

209 Their first encounter was also very urban: she noticed him while promenading in a public park, as he sat on the steps of the St Vladimir monument watching the passing girls with a group of students.

210 A horrified Olga wondered whether Radiuk indeed wanted that "both his wife and children spoke the language that our cook speaks" (334).

211 In the Russian Empire the intelligentsia became especially notorious for their contempt for townspeople and retail merchants, dismissing them as "philistines" or "petty bourgeoisie." Thus the Russian word for "townspeople" (*meshshane/meshchanstvo*) became synonymous with philistinism, bad taste, and social and political conservatism. Ukrainian intellectuals seemed to share these views with their Russian peers.

212 Nechui-Levyts'kyi, "Khmary," 397.

213 Andrzej Nowak, "Generała Bibikowa walka z „nierozsądną narodowością polską." (Dzieje jednego memoriału)," in Nowak, *Polacy, Rosjanie i biesy.*

214 Nechui-Levyts'kyi, "Khmary," 408.

215 Ibid., 224.

216 It is indicative of the play's popularity that in 1963 the Soviet filmmakers made a screen adaptation of *Za dvoma zaitsiamy*, which became one of the most popular films in the history of Soviet Ukrainian cinema and certainly the most popular of those set in Kyiv.

217 In Ukrainian, the term "mishchans'ka komediia" might have referred both to an actual social estate (*mishshany* or townspeople) and to the philistine way of life, often attributed to conservative and narrow-minded urban dwellers. Mykhailo Staryts'kyi's *Za dvoma zaitsiamy* can be found in his *Tvory u dvokh tomakh*, vol. 2, 88–157.

218 In his Ukrainian surname we hear the not very flattering metaphor *holyi khvist* (or "bare tail"), pointing to his lowly origins: his father was a barber "beyond the Ditch" – that is, in Plos'ka, the most plebeian area of the city.

219 Recently, Faith Hillis published a book devoted to this milieu and its politics. See her *Children of Rus'*.

220 Staryts'kyi, *Za dvoma zaitsiamy*, 93.

221 On social norms and cities see, Glaeser, *Triumph of the City*, 129.

222 See Sennett, *The Fall of Public Man*, esp. 161–76.

223 Sennett has pointed out that after the mid-nineteenth century, people started making enormous efforts to hide their "personalities" in public, for it was assumed that one could "involuntarily disclose" one's "personality" through the smallest details of one's clothes, manner of speech, gestures, and so on. See ibid., 159.

224 Staryts'kyi, *Za dvoma zaitsiamy*, 95.

225 Ibid. This is how urban economist Edward Glaeser comments on the relationship between clothing and the city: "In a diverse, complicated city, clothes indicate the interests and income of their wearer. Since cities have more social heterogeneity and more social interactions, clothing plays a somewhat more important role there than it does elsewhere." For example, today in large cities (with more than a million people), households spend 42 per cent more on women's clothing than rural households, as a share of total family expenditures. See Glaeser, *Triumph of the City*, 127.

226 Obviously, the barber was seeking to distance himself as far as possible from any associations with his lowly relations, whose very names referred to things not quite noble – "bare tail" (Holokhvostyi), and "pigsty" (Svynarenko).

2 Using the Past: The Great Cemetery of Rus'

1 Tolochko, "Kyievo-rus'ka spadshchyna," 310–18.

2 Hryhorii Hrabovych, *Do istoriï ukraïns'koï literatury*, 89.

3 Tolochko, "Kyievo-rus'ka spadshchyna," 331.

4 Levshin, *Pis'ma iz Malorossii*, 132.

5 Pushkin, *Sobranie sochinenii*, vol. 3, 7–87 (*Ruslan i Liudmila*); vol. 1, 185–9 (*Pesnia o veshchem Olege*). The entire publication is also available online: http://rvb.ru/pushkin/toc.htm.

6 Here and there, Pushkin throws in various "Oriental" allusions: Scheherazade, the "gardens of Armide," Tsar Solomon, khan of "Tauride," a Chinese nightingale, and so on.

7 On the epic hero, Oleg the Seer, see Pritsak, *The Origins of Rus'*, 142–53, 583.

8 Bilenky, *Romantic Nationalism*, 33–5; Megan Dixon, "Repositioning Pushkin," 49–74.

9 Kraszewski, *Latarnia czarnoksięska*, 286.

10 Muraviev, *Puteshestvie*, 6, 7.

11 Bulkina, "Antolohiia iak nahoda," 20.

12 Kozlov, *Polnoe sobranie stikhotvorenii*, 85.

13 Benediktov, "Kiev," 1.

14 Izmailov, *Puteshestvie v Poludennuiu Rossiiu*, 102.

15 The poem first appeared in *Al'bom severnykh muz. Al'manakh na 1828 god* (Saint Petersburg, 1828); I quote from: http://az.lib.ru/p/podolinskij_a_i/text_0120oldorfo-1.shtml .

16 Bulkina, "Kievskaia antologiia," in *Stat'i na sluchai: Sbornik v chest' 50-letiia R.G. Leibova*: http://www.ruthenia.ru/leibov_50/Bulkina.pdf, 3.

17 *Moskovskii Telegraf* 21 (1828), 71–4.

18 Tolochko, "Kyievo-rus'ka spadshchyna," 331–45.

19 Izmailov, *Puteshestvie v Poludennuiu Rossiiu*, 108.

20 Ibid., 109.

21 Tolochko, "Kyievo-rus'ka spadshchyna," 326.

22 Kraszewski, *Latarnia czarnoksięska*, 296.

23 Muraviev, *Puteshestvie*, 47, 75, 125, 139.

24 Ibid., 179.

25 Ibid., 123, 130.

26 Ibid., 32.

27 Ryleev, *Polnoe sobranie stikhotvorenii*, 226.

28 Bulkina, "Kievskaia antologiia," 4.

29 Ibid.

30 See Gluszkowski, *F.B. Bulgarin v russko-pol'skikh otnosheniiakh*, 113–31.

31 Bulgarin, *Dmitrii Samozvanets*, 148, 463.

32 Ibid., 171.

33 Bulkina, "Antolohiia iak nahoda," 19.

34 Kulish, *Tvory*, 56–7.

35 Ibid., 63.

36 Mitropolit Platon, "Puteshestvie…v Kiev…v 1804 g.," in Snegirev, *Zhizn' Moskovskogo Mitropolita Platona*, 37.

37 Dolgorukov, "Slavny bubny za gorami," 259.

38 Cited in Ikonnikov, *Kiev v 1654–1855 gg.*, 264.

39 On the aesthetics of ruins in imperial Russia, see Schoenle, *Architecture of Oblivion*.

40 Ananieva, "K voprosu ob arkheologicheskoi," 366–75. See also Ikonnikov, *Kiev v 1654–1855 gg.*, 265.

41 This discovery was well publicized in serialized publications as well as in separate works. Ievgenii himself published a groundbreaking study, *Opisanie Kievo-Sofiiskogo sobora i kievskoi ierarkhii* (Kyiv, 1825).

42 To the Caves Monastery, Ievgenii devoted another seminal work *Opisanie Kievo-Pecherskoi Lavry* (Kyiv, 1826).

43 Compare Tolochko, "Kyievo-Rus'ka spadshchyna," 330–1.

44 For the first complete edition see Berlyns'kyi, *Istoriia mista Kyieva*.

45 For example, Nikolai Karamzin started working on his *Istoriia gosudarstva Rossiiskago* in 1803; Joachim Lelewel began to work on his major historical project – *Dzieje Polski* – in the 1820s; and Dmytro Bantysh-Kamens'kyi published his four-volume *Istoriia Maloi Rossii* in 1822. *Istoriia Russov*, arguably the most famous Ukrainian historico-political pamphlet, began to circulate in handwritten copies in the 1820s and was first published only in 1846.

46 For example, he mentioned forty-seven royal privileges and decrees between 1544 and 1659, all preserved in the archives of Kyiv magistrate. He also enumerated all the charters issued by Russian rulers confirming or returning "rights and privileges" of Kyiv burghers, for 1654 to 1797. See Berlyns'kyi, *Istoriia mista Kyieva*, 180, 183.

47 Ibid., 168.

48 Ibid., 132.

49 Ibid., 160, and 267n88. The Magdeburg Law – a medieval urban law spread in much of Central and Eastern Europe – will be discussed in the next chapter.

50 Dolgorukov, *Slavny bubny za gorami*, 284.

51 On Kyiv's spatial imagination, see Bulkina, "Malorossiiskoe prostranstvo," http://www.ruthenia.ru/territoria_et_populi/ideogeograf.html.

52 Quoted in Bulkina, "Kievskaia antologiia," 3. The sentimental and romantic authors and travellers especially loved this mid-eighteenth-century

church, set on a picturesque hill overlooking Podil. By the early nineteenth century St Andrew's Hill had become the symbolic embodiment of Kyiv's "heavenly" landscape. See Bulkina, "'I pred Kievom, kak pred Troieiu …' Kiev v russkoi poezii," in her *Kiev v russkoi poezii*, 13–14.

53 Maslov, "Putevye zametki pri poezdke," 29–62.

54 In fact, Kyiv was chosen accidentally, and it was not even a first choice as a substitute for the closed Polish educational institutions. See Bilenky and Korotkyi, *Mykhailo Maksymovych*, 33–74, esp. 51. For a general survey of the first years of Kyiv University written by a Russian conservative but balanced author, see Shul'gin, *Istoriia universiteta sviatago Vladimira*. Nicholas's words sounded especially ominous after the brutal suppression of the Polish November uprising of 1830–1, which indirectly led to the foundation of Kyiv University in place of an abolished Polish-run lyceum in Krzemieniec (Ukranian Kremenets') and Wilno (Vilnius) University.

55 Obviously, historical research in Kyiv was the result of a general Romantic interest in history in Russia and in Europe; however, the specific geopolitical situation of Right-Bank Ukraine closely linked historical research in Kyiv with an imperial agenda, such as the "rediscovery" of Kyiv and the "southwestern region." See Kennedy-Grimsted, "Arkheohrafiia v tini impers'koï polityky," 11–33, esp. 23, 30, 31.

56 Cited in Ikonnikov, *Kiev v 1654–1855 gg.*, 266.

57 Maksymovych [Mikhail Maksimovich], *Pis'ma o Kieve*, p. 84.

58 On the commission and politics see Kennedy-Grimsted, "Arkheohrafiia v tini impers'koï polityky." For the views of an insider see Levyts'kyi (Levitskii), *Piatideseteletie Kievskoi kommissii*. The most recent publication on the history of the commission is O. Zhurba, *Kyïvs'ka arkheohrafichna komisiia*.

59 On the role of Ukrainians in this Russo-Polish historical struggle, see my *Romantic Nationalism*, esp. ch. 6.

60 See Makarov, "Kogda Bibikova sprosili."

61 Ikonnikov, *Kiev v 1654–1855 gg.*, 270.

62 On the Polish cultural and educational interests in Kyiv and Ukraine in general, see Epsztein, *Z piórem i paletą:*. On Poles in Kyiv University see Tabiś, *Polacy na Uniwersytecie Kijowskim*; and Remy, *Higher Education and National Identity*.

63 *Zapiska i rechi*, 14.

64 On the cult of Saint Vladimir and its reflection on Kyiv's monumental space and toponymy, see Bulkina, "Bor'ba za 'russkuiu' Malorossiiu pri Nikolae I," 88–9.

65 Uvarov, *Desiatiletie Ministerstva*, 39.

66 Maksymovych became a prolific student of Kyiv history, particularly
   its medieval monuments. On the historical research of Maksymovych
   in Kyiv during the 1830s and 1840s, see Bilenky and Korotkyi, *Mykhailo
   Maksymovych*, 177–89.

67 On the origins and contradictory logic behind Uvarov's notorious "triad"
   see Zorin, "Ideologiia 'pravoslaviia-samoderzhaviia-narodnosti,'" 71–104.
   On Maksymovych and his political historiosophy see my "Inventing an
   Ancient City."

68 Maksymovych, "Ob uchastii i znachenii Kieva," in his *"Kiev iavilsia gradom
   velikim*, 75.

69 Characteristically, Maksymovych himself, as a student and then professor
   at Moscow University, preferred Moscow to Saint Petersburg, but he
   sought not to part ways with official circles in Russia's political capital. On
   the views of Moscow intellectuals – specifically, on the opposition between
   Moscow and Saint Petersburg – see Knabe, *Moskva i "moskovskii tekst"
   russkoi kul'tury*, esp. the articles by D.P. Bak and Iu.M. Mann.

70 Fundukei, *Statisticheskoe opisanie Kievskoi gubernii*. In 3 vols. (Saint
   Petersburg, 1852–5).

71 In recognition of Funduklei's achievements as private donor and governor
   one of Kyiv's main streets bore his name between 1869 and 1919. For
   his biography and charitable activities see Kovalyns'kyi (Kovalinskii),
   Metsenaty Kieva, 5–28.

72 *Obozrenie Kieva v otnoshenii k drevnostiam* (Kyiv, 1847); and *Obozreniie mogil,
   valov i gorodishch Kievskoi gubernii* (Kyiv, 1848), the latter dealing more with
   the province rather than with the city.

73 He was a very wealthy man: in addition to the fortune he inherited from
   his father, he acquired very lucrative landed properties in Kyiv province
   and in the Crimea where he produced sugar and wine respectively. See
   Kovalyns'kyi, *Metsenaty Kieva*, 11.

74 Other Zhuravskii's works: *Plan statisticheskogo opisaniia gubernii Kievskogo
   uchebnoho okruga; O kreditnykh sdelkakh v Kievskoi gubernii; Ob istochnikakh
   i upotreblenii statisticheskikh svedenii*. Newest ed. (Moscow, 1946); on his
   biography see Ptukha, *D.P. Zhuravskii*.

75 Most local reports were sent to Kyiv between 1845 and 1850, and therefore
   the data reflected primarily the situation around 1845. The publication of
   three parts of the book began in 1849 but was completed only in 1852.
   See Funduklei's preface to *Statisticheskoe opisanie Kievskoi gubernii*, Vol. 1,
   iii. On the publication see Kovalyns'kyi, *Metsenaty Kieva*, 19–21.

76 Funduklei, *Statisticheskoe opisanie Kievskoi gubernii*, vol. 2, 151.

77 Ibid., 322.

78 Ibid., 323.
79 The periodical – *Chteniia v Imperatorskom Obshchestve istorii i drevnostei Rossiiskikh* – became a prominent venue for newly discovered historical sources, many of them pertaining to the history of Ukraine, which reflected the scholarly interests of the editor – Osyp Bodians'kyi, a native of Left-Bank Ukraine. In gratitude to his academic patron, Zakrevs'kyi praised his editorial work in his own book, in particular mentioning the publication of a few medieval sources in Bodians'kyi's periodical, and even quoting the editor.
80 On Zakrevs'kyi's biography see Fedorova, "Zakrevs'kyi Mykola Vasyl'ovych."
81 Zakrevskii, *Opisanie Kieva*, 7.
82 Ibid., 8n1.
83 Ibid., 26.
84 Ibid., 30.
85 It is assumed today that the Magdeburg Law was granted to Kyiv Podil burghers sometime between 1494 and 1498. It was mentioned in the 1499 charter given by a Lithuanian Grande Prince to Kyiv burghers as a *fait accompli*. See Bilous, *Kyïv naprykintsi XV-u pershii polovyni XVII stolittia*, 49–51. Zakrevs'kyi carefully reconstructed the origins of the Magdeburg Law in Kyiv, listing most important royal charters and correcting some mistakes in Berlyns'kyi's account. By 1649 there were forty-seven "royal privileges" securing Kyiv burghers' various rights, lands, separate court, freedom from military duties, and monopoly over the sale of alcohol. See Zakrevs'kyi, *Opisanie Kieva*, 36–9.
86 Zakrevs'kyi, *Opisanie Kieva*, 37.
87 Ibid., 39.
88 On Hrushevs'kyi and his "unmaking" of the dominant historiographical scheme, see Plokhy, *Unmaking Imperial Russia*, esp. ch. 3.
89 Zakrevs'kyi, *Opisanie Kieva*, 80.
90 After describing Catherine's famous visit to Kyiv in 1787, Zakrevs'kyi indeed mentioned certain "beneficial consequences," such as the beginning of industry, the rise of the entrepreneurial spirit among Kyivites, and the increase in population. But how all these benefits resulted from Catherine's policies remained unclear.
91 Ibid., 119.
92 Sementovskii, *Kiev i ego dostopamiatnosti*.
93 On the Ukrainian fashion see Bushkovitch, "The Ukraine in Russian Culture 1790–1860."
94 Sementovskii, *Kiev i ego dostopamiatnosti*, 10.
95 Ibid., 52.

96 Among the monuments, a major place was accorded to St Sophia, with its precious frescoes and graffiti, which just had been discovered and studied.

97 Ibid., 97.

98 Ibid., 257.

99 The full title of this seminal work by Sementovskii is *Kiev, ego sviatynia, drevnosti, dostopamiatnosti i svedeniia neobkhodimye dlia ego pochitatelei i puteshestvennikov*, 1st ed. (1st ed. Kyiv: 1864; 7th ed. Kyiv and Saint Petersburg: 1900). In the meantime, however, the prolific writer started a historical series titled *Galereia Kievskikh dostoprimechatel'nykh vidov i drevnostei*.

100 See, for example, two very popular illustrated albums: Zakharchenko, *Kiev teper' i prezhde* and Kul'zhenko, *Vidy Kieva*.

101 For his biography and major works translated into English, see Bilenky, *Fashioning Modern Ukraine*.

102 Antonovych's two major publications are *Sbornik materialov* and his lengthy article "Kiev, ego sud'ba i znachenie."

103 Paradoxically, by depriving Ukrainians of historical rights to Kyiv, Pogodin recognized their ethnic and cultural difference from Russians; meanwhile, Maksymovych implied that Ukrainians and Russians shared history and culture. On the Pogodin–Maksymovych debates and their wider ideological repercussions, see Tolochko, *Kievskaia Rus' i Malorossiia v XIX veke*, 205–325.

104 Plokhy, *The Origins of the Slavic Nations*, 10.

105 Ikonnikov, *Kiev v 1654–1855*.

106 On the meaning of the terms "imperial gaze" and "contact zone," see Pratt, *Imperial Eyes*.

107 Some prominent local historians, such as Orest Levyts'kyi and Mykola (Nikolai) Storozhenko, vacillated between the Russian nationalist and Ukrainian camps even after 1905. See Hillis, *Children of Rus'*, 144, 159, 170–1, 186, 189, 221.

108 V. Os'mak, "Drevnii gorod slovno vymer," *Kievskii al'bom* 1 (2001): 11.

109 On his biography and works see N.A. Khokhlova, "Muraviev, A.N.," in *Russkie pisateli*; on his time in Kyiv see Mykhailo Kal'nyts'kyi's preface to Muraviev, "Zapiska o sokhranenii samobytnosti Kieva," 259–61.

110 Kovalyns'kyi, *Kyiïvs'ki miniatiury*, vol. 4, 72–4.

111 Here he quotes from the Holy Scriptures (2 Corinthians 5:17).

112 Muraviev, "Zapiska o sokhranenii samobytnosti Kieva," 261.

113 Ibid., 264–5.

114 Ibid., 265.

115 These rules limited construction within the land belt – the so-called "esplanade" – surrounding the military fortress in Pechers'k. I will discuss this in greater detail in chapter 5.

116 See Kal'nyts'kyi and Kondel'-Perminova, "Pravovi zasady mis'koho budivnytstva," in their *Zabudova Kyieva*, 83.

117 Vortman, "Kyïvs'ka fortetsia," in *Entsyklopediia istoriï Ukraïny*, vol. 4 (Kyiv: 2007): http://www.history.org.ua/?termin=Kyivska_fortecya.

118 Paszkiewicz, *Pod berłem Romanowów*, 38.

119 See Kal'nyts'kyi's preface to Muraviev's "Zapiska o sokhranenii samobytnosti Kieva," 260.

120 A contemporary historian, Mykola Sementovs'kyi, in his extremely popular tourist guide, wrote that the procession of the cross to the St Vladimir (Magdeburg rights) monument was renewed between 1862 and 1865, when the monument itself was renovated. In 1865 the authorities even built a small house near the monument for an overseer from the ranks of novices of Kyiv Caves Monastery. See Sementovs'kyi [Nikolai Sementovskii], *Kiev, ego sviatynia, drevnosti, dostopamiatnosti*, 6th ed., 15.

121 *Kievlianin* 7 (1864), 28.

122 Berlyns'kyi, *Korotkyi opys Kyieva*, 29–30.

123 Buturlin, "Zapiski," 596.

124 On Gogol's split personality situated between Ukrainian "nationalism" and Russian imperial loyalty see Bojanowska, *Nikolai Gogol*.

125 Ponomarev, ed., *Podlinniki Pisem Gogol'a k Maksimovichu*, 4.

126 The image of Poles was hard to separate from that of a modern city. On the "iconography" of Poles and Jews see my article "Battle of Visions" at http://sites.utoronto.ca/tsq/13/bilenky13.shtml. The arrival of "new" Kyiv no doubt exacerbated a cultural alienation of Left-Bank Ukrainians ("Little Russians") from the modernizing city, to which economic interests and a newly founded university were attracting increasingly more Poles and Jews (although the latter were not allowed to reside legally in the city until after 1859). On the demographic movements and municipal politics in late imperial Kyiv, see Hillis, "Human Mobility."

127 This was a talk by Vladimir Tsykh, a newly appointed professor of history, during the ceremony of the solemn opening of Kyiv University in 1834. See *Zapiska i rechi*, 118–19. Characteristically, another observer, the above-mentioned traveller from Moscow Stepan Maslov, was sceptical about the prospects of Kyiv University, which was situated far from the city centre; he compared it unfavourably with Moscow University, which was located downtown. Maslov did not believe in the power of a new university to revitalize the surrounding area. See Maslov, "Putevye zametki," 57.

128 Maksymovych, "*Kiev iavilsia gradom velikim*," 71.

129 Maksymovych was perhaps too optimistic about the progress of modernization in the city. His contemporary, historian Nikolai (Mykola) Kostomarov, who arrived in Kyiv in 1844, *after* the beginning of the earliest urban renewal phase, was less than reserved about what he saw: his Kyiv was a dirty provincial town, filled with ugly clay huts and wooden houses, with almost no city infrastructure. See Kostomarov, *Istoricheskie proizvedeniia*, 462–3.

130 Maksymovych, "*Kiev iavilsia gradom velikim*," 71.

131 Zakrevskii, *Opisanie Kieva*, 131.

132 Ibid., 132.

133 Funduklei, *Statisticheskoe opisanie Kievskoi gubernii*, 317.

134 *Kievskie gubernskie vedomosti. Otdel vtoroi. Chast' neoffitsial'naia*, 39 (1853), 26 September, 302.

135 Ibid., 31 (1853), 1 August, 243–4.

136 *Kievlianin* 52 (1905), 3.

137 "Samyi vysokii dom v Kieve," *Zhizn' i iskusstvo*, 12 October (1897), 2. Quoted in Malakov, *Arkhitektor Horodets'kyi*, 63. In another instance, a newspaper article described both the "sky-scrapers" of New York and private houses across the country, emphasizing that even in Chicago, "more than a half of all residents live in separate [private] houses, almost a half of them owners." See *Kievlianin* 56 (1894), 3.

138 Pataleev, *Staryi Kyiv*), 153.

139 Ibid., 154.

140 *Kievlianin* 126 (1887), 2.

141 Druh, "Avtor spohadiv pro staryi Kyïv," in Pataleev, *Staryi Kyiv*, 9.

142 Vladimir Nikolaev was perhaps the most prolific architect that Kyiv ever knew. On his most important projects see Kal'nyts'kyi and Kondel'-Perminova, *Zabudova Kyieva*, 495–6.

143 Druh, "Avtor spohadiv pro staryi Kyïv," 12.

144 Pataleev mentions the most important families, some of whom he called "old rich firms." See Pataleev, *Staryi Kyiv*, 22, 146.

145 See notes by Olha Druh to Pataleev, *Staryi Kyiv*, 279nn22–3.

146 Taranets, *Staroobriadchestvo goroda Kieva*, 70–1.

147 Ibid., 48, 79–80.

148 The output of Rodion Dekhterev's pioneering plant grew steadily in the 1850s: in 1855 the plant produced various cast-iron and copper items to the amount of 123,912 roubles; in 1857 – 129,059 roubles; and in 1859 – 135,708 roubles, which made this industrial sector the fourth-largest in Kyiv, behind the sugar industry, tanning, and the manufacture of soap and candles. Ibid., 78, 86. Compare Hamm, *Kiev: A Portrait*, 33.

149 Taranets, *Staroobriadchestvo goroda Kieva*, 71–2.
150 The tsarist policies indeed managed to halt Kyiv's population growth: between 1840 and 1856 the city's population hovered around 44,700 to 56,000 people. Nicholas died in 1855; by 1861 the city's population had reached 65,000 and was beginning to grow rapidly. See Kudritskii, *Kiev. Entsyklopedicheskii spravochnik*, 30.
151 For example, the Iakhnenko brothers and Fedir Symyrenko were serfs from Cherkasy district, who, after buying their freedom, became the wealthy sugar producers. Artem Tereshchenko was a poor Cossack from Hlukhiv in northern Ukraine. They all had business headquarters in Kyiv. See Pritsak, "U stolittia narodyn M. Hrushevs'koho," 10–11.
152 On various projects and their benefactors see Kal'nyts'kyi, "Dzherela i formy investuvannia u zabudovu Kyieva," in Kal'nyts'kyi and Kondel'-Perminova, *Zabudova Kyieva*, 144–8; also a comprehensive study by Kovalyns'kyi (Kovalinskii), *Metsenaty Kieva*.
153 Ibid., 369.
154 Ibid., 247.
155 Ibid., 253.
156 Initially it was a three-storey house with forty-seven rooms, but soon Nikola had his house rebuilt as a Renaissance palace, also acquiring neighbouring properties until he owned an entire block along the prestigious Bibikovs'kyi Boulevard. See ibid., 254.
157 Ibid., 368.
158 Malakov, *Arkhitektor Horodets'kyi*, 77. Lazar' Brodsky was born in 1848 in the town of Zlatopil', into the family of wealthy entrepreneur Israel Brodsky, an owner of sugar refineries and the largest wheat mill in Kyiv. In 1876, Brodsky Senior moved to Kyiv. His son Lazar', together with his brother Lev (Leon), inherited his father's very lucrative sugar mill. See Meir, *Kiev, Jewish Metropolis*, 39.
159 They also participated together in such common causes as the Bacteriological Institute and Kyiv Polytechnic Institute. See ibid., 195–6. Compare Kovalyns'kyi, *Metsenaty Kieva*, 216–19.
160 On Khanenko see Kovalyns'kyi, *Metsenaty Kieva*, 357–84.
161 Ibid., 366, 369.
162 *Kievlianin* 85 (1872), 2–3.
163 On the changing costs of the project see the report compiled in 1894 preserved in TsDIAK, f. 442, op. 48, spr. 232a II, 150–61, 171.
164 *Kievlianin* 85 (1872), p. 3.
165 TsDIAK, f. 442, op. 48, spr. 232a II, 158 reverse.
166 Ibid., 163–7.

167 A long list of Ukrainian cultural causes financially supported by local
capitalists and aristocrats (many of them based in Kyiv) can be found in
Pritsak, "U stolittia narodyn M. Hrushevs'koho," 9–13.

168 For the history of the Russian nationalist movement in Kyiv see Hillis,
Children of Rus'.

169 On this subject see my article "Inventing an Ancient City."

Part II: Making the City

1 Around 1850 there were other European cities in which defensive works
of various kinds (Amsterdam, Barcelona, Copenhagen, Vienna) or legal
obstacles to building in particular areas (as in Berlin) hampered the cities'
expansion. But these cities largely freed themselves of these obstacles over
the next ten years. See Hall, *Planning Europe's Capital Cities*, 301.

2 Paszkiewicz, *Pod berłem Romanowów*, 14–39.

3 In the mid-eighteenth century, when Empress Elizabeth visited Kyiv, a
local Cossack chronicler described the festivities on her behalf "in *all three*
Kyiv towns" (emphasis added). Quoted in Erofalov-Pilipchak, *Arkhitektura
imperskogo Kieva*, 24. There has also been a tendency to attribute this
three-part urban structure to nature itself. For example, historian Mykola
Zakrevs'kyi wrote that "nature divided Kyiv into three parts." See
Zakrevskii, *Opisanie Kieva*, 140.

4 Kostof, *The City Shaped*, 59.

5 Ibid., 60.

6 On the workings of self-governing Kyiv under the Magdeburg Law in
medieval and early modern times see Bilous, *Kyïv naprykintsi*.

7 On the struggle between Kyiv burghers and Russian authorities see
Volodymyr Shcherbyna, "Borot'ba Kyieva za avtonomiiu," in *Kyïv ta ioho
okolytsia*. On the corruption scandal involving the leaders of the Kyiv
magistrate, which led to the abolition of municipal autonomy, see Ivan
Kamanin, *Poslednie gody samoupravleniia Kieva*.

8 Hamm, *Kiev, a Portrait*, 11–12.

9 Klymovs'kyi, *Sotsial'na topohrafiia Kyieva*, 91–3, 96–7.

10 Sarbei and al., *Istoriia Kieva*, 64.

11 Tonkiss, *Cities by Design*, 3.

12 Sutcliffe, "Introduction," in *The Rise of Modern Urban Planning*, 3.

13 Idem, *Towards the Planned City*, viii. In other words, urban planning
started as a "public intervention in the urban environment to intensify
and to extend itself," particularly in the sphere of "common facilities
such as thoroughfares, drains, sewers, water, and, towards the end of the

nineteenth century, gas, electricity and public transport." Another aspect of urban planning was "the imposition of obligations [by public authority] on the owners of urban property." Ibid., 5.
14 Lefebvre, *The Production of Space*, 42.

3 Municipal Autonomy under the Magdeburg Law, 1800–1835

1 "Iz zhizni Kieva v nachale iskhodiashchego stoletiia," *Kievskaia Starina* 54, no. 9 (1896): 65–9. See also the depiction of the event, with the historical context and valuable comments, in Ikonnikov, *Kiev v 1654–1855*, 84–6.
2 Shcherbyna, "Narysy z istoriï Kyieva, vidkoly pryiednano ioho do Moskovs'koï derzhavy, do pochatku Svitovoï viiny i Revoliutsiï," in his *Novi studiï z istoriï Kyieva*, 17. Curiously, Shcherbyna was one of the very few historians of Kyiv who not only was born in the city (in 1850) but also was a descendant of local burghers.
3 The city, however, for centuries absorbed foreigners, such as Tatars, Greeks, Poles, and Armenians, most of whom became assimilated into a Ukrainian-speaking Orthodox community of local burghers. Around the mid-eighteenth century we encounter more than twenty Greek merchants as parishioners of a Greek church (turned into a monastery) in Podil, among them the prominent families Lakerda and Karmalei. Russian merchants began to settle in the city in the early eighteenth century but largely remained a separate community, as many of them were Old Believers. Only a few Russians held any important positions in municipal self-government prior to 1835. Germans were invited by Catherine II and formed in Kyiv a rather distinct community, retaining their religion (Lutheranism) and speech. On Russians see Shcherbyna, "Narysy z istoriï Kyieva," 7; on Greeks and Germans see Ikonnikov, *Kiev v 1654–1855*, 29, 47, 73. On Kyiv's German community also see an older study: Neese, *Geschichte*.
4 The authority of the magistrate was, however, largely limited to the district of Podil, for centuries synonymous with the city of Kyiv. Yet Kyiv's self-governing organs used any opportunity to prohibit foreigners (unless they signed up for merchants' guilds) from trading in the city (as is seen from an 1811 petition to the police). See DAK, f. 165, op. 9, spr. 33.
5 On the solemn opening of Kyiv First Gymnasium see Ikonnikov, *Kiev v 1654–1855*, 112–13. See also TsDIAUK, f. 533, op. 1, spr. 1019, 122–3.
6 In fact, the first statue of Samson tearing open the lion's jaws appeared in 1749, designed by Ukrainian Baroque architect Ivan Hryhorovych-Bars'kyi, along with a new pavilion. This was on the spot of the first Kyiv water supply; water flowed into the reservoir through pipes from the Syrets' River.

7 Hamm, *Kiev: A Portrait*, 140.
8 See "Kievskoe predstavitel'stvo prezhnego vremeni," in *Kievskaia Starina* 2 (1882), 191.
9 Ibid., 141.
10 One example of an "invented tradition" was the burghers' procession towards the "Column of the Magdeburg Law," a monument erected between 1802 and 1808 to commemorate the restoration of Kyiv's self-government by Tsar Alexander I.
11 See Csendes and Opll, *Wien*, 217–18, 226.
12 For the anti-Jewish petition compiled by Kyiv's burghers see DAK, f. 1, op. 2, spr. 1386.
13 See Sarbei and al., *Istoriia Kieva*. 67, 126–7.
14 Those ramparts were relatively modern, largely created by Cossack and Russian authorities in the first half of the eighteenth century.
15 Yet the streets most probably did not correspond to the medieval layout – that is, from the time before the Mongol Invasion of 1240. See Klymovs'kyi, *Sotsial'na topohrafiia Kyieva*, 93.
16 The ramparts were levelled in 1832. See Sherotskii, *Kiev*, 19.
17 Kyiv's earliest historian Maksym Berlyns'kyi wrote around 1799 that this slope, "passing by St. Andrew's Church to Podil … due to the narrowness and steepness of the mountain is considered of little importance." It was also dangerous. See Berlyns'kyi, *Istoriia mista Kyieva*, 230.
18 Ibid., 244.
19 Erofalov-Pilipchak, *Arkhitektura imperskogo Kieva*, 22.
20 The Assumption Cathedral was Podil's main church, the place where the oath of office was taken by the newly elected city leaders such as *viit* (mayor) and *burhomistry* (burgomasters or members of the magistrate).
21 Popel'nyts'ka, "Naibil'shi zemlevlasnyky i pidpryiemtsi," 59.
22 Ibid., 60. Compare idem, "Istorychnyi rozvytok kyïvs'koho Podolu." Podil's social topography before the catastrophic fire of 1811 very much followed a European medieval pattern: artisans' and shopkeepers' livelihoods depended on their proximity to the marketplace. The area around the market was the most prized, followed by the streets leading to the town gates. See Kostof, *The City Shaped*, 48.
23 Popel'nyts'ka, "Naibil'shi zemlevlasnyky i pidpryiemtsi," 60.
24 Ibid., 60–1. A truly wealthy family might own as many as nine homesteads, some of which might have been used as manufacturing plants.
25 Kostof, *The City Shaped*, 44.
26 Bunin and Savarenskaia, *Istoriia gradostroitel'nogo iskusstva*, 368.

27 This order of Peter's was likely influenced by a contemporary German practice whereby local feudal princes, through the municipal police, exercised the right to establish the so-called *Fluchtlinien* (red or building lines) to mark the boundaries of lands to be used as new public thoroughfares in and around the towns. See Sutcliffe, *Towards the Planned City*, 11–12.

28 Catherine's urban vision was in accordance with Western ideals. She prophesied that the "glories [*znamenitosti*] of the architectural and street plan for one town would attract new inhabitants, and that the entire region would acquire a new life and take on a new appearance." Quoted in Brower, *The Russian City*, 9.

29 Ibid., 10.

30 Bunin and Savarenskaia, *Istoriia gradostroitel'nogo iskusstva*, 374. Saint Petersburg was probably the first city in Europe to be planned in accordance with the results of an international competition. See Peter Breitling, "The Role of the Competition in the Genesis of Urban Planning: Germany and Austria in the Nineteenth Century," in Sutcliffe, *The Rise of Modern Urban Planning*, 33.

31 Ikonnikov, *Kiev v 1654–1855*, 40.

32 With the implementation of the Charter to Towns in 1785, the magistrate had been reduced to a purely judicial organ; all municipal affairs were transferred to a new institution – the Kyiv city duma (consisting of "general" and "six-member" dumas). Kyiv's municipal elite joined the duma; even so, the institution was closely controlled by Russian governor. See Sarbei and al., *Istoriia Kieva*, 66–7. There is another opinion, however, regarding the extent of change in Kyiv following the 1785 Charter. Canadian historian Zenon Kohut notes that the provisions of the charter "were skillfully blended with local traditions. Magdeburg Law remained in force, and the Kievan patriciate maintained control over government and finances, even reinstituting a traditional part of Kievan administration, the militia." See his *Russian Centralism and Ukrainian Autonomy*, 288.

33 Erofalov-Pilipchak, *Arkhitektura imperskogo Kieva*, 30–1, with the plan reproduced on 28–9.

34 Ikonnikov, *Kiev v 1654–1855*, 57.

35 Erofalov-Pilipchak, *Arkhitektura imperskogo Kieva*, 31.

36 On his activities see ibid., 79–88, or online: http://alyoshin.ru/Files/publika/erofalov/imner_18.html.

37 Regarding the "organic" pattern as opposed to the grid as a city form see Kostof, *The City Shaped*, esp. ch. 1.

38 At that time Kyiv was split into four districts: I (Vladimir), II (Old Kyiv), III (Podil), and IV (Plos'ka). In terms of inhabited land, the largest was

Plos'ka (124 *dessiatin*), and the smallest was Podil (83 *dessiatiny*), although the latter was most populous and had the highest population density in the entire city. The new Vladimir district was the fastest-growing district in Kyiv. Of all the new land (119 *dessiatin*) allocated for private settlement in Kyiv between 1796 and 1805, almost all (112 *dessiatin*) was located in I district. Only Podil was administered by the magistrate. See Ivan Shchitkivs'kyi, "Do istoriï zabuduvannia m. Kyieva," 321–3.

39 According to other sources he died in 1791. However, he had accomplished all of his major projects before 1785.

40 See Shul'kevich and Dmitrenko, *Kiev*, 60.

41 Erofalov-Pilipchak, *Arkhitektura imperskogo Kieva*, 82.

42 This was a letter sent by the magistrate to the Kyiv governor-general, as quoted in Kovalyns'kyi, "Evropeis'ka ploshcha," in his *Kyïvs'ki miniatiury*, vol. 3, 212.

43 "Raznochintsy" ("people of diverse ranks") was a Russian legal category that referred to people who inhabited the changing social space between nobles and peasants in imperial Russia. Neither merchants nor clergy nor military men, they were by occupation petty officials, teachers, artists, retired soldiers, or street vendors. Mainstream society viewed them as outsiders. See Wirtschafter, *Structures of Society*.

44 For example, while in Podil there were 1,974 houses owned by the townspeople, in Pechers'k there were only 46; but when it came to more varied social categories such as soldiers, peasants, officials, and members of the nascent intelligentsia, Pechers'k (which included Old Kyiv) took the lead, with 632 soldier- and 172 peasant-owned houses. These were the data presented by Prince Rumiantsev to Empress Catherine II in 1785. The data are from Ikonnikov, *Kiev v 1654–1855*, 68.

45 Ibid., 79.

46 In course of ten to fifteen hours Podil lost 1,176 houses, including the magistrate, eleven stone churches, eight wooden churches, and three monasteries; this is not to mention the unimaginable loss of property – private and municipal. Losses resulting from the fire were estimated at millions of roubles in municipal funds. (Those funds, however, were more likely stolen.) See Ikonnikov, *Kiev v 1654–1855*, 87.

47 Zakrevskii, *Opisanie Kieva*, 117–18.

48 Erofalov-Pilipchak, *Arkhitektura imperskogo Kieva*, 82. The author also provides a depiction of Melens'kyi's plan.

49 DAK, f. 1, op. 1, spr. 474.

50 Kal'nyts'kyi and Kondel'-Perminova, *Zabudova Kyieva*, 29, 86. On city planning in early-nineteenth-century Kyiv, see Ignatkin, *Istoriia planirovki*

i zastroiki Kieva. On regularization in construction, see Sakovych, "Rehuliarni mistobudivni zakhody," 227.

51 Hamm, *Kiev: A Portrait*, 27–8.

52 DAK, f. 237, op. 2, spr. 9.

53 Ibid., 6.

54 Ikonnikov, *Kiev v 1654–1855*, 87n4.

55 These were the administrative headquarters of Kyiv province, built in 1805–9, with funds provided by the government. The Russian traveller Prince Dolgorukov, who visited Kyiv in 1810, noted that the "building of the Governmental Offices is big, [made of] stone, with columns, and constructed according to the new architecture." See Dolgorukov, "Slavny bubny za gorami," III, 261.

56 Erofalov-Pilipchak, *Arkhitektura imperskogo Kieva*, 34. As we will see later, Lypky became the first truly multiethnic area of the city, with Russian, Polish, Ukrainian, and "foreign" aristocrats residing side by side. Lypky, situated in central Vladimir (later Palace) district, experienced rapid growth beginning in the early nineteenth century, when imperial authorities began to distribute large landholdings among aristocrats, officers, and officials. Thus between 1796 and 1805, in the entire Vladimir district around 140 building plots were distributed (78 of them in upscale Lypky proper). See Shchitkivs'kyi, "Do istoriï zabuduvannia m. Kyïeva," 323.

57 Note that a long stretch of this road, today known as St Vladimir's Slope, became the first *paved* artery in the city in 1810. See Hyrych, *Kyïv v ukraïns'kii istoriï*, 243.

58 DAK, f. 165, op. 4, spr. 7 (Act on the formation of Municipal Commission), 2 reverse.

59 Shcherbyna, "Narysy z istoriï Kyïeva," 17.

60 On the commission's financial principles and on various corruption scandals that shook Kyiv at the time see Kamanin, *Poslednie gody samoupravleniia Kieva*, 30–42.

61 "Registered fellows" was a social category in Cossack Ukraine, in this case referring to Kyiv's municipal elite and municipal militia in particular. The group was first mentioned in sources around 1750. See Buzalo, "Reiestrovi tovaryshi," 63. Maksym Berlyns'kyi defined "registered fellows" as the "most distinguished and wealthiest of burghers." This group provided the cadres for the city's elected offices. It also formed the mounted guard – the elite of the traditional municipal militia – and enjoyed a status similar to that of the nobility. See Berlyns'kyi, *Istoriia mista Kyïeva*, 247.

62 DAK, f. 165, op. 4, spr. 7, 11–12. Among these burgomasters was Pylyp Lakerda, a highly influential "oligarch" of Greek descent, an interim *viit*

(1813–14), and a prominent figure in the corruption charges laid by the investigating authorities after 1821.

63 DAK, f. 165, op. 5, spr. 5 (on the debts of the magistrate to private persons in 1807), 2–3. The magistrate and the city commission eagerly sought approval from the Kyiv governor in each particular case involving a city debt to creditors. Yet I have the impression that the municipal leaders were given a free hand in managing most cases. Unless a creditor persisted, the governor chose not to get involved.

64 On the members of the magistrate between 1799 and 1817, see DAK, f. 1, op. 2, spr. 174. Ivan Kyselevs'kyi was a burgomaster in 1806.

65 Kamanin, *Poslednie gody samoupravleniia Kieva*, 24–6.

66 That year the governor formed a special committee to balance the city's revenues and expenses. This organ consisted of representatives of the Russian government and the autonomous city. The municipal commission seems to have failed to meet the expectations of the authorities; the government tried a few more times to deliberate with the city fathers, but apparently to no avail. See Kamanin, *Poslednie gody samoupravleniia Kieva*, 86–7. Regarding budget deficits, around 1799 the city's revenue did not exceed 50,000 roubles while the expenses were as high as 138,370 (in 1800 – more than 140,000 roubles!). See Ikonnikov, *Kiev v 1654–1855*, 80. It seems, however, that the budget was more balanced in subsequent years.

67 For example, in 1820 the city introduced a new "citizens" tax; the amount depended on the citizens' income but could not exceed 100 roubles. This new tax was to be collected when the name of a new "citizen" was recorded in the so-called "citizens' book," which had six categories: (1) city dwellers in general (including nobles and *raznochintsy*); (2) merchants of three guilds; (3) guild masters; (4) foreign merchants; (5) "renowned citizens" (professionals and most prominent merchants); and (6) burghers.

68 DAK, f. 239, op. 1, spr. 2 (the proposals of the Temporary Committee on the Reorganization of Kyiv), 28–28 reverse.

69 DAK, f. 239, op. 1, spr. 1 (on the city budget).

70 That year the local treasury board, after several unsuccessful requests, finally managed to obtain the financial reports for 1807, 1808, 1820, and 1821 (in addition to the reports for the years 1809 to 1819, which the board had already received). Still, two annual reports (for 1810 and 1822) were missing. See DAK, f. 239, op. 1, spr. 1, 26.

71 Kamanin, *Poslednie gody samoupravleniia Kieva*, 74.

72 DAK, f. 239, op. 1, spr. 1, 138–55.

73 DAK, f. 239, op. 1, spr. 2 (the file also summarized various measures that could be used to balance the city budget).

74 Compare Ikonnikov, *Kiev v 1654–1855*, 80–1. The magistrate, for example, in 1800 invested 4,562 roubles in the construction of the city's four drinking parlours, which it owned.

75 See Kamanin, *Poslednie gody samoupravleniia Kieva*, 42–6. See also Ikonnikov, *Kiev v 1654–1855*, 174–5.

76 DAK, f. 239, op. 1, spr. 1.

77 For example, the city owned vast lands with farmsteads (up to 700 *dessiatin* or 1,890 acres) in the suburbs of Priorka, Kurenivka, and Syrets'. See ibid., 92.

78 Ibid., p. 14 reverse.

79 As it turned out, some plutocrats (the Lakerdas, father and son) rented a store at *Hostynyi Dvir*, using the funds of the municipal commission while operating it as their own property.

80 DAK, f. 239, op. 1, spr. 2, 96–7.

81 Ibid., 19.

82 Ibid., 14 reverse.

83 This amount would be even bigger if we were to add a lump sum of more than 10,000 roubles to fill up a ravine in downtown Kyiv; more than 7,000 roubles for the maintenance of a bridge over the Dnieper; and a few smaller sums to renovate and maintain various city-owned buildings (the Contract Hall, the military and police quarters, two parish schools, etc.). See ibid., 155. Note that the costs allocated for the city beautification greatly exceeded those assigned for the police (around 15,000 roubles), a situation that would change dramatically in later decades. After the reign of Tsar Nicholas I, the maintenance of the police and the costs for billeting imperial troops would become major expenditures.

84 There is some evidence that the local imperial authorities were urging the city to pursue a city beautification policy. So, for example, in 1806, governor Pankratiev insisted that "road laying and regulation of streets … should be among the first subjects that [the city] must take notice of." See DAK, f. 1, op. 1, spr. 474, 2.

85 A number of archival files detail various street improvements and other city beautification schemes realized by municipal authorities. See, for instance, DAK, f. 165, op. 9, spr. 33 (on the boulevard near the royal palace); op. 11, spr. 6 (on the Dnieper bridge and a road leading to it); spr. 28 (on the construction of new pavements in Podil); op. 12, spr. 10 (on taking prompt action to repair the canal running through Podil); op. 19, spr. 9 (on acquisition for the I district of lanterns and poles); op. 29, spr. 38 (on renovation of gutters and drain pipes); op. 30, spr. 93 (on renovation of poles and street signs in Kyiv); and many others.

86 On this city beautification agenda as formulated in 1827, see DAK, f. 239, op. 1, spr. 2, 54–76.

87 Melens'kyi was also appointed a member of the municipal commission, and of other organs operated jointly by the Russian government and the city, such as the Provisional Committee for the Construction of Kyiv (1824–7).

88 These biographical facts can be found in Erofalov-Pilipchak, *Arkhitektura imperskogo Kieva*, 79.

89 Outside of Podil the land was usually distributed by the imperial authorities (often by the office of the Kyiv governor-general). See Shchitkivs'kyi, "Do istoriï zabuduvannia m. Kyieva," 323.

90 In this Podil quarter a plot for building a stone house was assigned to Melens'kyi himself. See DAK, f. 1, op. 1 (2), spr. 178, 5–6. It was Melens'kyi, as architect and land surveyor, who divided Podil into quarters (*kvartaly*) and streets. See Shchitkivs'skyi, "Do istoriï zabuduvannia m. Kyieva," 326.

91 Typically, this additional charge for acquiring a neighbouring plot varied from 50 kopeks to 5 roubles per square *sazhen*, depending on the location of the projected property.

92 See, for example, quarter no. 28 (where resided Kyiv's two most influential clans – the Balabukhas and the Rybal's'kyis), or quarter no. 7 (with the residence of Pylyp Lakerda). See DAK, f. 1, op. 1 (2), spr. 178, 25, 129. In general, in place of the 2,000 houses that had existed in Podil before the 1811 fire, only 600 were planned for the reconstruction.

93 DAK, f. 1, op. 2, spr. 301. As late as 1829, burgher Vasyl' Kravchenko (a legendary battler against the corruption of the Kyiv plutocrats) informed municipal authorities that he still had not received a building plot in compensation for his old home lost to the fire (his old plot later came into possession of the hay market). So he asked either for a new plot or for monetary compensation. See 56–56 reverse.

94 DAK, f. 1, op. 1, spr. 474, 9–45.

95 Since the beginning of the century, local imperial authorities had tried to enforce the following rule: all those who obtained empty plots were expected to complete their houses within three to five years (three for wooden and five for stone houses). Otherwise, "on government's instruction," the undeveloped plots "shall be given over to those who wish to build [new houses]." Ibid., 2–3. It appears, however, that this strict rule was rarely if ever enforced.

96 Ibid., 5.

97 On the political and strategic factors behind the replanning of Kyiv in the 1830s see Bulkina, "Bor'ba za 'russkuiu' Malorossiiu pri Nikolae I," 87.

98 DAK, f. 239, op. 1, spr. 1a. One of the experts was a military engineer from the Kyiv provincial building board; another was a provincial architect from neighboring Podolia; a third was a military architect employed by the Kyiv Arsenal.

99 On the plan of 1833 approved by the imperial authorities, Plos'ka was given a regular pattern similar to that of Podil, split into rectangular blocks. The plan is reproduced in Kudryts'kyi, *Kyïv: istorychnyi ohliad,* 76–7. I use the name Plos'ka for an urban district, although Plos'ke was also widely used, especially with respect to a larger rural locality adjacent to the city. The maps in the front matter use the second variant (Plos'ke) both for the urban district and the rural suburb.

100 DAK, f. 239, op. 1, spr. 75.

101 Ibid., 2-reverse.

102 On the circumstances leading to the creation of the Kyiv governorship-general in 1832 and on its structure and the activities of governor-generals, see Shandra, *Heneral-hubernatorstva v Ukraïni,* 265–76. The list of Kyiv governor-generals is on page 383.

103 For example, Levashov succeeded in obtaining tax privileges for Kyiv merchants. See ibid., 272.

104 DAK, f. 239, op. 1, spr. 33, 2.

105 Ibid., 3. Perhaps Savych's proposal influenced the statute on the reorganization of Kyiv (1834), which elaborated major principles of city beautification. See Zakrevskii, *Opisanie Kieva,* 104.

106 DAK, f. 239, op. 1, spr. 19, 1–3.

107 In November 1832, Levashov also approved a general plan for the reconstruction of Kyiv submitted by Colonel Savych, a plan that took into account the building of a new fortress in Pechers'k. See DAK, f. 239, op. 1, spr. 36.

108 DAK, f. 239, op. 1, spr. 102.

109 DAK, f. 239, op. 1, spr. 130, 1–2. The file contained Levashov's thoughts on "a few general directions as regards eleven subjects pertaining to the city organization."

110 Ibid., 15–27.

111 Ikonnikov, *Kiev v 1654–1855,* 160.

112 "Zapiski grafa M.D. Buturlina," *Russkii Arkhiv* 8 (1897), 595.

113 Shandra, *Heneral-hubernatorstva v Ukraïni,* 272.

114 There is no need to retell here the entire story of the corruption of Kyiv plutocrats and the series of investigations that followed. It has been well described by Kamaninin, *Poslednie gody samoupravleniia Kieva* (based on archival files), and by Ikonnikov in *Kiev v 1654–1855,* 173–6. Ikonnikov,

however, largely followed Kamanin's article. Therefore I will mention only a few major twists in this complicated story, following Kamanin's and Ikonnikov's accounts.

115 DAK, f. 1, op. 2 (2), spr. 977. On the elections in Kyiv of 1823, see page 17.
116 Ibid., 17–18.
117 As we will see in chapter 7, the municipal elite formed an even more exclusive club, counting fewer than two hundred men – those who participated in elections and held municipal offices. Compare Ikonnikov, *Kiev v 1654–1855*, 176n1.
118 The funds embezzled between 1813 and 1821 and those that had allegedly disappeared in 1811 fire totalled a staggering 1,400,000 roubles – a sum nine times that of the average annual city revenue of 144,635 roubles (in 1829).

4 Planning a New City: Empire Transforms Space, 1835–1870

1 Ikonnikov, *Kiev v 1654–1855*, 170–1.
2 The poem "Skorb' kievlian o potere Magdeburgskogo prava" (The Grief of Kyivites over the Loss of the Magdeburg Law), was published in *Kievskaia Starina* 5 (1882), 352–7.
3 For more about the change of elites in Kyiv after 1835, see chapter 7 of this book.
4 Here and below, the Ukrainian author of the poem plays on ethnographic differences between Russians and Ukrainians: the former (especially Old Believers) often sported beards and long hair, while the latter shaved their faces and cut their hair. Hence Russians were pejoratively called by Ukrainians *"katsapy"* or *"tsapy"* (goats).
5 Ivan Khodunov (1788–1853), a Russian merchant from Iaroslavl' province, settled in Kyiv in the early nineteenth century. He was the city head in 1838–41, 1844–7, and 1851–3. See DAK, f. 1, op. 2, spr. 1936. (On the elections of a city head and other officials in 1835, see 59–59 reverse. See also the commentaries of Olga Druh to O.V. Pataleev, *Staryi Kyiv: Zi spohadiv Staroho Hrishnyka*, 397n530.
6 Parfentii Dekhterev (1797–1837), Russian merchant, Kyiv's city head in 1835–7. His son Mikhail (1837–98) was a wealthy merchant and benefactor.
7 *Pylypon* was a reference to a sect among Russian Old Believers founded by one Filipov in the early eighteenth century in northern Russia. Here *Pylypon* means any Old Believer, or Russian in general.
8 Another reference to quasi-ethnography: contemporary Ukrainians mocked Russians for wearing blast shoes.

9 Yet the poet does mention, if only in passing, the *real* victims of the 1835 upheaval in Kyiv: the Jews, who had to leave the city altogether that year. The author's only regret was that instead of Jews came the Russians. See "Skorb' kievlian o potere Magdeburgskogo prava," 356.

10 Cited in Ikonnikov, *Kiev v 1654–1855*, 165.

11 On the functions of the magistrate after the 1835 transformation see Kamanin, *Poslednie gody samoupravleniia Kieva*, 1–2.

12 Shul'gin, "Iugo-Zapadnyi krai," 116–17.

13 DAK, f. 1, op. 2, spr. 1935, 7, 134.

14 On all of the most important planning projects in Europe's capitals and larger cities designed and implemented during the nineteenth century see Hall, *Planning Europe's Capital Cities*.

15 Thomas Hall has noted about Saint Petersburg: "During the second half of the nineteenth century no attempt appears to have been made at any kind of overall planning, and building controls were weak or non-existent." In addition, zoning rules and infrastructural measures were anything but consistent. See ibid., 2.

16 Kudritskii, *Kiev. Entsiklopedicheskii spravochnik*, 30.

17 On the differences between these two geographical settings see Hall, *Planning Europe's Capital Cities*, 9.

18 Kal'nyts'kyi and Kondel'-Perminova, *Zabudova Kyieva*, 17.

19 The tsar loved Kyiv and visited the city no fewer than fifteen times, the last time in 1852. See Makarov, *Kievskaia starina v litsakh*, 111. On Nicholas and Kyiv see also Kirkevich, *Vremia Romanovykh*, 92–123.

20 The most recent study of the grand transformation of Paris emphasizes the personal role of Napoleon III. See Kirkland, *Paris Reborn*. It seems that autocrats everywhere – from Babylon's Nebuchadnezzar II to France's Napoleon to China's Communist leaders – are "pro-growth" and like building. See Glaeser, *Triumph of the City*, 12.

21 Kostof, *The City Shaped*, 240.

22 Brower, *The Russian City*, 10.

23 Ibid., 11.

24 Wojciech Boberski, "Architektura ziem I zaboru rosyjskiego," in Konstantynow and Paszkiewicz, *Kultura i polityka*, 56.

25 Erofalov-Pilipchak, *Arkhitektura imperskogo Kieva*, 14. Spiro Kostof pointed to another function of regularizing planning: rational planning eradicates "traditional living arrangements, and with them loyalties that may be at odds with the policies of the state." See Kostof, *The City Shaped*, 258.

26 Opinions differ concerning the first coming of the duma to Kyiv. Historian Volodymyr Shcherbyna noted in the 1920s that Catherine's Town Charter

destroyed much of Kyiv's autonomy, economy, and distinct social order.
See his *Novi studiï z istoriï Kyieva*, 12–14. Later Soviet historians also
pointed out that the duma, as a new imperial institution, "unconditionally
depended on the governor," and that new "institutions of administrative,
judicial, and police character in city's administration almost totally
replaced [the former] Kyiv magistrate." See Sarbei and al., *Istoriia Kieva*,
66–7, 127. But Zenon Kohut, a North American authority on early modern
Ukraine, espoused a more optimistic vision: the 1785 Town Charter's
"provisions were skillfully blended with local traditions. Magdeburg
Law remained in force, and the Kievan patriciate maintained control over
government and finances, even reinstituting a traditional part of Kievan
administration, the militia." Quoted in Hamm, *Kiev: A Portrait*, 16.

27 Sarbei and al., *Istoriia Kieva*, 127.

28 Nardova, *Gorodskoe samoupravlenie v Rossii*, 13. For more on the history of city
dumas before 1870 see Ditiatin, *Ustroistvo i upravlenie gorodov Rossii*, 144–8.

29 Nardova, *Gorodskoe samoupravlenie v Rossii*, 13.

30 Ibid., 14.

31 Varadinov, *Istoriia Ministerstva vnutrennikh del*, 71–3.

32 Ikonnikov, *Kiev v 1654–1855*, 163.

33 Dmytro Malakov, an expert on Kyiv architecture, writes that Nicholas built
two fortresses in Kyiv: one military (in Pechers'k), and the other mental,
the latter consisting of new imperial institutions such as Kyiv St Vladimir
University, two male gymnasiums, a cadet corps (military school), the
Institute for Noble Maidens, and, later, the Luk'ianivka jail. See Malakov,
Prybutkovi budynky Kyieva, 7. Compare Ikonnikov, *Kiev v 1654–1855*, 241.

34 Shul'kevich and Dmitrenko, *Kiev. Arkhitekturno-istoricheskii ocherk*, 59. See
also Ihor Hyrych, "Do istoriï topohrafiï Pechers'koï chastyny Kyieva XIX
st.," in his *Kyïv v ukraïns'kii istoriï*, 167–78.

35 We have already seen how Leskov described these demolitions and
relocations in his literary memoir "Pecherskie antiki" (see ch. 1).

36 Ikonnikov, *Kiev v 1654–1855*, 157.

37 Funduklei, *Statisticheskoe opisanie Kievskoi gubernii*, 327–8.

38 With the completion of the *Cytadela Aleksandrowska* between 1832 and 1834
and the subsequent construction of a few external forts in 1847–53, the
city lost around 250 houses on both banks of the Vistula; 15,000 people
were resettled elsewhere. The emerging district of Żoliborz, adjacent to
the citadel, was almost completely destroyed. All of this prevented the city
from extending north along the river; at the same time, the city centre was
relocated towards the south, the area least affected by construction. See
Paszkiewicz, *Pod berłem Romanowów*, 21–2.

39 [Mykhailo Maksymovych], *Ocherk Kieva*, in Funduklei, ed., *Obozrenie Kieva*, xiii.

40 Seletskii, P.D. "Zapiski," *Kievskaia Starina* 10 (1884), 87–9. On other reminiscences left by Kyivites of Bibikov see "K kharakteristike D.G. Bibikova: Vospominaniia kievlian," *Kievskaia Starina* 3 (1882), 61–80.

41 On the Chain Bridge see Kovalyns'kyi, *Kyïvs'ki miniatiury*, vol. 7, 406–45.

42 Ibid., 410.

43 One contemporary anecdote featured a conversation between Bibikov and Pisarev during which the governor-general reproached his subordinate for allegedly taking bribes. To this Pisarev responded: "These are all inventions of people who envy me. One should not believe anything that is being said. For example, I'm being told that you, Your Excellency, are in the criminal liaison with my wife. I don't believe this. And you would do well if you, just like me, would not believe rumors circulating about myself." Bibikov reportedly stopped reproaching Pisarev for his corruption. See Makarov, *Kievskaia starina v litsakh*, 134.

44 Curiously, de Vignoles had excelled in building railways in the southern United States in the 1820s and in the United Kingdom in the 1830s, thus combining expertise in railway engineering with that in urban planning.

45 Ikonnikov, *Kiev v 1654–1855*, 163. However, the quality of the work, particularly that of the Kyiv street pavements, was, according to a contemporary expert, "quite negligent" (164).

46 Many German towns, for example, encountered problems with planned extensions and laying out the new streets owing to the conflicts with landowners and unclear guidelines for expropriation. See Sutcliffe, *Towards the Planned City*, 18. Another example was the capital of Russia's northwestern borderlands, the town of Vilnius, where the built-up area was so dense that the imperial planners encountered legal difficulties laying out the new "imperial" thoroughfare, Georgievskii prospect (St George's Avenue). See Weeks, *Vilnius Between Nations*, 26, 62.

47 On the judicial and financial history of the Russian imperial city in the context of the Russian interior ministry's policies, see Varadinov, *Istoriia Ministerstva vnutrennikh del*, 618.

48 Ibid., part III, vol. 1, 624. In fact, Kyiv's budget at that time was comparable to the budgets of other imperial cities of similar size. For example, in Kazan', with revenues of 197,033 roubles, expenditures were 188,371 roubles (hence the positive account balance of 8,628 roubles). Ibid., p.623. In Nizhnii Novgorod the revenues were 143,581, the expenditures 98,755 (with the surplus being considerably higher than that in Kyiv – 44,826 roubles). Ibid., 634. In Saratov the revenues were 141,840 roubles,

the expenditures were 85,279 (with a huge surplus of 56,560 roubles).
Ibid., 630. Among cities of similar size, only Astrakhan', an important
commercial centre in the south, had a much larger budget, with revenues
totalling 467,117 roubles, expenditures only 347,690 roubles, thus a
surplus nearing 120,000 roubles. Ibid., 619. Kyiv's budget in the 1830s, of
course, could not rival the budgets of empire's largest cities such as Saint
Petersburg, Moscow, or Odessa. For example, the latter's revenues in 1834
exceeded 1,000,000 roubles, with the surplus of 4,743 roubles. Ibid., 636.

49 These amounts appear much smaller because after 1838 the interior ministry
began counting in silver roubles instead of the so-called "assignation
roubles" (a paper currency). See Varadinov, *Istoriia Ministerstva vnutrennikh
del*, vol. 2, 572. On the population statistics, see ibid., 742–3.

50 Ibid., 574, 578. Kyiv, no doubt, received the bulk of that amount for its
costly public works.

51 Ibid. 701.

52 Ibid., vol. 3, 71. Another source confirms a large deficit that year – 7,750
silver roubles. See Funduklei, ed., *Statisticheskoe opisanie Kievskoi gubernii*,
402. In paper roubles (*assignatsii*), that amount would be around 27,125
(with the official exchange rate of 3.5).

53 For this year the numbers are based on budget estimates and are in silver
roubles. The revenues would have been even more substantial if they
included the arrears collected for a few previous years (29,757 silver
roubles). See ibid., 400.

54 This amount does not include 40,674 roubles spent by the city for
acquiring a private property on which to build the institutions of
municipal administration.

55 It is interesting to compare the expenditures in Kyiv with those made by
all Russian cities in 1848 (the aggregate amount was 7,665,125 roubles).
So, the largest portion of that aggregate budget was spent on municipal
administration, including police (both buildings and people – 3,630,974
roubles); the second-largest was allocated to maintain municipal
properties and for city beautification (2,049,194 roubles); then came
expenditures on charitable and educational institutions (670,418 roubles)
and on the billeting of troops and other military needs (415,744 roubles).
This structure of expenditures remained largely unchanged throughout
the 1850s. See Varadinov, *Istoriia Ministerstva vnutrennikh del*, vol. 3, 453
(1848), and vol 4, 73 (1853).

56 For instance, in 1859 the lump sum costs to maintain municipal property,
and for construction and beautification, were especially high – 54,454
roubles. See DAK, f. 17, op. 5, spr. 443.

57 The overall costs of city beautification – which ranged from road paving
to the maintenance of lanterns and barns to operating the city theatre and
maintaining the ruins of the medieval Golden Gate – grew from 34,037
roubles (1856) to 49,019 (1857) to 39,855 (1858) to a proposed 83,795 (1859).
The latter amount was probably never confirmed by the governor, for the
entire amount of building expenses in 1859, as shown in the annual financial
report, was about 54,000 roubles. See DAK, f. 17, op. 4, spr. 368, 17, 35. For an
actual figure of building expenses in 1859, see DAK, f. 17, op. 5, spr. 443.
58 Hall, *Planning Europe's Capital Cities*, 170.
59 Ibid., 323–5.
60 See Choay, *The Modern City*, 15–19. Paris, however, was not the only
European capital to have undergone an overall planning "make-over" in
the nineteenth century. Among other famous examples were Helsinki and
Athens, two newly minted capitals that were planned and substantially
built during the first decades of that century. See separate chapters on
each city in Hall, *Planning Europe's Capital Cities*. Note that the concepts
of "circulation" and "respiration" was first posited in the 1620s by the
physician William Harvey, in the context of his research on how the
human body worked. In the eighteenth century these physiological
notions were adapted by town planners, who "sought to make the city
a place in which people could move and breathe freely, a city of flowing
arteries and veins through which people streamed like healthy blood
corpuscles." See Sennett, *Flesh and Stone*, 256.
61 As the best-known example of "the unsystematic opening of main arteries"
in a nineteenth-century city, Choay points to the Viviani Plan for Rome,
whereby two axes – Corso Vittorio Emmanuele and Via Nazionale – were
constructed in the 1880s. See Choay, *The Modern City*, 21; compare Hall,
Planning Europe's Capital Cities, 295–6.
62 Kovalyns'kyi, "Vid Kozynoho bolota – do maidanu Nezalezhnosti," in
Kyïvs'ki miniatiury, vol. 3, 278.
63 Kostof, *The City Shaped*, 61.
64 A historian of Khreshchatyk writes that that street, owing to its
"geometrically central location in Kyiv," was from the start a prime
destination for traffic coming from all cross streets running to and from the
city's hilly areas. See Matushevych, *Khreshchatyk*, 48.
65 DAK, f. 19, op. 1, spr. 209.
66 Ibid., 3 reverse–4 (a coloured site drawing).
67 Ibid., 31–2.
68 Kal'nyts'kyi and Kondel'-Perminova, "Eksperymental'nyi maidanchyk
molodoho kapitalizmu," in their *Zabudova Kyieva*, 323.

69 Maksymovych, "Obozrenie Starogo Kieva," in *"Kiev iavilsia gradom velikim,"* 51.

70 Idem, *Ocherk Kieva*, in Funduklei, *Obozrenie Kieva*, xiii.

71 Sementovskii, *Kiev i ego dostopamiatnosti*, 160. Compare Funduklei, *Statisticheskoe opisanie Kievskoi gubernii*, 329.

72 See the assessment of private real estate in the Palace district in 1863: DAK, f. 17, op. 5, spr. 662. In the 1870s the municipal authorities began receiving numerous requests from homeowners for permission to add a third storey (or more) to existing houses or to build larger houses from scratch. See DAK, 163, op. 41(1), spr. 79–85, 232–3, 237–9, 441–3, and many others.

73 *Kievskie gubernskie vedomosti* 43 (1853), 24 October, 333.

74 These were the streets that ran towards Khreshchatyk from surrounding hills, which made it vulnerable to flooding.

75 Pataleev, *Staryi Kyiv*, 123.

76 DAK, fond 1, op. 2a, spr. 254.

77 Maksymovych, "Obozrenie Starogo Kieva," 71.

78 Idem, *Ocherk Kieva*, in Funduklei, *Obozrenie Kieva*, xiii.

79 See Kostomarov, *Istoricheskie proizvedeniia*, 462–3.

80 Most of the streets and blocks in today's Old Kyiv were planned in 1837–9, replacing the old defensive ramparts that had dominated the area. A further impetus for the rise of Old Kyiv was the building of the new Pechers'k fortress in the early 1830s and a subsequent relocation of many houses from Pechers'k to Old Kyiv. See Halaiba et al., *Prorizna*, 127.

81 Ikonnikov, *Kiev v 1654–1855*, 158.

82 First planned in 1837, initially it was called Bul'varne shosse (Bul'varnoe shosse or the Boulevard Highway), Bul'varna vulytsia (Bul'varnaia ulitsa or Boulevard Street), and Universytets'kyi bul'var (Universtitetskii bul'var or University Boulevard). In 1869 it was renamed Bibikovs'kyi bul'var to commemorate Dmitrii Bibikov. Today's legendary poplar trees were first planted in 1842. See Kal'nyts'kyi, "Nachalo bul'vara: galereia metamorfoz."

83 The idea of a straight street ending with an eye-catching marker – for instance, an obelisk, a column, a church, or some other monumental building – was born in late-sixteenth-century Rome and persisted in Europe until the late nineteenth century. See Hall, *Planning Europe's Capital Cities*, 28. In Kyiv, around the mid-nineteenth century there were only a few straight streets, and of these, only Khreshchatyk had some uniformity in structures.

84 My information about the meanings and functions of the boulevard in European cities come from Hall, *Planning Europe's Capital Cities*, 342.

85 Ibid., 367n4. A look at a map of Kyiv and its rural district tells us that Bibikovs'kyi Boulevard – or rather its western extension (Brest-Lytovs'ke Highway or *shosse*) – indeed served an important function as a radial road linking Kyiv's downtown with outer suburbs.

86 Such has long been a view of Parisian boulevards created by Baron Haussmann in the 1850s and 1860s, a view established by Walter Benjamin in the early twentieth century. Historian Patrice Higonnet, however, disputes the "militaristic" interpretation of Haussmann's intentions. Apparently Haussmann was already aware of the military uselessness of barricades, so the main idea behind his wide boulevards was political legibility, as a "proof of the creative power of the bourgeoisie," and also visibility. These two features of the Haussmannian project allowed "the visual as well as the military penetration of the city" and also offered a new way to organize the city's space – around communication, whereby individual monuments only emphasized the new straight and long perspectives. See Higonnet, *Paris, the Capital of the World*, 171–3. It is quite possible, however, that for Bibikov military concerns played a far greater role than for Haussmann.

87 Makarov, "Kogda Bibikova sprosili."

88 Erofalov-Pilipchak, *Arkhitektura imperskogo Kieva*, 92.

89 Zakrevskii, *Opisanie Kieva*, 124, 378.

90 See Alioshyn, "Bat'ko i syn Beretti," 39–40; see also Hrytsai, *Budynok universytetu*, 3. Note also that the author of the first publication, the famous Ukrainian architect Pavlo Alioshyn, led the work on the reconstruction of the university building in 1944–5, after it had been damaged during the war.

91 DAK, f. 241, op. 2, spr. 288, 3–3 reverse; compare Shul'kevich and Dmitrenko, *Kiev. Arkhitekturno-istoricheskii ocherk*, 73.

92 DAK, f. 241, op. 2, spr. 288, 6.

93 Ibid., 35–35 reverse.

94 Alioshyn, "Bat'ko i syn Beretti," 48. Recently, however, for some unknown reason, the building was repainted in caustic or rather acid red, to the detriment of tradition and taste.

95 Hall, *Planning Europe's Capital Cities*, 295–6.

96 Shul'kevich and Dmitrenko, *Kiev. Arkhitekturno-istoricheskii ocherk*, 74.

97 Hrytsai, *Budynok universytetu*, 4–5.

98 Maslov, "Putevye zametki," 57.

99 This was a quote from Mykola Bohatynov [Nikolai Bogatinov] (1833–96), a student in Podil noble school in the 1840s, later a teacher in Kyiv's elite First Gymnasium. His fascinating memoirs "Vospominaniia" were published in *Russkii Arkhiv* 1 (1899), nos. 2–12. The quote comes from *Russkii Arkhiv* 1 (1899), no. 3, 424.

100 Pataleev, *Staryi Kyiv*, 202–3.
101 Kostomarov, *Istoricheskie proizvedeniia*, 271–2.
102 Hrytsai, *Budynok universytetu*, 5–6.
103 Ibid.
104 Erofalov-Pilipchak, *Arkhitektura imperskogo Kieva*, 94.
105 Ibid.
106 DAK, f. 926 [The building committee of Kyiv University], spr. 400.
107 Ibid., 2–3.
108 This explanation has been suggested by Erofalov-Pilipchak in *Arkhitektura imperskogo Kieva*, 96.
109 The planning of Old Kyiv around the university was done by Beretti and Kyiv's municipal architect, Stanzani. See Ibid., 97.
110 Among the most famous examples of cities where a grid pattern was used for new sections of "organic" cities were Berlin and Amsterdam in Europe and Boston, Baltimore, and Richmond in the United States. The best example of a city where several grids representing different periods of urban history were linked smoothly together is Turin, Italy. See Kostof, *The City Shaped*, 99, 121, 136.
111 Koshman, *Gorod i gorodskaia zhizn'*, 64–7.
112 The copy of the plan can be found in DAK, f. 239, op.1, spr.1a, 10–12.
113 Ibid., 11.
114 In fact, in 1837 the Empire's interior minister issued a circular restricting the application of forced acquisition of private lands to "very rare cases" and only when it was dictated by "significant public benefit." The minister specifically elaborated on the circumstances where a new general plan required the demolition of private houses. No demolition of existing houses was to be enforced; however, any new construction on those plots was banned, except for minor repairs. As compensation, the authorities allotted the owners "other free plots, suitable for building, from municipal unoccupied [lands]." If no such lands could be found, the government had to issue monetary payments. Only when an owner *repeatedly* rejected an exchange of land or payment could the government enforce the acquisition of a plot. It seems, however, that the local administration, especially Governor-General Bibikov, did not care much about the rights of private owners. But in 1853, after his departure, the Ministry of Interior again urged local authorities to abstain from a forcible acquisition of private real estate. See DAK, f. 163, op. 41, spr. 134, pp. 47–9.
115 DAK, f. 239, op.1, spr.1a, 10.

5 Municipal Autonomy Reloaded: Space for Sale, 1871–1905

1 Nardova, *Gorodskoe samoupravlenie v Rossii*, 32 and Kal'nyts'kyi and Kondel'-Perminova, "Dzherela i formy investuvannia u zabudovu Kyieva," in Kal'nyts'kyi and Kondel'-Perminova, *Zabudova Kyieva*. Certainly the city dumas were quite narrowly focused on the wealthier elements, which got even narrower after Alexander III's counter-reforms.

2 A. Belomesiatsev, "Osoblyvosti zahal'noimpers'koï ta rehional'noï sytuatsiï u poreformenu dobu," in Kal'nyts'kyi and Kondel'-Perminova, *Zabudova Kyieva*, 25.

3 On the nature of the tax see Kal'nyts'kyi and Kondel'-Perminova, "Dzherela i formy investuvannia," 115–16. On the irregularities behind the real estate tax see *Zaria* (1881) 5, 2–3. Between 1870 and 1883 the "assessed property tax" was calculated based on the interest (percentage) from property's *relative value*. From 1885 through the 1890s, the principle behind the tax was changed, and it was exacted from the owner's *net income*. To illustrate the contradictions inherent in the tax, a reporter pointed to the two examples: a house in a remote suburb of Kurenivka valued at 5,000 roubles brought in an annual income of 100 to 200 roubles, while a wooden barn on Khreshchatyk might yield around 1,000 roubles. Whichever principle was used, the aggregate value of Kyiv's real estate grew steadily: from 5,575,300 roubles in 1872 to 12,979,600 roubles in 1882 and to 15,452,261 roubles in 1892. See *Kievlianin* (1892) 345, 2.

4 The costs of billeting troops sometimes were the single largest expense of the Kyiv city administration. For example, in 1899 the city spent 442,000 roubles for this purpose (of which 240,000 went for renting barracks). That year, Kyiv had to accommodate the Luts'k infantry regiment. See *Kievlianin* 77 (1900), 2.

5 Fedorov, *Istoriia Rossii*, 193–4.

6 The city also gave a subsidy of 300,000 roubles for the opening of Kyiv Polytechnic Institute, which brought the total expenses on education and charities to more than 600,000 roubles. See *Kievlianian* 319 (1898), 2.

7 A journalist from the liberal paper *Zaria* pointed out that on average the city spent 20 per cent of its budget on policing. He remarked ironically: "This is as if a family spent 20% of their budget on a night watchman." See *Zaria* (1881) 265, 2. Similarly, the conservative paper *Kievlianin*, quoting the city's budget commission, saw the growing cost of policing as a main reason for budget deficits in the city. See *Kievlianin* (1878) 11, 1.

8 The data about the cost of *uprava* appeared in *Zaria* (1882) 290, 2. The author of this report commented wryly that the costs of municipal self-government in Saint Petersburg, Moscow, and Warsaw were lower,

especially when juxtaposed with the growth of revenue. The data in table 5.2 were collected by the Senate audit commission and are slightly different, but they confirm the trend: the rise from 25,724 roubles in 1871 to 64,883 roubles in 1880. See DAK, f. 163, op. 47, spr. 18, 86.

9 *Zaria* 18 (1881), 2.

10 The total expenses for city improvements and beautification between 1871 and 1897 were considerable: 2,192,028 roubles for paving streets, 343,793 roubles for pipes and canals, 315,555 roubles for planning streets, squares, and hills. Smaller amounts were allocated for the construction of bridges and sidewalks. The total amount was 2,911,939 roubles. See *Kievlianin* 325 (1898), 2.

11 The total area under the streets in Kyiv in 1904 equalled 932,016 square *sazhen'*, of which only 332,754 were already paved. In Old Kyiv, Bul'varna, Palace, and Podil, most streets were paved, but in Lybid', Pechers'k, Luk'ianivka, and Plos'ka, between 75 and 80 per cent of the streets remained unpaved. Clearly, the city government was underfunding the improvement of peripheral areas, instead focusing on traffic in the city centre. See *Kievlianin* 28 (1904), 3.

12 In this Central European model, the dominance of the wealthiest voters was maintained by the three-class electoral system (*Dreiklassenwahlrecht*), which was first introduced in the Rhineland in 1845 and then in the state of Prussia in 1850. "Municipal taxpayers were ranked according to the size of their fiscal contribution and the resulting list was divided into three groups, each of which contributed one-third of the total tax revenues," wrote urban historian Anthony Sutcliffe. "Each group was then allowed to elect one-third of the council, subject to the proviso that at least half of those elected should be house-owners." See his *Towards the Planned City*, 17.

13 *Zaria*'s major rival, the conservative *Kievlianin*, while also criticizing Kyiv self-government, was much more reserved in doing so.

14 *Zaria* (1882) 194, 2.

15 For example, in 1900, instead of investing in the lighting of peripheries, the city government decided to divert 100,000 roubles to the new Municipal Theatre. See *Kievskoe slovo* 4317 (1900), 3. Another journalist bluntly accused Kyiv politicians of ignoring the interests of the poor. "Why," asked a local journalist, "do the cities spend fortunes on the luxurious municipal theaters, electric lights downtown, streetcars, etc., while leaving peripheries without schools, pavements, and lighting?" The answer he found was that the rich were preoccupied with their own well-being, whereas the poor could not even be elected to a duma. See *Kievskaia gazeta* 70 (1901), 3.

16 The best book on Kyiv's rented apartment houses (the so-called *dokhodnye doma* in Russian, or *prybutkovi budynky* in Ukrainian) is Malakov, *Prybutkovi budynky Kyieva*.

17 "Samyi vysokii dom v Kieve," *Zhizn' i iskusstvo*, 12 October (1897), 2. Quoted in Malakov, *Arkhitektor Horodets'kyi*, 63.

18 *Kievlianin* 2 (1872), 2.

19 *Kievlianin* 145 (1873), 2. In another account someone wrote about the ubiquitous "herds of cows" on the city's streets and sidewalks, roaming animals were accompanied by only one boy. The author insisted that at least the sidewalks should be reserved for people. *Kievlianin* 156 (1883), 2.

20 *Kievlianin* 15 (1880), 2.

21 These data are from the first comprehensive statistical survey conducted by Kyiv province's statistical committee in 1863 and published in *Kievlianin* 66 (1864), 266. For the full exposé see Dinovskii, "Zapiska sekretaria."

22 Malakov, *Prybutkovi budynky Kyieva*, 7.

23 For example, in 1845, out of forty-eight houses occupied by priests and other clergymen, twenty-eight had tenants. Specifically, the rent brought annually to the clergy of Old Kyiv 1,524 roubles, of Pechers'k 787 roubles, and of Podil 663 roubles. See Funduklei, *Statisticheskoe opisanie Kievskoi gubernii*, vol. 2, 219.

24 One plan from 1849 showed a large plot with a three-storey house, designed specifically to be a rental property. From the 1850s through to the 1870s, Khreshchatyk saw a surge in new rental housing. See T. Skibits'ka, "Arkhitektura kyïvs'koho zhytla," in Kal'nyts'kyi and Kondel'-Perminova, *Zabudova Kyieva doby klasychnoho kapitalizmu*, 370. On the building and rebuilding of individual rental properties on Khreshchatyk see the acts of Kyiv *uprava*'s Building Department: DAK, f. 163, op. 41 (1), esp. spr. 79–85, 441–3, 1629, and many others.

25 Malakov, *Prybutkovi budynky Kyieva*, 8–9.

26 Kostof, *The City Shaped*, 27.

27 Hall, *Planning Europe's Capital Cities*, 304.

28 These three notions –*town plan*, *land use pattern*, and *building fabric* – are from the vocabulary of urban geographer M.R.C. Conzen and designate the three elements in his analysis of urban fabric. For criticism of Conzen's approach see Kostof, *The City Shaped*, 25–6. Quote is from Conzen, "The Use of Town Plans."

29 Oskar Handlin, "Modern City as a Field of Historical Study," in Handlin and Burchard, *The Historian and the City*, 11.

30 Sutcliffe, *Towards the Planned City*, ix.

31 *Sputnik po Kievu*, Izdanie 8, S.M. Boguslavskogo (Kyiv, 1913), 7, as quoted in Malakov, *Prybutkovi budynky Kyieva*, 15.

32 Malakov, *Prybutkovi budynky Kyieva*, 15.

33 In late-nineteenth-century Kyiv there were at least three financial institutions
that invested in private construction: the Kyiv Mutual Credit Society
(founded in 1868), the Kyiv Land Bank (1872), and the Kyiv Municipal
Credit Society (1885), all of which issued short- and long-term loans to
all of those who wanted to build commercial real estate (primarily rented
apartment houses). Loans were usually secured with a land plot, an existing
house, or a newly started building. In 1898 just one of the aforementioned
institutions – the Kyiv Municipal Credit Society – issued 204 loans, with
a total worth of 6,049,000 roubles. Several city architects were among the
directors and active members of these institutions. See Kal'nyts'kyi and
Kondel'-Perminova, "Dzherela i formy investuvannia," 119–28.

34 *Kievlianin* 126 (1887), 2.

35 See the memoirs of merchant Pataleev, *Staryi Kyiv*, 151–2.

36 For example, from the late 1840s through the 1850s the lands controlled by
the military comprised around 1,776 *dessiatin*, while the traditional settled
areas of the city constituted 1,309 *dessiatin*. See Funduklei, *Statisticheskoe
opisanie Kievskoi gubernii*, 330.

37 Malakov, *Prybutkovi budynky Kyieva*, 57. On various changes in esplanade
rules see Kal'nyts'kyi and Kondel'-Perminova, "Pravovi zasady mis'koho
budivnytstva," in Kal'nyts'kyi and Kondel'-Perminova, *Zabudova Kyieva*,
83–5. The similar rules for another "fortress city," Warsaw, were abolished
in 1911. See Paszkiewicz, *Pod berłem Romanowów*, 39.

38 DAK, f. 163, op. 41, spr. 134, 53–55 reverse. In fact, the imperial
government vacillated between expanding and reducing the esplanade,
depending on actual external threats and their own phobias. For example,
ten years after liberating the city from the most burdensome esplanade
rules in 1859, the military authorities again decided to expand the
fortifications, so greatly that even the university quarter would have
been affected. See Kal'nyts'kyi and Kondel'-Perminova, "Pravovi zasady
mis'koho budivnytstva," 83. As late as 1892 the commandant of the Kyiv
fortress threatened the duma with legal action if the residents of Pechers'k
built or repaired their wooden houses "with the breach of the esplanade
rules." See *Kievlianin* 27 May (1892), 2.

39 See the account of the proceedings of the Kyiv city duma in *Kievlianin* 18
May (1880), 2.

40 *Kievlianin* 329 (1892), 2. In 1883 the government legalized this land grab
by sanctioning the "lease" (in reality, sale) of esplanade lands to the
owners of private homesteads, who were often military officers. So by
1912, of the total area of the military-held lands within the fortress and

its esplanades – 1,129 *dessiatin* (roughly 3,047 acres) – around 212 *dessiatin* (572 acres) had been leased to private landowners. See Kal'nyts'kyi and Kondel'-Perminova, "Pravovi zasady mis'koho budivnytstva," 84.

41 A city councillor complained that the state commission had assessed Kyiv's entire real estate at 60 million roubles, while in Odessa, a much larger and wealthier city, that figure was only 30 million roubles. See *Kievlianin* 351 (1892), 3.

42 Kal'nyts'kyi and Kondel'-Perminova, "Dzherela i formy investuvannia," 115. The author refers to the critical writing of Kyiv journalist M. Volynskii. See Volynskii, *Spravedlivo li raspredelenie naloga,* 9–16.

43 As the city's executive, the *uprava,* stated in 1898, the city could not afford to rent private apartments in newly built residential houses for the military; these were often very expensive. The city's solution was to build "new special quarters" (barracks) and to rent rooms from minor homeowners who could not arrange private apartments in their houses. See DAK, f. 163, op. 17, spr. 25, 50.

44 See a critical assessment of this practice published in Kyiv's liberal paper: *Zaria* 34 (1880), 2. The costs for billeting troops skyrocketed in 1899, reaching the astounding sum of 442,000 roubles (of which 240,000 were for renting barracks). See *Kievlianin* 77 (1900), 2.

45 Kyiv's mayor admitted that the city "builds barracks only because it is difficult to find entrepreneurs willing to offer their quarters to the troops." Also, developers were reluctant to build large quarters on the city outskirts, fearing that after the troops vacated these capacious properties, it would be impossible to find other tenants. In the city centre, land was too expensive. DAK, f. 163, op. 17, spr. 25, 108–111.

46 For example, the cost of building barracks rose and fell from 27,682 roubles in 1873 to 73,135 roubles in 1880 to 47,208 roubles in 1897, not including annual renovations worth at least a couple of thousand roubles. See DAK, f. 163, op. 17, spr. 25, 44–7. By 1902 Kyiv owned several barracks in Bul'varna and Luk'ianivka districts, financed through loans and assessed at 825,700 roubles. See *Kievlianin* 175 (1902), 3. Large cities were especially hard hit by the growing discrepancy between the "billeting pay" offered by the military and actual market prices. For example, between 1875 and 1884 Moscow received 3,097,320 roubles from the government for billeting troops but had to add much more from the city coffers – 5,710,494 roubles (excluding the costs of building the new barracks, which required a further 1,838,000 roubles). See the entry from *Entsiklopedicheskii slovar' F.A. Brokgauza i I.A. Efrona,* http://dic. academic.ru/dic.nsf/brokgauz_efron/50824/%D0%9A%D0%B2%D0%B0% D1%80%D1%82%D0%B8%D1%80%D0%BD%D0%B0%D1%8F.

47 Kal'nyts'kyi and Kondel'-Perminova, "Dzherela i formy investuvannia,"
   135–6.
48 The regulations were first introduced in Kyiv in September 1851, on the
   insistence of Tsar Nicholas I himself. By May 1852, his loyal lieutenant
   Dmitrii Bibikov reported that "in all parts of Kyiv there have been
   assigned the main and most significant streets, on which … there would
   be erected stone and wooden buildings with improved façades." Then on
   11 May 1861, Alexander II confirmed the new regulations, along with the
   new general plan of the city. The rules were again changed and confirmed
   in 1874, together with a new general plan of Kyiv. Both would remain in
   force until the 1910s. See Kal'nyts'kyi and Kondel'-Perminova, "Pravovi
   zasady mis'koho budivnytstva," 88–9.
49 The hierarchy of streets, however, had existed since antiquity. Planning
   historian Christopher Tunnard looked at ancient cities and discerned
   "a hierarchy of streets, with differentiation between important and less
   important arteries of interior communication." See Christopher Tunnard,
   "The Customary and the Characteristic," in Handlin, *The Historian and
   the City*, 221. Regarding the final version of imperial Kyiv's building
   regulations, see Appendix 1 of Kal'nyts'kyi and Kondel'-Perminova,
   Zabudova Kyieva, 525–8.
50 DAK, f. 163, op. 41, spr. 134, 19–21 (1861 ed.); 72–73 reverse (1872 ed.).
51 Ibid., 72.
52 In administrative terms, Khreshchatyk belonged to two districts – Old
   Kyiv (the street's right side) and Palace (its left side).
53 Ibid., 64–64 reverse.
54 But this tension was typical of non-Russian cities as well. According
   to Oscar Handlin, Paris, Rio de Janiero, and Rome "did not govern
   themselves" and even New York had to listen to the state governor. See his
   "Modern City as a Field of Historical Study," in Handlin and Burchard,
   The Historian and the City, 22. On the case of Vienna, see Breitling, "The
   Role of the Competition in the Genesis of Urban Planning," in Sutcliffe,
   The Rise of Modern Urban Planning, 39–44.
55 DAK, f. 163, op. 41, spr. 134, p. 61 reverse.
56 Ibid., 74–7.
57 For a monochromic copy of the 1874 plan see DAK, f. 163, op. 41,
   spr. 4545.
58 By the early twentieth century, Kyiv had been split into eight police
   districts – Old Kyiv, Pechers'k, Palace, Podil, Plos'ka, Lybid', Boulevard
   (Bul'varna), and Luk'ianivka. Some of these had absorbed entities once
   referred to as "suburbs," "outskirts," and "hamlets."

59 See Kal'nyts'kyi and Kondel'-Perminova, "Eksperymental'nyi maidanchyk molodoho kapitalizmu," in Kal'nyts'kyi and Kondel'-Perminova, *Zabudova Kyieva*, 325–6.

60 The initial proposal, made in 1871, was to locate Kyiv's city duma in the hilly park near Khreshchatyk's northern end (just off European Square). This idea was rejected by the duma's deputies, who argued against such "wasteful" spending. But a few years later, the deputies seemed to change their minds and voted for their new house to be located in the heart of Khreshchatyk Square. It was anticipated that some of the costs would be covered by renting out the duma's ground floor to various shopowners. The revenue from the rented spaces, however, would remain insignificant for years. See *Zaria* 18 (1881), 2.

61 See the first large-scale census of Kyiv: *Kiev i ego predmistiia*, 3.

62 DAK, f. 163, op. 41, spr. 134, 101–5.

63 Archaeologists have proven that in early medieval times, Greater Kyiv or the "Kyiv agglomeration" included the land between the three rivers – the Dnieper, the Lybid' and the Syrets' – a space filled again by the city in the mid-seventeenth century and yet again – more decisively – around 1870. On early moden Kyiv, see Klymovs'kyi, *Sotsial'na topohrafiia Kyieva*, 156–9, 185.

64 DAK, f. 163, op. 41, spr. 134, 105.

65 Ibid., 4–13.

66 Article 114 of the 1870 statute stated: "The confirmation of plans and façades of private buildings in the city, the issuance of permits for rebuilding, as well as the supervision over the correct execution of structures belong with the Municipal *Uprava*." See *Gorodovoe polozhenie s raz'iasneniiami i dopolneniiami* (Saint Petersburg: 1873), 19–20. In fact, only a few people were in charge of *all* building projects in Kyiv – the head of the *uprava*'s building department, and city architects (two from 1871 to 1898; three from 1898 to 1912). See Kal'nyts'kyi and Kondel'-Perminova, "Pravovi zasady mis'koho budivnytstva," pp. 69, 71–2.

67 Ibid., 73, 78. Homeowners often violated building regulations by covering their wooden houses with bricks, thus seizing some street space. See *Kievskoe slovo* 4308 (1900), 2.

68 Such was the case with Kyiv's legendary multistorey apartment house known as "Richard's castle." When it was almost completed in 1904, a municipal architect noticed that the developer had never received a building permit from the city *uprava*. The police then halted construction, but the developer somehow managed to get permission to continue. From the example of this particular property, we can see that the most lucrative rental apartment houses often changed hands: between 1904 and 1917,

"Richard's castle" was resold at least three times. See Kal'nyts'kyi and Kondel'-Perminova, "Dzherela i formy investuvannia," 197–9.

69 Malakov, *Prybutkovi budynky Kyieva*, 269.

70 Various building regulations and planning laws spread gradually all over Europe over the course of the century. For example, under Baron Haussmann, Paris was subjected to even more strenuous regulations with respect to the placement, forms, and ornamentation of new apartment houses. See Kostof, *The City Shaped*, 254, 262. Even in England, where building regulations and urban planning as such had hitherto been almost non-existent (except for a few local cases), in the second half of the century local and central authorities began to enforce various public health and building "acts," which culminated in London's Building Act of 1894. That act regulated the width of streets, the width of back lanes, and the open spaces behind buildings, all for the sake of hygiene and public health. See John Nelson Tarn, "Housing Reform and the Emergence of Town Planning in Britain before 1914," in Sutcliffe, *The Rise of Modern Urban Planning*, 83. Compare Sutcliffe, *Towards the Planned City*, 51.

71 Kal'nyts'kyi and Kondel'-Perminova, "Pravovi zasady mis'koho budivnytstva," 86.

72 Europe was not much different in this respect. Because of the persistence of fortifications and various legal obstacles regarding the exploitation of land, urbanization led to the more intense use of existing built-up areas, and new buildings were erected in people's courtyards, with fewer regularions in place than in Russia. See Hall, *Planning Europe's Capital Cities*, 49.

73 On this earliest Kyiv "skyscraper," see Skibits'ka, "Arkhitektura kyïvs'koho zhytla," 376.

74 On American cities, particularly New York and Los Angeles, see Kostof, *The City Shaped*, 121–4; on the terminology, see Conzen, "The Use of Town Plans."

75 Skibits'ka, "Arkhitektura kyïvs'koho zhytla," 371–5.

76 Sergei Witte, Russia's famous prime minister, quoted in Malakov, *Arkhitektor Horodets'kyi*, 54.

77 Kal'nyts'kyi and Kondel'-Perminova, "Dzherela i formy investuvannia," 186–7.

78 DAK, f. 163, op. 7, spr. 1361, 2.

79 Ibid., 55–6 reverse.

80 Ibid., 67.

81 On the history of this society see Moshenskii, *Finansovye tsentry Ukrainy*, 154.

82 DAK, f. 163, op. 7, spr. 1361, 35.

83 Malakov, *Arkhitektor Horodets'kyi*, 56.

84 Kal'nyts'kyi and Kondel'-Perminova, "Dzherela i formy investuvannia," 187–8.

85 Horodets'kyi also worked closely with architect Shleifer, a board member of the Kyiv Home Building Society, in the demolition of old and the building of new structures in the area. See Malakov, *Arkhitektor Horodets'kyi*, 55.

86 Moshenskii, *Finansovye tsentry Ukrainy*, 155.

87 Kal'nyts'kyi and Kondel'-Perminova, "Dzherela i formy investuvannia," 191.

88 DAK, f. 163, op. 41, spr. 134, 105 reverse–106.

89 Kal'nyts'kyi and Kondel'-Perminova, "Pravovi zasady mis'koho budivnytstva," 104. On London's leasehold estates see Olsen, *Town Planning in London*.

90 Borys Erofalov, "Mistobudivnyi rozvytok Kyieva," in Kal'nyts'kyi and Kondel'-Perminova, *Zabudova Kyieva*, 51.

91 Ibid.

92 Ibid., 52.

93 Hamm, *Kiev: A Portrait*, 122.

94 DAK, f. 163, op. 38, spr. 122, 61.

95 Demiïvka was finally annexed by the city in September 1918, when the cabinet of Hetman Pavlo Skoropads'kyi issued the Law on the Incorporation of Demiïvka and Saperna Slobidka into Kyiv. On this issue see Kal'nyts'kyi, "Kolyshnie peredmistia Demiïvka."

96 On the Russian government's more than troubled relationship with cities and urban populations see Koshman, *Gorod i gorodskaia zhizn'*, esp. ch. 2.

97 According to the data collected by the city duma, there were fifty smaller commercial and manufacturing establishments and one large plant – the Greter and Krivanek Machine Works, the largest machine-building plant in the city. Around 1895 the Orthodox were a narrow majority in Shuliavka. Out of 3,217 inhabitants, Jews numbered 597 (18.5%) and Catholics numbered 375 (or 11.6%). See DAK, f. 163, op. 38, spr. 122, 64. In the city itself (according to the 1897 census) the Orthodox were the dominant majority with 187,935 inhabitants (75.86%); the Jews came second at 32,093 (12.96%); and Roman Catholics came third at 19,230 (7.76%). See *Pervaia vseobshchaia perepis'*, 1904.

98 DAK, f. 163, op. 38, spr. 122, 4.

99 Ibid., pp. 53–5 (the report of the special Kyiv duma commission on the incorporation of Shuliavka).

100 The commission members calculated that the city would receive from the fifty local trading and manufacturing establishments only 1,500 roubles in taxes and the additional 600 roubles from real estate; these amounts would not cover expenses. See ibid., 55 reverse.

101 Ibid., 64.

102 Ibid., 70.

103 As late as 1910, Kyiv's governor demanded that the mayor respond to the concerns of Shuliavka's peasants, who continued to fight against the merger with the city. Ibid., 85–85 reverse.

104 Fiscal conservatives could be blamed for the failure to develop a social welfare system and for the city's reluctance to municipalize services and utilities. See Hamm, *Kiev: A Portrait*, 41–3, 201, 233. Yet in 1895, duma members, over strong opposition, voted for a proposal to help financially those homeowners who could not afford the new sewage system. See *Kievlianin* 158 (1895), 3.

105 DAK, f. 163, op. 7, spr. 1780.

106 By 1880 the Main Railway Shops were Kyiv's largest single employer, with 467 workers, a number that would rise to 2,500 by 1900. See V. Ievleva, "Transport, inzheneriia ta promyslova zabudova Kyieva kintsia XIX-pochatku XX stolit'," in Kal'nyts'kyi and Kondel'-Perminova, *Zabudova Kyieva*, 258. Compare Hamm, *Kiev: A Portrait*, 34, 231 (Kyiv's industrial workforce in 1897 numbered 13,000 people, much less than in Moscow (153,200) or even Odessa (24,200). Hamm's statistics come from Ryndziunskii, *Krest'iane i gorod*, 158–9.

107 Hall, *Planning Europe's Capital Cities*, 303.

108 See Ievleva, "Transport," 253. The story is briefly described by Erofalov in his "Mistobudivnyi rozvytok Kyieva," 56–7. A more detailed account is in Kal'nyts'kyi, Vitiuk, and Ievsieiev, *Solom'ians'kyi raion*, 19–20. Finally, the official materials pertaining to the incorporation of Solom'ianka in the early twentieth century can be found in DAK, f. 163, op. 57, spr. 2.

109 This explanation featured in the duma's own self-complementary publication *Obzor deiatel'nosti Kievskoi gorodskoi dumy za chetyrekhletie*, 11.

110 Erofalov, "Mistobudivnyi rozvytok Kyieva," 57–9. Characteristically, Dubelir's own project appeared in the Kyiv duma's own publication: "Zapiska professor D.G. Dubelira po voprosu o planirovke okrain g. Kieva," *Izvestiia Kievskoi gorodskoi dumy* (Kyiv: 1912).

111 This and other elements in Dubelir's innovative plan were in line with the progressive ideas about urban zoning and functional division of streets that had developed in Europe, especially in Germany in the early 1900s. See Sutcliffe, *Towards the Planned City*, 43.

112 Most projects in Europe and America that were influenced by Garden City philosophy did not realize Howard's main idea, which was to create clusters of economically self-contained small towns as a way to decentralize the metropolis. Most projects were realized not as garden *cities* but as garden *suburbs* of existing large cities. See Kostof, *The City Shaped*, 75–80,

89–91; Relph, *The Modern Urban Landscape*, 56–61; and Sutcliffe, *Towards the Planned City*, 41, 67, 76–8, 187. (The last page features two plans of a "garden city," one in Germany, near Munich, and the other in Italy, near Milan.)

113 As quoted in Erofalov, "Mistobudivnyi rozvytok Kyieva," 59.

114 The relationship between the city of Prague and its working-class suburbs such as the notorious Žižkov also generated a great deal of anxiety and fear, very much like that of central Kyivites vis-à-vis suburbanites. Franz Kafka, an urban mind as well as a mysterious soul, famously expressed similar feelings in his diary: "We accept foreign cities as a fact, the inhabitants live there without penetrating our way of life, just as we cannot penetrate theirs … The suburbs of our native city, however, are also foreign to us … Here people live partly within our city, partly on the miserable, dark edge of the city that is furrowed like a great ditch, although they all have an area of interest in common with us that is greater that any other group of people outside the city. For this reason I always enter and leave the suburb with a weak mixed feeling of anxiety, of abandonment, of sympathy, of curiosity, of conceit, of joy in travelling, of fortitude, and return with pleasure, seriousness, and calm, especially from Žižkov" (18 November 1911)." Franz Kafka, *Diaries*, 119.

115 Berlin also resembled Kyiv in that Prussia's capital until the very end of the nineteenth century was directly administered by the government. See Sutcliffe, *Towards the Planned* City, 12, 45.

116 Paszkiewicz, *Pod berłem Romanowów*, 38.

117 On Prague and Vienna see Melinz and Zimmermann, "Großstadtgeschichte und Modernisierung in der Habsburgermonarchie," in Melinz and Zimmerman, *Wien–Prag–Budapest*, 22–3. Curiously, in the United States, a country with a well-entrenched suburban lifestyle, the post-Civil War suburbs staunchly resisted annexation by central municipalities, which further complicated the task of administering urban areas. See Sutcliffe, *Towards the Planned City*, 91.

118 Erofalov, "Mistobudivnyi rozvytok Kyieva," 53.

119 Ibid.

120 Historians generally agree that Kyiv's urban space developed on the land between three rivers – the Dnieper in the east, and the Lybid' and the Syrets' in the west – a process that began in medieval times. See Hamm, *Kyiv: A Portrait*, 3; Klymovs'kyi, *Sotsial'na topohrafiia Kyieva*, 156–9, 185.

121 Erofalov, "Mistobudivnyi rozvytok Kyieva," 53.

122 Leshchenko, *Kievskaia sel'sko-khoziaistvennaia i promyshlennaia vystavka*, 11. Quoted in Ievleva, "Transport," 253. In the last quarter of the nineteenth century, in American cities, railways were also a major factor behind

the introduction of urban planning; before then, most cities had not experienced any significant planning at all, not even modest street beautification. See Sutcliffe, *Towards the Planned* City, 102–4.

123 Ievleva, "Transport," 256.

124 Ibid., 254–7 (a reconstructed plan of the Railway colony is reproduced on page 254).

125 Ibid., 260.

126 Hall, *Planning Europe's Capital Cities*, 325.

127 One of the most famous planners who championed radials (diagonals) was Daniel Burnham, an American. In his celebrated plan for the city of San Francisco he proposed "the superimposition of a number of new traffic streets on the existing grid, mainly in the outer districts. One was a ring boulevard but most of the others were 'radials' (diagonals) intended to shorten some cross-town journeys and create a number of star junctions." See Sutcliffe, *Towards the Planned City*, 106. Although significantly altered during their realization, Burnham's visually impressive plans for San Francisco and Chicago, and the revision of L'Enfant's design for Washington, D.C., have made a long-lasting contribution to modern urban planning in America and abroad. On Burnham and his plans see Hines, *Burnham of Chicago*.

128 Hamm, *Kyiv: A Portrait*, 15. Compare Rybakov, *Khreshchatyk vidomyi i nevidomyi*, 16.

129 Perhaps the most remarkable evidence of the failure to create a network of connecting arteries in the city was Besarabka Square, at the other end of Khreshchatyk. Initially planned as a transportation hub, in the 1860s and 1870s Besarabka re-emerged as trading place, the site of the legendary Besarabka market (until today). See Matushevych, *Khreshchatyk*, 22. Also compare Kal'nyts'kyi and Kondel'-Perminova, "Eksperymental'nyi maidanchyk," 358.

130 Hamm, *Kyiv: A Portrait*, 28.

131 Glaeser, *Triumph of the City*, 94.

132 Curiously, even social criticism from within the Kyiv city duma was largely the domain of the right-wing xenophobic populists. See Hillis, "Modernist Visions and Political Conflict."

Part III: Peopling the City

1 On the power of "naming" and official taxonomies, see Bourdieu, *Language and Symbolic Power*, 239–43.

2 Regarding social estates and trades, we know that a number of registered artisans did not practise their trade. Instead they were engaged in

domestic service, as guards, errand boys, and so on. Also, many poor townspeople sought work in the fields, either on private land around towns or on estates owned by municipalities. At the same time, peasants often worked as craftsmen in cities. Thus, the economic boundaries between burghers and peasants were blurred. See Brower, *The Russian City*, 27.

3 Izmailov, *Puteshestvie v Poludennuiu Rossiiu*, 210.

4 Stone's definition of "urban regime" as *"informal arrangements* that surround and complement the formal workings of governmental authority" can be quite useful for my purpose, although in the case of imperial Kyiv, "formal workings" and "informal arrangements" are not easy to detect. See Stone, *Regime Politics*, 3.

6 Counting Kyivites: The Language of Class, Religion, and Ethnicity

1 The term itself – the "all-Russian nation" – was coined by Russian historian Aleksei Miller as a means to specify the national community of Orthodox Eastern Slavs in the minds of many nineteenth-century observers; see his *The Ukrainian Question*. I examine the political history of the same term in the Romantic age in *Romantic Nationalism in Eastern Europe*.

2 Borges, *Selected Non-Fictions*, 229–33.

3 DAK, f. 1, op. 2, spr. 574, 3.

4 Funduklei, *Statisticheskoe opisanie Kievskoi gubernii*, 327.

5 This elite category, which referred to mounted municipal militia, disappeared after the city was stripped of its autonomy in 1835. The number of "registered fellows" had been steadily increasing over the years prior to 1835 (450 in 1817, 475 in 1818, 514 in 1819, 532 in 1820, 598 in 1829). See DAK, f. 1, op. 2, spr. 904, 3. Regarding the 1827 *reviziia* see DAK, f. 1, op. 2(b), spr. 1469, 2.

6 On the status of various urban groups in pre-revolutionary Russia, and especially on the inferior legal position of "burghers," see Koshman, *Gorod i gorodskaia zhizn'*. On social estates in Russia see Alison Smith's excellent study, *For the Common Good*, esp. 14–47.

7 Nardova, *Gorodskoe samoupravlenie v Rossii*, 10–13.

8 Brower, *The Russian City*, 23.

9 The State Archive of the City of Kyiv (DAK) contains a number of files with the election data, starting from as early as 1813 (the data from previous years was destroyed in the fire of 1811). See esp. f. 1, op. 2 2.

10 Quoted in Nardova, *Gorodskoe samoupravlenie v Rossii*, 13.

11 DAK, f. 1, op. 2a, spr. 253, 254, 261. A later section of this chapter on the "sociospatial form" of the city will attempt to reconstruct the social

composition of each neighbourhood based on real estate assessment lists and other statistical sources.

12 DAK, f. 1, op. 2a, spr. 263.

13 By the time the historian completed his manuscript in 1799, Kyiv had been placed under the supreme authority of the Russian military governor and, more immediately, the Kyiv civil governor. Simultaneously, Emperor Paul I restored major features of municipal self-government, with the Kyiv magistrate extending its authority beyond Podil to the burghers and merchants residing everywhere in the amalgamated city, including in Pechers'k and Old Kyiv.

14 Berlyns'kyi, *Istoriia mista Kyieva*, 262.

15 Ibid., 237 (Pechers'k), 243 (Old Kyiv), 256 (Podil).

16 Berlyns'kyi, *Korotkyi opys Kyieva*, 127–9.

17 Ibid., 129–30.

18 Mykhailo Maksymovych, *Ocherk Kieva*, in Funduklei, *Obozrenie Kieva*, xv.

19 Funduklei, *Statisticheskoe opisanie Kievskoi gubernii*.

20 Ibid., 325–6.

21 Ibid., 348.

22 Most of these soldiers and NCOs (8,000) resided in the barracks; the rest – generals and senior officers – were quartered in apartments owned by Kyiv residents.

23 I have allowed myself to simplify the complex social and economic categories used by the data compilers, excluding some less numerous groups. The percentages are based on the total population: 29,000 for 1835 and 56,971 for 1845, the latter figure including permanent and temporary civilian residents. For large groups (such as peasants, merchants, or nobles), neither the totals nor the percentages appeared in the original table.

24 Ibid., 351. It is worth comparing these Kyiv data with the overall picture for Russian imperial cities. So in 1840, nobles and officials comprised 5 per cent; clergy, 1 per cent; merchants, 4.5 per cent; burghers, 46.8 per cent; and the rest (mostly peasants and soldiers), 42.5 per cent. Around 1858 an imperial statistician estimated that the "urban estates" (merchants, burghers, guild artisans, and workers) had increased to 54.7 per cent, "rural estates" accounted for 20 per cent, and "military estates" comprised 14 per cent of Russia's urban population. See Rashin, *Naselenie Rossii za 100 let*, ch. 4, 119–20.

25 Yet the number of workers employed in Kyiv's seventy-three factories and plants remained small: just over 800 people, with most of the enterprises employing no more than five workers (including a master-artisan). By far the largest was Dekhterev's cast-iron foundry, which employed eighty-seven workers. Among other branches of industry, the largest ratios of

workers per factory could be found in brick making (33 to 1), pottery making (16 to 1), and tanning (10 to 1). See Funduklei, *Statisticheskoe opisanie Kievskoi gubernii*, 373–4.

26 Ibid., 356.

27 Ibid., 378–80. It seems that the numbers in the table did not correspond to the aggregates calculated afterwards. The author miscalculated the total number of artisans by undercounting the number of seasonal workers employed in construction. In my estimates I use the data from the table rather than the aggregates.

28 Compare these numbers with those from 1864. See Zakrevskii, *Opisanie Kieva*, 143.

29 The report about the census was presented by one of its principal authorities a year later, in the official periodical of the Kyiv provincial statistical committee: Dinovskii, "Zapiska sekretaria statisticheskogo komiteta," 25–38.

30 See ibid., 29. The paper *Kievlianin* provides slightly different numbers: 68,429 (47,479 permanent and 20,945 temporary). See *Kievlianin* 72 (1864), 290. Judging from the numbers in Funduklei's volume, the higher figures are preferable.

31 Dinovskii, "Zapiska sekretaria statisticheskogo komiteta," 27.

32 All of the numbers come from Dinovskii's account. In almost all cases the figures included both men and women. See ibid., 30.

33 This number included both men (11,542) and women – wives, daughters, and widows (6,273).

34 The social status of military families – soldiers' wives and children – was rather uncertain, but allowed for some measure of upward social mobility. Both soldiers and their wives became emancipated from serfdom, and their children belonged to the "military estate" rather than to the peasantry (or serfs prior to 1861) or the burghers. As free men with some education, soldiers' sons provided an important source of non-commisioned officers (*unter-ofitsery*) and could subsequently rise through the ranks. Legally free, soldiers' daughters acquired the social status of their husbands, although their livelihoods often remained precarious. After the new law on conscripts in 1867 and with the introduction of universal conscription in 1874, soldiers and their families would remain members of their inherited social estates, which still further confused the social status of low military personnel and their family members. This explains why the category of "military estate" gradually disappeared from censuses. See Wirtschafter, *Social Identity in Imperial Russia*, 44–5; idem, *From Serfs to Russian Soldier*, chs. 1–2; and idem, "Social Misfits."

35 In Russian practice, Orthodox were synonymous with "Russians" (the term also included Ukrainians), Catholics simply meant "Poles," Lutherans were "Germans" (often Baltic Germans), and Jews were obviously both a religion and an ethnicity. Muslims were the only category that could not be easily identified with a distinct ethnicity (although usually "Tatars" were the prime candidates).

36 Nardova, *Gorodskoe samoupravlenie*, 59.

37 The social composition of councillors in Russia's cities in the 1880s was as follows: 33.2 per cent belonged to the most privileged and educated group (nobles, officials, intelligentsia), 53.7 per cent were "merchants," and 13 per cent were burghers and artisans. This was out of roughly 2,940 city councillors in forty imperial cities.

38 Hamm, *Kiev: A Portrait*, 24–5, 34.

39 Historian and early socialist Mykhailo Drahomanov, a prominent member of the society's Kyiv branch, later recalled that it was the Ukrainian activists of the older generations ("mainly gymnasium teachers") who "composed the kernel of the newly established Southwestern Branch of the Russian Geographic Society." See Drahomanov, "Autobiographical Sketch," in Bilenky, *Fashioning Modern Ukraine*, 295.

40 On the scholars who conducted the 1874 census, see Shamrai, "Kyïvs'kyi odnodennyi perepys 2-ho berezolia 1874 roku," 352–84.

41 *Kiev i ego predmistia*, v. On the census, see also *Kiev po perepisi 2 marta 1874 goda*.

42 On Ziber's unusual biography, his Marxist "credentials," and his role in Russian statistics, see Shamrai, "Kyïvs'kyi odnodennyi perepys," 353–60. Ziber's early statistical work, *Opyt programmy dlia sobiraniia statistiko-ekonomicheskikh svedenii* (An Attempt of a Program for Collecting Statistical and Economic Data, 1875) was infused with Marxist ideas; according to Shamrai this "was a published plan of the statistical work and a Marxist approach which Ziber used for the organization of a one-day census of 2 March 1874." Ibid., 357.

43 Ibid., 361.

44 Like Ziber, his friend Drahomanov was a perfect example of a socialist (albeit of a pre-Marxist variety) with a strong national consciousness.

45 Criticisms by Russian conservative commentators appeared in the pages of *Kievlianin*, Kyiv's main conservative newspaper. See, for example, *Kievlianin* 139 (1874). Counter-arguments by one organizer of the census, Ziber, were published as a brochure: [Ziber], *Po povodu retsenzii "Kievlianina."*

46 A contemporary critic blamed the census takers for these excessive (in his opinion) details and also for excluding a significant portion of residents

from some of the census entries. See Shamrai, "Kyïvs'kyi odnodennyi perepys," 372.

47 The growing number of temporary residents – mainly peasants seeking short-term jobs – became a big problem for the police. For example, in Moscow by the 1870s, these temporary workers comprised two-thirds of the city's inhabitants. See Brower, *The Russian City*, 24.

48 In other cities, such as Odessa, women had the numerical advantage. An interwar expert on the census, Serhiy Shamrai, admitted that he could not explain such a heavy numerical superiority of men over women in Kyiv. In his view, the presence of soldiers and workers did not satisfactorily explain this imbalance. See his "Kyïvs'kyi odnodennyi perepys," 367.

49 *Kiev i ego predmistia*, 4–5 (table 2).

50 The latter term was coined recently by Steven Seegel in his impressive study of east-central European and Russian cartographies. See his *Mapping Europe's Borderlands*.

51 The census takers did not use the term "Ukraine." Instead the category read: "those born in Southwestern Region, Little Russia, and New Russia" – an obvious euphemism for an entity that was united only in the minds of Ukrainian activists. The greatest number of Kyivites – 32,633 people, or more than 25 per cent – were born in Kyiv province, a province that consisted mostly of ethnic Ukrainians.

52 Most ethnic Russians came from Great Russian provinces; some were born in Kyiv (a few thousand perhaps). By all accounts, ethnic Russians in Kyiv did not exceed 25 per cent of the total population and were often residing in the city temporarily. See Hamm, *Kyiv: A Portrait*, 103. A contemporary observer, the demographer Ivan Pantiukhov, admitted that "the influence of the pure Great Russian population on the contemporary character of Kyiv's population has been irrelevant." See Pantiukhov, *Opyt sanitarnoi topografii i statistiki Kieva*, 392.

53 In Kyiv proper, the Orthodox numbered 91,357; that was 78 per cent of 116,774 residents.

54 Bilenky, *Romantic Nationalism in Eastern Europe*, 53–4.

55 A later critic, however, suggested that it was not Ukrainian philologists but Russian officials who arrived at such an awkward language entry. See Shamrai, "Kyïvs'kyi odnodennyi perepys," 360.

56 Hamm, *Kiev: A Portrait*, 103.

57 In fact we do not know which criteria the organizers used – whether it was language spoken daily (vernacular), native language (spoken by parents), language spoken in public, or "literary" language.

58 The presence of both Great Russian and "common Russian" (*obshcherusskii*) may also have reflected Drahomanov's differentiation between those who spoke literary Russian as the common language of educated elites (of any ethnicity) and those who spoke the Great Russian dialect as their native language. See also his brochure *Literatura rosiis'ka, velykoruska, ukrainska i halyts'ka*. I am grateful to Dr Ostap Sereda for this observation.

59 *Kiev i ego predmistia*, 20–1 (table 8). Critics, however, doubted whether so many inhabitants of Kyiv were educated enough to know "common [literary] Russian," much less to be able to speak this mysterious Newspeak. See Shamrai, "Kyïvs'kyi odnodennyi perepys," 374.

60 *Kievlianin* 139 (1874), 1.

61 Ibid. Another critic went so far as to mock the very notion of an "all-Russian" language and people, for no one had yet seen a single "all-Russian." See Shamrai, "Kyïvs'kyi odnodennyi perepys," 373.

62 *Kievlianin*, 55 (1875), p. 1.

63 For example, *Kievlianin*'s chauvinistic editors called their major rival in Kyiv, the liberal newspaper *Zaria* (*The Dawn*, 1880–6), an organ that supported both Jewish and Ukrainian causes, a "Ukrainian-Jewish-Polonophile mouthpiece."

64 In the 1860s and 1870s some Russian administrators made a case for the recognition of "Russian"- (or rather Belarusian-) speaking Catholics, as a means to further undermine Polish influence on the western borderlands. But the strength of a traditional belief that equated Orthodoxy with Russianness and Catholicism with Polishness won the day, even though no legal definition of Russianness and Polishness ever developed in the Russian Empire. On the debates and legal practice, see Dolbilov, "Russification and the Bureaucratic Mind"; Weeks, "Religion and Russification"; and Staliunas, "Did the Government Seek to Russify Lithuanians."

65 *Kiev i ego predmistia*, 30–5 (table 11).

66 See Koshman, *Gorod i gorodskaia zhizn' v Rossii XIX stoletiia*, 29. On the weakness of economic classes in Russia, contrary to the pronouncements of Soviet historians, see Ivanova and Zheltova, *Soslovno-klassovaia struktura Rossii*.

67 Curiously, in the capital of the northwestern borderlands, Vilnius, the share of burghers in 1875 was much higher than in Kyiv – around 65 per cent, perhaps reflecting the numerical strength of Jews among the city residents (at least 46 per cent), almost all of whom belonged to the social estates of burghers and merchants. See Weeks, *Vilnius Between Nations*, 61.

68 *Kiev i ego predmistia*, 58–73 (tables 18–19).

69 Ibid., 58–63 (table 18).

70 For the social structure of Kyiv religious communities see *Kiev i ego predmistia*, 58–65 (table 18).

71 In fact, many plebeian Protestants were not Germans but more likely Latvians or Estonians or perhaps even local peasants, the followers of the Baptist-inspired movement known as "shtunda." On the latter see Zhuk, *Russia's Lost Reformation*, 153–201. Of Kyiv's Protestants, 249 spoke "Russian," 61 Polish, 133 "other West European languages," 22 Yiddish, and 8 "other [languages]." See *Kiev i ego predmistia*, 32–3 (table 11).

72 On the role in the Russian Empire played by Protestants and Baltic Germans in particular see Lieven, *Russia's Rulers under the Old Regime*, 20–83; and Armstrong, "Mobilized Diaspora in Tsarist Russia," 63–104. For a brief discussion of the Russian imperial elite see Kappeler, *The Russian Empire*, 126–53.

73 Shamrai, "Kyïvs'kyi odnodennyi perepys," 358.

74 *Kiev i ego predmistia*, 108–9 (table 1).

75 Ibid., 96–109 (table 1).

76 Ibid., 173–4 (table 5).

77 For example, the railway in Kyiv employed 502 "technicians," 287 "specialists-workers," and 348 "unskilled laborers" – 1,137 in total. The telegraph employed far fewer people (86), but the share of "technicians" here was even greater (43).

78 Ibid., 126–7 (table 3).

79 By contrast, the share of illiterates among the "first" class (master artisans of all kinds and workers) reached as high as 36 per cent, while among the "second" class (transport technicians, traders, shop owners, etc.) that figure was considerably lower – 15 per cent. One could easily imagine an illiterate tailor, carpenter, or butcher, but an illiterate railway technician, shopkeeper, or money lender was rather a rare bird. Even more unimaginable would have been an illiterate writer, printer, or painter.

80 *Kiev i ego predmistia*, 207 (table 13).

81 The critic, not surprisingly, worked for *Kievlianin*. See Shamrai, "Kyïvs'kyi odnodennyi perepys," 375.

82 To save space, I will ascribe numbers to the classes: 1 for the "industrial and artisanal class," 2 for "those engaged in transportation, trade, credit, and insurance operations," 3 for "those who serve popular enlightenment," and 4 for those who served the state and the church in various capacities.

83 *Kiev i ego predmistia*, 152 (table 4).

84 It is worth noting that another local branch of the society – set up in Vilnius, the capital of the northwestern borderlands – proved a total failure, a mere symbol of the futile attempts at Russification. See Weeks, *Vilnius Between Nations*, 66–7.

85 Drahomanov, "Autobiographical Sketch," 298.

86 Shamrai, "Kyïvs'kyi odnodennyi perepys," 379.

87 Ibid., 356.

88 Drahomanov, "Autobiographical Sketch," 299.

89 Nardova, *Gorodskoe samoupravlenie v Rossii*, 81, 151.

90 The educated public also held burghers in low esteem, hence the untranslatable word *meshchanstvo*, which was also an official name for the social estate. On all of these meanings of the word *meshchanstvo*, see Stepanov, *Konstanty*, 679–83. On the judicial and economic status of burghers see Wirtschafter, *Social Identity in Imperial Russia*, 130–40.

91 On this aspect of the 1897 census see Cadiot, "Searching for Nationality"; and idem, *Le laboratoire impérial*. On the preparation of the census and mistakes made by its organizers see Kotel'nikov, *Istoriia proizvodstva i razrabotki*.

92 Cadiot, "Searching for Nationality," 440.

93 Ibid., 442.

94 *Pervaia vseobshchaia perepis'*, 37–8.

95 Ibid., x.

96 These trends were studied by the noted Soviet demographer A.G. Rashin in his *Naselenie Rossii za 100 let*. (For peasants in Russian cities according to the 1897 census, see 122). In Odessa, for example, peasants comprised only 27 per cent of the population in 1897, which made this southern metropolis a far more "middle-class" city than Kyiv. See *Obzor Odesskago gradonachalstva za 1914*, 37.

97 *Pervaia vseobshchaia perepis'*, 171 (plate 21).

98 The same classification was used in the comprehensive 1902 census of the Moscow population. See Rashin, *Naselenie Rossii za 100 let*, 125–6.

99 Cadiot, "Searching for Nationality," 444.

100 *Pervaia vseobshchaia perepis'*, 260–261 (plate XXIV).

101 L. Lichkov, "Iugo-zapadnyi krai po dannym perepisi 1897 goda," *Kievskaia starina* 9 (1905), 327.

102 Ibid.

103 Ibid., 449–50.

104 *Pervaia vseobshchaia perepis'*, 98–9 (plate 24). The number of Russian-speaking Jews reflected a trend found throughout the entire Right-Bank Ukraine. For instance, in Kyiv province there were 3,097 Russian-speaking Jews and 345 Ukrainian-speaking; in Podolia province there were 887 Russian-speaking and 536 Ukrainian-speaking Jews; and in Volhynia there were 600 Russian-speaking and 537 Ukrainian-speaking Jews. The already quoted critic alleged that these numbers did not completely reflect reality. Many Jews, he wrote, could speak several

languages, and it was the arbitrary decision of census takers to include such Jews among Russian- and Ukrainian-speakers. See Lichkov, "Iugo-zapadnyi krai po dannym perepisi 1897 goda," 335.

105 From the other plates we learn that in 1897 there were 1,124 Poles in the military, which means that among the Polish speakers in Kyiv the military personnel comprised at least 7 per cent (most likely excluding their family members).

106 The social profile of language groups in Kyiv reflected a broader pattern in the three Right-Bank provinces. For instance, Polish speakers contained the highest share of nobles (16 per cent), with peasants and burghers comprising 38 and 27 per cent respectively. Great Russian speakers were the most balanced group: 14 per cent nobles; 43 per cent peasants; 30 per cent burghers; 5 per cent clergy; and 3 per cent merchants. Jews were the most urban group: 97 per cent burghers. Ukrainian speakers were the most rural community: 94 per cent peasants; 5 per cent burghers. These figures indicated that the nobility in Right-Bank Ukraine remained overwhelmingly Polish in culture. Also, note that perhaps a majority of Polish-speaking peasants had been once nobles who were relegated to the lower status by Russian authorities. See Lichkov, "Iugo-zapadnyi krai po dannym perepisi 1897 goda," 338.

107 *Pervaia vseobshchaia perepis'*, p. 171 (plate XXI).

108 Ibid. 198–9 (plate 22).

109 Moscow historically had a very large proportion of rural migrants. For example, around 1840 peasants and serfs accounted for 45 per cent of the city's population, while the percentage of nobles was only 4.7 per cent. By 1902 the proportion of nobles hovered at 5 per cent, while the share of peasants had risen dramatically to 67 per cent, with the percentage of burghers falling to 19.4 per cent (from 24 per cent in 1882). The social profile of Saint Petersburg was similar. The share of burghers there had always been low, while that of peasants was almost as high as in Moscow. For example, in 1831 the nobles comprised 9.6 per cent, burghers 12.5 per cent, peasants (including serfs) 48 per cent, and the military 10 per cent. In fact, the proportion of peasants in the city in 1800–31 was higher than in Russia's overall urban population. In 1843 the percentages of nobles (on service and retired), burghers, peasants, and "lower military ranks" were 11, 13.7, 35.6, and 21.3 respectively. Finally, by 1900 the proportion of nobles had decreased to 8 per cent, while that of burghers had slightly increased to 19 per cent, and peasants had become an overwhelming majority of the urban population with 63 per cent. See Rashin, *Naselenie Rossii za 100 let*, 124–9.

7 Municipal Elites and "Urban Regimes": Continuities and Disruptions

1 See Stone, *Regime Politics*, 3–13.

2 As quoted in Volodymyr Shcherbyna, "Kyïv v 20-kh rokakh XIX st., 116.

3 These were largely Polish landowners, who comprised an overwhelming majority of all nobles in Kyiv province. Those officials who were appointed by Russian government were mostly Ukrainian nobles from Left-Bank Ukraine. For almost two centuries, the latter served in the city as the representatives of either Cossack hetmans or Russian authorities.

4 Ibid., 117.

5 Ibid., 118.

6 A reconstruction of the functions and practices of Kyiv's self-governing institutions in the early nineteenth century can be found in Kamanin, *Poslednie gody samoupravleniia Kieva*.

7 On the municipal commission, especially its banking operations, see ibid., 30–1.

8 Kamanin gave an example from the mid-eighteenth century, when, against the request of Kyiv's Russian governor, the Senate barred Russian merchants from engaging in trade alongside local merchants. The Senate also forbade the Supreme Magistrate to send any decrees to Kyiv. See ibid., 83–4.

9 DAK, f. 1, op. 2 (2), spr. 174. The membership of the "most venerable society" could exceed 600 men when the magistrate needed the signatures of its supporters.

10 Kamanin, *Poslednie gody samoupravleniia Kieva*, pp. 7–9. A handful of plutocrats ran the banking operations. Although officially, the commission was operated by the *viit* and several elected officials, in reality it was run single-handedly by the *viit* and his closest allies among the plutocrats. For instance, on the eve of the fire of 1811 the commission was run by burgomaster Kostiantyn Balabukha and *ratsger* Oleksii Ostrovs'kyi. After 1817, the commission was headed by the *viit* Hryhorenko and two burgomasters – the notorious Pylyp Lakerda and Hryhorii Kyselevs'kyi. See idem, "Poslednie gody samoupravleniia Kieva," *Kievskaia Starina* 8 (1888), 159.

11 Kovalyns'kyi, *Kyïvs'ki miniatiury*, vol. 1, 138–9, 334–5. Another famous scion of the Kyiv municipal clan was Kalinik Mytiukov (1823–85), from the merchant family the Mytiuks, a professor of Roman law at Kyiv University and its rector in 1865. He was one of the very few local intellectuals who came from a burgher family

12 Ibid., 159, 334.

13 Ibid., 160, 336.

14 Kamanin, *Poslednie gody samoupravleniia Kieva*, pp. 23–4.

15 Ibid., 165.
16 The previously mentioned Balabukha family was among the oldest and
    wealthiest in Kyiv in the first decades of the nineteenth century. By 1790,
    Semen and Hryhorii Balabukha had been raised to the nobility. By 1803 the
    Balabukha family owned nine large homesteads in Podil. See Popel'nyts'ka,
    "Naibil'shi zemlevlasnyky i pidpryiemtsi kyïvs'koho Podolu," 59.
17 One remote example comes from the American South – especially before
    the Civil War – where municipal elites shared many characteristics with
    their Kyiv peers. See David R. Goldfield, "Planning for Urban Growth in
    the Old South," in Sutcliffe, *The Rise of Modern Urban Planning*, 13.
18 Ibid., 13–14.
19 Vasilii Pirazhkov (1768–1830) was a wealthy merchant of Russian ethnic
    background who owned a mansion in Pechers'k (still standing). He made
    a fortune from military supplies during the Patriotic War of 1812. On his
    death, his property included a number of luxury items – furniture, musical
    instruments, icons, silverware, paintings, and so on. He was also a famous
    financier, whose clients included Russian Decembrists. See Kovalyns'kyi,
    Kyïvs'ki miniatiury, vol. 1, 153, 155–6, 361.
20 Among them, *ratsger* Ivan Smorodinov in 1821; burgomaster Vasilii
    Pirazhkov in 1823; burgomaster Pirazhkov and *ratsger* Smorodinov in
    1827; *ratsger* Aleksei Bubnov in 1829; and *ratsger* Ivan Khodunov in 1835.
    See DAK, f. 1, op. 2(2), spr. 900 (1821); DAK, f. 1, op. 2(2), spr. 977 (1823);
    DAK, f. 1, op. 2(2), spr. 1289 (1827); DAK, f. 1, op. 2(2), spr. 1413 (1829);
    DAK, f. 1, op. 2(2), spr. 1773 (1835).
21 The chart is based on the lists of *eligible* voters, many of whom did *not*
    show up on election day. The figures are as follows: in 1813, out of 128
    voters, 20 were most likely Russians (15.6%); in 1815, out of 163, 34 (21%);
    in 1821, out of 171, 33 (19%); in 1823, out of 163, 40 (24.5%); in 1827,
    out of 209, 55 (26%); in 1829, out of 187, 46 (24.6%); in 1834, out of 190,
    48 (25%); in 1835, out of 165, 45 (27%); and in 1846, ten years after the
    abolition of Magdeburg autonomy, out of 278, 80 (30.5%). These figures
    are approximate, and it is quite possible that not all those counted here
    as "Russians" were ethnic Russians. There were quite a few individuals
    in whose case neither documents nor their last names allow for a reliable
    ethnic attribution. A few such voters were most likely of German or French
    descent. Yet the trend indicated the increasing presence of non-Ukrainians
    among Kyiv's municipal voters, especially among the elite groups of
    merchants and "citizens."
22 For example, in 1835, out of 164 merchants and citizens, 72 had Russian
    names (44.5 per cent); in 1847, out of 159 voters representing various social

groups – from merchants to nobles and officials – except for burghers there were 72 Russians (45 per cent). DAK, f. 17, op. 2, spr. 1171, 30–4.

23 DAK, f. 1, op. 2(2), spr. 1936, 57.

24 Ibid., 19–19 reverse.

25 The first of them was the merchant Ivan Khodunov. But his election was not confirmed by the governor-general, who preferred another Russian candidate – Parfentii Dekhterev, a wealthy merchant and Old Believer from Kaluga. See DAK, f. 1, op. 2(2), spr. 1936, 59 reverse–61. Two other Russian merchants from Kaluga in the office of the Kyiv city head were Pavel Eliseev (1837–8) and Semen Lychkov (1851–4). In the hiatus, a Protestant German merchant named Gottlieb Finke headed the city from 1844 to 1847. He was first elected a *ratsger* "for presence in the police" in 1832, and in 1835 he was elected a burgomaster. In 1832 Finke at his own expense supplied the new furniture for the magistrate chancellery. He also was an active member of the Kyiv Evangelical-Lutheran Society. See DAK, f. 17, op. 2, spr. 496, 10–16 reverse. On Protestant Germans in Kyiv in the nineteenth century see Hyrych, "Nimtsi v Kyievi," in his *Kyïv v ukraïns'kii istoriï*, 179–86. Another non-Russian city head was the Pole Józef Zawadzki, from 1860 to 1863.

26 Shcherbyna, *Novi studiï z istoriï Kyieva*, 7.

27 Pataleev, *Staryi Kyiv*, 22.

28 Merchant Oleksandr Pataleev, who came to Kyiv as a small child with his parents in 1855, perfectly grasped the attitudes of the local "old-time" burghers towards Russian newcomers. See his *Staryi Kyiv*, 263–4.

29 As a result of persecutions and the downward mobility of some prominent Old Believers, many of them were forced to join the official Church. See Taranets, *Staroobriadchestvo goroda Kieva i Kievskoi gubernii*, 78–80. On the most prominent figures, including Mikhail Parfentievich Dekhterev, the Popovs, and the Bugaevs, see ibid., 87–104. The Bugaevs were severely persecuted: in the 1840s they had enjoyed the status of first-guild merchants, but by 1900 their descendants had fallen to the status of simple burghers. See Olha Druh's comment no. 15 to Pataleev, *Staryi Kyiv*, 278.

30 DAK, f. 17, op. 2, spr. 1505, 5.

31 Kovalyns'kyi, *Kyïvs'ki miniatiury*, vol. 1, 334.

32 Ibid., vol. 2, 292.

33 Ibid., vol. 1, 334–5. The scions of the Kyiv plutocrats, unlike those of Russian merchants and burghers in other cities, often chose public service through higher education – a privilege they felt they enjoyed due to their higher social status in the autonomous city. On Semen Balabukha's son, who studied at Moscow University in 1815, see DAK, f. 1, op. 2, spr. 440.

On the children of other Kyiv merchants and burgers who pursued higher education see DAK, f. 17, op. 1, vol. 1, 1837 spr. 16; 1840 spr. 8 and 10.

34 Pataleev, *Staryi Kyiv*, 266–7. Voitenko did not come from a prominent family, but his father Illia Voitenko, a simple burgher, was elected to the city's deputy assembly in 1835. See DAK, f. 1, op. 2(2), spr. 1936, 74.

35 The family patriarch, Iakym Kobets' (d. 1822), was an influential *ratsger* and burgomaster in the magistrate and also the founder of a tannery. By the 1880s his descendants owned four of Kyiv's eight tanneries. Kobets' Brothers was one of the city's most successful commercial firms. One of its owners, Oleksii (1860–1920), was a first-guild merchant, a deputy in the Kyiv city duma (1898–1917), and a member of its executive. The Kobets' were the only old clan whose members in each generation participated in municipal governance, from the early 1800s until the end of the Old Regime in 1917. See Olha Druh's comment no. 341 to Pataleev, *Staryi Kyiv*, 353.

36 Glaeser, *Triumph of the City*, 79.

37 On his biography, see "Ivan Ivanovich Khodunov: Nekrolog," *Kievskie gubernskie vedomosti*, 28 July 1853, 221–3; "Vystavka sel'skikh proizvedenii, fabrichnykh i remeslennykh izdelii v g. Kieve v 1852 godu," *Kievskie gubernskie vedomosti*, 25 May 1853, 156–9; Kovalyns'kyi, *Kyïvs'ki miniatiury*, vol. 2, 290–3; Salii and Kovalyns'kyi, *Oblychchia stolytsi*, 30–2.

38 Khodunov received 225 votes, with only 23 against; his closest rival, Parfentii Dekhterev, a prominent Old Believer, received 118 votes, with 130 against. See DAK, f. 1, op. 2(2), spr. 1936, 57.

39 DAK, f. 17, op. 1(1), spr. 40, 6–6 reverse. In 1842 Kyiv trade commissioners from Podil and Pechers'k were ordered to assist the newcomers.

40 Ibid., 8.

41 DAK, f. 17, op. 2, spr. 1342, 3–5 reverse. The most expensive property was in Podil (a stone mansion priced at 25,000 silver roubles) and belonged to the widow of Vasilii Bugaev, a wealthy merchant from an Old Believer community in northern Ukraine (Chernihiv province).

42 Some sources suggest that intermarriage helped Russians gain a foothold in Podil. See Hamm, *Kiev: A Portrait*, 89.

43 It has been estimated that by the mid-1840s the overwhelming majority of skilled craftsmen, such as carpenters and stonecutters, came from Great Russia. Hamm notes that "contractors bypassed local craftsmen, and the massive construction needs of nineteenth-century Kiev were generally met by imported Russian workers with reputations for superior skills, work habits, and … comparative moderation in drinking." Ibid., 91. The 1874 census confirmed this assumption.

44 See Kovalyns'kyi, *Kyïvs'ki miniatiury*, vol. 3, 350–4. An early example of Jewish commercial success in Kyiv was Moisei Vainshtein (1825–1910), a merchant, sugar miller, and banker. See Pataleev, *Staryi Kyiv*, 25, and Druh's comment no. 26 on page 280.

45 On the reasons why Ukrainians were the least urbanized and successful urban community, see Krawchenko, *Social Change and National Consciousness*, 1–45.

46 Nardova, *Gorodskoe samoupravlenie v Rossii*, 43. In most cities, most voters belonged to the "homeowners" category; a minority (merchants and industrialists) paid taxes on trade and industries. Saint Petersburg was the only city in Russia where, among voters, traders and industrialists predominated.

47 Ibid., 59.

48 In 1871 the population of Kyiv was estimated at 76,979. See *Kievlianin* 82 (1871), 2.

49 On the populist deputies of the city duma see Hillis, *Children of Rus'*.

50 DAK, f. 163, op. 39, spr. 211. I cordially thank Faith Hillis for sharing with me the data from this file, which I was unable to obtain from Kyiv City Archive due to the file's "broken-down" state.

51 Nardova, *Gorodskoe samoupravlenie v Rossii*, 69–70.

52 More detailed results are in DAK, f. 163, op. 39, spr. 211, 88–90.

53 On the deputies: *Kievlianin* 10 (23 January 1871), 1; on the oligarchy: *Kievlianin* 6 (1871), 1.

54 *Kievlianin* 26 (1871), 1; 26 (1871), 1. Even in the 1880s, because of the massive absenteeism of nobles, merchants and burghers formed an overwhelming majority of all duma deputies in forty cities. Out of 2,940 deputies, 975 (33 per cent) were nobles and officials; 1,581 (53.7 per cent) were merchants; and 384 (13 per cent) were burghers, artisans, and peasants. See Nardova, *Gorodskoe samoupravlenie v Rossii*, 69–70, 80.

55 The paper's editor, Vitalii Shul'gin, commented that "a systematic exclusion [of Jews] from municipal governance" looked like "bigotry" (*fanatizm*). See *Kievlianin* 6 (1871), 2.

56 Kovalyns'kyi, *Metsenaty Kieva*, 113, 119. Demidov received 45 votes for and 24 against his candidacy.

57 The first donation (5,000 roubles) was made for the workhouse for the poor. After this, Demidov and his wife financed the opening of the two high schools – Kyiv-Podil Women's Gymnasium and the Third (Podil) Gymnasium. Perhaps the costliest project (73,266 roubles) was Kyiv real school (technical gymnasium) in 1872. He also supervised the building of the city duma's own house on Khreshchatyk Square. See ibid., 121–6.

58 Pataleev, *Staryi Kyiv*, 267.

59 Ibid.

60 *Kievlianin* 4 (1875), 1.

61 DAK, f. 163, op. 39, spr. 211, 43.

62 One of them, the renowned lawyer Lev Kupernik (1845–1905), was a relative of A.A. Kupernik, a prominent Kyiv merchant and Jewish writer. See Meir, *Kiev, Jewish Metropolis*, 50, 66, 74–5.

63 The data on 1871 are in *Kievlianin* 82 (1871), 2; the data on 1887 are in *Kievlianin* 11 (1887), 2.

64 *Kievlianin* 12 (1887), 2.

65 Nardova provides similar, albeit slightly different numbers of Kyiv voters in the early 1870s: 3,235, or 4.6 per cent of an overall population. See Nardova, *Samoderzhavie i gorodskie dumy v Rossii*, 20.

66 A number of Jews were indeed excluded from the first curia (primarily second-guild merchants who were banned from residing in Kyiv).

67 *Kievlianin* 12 (1887), 2.

68 *Kievlianin* 13 (1887), 3. Apparently, before this "reform," more then 600 voters from the third curia showed up on election day in 1879, while after the division of the curia into five groups in 1883 only 400 out of 3,800 voters showed up.

69 *Kievlianin* 12 (1887), 2.

70 Nardova, *Samoderzhavie i gorodskie dumy v Rossii*, 12–16.

71 Ibid., 20–2. Around 1897 the percentage of eligible voters in Russia's major cities was minuscule: in Saint Petersburg, 0.5 per cent, in Moscow, 0.6 per cent, in Odessa, 0.5 per cent, in Saratov, 1 per cent of all city dwellers. In 1901, in 132 cities of Russia with the population of 9.5 million people, only 100,000 people, or 1 per cent, enjoyed voting rights.

72 Ibid., 20. The data compiled by the Kyiv city duma are slightly different: around 2,245 voters. The Luk'ianivka quarter sustained the heaviest losses (155 voters in 1892 compared to 1,429 before), followed by the Lybid' district (358 voters vs 1,091). See *Kievlianin* 205 (1892), 2; 246 (1892), 2.

73 For example, in Vienna the percentage of voters grew from 5.7 per cent in 1891 to 18 per cent in 1912. In Budapest that figure rose from 5.58 per cent in 1899 to 8.69 per cent by 1910. In Prague the percentage of voters was lower – 5.5 per cent in 1896 and 7.6 per cent in 1910, but still much higher than in any Russian city. See Gerhard Melinz and Susan Zimmermann, "Großstadtgeschichte und Modernisierung in der Habsburgermonarchie," in Melinz and Zimmermann, *Wien–Prag–Budapest*, 26, 27, 247n38.

74 Nardova, *Samoderzhavie i gorodskie dumy v Rossii*, 35.

75 Ibid., 35–6. Nardova presented the data from each major city. The aggregate data from forty cities showed that of 1,917 duma members, most (1,070, or 55.8 per cent) were merchants and venerable citizens; nobles and officials numbered only 652 men, or 34 per cent. The rest – 187, or 9.8 per cent – were burghers and peasants. For instance, in Saint Petersburg the proportion of nobles and "raznochintsy" was 45.5 per cent, that of merchants and venerable citizens 53.5 per cent, and that of burghers and peasants 2 per cent; in Moscow those shares were 24.6, 66.2, and 9.2 per cent respectively; in Odessa, 54.4, 42.2, and 1.7 per cent; in Kharkiv, 13.7, 72.6, and 13.7 per cent.

76 The data from 1898 are in DAK, f. 163, op. 39, spr. 342; the data from 1902 are in DAK, f. 163, op. 39, spr. 416.

77 See the list of eighty elected members and three "candidates" in the 1902 elections: DAK, f. 163, op. 39, spr. 416, 7–177.

78 In fact, during each term of the city duma a few members – nobles, officials, or professionals – were engaged in various commercial activities as board members or chairmen in banks, credit unions, and industrial enterprises (above all sugar refineries) or were owners of commercial real estate. A case in point is jurist Gustav Eisman, or Vladimir Tolli – a prominent landowner, a justice of the peace, and a son of Kyiv's city head, the merchant Ivan Tolli. "Service nobility" refers to a Russian practice where nobles could enter civil service or stay on the land as landowners.

79 Kal'nyt'skyi, "Mis'kyi holova Gustav Eisman."

80 On the society see Moshenskii, *Finansovye tsentry Ukrainy*, 113–14.

81 On the Kyiv Credit Society see M.B. Kal'nyt'kyi, "Formuvannia ta diial'nist' systemy budivel'noho kredytu," in Kal'nyts'kyi and Kondel'-Perminova, *Zabudova Kyieva*, 123–5; compare Kal'nyts'kyi, "Ipoteka po-kievskii."

82 Kal'nyt'kyi, "Formuvannia ta diial'nist' systemybudivel'noho kredytu," 125.

83 Pataleev, *Staryi Kyiv*, 63.

84 *Zaria* 135 (1882), 2.

85 *Zaria* 288 (1882), 2.

86 He was a remarkable person. Yet another Protestant German, he was one of the very few Kyiv municipal politicians who eventually supported the Ukrainian Revolution as a legal scholar and statesman. On his pro-Ukrainian activities see Turchyn, *Otto Eikhel'man.*

87 Eichelman's essay was published in the mainstream paper *Kievskoe slovo*, 1 January 1902. I quote from Hamm, *Kiev: A Portrait*, 201.

88 On these right-wing populists see Hillis, "Human Mobility," 31–3.

89 Between 1871 and 1905 Kyiv had six city heads: Pavel Demidov (1871–2, 1873–4), Gustav Eisman (1872–3, 1879–84), Nikolai Rennenkampf

(1875–9), Ivan Tolli (1884–7), Stepan Sol'skii (1887–1900), and Vasilii Protsenko (1900–6). In terms of ethnicity, two were German Protestants (Eisman and Rennenkampf), two were local Ukrainians (Sol'skii and Protsenko), one was Russian (Demidov), and one was Greek from Odessa (Tolli). Regarding their occupations, three were professors (Eisman, Rennenkampf, and Sol'skii), two were merchants and industrialists (Demidov and Tolli), and one was a medical doctor (Protsenko). See Salii and Kovalyns'kyi, *Oblychchia stolytsi*, 35–40.

90 This was a term coined by the liberal paper *Kievskaia gazeta*. See Hamm, *Kiev: A Portrait*, 203.

Part IV: Living (in) the City

1 Sutcliffe, *Towards the Planned City*, 2–3.
2 Harvey, *The Urban Experience*, 119. Compare the cases of Paris and London in Sennett, *The Fall of the Public Man*, 134–5.
3 Harvey, *The Urban Experience*, 121.
4 Ibid., 123–4.
5 Yet the class structure of affluent and poor neighborhoods was different: while the wealthy required the (spatial) presence of numerous servants and workers, the working-class residents could do without middle-class dwellers in their midst. The social and functional segregation in large cities greatly increased in the last quarter of the nineteenth century. See Olsen, *The City as a Work of Art*, 133. Sennett also points out that "[now] each space in the city does a particular job." Sennett, *The Fall of the Public Man*, 297.
6 For a popular take on the term, see Coverley, *Psychogeography*.
7 Sutcliffe, *Towards the Planned City*, 3.
8 Lefebvre, *The Production of Space*, 38–9.

8 Sociospatial Form and Psychogeography

1 Lefebvre pointed out that while natural space is, like nature itself, "on the decline," the social character of space – "those social relations that it implies, contains, and dissimulates – has begun *visibly* to dominate." See Lefebvre, *The Production of Space*, 83.
2 Ibid., 82–3.
3 Ibid., 85. Urbanist Fran Tonkiss also emphasizes that urban forms are determined above all by "economic arrangements, social relations, and divisions, legal constructions and political systems." See her *Cities by Design*, 2.
4 Harvey, *Paris, Capital of Modernity*, 39.

5 Tonkiss, *Cities by Design*, 20.
6 For example, in the American South, especially in urban Virginia, property holding was remarkably widespread, "with more than forty per cent of the white householders in Richmond … possessing some form of real property." See Goldfield, "Planning for Urban Growth in the Old South," in Sutcliffe, *The Rise of Modern Urban Planning*, 13. In more developed capitalist cities the rate of homeownership was significantly lower (for example, in American northern metropolises, the figure was less than one-quarter that of Richmond).
7 DAK, f. 1, op. 2a, spr. 261–2. Paradoxically, while some adult males were not listed as property owners, a few minors were. These were the underage heirs to their relatives' real estate.
8 See Harvey's *Paris, Capital of Modernity*, esp. chs. 4 and 5.
9 On Prague see the excellent study by Cohen, *The Politics of Ethnic Survival*.
10 See Maderthaner and Musner, *Unruly Masses*, 22–30; Barea, *Vienna*, 251–2; Csendes and Opll, *Wien*, 176–7.
11 Anthony Sutcliffe linked social segregation with the segregation of uses in industrial cities: "This was paralleled, in residential areas, by the segregation of socio-economic groups which resulted from their differing economic capacities to compete for desirable land. Thus under the impact of industrialization the town came to express in spatial form the major components of its economic and social structures, a process which encouraged, and was encouraged by, a much more efficient land market than had existed in the pre-industrial period." Sutcliffe, *Towards the Planned City*, 3.
12 On the social status and informal prestige of the state service in imperial Russia see Shepelev, *Chinovnyi mir Rossii*, 113–30.
13 More than half of this number were artisan-soldiers employed by Kyiv Arsenal, a fact that reflects the links between the neighbourhood's new residents with Pechers'k, from which they had just been relocated.
14 This group also includes some people, often "foreigners," whose status is impossible to define or who cannot be squeezed into either category. For example, in 1835–6, foreigners and unknowns among homeowners in Old Kyiv numbered nine, in Podil ten, in Lybid' five.
15 The data from 1845 can be found in Funduklei, *Statisticheskoe opisanie Kievskoi gubernii*, 346–7. For data from 1849 see DAK, f. 17, op. 4, spr. 2805 (Old Kyiv); spr. 2806 (Pechers'k), spr. 2807 (Palatsova or Palace), spr. 2808 (Podil), spr. 2809 (Plos'ka), and spr. 2810 (Lybid').
16 At least 533 houses were demolished in Pechers'k between 1832 and 1846. See Funduklei, *Statisticheskoe opisanie Kievskoi gubernii*, 328.
17 Hamm, *Kiev: A Portrait*, 27.

18 It was not Plos'ka but a growing suburb of Kurenivka that had the highest
    share of burghers (406, or 78% out of 520 homeowners). See DAK, f. 17,
    op. 4, spr. 2803 (Zvirynets' quarter); spr. 2804 (Kurenivka quarter).

19 Ibid., 344.

20 The number in this category seems to be low because officials were listed
    inconsistently, in most cases without indicating their service rank. Ranks
    between VI and IX class on the Table of Ranks are given for only seventeen
    people, but the actual number of these middle-range officials must have
    been much higher. So a number of these officials (or their widows) are
    included in category III.

21 For a general overview of Khreshchatyk's history see Rybakov,
    Khreshchatyk vidomyi i nevidomyi, 11–42.

22 DAK, f. 17, op. 5, spr. 662, 11 reverse.

23 Ibid., 4 reverse.

24 DAK, f. 17, op. 5, spr. 666, 40.

25 Kovalyns'kyi, "Evropeis'ka ploshcha," in *Kyïvs'ki miniatiury*, vol. 3, 218–20.

26 For the list of merchants with descriptions of their properties on
    Khreshchatyk see DAK, f. 17, op. 5, spr. 666 (Old Kyiv), 44–6, and
    spr. 662 (Palace).

27 DAK, f. 17, op. 5, spr. 666, 42. He owned at least two other properties on
    other streets.

28 On these and other Russian moguls see DAK, f. 17, op. 5, spr. 467, 3–8, 11–28.

29 Ibid., 52, 57.

30 See DAK, f. 17, op. 5, spr. 668.

31 Ibid., 7. On this legendary brewery and on the Marr family see
    Kovalyns'kyi, "Kyïvs'ke pyvo," in *Kyïvs'ki miniatiury*, vol. 3, 81–105.

32 DAK, f. 17, op. 5, spr. 668, 15. Koeln owned several lucrative properties in
    Kurenivka.

33 DAK, f. 17, op. 5, spr. 662, 6 reverse–9.

34 DAK, f. 17, op. 5, spr. 666, 55.

35 The census was conducted by the Kyiv provincial statistical committee.
    The data were published in Dinovskii, "Zapiska sekretaria statisticheskogo
    komiteta," 25–38.

36 Lefebvre, *The Production of Space*, 129.

37 Dinovskii, "Zapiska sekretaria statisticheskogo komiteta," 28. The
    population of each district (including permanent and temporary
    residents) was as follows: Plos'ka, 9,883; Podil, 11,161; Old Kyiv, 9,635;
    Palace, 4,489; Pechers'k, 14,856; Lybid', 11,430; Kurenivka, 4,253;
    Luk'ianivka, 4,634.

38 These data can be found in *Kievlianin* 72 (1864), 290.

39 Tonkiss, *Cities by Design*, 37. The residential densities will be considered
   later, based on data from the early twentieth century.
40 Among all Kyiv neighborhoods, Pechers'k had the largest gap between
   male and female residents: 10,210 males to 4,647 females, at a ratio of
   2.2:1. See Dinovskii, "Zapiska sekretaria statisticheskogo komiteta," 30.
41 Ibid.
42 The population of the city proper was 116,774. See *Kiev i ego predmistiia*, 3
   (plate I).
43 The term was coined by American urbanist E.W. Soja and quoted by
   Tonkiss in *Cities by Design*, 23.
44 *Kiev i ego predmistiia*, 50–1 (plate XVI).
45 Ibid., 277 (plate I). Most houses still had one or two stories (9,112
   excluding suburbs); only 160 had three stories; 18 had four and 3 had five.
46 Ibid., 261 (plate XXX). The sources, however, referred to any real estate
   owner as *domovladelets* – literally "homeowner" (although this concept
   presupposed that a person owned an urban homestead, which often
   contained more than one residential structure).
47 *Kiev i ego predmistiia*, 262–9 (plate XXXI).
48 Ibid., 324–5 (plate X); on the number of rooms see 326 (plate XI).
49 These data probably come from the census materials, but the numbers did
   not correspond to the data published by the census takers. Perhaps these
   were raw data, leaked to the newspaper before the official results were
   published. See *Kievlianin* 51 (1874), 2.
50 *Kiev i ego predmistiia*, 306–7 (plate I).
51 Ibid., 360–2.
52 Similarly, most of the city's 9,795 Roman Catholics resided in Old Kyiv
   (2,944, or 30%) and Lybid' (2,543, or 26%). In 1863, Roman Catholics (8,604)
   also resided predominantly in Lybid' (2,534, or 29%), Old Kyiv (2,002,
   or 23%), and Podil (2002, or 23%). See Dinovskii, "Zapiska sekretaria
   statisticheskogo komiteta," 30.
53 The numbers of Catholics in Kyiv grew between 1863 and 1897 from 8,604
   to 19,230, but their share of the urban population was falling: from 12
   per cent in 1863 to 8 per cent in 1874 to 7.7 per cent in 1897. Nonetheless,
   Roman Catholics were still overrepresented among the students of Kyiv's
   elite high schools. In 1893 they comprised 19 per cent of students in the
   elite First Gymnasium and 20 per cent in the Second Gymnasium (both in
   Old Kyiv). See *Kievlianin* 284 (1893), 2; 297 (1893), 2.
54 Compare this to the city of Vilnius, where Jews could legally purchase
   real estate and reside anywhere. See Weeks, *Vilnius between Nations*,
   44–6.

55 For this year the numbers are the assessed *value* of real estate, not the amount of taxes collected.

56 Historian Nathan Meir has written that "[after 1874] in no neighborhood did Jews constitute more than a third of the population. There were clear concentrations of Jews in particular parts of the city, but no district could be called exclusively Jewish." See Meir, *Kiev, Jewish Metropolis*, 120.

57 Ibid.

58 An interesting application of residential assessments to the study of spatiality and social mobility in a nineteenth-century city can be found in Stuart Blum, "Mobility and Change in Ante-Bellum Philadelphia," in Thernstrom and Sennett, *Nineteenth-Century Cities*, 125–208. The author establishes a relationship between high average assessment and a neighbourhood's centrality (186–90).

59 As noted in chapter 5, the assessed property tax remained a controversial matter for decades, for it was unclear what the tax was based on: was it market value or net profit of real estate? The total tax equalled 27,243 roubles in 1871; 74,509 in 1876; 106,487 in 1879; and 192,102 in 1887. Through the 1890s it continued to rise. See *Zaria* 166 (1882), 2; *Kievlianin* 127 (1888), 2; compare slightly different figures in DAK, f. 163, op. 47, spr. 18, 83–4. The total value of Kyiv real estate grew from 5,575,300 roubles in 1872 to 12,979,600 roubles in 1882 to 15,452,261 roubles in 1892. See *Kievlianin* 345 (1892), 2.

60 The assessments of municipal property showed a very similar picture. The most expensive real estate owned by the city was in Palace district (priced at 659,504 roubles), followed by Old Kyiv (505,666), and Lybid' (471,319). The most expensive municipal building by far was the Kyiv City Duma (assessed at 327,065 roubles) in Old Kyiv, followed by Alexander Hospital (411,741) in Palace, the municipal slaughterhouse (284,073) in Lybid', and the military barracks (209,435) in Luk'ianivka. The earliest municipal properties, such as the Contract House and the Trade Hall (Hostynyi Dvir) in Podil, were of relatively low value – 70,000 and 30,000 roubles respectively – lower than Podil district police quarters, which was assessed at 67,747 roubles. See *Kievlianin* 325 (1898), 3.

61 *Kievlianin* 94 (1898), 3.

62 *Kievlianin* 106 (1898), 3.

63 Population densities in other districts would be higher if their suburbs were excluded. The population figures are taken from Nikolai Sementovskii, *Kiev, ego sviatynia*, 7th ed. (1900), 19.

64 We can assume that while population figures changed substantially between 1897 and 1905, the area under urban homesteads in each district

remained largely unchanged due to the lack of available land for private use. Of the four districts with the highest population increase by 1905, only Luk'ianivka contained vast municipally held lands that could be developed. On city-owned lands see *Kievlianin* 94 (1903), 3. On the lands in Luk'ianivka see Mashkevich, *Ulitsy Kieva*, 178–9.

65 The population of Kyiv was estimated for 1900 at 300,000; for 1905, at 332,987. According to Russia's Central Statistics Committee, Kyiv's population in 1903 was 319,000, which made it the sixth-largest city in the empire after Saint Petersburg, Moscow, Warsaw, Odessa, and Lodz. See *Kievlianin* 335 (1903), 3. Around 1900 an entire new district – Bul'varna, west of Lybid' and south of Luk'ianivka – was added, with a population of 23,099. A suburb of Kurenivka merged with Plos'ka, and together they became the largest single district by population and area.

66 *Dessiatina* was a land measurement used in imperial Russia. A *dessiatina* is equal to 2,400 square *sazhens* and is roughly equivalent to 2.7 English acres, 1.09 hectares, or 10,925 square metres.

67 Some districts also included capacious suburbs, which considerably increased the total area under homesteads. Thus Plos'ka included the large suburbs of Kurenivka and Priorka; Lybid', the small communities of Protasiv Iar and Baikova Hora; Pechers'k, the populous suburb of Zvirynets'; Bul'varna, the large village of Shuliavka and the smaller communities of Upper and Lower Solomianka. Without some of these suburbs the population densities in core districts would have been much higher. For example, the settled area of Bul'varna proper was only 52 *dessiatinas*, while that of Shuliavka was 112. *Dessiatinas* refer here to the residential component of the land area – that is, the area under private homesteads. Around the same time, the city owned a number of homesteads with a total area of 63 *dessiatinas* assessed at 1,624,000 roubles. The total value of the city-owned buildings in these homesteads was 4,460,000 roubles, the most valuable of them all being the new Municipal Theatre, priced at 815,439 roubles. The city also owned a lot of "natural" space – a forest, farmlands, city parks, gardens, and so on – 8,224 *dessiatinas* in total, with an estimated value of 11,600,236 roubles. The priciest item was the city forest (in Pushcha Vodytsia) with 3,128 *dessiatinas* assessed at 3,208,125 roubles. Of the "empty spaces" located within the city limits, the largest were in Luk'ianivka district (550 *dessiatinas*). See *Kievlianin* 175 (1902), 3; 180 (1902), 3.

68 On the benefits of higher densities in various spatial forms, even for the poorest residents, see Tonkiss, *Cities by Design*, 37–50.

69 Even if we assume that 49,455 people lived on 235 *dessiatinas* (in Plos'ka proper) – excluding large areas of Kurenivka and Priorka – the population

density of Plos'ka (210 residents per *dessiatina*) would still have been lower than in Podil, Old Kyiv, and Palace. The figure of 49,455, however, almost certainly included the residents of Kurenivka and Priorka.

70 Iievlieva, "Transport," in Kal'nyts'kyi and Kondel'-Perminova, *Zabudova Kyieva*, 274.

71 Meir, *Kiev, Jewish Metropolis*, 35, 120.

72 What matters is not so much overall density but *perceived* density. See Tonkiss, *Cities by Design*, 44–5.

73 Here, a homestead referred to both a single-family house with utility structures and a new multi-storey apartment house built on the site of one or more traditional homesteads. Obviously, in these two cases population and residential densities would have been quite different.

74 As late as 1902, homeowners were lobbying for a streetcar line along Moskovs'ka Street, a major artery in Pechers'k. They felt, rightly so, that their neighbourhood was isolated.

75 Malakov, *Prybutkovi budynky Kyieva*, 19. The local press reported that there was no demand for bricks in the first years of the twentieth century. See *Kievlianin* 188 (1900), 3; 107 (1902), 2.

76 During these years more than eight hundred large apartment buildings were built, most of them in Lybid', on streets such as Velyka Vasyl'kivs'ka, Kuznechna, Mariïns'ko-Blahovishchens'ka, and Tarasivs'ka. See Malakov, *Prybutkovi budynky Kyieva*, 21.

77 It has been estimated that around 1900 the average size of a land allotment per man capita in all provinces of European Russia equalled 2.6 *dessiatin* (roughly 2.85 hectars) – well above the average size of an urban homestead in Kyiv.

78 The number of persons per homestead in Palace district was 45.8, followed by Old Kyiv (30.8), Podil (25.4), Lybid' (22), Plos'ka (18), Luk'ianivka (15.6), Pechers'k (15.4), and Kurenivka (6.4). See *Kievlianin* 51 (1874), 2.

79 As an example, see the annual address book *Ves' Kiev za 1905*, 140–210.

80 *Kievlianin* 246 (1892), 2. See also Nardova, *Samoderzhavie i gorodskie dumy v Rossii*, 20.

81 These figures can be found in *Kievlianin* 4 (1902), 3.

82 One square *sazhen* equalled 2,1336 square metres.

83 The above valuation was done by Kyiv Municipal Credit Society around 1910. See Skibits'ka, "Arkhitektura kyïvs'koho zhytla," 370; the data on 1907 can be found in Druh, " Do istoriï kyïvs'koïsadyby," 83 (the original figures come from *Ves' Kiev na 1907 god*, xxxiv).

84 Gamolia and Mokrousova, "Kamennye 'kopilki'"; compare Malakov, *Prybutkovi budynky Kyieva*, 23.

85 Druh, *Vulytsiamy Staroho Kyieva*, 24.

86 Shcherotskii, *Kiev. Putevoditel'*, 319.

87 Vigel', *Vospominaniia*, 208–9.

88 On this gentleman's property in the heart of the prestigious Lypky neighbourhood see Druh, "Do istoriï kyïvs'koï sadyby XIX–XX stolit'," 79–87.

89 Ibid., 81.

90 On this affair see DAK, f. 19, op. 1, spr. 86. The story was reconstructed by Druh in "Do istoriï kyïvs'koïsadyby," 81.

91 It consisted of "a wooden one-storey house, with a wooden one-story annex … and garden; it takes up a square bordered by streets: Lyps'ka, Shovkovychna, and Himnazychna." See DAK, f. 17, op. 5, spr. 662, 25.

92 On this type of dwelling in late imperial Kyiv see Druh and Malakov, *Osobniaky Kyieva*.

93 Pataleev, *Staryi Kyiv*, 191.

94 T. Skibits'ka, "Arkhitektura kyïvs'koho zhytla," in Kal'nyts'kyi and Kondel'-Perminova, *Zabudova Kyieva*, 378–9.

95 Zakharchenko, *Kiev teper' i prezhde*, 161–2.

96 See Malakov and Druh, *Osobniaky Kyieva*.

97 Pataleev, *Staryi Kyiv*, 197.

98 Alfred Von Junk, "Kievskaia letopis'," in *Kievskii Telegraf* 28 (1861), 113.

99 Such was the perception of the liberal press – often accused by Russian right-wingers of fomenting a common Ukrainian–Jewish political agenda. See *Zaria* 101 (1881), 2.

100 *Zaria* 94 (1881), 2.

101 *Kievlianin* 96 (1881), 2.

102 In their letter to the Kyiv city duma a number of prominent Shuliavka residents (nobles, merchants, and officials) pointed to rising crime – thefts, robberies, hooliganism, murders – as the main argument for merger with the city. See DAK, f. 163, op. 38, spr. 122, 66. Many residents felt besieged in their homes: "when twilight comes, residents are forced to stay inside, locking themselves up, fearing and expecting all kinds of assaults." See *Kievlianin* 311 (1895), 2.

103 *Kievlianin* 112 (1886), 1.

104 The most famous example is post-Haussmannian Paris, in which the image of the city (with a clear centrality) as an ideology, utopia, and myth was conditioned by the relocation of the lower classes from the city centre to the periphery. See Stanek, *Henri Lefebvre on Space*, 191. For a general discussion of centrality by Lefebvre, see his *Production of Space*, 331–5.

105 *Kievlianin* 138 (1885), 2.

106 *Kievlianin* 34 (1871), 2.

107 The centrality of streets was also reflected in certain street improvement measures. For example, in 1902, the city duma decided to pave with fashionable asphalt several *central* streets: Khreshchatyk, Velyka Vasyl'kivs'ka (its central part), Volodymyrs'ka, Fundukleïvs'ka, and Oleksandrivs'ka (from Podil to European Square). These streets delineated Kyiv's new centre. See *Kievlianin* 166 (1902), 2.

108 *Kievlianin* 183 (1892), 2.

109 *Kievlianin* 60 (1895), 3.

110 A pioneering work on sanitary conditions in Kyiv was compiled by the famous medical doctor and hygienist Ivan Pantiukhov, *Statisticheskie i sanitarnye ocherki Kieva.*

111 *Kievlianin* 77 (1869), 304.

112 *Kievlianin* 103 (1886), 2.

113 Pantiukhov, *Statisticheskie i sanitarnye ocherki Kieva*, 42.

114 Ibid., 43.

115 *Kievlianin* 103 (1888), 2.

116 *Kievlianin* 132 (1872), 2.

117 *Kievlianin* 93 (1869), 368.

118 On the geography of prostitution see Kovalyns'kyi, *Kyïvs'ki miniatiury*, vol 4, 80–2, 95–8, 128–31, 154–5. In the early twentieth century the most expensive brothels were located downtown, where monthly rents reached 50 to 55 roubles (Mykhailivs'ka and Sofiïv'ska Streets); the rent for brothels farther from downtown – for example, on Mariïns'ko-Blahovishchens'ka street in Lybid' – was about 25 roubles. See ibid., 155.

119 Sylvester, "City of Thieves: Moldavanka," 150.

120 See Pataleev, *Staryi Kyiv*, 153.

121 Pantiukhov, *Statisticheskie i sanitarnye ocherki Kieva*, 58–9.

122 Sennett, *The Fall of the Public Man*, 135.

9 What Language Did the Monuments Speak?

1 See Lefebvre, *The Production of Space*, 142–4.

2 Gary Cohen has famously shown this, using the example of pre–First World War Prague. See Cohen, *The Politics of Ethnic Survival.*

3 Pataleev, *Staryi Kyïv*, 93.

4 Meir, *Kiev, Jewish Metropolis*, 195.

5 Lefebvre, *The Production of Space*, 33.

6 Schorske, "The Idea of the City in European Thought," 104–5.

7 Also in the 1860s, government officials and local experts took part in an ambitious plan to name and rename city streets; many of these were given

"historical" names. Kyiv's space was thus historicized in the second half of the century. See Mashkevich, *Ulitsy Kieva*, 24–32. Also, in 1899 the Kyiv governor-general proposed renaming streets by giving them "historical names." He even suggested renaming Il'ïns'ka street as Sahaidachnyi (after Hetman Petro Konashevych-Sahaidachnyi); a unnamed passage alongside the Government Offices as Bohdan Khmel'nyts'kyi Square (after the famous Hetman Bohdan Khmel'nyts'kyi); and Naberezhno-Nykil'ska as Petro Mohyla street (after Metropolitan Petro Mohyla). This time, however, the duma voted down the proposal. See *Kievlianin* 314 (1898), 3.

8 Kalnyt'skyi and Kondel-Perminova, "Eksperymental'nyi maidanchyk," in Kalnyt'skyi and Kondel-Perminova, *Zabudova Kyieva*, 325.

9 Needless to say, the "Russian style" affected ecclesiastical architecture across the western borderlands. See Wojciech Boberski, „Architektura ziem I zaboru rosyjskiego," in Konstantynow and Paszkiewicz, *Kultura i polityka*, 50–1.

10 Erofalov-Pilipchak, *Arkhitektura imperskogo Kieva*, 101–14.

11 On architectural style in late imperial Kyiv see T. Skibits'ka, "Stylistyka zabudovy," in Kal'nyts'kyi and Kondel'-Perminova, *Zabudova Kyieva*, 389–94; compare Malakov, *Prybutkovi budynky Kyieva*, 95–151.

12 Henri Lefebvre aptly called buildings "the prose of the world" that "effects a brutal condensation of social relationships," in contrast to the "poetry of monuments." Buildings stand for everyday life, products, and lived experience; monuments point to festivals, works, and perceived experience. See Lefebvre, *The Production of Space*, 223, 227.

13 Ibid., 221. It must be said that Lefebvre was referring to monumental or representational spaces, such as temples or governmental complexes, rather than to statues to great men. But much of what he wrote about the former can also be applied to the latter.

14 These quotes from Lefebvre's other works come from Stanek, *Henri Lefebvre on Space*, 118.

15 Nora, "Between Memory and History."

16 Higonnet, *Paris, Capital of the World*, 157. He also compared monumental spaces in Paris with those of other cities, pointing out that while in Munich, Barcelona, Hamburg, and Venice monuments were largely municipal and regional, in Paris they have proposed a broader message – simultaneously civic and universal. Ibid., 158.

17 On the national competition for Lviv's public space see the excellent monograph by Markian Prokopovych, *Habsburg Lemberg*.

18 While it is certain that the monument was funded by the "Kyiv citizens," it is still unknown who was its architect. It was long believed that it

had been Andrii Melens'kyi, but recently it has been suggested that the monument's author was Aleksei Eldezin, a Russian military engineer employed as Kyiv province's chief architect between 1798 and 1804. See Kadoms'ka, "Pam'iatnyk Magdeburz'komu pravu," 42–3.

19 See the interview with Mykhailo Kal'nyts'kyi, "Orthodoxy," http://2010.orthodoxy.org.ua/node/78219. Compare Kadoms'ka, "Pam'iatnyk Magdeburz'komu pravu," 43.

20 Ironically, Tsar Alexander I was angry at the Kyiv military governor who had allowed the erection of the monument without first asking permission from the tsar himself. Alexander then fired the governor and issued a decree banning the building of any monument without a prior consent from the tsar. See ibid., 43–4.

21 The most comprehensive study of the monument – its origins and completion – is a short monograph by Tolochko and Hrybovs'ka, *Pam'iatnyk Sviatomu Kniaziu Volodymyru v Kyievi*.

22 Only its pedestal was 16 metres high.

23 Hyrych, *Kyïv v ukraïns'kii istoriï*, 92.

24 Ibid.

25 *Kievlianin* 12 February (1872), 2.

26 Kal'nyts'kyi, "Monumenty iak skladova chastyna mis'koho seredovyshcha," in Kalnyt'skyi and Kondel-Perminova, *Zabudova Kyiva*, 226.

27 Articles on the history of the monument include: Levitskii, "Pamiatnik Bogdanu Khmel'nitskomu"; idem, "Istoriia budovy pam'iatnyka"; Vatulia and Poznanskii, "K istorii sooruzheniia"; Demchenko, "Dokumenty pro istoriiu sporudzhennia."

28 Zakrevskii, *Opisanie Kieva*, vol. 1, 58.

29 The original materials can be found in "Istoricheskii ocherk sooruzheniia pamiatnika Bogdanu Khmel'nitskomu, " in Central State Historical Archive of Ukraine in Kyiv (TsDIAUK), f. 442, op. 48, spr. 232, part II, 150–61.

30 Ibid., 152–3.

31 Ibid., 155–155 reverse; compare Kal'nyts'kyi, "Monumenty," 227.

32 The initial estimate calculated by Mikeshin himself amounted to 145,200 roubles, with public donations not exceeding 25,000. According to some reports, local Ukrainians did whatever they could – mostly engaging in behind-the-scenes sabotage – to block the erection of the monument. See Hyrych, *Kyïv v ukraïns'kii istoriï*, 94.

33 DAK, f. 301, op. 1, spr. 8, 51.

34 "All in all, the indifference towards the monument on part of Little Russia appeared complete." So complained a zealous Russian patriot from the newspaper. See *Kievlianin* 85 (1872), 2.

35 DAK, f. 301, op, 1, spr. 8, 197–8.

36 As late as 1909 this name – Bohdan Khmel'nyts'kyi Square – could still
    be found on building plans in the Besarabka area approved by city
    authorities. SeeKal'nyts'kyi, "Dzherela i formy investuvanniau zabudovu
    Kyieva," in Kalnyt'skyi and Kondel-Perminova, *Zabudova Kyieva*, 184.

37 DAK, f. 163, op. 38, spr. 102, 14 (on the choice of a site on St Sophia's
    Square for the monument to Bohdan Khmel'nyts'kyi).

38 Ibid., 17.

39 This was in sharp contrast to the first half of the nineteenth century, when
    urban land had not yet become a prime commodity, and therefore in a
    number of cities (among them Bremen and Frankfurt), spacious parks and
    green belts were laid out on land previously occupied by earthworks or
    glacis. See Breitling, "The Role of the Competition in the Genesis of Urban
    Planning: Germany and Austria in the Nineteenth Century," in Sutcliffe,
    The Rise of Modern Urban Planning, 41.

40 *Kievlianin* 42 (1871), 2; 60 (1872), 2. For justice's sake, it should be
    mentioned that other prominent councillors (among them Eisman's
    German Protestant peers Nikolai Bunge and Nikolai Rennenkampf)
    rejected anti-Jewish arguments outright, arguing that no law prevented
    Jews from acquiring plots downtown.

41 This apocryphal story appeared in the memoirs of Kyiv Ukrainian
    intellectual Maksym Slavyns'kyi; see his *Zakhovaiu v sertsi Ukraïnu*,
    218–19. On the raising of the monument to Nicholas I see Kal'nyts'kyi,
    "Monumenty," 230–2.

42 "Otkrytie pamiatnika Imperatoru Nikolaiu I," *Kievlianin*, 22 August (1896), 2.

43 Bublik, *Putevoditel' po Kievu*, 139.

44 Alexander II, popularly known as the Tsar-Liberator, boasted the greatest
    number of monuments dedicated to him all over Russia. Between 1911 and
    1916 several thousand monuments to him appeared across the empire. See
    Kal'nyts'kyi, "Monumenty," 235.

45 On this imperial historical showcase see I. Shchitkivs'kyi, "'Istoricheskii
    put' u Kyievi." Another comprehensive account is in Kal'nyts'kyi,
    "Monumenty," 232–5.

46 As quoted in Shchitkivs'kyi, "'Istoricheskii put' u Kyievi," 386.

47 As quoted in Kal'nyts'kyi, "Monumenty," 234.

48 Ibid., 236.

49 The description of the monument is in ibid., 237.

50 Ibid., 243.

51 On the assessment of the statue's poor quality see DAK, f. 93, op. 4, spr. 2, 4.
    On the story in general see Kal'nyts'kyi, "Monumenty," 245.

52 *Narodnyi dom Kievskogo Obshchestva Gramotnosti v g. Kieve*, 20. See also Kal'nyts'kyi, "Dzherela i formy investuvannia," 200–2.

53 For example, the Jewish entrepreneur Lazar' Brodsky donated 12,000 roubles for the society's library, while the contractor L.B. Ginzburg completed some interior works on a charitable basis. The society was led by the prominent Ukrainian intellectual Volodymyr Naumenko. Regarding the broader context of Ukrainian–Jewish cooperation in the Kyiv Literacy Society see Meir, *Kiev, Jewish Metropolis*, 102, 194–5, 198, 204, 304.

54 Kal'nyts'kyi, "Monumenty," 244.

55 Vynnychenko, "A Zealous Friend," 86–94.

56 Paszkiewicz, *Pod berłem Romanowów*, 169. On how the image of Paskevich was celebrated by some Ukrainian authors see my "The Clash of Mental Geographies," 90. Another major city in Russia's western borderlands, Vilnius, had its share of Russian imperial monuments. These included a statue of the notorious "hangman" of Polish patriots Governor General Mikhail Muraviev (1898); a small bust of Russian poet Aleksandr Pushkin (1899); and a bombastic memorial to Catherine the Great (1904). See Weeks, *Vilnius Between Nations*, 69–72.

57 Faith Hillis has brilliantly shown how Russian right-wing populists and nationalists and the successive coalitions of anti-liberal forces became increasingly dominant in Kyiv in the early twentieth century. See her *Children of Rus'*, esp. chs. 4, 6, 7, and 8.

Conclusions: Towards a Theory of Imperial Urbanism in the Borderlands

1 Vilnius, the capital of the northwestern borderlands, was also strategically important because of its position on the rail line from Saint Petersburg to Warsaw. Vilnius, however, never experienced large-scale "imperial" redevelopment, save for a few arteries constructed in the late nineteenth and early twentieth centuries. These new streets bore the names of Russian cities and housed Russian officials and professionals as well as acculturated Jews. See Weeks, *Vilnius Between Nations*, 59, 61–3.

2 Paszkiewicz, *Pod berłem Romanowów*, 14–39.

3 Driver and Gilbert, *Imperial Cities*, 4.

4 Brower, *The Russian City*. Two other types of Russian city, according to Brower – "intermediate cities" and "stagnant cities" – remained outside his analysis.

5 By the end of the century merchants were a minority among city duma members in Kyiv but accounted for most city duma members (53.7%) in Russia's forty major cities. Merchants were a small minority among city

heads in Ukraine but accounted for 47 per cent in Russia's Central Black Soil region, 50 per cent in the Ural region, 72 per cent in Siberia, and 93 per cent in the North. See V.A. Nardova, *Gorodskoe samoupravlenie v Rossii*, 71, 80, 139.

6 Here I will mention only a few notable works dealing with planning and building Saint Petersburg and Odessa. On Odessa: Skinner, "Trends in Planning Practices"; Patrice Herlihy, *Odessa: A History, 1794–1914* (Cambridge, MA: Ukrainian Research Institute of Harvard University, 1991). On Saint Petersburg: Bruce Lincoln, *Sunlight at Midnight: St. Petersburg and the Rise of Modern Russia* (New York: Basic Books, 2002).

7 A special place among local agents of change belonged to a few newspapers, such as the conservative *Kievlianin* and the liberal *Zaria*.

8 The culture of imperial urbanism of course varied across places and times, so the experience of imperial Kyiv was fairly different from that of Paris, Glasgow, or Prague. For a comparative study of imperial culture and urban space, mainly in Britain and continental Western Europe, see Driver and Gilbert, *Imperial Cities*.

9 Urbanist Spiro Kostof mentioned other common topographical settings: natural harbour, defensive site, linear ridge, and sloped terrain; notable examples of these were Naples, ancient Troy, Perugia, and Assisi respectively. See Kostof, *The City Shaped*, 54–5.

10 On the different "city-generating" areas in Kyiv until the mid-seventeenth century see a pioneering study of the city's social topography: Klymovs'kyi, *Sotsial'na topohrafiia Kyieva*, especially several colour inserts in the end of the book showing topographical maps of medieval and early modern Kyiv.

11 See Patricia Herlihy's review of Brower's *The Russian City* in *American Historical Review* 97, no. 1 (1992): 254–5.

12 An alternative concept of making Kyiv a Ukrainian city was ostensibly also incompatible with an imperial cosmopolitan metropolis. But because this Ukrainian vision was advanced largely from the left and by a disadvantaged minority, it never became a real threat to the city's diverse demographics, not until the Second World War

13 Hillis, *Children of Rus'*, 170.

14 On early Soviet experiments in arts and literature in Kyiv see Makaryk and Tkacz, *Modernism in Kyiv*.

15 For a critical assessment of post-Communist urbanism and municipal issues in Kyiv see Cybriwsky, *Kyiv, Ukraine*.

Selected Bibliography

Archival Sources

Derzhavnyi arkhiv mista Kyieva [State Archive of the City of Kyiv] (DAK), Kyiv.

Fond 1 (Kyiv Magistrate, 1800–1835), op. 1–5

Fond 17 (Kyiv City Duma, 1835–1872), op. 1–6

Fond 19 (Interim Committee on city's improvement at Kyiv Provincial Board, 1834–1842), op. 1–2

Fond 163 (Kyiv City *Uprava*, 1870–1919), op. 6 (financial department), op. 7 (economic department), op. 8 (secretariat), op. 39 (secretarial department), op. 40 (public health), op. 41 (construction department), op. 42 (sanitary department), op. 46 (property assessment department), op. 47 (bookkeeping department)

Fond 165 (Kyiv Municipal Commission on managing revenues and expenditures, 1802–1837), op. 1–34.

Fond 239 (Interim Commission on Kyiv's improvement, 1824–1834)

Fond 240 (Commission on rebuilding Podil, 1812–1835)

Fond 241 (Interim Committee on building Kyiv University), op. 1–2

Fond 301 (Committee on building Bohdan Khmel'nyts'kyi monument, 1870–1890)

Fond 926 (University building committee)

Tsentral'nyi derzhavnyi istorychnyi arkhiv Ukrainy u m. Kyievi [Central State Historical Archive of Ukraine in Kyiv] (TsDIAUK), Kyiv.

"Istoricheskii ocherk sooruzheniia pamiatnika Bogdanu Khmel'nitskomu," fond 442 (Chancellery of Kyiv

governor-general), op. 48, spr. 232, part II.

Fond 533 (Kyiv military governor, 1796–1832), op. 1.

Rossiiskaia Natsional'naia biblioteka. Otdel rukopisei [Russian National Library, Manuscript Division] (RNB OR), Saint Petersburg, V.G. Anastasevych, "Zapiska iz Polotska v Krym i Peterburg," fond 18 (of V.G. Anastasevich).

Published Primary Sources

Newspapers and journals

Izvestiia Kievskoi gorodskoi dumy
Kievlianin (1840–50)
Kievlianin (1864–1917)
Kievskaia gazeta
Kievskaia starina
Kievskie gubernskie vedomosti
Kievskii telegraf
Kievskoe slovo
Zaria

Books, pamphlets, and memoirs

Aleichem, Sholem. *The Letters of Menakhem-Mendl and Sheyne-Sheyndl* and *Motl, the Cantor's Son*. New Haven: Yale University Press, 2002.
Antonovych, V.B., ed. "Kiev, ego sud'ba i znachenie s XIV po XVI stoletie." In *Moia spovid': vybrani istorychni ta publitsystychni tvory*, 535–78. Kyiv: Lybid', 1995.
– *Sbornik materialov dlia istoricheskoi topografii Kieva i ego okrestnostei.* Kyiv: Tipografiia A.Ia. Fedotova, 1874.
Benediktov, V. "Kiev," *Kievlianin* 1 (Kiev, 1840), 1–3.
Berlyns'kyi, Maksym. *Korotkyi opys Kyeva.* Reprynt. Kyiv: b.v., 1990.
– *Istoriia mista Kyieva.* Kyiv: Naukova dumka, 1991.
Bilenky, Serhiy, ed. *Fashioning Modern Ukraine: Selected Writings of Mykola Kostomarov, Volodymyr Antonovych, and Mykhailo Drahomanov.* Toronto and Edmonton: Canadian Institute of Ukrainian Studies Press, 2013.
Bogatinov, Nikolai. "Vospominaniia." *Russkii Arkhiv* 1, no. 3 (1899): 410–40.
Bublik, V.D. *Putevoditel' po Kievu i ego okrestnostiam*, 4th ed. Kyiv: Tipografiia S.V. Kul'zhenka, 1897.
Bulgarin, Fadei. *Dmitrii Samozvanets.* Vologda: Poligrafist, 1994.
Bulkina, Inna, ed. *Kiev v russkoi poezii. Antologiia.* Kyiv: Laurus, 2012.
Buturlin, M.D., ct. "Zapiski. Chast' VIII 1834–1836," *Russkii arkhiv* 8 (1897): 529–601.

Chołoniewski, Stanisław, ks. *Opis podróży kijowskiej odbytej w 1840 roku*. L'viv: Nakładem Gubrynowicza i Schmidta, 1886.

Dinovskii, F.I. "Zapiska sekretaria statisticheskogo komiteta o narodonaselenii v g. Kieve (1863)." In *Sbornik statisticheskikh svedenii o Kievskoi gubernii*, 25–38. Kyiv: 1864.

Dolgorukov, I.M., prince. "Slavny bubny za gorami, ili moe puteshestvie koe-kuda v 1810 g." In *Chteniia v obshchestve istorii i drevnostei Rossiiskikh*, vol. 2 (April–June), 1–170; vol. 3 (July-September), 171–352. Moscow: 1869.

Drahomanov, Mykhailo. *Literatura rosiis'ka, velykoruska, ukrainska i halyts'ka*, Lviv: Tov-vo im. Shevchenka, 1874.

Drzewiecki, Józef. *Pamiętniki*. Cracow: G. Gebethner, 1891.

Drzewiecki, Karol. *Kontrakty*. Vilnius: J. Zawadzki, 1842.

Działyńska z Błędowskich, Henrieta. *Pamiątka przeszłości*. Warsaw: Państwowy instytut wydawniczy, 1960.

Funduklei, Ivan, ed. *Obozrenie Kieva v otnoshenii k drevnostiam*. Kyiv: V tipografii I. Val'nera, 1847.

– ed. *Obozreniie mogil, valov i gorodishch Kievskoi gubernii*. Kyiv: V tipografii I. Val'nera, 1848.

– ed. *Statisticheskoe opisanie Kievskoi gubernii*. Saint Petersburg: Ministerstvo vnutrennikh del, 1852.

Gogol, N.V. *Polnoe sobranie sochinenii i pisem*. 23 vols, vol. 1. Moscow: Nasledie, 2001.

Goldstein, M.L. *Vpechatleniia i zametki (Iz fel'etonov, napechatannykh v "Kievskom slove" i "Kievlianine" za 1887–1892 gg)*. Kyiv: Tipografiia gazety "Kievskoe slovo," 1895.

Gorodovoe polozhenie s raz'iasneniiami i dopolneniiami. Saint Petersburg: 1873.

Goszczyński, Seweryn. *Zamek Kaniowski*. Cracow: Towarzystwo Autorów i Wydawców Prac Naukowych "Universitas," 2002.

Hrebinka, Ievhen. "Machekha i Pannochka. Malorossiiskoe predanie." In his *Tvory*. 3 vols. 1: 315–23. Kyiv: Radians'kyi pys'mennyk, 1980.

Ievgenii (Bolkhovitinov), metropolitan. *Opisanie Kievo-Pecherskoi Lavry*. Kyiv: V tipografii Kievopecherskoi lavry, 1826.

– *Opisanie Kievo-Sofiiskogo sobora i kievskoi ierarkhii*. Kyiv: V tipografii Kievopecherskoi lavry, 1825.

Ikonnikov, V.S. *Kiev v 1654–1855. Istoricheskii ocherk*. Kyiv: Tipografiia Imperatorskogo Universiteta sv. Vladimira, 1904.

Innokentii (Borisov). "Zapiska o Kievskom universitete Sv. Vladimira v 1838 g." In *Z imenem Sviatoho Volodymyra*, ed. Viktor Korotkyi and Vasyl Ulianovs'kyi. 2 vols, vol. 1. Kyiv: Zapovit, 1994.

Istoriia Russov. Moscow: V universitetskoi tipografii, 1846. Reprinted, Kyiv: Dzvin, 1991.

Izmailov, Vladimir. *Puteshestvie v Poludennuiu Rossiiu. V pis'makh*. Moscow: V universitetskoi tipografii, 1800.

Jełowicki, Alexander. *Moje wspomnienie*. Cracow: Nakładem Księgarni Spółki wydawniczej Polskiej, 1891.

Kafka, Franz. *Diaries, 1910–1923*. New York: Schocken, 1988.

Karlgof, Vil'gel'm. *Povesti i rasskazy*. 2 vols. Saint Petersburg: Tipografiia Departamenta narodnogo prosveshcheniia, 1832.

– (A.V. Ve—skii). "Sila privychki." *Kievlianin* 1 (1840): 177–99.

Khomiakov, Aleksei. *Stikhotvoreniia i dramy*. Leningrad [Saint Petersburg]: Sovetskii pisatel', 1969.

Kiev i ego predmistiia: Shuliavka, Solomenka s Protasovym Iarom, Baikova Gora i Demievka s Sapernoiu slobodkoi po perepisi 2 marta 1874 goda. Kyiv: V tipografii imperatorskogo universiteta sv. Vladimira, 1875.

Kiev po perepisi 2 marta 1874 goda. Kyiv: 1875.

Korzeniowski, Józef. "Emeryt." In his *Dzieła*, vol. 2. Warsaw: S. Lewental, 1871.

Kostomarov, N.I. *Istoricheskie proizvedeniia. Avtobiografiia*. Kyiv: Lybid', 1990.

Kozlov, I.I. *Polnoe sobranie stikhotvorenii*. Moscow: Sovetskii pisatel', 1960.

Kraszewski, Józef Ignacy. *Latarnia czarnoksięska*. Series I. Cracow: Wydawnictwo Literackie, 1964.

– *Listy do rodziny 1820–1863*, pt 1: *W kraju*. Cracow: Wydawnictwo Literackie, 1982.

Kulish, Panteleimon. *Tvory*. 2 vols. Vol. 1. Kyiv: Naukova dumka, 1998.

Kul'zhenko, S.V. *Vidy Kieva*. Kyiv: Svetopechat', 1900.

Kuprin, Aleksander. "Iama." In his *Izbrannoe*. Kharkiv: Vyshcha shkola, 1988.

– *Yama [The Pit]. A novel in three parts by Alexandre Kuprin*. Trans. Bernard Guilbert Guerney. New York: 1922.

Leshchenko I., ed. *Kievskaia sel'sko-khoziaistvennaia i promyshlennaia vystavka 1897 goda i ee uchastniki*. Kyiv: 1898.

Leskov, N.S. "Pecherskie antiki." In his *Sobranie sochinenii*. 12 vols. 10: 248–327. Moscow: Pravda, 1989.

Levshin, Aleksei. *Pis'ma iz Malorossii*. Kharkiv: V universitetskoi tipografii, 1816.

Levyts'kyi (Levitskii), Orest. *Piatideseteletie Kievskoi kommissii dlia razbora drevnikh aktov (1843–1893)*. Kyiv: 1893.

– "Istoriia budovy pam'iatnyka B. Khmel'nyts'komu v Kyievi." *Literaturno-naukovyi visnyk* 62 (1913): 467–83.

– "Pamiatnik Bogdanu Khmel'nitskomu: istoricheskii ocherk ego sooruzheniia." *Kievskaia Starina* 7 (1888):145–56.

Łukaszewicz, W., W. Lewandowski, et al., eds. *Postępowa publicystyka emigracyjna: Wybór źródł.* Wrocław: Zakład Narodowy im. Ossolińskich, 1961.

Maksimovich, M.A. [M.O. Maksymovych]. "Mysli ob universitete Sv. Vladimira v kontse 1838 g." In *Z imenem Sviatoho Volodymyra,* ed. Viktor Korotkyi and Vasyl Ulianovs'kyi. 2 vols. Vol. 1. Kyiv: Zapovit, 1994.

– *Pis'ma o Kieve i vospominaniia o Tavride.* Saint Petersburg: Tipografiia A. Transhela, 1871.

– *"Kiev iavilsia gradom velikim … " Vybrani ukraïnoznavchi tvory.* Kyiv: Lybid', 1994.

Maslov, "Putevye zametki pri poezdke iz Moskvy v Kiev, Khar'kov i Voronezh," *Zemledel'cheskii zhurnal* 4 (1839): 50–60.

Muraviev, Andrei. *Puteshestvie po sviatym mestam russkim. Kiev.* Saint Petersburg: V tipografii III otdeleniia Ego Imperatorskogo Velichestva kantseliarii, 1844.

– "Zapiska o sokhranenii samobytnosti Kieva." *Jehupets* 5 (1999): 259–67.

Narodnyi dom Kievskogo Obshchestva Gramotnosti v g. Kieve. Kyiv: 1902.

Nechui-Levyts'kyi, Ivan. "Khmary," in his *Tvory v dvokh tomakh,* vol 1. Kyiv: Naukova dumka, 1985, 101–414.

– *Tvory v dvokh tomakh.* Kyiv: Dnipro, 1977.

Obzor deiatel'nosti Kievskoi gorodskoi dumy za chetyrekhletie 1906–1910. Kyiv: 1910.

Obzor Odesskago gradonachalstva za 1914. Odessa: 1916.

Olizar, Gustaw. *Pamiętniki.* Lviv: Księgarnia Gubrynowicza i Schmidta, 1892.

Pantiukhov, Ivan. *Statisticheskie i sanitarnye ocherki Kieva.* Kyiv: V universitetstkoi tipografii, 1877.

– *Opyt sanitarnoi topografii i statistiki Kieva.* Kyiv: Izd. Kievskogo gubernskogo statisticheskogo komiteta, 1877.

Pataleev, O.V. *Staryi Kyiv: Zi spohadiv Staroho Hrishnyka.* Kyiv: Lybid', 2008.

Pervaia vseobshchaia perepis' naseleniia Rossiiskoi imperii, vol. 16: *Kievskaia guberniia.* Saint Petersburg: Tsentral'nyi statisticheskii komitet MVD, 1904.

Podolinskii, Andrei. *Sochineniia.* 2 vols. Saint Petersburg: Tipografiia V. Bezobrazova, 1860. Also available online: http://az.lib.ru/p/ podolinskij_a_i/text_0120oldorfo-1.shtml

Ponomarev, S., ed. *Podlinniki Pisem Gogol'a k Maksimovichu.* Saint Petersburg: Tipografiia imperatorskoi akademii nauk, 1877.

Pushkin, A.S. *Polnoe sobranie sochinenii.* 10 vols, vol. 3, pt 1. Leningrad: Pechatnyi dvor: 1948.

– *Sobranie sochinenii.* 10 vols. Moscow: Gosudarstvennoe izdatel'stvo khudozhestvennoi literatury, 1959 (vol. 1), 1960 (vol. 3).

Ryleev, Kondratii. *Polnoe sobranie stikhotvorenii.* Leningrad [Saint Petersburg]: Sovetskii pisatel', 1971.

Sbitnev, M. "Zapiski." *Kievskaia starina* 2 (1884): 285–312.

Sbornik statisticheskikh svedenii o Kievskoi gubernii. Kyiv: Kievskii gubernskii statisticheskii komitet, 1864.

Seletskii, P.D. "Zapiski." *Kievskaia starina* 8 (1884): 276–445.

Sementovskii, Nikolai. *Galereia Kievskikh dostoprimechatel'nykh vidov i drevnostei.* Kyiv: V gubernskoi tipografii, 1857–8.

– *Kiev i ego dostopamiatnosti.* Kyiv: 1852.

– *Kiev, ego sviatynia, drevnosti, dostopamiatnosti i svedeniia neobkhodimye dlia ego pochitatelei i puteshestvennikov.* 1st ed. Kyiv: Tipografiia Sementovskogo, 1864.

– *Kiev, ego sviatynia, drevnosti, dostopamiatnosti.* 6th ed. Kyiv: Izdanie knigoprodavtsa N.Ia. Ogloblina, 1881.

– *Kiev, ego sviatynia, drevnosti, dostopamiatnosti i svedeniia neobkhodimye dlia ego pochitatelei i puteshestvennikov.* 7th ed. Kyiv and Saint Petersburg: Izdanie knigoprodavtsa N.Ia. Ogloblina, 1900.

Sherotskii, K.V. *Kiev. Putevoditel'.* Kyiv: V.S. Kul'zhenko, 1917.

Shevchenko, Taras. *Povne zibrannia tvoriv.* 6 vols. 2: *Poeziï 1847–1861.* Kyiv: Vydavnytstvo Akademiï nauk URSR, 1963.

Shmakov, A. *Pogrom evreev v Kieve. Ocherk.* Moscow: 1908.

Shul'gin, V.Ia. *Istoriia universiteta sviatago Vladimira (1834–1839).* Saint Petersburg: V tipografii Riumina, 1860.

Serdiukov, I.I. "Avtobiograficheskaia zapiska." *Kievskaia starina* 12 (1896): 337–73.

Slavyns'kyi, Maksym. *Zakhovaiu v sertsi Ukraïnu: Poeziia. Publitsystyka. Spohady.* Kyiv: Iunivers, 2002.

Słowacki, Juliusz. *Dzieła,* vol. 11: *Listy do matki.* Wrocław: Wydawnictwo Zakładu Narodowego im. Ossolińskich, 1949.

"Skorb' kievlian o potere Magdeburgskogo prava" (The Grief of Kyivites over the Loss of Magdeburg Law). *Kievskaia Starina* 5 (1882): 352–7.

Snegirev, I.M. *Zhizn' Moskovskogo Mitropolita Platona,* vol. 2. Moscow: Spaso-Vifanskii monastyr', 1891.

Staryts'kyi, Mykhailo. *Za dvoma zaitsiamy.* In his *Tvory u dvokh tomakh,* vol. 2: *Dramatychni tvory,* 88–157. Kyiv: Dnipro, 1984.

Sulima, S. "Zametki starogo kievlianina (Kiev v 1812 и 1824 g.)." *Kievskaia starina* 12 (1882): 614–24.

Uvarov, S.S. *Desiatiletie Ministerstva narodnago prosveshcheniia.* Saint Petersburg: V tipografii imperatorskoi akademii nauk, 1864.

Varadinov, V.V. *Istoriia Ministerstva vnutrennikh del,* pt 3, vols. 1–3: *Period tretii: s 19 noiabria 1825 po 20 avgusta 1855.* Saint Peterburg: Tipografiia Ministerstva vnutrennikh del, 1862.

Ves' Kiev na 1905: adressnaia i spravochnaia kniga. Kyiv: Tipografiia "Pechatnoe delo v Kieve," 1905.

Vigel', F.F. *Vospominaniia*, pt 1. Moscow: V universtitetskoi tipografii, 1864.

Volkonskii, S.G. *Zapiski.* Saint Petersburg: Sinodal'naia tipografiia, 1901.

Volynskii, M. *Spravedlivo li raspredelenie naloga mezhdu nedvizhymymi imushchestvami v g. Kieve?* Kyiv: 1905.

Vynnychenko, Volodymyr. "A Zealous Friend." Trans. Theodor Prokopov. In his *Selected Short Stories*, 86–94. Wakefield: Longwood Academic, 1991.

Zakharchenko, M.M. *Kiev teper' i prezhde.* Kyiv: S.V. Kul'zhenko, 1888.

Zakrevskii, Nikolai. *Opisanie Kieva*, vol. 1, pt 1: *Letopis' goroda Kieva.* Moscow: V tipografii V. Gracheva, 1868.

Zapiska i rechi, chitannye pri otkrytii imperatorskago universiteta sviatago Vladimira 15 iiulia 1834 g. Kyiv: V universitetskoi tipografii, 1840.

Zhuravskii, D.P. *Plan statisticheskogo opisaniia gubernii Kievskogo uchebnoho okruga.* Kyiv: V universitetskoi tipografii, 1851.

– *O kreditnykh sdelkakh v Kievskoi gubernii.* Kyiv: 1856.

[Ziber, Nikolai]. *Po povodu retsenzii "Kievlianina" na perepis' 2-go marta 1874 goda. Soobrazheniia i zametki odnogo iz prinimavshikh uchastie v razrabotke perepisi.* Kyiv: Tipografiia M.P. Fritsa, 1875.

Secondary Sources

Alfonsin, Anthony. *When Buildings Speak: Architecture as Language in the Habsburg Empire and Its Aftermath, 1867–1933.* Chicago: University of Chicago Press, 2008.

Alioshyn, Pavlo. "Bat'ko i syn Beretti (z arkhitekturnoï spadshchyny)." *Arkhitektura Radians'koï Ukraïny* 3 (1938): 39–40. http://www.alyoshin.ru/Files/publika/pfa/pfa_beretti.html.

Ananieva, Tatiana. "K voprosu ob arkheologicheskoi deiatel'nosti Kievskogo mitropolita Ievgeniia Bolkhovitinova." *Tretia akademiia pam'iati profesora Volodymyra Antonovycha*, 366–75. Kyiv: 1996.

Armstrong, John. "Mobilized Diaspora in Tsarist Russia: The Case of the Baltic Germans." In *Soviet Nationality: Policies and Practices*, ed. Jeremy R. Azrael, 63–104. New York: 1978.

Barea, Ilsa. *Vienna.* New York: Alfred A. Knopf, 1966.

Bilenky, Serhiy. "Battle of Visions: How Was Kiev Seen in the 1780s–1840s?" *Toronto Slavic Quarterly* 13 (2005): 1–13. http://sites.utoronto.ca/tsq/13/bilenky13.shtml.

– "The Clash of Mental Geographies: Poles on Ukraine, Ukrainians on Poland in the Time of Romanticism." *Polish Review* 53, no. 1 (2008): 73–95.

– "Inventing an Ancient City: How Fiction, Ideology, and Archeology Refashioned Kyiv during the 1830s and 1840s." In *Festschrift for George G. Grabowicz*, a separate issue of *Harvard Ukrainian Studies* 32–3, pt 1 (2011–14): 107–26.

– *Romantic Nationalism in Eastern Europe: Russian, Polish, and Ukrainian Political Imaginations*. Stanford: Stanford University Press, 2012.

– "Spohliadannia mista. Kyïv i Universytet Sv. Volodymyra u 30-40-vi roky XIX st." *Kievskii al'bom* 1 (2001): 13–30.

Bilenky, Serhiy, and Korotkyi Viktor. *Mykhailo Maksymovych ta osvitni praktyky na Pravoberezhnii Ukraïni v pershii polovyni XIX stolittia*. Kyiv: Kyïvs'kyi Universytet, 1999.

Bilous, Natalia. *Kyïv naprykintsi XV-u pershii polovyni XVII stolittia: mis'ka vlada i samovriaduvannia*. Kyiv: Vydavnychyi dim "Kyievo-Mohylians'ka Akademia," 2008.

Blum, Stuart. "Mobility and Change in Ante-Bellum Philadelphia." In *Nineteenth-Century Cities: Essays in the New Urban History*, ed. Stephan Thernstrom and Richard Sennett, 125–208. New Haven: Yale University Press, 1969.

Bojanowska, Edyta. *Nikolai Gogol: Between Ukrainian and Russian Nationalism*. Cambridge, MA.: Harvard University Press, 2007.

Borges, Jorge Luis. *Selected Non-Fictions*, ed. Eliot Weinberger. New York: Penguin, 2000.

Bourdieu, Pierre. *Language and Symbolic Power*. Cambridge, MA.: Harvard University Press, 1999.

Brower, Daniel R. *The Russian City between Tradition and Modernity, 1850–1900*. Berkeley: University of California Press, 1990.

Bulkina, Inna. "Antolohiia iak nahoda." *Krytyka* 12 (2001): 3–5.

– "Kievskaia antologiia." In *Stat'i na sluchai: Sbornik v chest' 50-letiia R.G. Leibova*. http://www.ruthenia.ru/leibov_50/Bulkina.pdf

– "Bor'ba za 'russkuiu' Malorossiiu pri Nikolae I." In *"Ideologicheskaia Geografiia" Rossiiskoi imperii: Prostrantstvo, granitsy, obitateli*, ed. L. Kiseleva, 71–89. Tartu: Universitas Tartuensis, 2012. http://www.ruthenia.ru/territoria_et_populi/texts/1.2.Bulkina.pdf

– "Malorossiiskoe prostranstvo." In *"Ideologicheskaia Geografiia" Rossiiskoi imperii: Prostrantstvo, granitsy, obitateli*, ed. L. Kiseleva, 224–60. Tartu: Universitas Tartuensis, 2012. http://www.ruthenia.ru/territoria_et_populi/ideogeograf.html

Bunin, A.V., and T.F. Savarenskaia. *Istoriia gradostroitel'nogo iskusstva. Gradostroitel'stvo rabovladel'cheskogo stroia i feodalizma*, vol. 1. Moscow: Stroiizdat, 1979.

Bushkovitch, Paul. "The Ukraine in Russian Culture 1790–1860: The Evidence of the Journals." *Jahrbücher für Geschichte Osteuropas*, Neue Folge, 39, no. 3 (1991): 339–63.

Buzalo, V. "Reiestrovi tovaryshi." *Pam'iatky Ukraïny* 2 (1990): 63.

Cadiot, Juliette. *Le laboratoire impérial: Russie–URSS, 1860–1940*. Paris: CNRS Éditions, 2007.

– "Searching for Nationality: Statistics and National Categories at the End of the Russian Empire (1897–1917)." *Russian Review* 64 (July 2005): 440–55.

Choay, Françoise. *The Modern City: Planning in the 19th Century*. New York: George Braziller, 1969.

Cohen, Gary. *The Politics of Ethnic Survival: Germans in Prague, 1861–1914*. West Lafayette: Purdue University Press, 2006.

Conzen, M.R.C. "The Use of Town Plans in the Study of Urban History." In *The Study of Urban History*, ed. H.J. Dyos, 113–30. London: Edward Arnold, 1968.

Coverley, Merlin. *Psychogeography*. London: Pocket Essentials, 2010.

Csendes, Peter, and Opll, Ferdinand, eds. *Wien: Geschichte einer Stadt*, Bd 3: *Von 1790 biz zur Gegenwart*. Wien, Koln, Weimar: Böhlau Verlag, 2006.

Cybriwsky, Roman Adrian. *Kyiv, Ukraine: The City of Domes and Demons from the Collapse of Socialism to the Mass Uprising of 2013–2014*. Amsterdam: Amsterdam University Press, 2014.

Dauber, Jeremy. *The Worlds of Sholem Aleichem*. New York: Schocken Books, 2013.

Demchenko, L. "Dokumenty pro istoriiu sporudzhennia pam'iatnyka B. Khmel'nyts'komu v m. Kyievi." *Arkhivy Ukraïny* 4 (1988): 39–49.

Ditiatin, I.I. *Ustroistvo i upravlenie gorodov Rossii*, vol. 2: *Gorodskoe samoupravlenie do 1870 g*. Yaroslavl: Tipografiia G.V. Falk, 1877.

Dixon, Megan. "Repositioning Pushkin and the Poems of the Polish Uprising." In *Polish Encounters, Russian Identity*, ed. David L. Ransel and Bozena Shallcross, 49–74. Bloomington: Indiana University Press, 2005.

Dolbilov, Mikhail. "Russification and the Bureaucratic Mind in the Russian Empire's Northwestern Region in the 1860s." *Kritika* 5, no. 2 (2004): 245–71.

Driver, Felix and Gilbert, David, eds. *Imperial Cities: Landscape, Display, and Identity*. Manchester: Manchester University Press, 2003.

Druh, Olha. "Do istoriï kyïvs'koï sadyby XIX-XX stolit': vulytsia Lyps'ka No. 16." *Kievskii al'bom. Istoricheskii al'manakh 2001 god* 1 (2001): 79–87.

– *Vulytsiamy Staroho Kyieva*. Lviv: Svit, 2013.

Druh, Olha, and Malakov, Dmytro. *Osobniaky Kyieva*. Kyiv: Kyi, 2004.

Epsztein, Tadeusz. *Z piórem i paletą: zainteresowania intelektualne i artystyczne ziemiaństwa polskiego na Ukrainie w połowie XIX wieku*. Warsaw: "Neriton," Instytut Historii PAN, 2005.

Ernst, Fedir. *Kontrakty ta kontraktovyi budynok u Kyievi, 1798–1923.* Kyiv: Drukarnia VUAN, 1923.

Erofalov-Pilipchak, Boris. *Arkhitektura imperskogo Kieva.* Kyiv: Izdatel'skii dom A.S.S/NDITIAM, 2000.

Fedorov, V.A., ed. *Istoriia Rossii XIX-nachala XX v.* Moscow: Vysshaia shkola, 2006.

Fedorova, L. "Zakrevs'kyi Mykola Vasyl'ovych." In *Entsyklopediia istorii Ukraïny,* vol. 3, 225–6. Kyiv: Naukova dumka, 2005.

Gamolia, Nataliia, and Elena Mokrousova. "Kamennye 'kopilki.'" *Interesnyi Kiev:* https://www.interesniy.kiev.ua/kamennyie-kopilki.

Glaeser, Edward. *Triumph of the City: How Our Greatest Invention Makes Us Richer, Smarter, Greener, Healthier, and Happier.* New York: Penguin Books, 2012.

Gluszkowski, Piotr. *F.B. Bulgarin v russko-pol'skikh otnosheniiakh pervoi poloviny XIX veka: evoliutsiia identichnosti i politicheskikh vozzrenii.* Saint Petersburg: Aleteiia, 2013.

Grossman, Leonid. "Balzak v Rossii," *Literaturnoe nasledstvo* 31–2 (Moscow: 1937): 149–372.

Halaiba, Vasyl' et al., *Prorizna. Iaroslaviv val: kul'turolohichnyi putivnyk.* Kyiv: Amadei, 2010.

Hall, Thomas. *Planning Europe's Capital Cities: Aspects of Nineteenth Century Urban Development.* London: Routledge, 1997.

Hamm, Michael. *Kiev: A Portrait, 1800–1917.* Princeton: Princeton University Press, 1993.

Handlin, Oscar, and John Burchard, eds. *The Historian and the City.* Cambridge, MA: MIT Press and Harvard University Press, 1963.

Harvey, David. *Paris, Capital of Modernity.* New York: Routledge, 2006.

– *The Urban Experience.* Baltimore: Johns Hopkins University Press, 1989.

Higonnet, Patrice. *Paris: Capital of the World.* Cambridge, MA: Harvard University Press, 2002.

Hillis, Faith. *Children of Rus': Right-Bank Ukraine and the Invention of a Russian Nation.* Ithaca: Cornell University Press, 2013.

– "Human Mobility, Imperial Governance, and Political Conflict in Pre-Revolutionary Kiev." In *Russia in Motion: Cultures of Human Mobility since 1850,* ed. John Randolph and Eugene M. Avrutin, 25–42. Urbana: University of Illinois Press, 2012.

– "Modernist Visions and Political Conflict in Late Imperial Kiev." In *Races to Modernity: Metropolitan Aspirations in Eastern Europe, 1890–1940,* ed. Jan C. Behrends and Martin Kolrausch, 49–72. New York: Central European Press, 2014.

Hines, Thomas S. *Burnham of Chicago: Architect and Planner*. Chicago: University of Chicago Press, 2009.

Hrabovych, Hryhorii. *Do istorii ukrains'koï literatury*. Kyiv: Osnovy, 1997.

Hrushevs'kyi, Mykhailo, ed. *Kyiv ta ioho okolytsia v istorii ta pam'iatkakh*. Kyiv: Derzhavne vydavnytsvo Ukraïny, 1926.

– ed. *Kyïv ta ioho okolytsia v istorii ta pami'atkakh*. Kyiv: Derzhavne vydavnytstvo Ukraïny, 1926.

– ed. *Kyïvs'ki zbirnyky istorii i arkheolohii, pobutu i mystetstva*. Kyiv: Vydannia komisii istorii Kyieva VUAN, 1931, vol. 1.

Hrytsai, M. *Budynok universytetu im. T.H. Shevchenka v Kyievi (pam'iatnyk arkhitektury XIX st.)*. Kyiv: Derzhavne vydavnytstvo literatury z budivnytstva i arkhitektury URSR, 1959.

Hyrych, Ihor. *Kyïv v ukraïns'kii istorii*. Kyiv: Smoloskyp, 2011.

Ignatkin, I. *Istoriia planirovki i zastroiki Kieva v nachale XIX veka*. Avtoreferat dissertatsii. Kyiv: 1962.

Interesnyi Kiev (webportal on Kyiv's history). https://www.interesniy.kiev.ua.

Ivanova, N.A. and V.P. Zheltova. *Soslovno-klassovaia struktura Rossii v kontse XIX-nachale XX veka*. Moscow: Nauka, 2004.

Kadoms'ka, Mariia. "Pam'iatnyk Magdeburz'komu pravu," *Pam'iatky Ukrainy* 5 (2014): 42–53.

Kal'nyts'kyi, Mykhailo. *Zruinovani sviatyni Kyieva: vtraty ta vidrodzhennia*. Kyiv: Vydavnychyi dim Dmytra Buraho, 2012.

– "Nachalo bul'vara: galereia metamorfoz," *Interesnyi Kiev*. https://www. interesniy.kiev.ua/nachalo-bulvara-galereya-metamorfoz

– "Kolyshnie peredmistia Demiïvka," *Interesnyi Kiev*. https://www.interesniy. kiev.ua/kolishnye-peredmistya-demiyivka

– "Mis'kyi holova Gustav Eisman," *Interesnyi Kiev*. https://www.interesniy. kiev.ua/miskiy-golova-gustav-eysman

– "Ipoteka po-kievskii," *Interesnyi Kiev*. https://www.interesniy.kiev.ua/ ipoteka-po-kievski

Kal'nyts'kyi, Mykhailo, and N.M. Kondel'-Perminova, eds. *Zabudova Kyieva doby klasychnoho kapitalizmu, abo koly i iak misto stalo ievropeis'kym*. Kyiv: Stylos, 2012.

Kal'nyts'kyi, Mykhailo, N. Vitiuk, and S. Ievsieiev. *Solom'ians'kyi raion mista Kyieva vchora, siohodni, zavtra*. Kyiv: Drukarnia Diaprynt, 2010.

Kamanin, Ivan. *Poslednie gody samoupravleniia Kieva po Magdeburgskomu pravu*. Kyiv: Tipografiia G.T. Korchak-Novitskago, 1888. (An offprint from *Kievskaia starina*, 1888, vol. 5: 157–95, vol. 8: 597–622, and vol. 9: 140–68.)

Kappeler, Andreas. "*Mazepintsy, Little Russians, Khokhly*: Ukrainians in the Ethnic Hierarchy of the Russian Empire." In *Culture, Nation, and Identity*:

The Ukrainian–Russian Encounter (1600–1945), ed. Andreas Kappeler et al, 162–82. Toronto and Edmonton: Canadian Institute of Ukranian Study Press, 2003.

– *The Russian Empire: A Multiethnic History*. Harlow: Pearson Education, 2001.

Kennedy-Grimsted, Patricia. "Arkheohrafiia v tini impers'koï polityky: Kyïvs'ka arkheohrafichna komisiia ta utvorennia Kyïvs'koho tsentral'noho arkhivu davnikh aktiv," 11–33. In *Materialy iuvileinoï konferentsiï, prysviachenoï 150-richchiu Kyivs'koï arkheohrafichnoï komisiï*. Kyiv: Instytut ukrains'koï arkheohrafiï, 1997.

Kirkevich, Viktor. *Vremia Romanovykh: Kiev v imperii*. Kyiv: Kievlianin, 2004.

Kirkland, Stephane. *Paris Reborn: Napoléon III, Baron Haussmann, and the Quest to Build a Modern City*. New York: Picador, 2013.

Klymenko, Olga. "The Urbanization of Kiev from the End of the Eighteenth to the Middle of the Nineteenth Century: The Distinguishing Features and the Impact of the Integration into the Russian Empire," MA thesis, Central European University, Budapest, 1998.

Klymenko, P.V. *Kyïvs'ka mis'ka kapela v pershii chverti XIX st.* Kyiv: Muzyka, 1925.

– *Tsekhi na Ukraine*. Kyiv: 1929.

Klymovs'kyi, Serhii. *Sotsial'na topohrafiia Kyieva XVI-seredyny XVII storichchia*. Kyiv: Stylos, 2002.

Knabe, G.S., ed. *Moskva i "moskovskii tekst" russkoi kul'tury*. Moscow: Rossiiskii gosudarstvennyi gumanitarnyi universitet, 1998.

Kohut, Zenon. *Russian Centralism and Ukrainian Autonomy: Imperial Absorption of the Hetmanate 1760s–1830s*. Cambridge, MA: Harvard University Press, 1988.

Kondufor, Iurii, ed. *Istoriia Kieva*, vol. 2: *Kiev perioda pozdnego feodalizma i kapitalizma*. Kyiv: Naukova dumka, 1984.

Konstantynow, Dariusz, and Piotr Paszkiewicz, eds. *Kultura i polityka. Wpływ polityki rusyfikacyjnej na kulturę zachodnich rubieży Imperium Rosyjskiego (1772–1915)*. Warsaw: Instytut sztuki polskiej akademii nauk, 1994.

Koshman, L.V. *Gorod i gorodskaia zhizn' v Rossii XIX stoletiia. Sotsial'nye i kul'turnye aspekty*. Moscow: ROSSPEN, 2008.

Kostof, Spiro. *The City Shaped: Urban Patterns and Meanings through History*. New York: Little, Brown, 1991.

Kotel'nikov, A. *Istoriia proizvodstva i razrabotki vseobshchei perepisi naselenia 28-go ianvaria 1897 g.* Saint Petersburg: Knizhnyi magazin "Nasha zhizn'," 1909.

Kotenko, Anton, Olga Martyniuk, and Aleksei Miller. "Maloros." In *Poniatiia o Rossii. Kliuchevye obshchestvenno-politicheskie poniatiia v Rossii imperskogo perioda*, ed. A. Miller, D. Sdvizhkov, and I. Shirle, 392–444. Moscow: 2012.

Kovalyns'kyi, Vitalii. *Kyïvs'ki miniatiury*. 9 vols. Kyiv: Kupola, 2006–11.

– *Metsenaty Kieva*. Kyiv: Kyi, 1998.

Koznarsky, Taras. "Three Novels, Three Cities." In *Modernism in Kyiv: Jubilant Experimentation*, ed. Irena Makaryk and Virlana Tkach, 98–137. Toronto: University of Toronto Press, 2010.

Krawchenko, Bohdan. *Social Change and National Consciousness in Twentieth-Century Ukraine*. New York: Palgrave Macmillan, 1985.

Kudritskii, A.V., ed. *Kiev. Entsyklopedicheskii spravochnik*. Kyiv: Glavnaia redaktsiia Ukrainskoi Sovetskoi Entsiklopedii, 1985.

– ed. *Kyïv: Istorychnyi ohliad (karty, iliustratsiï, dokumenty)*. Kyiv: Vydavnytstvo Kyïv, 1982.

Lefebvre, Henri. *The Production of Space*. London: Blackwell, 1991.

– *Urban Revolution*. Minneapolis: University of Minnesota Press, 2003.

Lieven, Dominic. *Russia's Rulers under the Old Regime*. New Haven: Yale University Press, 2000.

Lindner, Christoph. *Imagining New York City: Literature, Urbanism, and the Visual Arts, 1890–1940*. Oxford and New York: Oxford University Press, 2015.

Lynch, Kevin A. *The Image of the City*. Cambridge MA: MIT Press, 1960.

Maderthaner, Wolfgang, and Lutz Musner. *Unruly Masses: The Other Side of Fin-de-Siècle Vienna*. Oxford and New York: Oxford University Press, 2008.

Makarov, Anatolii. *Kievskaia starina v litsakh: XIX vek*. Kyiv: Dovira, 2005.

– *Malaia entsiklopediia Kievskoi stariny*. 2nd ed. Kyiv: Dovira, 2005.

– "Kogda Bibikova sprosili, zachem delat' takimi shirokimi ulitsy Vladimirskuiu i Kreshchatik, on otvetil 'Chtoby nel'zia bylo stroit' barrikady.'" *Interesnyi Kiev*. https://www.interesniy.kiev.ua/kogda-bibikova-sprosili-zachem-delat

Makaryk, Irena, and Virlana Tkacz, eds. *Modernism in Kyiv: Jubilant Experimentation*. Toronto: University of Toronto Press, 2010.

Malakov, Dmytro. *Arkhitektor Horodets'kyi*. Kyiv: Kyi, 1999.

– *Prybutkovi budynky Kyieva*. Kyiv: Kyi, 2009.

Malakov, Dmytro, and Olha Druh. *Osobniaky Kyieva*. Kyiv: Kyi, 2004.

Mashkevich, Stefan. *Ulitsy Kieva. Retroputeshestvie*. Kyiv: Folio, 2015.

Matushevych, Adrian. *Khreshchatyk*. Kyiv: Vydavnytstvo Akademiï arkhitektury URSR, 1950.

Mazower, Mark. *Salonica, the City of Ghosts: Christians, Muslims, and Jews, 1430–1950*. New York: Vintage Books, 2006.

Meir, Natan M. *Kiev, Jewish Metropolis: A History, 1859–1914*. Bloomington: Indiana University Press, 2010.

Melinz, Gerhard, and Susan Zimmermann, eds. *Wien–Prag–Budapest: Blützeit der Habsburgermetropolen; Urbanisierung, Kommunalpolitik, gesellschaftliche Konflikte (1867–1918)*. Vienna: Promedia, 1996.

Miller, Aleksei. *The Ukrainian Question: The Russian Empire and Nationalism in the 19th Century*. Budapest: Central European University Press, 2003.

Moshenskii, S.Z. *Finansovye tsentry Ukrainy i rynok tsennykh bumag industrial'noi epokhi*. London: Xlibris, 2014.

Nardova, V.A. *Gorodskoe samoupravlenie v Rossii v 60-kh – nachale 90-kh godov XIX veka*. Leningrad [Saint Petersburg]: Nauka, 1984.

– *Samoderzhavie i gorodskie dumy v Rossii v kontse XIX-nachale XX veka*. Saint Petersburg: Nauka, 1994.

Neese, N. *Geschichte der Evangelisch-lutheranische Kirche und Gemeinde in Kiew*. Kyiv: 1882.

Nora, Pierre. "Between Memory and History: Les Lieux de Memoire," in *Representations* 26 (Spring 1989): 7–24.

Nowak, Andrzej. *Polacy, Rosjanie i biesy. Studia i szkice historyczne z XIX i XX wieku*. Kraków: ARCANA, 1998.

Olsen, Donald J. *Town Planning in London: The Eighteenth and Nineteenth Centuries*. New Haven: Yale University Press, 1982.

– *The City as a Work of Art: London, Paris, Vienna*. New Haven: Yale University Press, 1986.

Os'mak, Vladyslava. "Drevnii gorod slovno vymer." *Kievskii al'bom* 1 (2001): 11–13.

Paszkiewicz, Piotr. *Pod berłem Romanowów: Sztuka rosyjska w Warszawie, 1815–1915*. Warsaw: Instytut Sztuki-Polska Akademia Nauk, 1991.

Plokhy, Serhii. *The Origins of the Slavic Nations: Premodern Identities in Russia, Ukraine, and Belarus*. Cambridge: Cambridge University Press, 2006.

– *Unmaking Imperial Russia: Mykhailo Hrushevsky and the Writing of Ukrainian History*. Toronto: University of Toronto Press, 2005.

Popel'nyts'ka, Olena. "Istorychnyi rozvytok kyïvs'koho Podolu (XVII – pochatok XIX st.)," *Ukraïns'kyi istorychnyi zhurnal* 3 (2002): 104–19.

– "Naibil'shi zemlevlasnyky i pidpryiemtsi kyïvs'koho Podolu XVII-XVIII st." *Kievskii al'bom* 1 (2001): 59–63.

Popov, Oleksandr, ed. *Iliustrovana istoriia Kyieva*. Kyiv: Feniks, 2012.

Pratt, Mary Louise. *Imperial Eyes: Travel Writing and Transculturation*. New York: Routledge, 2008.

Pritsak, Omeljan. *The Origins of Rus'*, vol. 1. Cambridge, MA: Harvard University Press, 1981.

– "U stolittia narodyn M. Hrushevs'koho." *Lysty do Pryiateliv / Letters to Friends* 14, nos. 5–7 (1966): 1–18.

Prokopovych, Markian. *Habsburg Lemberg: Architecture, Public Space, and Politics in the Galician Capital, 1772–1914*. West Lafayette: Purdue University Press, 2008.

Prymak, Thomas. "Honoré de Balzac's Ukrainian Dreamland." http://www.academia.edu/29765117/HONOR%C3%89_DE_BALZACS_UKRAINIAN_DREAMLAND

Ptukha, M.V. *D.P. Zhuravskii. Zhizn', trudy, statisticheskaia deiatel'nost'*. Moscow: Gosstatizdat, 1951.

Rashin, A.G. *Naselenie Rossii za 100 let (1813–1913)*. Moscow: Gosstatizdat, 1956.

Relph, Edward. *The Modern Urban Landscape: 1880 to the Present*. Baltimore: Johns Hopkins University Press, 1987.

Remy, Johannes. *Higher Education and National Identity: Polish Student Activism in Russia 1832–1863*. Helsinki: Finnish Literature Society, 2000.

Russkie pisateli, 1800–1917. Biograficheskii slovar', vol. 4. Moscow: Bol'shaia sovetskaia entsiklopediia, 1999.

Rybakov, Mykhailo. *Khreshchatyk vidomyi i nevidomyi*. Kyiv: Kyi, 2003.

Ryndziunskii, P.G. *Krest'iane i gorod v kapitalisticheskoi Rossii vtoroi poloviny XIX veka*. Moscow: Nauka, 1982.

Sakovych, L. "Rehuliarni mistobudivni zakhody pochatku XIX v. u Rosiï i na Ukraïni." In *Pytannia istoriï arkhitektury ta budivel'noï tekhniky Ukraïny*, ed. Iu. Nel'hovs'kyi, 283–4. Kyiv: 1959.

Salii, Ivan, and Mykola Kovalyns'kyi. *Oblychchia stolytsi v doliakh iï kerivnykiv*. Kyiv: Dovira, 2008.

Sarbei, V.G., et al. eds. *Istoriia Kieva*, vol. 2: *Kiev perioda pozdnego feodalizma i kapitalizma*. Kyiv: Naukova dumka, 1984.

Savchenko, Fedir. "Balzak na Ukraïni (1847–1850)," *Ukraïna* 1 (Kyiv, 1924): 134–51.

Schoenle, Andreas. *Architecture of Oblivion: Ruins and Historical Consciousness in Modern Russia*. De Kalb: University of Northern Illinois Press, 2011.

Schorske, Carl. *Fin-de-Siècle Vienna: Politics and Culture*. New York: Vintage Books, 1981.

– "The Idea of the City in European Thought: Voltaire to Spengler." In *The Historian and the City*, ed. Oscar Handlin and John E. Burchard, 95–113. Cambridge, MA: MIT Press, 1966.

Seegel, Steven. *Mapping Europe's Borderlands: Russian Cartography in the Age of Empire*. Chicago: University of Chicago Press, 2012.

Sennett, Richard. *The Fall of Public Man*. New York: W.W. Norton, 1992.

– *Flesh and Stone: The Body and the City in Western Civilization*. New York: W.W. Norton, 1994.

Sereda, Ostap. "Nationalizing or Entertaining? Public Discourses on Musical Theater in Russian-ruled Kyiv in the 1870s and 1880s." In *Oper im Wandel der Gesellschaft. Kulturtransfers und Netzweke des Musiktheatres im modernen Europa*, ed. Sven Oliver Mueller, Philipp Ther, Juta Toelle, and Geza zur. Nieden, 33–58. Wien: Boehlau Verlag, 2010.

Shamrai, Serhiy. "Kyïvs'kyi odnodennyi perepys 2-ho berezolia 1874 roku (Storinka z istorii marksyzmu v Ukraïni)." In *Kyïv ta ioho okolytsia v istorii i pam'iatkakh*, ed. Mykhailo Hrushevs'kyi, 352–84. Kyiv: Derzhavne vydavnytstvo Ukraïny, 1926.

Shandra, V.S. *Heneral-hubernatorstva v Ukraïni: XIX-pochatok XX st.* Kyiv: NAN Ukraïny. Instytut istorii Ukraïny, 2005.

Shcherbyna, Volodymyr. "Narysy z istorii Kyieva, vidkoly pryiednano ioho do Moskovs'koï derzhavy, do pochatku Svitovoï viiny i Revoliutsii." In his *Novi studii z istorii Kyieva*, 3–20. Kyiv: Vydavnytstvo UAN, 1926.

– "Kyïv ta Kyïvshchyna na pochatku XIX viku." *Ukraïna* 3–4 (1929): 54–9.

– "Kyïv v 20-kh rokakh XIX st. (Z materiialiv zhandarms'koho arkhivu)." *Ukraïna* 3 (1925): 112–18.

Shchitkivs'kyi, Ivan. "Do istorii zabuduvannia m. Kyieva na pochatku XIX stolittia." *Kyïvs'ki zbirnyky istorii i arkheolohii, pobutu i mystetstva* 1 (1931): 315–23.

– "'Istoricheskii put' u Kyievi." In *Kyiv ta ioho okolytsia v istorii ta pam'iatkakh*, ed. Mykhailo Hrushevs'kyi, 385–92. Kyiv: Derzhavne vydavnytstvo Ukraïny, 1926.

Shepelev, L.E. *Chinovnyi mir Rossii, XVIII-nachalo XX v.* Saint Petersburg: Iskusstvo, 1999.

Shul'gin, V.Ia. "Iugo-Zapadnyi krai pod upravleniem D.G. Bibikova." *Drevniia i novaia Rossiia* 2, nos. 5–6 (1879): 5–32.

Shul'kevich M.M., and T.D. Dmitrenko. *Kiev. Arkhitekturno-istoricheskii ocherk*, 6th rev. ed. Kyiv: Budivel'nyk, 1982.

Skinner, Frederick. "Trends in Planning Practices: The Building of Odessa, 1794–1917." In *The City in Russian History*, ed. Michael Hamm, 139–59. Lexington: University Press of Kentucky, 1976.

Smith, P.D. *City: A Guidebook for the Urban Age.* London: Bloomsbury, 2012.

Smith, Alison K. *For the Common Good and Their Own Well-Being: Social Estates in Imperial Russia.* New York: Oxford University Press, 2014.

Staliunas, Darius. "Did the Government Seek to Russify Lithuanians and Poles in the Northwest Territory after the Uprising of 1863–1864?," *Kritika* 5, no. 2 (Spring 2004): 273–91.

Stanek, Lukasz. *Henri Lefebvre on Space: Architecture, Urban Research, and the Production of Theory.* Minneapolis: University of Minnesota Press, 2011.

Stepanov, Iurii S. *Konstanty: slovar' russkoi kul'tury*, 3rd ed. Moscow: Akademicheskii proekt, 2004.

Stone, Clarence. *Regime Politics: Governing Atlanta, 1946–1988*. Lawrence: University Press of Kansas, 1989.

Straszewska, Maria. *Czasopisma literackie w Królewstwie Polskim w latach 1832–1848*. Wrocław: Zakład narodowy im. Ossolińskich, 1953–9.

Sutcliffe, Anthony, ed. *The Rise of Modern Urban Planning, 1800–1914*. Mansell, 1980.

– *Towards the Planned City: Germany, Britain, the United States, and France, 1780–1914*. London: St Martin's Press, 1981.

Sylvester, Roshanna P. "City of Thieves: Moldavanka, Criminality, and Respectability in Prerevolutionary Odessa." *Journal of Urban History* 27, no. 2 (January 2001): 131–57.

Tabiś, Jan. *Polacy na Uniwersytecie Kijowskim: 1834–1863*. Kraków: Wydawnictwo Literackie, 1974.

Taranets, S.V. *Staroobriadchestvo goroda Kieva i Kievskoi gubernii*. Kyiv: 2004.

Tarnawsky, Maxim. *The All-Encompassing Eye of Ukraine: Ivan Nechui-Levyts'kyi's Realist Prose*. Toronto: University of Toronto Press, 2015.

Thernstrom, Stephan, and Richard Sennett, eds. *Nineteenth-Century Cities: Essays in the New Urban History*. New Haven: Yale University Press, 1969.

Tolochko, Oleksii. "Kyievo-rus'ka spadshchyna v istorychnii dumtsi Ukraïny pochatku XIX st." In *Ukraïns'ki proekty v Rosiis'kii imperiï*, ed. V.F. Verstiuk, V.M. Horobets', and O.P. Tolochko, 250–331. Kyiv: Naukova dumka, 2004.

– *Kievskaia Rus' i Malorossiia v XIX veke*. Kyiv: Laurus, 2012.

Tolochko L.I., and O.V. Hrybovs'ka. *Pam'iatnyk Sviatomu Kniaziu Volodymyru v Kyievi*. Kyiv: Tekhnika, 2007.

Tonkiss, Fran. *Cities by Design: The Social Life of Urban Form*. Cambridge: Polity Press, 2014.

Turchyn, Ia. B. *Otto Eikhel'man, postat' na zlami stolit': politolohichnyi dyskurs*. Lviv: Vydavnytstvo L'vivs'koï politekhniky, 2010.

Ułaszyn, Henryk. *Kontrakty Kijowskie. Szkic historyczno-obyczajowy 1798–1898*. Saint Petersburg: Nakładem księgarni K. Grerdyszyńskiego, 1900.

Vatulia B., and V. Poznanskii. "K istorii sooruzheniia v Kieve pamiatnika B. Khmel'nitskomu: obzor dokumentov." *Nauchno-informatsionnyi biulleten' Arkhivnogo upravleniia* [since 1965 *Arkhivy Ukrainy*] 1 (1954): 49–58.

Vortman, D. "Kyïvs'ka fortetsia." In *Entsyklopediia istoriï Ukraïny*, vol. 4. Kyiv: Naukova dumka, 2007.

Weeks, Theodore. *Vilnius between Nations, 1795–2000*. DeKalb: University of Northern Illinois Press, 2015.

– "Religion and Russification: Russian Language in the Catholic Churches of the 'Northwest Provinces' after 1863." *Kritika* 2, no. 1 (Winter 2001): 87–111.

Wirtschafter, Kimerling Elise. *Social Identity in Imperial Russia*. DeKalb: University of Northern Illinois Press, 2015.
– *From Serf to Russian Soldier*. Princeton: Princeton University Press, 2014.
– "Social Misfits: Veterans and Soldiers' Families in Servile Russia." *Journal of Military History* 59 (1995): 215–35.
– *Structures of Society: Imperial Russia's "People of Various Ranks."* DeKalb: University of Northern Illinois Press, 1994.
Wolff, Larry. *Inventing Eastern Europe: The Map of Civilization on the Mind of the Enlightenment*. Stanford: Stanford University Press, 1995.
Zhuk, Sergei. *Russia's Lost Reformation: Peasants, Millennialism, and Radical Sects in Southern Russia and Ukraine, 1830–1917*. Washington, DC: Woodrow Wilson Center Press, 2004.
Zhurba, Oleh. *Kyïvs'ka arkheohrafichna komisiia, 1843–1921*. Kyiv: Naukova dumka, 1993.
Zorin, Andrei. "Ideologiia 'pravoslaviia-samoderzhaviia-narodnosti': opyt rekonstruktsii. (Neizvestnyi avtograf memoranduma S.S. Uvarova Nikolaiu I)." *Novoe literaturnoe obozrenie* 26 (1997): 71–104.

Index

www.ingramcontent.com/pod-product-compliance
Lightning Source LLC
Chambersburg PA
CBHW030007131025
33395CB00025B/93/J